For P. R. H. and J. D. H.
(MY MOTHER AND FATHER)

PIMLICO

719

MARY MAGDALEN

Susan Haskins read English and Art History at University College London. She lived for several years in Italy and worked at Harvard University's Villa I Tatti. She is co-author with Anthony Burton of *European Art in the Victoria & Albert Museum* (1983), and translator of *The Papal Prince* by Paolo Prodi (1987). She lives in London.

Mary Magdalen announcing the Resurrection to the Disciples. From the Albani Psalter, dating from before 1123, possibly made for Christina of Markyate. Pfarrkirche St Godehard, Hildesheim.

MARY MAGDALEN

Myth and Metaphor

———

SUSAN HASKINS

PIMLICO

Published by Pimlico 2005

2 4 6 8 10 9 7 5 3 1

First published in Great Britain in 1993 by
HarperCollins*Publishers.*

Pimlico edition 2005

Pimlico
Random House, 20 Vauxhall Bridge Road,
London SW1V 2SA

Random House Australia (Pty) Limited
20 Alfred Street, Milsons Point, Sydney,
New South Wales 2061, Australia

Random House New Zealand Limited
18 Poland Road, Glenfield,
Auckland 10, New Zealand

Random House South Africa (Pty) Limited
Endulini, 5A Jubilee Road, Parktown 2193, South Africa

Random House UK Limited Reg. No. 954009

A CIP catalogue record for this book
is available from the British Library

ISBN 1-8459-5004-6

Papers used by Random House UK Limited are natural,
recyclable products made from wood grown in sustainable forests.
The manufacturing processes conform to the environmental
regulations of the country of origin

Printed and bound in Great Britain by
Bookmarque Ltd, Croydon, Surrey

Contents

Preface

An Arundel Society print of a Trecento Florentine crucifixion, which hung on a wall of a class-room in my convent school, was my first introduction to Mary Magdalen. On asking who the red-cloaked golden-haired figure was at the foot of the cross and why she wept, I was told that it was Mary Magdalen and that she was weeping for her own sins and for those of mankind which had put Christ on the cross. Further questions elicited the stiff reply that her sins were 'those of the flesh' and that I would understand what these were when I was older. Other than this we learned only that Mary Magdalen had been a sinner who had become a follower of Christ – a kind of servant who, along with the other women, ministered to him and the twelve male disciples. Our attention was turned rather to the Virgin Mary, the mother of Christ, of whose presence we were made constantly aware through prayers and hymns, paintings, statues and holy cards. The year was marked out by the major feasts of the Virgin. It was she whom we were enjoined to emulate, and Mary of Magdala was for a time entirely forgotten. She became part of what is now called the forgotten history of women.

It was not until several years later that I encountered the beautiful weeping penitent of seventeenth-century art and, above all, Bernini's anguished figure in Siena Cathedral. Now, however, she was usually portrayed semi-naked. It was clear that she was more important than we had learned at school, but other questions also came to mind. Where was her story told, of her sinfulness, and how and why had she become the Church's symbol of penance? I little thought that the answers to these questions, first planned as a thesis on her seventeenth-century image, would have led me into such matters as the role of women in the early Church, Gnosticism, ecclesiastical misogyny, medieval piety, prostitution and the ministry of women. I realised that her image embodied the perceptions of every era, being refashioned again and again to suit the needs and aspirations of the times. The result is a book in which I have tried to draw together all the disparate elements which have gone into creating her different personae. It does not pretend to be all-inclusive; a great deal more material has had to be left out than could be contained in a necessarily short history of this ubiquitous saint. This study concentrates on the western Church's treatment of her, with only occasional glances to the Orthodox Churches' tradition in which she figures as her gospel self. I have been more concerned to discover why in the western tradition she has been seen as a repentant prostitute, and what this means in the context of women's place within that tradition.

Mary Magdalen is everywhere, as a friend and I recently discovered on a short trip through France – taken to celebrate the delivery of the final text. An hour into France, we had passed a farm called 'La Madeleine', and a few miles on a modern housing estate called the 'Lotissement de la Madeleine'. Outside the line of the medieval walls of the city of Tours, we parked by chance near a 'Clinique des Dames Blanches', a hospital on the site of a medieval convent for repentant women, some prostitutes and some not, under the patronage of Mary Magdalen, round the corner from a street called 'rue de la Madeleine'. A day later, we came across a 'Relais de la Madeleine', near St-Pierre de Loubrissac (Quercy), and fifty miles north a camping site called 'La Magdelaine'. En route for Fontevrault, where in the twelfth century a wandering preacher, Robert of Arbrissel, established the foundations of what became an abbey, with a house for repentant women under the aegis of Mary Magdalen, I saw on the map a spot marked 'La Madeleine', near a village called Cizay-la-Madeleine, which turned out to be a tiny twelfth-century chapel. It was all that remained of a small convent dedicated to the saint. Here we were met by an irate farmer; the chapel was his, it was full of hay, and there was nothing for us to see. Churches and streets named after her are often to be found outside medieval city and town walls as her cult was a phenomenon of the later Middle Ages. But they were also placed thus as they were often associated with leper hospitals, of which Mary Magdalen, with her supposed sisterly relationship with Lazarus, was a patron, such as the tiny, early twelfth-century chapel of St Mary Magdalen at Stourbridge, outside Cambridge, or the Magdalen hospital at Norwich. Ruins of magnificent ecclesiastical buildings in deserted places such as the Augustinian priories of Pentney in Norfolk, founded before 1135, and Lanercost, in Cumberland – where a statue of Mary Magdalen with a donor monk (c.1270) is still extant in the west gable – witness her stature within the medieval monastic world.

Mary Magdalen's name has been given to such disparate things as a Palaeolithic era, known as the Magdalenian Culture (from the discovery of remains below a troglodite village containing a medieval chapel under the patronage of the saint), an island off the north of Sardinia, mountain ranges in northern and southern Italy, towns in Austria and Estonia, and numerous towns and villages across Europe with churches dedicated to her. Colleges in Oxford and Cambridge bear her name, preserving a variation on the medieval French pronunciation in 'maudlin', a word which has also gone into the English language to denote tearfulness, sometimes drunken. It has been taken to the New World, given to a major river in Colombia and the state named after it, to a river in Bolivia, and towns in Argentina and Venezuela; to a group of islands between Nova Scotia and Newfoundland, and also to an island in the Marquesas in the South Pacific. Her doll-like image, gilded and brightly coloured, decorates the vaults of a baroque church in Mexico, and she is unexpectedly to be found, naked and weeping, in a Mughal miniature of the seventeenth century. She is associated with a bakery called 'Le Tre Marie' which claims to have been established in the mid-twelfth century by crusaders in Milan, and is still making the traditional Easter dove-shaped cakes or *colombe*; the *madeleines* made famous by Proust in his *A la recherche du temps perdu* are, however, named after the woman who first baked them. In the end, I can only hope that I have done Mary of Magdala the justice she deserves.

My subtitle, 'Myth and Metaphor', was in my mind for some time before I remembered that it was the title of a collection of essays by Northrop Frye (*Myth and Metaphor: Selected Essays, 1974–1988*, 1990); its suitability to the subject of Mary Magdalen, however, remains, as my book is, for the most part, about the mythical aspects of her figure and their meaning.

As it is impossible to illustrate all the works of art to which I have referred, I have given references to two works where the majority of images is reproduced, under the name of the author – Schiller (Gertrud Schiller, *Ikonographie der christlichen Kunst*, Gütersloh, 1966–91; I have used the German edition as it is more complete than its English translation), and the exhibition catalogue title *La Maddalena* (*La Maddalena tra Sacro e Profano*, ed. Marilena Mosco, Milan-Florence, 1986). An iconographical reference work, Louis Réau's *Iconographie de l'art chrétien* (Paris, 1958), is also cited by the author's surname. I have chosen the spelling 'Magdalen' for my own use, but have followed the various spellings of my sources in quotation.

I have used the King James Authorised Version of the Bible because of its beautiful language and imagery, but have referred when necessary, to make meanings clearer, to the New Jerusalem Bible, the *RSV Interlinear Greek-English New Testament*, and the *Theological Dictionary of the New Testament*.

Anyone working on the figure of Mary Magdalen cannot fail to be indebted to the researches of Monsignor Victor Saxer, director of the Istituto Pontificale d'Archeologia Cristiana, Rome, doyen of Magdalenian studies, who, since 1954, has published two substantial volumes and several articles on the saint. I would like to acknowledge my debt to him, without whose labours my own would have been impossible.

I could not have written this book without the help and encouragement of many friends and colleagues and some who have become both friends and colleagues in the course of my research. I am profoundly grateful to Evelyn Welch, who read the final draft of the entire manuscript, whose enthusiasm and knowledge have been indispensable to me. I have had most helpful discussions with Father Robert Murray SJ and Professor Mary Grey, both of whom have read chapters, made comments, corrections and suggestions. Professor Elaine Pagels most kindly gave me of her time, and also directed me to useful sources. Veronica Sekules' medieval expertise helped me to avoid a number of pitfalls, whilst Jan Johnson and Elizabeth McGrath greatly improved my seventh chapter with their knowledge and critical acumen. The errors that have crept in are mine and mine alone. Adele Airoldi patiently translated and also corrected my translations of many of the Latin, medieval French and Italian texts, and has indefatigably brought to my attention, and obtained copies of, the latest books on Mary Magdalen and related subjects. I have also been enormously helped by information freely given by Nicolas Barker, Renzo Bragantini, Anthony Burton, Salvatore Camporeale, Joanna Cannon, James Davis, Ellen D'Oench, Sabine Eiche, Chris Fischer, M. R. D. Foot, Richard Fremantle, Liesbeth Heenk, Sandy Heslop, Christopher Hogwood, Charles Hope, Deborah Howard, Peter Humfrey, Gabriel Josipovici, Jill Kerr, Jacques Lalubie, Norman Land, Christopher Lloyd, Rosamond and David McKitterick, Christopher Mendez, the Revd Ulla Monberg, Nigel Morgan, Katharine F. Pantzer, Melinda Lesher Parry, Daria Perocco, Guy Petherbridge, Véronique Plesch, Aldo De Poli, Cesare Poppi, Thomas Puttfarken, Virginia C. Raguin, Dennis Romano, Dana Goodgal Salem, Dorothy Shepard, Susan Tattersall, Dora Thornton,

Nicholas Turner, David Wakefield, Robert Williams and Peter van Wingen. My thanks also go to Paul Hills whose idea it was that I turn my initial study into a book.

I have also to thank the following: Kyle Cathie for her wisdom and support, to which I was able to turn time and again over the years; the encouragement of Catharine Carver whose renowned blue pencil was the first to strike through my infelicities of style. JoAnne Robertson has been an unfailing source of moral and practical support, as has been Judy Spours. Robert Baldock, Ellen Grout and Gillian Malpass have all, amongst other things, helped me to iron out publishing problems. Other friends who have in one way or another contributed to this book are Rita Adam, Rosalind Barker, Graham Beck, Julia Brown, Alan Crawford, Sue Crockford, Jean Farr, Jean Fraser, Claire Glasspoole, Mary Goodwin, Nicholas Hadgraft, Edith Hazen, Celia Jones and Malcolm Wilson, Elizabeth Keay, Philip Leonard, Suzanne O'Farrell, Diana Ruston, Preman Sotomayor, Neil Thomson and Alfredo Vig. My sister, Nicola, helped with translations, and had to put up with frequent sororial visits to Paris. My researches abroad, always enjoyable, were further enhanced by the hospitality of David Ellwood, Nancy Isenberg and David Hart, Magdalen Nabb, Marica Redini and Candida and Maurizio Vig Ranieri. To Bill and Marie-Ange Underwood I owe much affection and gratitude for their many kindnesses. Working at I Tatti in 1988 renewed ancient friendships with members of the staff there. I should also like to thank Father Leonard E. Boyle OP of the Vatican Library and Professor Gerhard Ewald of the Kunsthistorisches Institut in Florence for particular help. I am also indebted to those members of the staffs of the Index of Christian Art at Princeton, the Pierpont Morgan Library, New York and the British Library, who have given me assistance.

I owe a special debt of gratitude to Eric Hobsbawm, Paolo Prodi and William Vaughan, for their kindness and support. I am grateful to the Italian Government for a grant given in 1988; to the Gladys Krieble Delmas Foundation for a grant which enabled me to carry out research in Venice in 1989; to Douglas Blyth who put me in the way of receiving a grant from the Hélène Heroys Literary Foundation in Geneva, through the auspices of the Society of Authors; and to Douglas Matthews and his fellow trustees for seemingly endlessly renewed London Library grants.

Finally, my thanks go to Anthony Goff, and to Philip Gwyn Jones for his enthusiasm for the book, sympathetic editing and patient handling of last-minute additions. Philip Lewis has made it look better than I could ever have hoped for. My debt to all those who have fed, clothed and consoled me during the last two penurious years should also be recorded: they will know who they are. My most enormous debt of gratitude is, however, to Nicholas Pickwoad, whose being there, help beyond all bounds of duty and very strong shoulder, have contributed to the writing, and particularly finishing, of this book. Without his unfailing generosity, it would never have been.

S. H., September 1992

Foreword to the Pimlico edition

Since finishing my book in 1992, an enormous amount of literature has proliferated concerning Mary Magdalen. Films and television programmes have been made, plays performed. As the most recent monograph (Katherine Ludwig Jansen's *The Making of the Magdalen: Preaching and Popular Devotion in the Later Middle Ages*) noted in 2000, the 1990s proved a most fruitful decade for Magdalen studies. Jansen surveys in detail the medieval Magdalen, drawing on a wealth of manuscript and archival sources, showing how the mendicants created their own Magdalen. Edith de Boer's *Mary Magdalen: Beyond the Myth* (1997) discusses the disciple and apostle, focusing on the Gnostic Gospel of Mary, suggesting that, after Christ's death, she carried out her own apostolate. Elisabeth Pinto-Mathieu's *Marie-Madeleine dans la littérature du Moyen Age* (1997) discusses ecclesiastical writings and literature, and the legends. Ingrid Maisch's *Mary Magdalene: The Image of a Woman through the Centuries* (1998) traces the history of interpretations of Mary Magdalen, particularly in German-speaking countries, and Antti Marjanen's *The Woman Jesus Loved: Mary Magdalen in the Nag Hammadi Library and Related Documents* (1996) examines the figure in the Gnostic gospels.

In that time two important conferences were held in Italy and France, the proceedings of which were published in the *Mélanges de l'Ecole française de Rome: Moyen Age* (tome 104-1-1992), with many excellent essays about the medieval Magdalen, and *Marie-Madeleine: Figure mythique dans la littérature et les arts* (ed. A. Montandon, Paris, 1999). There are many other publications, I am sure, but the above will go a long way to providing bibliographies and references to other works that discuss Mary Magdalen. Mary Magdalen was the subject of a section ('Teaching the Faithful to Fly: Mary Magdalene and Peter in Baroque Italy') of the exhibition *Saints and Sinners: Caravaggio and the Baroque Image*, curated by Franco Mormando, held at the McMullen Museum of Art, Boston College, Boston, MA, in 1999; and the exhibition *Maria Magdalena: Extasis y arrepentimiento* was held in Mexico City in 2001. The exhibition *Maria Magdalena: Zondares van de Middeleeuwen tot vandaag*, curated by Barbara Baert, was at the Museum voor Schone Kunsten, Ghent, 2002-2003.

On 21 May 1997 the late Pope John Paul II caused consternation when he told a general audience of pilgrims that the Virgin Mary and not Mary Magdalen was the first to see the Risen Christ ('Giovanni Paolo II corregge i Vangeli: "Fu Maria la prima a vedere Cristo risorto"', *La Repubblica*, 22 May 1997, p. 25); three years earlier he had similarly shocked pilgrims in St Mark's Square when he said: 'Even if the gospels do not refer to it there is a belief that the first announcement [of the Resurrection] was made to the Virgin.' Two days later, clearly to calm the souls of the faithful, he retreated from this standpoint, saying, 'The first person to whom the risen Christ appeared was Mary Magdalen' (*La Repubblica*, 7 April 1994, p. 22).

Mary Magdalen's relationship to Christ still causes furore: at Easter 2000 the Greek Orthodox Church moved to ban a best-selling novel, *M to the Power of N* by Mimis Androulakis (published in Greece in 1999 by Kastaniotis), for blasphemy in portraying Christ as a philanderer who finds it hard to resist Mary Magdalen (*Guardian*, 25 April 2000). Norman Mailer's *Gospel According to the Son* (1997) similarly caused a stir in its depiction of Christ being tempted by the beautiful Mary Magdalen. An article in the *Los Angeles Times* of 24 July 1999 ('Women Celebrate a Christian Heroine') heralded a nation-wide movement in the United States to rehabilitate the image of Mary Magdalen; to celebrate Jubilee Year 2000's Easter Monday, a 'biopic' *Maria Maddalena* was shown on Italian television's Canale 5, its heroine repudiated by her husband because of her infertility, who then becomes pregnant by another but loses the child, attempts suicide, all before being redeemed by Christ. Mary Magdalen continues to exert her fascination over us, and will do so clearly for some time.

Susan Haskins
April 2005

Acknowledgements

The Author and Publishers would like to thank the following for permission to use the illustrations listed below:

Plates 6 and 12, The Master and Fellows of Corpus Christi College, Cambridge; Plate 81, The Master and Fellows of Trinity College, Cambridge; Plates 55, 82 and 88, The Syndics of the Fitzwilliam Museum, Cambridge; Plate 89, David Wynne Esq.

Whilst every effort has been made to trace the owners of copyright in the photographs, the Author and Publishers regret that this has not always been possible.

The woodcut at the beginning of each chapter is taken from the homily for St Mary Magdalen's feast-day, 22 July, from Antonius Corvinus, *A Postill or Collection of Moste Godly Doctrine upon every gospell through the yeare, as well for Holye dayes*, etc., London, 1550.

List of Illustrations

Frontispiece: Mary Magdalen announcing the Resurrection to the Disciples. From the Albani Psalter, folio 31b. Pfarrkirche St Godehard, Hildesheim/ Herzog August Bibliothek, Wolfenbüttel. Before 1123.

MARY MAGDALEN

DE UNICA MAGDALENA[1]

Her of your name, whose fair inheritance
  Bethina was, and jointure Magdalo:
An active faith so highly did advance,
  That she once knew, more than the Church did know,
The Resurrection; so much good there is
  Deliver'd of her, that some Fathers be
Loth to believe one Woman could do this;
  But, think these Magdalens were two or three.

JOHN DONNE, 'To the Lady Magdalen Herbert:
of St Mary Magdalen'[2]

 WE KNOW VERY LITTLE about Mary Magdalen. The predominant image we have of her is of a beautiful woman with long golden hair, weeping for her sins, the very incarnation of the age-old equation between feminine beauty, sexuality and sin. For nearly two thousand years, the traditional conception of Mary Magdalen has been that of the prostitute who, hearing the words of Jesus Christ, repented of her sinful past and henceforth devoted her life and love to him. She appears in countless devotional images, scarlet-cloaked and with loose hair, kneeling below the cross, or seated at Christ's feet in the house of Mary and Martha of Bethany, or as the beauteous prostitute herself, sprawled at his feet, unguent jar by her side, in the house of the Pharisee. Her very name evokes images of beauty and sensuality, yet when we look for this creature in the New Testament, we look for her in vain. All we truly know of her comes from the four gospels, a few brief references which yield an inconsistent, even contradictory vision. These shifting reflections converge, however, on four salient aspects: that Mary Magdalen was one of Christ's female followers, was present at his crucifixion, was

a witness – indeed, according to the gospel of St John, *the* witness – of
his resurrection, and was the first to be charged with the supreme ministry, that of proclaiming the Christian message. She brought the knowledge that through Christ's victory over death, life everlasting was
offered to all who believe.

In the Christian story, Jesus Christ, son of God made man, was born
of a virgin, crucified, died and was buried for the salvation of the human
race, and in fulfilment of the Scriptures. Three days after the crucifixion,
he rose from the dead, signifying his triumph over death. Belief in the
resurrection, the central message of Christianity, is reiterated in the
beautiful words of the Nicene Creed, originally formulated in Greek in
the fourth century, and chanted at every mass or service ever since:

> *Qui propter nos homines, et propter nostram salutem descendit de caelis.*
> *Et incarnatus est de Spiritu Sancto ex Maria Virgine; Et homo factus*
> *est. Crucifixus etiam pro nobis: sub Pontio Pilato passus, et sepultus est.*
> *Et resurrexit tertia die, secundum Scripturas . . .*

> (Who for us men, and for our salvation, came down from heaven,
> And was incarnate by the Holy Ghost of the Virgin Mary, And
> was made man. And was crucified also for us under Pontius Pilate.
> He suffered and was buried. And the third day he rose again
> according to the Scriptures . . .)

Every Easter, Christians celebrate the Passion, death, and especially the
resurrection of Christ, seeing in the festival not only a commemoration
of the events of the gospels, but also their own spiritual regeneration,
through their baptism into the Church, with Christ, and their delivery
from time, sin and death.[3] Easter was the earliest and most important
of all the Christian feasts, lauded by Pope Leo the Great (*c.*400–61) as
the *festum festorum*,[4] although in modern times it has been overshadowed
by the celebration of Christmas. In its earliest years, it may have been
observed in conjunction with the Passover, the chief Jewish festival at
the time of Christ, which celebrated Israel's delivery from Egyptian
slavery and her exodus to the Promised Land, but, by the end of the
second century, all Christians, except those of Asia Minor, commemorated Christ's resurrection on the Sunday after the Jewish feast.[5]

The Easter story is where the story of Mary Magdalen begins, for it
is here, at the climax of Christ's life on earth, that she makes her first
appearance. Accounts of Christ's life and death were passed down orally

from those who had been witnesses of the events or, as Luke tells us, 'which from the beginning were eyewitnesses, and ministers of the word' (1:2), until the point when, some time before the beginning of the second century, and probably within fifty years of Christ's death, they were written down in what were to become the four canonical books of the New Testament, the gospels.[6] Three of these accounts, by Matthew, Mark and Luke, are so close in form and content that they are called the 'synoptics', from the Greek word *synoptikos*, meaning from the same point of view. The authorship of the fourth and later gospel, which is entirely different in style and approach, is still a matter of scholarly dispute, although it is traditionally attributed, together with that of the Book of Revelation, to the apostle John, who is also identified with the 'beloved disciple' who leant against Christ's breast at the Last Supper (John 13:23). According to a much later myth, this figure was to have a remarkable part to play in the legendary life of Mary Magdalen.[7]

It is to these earliest of Christian writings that we have to turn in order to discover the true identity, and consequently the prominence and importance, of the historical figure who very quickly gave way to the mythical creature we know today.

Mary Magdalen is first referred to by name in Chapter 15 of St Mark's gospel, towards the end of his account of Christ's crucifixion on Golgotha, 'the place of a skull', the Hebrew name for Calvary, just outside Jerusalem. Mark's gospel, probably written about AD 66–8, is now agreed by most scholars to be the source for those of Luke and Matthew, the latter traditionally thought to have been written first.[8] Mark describes the scene: Christ, crucified between the two thieves, forsaken by his male disciples (14:50), and alone except for the 'women looking on afar off', has just died on the cross in that desolate place. Among the women who stayed after the men had fled were 'Mary Magdalene, and Mary the mother of James the less and of Joses, and Salome' (15:40). These women had followed Christ in Galilee and had 'ministered unto him' (v.41), and they now stood together with the 'many other women which came up with him into Jerusalem'. Christ's body is then taken down from the cross, and Joseph of Arimathaea, 'an honourable counsellor' of the Sanhedrin (v.43),[9] who had earlier refused to condemn Christ (Luke 23:51), requests it of Pontius Pilate, the Roman governor of Judaea. He wraps it in fine linen, and lays it in a sepulchre which he closes with a stone. As the following day is the Sabbath, during which all Jews have to rest, the burial ceremony cannot take place until the day after, when, according to Jewish custom, the body will be buried outside the city walls in a tomb hewn out of rock.[10] At the end of the chapter, Mark tells us that Mary Magdalen and Mary the mother of Joses 'beheld where he was laid' (15:47).

Immediately following this, in Chapter 16, the evangelist describes the events central to Christian belief, in which Mary Magdalen has an integral role, one often ignored and eclipsed when seen in relation to the legendary aspects of her 'life'. Early on the morning after the Sabbath, she and Mary the mother of James, and Salome, take to the sepulchre sweet spices bought before the Sabbath to anoint Christ's body in preparation for burial, a ritual traditionally carried out by Jewish women. Mark's description of the women rising 'very early in the morning the first day of the week', to reach the sepulchre 'at the rising of the sun', became from the earliest centuries of Christianity a focal point for artists and sculptors who sought to represent the drama of the resurrection. Arriving at the tomb, the women discover that the stone placed in the tomb's entrance has been rolled away, and that a young man clad in a long white garment is sitting within. They are terrified, but he tells them not to be afraid as Christ has risen, and that they should relay the message to the disciples 'and Peter' that they will see Christ again in Galilee. According to Mark, the women flee 'quickly', and trembling, so frightened that they tell no-one. However, in verse 9, in what is now known to be a later addition,[11] further information is given about Mary Magdalen, which introduces an element, her 'possession' by devils, used later in the creation of her mythical character:

Now when Jesus was risen early the first day of the week, he appeared first to Mary Magdalene, out of whom he had cast seven devils.

And she went and told them that had been with him, as they mourned and wept.

And they, when they had heard that he was alive, and had been seen of her, believed not (16:9–11).

Matthew tells much the same story: Mary Magdalen is among the many women watching the crucifixion 'which followed Jesus from Galilee, ministering unto him' (27:55), together with 'Mary the mother of James and Joses, and the mother of Zebedee's children' (v.56). Joseph of Arimathaea, this time described as a rich man and one of Christ's disciples, takes the body, wraps it in linen cloth, and places it in his own tomb, against which he places a great stone. Mary Magdalen and a woman described as 'the other Mary'[12] sit beside the sepulchre (v.61).

In Matthew's account, the chief priests and Pharisees, afraid that Christ's disciples might steal the body to claim a false resurrection, ask Pilate to set a watch until the third day, the day that Christ had prophesied that he would rise from the dead (16:21; 17:23; Mark 8:31; 9:31). In Chapter 28, Mary Magdalen and 'the other Mary' come to the sepulchre. Unlike Mark's account, there is no mention of spices or anointing; the women have come to look. There is an earthquake, and an angel, his countenance 'like lightning, and his raiment white as snow' (v.3), descends, removes the stone from the grave opening and seats himself upon it. Like the young man in white in Mark's account, the angel tells the women not to be afraid, that Christ has risen and that they will meet him in Galilee. But again unlike Mark's account, we hear that on their way back to tell the disciples, in 'fear and great joy', the women meet Christ himself, who greets them with the words, 'All hail', and they fall to the ground, clasping his feet and worshipping him. He too bids them not to be afraid and to tell the disciples that they will meet him in Galilee (v.10).

Luke's first reference to Mary Magdalen occurs earlier, in Chapter 8 of his narrative, during his account of Christ's travels around the countryside preaching, accompanied by the twelve disciples, and 'certain women, which had been healed of evil spirits and infirmities'. Among these are 'Mary called Magdalene, out of whom went seven devils, And Joanna the wife of Chuza, Herod's steward, and Susanna, and many others, which ministered unto him of their substance' (vv.2–3). In Chapter 23, in Luke's account of the crucifixion, the number of people around the cross has grown to include: 'all his acquaintance, and the women that followed him from Galilee, [who] stood afar off, beholding these things' (v.49). Again Joseph of Arimathaea takes the body, 'And the women also, which came with him from Galilee, followed after, and beheld the sepulchre, and how his body was laid. And they returned, and prepared spices and ointments; and rested the sabbath day according to the commandment' (vv. 55–6).

In Chapter 24, these women – so far unspecified – go to the sepulchre with their spices very early in the morning. In place of the single angel of the earlier accounts, they find two 'men [standing] by them in shining garments' (v. 4), who ask them why they seek the living among the dead, showing that the women had not truly understood when Christ had foretold his resurrection (vv. 5–7). Luke now confirms that 'It was Mary Magdalene, and Joanna, and Mary the mother of James, and other women that were with them, which told these things unto the apostles' (v. 10). As in Mark, the women's words 'seemed to them as idle tales, and they believed them not' (v. 11). Some lingering doubt, however, seems to impel Peter to go to the sepulchre and see for himself the discarded grave-clothes, where he is amazed, and wonders what has taken place.

The story of the events after the crucifixion as told by Mark, Matthew and Luke are thus synoptic – narrated, with variations, from more or less the same point of view. With minor variations, the same women are present, and the body is taken by Joseph of Arimathaea, who appears in no other episode in the New Testament.[13] In Mark and Luke, the women go to the tomb with the purpose of anointing the body, and in Matthew they come to visit the tomb only as it has been sealed and guarded under Pilate's orders. In Mark, initially Mary Magdalen alone sees the risen Christ (and no-one believes her); in Matthew, Mary Magdalen and the 'other Mary' return to the disciples and meet Christ on the road; and in Luke, the women tell the disciples and are not believed.

In the gospel of John the story is quite different. Gone are the women mourners who watch from afar, and in their place, in Chapter 19, the fourth evangelist states clearly, 'Now there stood by the cross of Jesus his mother, and his mother's sister, Mary the wife of Cleophas, and Mary Magdalene' (v. 25).[14] The body is taken down and Joseph of Arimathaea, this time with Nicodemus, who has brought myrrh and aloes and appears in no other account, winds linen round Christ's body and lays it in the sepulchre.

In the following chapter, John writes: 'The first day of the week cometh Mary Magdalene early, when it was yet dark' (v. 1). On discovering that the stone has been moved and that the sepulchre is empty, and fearing that the body has been stolen, or removed by the Jews,

Mary Magdalen 'then [. . .] runneth, and cometh to Simon Peter, and to the other disciple, whom Jesus loved', to tell them of her discovery. Here, she is quoted as saying, 'They have taken away the Lord out of the sepulchre, and we know not where they have laid him', making it ambiguous as to whether at this point she went to the sepulchre alone, or with the other women. The two men run to the sepulchre, and the 'other' disciple outruns Peter, reaches the tomb first, and stoops down to look in, and sees the cloths in which the body has been wrapped, but does not go in. Peter, however, enters, sees the wrappings and the sudarium, and is then followed by 'that other disciple' who in John's words 'saw, and believed'.[15] This incident, known as the 'race' to the tomb, was to be re-enacted as part of the Easter ceremony in the Middle Ages, and became one of the 'witness' themes of medieval mystery plays. It was John's emphasis on the word 'believed' which, according to later commentators, distinguished the 'other' disciple's belief in the resurrection from the doubts of the rest of the group of followers.

The disciples then return to their houses, leaving Mary Magdalen to a lonely vigil by the sepulchre. As she stands weeping outside, she stoops down to look into it and sees two angels in white sitting at either end of the place where Christ's body has lain. When asked by them why she weeps, she replies, 'Because they have taken away my Lord, and I know not where they have laid him' (v.13). In her grief she seems not to have noticed the grave-clothes left lying in the tomb, and assumes that the body has been taken away. Then comes the beautiful and dramatic scene of recognition in the garden, so often depicted in paintings and sculpture from the early Middle Ages onwards:

> And when she had thus said, she turned herself back, and saw Jesus standing, and knew not that it was Jesus. Jesus saith unto her, Woman, why weepest thou? whom seekest thou? She, supposing him to be the gardener, saith unto him, Sir if thou have borne him hence, tell me where thou hast laid him, and I will take him away. Jesus saith unto her, Mary. She turned herself and saith unto him Rabboni; which is to say, Master (20:14–16).

In recognising Christ, Mary Magdalen calls him *Rabboni*, the Hebrew for 'teacher', a word which had a more solemn resonance than the usual term 'rabbi', and which was usually reserved for God; John thereby infers that she was acknowledging Christ's new role within the Christian

story of salvation.[16] Joyfully, she obviously then attempts to embrace
him or to seize his feet (as in Matt. 28:9, and as she is later usually
shown in the numerous depictions of the scene) for his next words are
'Touch me not' or, as they are better known in the Latin of the Vulgate,
'Noli me tangere'. However, the words of the Greek text, 'me mou
aptou', imply rather the sense of 'do not seek to hold onto, cling to, or
embrace me', and sound less brusque or unkind than do their Latin and
terse English translations.[17] Christ explains why she should desist from
holding him with the words 'for I am not yet ascended to my Father',
from which Mary Magdalen is to infer that her relationship with him
has now changed, that any kind of physical contact which she might
have had with him formerly is no longer appropriate, and that she
should cease from worshipping him in a human, corporeal sense. Christ
then tells her to tell his 'brethren', 'I ascend unto my Father, and your
Father; and to my God, and your God.'[18] The sequence ends with Mary
Magdalen telling the disciples that she has seen Christ, and delivering
his message. Only John gives words to her speech: the Greek New
Testament reports that 'Comes Mary the Magdalene announcing to the
disciples, I have seen the Lord, and these things he said to her.'[19] In
John's gospel, there is, however, no intimation that her word is disbelieved; the episode is followed by Christ's appearances to the disciples
and then to doubting Thomas (vv. 19–29). It is, however, here, in the
gospel of John, that Mary Magdalen appears as one of the several women
of faith, and unequivocally as the first witness of the Empty Tomb and
of the Risen Christ, the cornerstone of Christian belief; the first recipient
of an apostolic commission, she becomes not only the herald of the
'New Life', but also the first apostle.[20]

These few accounts in the gospels tell us all we can claim to know about
Mary Magdalen. Elsewhere in the New Testament, Acts I tells us that
after the resurrection, Christ showed himself 'to many during forty
days'; after the ascension, the disciples meet in an upper room to pray
and supplicate (v. 14), 'with the women, and Mary the mother of Jesus
and with his brethren', and we may infer, although she is not specifically
named, that Mary Magdalen was included in the group of women. But
it is immediately clear from the gospels that the evangelists are careful
to name her precisely, setting her apart from the several other Marys in
their texts and, in every account of the crucifixion except John's, placing
her at the head of the list of Christ's female followers. This prominent

position has naturally engendered much speculation about Mary Magdalen's exact role and place within the group of women followers, but there has recently been a growing tendency to see her as its leader.[21] And, of course, it has given rise to the tantalising mystery of Mary Magdalen's precise relationship to Christ himself, which has been a source of fascination from the very beginning of the Christian era. But the texts themselves yield nothing more than the barest of bones; every interpretation which has accumulated around her reflects only the imagination of subsequent writers and their own historical context. From the gospels, however, we can at least deduce her importance to the evangelists themselves, and therefore to the small Christian community in the century following their leader's death. It is a prominence more readily attributable to the unequivocally significant part she played as a devoted disciple in the Easter events and as first witness to the resurrection than to the faith and the service she rendered Christ in his lifetime, or to her importance, whatever that might be, within the group of women. That said, judging from the way she is introduced by name first, she seems to have been the most important woman follower, but the fact that the women only appear at the *end* of all the gospel narratives – except Luke's – at the crucifixion and after the burial, would suggest that their relevance and importance, and particularly that of Mary Magdalen herself, is as witnesses, believed or not, to the resurrection, the central tenet of Christianity.

One of the most striking aspects about the gospel accounts is the role given to Christ's female followers as supporters and witnesses during the events of that first Easter. Their faith and tenacity were acknowledged by early Christian commentators, but later cast into the background as new emphases and interpretations increasingly reduced their importance. The true significance of their witness was for the most part ignored, while Mary Magdalen herself was in the late sixth century recreated as an entirely different character to serve the purposes of the ecclesiastical hierarchy. This refashioning by the early Church Fathers has distorted our view of Mary Magdalen and the other women; we need therefore to turn again to the gospels in order to see them more clearly.

Mark tells us that Mary Magdalen was among the women who when Christ was in Galilee 'followed him and *ministered* unto him' (my italics; 15:41; see also Matt. 27:55). 'To minister' is translated from the Greek verb *diakonein*, to serve or to minister. It is also the root of the word 'deacon', which establishes the important function given to the women within the group of both female and male disciples.[22] Luke, from whom we also hear that the group has been part of Christ's entourage for some considerable time before the crucifixion (8:1–4), corroborates their ministering role, and amplifies it with the words 'of their own substance' (v.3). This role has often been assumed to have been domestic, as women's lives in Jewish society of the first century AD were circumscribed within their traditional household environment. They carried out such tasks as grinding flour, baking and laundering, feeding children, bed-making and wool-working.[23] Until modern times the role of the women amongst Christ's followers has also been taken to have been merely domestic, and therefore less important, an assumption which has only recently been questioned by scholars. But 'of their own substance' indicates that the women contributed the means to enable the travelling preachers to carry out their work. Whilst women are known to have supported rabbis with money, possessions and food, their participation in the practice of Judaism was negligible.[24] Although they were allowed to read the Torah at congregational services, they were forbidden to recite lessons in public in order to 'safeguard the honor of the congregation'.[25] In the first century AD, one Rabbi Eliezer was quoted as saying, 'Rather should the words of the Torah be burned than entrusted to a woman!'[26] It was for much the same reason that in the synagogue itself, women were seated apart from the men. They were restricted to a gallery above, unable to wear the phylactery – the small leather box containing verses from the Old Testament attached to the head and arm by leather thongs – or to carry out any liturgical functions. Their exclusion from the priesthood was based on their supposed uncleanness during menstruation, as defined in a Temple ordinance (Leviticus 15), a taboo which was also invoked by the Christian Church and still used until recently as a powerful weapon against the entry of women into ecclesiastical office. A priest, according to Leviticus 21 and 22, was to be clean and holy at all times to offer sacrifice.[27] Women were, nonetheless, allowed to be prophetesses, as the Old Testament bears witness, and even, as in the case of Anna, daughter of Phanuel, celebrated as such in Christ's day (Luke 2:36–8).

It is in this context that Luke's phrase has a special significance, as it suggests that Christ's women followers were central to the group as a whole, in that they donated their own property and income to provide Christ and the male disciples with the means to live as they travelled around the countryside preaching and healing. This, in turn, sheds further light on the women, since their ability to dispose of their money presupposes their financial independence, and possibly their maturity, which is corroborated by the statement that one of the Marys is the 'mother of James', presumably referring to the apostle (Mark 15:40 and 16:1). Even more important is the recent suggestion that, contrary to a general assumption that the women disciples did not preach, and in this way differed from their male counterparts, they may well have done so, since the term 'to follow' as used by Mark to describe those at the crucifixion – 'who also when he was in Galilee followed him, and ministered unto him' (15: 41) – was used technically to imply their full participation, both in belief and in the activities of the travelling preachers, as is borne out by the accounts in Acts and in Paul's letters of the women's involvement.[28] Nowhere in the texts is there any indication that Christ regarded the women's contribution as inferior or subsidiary to that of his male disciples. Indeed, it could be argued that the women's contribution both during and after the crucifixion showed greater tenacity of purpose and courage, though not necessarily greater faith, than that of the men who fled. Unlike the eleven male disciples who feared for their own lives, the women disciples followed, were present at the crucifixion, witnessed the burial, discovered the empty tomb and, as true disciples, were rewarded with the first news of the resurrection and, in the case of Mary Magdalen, the first meeting with the risen Christ.

Christ's disinterest in the conventions of his day, and his desire to radically alter certain social *mores*, are made manifest in his treatment of women, not least because they actually formed part of his retinue. Although women might assist rabbis financially, it was certainly uncommon for them to accompany preachers as travelling disciples.[29] Christ also welcomed into the group the kind of women whom Luke describes as having been healed of 'evil spirits and infirmities' (8:2–3), those who might otherwise have been regarded as social outcasts. Of the few women in the community who are named, one, Joanna, is or has been married to Chuza, Herod's steward, and must therefore have left her family and the royal court to follow Christ. It perhaps should be noted that the reference to Joanna's social status, as a married woman, has the effect of further determining that of Mary Magdalen: of the women described, she alone stands out undefined by a designation attaching her to some male as wife, mother or daughter; and she is the only one to be identified by her place of birth. It is therefore as an *independent* woman that she is presented: this implies that she must also have been of some means, to have been able to choose to follow and support Christ.

From the gospel accounts it would appear that the women formed a heterogeneous group, some of whom in conventional Jewish terms might also have been seen as marginalised. That social status and other socio-religious considerations are unimportant to Christ is shown by his rejection of the traditional Jewish ideas about taboo and impurity found in the Old Testament, as in the case of the woman with an issue of blood (Matt. 9:20–2; Luke 8:43–8), whom he cures of her physical ailment, thereby denying any connotation of uncleanness. In the story, she comes from behind him in a crowd to touch the hem of his garment so that she may be healed of the complaint she has had for twelve years, and upon which she has spent all her money. When Christ asks who has touched him, she tremblingly admits to it, giving her reason, and the result, her immediate cure; he tells her to go in peace as her faith has made her whole (Matt. 9:22; Luke 8:48). She is cured by touching him and believing, whereas in Jewish society of the time she would normally have been considered as having polluted the person she touched.[30]

Mary Magdalen's 'seven devils' to which both Luke and Mark refer were a focus for speculation amongst early Christian commentators; their link with the 'evil spirits and infirmities' ascribed to some of the women may well have led to their identification with the seven deadly sins. It has been suggested that Mary Magdalen was the best known of the women because her 'healing was the most dramatic', as the seven demons may have indicated a 'possession of extraordinary malignity'.[31] However, nowhere in the New Testament is demoniacal possession regarded as synonymous with sin.[32] That Mary Magdalen's condition might have been psychological, that is, seen as madness, rather than moral or sexual, seems never to have entered into the considerations of the early biblical commentators, although it preoccupied her interpreters from the nineteenth century onwards. There is, after all, no implication in the story of the *man* possessed of devils that his 'unclean spirit' is sexual (Luke 8:26–39), nor in that of the demoniacs whose 'devils' went into the swine which 'ran violently down a steep place into the sea' (Matt. 8:28–34). Nor, indeed, in the story of the daughter of the Syro-Phoenician woman who was cured of her unclean spirit (Matt. 15:21–8). Mrs Balfour, the noted nineteenth-century Evangelical, was one of the first to deny that Mary Magdalen's malaise was anything other than psychological, and more recently one scholar has written that rather than being in a state of sinfulness, she probably suffered from a 'violent and chronic nervous disorder'.[33]

To the ascription to her of the ambiguous 'seven devils' was added the putative disadvantage of her birthplace: Mary Magdalen's second name, *Magdalini* in Greek, signified her belonging to el Mejdel, a prosperous fishing village on the north-west bank of the lake of Galilee, four miles north of Tiberias. Its apparent notoriety in the early centuries of Christianity – it was destroyed in AD 75 because of its infamy and the licentious behaviour of its inhabitants – may have helped later to colour the name and reputation of Mary Magdalen herself.[34] (Today, a rusting sign by the lake tells the passing tourist that Magdala, or Migdal, had been a flourishing city at the end of the period of the Second Temple, and was also the birthplace of Mary of Magdala who 'followed and ministered to Jesus'.[35])

It might be argued that none of the elements detailed above offers sufficient grounds in itself for proving that Mary Magdalen was a sinner or prostitute. Indeed, these assertions might never have achieved currency – at least not to the extent they did – had she not also been confused with other female characters from the gospels, some of whom are explicitly described as sinners; and one who, from her story, appears to have been a prostitute. To later commentators, and in an ecclesiastical environment which was becoming more entrenched in its attachment to the ideal of celibacy, her femaleness would only have served to lend credence to this misidentification. By such means could the seven devils with which she was possessed assume the social and moral stigma, and the monstrous proportions, of lust and temptation – those vices which early interpreters of Genesis traditionally associated with the Female – that they did. Mary Magdalen, chief female disciple, first apostle and beloved friend of Christ, would become transformed into a penitent whore.

*　　　*　　　*

Mary Magdalen was, from the earliest centuries of Christianity, closely linked to and ultimately conflated with two other New Testament figures – a woman described by Luke as a 'sinner', and Mary of Bethany, who appears in Luke's gospel and in John's account of the Passion. To a lesser extent, she was also associated with the woman from Samaria (John 4:6–42), and the woman taken in adultery (John 8:3–11). Her identification with Luke's 'sinner' and Mary of Bethany was so pervasive that for the greater part of the Christian era the persona created for her by exegetes has overshadowed her biblical role as disciple of Christ and herald of the 'New Life'. Confusion about the identity of these women dates from at least the third century, but it was not until the end of the sixth century that Pope Gregory the Great (c. 540–604) was to settle the question by declaring that Mary Magdalen, Mary of Bethany and the sinner in Luke were one and the same. A close examination of these figures will show clearly their very different individual character traits, their actions and their significance, and that, in the case of Luke's sinner and of Mary of Bethany, their only point of convergence with Mary Magdalen is in their association with anointing Christ. How and why the process of conflation took place will be examined in more detail in Chapter Three, but it is necessary to establish the different identities as they appear in the gospels so that they can be recognised when they are subsumed into that of Mary Magdalen.

At the end of Chapter 7, just before Luke introduces Mary Magdalen by name for the first time as a follower of Christ in Chapter 8, he describes the episode where a woman 'which was a sinner' (v. 37) comes to seek forgiveness from Christ. The evangelist's marvellous story-telling powers vividly dramatise the events which take place in the town of Nain early in Christ's ministry, a scene which has provided us with one of the most enduring images of the mythical Magdalen (see Plate 1):

> And one of the Pharisees desired him that he would eat with him. And he went into the Pharisee's house, and sat down to meat. And, behold, a woman in the city, which was a sinner, when she knew that Jesus sat at meat in the Pharisee's house, brought an alabaster box of ointment, And stood at his feet behind him weeping, and began to wash his feet with tears, and did wipe them with the hairs of her head, and kissed his feet, and anointed them with the ointment. Now when the Pharisee which had bidden him saw

it, he spake within himself, saying, this man, if he were a prophet, would have known who and what manner of woman this is that toucheth him: for she is a sinner (7:36–9).

To the modern reader, the geography of the events may seem a little strange: the unnamed woman has entered the house, and appears to be behind Christ's feet and therefore not in his vision, but within the Pharisee's. The Greek, however, reads that on 'entering into the house of the Pharisee, [Christ] reclined', a description which suggests that the household adopted the Graeco-Roman fashion of banqueting, where sandals were left at the door, and where the host and his guests lay on couches to eat.[36] The woman would have been able to enter freely as Jewish houses were open; that the Pharisee, named Simon, does not seem surprised by her presence may have been due to the fact that it was not unusual for poor people to enter the houses of rich men in order to beg.[37] When the woman comes in, Christ's back is turned towards her, preventing him from witnessing her arrival. Until the sixteenth century, depictions of the scene almost always showed Christ, the Pharisee and other guests seated in the traditional European fashion,

1 Luke's sinner at Christ's feet in the House of Simon the Pharisee. From the Gospel Book of Henry the Lion of c.1180. Wolfenbüttel, Herzog August Bibliothek.

deriving from the Latin text which described them as '[sitting] down to meat'. In such images, Christ appears to ignore the woman's action, whilst she grovels at his feet. In 1648, Nicolas Poussin painted the scene to illustrate the theme of the Sacrament of Penance, in his series of paintings of the *Seven Sacraments* made for the sieur de Chantelou, perfectly portraying the *triclinium* as it appeared in the original Greek of Luke's gospel, where the sinner rushes in behind Christ to pour ointment on his feet, in her act of homage and supplication.[38] It is, as we shall see, the act of anointing which opened the way to the confusion about the figures which were conflated to create the image of Mary Magdalen.

The Pharisee's words imply that the woman is notorious as a 'sinner' in the city, and he consequently assumes that Christ too will be aware of her 'evil ways and reputation'.[39] The Greek word for 'sinner', *hamartolos*, used here in Luke 7, has various connotations in the New Testament: in a Jewish context, it could be applied to someone who had forfeited his or her proper relationship with God by disobeying the Law; it could also refer to anyone who lived an immoral life, such as a murderer or thief, or who followed a dishonourable profession.[40] Although the Greek word for a harlot, *porin*, which appears elsewhere in Luke (15:30), is not used in this account, the emphasis given to Luke's phrase 'a sinner in the city', and the word 'sinner' used by the Pharisee, both seem to indicate the latter's conviction that the woman's 'sin' is sexual, that she is a prostitute. That the woman apparently wears her hair loose is another sign of her fallen status, as only prostitutes wore their hair thus in public. Loosening the hair was also one way of disgracing a suspected adulteress;[41] a good Jewess allowed none but her spouse to see her hair unbound, and by loosing it in public she gave grounds for mandatory divorce.[42] No reference is made to the woman's marital position, but it seems unlikely that she was an adulteress as, had she been so, she would doubtless have been punished by stoning in accordance with Mosaic law.[43] At all events, it has always been assumed that the sins of the 'sinner in the city' were those of her sexuality, and as such she was to provide the Church with a useful paradigm.

The woman has come to ask for forgiveness for the sins of her past life; in verse 37 Luke makes it quite clear that he wishes his audience to know that her purpose is to anoint Christ with an expensive ointment which she carries in an alabaster box, an *alabastron*. She weeps on his feet, drying them with her hair as a sign of repentance, and in doing so clearly violates rabbinic codes of seemly behaviour. In kissing Christ's feet, she also breaks the laws of clean and unclean: defiled by her trade and therefore ritually impure, her touch would pollute others. Christ's acquiescence in the woman's dramatic behaviour proves to the Pharisee what he wishes to know – his guest is not a prophet, otherwise he would have known of her unclean state and would never have allowed such a creature to touch him. Christ then tells him a parable about a creditor and his two debtors, one of whom owes him a large sum and the other a lesser sum, and whom he releases from their obligations. Which debtor, he asks Simon, 'will love him the most?' The Pharisee has to confess reluctantly that the one who is forgiven most will be the one who loves most. Christ then curtly criticises his host for failing to carry out the normal rituals of hospitality towards his guest, those of washing his feet, kissing him in greeting, and anointing him with precious oil, all of which the woman has done, although as acts of intense humility and gratitude rather than as matters of convention.

The parable is intended to illustrate to the Pharisee the way in which Christ himself regards the woman: she is the debtor who owes more, and naturally loves more. Christ accepts the touch of the sinner, and implies that her action is more welcome to him than his host's. Although Simon's attitude is, according to Pharisaic law, correct, the sinner, 'whose sins are indeed many', is forgiven because she loves much, and out of gratitude. The Pharisee, by adhering to the Law strictly, and showing less gratitude and love towards Christ, is compared to his detriment with someone whom he had himself considered a social pariah. Christ tells her that her many sins are forgiven, for she has loved much: a phrase which has often been taken to refer to her sexual past, and not, as Christ's words indicate, to her love for him and to her faith, which are what save her.[44] He then tells her to go in peace (v. 50).

Because of the beautiful, edifying story of the unnamed sinner, the most pervasive image we have of Mary Magdalen is one of a weeping woman with long loose hair, holding an ointment jar. It may have been because the sinner rushed into the Pharisee's house with her *alabastron* to ask forgiveness for her sins and to anoint Christ in gratitude that she was associated with the female disciple who had seven devils cast from her, and who went to anoint Christ in his death. That the second woman, Mary Magdalen, is first described by Luke immediately after the scene in the Pharisee's house may have given rise to the idea that they were one and the same woman, and the fact that she was also numbered amongst the women 'healed of evil spirits and infirmities' could have reinforced her identification with a sinner, despite the fact that possession by evil spirits is nowhere else equated with sin. It is because Mary Magdalen went to anoint Christ that she is also associated, as we shall see, with Mary of Bethany.

The gospels tell us that Christ had two friends called Mary and Martha (Luke 10:38–42; John 11:1). In Luke's brief story, Christ, wearied by his journeys, enters an unnamed village where 'a certain woman named Martha received him into her house. And she had a sister called Mary, which also sat at Jesus' feet, and heard his word' (vv. 38–9). The setting is domestic, clearly a place Christ has visited before on his travels; and it would appear, since she receives Christ 'into her house', that Martha is the elder sister. She fusses around fulfilling her role as hostess, and is quite understandably incensed when Mary does not help her. According to Jewish custom, a woman's role was to serve: it is therefore the younger sister's duty to assist.[45] Martha appeals to their guest, asking him to reprimand Mary, but he calms her, at the same time as defending her sister, 'Martha, Martha, thou art careful and troubled about many things.' He reminds her that although her own hospitable actions are important, Mary's apparent inaction, her choice of 'that good part', as he describes it, is equally necessary. By this he means that in performing the role of a disciple who listens and learns, Mary has come to understand, and as such is a model for his audience. (The story of Mary and Martha of Bethany was often quoted in medieval sermons as an edifying example to noisy, and particularly female, congregations.) Martha too has her good side, for she and Mary may well have come from the kind of background where servants were employed, and in assuming that role, in preparing a meal for their visitor, she has done it out of love and a desire to serve. In using the metaphor of a disciple sitting at a master's feet, Luke does not necessarily imply that Mary was physically sitting by Christ's feet, but may simply be stating that she is already a disciple. He establishes the fact that Mary has understood Christ's words, and is therefore a follower, something – 'the one thing needful' – which Martha should try to understand and emulate.[46]

The episode of Mary and Martha leads us to John 11:1–45, where we have the climactic story of the raising of Lazarus, the event which precipitates the Passion and death of Christ. For with the miracle of Lazarus' return from the dead, the Pharisees and chief priests know that they can no longer allow Christ to continue his work without his threatening their own authority and their relations with the Roman officials. In this chapter, we hear that a 'certain man was sick, named Lazarus, of Bethany, the town of Mary and her sister Martha', and that 'Jesus loved Martha, and her sister, and Lazarus' (v. 5). Mary and Martha are the central characters, Lazarus' grieving sisters, who send for Christ when their brother is sick. On hearing of his friend's illness, Christ, seemingly inexplicably, tarries for a further two days, so that by the time he arrives, he finds that Lazarus has already been dead for four days. Martha, who again seems to be the elder sister, goes out to meet him on his arrival, and to reproach him for not having come sooner. In the ensuing conversation, she confesses to her belief in the resurrection of the dead, and also in him as Jesus Christ, the son of God, the Messiah. Mary, meanwhile, has remained quietly in the house, presumably because of her great sorrow. Christ sends Martha in to request her presence. When Mary comes out, she too falls at his feet, weeping, reproaching him for allowing their brother to die. On seeing Mary, and the Jews about her who have come to comfort the bereaved sisters, weep, Christ joins in their grief. He then performs the miracle, bidding Lazarus to come forth from the grave, saying to Martha, 'Said I not unto thee, that, if thou wouldest believe, thou shouldest see the glory of God?' (see Plate 2). This miracle ensures Christ's death: some of the Jews present go to the Pharisees who, fearing the loss of their nation and their importance, decide that Christ's death is the only way to maintain their authority.

Ambiguities abound in these two stories, not least in the relationship between the two sets of sisters with their identical names. In neither account do they appear to be members of Christ's immediate entourage, but a close relationship seems to exist already, as is evident from both accounts, the major difference being that in John the sisters have a brother called Lazarus. (The Lazarus in Luke [16:20–31] is quite another character.) John's strange emphasis in his description, that 'Jesus loved Martha, and her sister, and Lazarus', has been seen to imply that the relationship between the sisters and Christ was closer than that between Christ and Lazarus, or that they were somehow more important in the

2 The Raising of Lazarus. From the Codex Egberti (*c*.990), named after Egbert, archbishop of Trier between 977 and 993. Trier, Stadtbibliothek.

eyes of the evangelist. A further dissimilarity, and one which is quite telling, exists between the two Marys – in Luke's story she is already a disciple, but according to John she clearly has doubts in her faith. In Luke's story, it is Mary who has the more important role as believer, but in John, it is Martha, as the recipient of dogma. In spite of these differences, the coincidence of the names has allowed the accounts to be regarded as different episodes in the same women's lives, so that the Mary who sits at Christ's feet has always been known as Mary of Bethany. Early in the third century, Origen (*c*.185–254), the great biblical scholar and theologian, was to identify Martha and her sister Mary as the active and contemplative forms of the religious life on the basis

of Luke's account. Through the accretion of Luke's Mary to Mary
Magdalen by way, as we shall see, of Mary of Bethany, the Magdalen
would become the symbol of the contemplative life and be regarded as
such throughout the Middle Ages and again, with further emphasis, in
the seventeenth century. To the early Christians, the story of the raising
of Lazarus – like the Old Testament story of Jonah[47] – prefigured and
represented Christ's own death and resurrection, with the result that it
was depicted frequently from the earliest years of Christianity. Forty
paintings of the scene survive in the catacombs alone,[48] and in later
images the shrouded figure of Lazarus appears, being bidden from the
grave, watched in astonishment by onlookers holding their noses against
the terrible stench of death, and with Mary of Bethany and her sister
often kneeling at Christ's feet. With the conflation of Mary of Bethany
and Mary Magdalen, the episode of Lazarus' resurrection was to be
included in the medieval and later legends of Mary Magdalen's life, and
became part of the extensive imagery which built up around her.

John may have known Luke's story of the unknown sinner, and have
applied it to Mary of Bethany for, at the beginning of the Lazarus
episode, he tells us very clearly, apparently anticipating his account of
the event in his next chapter, that 'It was *that* Mary which anointed the
Lord with ointment, and wiped his feet with her hair, whose brother
Lazarus was sick' (11:2). It has also been suggested that the relevant
chapters in John have been transposed, and that John is referring to the
Mary of his own story.[49]
   Either way, his account compounds the confusion about the various
women, and has helped the composite Magdalen on her way. The
anointing takes place in John 12:1–8, in the house of Mary and Martha
at Bethany, six days before the Passover, where 'they made him a
supper', and the resuscitated Lazarus 'was one of them that sat at the
table with him' (v.2). Again Martha serves, but in this case does not
complain, assuming the role of servant as an act of thanksgiving and
love. Then Mary takes a 'pound of ointment of spikenard, very costly',
and anoints Christ's feet, and wipes them with her hair: 'and the house
was filled with the odour of the ointment' (v.3) (see Plate 3). This
scented imagery, when applied to Mary Magdalen in later allegorical
commentaries, contributed to the aura of femininity and eroticism
which was to envelop her.
   Among the disciples is Judas Iscariot, later to betray Christ to the

chief priests, who criticises Mary for wasting the ointment rather than selling it for 'three hundred pence' which could have been given to the poor. John, far from seeing this as evidence of Judas' charitable ideals, regards this episode – the loss to Judas of three hundred pence – as the reason why he sells Christ to the Jews. Here, Mary as anointer may also take on the role of servant: her act, performed in homage (as in Christ's washing of the feet at the Last Supper, anointing the feet was symbolic for anointing the whole body[50]), is perhaps also performed in thanksgiving for the restoration of her brother's life, and even as an apology for her lack of faith at the moment of his death.[51] Mary not only anoints Christ's feet but also, in common only with the sinner in Luke 7, wipes them with her hair. This action may also be related to the custom of masters wiping or drying their hands on the heads or hair of their servants, which again implies that Mary has adopted the role of servant.[52] Christ then replies, 'Let her alone: against the day of my burying hath she kept this' (v.7), thus establishing Mary of Bethany's prophetic and prescient role: in anointing him in his lifetime, she witnesses her knowledge of his death and resurrection. She is, moreover, the only disciple to know of Christ's soteriological, or redemptive, death before it takes place.[53]

Pouring balm has an important role in the gospels and since it is performed by women on each occasion, it has led to the theory that the same woman carries out the ritual. Echoes of the proleptic anointing for Christ's burial are to be found in two further episodes, in Mark 14:3–9 and Matthew 26:6–13. Both take place two days before the feast of the Passover, at the height of the machinations of the chief priests and scribes in their attempt to trap Christ. In both accounts Christ is in Bethany, in the house of Simon the Leper, and the woman who anoints him is unnamed. Matthew 26 records: 'There came unto him a woman having an alabaster box of very precious ointment, and poured it on his head, as he sat at meat.' The costliness of the balm is echoed in the 'spikenard very precious' of Mark 14:3, and in Mary of Bethany's 'very costly' 'pound of ointment of spikenard' in John 12. The disciples criticise the woman, and again, as in the case of Mary of Bethany, Christ defends her action, pointing to the fact that she has done it in anticipation of his death. In anointing Christ's head, the woman, in both Mark and Matthew, acknowledges and celebrates Christ's royal and priestly nature. (According to both evangelists, this incident acts as a catalyst for Judas to seek out the chief priests, offering to deliver Christ up to

3 Mary, sister of Lazarus, wipes Christ's feet with her hair while Judas criticises her. From the Codex Egberti (c.990). Trier, Stadtbibliothek.

them in return for money.) These anointings, helped by the fact that three took place in the houses of men called Simon (Luke 7:36–50; Mark 14:3–9; Matt. 26:6–13), were to be the principle by which later exegetes, commenting on the various characters who appeared in the New Testament, were to conflate the women into a single figure (see Chapter Three). Whether there was one anointing or two, and whether it was carried out by one woman or different women, is a problem which has teased, and still teases, the imaginations of scholars and commentators; the theory of two anointings by one woman, later identified as Mary of Magdala, sister of Martha and Lazarus, was called by exegetes the theory of unity; its antithesis, the theory of plurality, claimed that two, if not three, different women anointed Christ, and distinguished Mary Magdalen from Mary of Bethany, Luke's sinner and the anointings in Bethany. From the time of Gregory the Great until 1969, when changes were made to the Roman calendar, the western Church tended to treat the three as one, celebrating them as Mary Magdalen on 22 July. This despite the fact that in the sixteenth century Jacques Lefèvre d'Etaples ruffled the until-then untroubled waters of consensus by daring to suggest that Mary Magdalen was a separate character from Mary of Bethany and Luke's sinner, and was duly excommunicated for his pains.[54] The eastern Church, however, followed St John Chrysostom in distinguishing the two different Marys of Bethany and Magdala, and Luke's sinner, and celebrates their feasts on separate days.[55]

The purposes of the women's anointing of Christ are as various as their characters: Luke's sinner anoints Christ out of gratitude and love; Mary of Bethany out of homage and foreknowledge of his death (and possible thanks for Lazarus' return to life), as do the unnamed women of Matthew 26 and Mark 14; and Mary Magdalen goes to seek Christ in order to embalm him after his death. Mary Magdalen's role as an active, courageous follower of Christ differentiates her from Luke's sinner, whose dramatic act is inconsistent with the gospel character of Mary Magdalen. Although Mary of Bethany is also a disciple, she symbolises the essentially contemplative aspect of the spiritual life and, as the sister of Lazarus, has a mystical premonition of Christ's death, whereas the Magdalen mourns the dead Christ, and seeks 'the living among the dead' in order to anoint him. To the extent that Mary Magdalen was subsequently identified with these figures, she also inherited their characteristics in her composite form, so that through the centuries she was to become the symbol of the contemplative life and model of repentance, while the significance of her actual role in the New Testament as disciple and primary witness to the resurrection receded into the background.

The links between Mary Magdalen and both the woman of Samaria and the woman taken in adultery are even more tenuous than those between the Magdalen and Luke's sinner and Mary of Bethany. They owe their origins, however, to the conflated creature which Mary of Magdala became from the sixth century on – the repentant whore. For both the Samaritan woman and the adulteress epitomise aspects of the female sexuality which the rabbis and, as we shall see, the early Church Fathers so feared and despised.[56]

In John 4, Christ, wearied with his travels, rests by a well in Samaria (see Plate 4). There he asks a woman drawing water for something to drink. His request surprises her since 'the Jews have no dealings with the Samaritans' (v.9).[57] Then Christ speaks to her about the healing waters of everlasting life, and the woman questions him, showing her receptivity to his teaching. The beautiful imagery of water often appears in the Bible, in both the Old and New Testaments, where wells and springs symbolise the life given by God, and in the New Testament symbolise the life given by divine Wisdom and by the Law, and also signify the spirit. Christ tells the woman to call her husband; she replies that she has none. He then says he knows of her five husbands, and that the man she is presently with is not her legal husband. She is astonished, and confesses her belief in the Messiah, and departs to tell her people in the city, wondering if the man she is speaking with is indeed the Christ (vv.16–29). The disciples who have been away buying food return, amazed to see their master talking with a woman, and one who is a foreigner. When she comes back, the woman is accompanied by many

4 Christ and the Samaritan Woman. From the Codex Egberti (c.990). Trier, Stadtbibliothek.

of the townspeople who through her agency have come to believe that
Christ is the Messiah they have been awaiting (v.42). In early Christian
commentaries on the story, the woman of Samaria was to be regarded
as the first apostle to the Gentiles for her role in bringing truth to the
unconverted.[58] The story also illustrates Christ's radical views concerning women: not only was the woman not a Jew, but her social status,
living with a man out of wedlock, meant that in Jewish eyes she was
unclean. As with Luke's sinner, Christ makes no judgement on her
moral position, and this, together with the fact that Jewish men and, in
particular, rabbis were not allowed to speak with women in public
places, demonstrates not only his acceptance of women, of all kinds,
but also that he considered women equal with men, regardless of their
race or creed.[59] And once again, as in the case of the Lazarus episode,
he has used a woman as a vehicle in discussing a tenet of faith; indeed
it is to her that he reveals himself as the Messiah for the first time (in
John's gospel), 'I that speak unto thee am [the Messiah]' (v.26). Despite
her very different role, the woman of Samaria has been confused with
Mary Magdalen, solely on the basis of her own admitted sexual sins,
and those imputed to Mary Magdalen, an association which appears in
some medieval texts, and is still to be found today.

In John 8:3, the scribes and Pharisees bring a woman before Christ
whilst he is teaching in the temple.[60] Apparently caught in the act of
committing adultery, she is to be stoned to death, the punishment meted
out under Mosaic law to adulterous married women. Eager to trap
Christ into denying the teachings of the Torah, or Law, the scribes and
Pharisees challenge him, asking whether he regards stoning as the correct penalty for such a crime. Christ's response is to bend down and
write something in the sand, implying that he wishes to dissociate himself from the situation (see Plate 5). The Jews persist, and he finally
replies: 'He that is without sin among you, let him first cast a stone at
her' – by which he neither contradicts Mosaic law nor encroaches upon
Roman law. Here again, he passes no judgement on the woman, but
rather questions the motives of her accusers. The Jews, understanding
his meaning, and 'being convicted by their own conscience', go away,
leaving Christ alone with the woman. On his questioning her, she tells
him that no-one has condemned her (v.11), and his reply is that neither
does he, and that she should 'go and sin no more'. What the episode
most sharply brings into focus are the motives of the Jews and the

5 Christ and the Adulteress. From the Codex Egberti (*c*.990). Trier, Stadtbibliothek.

witnesses, rather than the woman's adultery *per se*. Christ himself does not stand in judgement on the woman; instead, he rejects her accusers' methods as being hypocritical and discriminatory in a social context where a woman's seduction, or sexual sin, was regarded as far more heinous than a man's lust. The woman's association with Mary Magdalen, remote though it is, centres on the fallenness of the mythical Magdalen and their sistership in sexual crime.

Mary Magdalen stands out from among the group of women in the gospel texts for her role at Easter. This has been noted in recent studies about the origins of the early Church, and in particular those concerning the position of women within it, which have led to a re-evaluation of their roles and functions. Until quite recently, these women followers have often been relegated to the status of mere hangers-on and helpers at a subsidiary level, even though, as we have seen, Christ is shown throughout his ministry as positive and egalitarian in his attitude towards women, in having them as friends and followers, talking with them freely, making them recipients of what was later to become Christian dogma, and assigning them roles in parables and stories. His attitude towards women constitutes, as one commentator has observed, 'a highly original and significant feature of his life and teaching'.[61] Just how radical his approach was can be evinced from the gospels themselves, in the reactions of the Pharisees, and of the male disciples who 'wondered among themselves' when they saw Christ talking to the foreigner and social outcast, the woman of Samaria. That he was open to all comers is manifest in the ragged assortment of followers which gathered around him, and included sinners and publicans, prostitutes, and the sick and poor, all marginalised in one way or another by society. Christ accepted all of these, while simultaneously rejecting those stereotypes in which women were treated as scapegoats for the ills of society. His approach is epitomised in his debate with the chief priests and elders in the temple where reference is made once more to that most degraded and despised of creatures, the prostitute, who, together with the tax collector, another ignoble, will, through repentance, enter into heaven before the righteous (Matt. 21:23, 31–2). (The phrase 'Jesus saith unto them, Verily I say unto you, that the publicans and the harlots go into the kingdom of God before you' (v.31) was constantly quoted by medieval preachers to precede sermons and homilies about Mary Magdalen.) He also criticises the conventional idea of women as temptresses, shifting the blame onto the beholder, rather than onto the object beheld, as in his sermon on the mount (Matt. 5:28) where, contrary to rabbinical sources which warned men against women's blandishments, he states clearly that anyone looking lustfully on a woman has already committed adultery with her in his heart. Christ's overturning of conventional Jewish and Hellenistic values, at least within his own group of followers, was to be reversed within only a few generations of his death, while the rabbinical prejudices concerning the nature and role of women were absorbed into Christian thinking, and have lasted into the twentieth century.

The gospels show clearly that Christ regarded his women followers as disciples in their own right, capable of receiving unique revelation, and worthy of being valid witnesses of his death, burial and resurrection. Yet, at the same time, there are intimations in the narratives that a more conventional view will prevail. Although Mary Magdalen is mentioned in the four canonical gospels as the primary witness to the resurrection, and, in John's gospel, is sent by Christ to tell the disciples what she has seen, thereby becoming the first apostle, this crucial role is already diminished in Luke by the emphasis he places on his account of the women's witness: the women 'told these things unto the eleven, and all the rest . . . And their words seemed to them as idle tales, and they believed them not' (24:9–11). In fact, Peter is prompted to look for himself, possibly through curiosity, and possibly because of conventional Jewish male prejudice against the women's witness (v. 12). Luke's gospel ends in a climax which totally eclipses the women's testimony: here Christ appears to Peter (v. 34), and the evangelist entirely excludes any reference to his appearance to the female disciples; instead he lays emphasis on the final appearance of Christ to the 'eleven' (vv. 36–53). And in the first account of Christ's appearances after the resurrection to be written, in Paul's first epistle to the Corinthians, Chapter 15:5–8, Mary Magdalen's meeting with him in the garden is entirely omitted.[62]

When the gospel Mary Magdalen is distinguished from the other New Testament figures who have over the centuries coloured her persona, it is possible to recognise the extraordinary role which was assigned to her and to the other women disciples during the Paschal events. Yet her disappearance and transformation remain to be explained. There is still the question of why it was to her that Christ appeared after his resurrection, and why, if a fundamental part of Christian *kerygma* (Greek, preaching) is based on the witness of Mary Magdalen and the other women, its importance and meaning has been played down in the Christian tradition. Perhaps more interesting still is that, for almost fourteen hundred years, she has primarily been represented as a repentant whore. Finally, there is the question of why the New Testament tradition of the women as disciples is maintained and emphasised in apocryphal texts from the late first century onwards, all but a few of which have vanished, and which have been regarded by the Church as heretical.

The few New Testament references to Mary Magdalen yield a character both enigmatic and powerful; the limited biographical evidence with which we are presented creates a tangible personality and yet, at the same time, allows of interpretation. Her role at Easter and her closeness to Christ in John's gospel are tantalising but obscure elements which beg further exploration. Her very mysteriousness has inspired elaborate legends, which have taken her to places such as Rome and Ephesus, and to a hermit-like existence in the south of France. Her metamorphosis into a composite character who represents womankind in the Christian tradition takes us beyond the gospel figure, and is the subject of this book.

CHAPTER II

COMPANION OF THE SAVIOUR

> There were three who always walked with the Lord: Mary
> his mother and her sister and Magdalene, the one who was
> called his companion.
>
> *Gospel of Philip*[1]

 IN DECEMBER 1945 some Arab *fellahin*, digging for soft soil with which to fertilise their crops in the desert near the town of Nag Hammadi (Chenoboskion) in Upper Egypt, unearthed an ancient jar hidden under a boulder. Fearful that a *djinn*, or evil spirit, might be lurking inside, they hesitated to break it open, but curiosity and the thought that it might also harbour gold persuaded one of them, Muhammad Ali al Samman, to smash the jar and reveal its contents. Inside were several papyrus books, some of which were later burned by Muhammad Ali's mother, others of which were lost and still others made their way onto the black market through dealers in antiquities in Cairo; and one came onto the American market to be bought eventually by the Jung Foundation in Zürich. Muhammad Ali had found a Coptic Gnostic library, which had been buried sometime around AD 400,[2] thirteen codices of which, containing fifty-two tractates, or treatises, still survive. After thirty years, they have been reassembled and are now housed in the Coptic Museum in Cairo. The proximity of the site of their discovery to the monastery at Pabau established by St Pachomius, the founder of Christian monasticism, offers the tantalising possibility of a link between the early Christian Church and the framework of disparate beliefs it came to regard in the second and third centuries as its most dangerous enemy – Gnosticism. On the walls of the now empty caves which had once housed the tombs of sixth-dynasty pharaohs (2350–2200 BC) are traces

of prayers, Coptic psalms and Christian crosses, painted by the hermits or monks who had subsequently inhabited them.[3] The manuscripts were hidden nearly sixteen hundred years ago, possibly because of their heretical nature during a period of persecution, or for safe-keeping by believers. The texts themselves are, in fact, copies, made in a monastery, of Greek originals, some of which, written as early as the second half of the first century, were contemporary with the gospels of the New Testament. Some of the writings are 'gospels' attributed to the apostles and disciples of Christ which purport to contain secret teachings revealed by him only to these chosen few, and concern the origins and disposition of the universe, the nature of sin and evil in the world, and the need for repentance – mysteries which will admit those who have such *gnosis* (Greek, knowledge) to heaven. Apart from revealing the varied and various beliefs which flourished contemporaneously with those which became orthodox Christianity, some of the documents are remarkable for their unique interpretations of the role of Mary Magdalen. Among the groups of disciples who appear in these Gnostic writings are characters who also appear in the New Testament, so that one quite naturally finds Peter, Thomas, Philip or James as revealers of Christ's mysteries; but, in an extraordinary contrast with the presentation of the community around Christ in the synoptics, and in subsequent interpretations, these groups incorporated women – such as Salome and Martha and, especially, Mary Magdalen – and do not appear to have differentiated sexually between their roles. In the Gnostic writings the women's importance is also stated, rather than merely hinted at as in the New Testament: they are disciples. It is a woman, Mary Magdalen, who has a major role in several of these writings, and is the only female figure from the New Testament to have one of these apocryphal texts, the *Gospel of Mary*, named for her. The Gnostic Mary Magdalen contrasts strongly, therefore, with the figure that emerges from conventional interpretations of the New Testament.

Gnosticism is the collective name given to a variety of religious teachings which both existed before and were very much alive during the early centuries of the Christian era, teachings which emphasised salvation through secret knowledge, or *gnosis*.[4] The name Gnosticism does not, in fact, refer to a particular group of believers, but rather to the various sects whose names derived from those of their founders, such as the Valentinians, Marcionites, or Basilideans; or, as in the case of the Phrygians, their place of origin; or, in that of the Ophites, from their worship of the snake (*ophis* in Greek).[5] Multifarious and eclectic as their ideas and beliefs were – 'Every day every one of them invents something new', the heresy-hunting bishop Irenaeus of Lyon (*c.*130–200) was to say scornfully[6] – the different Gnostic systems all shared a deep-seated conviction that the world – and the flesh and matter of which it was made – was irredeemably corrupt and controlled by evil forces; only the spirit was good. By the beginning of the third century, Gnostic belief and orthodox Christianity were so enmeshed that large Gnostic Christian sects flourished all over the Roman Empire.[7] The Gnostic desired to transcend all the evils of the world of humanity, and this he achieved through true knowledge, intelligible, and thus accessible, only to a select few, who were called 'spirituals'.[8] This *gnosis* was essentially mystical, concerning the nature of God and human existence, and the divine realm of being; it was revealed to initiates through secret writings and inner enlightenment. The Gnostics' claim to have a superior comprehension of God and of their own spiritual nature, together with their claim that this came to them through personal revelation, set them apart from the other Christians who accepted their beliefs through the mediation of bishops and clergy; for this reason, the orthodox Church regarded them with the utmost suspicion. They were heretics of the true faith.

How Gnosticism arose is still a matter of much debate, but modern scholars now tend to agree that its roots lie in late Hellenistic, particularly Platonic, philosophy, with elements which derive from Jewish, oriental and Christian beliefs.[9] Until the nineteenth century, Gnosticism itself and its adherents were only known from the reports written by their orthodox opponents, particularly Irenaeus, Tertullian (*c.*160–*c.*225), Origen (*c.*185–254), Hippolytus of Rome (*fl.*200) and Epiphanius (*c.*315–403), who, since they regarded the various Gnostic sects as heretical perversions and therefore as highly dangerous, were careful to describe them precisely, but with an inevitable bias, in order to refute their beliefs.[10] (The title of the first book of Irenaeus' treatise, 'On the Detection and Refutation of *gnosis* falsely so-called',[11] allows us to savour orthodox sentiments towards the creeds which threatened them.) After the victory of the orthodox Church in the fourth century, Gnosticism lay almost forgotten, except in the writings of its early detractors, for fifteen centuries. But elements of its dualistic precepts, above all in the equation of the spirit with good, and matter, or the flesh, with evil, are still present in Christian thinking today, traceable through early orthodox Christianity, and in the later ideals of western monasticism, which particularly affected the medieval concept of virginity, and culminating in the apotheosis of the Virgin Mary and the creation of the mythical Mary Magdalen.[12] It was not until the publication towards the end of the nineteenth century of two primary and authentic Gnostic texts, one from an archaeological excavation in Upper Egypt, the other from a late eighteenth-century collection in London, that the voice of the Gnostics themselves was heard once again. The first manuscript, now known as the Codex Brucianus, was discovered by the great Scots traveller James Bruce, in 1769, near Thebes, the modern Luxor, in Upper Egypt;[13] the second, the *Pistis Sophia*, in which Mary Magdalen appears, was sold in 1785 to the British Museum from the collection of the antiquary Dr Anthony Askew.[14] A further manuscript, which includes the *Gospel of Mary*, whose central 'character' is Mary Magdalen, was bought in Cairo in 1896.[15] The discovery and translation, by members of the Institute for Gnostic Studies, of the texts found at Nag Hammadi have revealed something of the richness and diversity of beliefs co-existing in the often unhappy alliance with early Christianity, at a time when the Christian sect was merely one group among many which hoped for salvation. And they have unveiled in Mary Magdalen a figure both ambiguous and sharply defined, whose importance in the early centuries of Christianity may only be hazarded at, but nevertheless should not be disregarded. For, as M. R. James (1862–1936), the biblical scholar, antiquary, palaeographer and ghost-story writer, wrote:

[even] if these writings are good neither as books of history, nor of religion, nor even as literature . . . they have a great and enduring interest . . . They record the imaginations, hopes, and fears of the men who wrote them; they show what was acceptable to the unlearned Christians of the first ages, what interested them, what they admired, what ideals of conduct they cherished for this life, what they thought they would find in the next . . . They have, indeed, exercised an influence (wholly disproportionate to their intrinsic merits) so great and so widespread, that no one who cares about the history of Christian thought and Christian art can possibly afford to neglect them.[16]

In the Gnostic cosmology, a huge and unbridgeable chasm divides heaven from the world of matter, and the opposites of light and dark are reflected in the concepts of a divine realm of light and a world or cosmos which is the realm of darkness. According to many Gnostic sects, God is neither creator nor governor of the world, from which he is separated by a vast abyss, and remains always alien and unknowable to man, unless man should become the recipient of supernatural revelation. To the Gnostic mind, the supreme being and God of love could never have created the universe of chaos and evil; it was something which could only have been caused by a lesser, imperfect, deity, to whom the name of Demiurge was given.[17] Man, by definition being imperfect, was also a creation of the Demiurge, and formed of flesh, soul and spirit; it was his ignorance and sin which had been responsible for the corruption of the world. (Somewhat confusingly, the soul is not seen by Gnostics as it is in modern times – as the divine element in man – but rather as the force which motivates and gives appetite to his body.) However, imprisoned within the soul of some 'elect' men was the divine spark, the *pneuma* or spirit, which itself was alien to the world of matter, and was capable of being saved. Salvation took place when the *pneuma* came to know the Supreme Being, and to understand itself, its divine origins and its ultimate destiny – reunion with the supreme deity in the realm of light. In many Gnostic writings, the Redeemer, or Saviour as he is often described, is sent by the Supreme God as an emissary to give *gnosis*, which is in itself redemption, to those capable of salvation. This feature, a central component in Gnostic myths, was derived from the orthodox Pauline argument that Christ had been sent by God the Father to save the world.

It is here that Mary Magdalen enters the Gnostic cosmos, as the 'mysterious figure called Mariam, of uncertain identity' described by one modern writer,[18] who is given unparalleled prominence in several of these apocryphal writings; in Greek this name is rendered as Mariamne or Mariamme, and in Coptic as Mariham. Although a categorical identification of this Mary is impossible, there is little doubt that this figure is Mary Magdalen herself.[19] In some texts she is specifically referred to by name: in the *Gospel of Philip*, Jesus calls her 'Mary Magdalene', and, in *Pistis Sophia*, he calls her 'Maria the Magdalene'. Elsewhere, in the *Gospel of Mary*, and in the *Dialogue of the Saviour* and the *Gospel of Thomas*, her prominent role as disciple, visionary, mediatrix and messenger of esoteric revelations continues and even transcends the implications inherent in Mark and John of the importance of her function in the gospels. In the *Gospel of Peter*, the earliest account of the Passion apart from those found in the synoptic gospels, she is also described as

a 'disciple [Greek, *mathētria*] of the Lord'.[20] In the Gnostic writings Mary
Magdalen is the subject of the most extraordinary apophthegms, all
inconceivable within the context of mainstream Christianity. It is also
interesting to note that there is no reference to her in the writings as a
sinner or a prostitute, which would suggest that this was a later tradition. She is Mariam, the 'woman who knew the All' who 'reveal[s]
the greatness of the revealer' in the *Dialogue of the Saviour*.[21] She is also
the chief interlocutrix of the Saviour, who brings *gnosis* to the other
disciples. In the *Pistis Sophia*, she is the 'one who is the inheritor of
Light' and, as revealer of the words of Pistis Sophia, becomes absorbed
into, or becomes an aspect of, the *Sophia* or Wisdom of God.[22] As chief
female disciple, the first witness and herald of the New Life, and thus
revealer of salvific knowledge in the New Testament, her role bears a
strong similarity to that of chief questioner, the 'privileged interlocutrix'
of the *Pistis Sophia*;[23] in the *Gospel of Philip*, she is the most important
of the three women 'who were always with the Lord', and the one who
'is called his companion'.[24] She has been described as the 'Saviour's
terrestrial companion, counterpart of the celestial Sophia'.[25] The Gnostic
writings echo and augment the hints about her in the New Testament,
and give us some idea of the importance in which she, as well as some
of the other women such as Martha, Salome and, to a lesser extent,
Mary the mother of Jesus, were held by at least some sections of the
early Christian community.

In the *Gospel of Mary*, written sometime during the second century,[26]
the risen Christ has been conversing with the disciples, encouraging
them to continue his work in preaching the kingdom of heaven. He
then departs, leaving the grieving disciples fearing for their lives, for if
the Gentiles have not spared their leader, how can they then expect to
escape death when they go out to preach? Mary then takes the initiative.
She consoles them, and tells them not to waver from their purpose as
Christ's spirit is still with them, protecting them, for, she says, 'he has
prepared us [and] made us into men'. From this point in the text, she
appears to be in charge of the disciples, her authority apparently deriving
from her closeness to Christ, a relationship which Peter acknowledges
when he says, 'Sister, we know that the Saviour loved you more than
the rest of the women.'[27] He then urges her to tell them of the Saviour's
words which she alone, and separately, has been privileged to hear and
understand. She accordingly relates the vision of the Lord which she
has just received in which he has told her that she is blessed as she did

not waver at the sight of him: 'For where the mind is,' he says, 'there is the treasure.' There then follows a discussion of the nature and perception of visions where Mary asks, 'Lord, how does he who sees the vision see it, through the soul or through the spirit?', to which the Saviour replies, 'He does not see through the soul nor through the spirit, but the mind which is between the two – that is what sees the vision and it is [. . .]', thus implying that visions are apprehended through the mind, *nous*, or understanding, of the initiate.[28] (At this point, the text of the 'gospel' breaks off, and the following four pages are missing.) Mary Magdalen's function in this part of the dialogue is to stress the visionary aspect of Gnosticism, one of the central components so roundly condemned by the heresiologists. Elaine Pagels has suggested that Peter represents the orthodox position which rejected 'inner vision', regarded by the Church – which claimed to be the successor to Peter – as threatening its authority, while Mary Magdalen represents the Gnostic claim of Christ's continued presence and the value of individual visionary experience.[29]

Mary next describes the soul's journey through the spheres, and when she has finished her account of her vision, she falls silent. Andrew, however, refuses to believe what she has said, and Peter appears to do a volte-face as he now seems unable to credit the fact that Christ spoke 'privately with a woman', and not openly with the other, by implication male, disciples: 'Are we to turn about and all listen to her?' he demands. 'Did he prefer her to us?' Mary weeps, hurt that they should believe that she has invented her vision, and that she is lying. Levi, the tax-gatherer called by Christ to become a disciple and identified with Matthew, establishes calm, accusing Peter of falling prey to his customary irascibility. If the Saviour has made her worthy, who is he indeed to reject her? He adds, 'Surely the Saviour knows her very well. That is why he loved her more than us.' He reproves his fellow apostles, telling them that they should be ashamed and should 'put on the perfect man',[30] and go out to preach the gospel, imposing no other law than that of the Saviour. The gospel ends with the words, 'and they began to go forth to proclaim and to preach'.[31]

The *Gospel of Mary* contains several different features which are common to other writings, which also help to throw light on the Gnostic perception of Mary Magdalen. She is here depicted not only as the beloved of the Saviour, but also as the leader of the group of apostles, even though this position does not, as we have seen, go unchallenged. It is neverthe-less a status dramatically dissimilar to that of the New Testament Mary Magdalen who was never accorded such a position of leadership by the orthodox Church, except in an honorific fashion, as the 'Apostle to the Apostles'.[32] She is the one privileged to receive visions, has greater comprehension than Peter, and acts as a conduit for the Lord's teachings. While she is loved more than the other apostles, and perhaps because of it, she is also the object of male–female antagonism and resentment, as in the passage just quoted. Her dominant position is also clearly expressed in, for example, the *Dialogue of the Saviour*, where she appears as the 'apostle who excels the rest', superior to Thomas and Matthew and, as we have seen, the 'revealer of the greatness of the revealer', and a woman 'who knew the All'. And her close relationship to Christ is emphasised in the *Gospel of Philip* where she is depicted as one of the 'three who always walked with the Lord: Mary his mother, her sister and Magdalene [*sic*], the one who was called his companion. His sister and his mother and his companion were each a Mary. And the com-panion of the Saviour is Mary Magdalene.'[33] The Greek word *koinonōs* used to describe Mary Magdalen, whilst often rendered as 'companion', is more correctly translated as 'partner' or 'consort', a woman with whom a man has had sexual intercourse.[34] Two pages on is another passage, which amplifies in sexual imagery the relationship already described:

> But Christ loved her more than all the disciples and used to kiss her often on the mouth. The rest of the disciples were offended by it and expressed disapproval. They said to him, 'Why do you love her more than all of us?' The Saviour answered and said to them, 'Why do I not love you like [I love] her?'[35]

Erotic love has often been the vehicle used to express mystical experi-ences, perhaps most notably in that great spiritual epithalamium, the *Canticle of Canticles*, or *Song of Songs*, which describes in the most sensual and voluptuous imagery what the rabbis were to read as an allegory of Yahweh's love for Israel, and early Christian commentators to interpret as Christ's love for the Church, for the Christian soul – sometimes in the person of Mary Magdalen – and for the Virgin Mary.[36] In the *Gospel of Philip*, the spiritual union between Christ and Mary Magdalen is couched in terms of human sexuality; it is also a metaphor for the reunion of Christ and the Church which takes place in the bridal chamber, the place of fullness or *pleroma*. While the tractate itself deals with sacramental and ethical arguments, its main theme is the idea, common to many Gnostic and later Christian writings, that mankind's woes had been brought about by the differentiation of the sexes caused by the separation of Eve from Adam, which destroyed the primal androgynous unity found in Genesis 1:27, after which the Gnostic spirit would forever yearn. As the author of the *Gospel of Philip* explains: 'When Eve was still in Adam death did not exist. When she was separated from him, death came into being. If he again becomes complete and attains his former self, death will be no more.'[37] The *Gospel of Philip* uses the bridal chamber as a metaphor for the reunion between 'Adam' and 'Eve', in which the polarities of male and female would be abolished, and androgyny, or the spiritual state, would be effected through the coming of Christ, the Bridegroom.[38] The relationship between Christ and Mary Magdalen symbolises that perfect spiritual union. Some Gnostics, however, were believed by their adversaries to put erotic concepts into practice, and to take part in sexual orgies which were profane re-enactions of Christian ritual: according to Epiphanius, the Gnostics had a book called the 'Great Questions of Mary' which represented Christ as a revealer to Mary Magdalen of obscene ceremonies which a sect had to perform for its salvation. He wrote indignantly:

> For in the Questions of Mary which are called 'Great' . . . they assert that he [Jesus] gave her [Mary] a revelation, taking her aside to the mountain and praying; and he brought forth from his side a woman and began to unite with her, and so, forsooth, taking his effluent, he showed that 'we must so do, that we may live'; and how when Mary fell to the ground abashed, he raised her up again and said to her: 'Why didst thou doubt, O thou of little faith?'[39]

The sequence in the *Gospel of Philip* can be seen at two different levels, one symbolic of the love of Christ for the Church – in the person of Mary Magdalen – and the other as representing an historical situation in which she symbolises the feminine element in the Church. As we have seen, the preferential treatment that Mary Magdalen receives from Christ in both the *Gospel of Mary* and the *Gospel of Philip* gives rise to jealousy among the other disciples, notably Peter. In the *Pistis Sophia*, one of the few tractates found before the writings at Nag

Hammadi, a similar argument breaks out between Mary and Peter, who complains on behalf of the male disciples that Mary dominates the conversation about Pistis Sophia's fall from the realm of Light, and so prevents them from speaking. Jesus rebukes him.[40] Mary later tells Jesus that she fears Peter, 'because he is wont to threaten me, and he hateth our sex'.[41] (Jesus tells her that anyone who is inspired by the divine spirit may come forward to speak, implying that inspiration nullifies sexual differentiation, and reiterating the theme of androgyny found in the *Gospel of Philip*.) It has been suggested that Peter's antagonism towards Mary Magdalen may reflect the historical ambivalence of the leaders of the orthodox community towards the participation of women in the Church.[42] But by the end of the second century, the egalitarian principles defined in the New Testament, and adhered to in this context by St Paul, had been discarded in favour of a return to the patriarchal system of Judaism which had preceded them.[43] Thus at the level of historical interpretation, the Gnostic texts may have referred to a political tension in the early Church. It is a situation inferred in the synoptics through the disciples' disbelief of the women's account of the resurrection, and in Paul's omission of the women's witness of the resurrection, but never alluded to directly by the orthodox Christians, namely the suppression of the feminine element within the Church which had gradually been taking place from the second century.

Despite the importance given to Mary Magdalen and the other women in some Gnostic writings, there is little suggestion in them of what the twentieth century might regard as a feminist stance. The figure of Pistis Sophia herself, indeed, is portrayed as another Eve, who, separating from her divine spouse, through presumption transgresses against God's will, bringing in her wake the creation of matter and evil, and chaos and destruction to mankind.[44] Whilst both sexes seem to have been allowed to play an equal part in religious practice and discussion, the ultimate aim of the Gnostic was to achieve a state which eliminated sexual difference – which in effect meant that women had to lose their femaleness in order to be subsumed into the larger 'male' group, whose actual sex was no longer significant. The Gnostics' use of the terms male and female to describe the division between spirit and matter, and their further equation of these terms with good and evil, inevitably leads to the association of woman and sexuality with evil. If woman and femaleness represented human nature and sexuality, then by rejecting these, and in particular sexual intercourse and procreation, Gnostics, as well as certain orthodox Christians influenced by this dualistic outlook, believed they could reach great spiritual heights. The Magdalen of the Gnostics has achieved a spiritual greatness which allows her to have such a prominent role. Even in the texts which extol her, and where she herself represents the feminine element, anti-female ideas abound. In the *Gospel of Mary*, her cryptic utterance when consoling the grieving disciples, 'for he has prepared us [and] made us into men', is, as we have seen, echoed later by Levi's call to the disciples to 'put on the perfect man', and in the *Gospel of Thomas* when Simon Peter, once again the spokesman for the anti-feminist party, says, 'Let Mary leave us, for women are not worthy of Life', Jesus replies, 'I myself shall lead her in order to make her male, so that she too may become a living spirit resembling you males.' He then adds, 'For every woman who will make herself male will enter the Kingdom of Heaven.'[45] These sentiments reflect the radical dualism at the core of Gnostic belief, which manifests itself both as a metaphysical concept and, with far greater implications, in an anthropological sense. Man, in the Gnostic universe, like his Platonic counterpart, is tripartite, and made up of spirit, soul and matter. In the material world, into which he has fallen from the perfect state of the spirit, he consists of the *pneuma* which is enveloped in seven 'soul-vestments' – the appetitive 'fleshly garment' which is the 'female' principle. Only by discarding this fleshly garment can he regain his spiritual self, or the 'male' principle, paradoxically the primordial asexuality, or androgyny, to which Gnostic adherents aspired to return. In the *Gospel of Thomas*, the disciple has to strip off his fleshly garment and 'pass by' his mundane existence in order to participate in the spiritual world. Jesus says that Mary Magdalen too may become male, that is to say, 'spiritual', under his tutelage; and that she has evidently become so is reflected in her mysterious pronouncement in the *Gospel of Mary*: 'he has prepared us [and] made us into men.'

Of the Gnostic writings which refer to Mary Magdalen, the longest and most elaborately developed is the *Pistis Sophia*, known in a Coptic translation dating from the second half of the fourth century, and made

from an earlier original which was probably written in Greek. This tells
the story, in four documents, of the resurrected Saviour who returns to
spend twelve years teaching his disciples before his final ascension. The
Pistis Sophia (or Faith Wisdom) again takes the form of a dialogue with
the disciples and holy women, among whom are Salome, Martha,
Mary 'the mother of Jesus', and Mary Magdalen, who appears once
more as chief questioner. She is the 'happy one, beautiful in her speaking', 'pure spiritual Mariham' and 'inheritor of the Light', a figure who,
even if not actually here the symbol of divine Wisdom, in seeking and
imparting knowledge about the Pistis Sophia, becomes handmaiden and
sometimes *alter ego* to the symbol of divine Wisdom herself.[46]

Although it is not difficult to understand why the orthodox hierarchy
might have wanted to suppress this image of a powerful female
mediator, it is less easy to discover why it was created by the Gnostics
in the first place, and whether it might not have derived from a tradition
now lost to us. Unlike other ancient religious cults of the world such
as those of Egypt, Babylonia, Greece, Rome, and Africa, India and
North America, the Christian religion, like its Jewish and Islamic
counterparts, is conspicuous for its lack of a feminine deity. The Virgin
Mary, though celebrated as the *mother* of God by Christians and particularly by Catholics, has never been regarded as divine; in fact Catholics
are particularly careful to stress her very non-divinity and inferior
human and feminine status, and her essential exclusion from the masculine godhead. Young Catholic girls, whilst brought up to venerate her,
and to set her before them as role model, to become the 'Little Children
of Mary' and to join sodalities, or societies, where they are called
'Marians', have always had it impressed upon them that Mary was the
humble 'handmaid of the Lord' who, although she could become the
mother of God, was a mere mortal whose humility and sense of 'inferior
otherness' they should always seek to emulate. Nowhere in the New
Testament is there any intimation that she should be regarded in any
other light than as the young girl whose *fiat* ushered in the son of God
made man, and whose sorrowing motherhood at the crucifixion was
stressed only by John. It was later commentary only which gave Mary
the titles of 'Queen of Heaven' (a title already given to the pre-Christian
goddess Ishtar [Jer. 7:18]), 'God-bearer' (Greek, *Theotokos*), 'mother of
God' and 'divine Wisdom', attributes which derived from the Church's
conflicts during the early centuries in establishing both the divinity and
humanity of Christ.

Among some Gnostic sects, particularly the Valentinians, who borrowed the myth from the Ophites, there may have been some attempt to compensate for this lack of a feminine element in their worship by turning back to the potency of the ancient pre-Christian mother-goddesses who had peopled the lands of the near East and the Mediterranean littoral. From Mesopotamia came Ishtar, who was sister and lover to the shepherd Tammuz; from Egypt, Isis, mother of the gods, wife of Osiris, who ruled the sea, the fruits of the earth and the dead; from Canaan came Astarte, the bride of Baal, god of the Canaanites; and from Phrygia came Cybele, the Great Mother, worshipped in the mountains of Asia Minor, whose companion and lover was Attis. To this illustrious cohort could be added the goddess of the grey eyes, Athena – goddess of wisdom, and warrior maiden. These feminine deities, who migrated from the near East and west Asia to Mesopotamia, spread further still to Egypt, Syria, Asia Minor and to the Aegean, and were the seeds from which Pistis Sophia, the Gnostic Christian goddess of wisdom, would be born.[47]

The land of Canaan, later known as Palestine, was the country amongst whose native peoples, about thirteen hundred years before the birth of Christ, the forebears of the Israelites – nomads and shepherds – came to settle. These latter tribes, as agriculturists, naturally celebrated the gods who would help them in their way of life; as the seasons of the year came and went, and the vegetation withered and regenerated, so too did their gods – amongst them Osiris and Tammuz – to be revived by their lovers, Isis and Ishtar, brought to Canaan from Egypt, Babylon and elsewhere. The death of a god, his revival and joyful reunion with his goddess were personified in the ritual of the sacred marriage, which also symbolised the union of the sky and earth. Composed of different tribes, each with their own tribal god, the Israelite nation proceeded to absorb the deities and rituals by which it found itself surrounded.[48] By the time of King David, who probably died c.930 BC, the northern and southern tribes had become a conglomerate of city-states, and in the temple at Jerusalem a pantheon of gods and goddesses was worshipped, including Yahweh, who had by then emerged. Yahweh became the only god of Israel by the end of the Babylonian captivity (586–38 BC). Thenceforth his name was never to be uttered except by the high priest as he entered the holy of holies, and then inaudible to all others, the very non-utterance of his name symbolising his transcendence.[49]

Viewed from the perspective of modern Judaism, it might now seem inconceivable that the Hebrew god should have ever taken to himself a consort. But we do know that the prophet Hosea (before 721 BC) saw Israel as Yahweh's faithless wife,[50] and that the rabbis interpreted the *Canticle of Canticles* as the bridal song of Yahweh and his spouse, both using imagery borrowed from another existence. The idea of a feminine deity in Jewish lore is anathema when seen in the light of the all-male Yahweh of the Old Testament and his Christian derivative, God. But the idea that the god of Israel might have had a feminine aspect, or had a feminine spouse, appears in a Hebrew inscription of the eighth century BC, found in the Negev desert, which reads, 'the Lord and his Asherah'. (Asherah or Athirath is the name of the Canaanite goddess of love, fertility and war.)[51] At Elephantiné, near Aswan, in the fifth century BC Jews in exile venerated Anat Jahu, another Canaanite deity, possibly as the 'spouse of the Lord', taken by them into Egypt from Palestine.[52]

The fertility cults, and the goddesses who presided over them, which had co-existed with Yahweh in the early days, vanished from the land of Canaan sometime after the Exile. Yahweh, the one true god, became universal creator, transcendent beyond, and superior to, the sphere of nature. Patriarchy and the advent of monotheism are often cited as the causes of this disappearance, but a recent study has argued persuasively that cultic rivalry between the followers of Yahweh and those of the nature religions provides a more plausible explanation.[53] To the Jews, a religion which worshipped fertility, personified in gods and goddesses, but at the same time offered no ethical framework, was valueless. To the great prophet Jeremiah, Yahweh thundered, condemning and threatening the Jews for their idolatry: 'The children gather wood, and the fathers kindle the fire, and the women knead their dough, to make cakes to the queen of heaven [Ishtar], and pour out drink offerings unto other gods, that they may provoke me to anger' (Jer. 7:17–18). King Asa of Judah expelled followers of these alien cults, removed the idols of his forebears and divested his mother of her position as queen mother for erecting a statue ('and Asa destroyed her idol and burnt it by the brook Kidron'; I Kings 15:11–13). Several goddesses fell victim to the onslaught against the cults in the assertion of monotheism, as did a large number of Old Testament mothers, sisters, wives and lovers, in the attempt to expunge all traces of the feminine element during the editing of the texts into their canonical form which began around the third century BC, and lasted for several centuries. Yahweh was endowed with masculine traits, probably mirroring the power structures of early

Israelite society.[54] So, for whatever reason, the world of nature gods and goddesses retreated, leaving traces to be resumed at a later date, above all in the parallels with the story of the Christian god who was slain and rose again from the dead, and the goddess who found him again in the garden at Gethsemane.

The Canaanite goddesses Anat and Asherah, spouses of Yahweh in a golden age, lived on too, but in another guise, which links them with Pistis Sophia. But prior to that association is yet another which involves Mary Magdalen. This is in the Old Testament story of Miriam the prophetess, traditionally known as the sister of Moses and Aaron. Exodus 15:20–1 describes how Miriam took a 'timbrel in her hand' and led all the women 'with timbrels and with dances' in a hymn of victory to Yahweh, after he had divided the Red Sea, allowing the Hebrews to pass through and escape the Egyptians. Here she is seen as equal in status with Aaron and Moses. In Numbers 12:1–15, Miriam and Aaron criticise Moses for marrying an Ethiopian woman. For such temerity, Miriam is punished by the Lord with leprosy; Aaron however is not chastised. Through Moses' mediation with Yahweh, Miriam is cured. But she has been demoted from being on a par with the great leader, prophet and law-giver Moses. In the story of Moses' birth (Exodus 2: 2–7), the baby is hidden away in the bulrushes as Pharaoh had decreed that all male children be killed. Moses' sister, later thought to be Miriam (Numbers 26:59), witnesses the discovery of the baby by Pharaoh's daughter, and thus becomes the mother of his second birth. In the mythological sequence, Moses' sister/Miriam succeeds Isis/Asherah whose brother/husband Osiris is murdered by his brother Seth. Isis reassembles the pieces of Osiris and conceives Horus; and Mary Magdalen, a still later incarnation, in witnessing the resurrection of Christ also witnesses his rebirth, and in a mythic sense can be seen as his second mother.[55] The parallel between Miriam and Mary Magdalen is maintained in later imagery: Miriam, triumphant with her tambourine, or timbrel, identified as 'Miriam soror Moyses', appears in the chapel dedicated to Mary Magdalen at Assisi, together with St Mary of Egypt, as examples of penitence; in the *Biblia Pauperum* of *c*.1460, the scene of Luke's sinner is flanked on one side by Miriam being cured of leprosy (see Plate 6).[56] Both characters, prophetesses of the Old Testament and the New, shared the same fate – demotion from their original prominence to a position of repentance.

6 Miriam, cured of leprosy through the mediation of Moses, the type, together with Nathan and David, of Luke's repentant sinner. From a mid-fifteenth century *Biblia Pauperum*. Cambridge, Corpus Christi College.

In the Old Testament, the figure of Wisdom is personified as a woman, Ḥokhmah. The *Book of Proverbs* tells us that Wisdom 'standeth in the top of high places, by the way in the places of the paths. She crieth at the gates' (8:2–3) to proclaim that the Lord has brought her forth before all else and, after the Creation, she 'was by him, as one brought up with him: and [she] was daily his delight, rejoicing always before him; rejoicing in the habitable part of his earth; and [her] delights were with the sons of men' (vv. 30–1). When the Old Testament came to be translated into Greek, in what is now known as the Septuagint Bible, sometime between the third and second centuries B C, *ḥokhmah*, the Hebrew word for wisdom, became *sophia*.[57] In the *Wisdom of Solomon*, written in Alexandria during the first century A D, Sophia (Wisdom) is said to be the emanation of God's glory, the Holy Spirit, the immaculate mirror of his energy, *and* spouse of the Lord (Sept. 8:3).[58] It is this figure, which the Gnostics revived as Pistis Sophia, that links Mary Magdalen to a long, unbroken tradition of feminine deities.

The *Pistis Sophia*, the central myth of the Valentinian system, tells of the fall, repentance and restoration of Sophia, the first feminine principle which emanates from the Supreme Being or God. Like the story of Eve, it is a tale of feminine *hubris* which wreaks havoc and leaves disaster in its wake. Deserting her spouse, or *suzugos*, Pistis Sophia follows a light which she thinks will take her from the realm of Light to the highest place, the Treasure House, where she hopes to find greatness.[59] Her punishment for this presumption is to be set upon by the material powers who deprive her of her own light, and she falls into the darkness of the Aeons below, the world of matter or Chaos, unable to return to her place in the thirteenth Aeon until she repents and is redeemed by the Saviour. The story of Pistis Sophia's punishment and repentance was a warning to all those who transgressed, and illustrated the need for repentance and redemption, baptism and forgiveness, to a world which through its own propensity for evil had become divorced from its maker.

In the *Pistis Sophia* Jesus has travelled through the almost incomprehensibly complex cosmos of the Valentinian system, his mission to bring enlightenment to the universe, and to banish the evil powers of fate, magic and astrology. To this end he has assumed 'vestures' which have enabled him to travel through the boundaries of the upper and lower spheres. Providing for his own incarnation by taking on the form of Gabriel, he tells his disciples, 'I looked down upon the World of the mankind [*sic*] and I found Maria this whom they are wont to call my mother according to the body of matter . . . and I . . . cast in unto her the first power . . . the body which I wear in the Height.' (The somewhat dismissive way in which Jesus describes his 'mother' in this passage offers an intriguing contrast to the prominence and many expressions of favour given to Mary Magdalen throughout the text.) In this way too he has impregnated ('sowed a power into') the mother of John the Baptist so that the latter may 'prepare my road and baptise in water for forgiving sin'. In a war of flashing light and darkness, he has then overcome the transgressing Angels and Tyrants in the Aeons and reduced their power. He has then ascended to the Height, and reached the thirteenth Aeon.[60]

It is here, below the thirteenth Aeon, that Jesus has found Pistis Sophia 'quite alone', 'distressed and mourning', whom he then saves and restores to her place in the realm of the light.[61] Before relating this episode, however, as he closes with his account of how he has overthrown the evil powers, Mary Magdalen, or Mariham as she is called in the *Pistis Sophia*, begins to speak, having gazed 'in the air for the time of an hour'. Her role is to question, elucidate and elaborate upon Jesus' words as he recounts the fall and redemption of Pistis Sophia. When she asks him if she may speak 'in boldness', Jesus' reply immediately distinguishes her from the rest of the disciples: 'Mariham, Mariham, the happy, this whom I shall complete in all the mysteries of the things of the Height. Speak in boldness, because thou art she whose heart straineth toward the Kingdom of the heavens more than all thy brothers.' Because of her knowledge and intuition, she will become 'happy beyond every woman who is upon the earth, because thou art she who will become the Pleroma of the Pleromas', and he further praises her for 'giving light upon everything in accuracy and in exactness'.[62] She therefore receives *gnosis* from him at the same time as imparting it to the other disciples. She is the first to question him about the nature of Pistis Sophia, who, along with her spouse or 'partner', is one of the twenty-four emanations or principles flowing out of the Supreme Being and who, through disobedience, finds herself deprived of her own light, in the darkness of Chaos, below the Aeons. In this plight, Sophia sings twelve hymns of repentance to the 'Light of the Truth' or Light of the Treasure House which Jesus recites to the disciples, the words of which Mariham and the other disciples interpret.

In view of the fact that Mariham dominates the first two of the four documents of the *Pistis Sophia*, asking thirty-nine of the forty-six questions, it is scarcely surprising that she upsets the male disciples, and provokes Peter's outburst (similar to his attack against Mary Magdalen in the *Gospel of Mary*), after Jesus' account of Sophia's second repentance: 'My Lord, we are not able to bear with this woman, saying instead of us; and she lets not any of us speak, but she is speaking many times.' Somewhat in the tones of an indulgent father pacifying a petulant child, Jesus tells him that anyone who is inspired should not hesitate to speak, and then asks Peter to interpret the second hymn.

The first document of the *Pistis Sophia* ends with Sophia, her head surrounded by light sent by Jesus to protect her from her enemies, and Jesus both approving of Mariham's description of how the powers, Mercy and the Truth, met with one another, and the 'righteousness with the peace kissed one another'.[63] Mariham then interprets his 'power of light' as being the mercy sent by the First Mystery to help Pistis Sophia in her afflictions, and the truth, being Jesus' delivery of her, as having been foretold 'once by David in the eighty-fourth psalm'. Righteousness will 'steer' Sophia, and peace will redeem the lights which her enemies took from her, and restore them to her. For this interpolation, Mariham will 'inherit all the kingdom of the Light', and Jesus further celebrates her as the 'inheritor of the Light'.

The rescue of Pistis Sophia is related in the second document where, again, Mariham/Mary Magdalen is chief interlocutor in the story of the mission of Gabriel and Michael, who are sent to help the fallen Sophia, and her second attack by the powers of Chaos. Michael and Gabriel then bring her out of Chaos, and having dealt with her tormentors, Jesus takes her up to the place 'below the thirteenth Aeon', warning her she will be tormented again; this has apparently taken place just before he ascends in the vesture of light. He then finally routs her enemies and restores her to her original place in the thirteenth Aeon. It is when 'Maria the Magdalene', as Jesus now calls Mariham, tells him that she 'comprehend[s] every word which [he] sayest' that he 'wonder[s] greatly' at her words 'because that she had become spirit quite pure', and praises her: 'Well done, O pure spiritual Maria, this is the explanation of the word.'[64] And thus, through a series of questions and answers, the mysteries of the Gnostic universe – its disposition, and the process by which those who will come to receive the 'highest' mystery of all, the 'Mystery of the Ineffable One', will be absorbed into his being – are revealed. When the millennium occurs, the twelve disciples will be placed with Jesus as joint kings reigning over those who receive the mysteries of the Ineffable in the 'midst of the Last Helper'. In the most exalted place among his 'twelve Deacons', Jesus strangely tells them, 'Maria the Magdalene with Iohannes the Virgin will become excelling all my disciples',[65] thus, for the first time since John's gospel account, linking the two who, according to legend in the Middle Ages, would become betrothed, as preferred disciples. Although Pistis Sophia herself has disappeared from the scene halfway through the second document, to re-emerge briefly in the fifth, the dialogue between Jesus, Mary Magdalen and the disciples continues in the third and fourth documents, ranging from punishment after death to the topography of terrors to be undergone in four hells of increasing intensity. Hell's torments are the subject of the fifth book also, a book populated by a panoply of pagan deities such as the Syrian Adonis, Egyptian Typhon, and Greek Persephone and Hecate, a cast indicating Gnosticism's debt to the various ideas and beliefs current during the period of early Christianity. Jesus' celebration of Mary Magdalen as 'inheritor of the Light' seems to complement his description of her as 'straining towards the heavens *more than all thy brothers*', and this combines with the statement that she will become the 'Pleroma of the Pleromas' to reinforce the link between her and the symbol of divine Wisdom.

The *Pistis Sophia* is not the only Gnostic source to interpret Mary Magdalen in this special way. She is also identified as the 'Spirit of Wisdom', or Sophia, by another 'heretical' sect, in a Coptic psalm attributed to Heracleides, a follower of the Persian Manes (*c.*216–76). Equally important in this case is the fact that she also has the role, as in the *Gospel of Mary*, of chief disciple who holds the group together. The psalm begins with a lovely meditation on the *Noli me tangere* in which Christ says tenderly to Mary Magdalen:

> Mariam, Mariam, know me: do not touch me . . . stem the tears of thy eyes and know me that I am thy master. Only touch me not, for I have not yet seen the face of my Father.
> Thy God was not stolen away, according to the thoughts of thy littleness: thy God did not die, rather he mastered death.
> I am not the gardener . . . I appeared not to thee, until I saw thy tears and thy grief for me.[66]

Thus reassured that the Lord's body had not been stolen, that he has risen from the dead, Mary Magdalen is then sent to find the Eleven, 'these wandering orphans', to bring them back from the banks of the Jordan where, persuaded by the 'traitor',[67] they have laid down their nets, and are no longer fishers of men, carrying out their tasks as disciples of Christ. 'Say to them,' Jesus commands her, ' "Arise, let us go, it is your brother that calls you." If they scorn my brotherhood, say to them, "It is your master." If they disregard my mastership, say to them, "It is your Lord." Use all skill and advice until thou hast brought the sheep to the shepherd.'[68] Magdalen the faithful is to return the straying sheep to the shepherd (l.23), and, as she seeks them, she takes on their role – 'a net-caster is Mariam' – the prerogative of the male disciples in the New Testament. Furthermore, the psalm tells us, God, in becoming man, had taken on 'a slave's vesture', and had chosen among his disciples – the 'beginning of his fold' – Peter, 'the foundation of his Church', Andrew, 'the first holy statue', John, 'the flower of virginity', James 'the spring of new wisdom', Levi 'the throne of faith' and (l. 19) 'Mariam the Spirit of Wisdom'. This inclusion of the attributes of a feminine deity shows that among some Christians at least there was an awareness of the need for a feminine element in their religious beliefs. Mary Magdalen is also the faithful one, in contradistinction to the male disciples, an attribute which applies to her in all contexts, both biblical and apocryphal, and although Peter is described as the 'foundation of [God's] church', Mary Magdalen, in this Coptic psalm, takes on the traditional male apostolic role, as a 'fisher of men'.

The Gnostic gospels were written between the late first and fourth centuries, against a background of growing institutionalisation within the Church. During the second century, the Church was evolving into a three-tiered organisation with a hierarchy of male bishops, priests and deacons, reflecting the triune divine authority in heaven, who claimed their authority derived directly from the apostles.[69] According to a letter believed to have been written by Clement of Rome to the Corinthians in the last decade of the first century, those first apostles had provided for succession to their own ministry by establishing bishops, together with a rule that other proven 'men' should take over that ministry.[70] In the Acts of the Apostles, written by Luke, the male apostles were given the role of witnesses, to go out and spread Christ's words (1:8); also in Acts, Paul, in the first major sermon attributed to him, insists that God raised Christ from the dead, and that the apostles, unquestionably male, were witnesses (13:16–31). However, as we learn from Acts and Paul's own epistles, women were able, like Phoebe and Junia, to have important functions as bishops and deacons in the fledgling Church, earning the admiration of Paul himself.[71] It was a state of equality that was to last only a few generations after Christ's death. Towards the end of the second century, the African Church Father Tertullian was to write, 'It is not permitted for a woman to speak in the church, nor is it permitted for her to teach, nor to baptise, nor to offer [the eucharist], nor to claim for herself a share in any *masculine* function – not to mention any priestly office', echoing the passage in I Timothy attributed to Paul.[72]

Among the Gnostics, however, it seemed that no such hierarchy, and no such sexual discrimination, existed: all were equal, and all might function as bishop, priest or prophet. Women in the Gnostic sects were able, according to the amazed Tertullian, to teach, 'engage in discussion', exorcise, cure, and possibly baptise.[73] He also criticised them for their lack of modesty and boldness in carrying out these roles which of course were now denied to orthodox women for fear of shaming their menfolk.[74] (Tertullian's harsh asceticism and rigorism, far from preventing him from espousing Montanism, in fact drew him to this the radical prophetic sect which celebrated two prophetesses, Prisca and Maximilla, as its founders.[75]) Irenaeus of Lyon noted that women were particularly drawn to the heretical sects (as they would be in the Middle Ages), and were even allowed by the Gnostic teacher Marcus to prophesy and, worse, to function as priests when celebrating communion with him, and to say the prayer and words at the consecration of the host.[76]

Despite the inclusion of women within their ranks, and the strong presence of a feminine element, the Gnostics could never be described as pro-female: women and femaleness were associated with sexuality, procreation and evil, as they came to be within the Church itself. In the *Dialogue of the Saviour*, for example, Jesus tells his followers to pray in the place where there is no woman, and that the works of femaleness (intercourse and procreation) are to be destroyed.[77] And, as we have seen, in the *Gospel of Thomas*, Mary Magdalen could only become a living spirit, 'resembling you males', by becoming male, that is to say, spiritual and asexual, and transcending her feminine self. Gender bias prevailed among the Gnostics in what was still a patriarchal ambience. As Peter Brown has written:

> Gnostic circles treasured those incidents in the Gospels that had described the close relations of Christ with the women of His circle, and most especially those with Mary Magdalen. For a second-century writer, such anecdotes were an image of the sweet and irresistible absorption of the woman, the perpetual inferior other, into her guiding principle, the male.[78]

The gospels of Mark and John describe how, after his resurrection, Christ first appeared to Mary Magdalen. Yet within only a few generations of Christ's death, the orthodox Church was emphasising, following Luke's account of the resurrection, that Christ had appeared first to Simon Peter (24:34: 'The Lord has arisen indeed, and hath appeared to Simon'); the pope to this day traces his succession to Peter himself, the 'first apostle', who was 'first witness' to the resurrection. This first 'sighting' of the risen Lord was to justify the system which evolved during the latter part of the first century, in which those who claimed to be direct successors to the first apostles also laid claim to have the unique right and sacred power to teach, rule and sanctify, apparently conferred upon them by Christ in his lifetime ('Thou art Peter, and upon this rock I will build my church. And I will give unto thee the keys of the kingdom of heaven'; Matt. 16:18–19).[79] But the assertion that it was to Peter that Christ first appeared, in face of the Mary Magdalen tradition, had, it has been argued,[80] an essentially political end: it legitimised the claims of these men to assume authority within the Church, thereby subsequently excluding women from any such functions, reverting to the patriarchal system which prevailed before Christ's time, a system which has since pertained for almost two thousand years.

Mary Magdalen was accorded a far greater importance by the Gnostics and Manichees than she ever was by those who saw themselves as the true successors to Peter, and she was chosen by them to represent their doctrines, to be the mouthpiece for thinking very different from that of the Church. The fact that we see this as an extraordinary role for a woman is evidence of the influence of mainstream Christian thinking on our image of Mary Magdalen's and women's roles in general in the Church, and by extension in society as a whole. If, in fact, the Gnostic accounts of Mary Magdalen reflect a surviving historical tradition from Christ's life excluded from the orthodox accounts of his ministry, then the latter may be seen as the result of a political decision, whose precise form may never be known, to reduce the role of women, and Mary Magdalen as their representative.[81] In the late twentieth century, the Church of Rome has been forced to acknowledge the crucial role of Christ's female followers, and particularly that of Mary Magdalen, but yet, in its steadfast adherence to male symbolism and supremacy, refuses to accept its enormous significance.[82]

When the goddesses of the near East began to vanish sometime during the Bronze Age, about two thousand years before the birth of Christ, and, in the case of Palestine, during the last millennium, they took with them all elements of feminine symbolism within the divine pantheon. We have seen that Ishtar, Anat and Cybele went, together with the celebration of fertility – their domain – and feminine sexuality, to be replaced by exclusively masculine deities. Here and there the old goddesses did survive, long enough for Paul and even, in the fourth century, St Augustine to deplore their cults. Among the Israelites, however, the goddesses who had impregnated the land of Canaan vanished completely, to be replaced by Yahweh with his male attributes of wrath and vengeance – although it should perhaps not be forgotten that the goddesses could be wrathful and vengeful themselves.[83] While Yahweh may have had a spouse in the eighth and fifth centuries before Christ's birth, he soon becomes sole creator, *fons et origo*. In Genesis, the creative principle is male, the Lord God our Father, who has succeeded the mother goddess, originally the source of fecundity. Yahweh was therefore the god whom Christians were to inherit, the Almighty Father, creator of both heaven and earth, and all things in them, thereby relegating the feminine procreative role to an inferior position for nearly two thousand years. When Christianity decided to reinstate the mother-goddess, in the form of the Virgin Mary, she brought in her wake the very antithesis of the fruitfulness borne by her predecessors. With her also came not the prestige of real women which seems to have co-existed with the lauding of the goddesses of fertility in a period of complementarity,[84] but rather a hatred and fear of female sexuality, concomitant with similar feelings towards her human representatives, out of which the idea of her had been born. The mother-goddess's once all-powerful being was relegated, in the Virgin Mary, to that of passive and inferior 'otherness', always excluded from the divine triad, and always subservient to her son.

The Gnostic texts, several of which have Mary Magdalen as a central figure, also vanished, sometime during the fourth century, suppressed by the orthodox Church for their heretical ideas. By the third century, the Church had imposed a common system of teaching and ritual on the scattered Christian communities, to bind them together in the 'one, Catholic and apostolic church'. It was during this period that the New Testament canon came to be edited, and the many texts which failed to toe the orthodox line were eliminated; those which lauded Mary

Magdalen were among the ones to fall victim. The Church of Rome directed that only those writings which had the stamp of apostolicity, that is to say, had the authority of Peter and Paul, could form part of the scriptural canon. These included the words of the Lord written in the gospels according to Mark, Matthew, Luke and John. Others previously incorporated into the canon were rejected. According to Eusebius (c. 260–c. 340), the 'Father of Church History', it was the policy of the triumphant Church after the pact with Constantine to destroy all the writings of the heretics. It was a policy that Augustine sustained when he advised that all Manichaean writings be burned, having once been an adherent to that sect himself.[85]

The early Israelites removed all elements of the feminine from the religion of the land of Canaan; in the Christian religion, the same situation prevails. The Gnostics incorporated the Jewish myth of Ḥokhmah, symbol of divine Wisdom, into their own system, in the figure of Pistis Sophia. As handmaiden and occasional *alter ego* to the fallen Sophia, creator of the world, Mary Magdalen clearly assumes the role of symbol of divine Wisdom, an appellation attributed to her before it was wholly absorbed into the figure of the Virgin Mary. With the disappearance of these 'heretical' writings, Mary Magdalen, heroine of the Gnostics, chief disciple, 'companion of the Saviour', his 'spouse', 'consort', and 'partner', vanished too, to re-emerge in orthodox eyes briefly as a witness to the resurrection, and 'apostle to the apostles', but, more significantly for the history of Christianity, and women, more enduringly as a repentant whore.[86]

CHAPTER III

APOSTOLA APOSTOLORUM

> . . . and especially, how Mary of Magdala received the
> epithet 'fortified with towers' because of her earnestness
> and strength of faith, and was privileged to see the rising
> Christ first before even the apostles.
>
> ST JEROME, *Epist. CXXVII ad Principiam virginem*[1]

apostello, to send away, to dispatch on service; prop., *to send*
with a commission, or on service;[2]

In the New Testament, *apostello* can also mean delegate,
envoy, messenger. It is used predominantly for the group
of highly honoured believers who had a special function.
At first it denoted one who proclaimed the gospel.[3]

IN A WALL PAINTING from the nave of an early
Christian chapel, three female figures process towards a large sarcophagus, each carrying a burning
torch and a bowl of myrrh (see Plate 7). The figures,
one of which is the earliest surviving image of Mary
Magdalen, also appear in the earliest extant example
of a frescoed house-church, found in 1929 at Dura-
Europos, on the west bank of the Euphrates, in what is now Syria. (The
wall painting is now in the Yale University Art Gallery at New Haven.)
Because of its rich decoration, now, sadly, mere fragments, the room is
believed to have been a baptistery of the new Christian faith. From the
earliest days of Christianity until the late fourth century when, on his
conversion, Constantine established Christianity as the official religion
of the Roman Empire, Christians met to celebrate their cult in their
own houses. By the second century, some of these houses had been
given to congregations and converted into churches. In the case of
Dura-Europos, a Roman garrison town, two rooms of a first-century

7 Two Marys approaching the Tomb. Detail of a wall painting (*c.* AD 240) from Dura-Europos, photographed *in situ*. New Haven, Yale University Art Gallery.

house were knocked together to form the chapel. The date of AD 232, found scratched into the plaster, refers either to the building of the house or to the period when the rooms had been made into one, and provides an approximate date for the frescoes, just two centuries after the crucifixion itself.[4] These paintings illustrate some of the New Testament themes favoured by early Christians – the healing of the paralytic, Christ walking on the water, the Samaritan woman at the well and the visit of the holy women to Christ's sepulchre.[5]

Mary Magdalen appears in the main scene on the north wall, one of the three figures (the third almost invisible now) moving to the left towards the huge yellowish-white sarcophagus. She holds a burning torch upright in her right hand, while the torch of the second female figure, presumably the second of the three Marys, is held diagonally. Because of the fineness of its execution, this painting is believed to be the most important in the series. The two women nearest the tomb, in graceful white pallae – the first with a red neckband and girdle, the second with a green neckband – and long white veils, wear their hair waved in front and falling down at the sides in little tufts, a style popularised by Julia Mamaea, the mother of Emperor Alexander Severus who ruled from AD 222 to 235.[6] Beyond the women, in the niche where the baptismal font once stood, are fragments of the central figures of the Good Shepherd, and below, mankind's ancestors, Adam and Eve, the perpetrators of the primal sin, for whose redemption God was made man and sacrificed himself. The healing waters of baptism, symbol of spiritual rebirth, are reflected on the walls leading up to the font, and the scene of the three women at the tomb itself illustrates mankind's spiritual rebirth through Christ's resurrection.

The painting of the holy women at Dura-Europos is important not simply by virtue of its early date but also for its choice of subject-matter. In a direct reference to the gospel accounts where the women rise at dawn, the artist shows them carrying torches, a detail found in this painting and only one other.[7] Lit by the flame from those torches, they thread their way to the sarcophagus, against a red-purple background which represents the subterranean darkness. The spice bowls – another unique feature – which they carry identify them as the myrrhophores, or ointment bearers, described by Mark and Luke, who, in going to anoint Christ's body, became first witnesses of his resurrection. The painter seems to have chosen to depict the moment the women enter the

8 Two Marys finding the Angel at the Empty Tomb. Above: the Crucifixion. On a sixth-century ampulla. Monza Cathedral.

hypogeum, or underground vault, containing the still-closed sepulchre, before the angels have told them of the resurrection. This imagery places the emphasis on what the sarcophagus is about to reveal, and on the women's actual act of witness. In so doing it provides evidence of the early Church's belief in the women's direct witness of the empty tomb as proof of Christ's bodily resurrection. With the absence of any written description of the resurrection itself, early Christian artists used the scene of the discovery of the empty tomb to illustrate it.[8] It was not until much later, in about the tenth century in Ottonian Germany, that the Christian imagination dared to portray the risen Christ, in the pose which we now know so well, actually leaping out of his tomb, graveclothes swirling around him, while the soldiers keeping guard sleep on.

As the result of such literalism, the women's testimony of the empty tomb became one of the most frequently depicted images in early Christian art. It appeared on souvenirs bought by pilgrims visiting Jerusalem in the first centuries, on ampullae for carrying holy oil (see Plate 8), on ivory book covers and caskets, and on embroidered church vestments. The number of women varies, just as it does in the gospel accounts, between two and three. In the eastern Church, where the scene seems to have appeared most often, Matthew's text, which describes 'Mary Magdalen and the other Mary', was used for the Easter liturgy, and two women therefore usually appear in eastern and Byzantine art, carrying incense burners or boxes of ointment. In the west, too, early images usually showed two women, but from the Middle Ages, when Mark's version (16:1–11) became the norm, three women were depicted, and were popularly known as the 'three Marys' (see Plate 9). Sometimes four women appear; this fourth figure was the Virgin Mary, and may reflect the Syrian Marian tradition – where she makes several apocryphal appearances – which attempted to transform Christ's mother into first witness to the resurrection (see Plates 10 and 13; and pp. 92–3).[9]

From about AD 400, the Marys are almost invariably accompanied by the angel or angels whose pneumatic presence may well have been added to lend further credence to their story, and it is this version which is used almost without exception from then on, sometimes with the addition of the sleeping soldiers set to guard the tomb. Just how important the episode was to the early Church is corroborated by the numerous examples of the scene which survive: two of the earliest appear in the beautiful panels on the doors of the church of S. Sabina in Rome,

9 Three Marys at the Tomb. Above: the Ascension. Ivory plaque. Salian. Eleventh century. London, British Museum.

carved before 432, and show the little Late Antique figures of the two women – Mary Magdalen and 'the other Mary' – being greeted by the angel and, in the second panel, their meeting with Christ on Easter morning (see Plate 11). In early depictions of the scene, the women usually carry nothing, and therefore appear as witnesses rather than as myrrhophores, with the inference that this aspect was more important than their intention to anoint Christ. In the fifth century St Augustine was to emphasise the literal sense of Mary Magdalen's visit to the tomb as 'ocular proof' of the resurrection.[10]

This, therefore, was the way in which Mary Magdalen first appeared to the early Christians, as one of the myrrhophores, anointers of Christ or ointment bearers, and witness to the central tenet of their beliefs. It was one of the first images in Christian art, an art whose function was to celebrate and set before the faithful the events of the Old and New

Testaments, and to be, as Gregory the Great later wrote, the Bible of the illiterate.[11] It is perhaps no coincidence that this first pictorial representation at Dura-Europos of Mary Magdalen as one of the holy women should have as its literary counterpart the near-contemporary celebration of her as a myrrhophore by Hippolytus of Rome (c.170–c.235), a bishop of Rome, heresiologist and a staunch defender of the faith for which he ultimately died. The description appeared in his commentary – the first such Christian exposition to come down to us – on the *Canticle of Canticles*, the ancient allegory ascribed to Solomon and his beloved, the Shulamite. To Hippolytus, the Bride, or Shulamite, as she sought the Bridegroom, was Mary Magdalen, the myrrhophore, seeking Christ in the garden to anoint him. Hippolytus oddly names her Martha and Mary, but it is clear from the context that he is referring to the figure of Mary Magdalen.[12]

In the loving, searching figure of the Shulamite, Hippolytus sees the holy women who went to the sepulchre at night, seeking Christ's body,

10 Four Marys at the Tomb. Above: the Resurrection and Soldiers. From the Farfa Bible. First half of the eleventh century. Catalan. Vatican City, Biblioteca Apostolica Vaticana.

11 Two Marys meeting
Christ on Easter morning
(c.430). Rome, S. Sabina.

and who, on finding the tomb empty, heard of the resurrection from
the angel (cf Luke 24:22). He introduces the theme of the women, whom
he calls Martha and Mary, visiting the sepulchre, with the Shulamite's
words from the opening lines of the third canticle, which describe the
Bride searching for the Bridegroom:

> 'By night, I sought him whom my soul loveth': See how this is
> fulfilled in Martha and Mary. In their figure, zealous Synagogue
> sought the dead Christ . . . For she teaches us and tells us: By
> night, I sought him whom my soul loveth. It is told in a gospel:
> 'The women came by night to see the sepulchre.' 'I sought him
> and found him not,' she says.[13]

It is not known why Hippolytus introduces Martha in these scenes in his
many-layered, and often highly confusing, elaboration of the beautiful
Old Testament poem, but it is clear that Martha and Mary also represent
Synagogue, the Church of the Jews, who are first witnesses of the Church
of Christ. They seek truth, in Christian terms, in the garden of Gethsemane. Again, in the Shulamite's words, 'The watchmen that go about
the city found me'; but it is now the women who ask, 'Saw ye him whom
my soul loveth?', to which the watchmen of the *Canticles*, now seen as the
angels guarding the tomb, reply, 'Whom do you seek? Jesus of Nazareth?
See he has risen.' Hippolytus then conflates the meeting between Christ
and the two Marys and the recognition scene in the garden between
Christ and Mary Magdalen in John's gospel:

It was but a little that I passed from them, and as they [Mary and Martha] went away then they met the Saviour. Thus they fulfilled the saying: 'It was but a little that I passed from them, but found him whom my soul loveth.' But the Saviour answered and said: 'Martha, Maria!' They replied, 'Rabboni.'[14]

In the joyful words of the Bride, Mary Magdalen/Martha-Mary finds 'him whom my soul loveth and I would not let him go' (v.4). And then in a parallel which will become increasingly important, having found Christ in the garden, Mary Magdalen becomes the New Eve. As the old Eve had forfeited her right to the tree of life in the Garden of Eden, Mary Magdalen/Martha-Mary now cling passionately to Christ having found him, the Tree of Life, in the Easter garden where life rises anew. In Genesis, man had been put in the Garden of Eden to 'tend' it; there Satan had betrayed him, through the agency of Eve's temptation, to everlasting death. In John's garden, Satan, in the form of Judas, again attempts to betray man but fails. Mary Magdalen mistakes Christ for the gardener, and then recognises him, thereby repairing Eve's fault.

And here in Hippolytus is possibly the first appearance of the title which recognises the importance of Mary Magdalen's (or Martha-Mary's) role in announcing the resurrection to the apostles: for bringing mankind hope of eternal life and for compensating for the first Eve's sin, the New Eve becomes 'Apostle to the Apostles'. 'Oh consolation,' Hippolytus exclaims, 'Eve was called Apostle':

[And] so that the apostles [the women] did not doubt the angels, Christ himself appeared to them, so that the women are Christ's apostles, and compensate through their obedience for the sin of the first Eve . . . Eve has become apostle . . . So that the women did not appear liars but bringers of the truth, Christ appeared to the [male] apostles and said to them: It is truly I who appeared to these women and who desired to send them to you as apostles.[15]

Now, Hippolytus ends triumphantly, Synagogue, the Church of the Jews, represented by the first Eve, has been overcome, and the Church of Christ – symbolised by Mary Magdalen, or Martha-Mary, the New Eve, and Apostle to the Apostles – has been glorified.

Hippolytus' association of the Bride of the *Canticles* with Mary Magdalen, forged in the third century, has lasted until today (see Plate 12):

a verse from the *Canticles* forms part of the liturgy which commemorates the saint's feast-day on 22 July. Hymning the love of the Bride for the Bridegroom, it also celebrates Mary Magdalen's passionate and undying love for Christ, and, allegorically, the love of the Church for Christ:

> Set me as a seal upon thine heart, as a seal upon thine arm: for love is strong as death; jealousy is cruel as the grave: the coals thereof are coals of fire, which hath a most vehement flame.
>
> Many waters cannot quench love, neither can the floods drown it: if a man would give all the substance of his house for love, it would utterly be contemned.

(Canticles 8:6–7)

Hippolytus' commentary established ideas about Mary Magdalen which were to become tradition. Perhaps the most important of these were to see her as the Bride of Christ and symbol of the Church, titles which

12 The Bride finds the Bridegroom in the *Canticle of Canticles*, the type of Mary Magdalen finding Christ in the garden, together with King Darius finding Daniel alive in the lions' den. From a mid-fifteenth century *Biblia Pauperum*. Cambridge, Corpus Christi College.

became more usually associated with the Virgin Mary.[16] The commentary's effect has endured, however, leaving its trace in the erotic element which has always been part of the mystical relationship attributed to Christ and Mary Magdalen. But the title which recognised her importance, or that of the women who witnessed the resurrection – the 'Apostle to the Apostles' – could be seen to have equal significance, and one which is perhaps ironic, when viewed in the light of the subsequent role women were to play in the Church. Although later commentators were to laud Mary Magdalen as 'Apostle to the Apostles', the title was to fade into insignificance, despite a brief resurgence in the Middle Ages, to make way for the appellation of 'New' or 'Second' Eve,[17] and for her subsequent role as symbol of penance, the *raison d'être* for which derived directly from that title and was to have a far greater resonance. For in it was embodied the Church's thinking on the nature of human existence, sexuality, sin and death which, it was deemed, were all due to the perfidy of the first Eve. The story in Genesis of mankind's origins, and the interpretations of the Fall, have had so fundamental an impact on the status of women in Christianity that we should examine them in some detail. Only then can we understand fully how the figure of Mary Magdalen developed as it did, and comprehend its significance within the Christian economy.

The first Eve, as most people know, was created from the side of Adam, as it is recorded in Genesis 2:

> And the Lord God caused a deep sleep to fall upon Adam, and he slept: and he took one of his ribs, and closed up the flesh instead thereof; And the rib, which the Lord God had taken from man, made he a woman, and brought her unto the man. And Adam said, This is now bone of my bones, and flesh of my flesh: she shall be called Woman, because she was taken out of Man . . . And they were both naked, the man and his wife, and were not ashamed.

(Genesis 2:21–5)

Yahweh, having already created Adam (*'adam*, the Hebrew for 'man', or 'mankind'), in his providence had earlier said, 'It is not good that the man should be alone; I will make him an help meet for him' (v.18). This description of Eve's role was used later to justify womankind's subordinate role in relation to man, together with her secondary creation from Adam's rib.[18] The brief account of the Creation which appears in Genesis I (vv.26–8), written a century or so later than Genesis 2, in the eighth century BC, describes Yahweh as creating man in 'his own image, in the image of God created he him; male and female created he them'. This more egalitarian version was usually overlooked in favour of the earlier and longer one.[19] In Michelangelo's *Creation of Man* in the Sistine chapel, one of countless depictions of the scene, Yahweh's right arm stretches out, almost touching the outstretched hand of the beautiful-bodied Adam into whom he is about to breathe life. That Eve is already present in the Creator's mind, but as a secondary thought, is quite evident, as the Lord God's left arm encircles an apprehensive-looking Eve who is also on a smaller scale than the other two figures. (It is not until the next scene that her own creation takes place, as Yahweh commands a rather ungainly Eve to climb out of the side of the recumbent Adam.)

Eve's temptation by the 'subtil' serpent is also a story we know well. Earlier in Genesis, Yahweh had commanded man not to eat of the tree of knowledge of good and evil, on pain of death (v.17). Portraying Yahweh as a jealous god, desirous of keeping his knowledge to himself, the serpent guilefully persuades Eve that knowledge rather than death will be hers. Partake of the fruit, he advises her, and 'ye shall be as gods, knowing good and evil' (3:5). Spurred by the serpent's alluring words, and seeing that 'the tree was good for food, and that it was pleasant to the eyes, and a tree to be desired to make one wise' (v.6), Eve, desirous of greater wisdom, 'took of the fruit thereof, and did eat, and gave also unto her husband with her'. Having been hitherto blissfully unaware of their nakedness, and therefore apparently of their sexuality, they are now horribly cognisant of it, and rapidly sew figleaves together to cover themselves.

Hearing the voice of Yahweh as he takes a walk in the garden 'in the cool of the day', Adam and Eve hide and, on being summoned by their Creator, Adam tells him that they have hidden themselves away because of their nakedness. Yahweh then asks how they know of their nakedness, and if they have eaten of the tree. Adam whimpers, 'The woman whom thou gavest to be with me, she gave me of the tree, and I did eat' (v.12). Eve in turn replies that the 'serpent beguiled' her. Yahweh's wrath is so great that to the woman, he says, 'I will greatly multiply thy sorrow and thy conception; in sorrow thou shalt bring forth children; and thy desire shall be to thy husband, and he shall rule over thee.' To Adam, Yahweh imposes a somewhat lighter lot, everlasting toil, and the promise of death, 'for dust thou art, and unto dust shalt thou return'. He then drives them out of Paradise, providing them with coats of skins to cover their shame. Seldom shown in this divine garb in art, mankind's ancestors usually appear being driven forth in their nakedness, their arms raised to protect themselves from the angel's sword (as in the Sistine chapel), or hands clasped to their genitals and breasts, as in the Eve of Masaccio's fresco of the *Expulsion* in the Brancacci chapel in Florence – the loci, as later biblical commentators would interpret them, of their misdeed. In their wake trail all the horrors and chaos of existence, sin and death, which will replace the primal innocence and felicity they enjoyed in the Garden of Eden.

While some may still believe the Fall of Adam and Eve to have been an historical event, most now see the story of the Creation as an aetiological myth, invented by Yahwist writers some ten or nine centuries before the birth of Christ, to explain the causes of the world and the way in which it had come into being. These descendants of the nomadic tribes who had settled in Canaan a thousand years earlier – those very tribes who had dislodged the deities of their agriculturist predecessors – took the world, or the social structures within it, as they found it, and created a myth to explain how it had evolved. In so doing, the writers revealed their own understanding of the human condition in general, and human sexuality in particular. Man toiled, and woman, her lot still worse, was subject to man; she suffered in childbirth, and her status was inferior, mitigated only by her childbearing powers. Somewhere along the line too, nakedness had become synonymous with shame. All these things, the writers believed, had come about because man had turned his back to God, and lost what had been deemed to be the originally perfect creation of Yahweh, a good God.

The book of Genesis contains the biblical basis for much Christian, as well as Jewish, teaching, particularly concerning the Creation and Fall. For nearly two thousand years, the myth of man's origins was taken at face value. It was not until Charles Darwin, in the middle of the nineteenth century, put forward his rationalist and scientific theories about the evolution of man that the bubble burst. Although both Creation and Fall are now held to be inconsistent with the scientific facts of man's development, many theologians still regard the story in Genesis 2 and 3 as a fundamental truth about man's alienation from God, albeit in legendary form. Out of the Fall narrative – originally the story of moral choice – grew the doctrine of Original Sin, the state in which, according to later Christian commentators, man found himself captive as the result of Adam's transgression. In Genesis 3 also was the outline of the parameters within which the concept of woman and her role in both Judaism and Christianity was to evolve, based on that of the first Eve, whose own subordinate position reflected woman's lowly lot in early Judaic society. But as Chapter 3 of Genesis shows us, Eve's sin was not to tempt, but to aspire to greater, if forbidden, wisdom, to be 'equal with the gods'.

Presumption, as Augustine was to say in the fourth century, was therefore man's first transgression of God's law. Eve's part in mankind's tragedy became the subject of much reflection on the part of the early Fathers as they pondered upon the way the Fall had come to pass. And it was out of these deliberations that Eve came to assume the role of deceiver and temptress to sexual sin, and sexuality itself to assume the enormous significance it has within Christianity. The ideas about the origins of sin and death, and Eve's role as the scapegoat for the Fall, were to have a direct bearing on the development of the figure of Mary Magdalen as 'Second Eve'.

Christianity also inherited, and manipulated, other notions of the origins of evil found in later Jewish writings, many of them extra-biblical, written during the five centuries before Christ's birth. Of these, two concern Adam and Eve in that the source of evil is seen as the inherited sinfulness derived from the Fall; and the idea that mankind had also been corrupted by this sin came from folklore which told of Eve's physical pollution by the serpent or Satan.[20] In Genesis 6 another story with sexual elements is that of the fall of the angels, the 'sons of Elohim', or gods, who had looked down from heaven and lusted after the 'daughters of men', or earthly women. The unnatural unions which then ensued had resulted in a progeny of giants, the 'Nephalim', 'mighty men which were of old, men of renown' (v.4). This unhappy state of affairs provoked Yahweh to rue the day he had created the world and to cause the Flood, which only Noah, and his wife, and a pair of each species, were to survive.[21] In yet another story, which appears in the Ethiopic *Book of Enoch*, written between the end of the third century and 150 BC, mankind is corrupted even further by the apostate angels, or 'watchers', who bring them knowledge which Yahweh had not intended them to have.

Man, these apocalyptic stories implied, had inherited a moral taint or weakness which was transmitted to posterity by physical heredity. A very different, and psychologically orientated, theory was propounded by the rabbis about two hundred years before the birth of Christ. This was the *yēçer ha-ra'*, or 'evil impulse'. Unlike the earlier Hebrews, who had blamed themselves for their woes, the rabbis showed no hesitation in attributing to God the ultimate source of the *yēçer*, which they believed he had implanted in the 'heart', the Hebrew place of the modern 'unconscious', of each individual at his birth or conception. The *yēçer* was therefore not hereditary. As a creation of God, it was intrinsically good; it was also the source of creative energy, but since appetite too was involved, it had a strong potential for evil, particularly where sexual matters, or man's relationship with God, or other human beings, were concerned. Only strict observance of the Law could keep the strong drives it engendered under control. (The belief that it was placed in the 'heart' or 'unconscious' relates the *yēçer* to a much later concept, in twentieth-century psychology, the theory of *libido*.[22])

To the commentators in the five centuries before Christ, Adam's death was due to his own sins, and not to any sin innate in the race of man. In Christian hands, the *yēçer* would become the debilitating corrupting condition known as 'concupiscence', which each human being would inherit at birth, and which was transmitted through the sexual act, through the 'libido' which accompanied it, and which infected his every action, and was commutable in part only through baptism. These ideas about evil and sin were constants in the early Christian period, but no unified concept was formulated by the Jews themselves; that was, as N. P. Williams wrote, 'a task which Providence reserved for Christian thought'.[23]

Adam's transgression became a central topic of theological controversy in the churches of both east and west from the second century; it was to take two further centuries before St Augustine made his pronouncements on original sin and the Fall, which would forever weld together the Christian notions of sin, sexuality and death. Christians were born into a sinful world, a fact which Christ himself constantly reiterated when he called for sinners to repent,[24] but he never referred either to the Fall itself, except to say that mankind was fallen, or to original sin, and alluded only once to Adam and Eve when replying to the Pharisees' question about putting away wives, and the legal grounds for divorce (Matt. 19:4).

The first intimation in the New Testament that Adam bequeathed sin to mankind is to be found in the lapidary pronouncement by St Paul, the Hellenised Jew who so dramatically converted to Christianity, in his first letter to the Corinthians: 'For as in Adam all die, even so in Christ shall all be made alive' (15:22). Linking the idea of original sin with the story in Genesis 3, Paul worked retrospectively, seeing Christ's death as the salvific act which made necessary a real sin by an historical Adam, in which all mankind, corrupted and lost as a result, were integrally involved. This definition, the only reference to original sin in the New Testament, was to have far-reaching consequences when it came to be interpreted by St Augustine at the end of the fourth century. Paul's act was to cement a bond between Adam, the first father, and the rest of mankind. Adam's descendants now became the 'children of disobedience' (Eph. 2:2), who were 'by *nature* the children of wrath, even as others' (v.3; my italics). In his letter to the Romans, Paul added the phrase which was to condemn mankind forever in Christian teaching: 'Wherefore, as by one man sin entered into the world, and death by sin; and so death passed upon all men, for that all have sinned' (5:12). Sin and death had entered all men through the sin of the first man, and through one man's disobedience the rest were rendered sinners. But God in his mercy had offered up his own son to atone for Adam's sin, and it was through Christ and 'by grace [that] ye are saved' (Eph. 2:5).

For Paul, Adam's transgression had resulted in sin and death, and man was doomed to a sinful state. To the rabbis, evil had been the cause of sin in the world; to Paul, it had been the result: he was therefore turning the *yēçer* upside down, and shifting its emphasis. He was also altering its locus within human physiology: the rabbis' *yēçer* was implanted in the 'heart' or psyche, but Paul radically transferred its location: man's inherited disease, corruption, or weakness was rooted in the 'flesh', that is, in the body and its members. In mankind's corrupted state, spirit and flesh constantly warred against each other, as he wrote to the Galatians in his inflammatory style: 'For the flesh lusteth against the Spirit, and the Spirit against the flesh: and these are contrary the one to the other: so that ye cannot do the things that ye would'

(5:17). Man was no longer in control of himself, but a prey to his flesh; and the works of the flesh, he further explained, were, firstly, 'Adultery, fornication, uncleanness [and] lasciviousness', followed by such sins as 'idolatry, witchcraft, . . . wrath, . . . envyings and murders' (vv. 19–21), thus demonstrating for the first time the prime place of sexuality, or sexual 'sins', within the Christian catalogue of evils. Paul's stress indicates the significance of Mary Magdalen's sin as repentant whore when she came to be associated with the sinner in Luke 7. How Adam's sin came to be transmitted to his descendants, Paul did not say. Nor does he anywhere link sexuality (although he has much to say about it, see below) with original sin. Nor does he mention Eve, or her role in mankind's fall. But from the second century, the story of Adam and Eve was, in the words of Peter Brown, to 'remain very wide awake indeed',[25] and as the generations of Christians grew, Eve's name fell ever more frequently from the lips of the early Christian Fathers.

The various theories about Adam and Eve and the nature of that first sin, and of those who had perpetrated it, therefore, came to rest on their sexuality, and more specifically on the very nature of sexual intercourse itself – whether and how it had taken place in Eden; whether it had taken place before the Fall, and if so, how; or whether, as it in fact came to be seen, it was a consequence of the Fall. The views of the interpreters of the Genesis story differed radically, and depended largely on whether they were of the eastern or western Church, although they ultimately all but concurred in their deliberations regarding sexuality and sin. In the eastern Church, the myth was seen as an allegory of the evolution of man, whilst in the west, following Paul, it tended to be treated as an historical fact. The eastern interpretation,[26] influenced by Greek thought, in part Plato, and later by the Neoplatonist Plotinus (d. 270), viewed the world of matter darkly: man and evil had evolved through the descent of the pre-existing spiritual substance, or soul, into matter. When this theory came to be applied to the story of Adam and Eve by second- and third-century exegetes of the Alexandrian school, the Garden of Eden was seen to symbolise man's primeval and pristine state in which his forebears together represented the sinful union of spirit (Adam, the male principle) and flesh (Eve, the female principle).[27] Man's first nature was generally believed to have been spiritual and bodiless, without and incapable of sexual differentiation; he had become a physical being, and sexed, through his soul's sin, which had been to desire the mundane. According to Gregory of Nyssa (c. 330–c. 395), a Cappodocian, procreation – since there had been no reference to sexuality in Eden in Genesis – depended on some kind of spiritual emanation, achieved in Stoic *apatheia*, a passionless quality belonging to the angels, between physically asexual beings. (The idea that Adam had been the possessor of the *vita angelica* before the Fall appealed greatly to Augustine when he came to make his final pronouncements on the subject of original sin.) Furthermore, according to Gregory, in his terrible indictment of marriage, the treatise *De Virginitate*, this first sin had contaminated man's spiritual essence, and the wages of his sin had been sexuality and death.[28]

To the western Fathers, however, Adam and Eve were only too real, the ancestral authors of mankind's woes. The world, because it had been created by God, had originally been good, and by rebelling, man had forfeited his rightful place in it. The form this rebellion had taken began to assume ever more sexual overtones. Tatian (b.*c.*120), an apologist, and possibly the founder of the Encratites, and other writers had earlier taught that the fruit of the tree conveyed carnal knowledge.[29] Clement of Alexandria (*c.*150–*c.*215), head of the theological school at Alexandria, though imbued with Gnostic Christian thinking which saw the soul as being imprisoned in the body, was able to defend marriage against the Gnostic Julius Cassianus, stating clearly that the first sin had not, in point of fact, been the act of generation itself, but that Adam and Eve had capitulated to their lustful feelings for each other,[30] and had had intercourse before the time God had appointed for their nuptials. It was the 'weakness of matter' – man's material body and involuntary impulses of ignorance – which had led to this over-hasty consummation, which otherwise would have been perfectly in order and in accordance with God's commandment to go forth and multiply. 'For [human] generation', Clement wrote,

> is a created thing, and a creation of the Almighty . . . The Saviour came unto us who had gone astray as to our *minds*, which had been *corrupted* as a result of the disobedience committed by us, pleasure-loving as we were, against the commandments . . . the first-formed man perchance . . . before the time of the grace of matrimony having experienced desire and committed sin.[31]

A Hellenised Christian much influenced by Stoic thinking, Clement's less positive legacy to western Christendom was elucidated in the

Paedagogus, his treatise on the Christian life, where he stressed that although marriage was divinely ordained, sexual intercourse had to be divorced from passion, and was solely for the purpose of begetting children in the service of God. It was to be approached 'with a chaste and controlled will',[32] in a 'Stoical manner', and was certainly not to be undertaken for pleasure. It was also to be regulated: never to take place in the morning, daytime or after dinner, and never with menstruating, barren, or menopausal wives.[33] Many of Clement's theories, which mirror the profound ambivalence towards sexuality which became a marked characteristic of Christianity, were to become accepted Christian ideals and practice for the next two thousand years.

To Irenaeus, the irascible bishop of Lyon, Adam and Eve had been under age. Adam's lust had led them into pre-empting God's command, and their guilty reaction had been to cover themselves immediately in scratchy figleaves, thus chastising those organs which had led them to sin.[34] But Irenaeus could also see that the Fall had not been entirely calamitous, for had mankind's ancestors not committed the misdeed, man himself would have had a less full and rich moral evolution;[35] this view came to be known as the doctrine of the 'Fortunate Fall'.

The idea that mankind had been positively corrupted as the hereditary consequence of the Fall, and that the corruption itself was passed through propagation, came from another convert, the great African orator and Church Father Tertullian. Man was not merely weakened, he believed, but *depraved* as a consequence of Adam's sin, an idea which Calvin espoused heartily in the sixteenth century. Tertullian also coined the word 'concupiscence' (from the Latin, *concupiscere*, to long for, to be desirous of, to covet), which signified Adam and Eve's fatal flaw and the loss of integrity which had resulted from their disobedience to God, and which ever since has played an integral part in the western theology of sin. A variation on *yeçer*, its counterpart in English is 'desire' or 'libido', which, under Augustine's tutelage, would become equated with 'lust' and sin, thus imputing a sinful connotation to a previously morally neutral word.

Augustine had originally held Adam's body to be transparent and celestial; the union of the first parents had been purely spiritual. Later, however, he came to view the story in Genesis in a strictly literal sense. It was his reading of St Paul, in particular of the letter to the Romans, which had led him to see man's condition as one of human bondage. To Augustine, death had come upon all human beings by their union with Adam, and they also shared in the responsibility for the Fall; he thereby denied that humanity had a free moral choice. Mankind's nature was irreversibly damaged by sin, he believed, 'For we were all in that one man, seeing that we all *were* that one man who fell into sin through the woman who was made from him . . .'[36] The penalties for that first sin were also borne by each human being as descendants of Adam. These were concupiscence and death.

Augustine took up Tertullian's idea of concupiscence with all the enthusiasm of a 'twice-born'.[37] Born in North Africa in 354 of a pagan father, Patricius, and a Christian mother, Monica, he at first rejected the Christianity of his childhood and lived for fifteen years with a concubine, by whom he had a son, Adeodatus. His passionate attachment to his mistress, and the 'sharp and searing pain' he felt when he had to reject her in order, on his mother's insistence, to make a good marriage, make for moving reading in his *Confessions*.[38] (In fact, he never married his prospective bride; she had been under the legal age for marriage, and he took another concubine with whom to while away the time, and later dramatically converted.) During the early period, he had espoused Manichaeism, a radical offshoot of Gnosticism, which saw light and dark, or good and evil, as two principles locked in permanent conflict within the psyche, in which the soul, a spark of light, sought to escape from the darkness of the physical world. These dualistic tenets never entirely left him, although after nine years he grew disillusioned with the sect itself. In 383 he went to Rome, and thence to Milan, where he met the bishop Ambrose who was to have a profound influence on him, and who in turn introduced him to Christian Neoplatonism and the writings of St Paul, three factors which led to his conversion in 387. Ambrose, a champion of orthodoxy, an ardent advocate of the Virgin Mary, and yet another 'twice-born', regarded Adam in Paradise as a 'heavenly being', his sin not merely a transgression but a *lapsus*, or fall.

Ambrose taught that Adam and Eve had fallen from a state of 'original perfection', and adopting this thesis, Augustine wrote in glowing terms of the life that Adam had originally had in Paradise, exempt from all physical evils or sickness, endowed with immortal youth, and with the possibility of immortality, which would come to him through eating of the tree of life. Adam's intellect and moral character had been equally elevated. He had, however, misused the free will given him by his Creator, succumbed to temptation, and lost original justice, by which

God had given him physical immortality and happiness.[39] As a punish-, ment, he had acquired a moral debility, concupiscence, which was transmitted through physical heredity to his descendants, who were thus rendered a *massa damnata*. It was in the face of sharp criticism for his gloomy stand on free will and the Fall from the British monk Pelagius that Augustine formulated his ideas. Pelagius also held that the Fall had come about through God's gift of free will, but denied that the sin of Adam and Eve had been passed on to their descendants – it had been theirs alone – and thus rejected St Paul's pronouncement in his letter to the Romans. God's grace was not necessary for man's redemption since, as he was unimpaired by the Fall, none was needed, although it was helpful. Man himself, Pelagius further believed, in a manner which seems remarkably sane and modern, was entirely free to choose to do good or evil. For his assertion that man was independent of God, and responsible for his own salvation, Pelagius was twice accused of heresy, and vanished from history in 418.

To Augustine, the sin of Adam and Eve had not been sexual intercourse itself; it had been their presumption, in their desire for knowledge, to rival their Creator, which had resulted in their loss of *psychological* integrity. Concupiscence affected the whole being, as man in his fallen state no longer had control over himself, and was prey to agitations of the flesh. Adam and Eve's sin lay not in their indulgence in the sexual act, but in the *lust* which accompanied it, lust which was now a prerequisite to the procreative process, which would otherwise have been achieved in angelic *apatheia*. Augustine's debt to Gnosticism is clear in his equation of concupiscence, or sexual desire, with sin.

In the *City of God*, written in 413–26, Augustine dwells long and thoughtfully on the subject of how intercourse might have taken place in Paradise before the Fall. There was every reason to believe God had instituted marriage before the Fall. Why else had he created male and female except to 'increase and multiply, and fill the earth and hold sway over it'?[40] In Chapter 22, he notes that it would be 'a manifest absurdity to deny' that the sexual differences were created for begetting children. But marriage would have taken place in Paradise without the accompanying 'lust' required for post-lapsarian procreation, although he has the grace to admit 'as it is, we have no example to show how this could have come about'. He then returns to the idea of Stoic *apatheia*. No lust would have been necessary to fulfil the Paradisal sexual act, which would have been achieved merely by a pure act of will, without the slightest concupiscent, and *ergo* sinful, passion, and without even losing the physical virginity which his earlier espousal of Manichaeism would never allow him to forget. Further, Augustine tells us, before the Fall, Adam had been capable of moving his sexual member with as much control as fallen man might exercise over a finger, arm or foot.[41] But now, infected by the stain of original sin, the sexual organs functioned with no regard to their owner, in retribution for their sin of disobedience. Paradise was lost, and the seed of children was to be sown in lust, quite contrary to the way it should have been, when 'without the allurement of passion goading him on, the husband would have relaxed on his wife's bosom in tranquillity of mind and with no impairment of his body's integrity'.[42] As it was, 'after their sin our first parents were ashamed of their nakedness and . . . they covered their parts of shame – their *pudenda*' (Latin, *pudendus*, shameful). Eve's formation from Adam's rib rendered her the weaker part of the couple,[43] and she compounded her subordinate role as helper by tempting Adam to fall. Adam's culpability lay in his uxoriousness: undeceived by the serpent, he had wished merely to please his spouse. Augustine, the redeemed licentiate, who had once, in his Manichaean days, prayed for chastity and celibacy, that they might come, 'only not yet', enabled sexuality to be associated with original sin through the workings of lust, whilst still allowing the physical creation of God to be essentially good – a point strongly denied by Gnostics. Such was Augustine's later reputation that this was to permanently colour the Christian view of sin, sexuality and the female, responsible for the Fall.

In all these deliberations, Eve naturally comes off rather badly: for her secondary and subordinate creation, for her weakness in being tempted, and for her role as temptress and protagonist of the Fall. The earliest Christian document to 'blame' her for the Fall is the anonymous *Epistle of Barnabas* of *c.* AD 130, which describes the 'transgression wrought in Eve', although guilt had been laid squarely on her shoulders about three hundred years earlier in the apocryphal 'Wisdom of Jesus ben Sirach' which had declared, 'From a woman was the beginning of sin, and because of her we all die.'[44] It was Tertullian, however, who summed up most pithily what he thought about Eve and her successors when he roundly castigated the feminine sex for bringing death to mankind, and for necessitating Christ's sacrifice:

And do you not know that you are [each] an Eve? The sentence of God on this sex of yours lives in this age: the guilt must of necessity live too. *You* are the devil's gateway: *you* are the unsealer of that [forbidden] tree: *you* are the first deserter of the divine law: *you* are she who persuaded him whom the devil was not valiant enough to attack. *You* destroyed so easily God's image, man. On account of *your* desert – that is, death – even the Son of God had to die.[45]

(His accusation particularly appealed to, and was echoed frequently by, medieval preachers, when they came to excoriate the foibles of the weaker sex.)

The idea that sexuality and marriage had been brought about by the Fall appears in St Jerome's famous letter to Eustochium where he describes Eve in Paradise as a virgin: 'it was only after she put on a garment of skins that her married life began', he wrote, clearly equating marriage and human sexuality with sin. 'That you may understand that virginity is natural and that marriage came after the Fall, remember that what is born of wedlock is virgin flesh and that by its fruit it renders what in its parent root it had lost.'[46] Similar sentiments are to be found in the treatise *On Virginity* written by the 'golden-mouthed' John Chrysostom, bishop of Constantinople, an adherent of the Gnostic Christian eastern Church:

Scarcely had they [Adam and Eve] turned from obedience to God than they became earth and ashes and, all at once, they lost the happy life, beauty and the honour of virginity: thereupon God took virginal chastity from them . . . they were . . . made subject to death and every other form of imperfection; then did marriage make its appearance with the mortal and servile garment of human nature . . . Do you see where marriage took its origin? How it had of necessity to be preceded by the breaking of the divine commandment, by malediction and death? For where there is death, there too is sexual coupling; and where there is no death, there is no sexual coupling either.[47]

If human sexuality had come about through sin, these churchmen argued, its moral opposite was innocence embodied in virginity. Now seen in explicitly sexual terms, the Fall's counterpart had necessarily to be a redemption predicated upon virginity. (Herein also lies the significance of Mary Magdalen's appellation, the 'Second Eve', which she earns through repairing the work of the first Eve, at the resurrection; the sin with which she was endowed as the symbol of penance, her sexuality, was also, as it was believed, that of Eve.) It followed therefore that a perfect, sexless virginal vessel should carry the perfect virgin son of God, sent to redeem mankind. It was during the first five centuries of Christianity that the Virgin Mary came to take a more prominent position and to assume greater importance, as her role as mother of God came to be defined as a result of the various controversies over the nature of Christ. As the Church combated against the heretic Docetists, Arians and Nestorians, it asserted her unbroken virginity which by suspending the law of nature manifested the divine, while her giving birth to Christ stressed his humanity. Her virgin motherhood was proclaimed at the First Council of Constantinople, and she was proclaimed *Theotokos* at the Council of Ephesus in 431. She received the title *Aeiparthenos* (ever-virgin) at the Council of Chalcedon in 451, and at the First Lateran Council in 649 her perpetual virginity became a dogma of the Church.[48]

The Virgin Mary's importance stemmed from the growing asceticism which had been steadily gaining ground within the Church from the second century. By the time Augustine came to formulate his doctrine of original sin, and Jerome, Ambrose and Chrysostom, amongst others, to propound the supremacy of virginity, asceticism and celibacy – elements of Gnostic belief which stubbornly resisted eradication by the western Church – had become Christian ideals. Virginity was their supreme manifestation.

The origins of Christian asceticism have been identified with the Essenes (the sect to which John the Baptist may have belonged), who lived in Judaea, at Engeddi in the desert by the Dead Sea, before the birth of Christ. They lived austere celibate lives, practising frequent ritual ablutions to cleanse their despised flesh; a similar community also existed at Wadi Qumran during the first century. Both groups rejected the world around them, a land under the yoke of the Roman Empire, to live instead in 'the house of perfection and truth in Israel',[49] dedicating their lives to God. Sexual abstinence was considered an integral part of the life of the soldier of God. Pliny the Elder described the Essenes as being 'remarkable among all other tribes in the whole world, as it has no women and has renounced sexual desire, a race in which no-one is born [nevertheless] lives on forever'.[50] The Dead Sea Scrolls, found in 1947 in a cave at Qumran, show that a number of the males of the community, which included married householders also, were required to live under a vow of celibacy for a time.[51] Why both these groups chose continence as a way of life is unknown, but Brown has pointed to an ancient tradition which linked prophecy with sexual abstinence in Jewish folklore.[52]

The notion of celibacy within Christianity seems to have derived more immediately from St Paul whose major preoccupations were eschatological rather than mundane, as he awaited salvation and the Second Coming promised by Christ. This is most clearly stated in his letter to the Corinthians, of AD 54, apparently written in reply to a query from the church at Corinth ('Now concerning the things whereof ye wrote unto me'), which begins with another inflammatory flourish, particularly when read in isolation: 'It is good for a man not to touch a woman' (I Cor. 7:1), which is followed by another, 'for it is better to marry than to burn' (v.9). The argument in between tells us that the original question concerned marriage, and it is soon clear that marriage comes a poor second best, a prophylactic against fornication (sexual relations outside marriage, or with a married person), for those who are unable to be celibate, like himself. But, says Paul, there is no divine law concerning virginity, which he himself sees as good for 'the present distress' (v.26). Marriage and the things of the world distract from the true goal of the Christian, the things that belong to the Lord. Although he is aware that each is made differently, and that all have their 'proper gift of God', he would prefer that all were celibate ('For I would that all men were even as I myself', v.7), to devote their lives to God. In verse 38, he seeks to redress this argument, having previously denied that marriage was sinful (v.28), by saying that marriage is good, but that it is equally good, if not better, not to marry. This oddly phrased letter, or selected and pithy phrases from it, were used later to justify the superiority of the single state, and helped to set the seal on the Christian view of celibacy and marriage for the coming generations.

But in this view of the priority of the kingdom of heaven, Paul was merely reiterating the words of Christ which had, in fact, sounded a good deal more stringent, when he commanded, 'If any man come to me, and hate not his father, and mother, and wife, and children, and brethren, and sisters, yea, and his own life also, he cannot be my disciple'

(Luke 14:26–7); in Matthew's gospel, he says much the same thing, 'If any man will come after me, let him deny himself, and take up his cross, and follow me. For whosoever will save his life shall lose it: and whosoever will lose his life for my sake shall find it' (16:24–5). He was also to make the remark which some Christians were to later take quite literally, 'There be eunuchs who have made themselves eunuchs for the kingdom of heaven's sake' (Matt. 19:12). He appears in the gospel accounts to have eschewed family ties himself (*vide* his curt reply to his mother on having been found by her in the temple, 'I am about my Father's business' [Luke 2:49]) to take up the single-minded labours of a radical. The New Testament contains no reference to Christ's sexual status; some modern theologians have suggested that he may even have been married, as a rabbi of his age in orthodox Judaism is more than likely to have been, since uxoriousness and procreation had been divinely instituted to sustain the Chosen Race.[53] But even if Christ himself were celibate, married people were included in his group – for example, and in particular, Peter, who was to become leader after Christ's death.[54] (In the fourth century Jerome's contempt for marriage was such that he considered Peter, despite his primacy, to be infinitely inferior to John the Evangelist, since one was married and the other a virgin.[55]) Despite this dismissal of blood relationships, there is in Christ no hint of any hatred of the flesh. The revulsion towards Eve and her descendants, which would accompany the path of asceticism and celibacy in the Church founded in his name, cannot be located in his recorded words. For Christ, a devoted follower such as Mary Magdalen suffered no subordination on account of her sex; indeed, she received the supreme accolade in being the witness of his resurrection. That the equal position of women was, in the following centuries, called into question shows how closely that Church was prepared to follow the example of its own founder.

During the second century, celibacy became the hallmark of Christianity, and writers both Christian and pagan remarked upon the phenomenon. The Greek doctor Galen noted of the Christians during the second half of the century: 'Their contempt for death is patent to us every day, and likewise their restraint from intercourse. For they include not only men but also women who refrain from intercourse all through their lives.'[56] All across the Roman Empire, small communities of Christian men and women who had resigned their natural lives to take up the harsh rigours of asceticism saw liberation in the denial of their sexuality, in total self-abnegation, in order to give themselves up to God. Virginity could represent freedom from domination by things of the world, such as foreign tyranny and, in the case of women, from subjection within marriage, or even from marriage itself. It also symbolised a singular closeness to God, a closeness, it was argued, which could not be achieved by ordinary married persons. In the fourth century, hermits like St Anthony (c.250–356) and Pachomius retired to the Thebaid, the desert of Egypt, to live lives of extraordinary austerity – in the case of Anthony, eating only bread and water once a day in his denial of the flesh (an aspect of asceticism which would affect the legendary life of Mary Magdalen), and tempted by terrible assaults by the devil to give up his rigorous life. (Anthony's biography, written by St Athanasius about a year after his death, was the first handbook to the ascetic life, and was to have a profound effect on later western monasticism.) Some ascetics carried their mortifications to extremes, such as the holy men who lived on columns in Syria like Simon Stylites (d.459), or even castrated themselves in their passionate desire to dedicate themselves to God. Seen as both the remedy for and cause of death, sexuality was abhorrent. Married Christians became continent and even the young renounced their desires, carrying out a 'boycott of the womb'.[57] Such sentiments were to contribute to the shaping of Mary Magdalen's symbolic function.

Augustine had developed his ideas through the different beliefs he came across during his spiritual and intellectual journey towards Christianity. These were Stoicism, Manichaeism and Neoplatonism, which all contributed to his world-view. Plotinus influenced him as he had Origen; Clement also owed his credo to the Graeco-Judaic philosophy expounded at Alexandria. Common to these ideologies which were flourishing in the Roman Empire as Christianity emerged was the life-negating view that the world and matter, or flesh, were evil, and that good resided only in the spirit: this dualistic outlook permeated the orthodox Church, which was simultaneously battling against it, to the point where the Church itself soon overtook the heretics in its revulsion towards the world and the flesh and, by extension, woman.[58] Sexuality represented the staving off of death through procreation; marriage, and all its appurtenances, evil. Jerome prayed hopefully that all mankind might abstain from marriage so that the human race might soon come to an end.[59] Elsewhere, he saw it as the means of furnishing him with virgins.[60]

Virginity became the subject of treatise after treatise, from the second century onwards. The story of Tecla, the 'imagined inviolate virgin' who chastely loved St Paul,[61] became the paradigm for both males and females. Physical virginity represented the unsullied soul, and *par excellence* it was that of the young female virgin which embodied it. In one of the first treatises, *The Banquet* of Methodius (d.*c*.311), a panegyric on virginity influenced by Plato's *Symposium*, ten virgins replaced the ten sexually experienced Athenians, celebrating the incomparability of their high calling. The Christian world had everywhere become peopled with noble consecrated virgins, daughters of the wealthy, or widows, who supported less wealthy holy men like St Jerome – who himself encouraged great Roman ladies such as Paula and Marcella to take up the ascetic life – in their scholarly enterprises. Ambrose of Milan, author of yet another treatise on virginity, also saw the economic benefits to his church of rich virgins as he promoted the cause of Mary's perpetual virginity.[62] Against such an ideal, Mary Magdalen, as the reformed prostitute she was to become, could only occupy a subordinate position. Had the Church set out to neutralise her importance as a disciple of Christ, it could scarcely have found a more powerful weapon for doing so.

A paradoxical effect of the lauding of virginity was in fact the gradual erosion of feminine participation within the higher echelons of the Church from the fourth century. In an institution which treasured the idea of the Virgin, it might have been thought that her feminine representatives would have been highly esteemed; they might have been expected to maintain the status given to them by Christ, and extended during St Paul's lifetime. As we have already seen, Christ's own attitude towards women was, particularly given his rabbinical background, remarkably egalitarian compared with the Jewish context in which he lived. There, a woman could only become a disciple if her husband or master were a rabbi,[63] whereas the women who followed Christ, some of whom are named, such as Salome, Joanna and Mary Magdalen herself, had been treated as disciples in their own right, and with men, been regarded equally as his followers. This elevated them from the passive role they were allowed to play in the synagogue, and allowed them to become not only disciples but also witnesses of the new faith. And, of course, according to the gospels, he chose a woman, Mary Magdalen, to be his 'first apostle', in the true sense of the words.

Christ's liberation of women from their conventional familial position within Jewish society prevailed in the twenty to thirty years after his death, and may well have been some part of the reason why women seem to have been drawn to the Christian movement, a fact which was corroborated by pagan writers like Celsus, writing in the late second century, who scoffed at Christianity for being a religion of women, capable only of appealing to the simple and lowly and those without understanding, such as women, slaves and children. (He further mocked Christianity by claiming that the resurrection itself had been based on nothing more than the reports of hysterical women.)[64] As it was, and as Paul's epistles and various references in Acts also inform us, women from every stratum of life, such as the Gentile Lydia, the 'seller of purple' at Philippi and a god-fearer, prominent women like the Greeks in Thessalonika and Boroea (Acts 16:14–15; 17:4, 12–13), and well-off middle-class women like Mary, the mother of John Mark (12:12–17), as well as those who by the mere fact of being women were prevented from active participation in other religious spheres, were absorbed into the new religion which, for a time, valued and esteemed them, and offered them purpose and status otherwise denied them in a patriarchal society.

Mary Magdalen's task as witness and messenger of the true faith was unique within the context of what may now seem an equally unique period in the growing Christian community. She appears to have been among the first, and certainly the most important, of the women disciples around Christ; but in the post-resurrection generation, we may be surprised to discover just how important were some of the roles women were able to undertake. In Paul's letters, written before the synoptics themselves in *c.* AD 50–60, and in Acts, produced in the last decade of the first century, we hear not only how women of means continued to support the missionaries financially, in the way that Mary Magdalen and the other women disciples had contributed to the upkeep of Christ's retinue, but how some, like Phoebe (Rom. 16:1–2), were also able to be leaders and missionaries in their own right, and how she in particular had been in a position to give Paul succour (v.2). A picture emerges of women assuming important functions as apostles, deacons, leaders of communities, prophetesses and teachers, women whom the apostle Paul, often regarded as the author of misogyny in the Christian Church, praises as 'fellow-labourers' and 'sisters in the Lord'. With such appellations he seems to suggest their equal value, and some of them he acknowledges, such as Phoebe and Junia (Rom. 16:7), as having converted before himself. In these labours, as missionaries preaching Christ among the Gentiles, all were equal, 'For', Paul said, 'as many of you as have been baptised into Christ have put on Christ. There is neither Jew nor Greek, there is neither bond nor free, there is neither male nor female: for ye are all one in Christ Jesus' (Gal. 3:27–8), witnessing that in the Christian communities of his time baptism removed all ethnic, social and sexual differences, an attitude which distinguished the Christians from their Hellenistic and Jewish contemporaries.

Women often founded and maintained house-churches like that at Dura-Europos, which functioned as centres of the Christian communities, giving hospitality and support to the missionaries who, in the footsteps of Christ, travelled around the countryside spreading the gospel. Lydia's household converted to Christianity with her (Acts 16:14–15), and the establishment in Jerusalem of Mary the mother of John Mark included servants and was presumably large enough to put up guests (Acts 12:12–15).[65] The important part which women took in the establishment of the early Church marked a radical departure from the negligible role in the synagogue of their sisters in Judaism, to whom leadership positions were denied, and it is an importance which has until recently been either misunderstood or deliberately and conveniently ignored.

Recent studies of the early Church have shown that contrary to the general assumption that the women's roles as disciples were both subsidiary and auxiliary, their true significance lies in the fact that, far from denoting inferior functions when applied to women, the word 'follower' meant precisely the same as it did when applied to the male disciples. Similarly, the bias of later exegesis has coloured the interpretation of other words and therefore roles.[66] When Paul wrote of Phoebe, 'deaconess' of the church of Cenchraea, he gave her three titles: sister, *diakonos* and *prostatis* (Rom. 16:1). When applied to either Paul himself or another male leader, *diakonos* is translated as missionary or servant,[67] but when referring to Phoebe it has usually been translated as 'deaconess', which imposes upon her role in the first century the less important duties of later deaconesses whose authority was restricted to caring for the sick and poor, and baptising women and children. But its use in the masculine form in the Greek in Romans implies that absolutely no distinction was made between male and female deacons. Phoebe's third title, *prostatis*, is usually translated as 'helper' or 'patroness', but contemporary use of the word implied such high-ranking functions as governor or superintendent, and in I Tim. 3:4–13 and 5:17, it signifies a bishop, deacon or elder.[68] Phoebe's function therefore, as missionary, minister and possibly bishop of her church, had far greater significance in the first century than its translation has led us subsequently to believe. Women deacons survived until the mid-fourth century in the west,[69] the previous century having been the 'heyday of the diaconate of women',[70] and continued later in the eastern Church.

Yet within only one generation of Paul, early in the second century, there are intimations of change. Women were no longer allowed to teach, or to have authority over men (I Tim. 2:12). This we learn from the letters addressed to Timothy known, along with the one to Titus, as the Pastoral Epistles, and purporting to have been written by, and still erroneously attributed to, Paul. Justification is found in Eve's secondary creation, and through her deception by the serpent she is the first to sin ('For Adam was first formed, then Eve. And Adam was not deceived, but the woman being deceived was in the transgression', vv.13–14). The writer further demands that woman is 'to learn in silence with all subjection' (v.11). She is, if she is to profess godliness, to adorn herself suitably 'in modest apparel, with shamefacedness and sobriety; not with broided [plaited] hair, or gold, or pearls, or costly array' (v.9). Her salvation is through childbearing, the author continues, reverting to Jewish tradition, based on the orthodox reading of Genesis 1, where Yahweh commands Adam and Eve to go forth and multiply. A further hint of the change in direction and return to traditional patriarchal values comes later in the letters where it is suggested that widows under sixty should be dissuaded from enrolling in the special groups of widows set up to pray and care for the sick, as they might wish to remarry, and were also idlers, gadders-about, gossips and busybodies, and it was therefore preferable that they marry and have children. It has been suggested that the Christians had been forced to return to patriarchal values by criticism from outside as the active role women played came to be seen as shameful.[71]

Much the same thing happened to the role of apostle, the role which Mary Magdalen was the first to receive, and which Hippolytus was the first orthodox Christian commentator to celebrate. The original Greek word signified one who had witnessed and had been sent to preach the Word. Mary Magdalen fulfilled these criteria, witnessing both the empty tomb, and the risen Christ, and proclaiming the news to the other disciples, although it has been claimed that the fact that she took

the news no further, and it was apparently left to the male disciples
to spread the message to the world at large, rendered her merely a
'quasi-apostle'.[72] It seems, though, hard to deny that she was the first
apostolic witness to the resurrection, corroborated by Matthew, John
and Mark. Although until recently the Catholic Church has consistently
played down the role of the female witnesses, or quietly ignored it, her
incontestable appearance as primary witness in the canonical accounts
simply cannot be ignored. It was the supposed fact of being first witness
of the resurrection, according to I Cor. 15:3–8, Luke 24:34, and Acts
2:32; 3:15, which allowed Peter to claim his succession to Christ, and
which was to justify subsequent male apostolic succession in the Church.
By the time Acts came to be written in the last decade of the first
century, although there were still male apostles, women no longer
counted among their number, just as none is mentioned as a missionary
or preacher. The women who do appear there are rich proselytes or
god-fearers who function as patrons and collaborators within the
Church. But just how highly the early Church had regarded the role of
apostle was made palpable in his commentary on Romans by St John
Chrysostom, when he extolled Junia, the woman greeted with her
husband Andronicus, and together described as 'of note among the
apostles', and who had converted before him, by Paul:

> There is something great about being an apostle. But to be pre-
> eminent among the apostles – think what marvellous praise that
> is. They were pre-eminent by virtue of their work and their honest
> tasks. How great the wisdom of this woman must have been for
> her to have been found worthy of the title apostle.[73]

Chrysostom might well have been speaking of Mary Magdalen herself.
But already by the time Hippolytus came to celebrate the Magdalen as
the 'apostle to the apostles' in the second or third decade of the third
century, the rolé and title were already anachronisms, harking back to
a period of equality in the Christian community which no longer pertained. By the third century the Church was already in the process of
evolving as an ecclesiastical hierarchy, dominated by the successors to
St Peter, in the roles of bishops, deacons and priests. In those churches
which had once accommodated male and female together, segregation
now became the norm, as it was in the synagogue. In the gradual
depression of women's status, they were no longer able to preach and

baptise. It became more common for holy women to minister to other women than to the general community, and the positions of power and authority which they had enjoyed in the earlier period were no longer open to them.

From the fourth century, the Church was also in the process of becoming the church of the celibate, the male celibate. Marriage had originally been allowed to the clergy, indeed wives of priests and bishops had assisted their spouses in their pastoral duties, but in 305 the Council of Elvira instructed those involved in the ministry of the altar to maintain entire abstinence from their wives under pain of forfeiting their positions. This was in effect a reversion to the Temple laws in Leviticus which were to ensure the purity at all times of the holy of holies, which contact with women, unclean from menstruation, would pollute.[74] In 352 the Council of Laodicea forbade women to serve as priests or to preside over churches, a ruling which implies that, contrary to modern assumptions, women had been able to assume the sacerdotal role and function in the early Church.[75] (In the Gentile world, priestesses took part everywhere in the duties of worship and the sacraments, and in the first century AD some women had such powers as priestess-magistrates.[76]) In the Christian Church, the higher echelons of the clergy were the first to be forbidden to marry, and this ruling was extended ultimately to include all who entered holy orders. The Church had its critics on the point of celibacy, one of whom was Jovinian, an unorthodox monk who, in his argument with Jerome, denied its efficacy, and that virginity was a higher state than marriage. In 412 he apparently made enough of an impression to lead a number of virgins to abandon their vows and marry. For his pains, he was scourged and banished to Boa.[77] At the Fifth Council of Carthage in 401, at which Augustine was present, it was decreed that married clergy in the higher grade should be separated from their wives under pain of being deprived of their office.[78] Clerical continence in the Catholic Church had come to stay. It was against this background that Mary Magdalen's role as 'apostle to the apostles' came to have merely an anachronistic significance – a victim, like the rest of her sex, to the waves of asceticism which engulfed the Church. With the growing male dominance within the ecclesiastical hierarchy, a climate was created in which such a prominent role could no longer be sustained. With Eve constantly held responsible for the Fall, her 'daughters', ever embodying the sexuality so abhorred by the Church, and unable to match up to the defeminised 'Queen of Heaven', became the objects of extraordinary hatred by the men of the Church. It was therefore inevitable, and necessary, that Mary Magdalen's sin became that of her sexuality.

Hippolytus of Rome had linked Mary Magdalen with Eve; he had also described her as one of the myrrophores and was the first to designate her the 'apostle to the apostles'. The Gnostics and Manichees had also celebrated her as an apostle and as a spokeswoman for their arcane doctrines, the female figure more important in many of their writings than the male apostles – and certainly often more important than the Virgin Mary. Within the Church, too, the identity of Mary Magdalen and the other female characters in the New Testament who came to be associated with her continued to be a source of fascination, exercising the ingenuity of the early commentators. As has already been mentioned, the Fathers of the east and west viewed the women very differently, following two traditions: in the east they were seen as separate characters, and in the west they gradually came to be treated as one.

Apart from Hippolytus' commentary, few Christian writers in the third century referred to Mary Magdalen, and when they did it was merely to allude to her. It has been suggested that this reticence may have been due to the extraordinary prominence given to her from the second century by the Gnostics whose own writings were suppressed in the fourth century for their heretical contents.[79] From the fourth century, however, Mary Magdalen, Luke's sinner and Mary of Bethany became the objects of close scrutiny by orthodox writers. As all their attributes would at some time accrete to Mary Magdalen herself, in particular those of Luke's sinner, it is perhaps worth looking at what the commentators had to say about the latter two figures. In a Church whose asceticism and stress on penance was growing in the early centuries, Luke's story about the beautiful sinner fired poetic souls, particularly those of the writers of the east. In his sermon on the sinful woman, Ephrem the Syriac (d. 373), who commented on her several times, noted with admiration the 'supreme and honest impudence' with which she had entered the house of the Pharisee: she was even more daring than the angels in the way she had come close to God. He conjures up an entire life for her, one which involves her in a long dialogue with a scent-seller who interrogates her about her lover, the identity of whom she keeps a secret until almost the end of the episode. She has been seized by the Lord's beauty, and vows to give him the perfume regardless of how much it may cost.[80] (This scene, clearly thought to be too useful to lose, appears, reworked, in the thirteenth-century Passion plays of Benediktbeuern and Vienna, and in later French *mystères* where it forms part of the dissolute life of Mary Magdalen.[81]) To Severinus of Gabala (d.c.408), the sinner becomes the faithful prostitute who goes in search of the one who has set her on fire with such love;[82] and to Amphilocus (d.403), the sinner, the prostitute, 'has been adjudged by the supreme judge as the one who through her tears has compensated for Eve's sins'.[83] To the eastern Fathers, Luke's sinner represented love profane, at once erotic and mystical, and transformed into spiritual love through penance and forgiveness, expressed in language with always that little *frisson* with which the celibate delights in describing the erotic, as something forbidden and unexperienced, and all the more tantalising for that.

When Origen, who had heard Hippolytus preach in Rome in c.212, came to write his own commentary and homilies on the *Canticle of Canticles*, he too was moved by the erotic power of its poetry, but felt it necessary to qualify it as being a 'drama of mystical meaning' rather than a 'hymn to fleshly union'. Quite willing to accept that it was an epithalamium, he advised 'everyone who is not yet rid of the vexations of flesh and blood, has not yet ceased to feel the passion of his bodily nature, to refrain completely from reading this little book'.[84] According to Origen, the arch-exponent of the threefold allegorical method of biblical exegesis, the Bride (or Soul) was Mary of Bethany, and the ointment used by the Bride was that used by Mary to anoint the feet of Jesus (the Bridegroom or Eros), before wiping them with her hair in the gospels of Luke and John.[85] Although he was to comment on her role in Christ's Passion, he was to have a far greater effect on her composite career when he identified the active life with Martha and the contemplative with her sister Mary, which was to have such importance in the religious life of the Middle Ages, and again in the sixteenth and seventeenth centuries.

Several of the eastern writers lauded Mary Magdalen for her Easter role, seeing in it a reason for honouring women, otherwise cursed for Eve's sin. To Cyril of Alexandria (d.444), most famous for his defence of Catholic orthodoxy against Nestorius (who had taught that there were two separate and distinct persons in Christ, one divine and one human), women were doubly honoured: through Mary Magdalen, their representative, all women were forgiven for Eve's transgression, and she was witness to the resurrection.[86] Proclus (d.*c.*446), patriarch of Constantinople, however, saw an inversion of the natural order – to a man of the Church, it was a world turned quite upside down – in that it was the myrrhophores who told the apostles of the resurrection, and not the other way around but, he concluded, that was reason in itself to honour women.[87] And on much the same theme, and certainly from the same point of view, is the imaginative speech Gregory of Antioch (d.593) put into Christ's mouth when he appeared to the women: 'Be the first apostles to the apostles. So that Peter . . . learns that I can choose even women as apostles.'[88] To Modestus, patriarch of Jerusalem in 630, who believed that Mary Magdalen had died both a virgin and martyr, she was leader of the women disciples, an idea which has clear resonances with the writings of the Gnostics.[89] In Syria, an extraordinary phenomenon evolved in which in the typology of the Church the figure of the Virgin Mary was conflated with that of Mary Magdalen in the scene of the resurrection, in a deliberate and systematic 'superimposition' of the Marys, which reflected the confusion over the Marys in the gospels in which the early Church found itself.[90] This may well have been part of a deliberate 'conspiracy' by the Syriac Church, which had a particular devotion to the Virgin, to find or create for itself an appearance of Christ to his mother. In a beautiful poetic homily, or *memrâ*, for the night of the resurrection, Ephrem, or an author close to him, wrote:

> He drew Mary Magdalen/ to come and see his resurrection./ And why was it first to a woman/that he showed his resurrection, and not to men?/ Here he showed us a mystery/ concerning his Church and his mother./ At the beginning of his coming to earth/ a virgin was first to receive him,/ and at his raising up from the grave/ to a woman he showed his resurrection./ In his beginning and in his fulfilment/ the name of his mother cries out and is present./ Mary received him by conception/ and saw an angel at his grave.[91]

A little later, the same author wrote: 'But Mary, type of the Church/ looked into the sepulchre', showing that for him the name Mary or 'Maryam', which belongs both to the Virgin and to the Magdalen, as personifications of the Church as mother of Christ's members, and in the case of Mary Magdalen, as bride of Christ and herald of the New Life, had become a functional title in the way that the name Peter, as in the case of Simon Peter, was sometimes used.[92] This literary tradition was given its first known visual expression in the Syriac gospel codex of the monk Rabbula, dated 586 (see Plate 13).[93] In the upper scene of the crucifixion, the Virgin stands on the left, dressed in violet, haloed and weeping, and the three Marys stand to the right. In the scene below, of the women at the sepulchre, the Virgin again appears in identical clothes, and with a halo, which the other Mary does not have, and enters from the left carrying a censing vessel. In the scene of the Marys meeting Christ, the Virgin is similarly clad, and holding a censer. There is no indication that any of these female figures is Mary Magdalen. This eastern tradition was known in the Middle Ages in the west where it was taken up and used by homilists, playwrights and artists who saw that it was only appropriate that Christ should first appear to his mother.

In the west, commentators at first treated Mary Magdalen, Mary of Bethany and Luke's sinner separately, but confusion soon set in over their identities, united as they were by their aura of incense and weeping. Ambrose voiced the question in the fourth century: 'Were there Mary, the sister of Lazarus, and Mary Magdalen, or more people?',[94] but a categorical reply was not given for a further two hundred years. He also noted Mary Magdalen's weak faith at the tomb, but altered the story somewhat: 'Also, she is sent to those stronger than herself so that they preach the resurrection to her, whose example will teach her to believe.'[95] (This contrasts with Jerome's celebration, quoted at the beginning of this chapter, of her zeal and great fidelity for which she was rewarded with the first sighting of the resurrected Lord.) In his commentary on Luke 10 Ambrose allows the possibility of a link between Mary Magdalen and Mary of Bethany,[96] and like Hippolytus he also associated Eve and Mary Magdalen, encouraging his audience to cling to Christ, the Tree of Life, even though Christ had said, 'Do not touch me.' Women, ever weak vessels in Ambrose's eyes, he advised further, 'Do not leave Eve for fear that she may fall again; take her with you, so that she no longer errs but holds on to the Tree of Life.'[97]

To Augustine, Luke's sinner could have been Mary of Bethany who anointed Christ on two occasions;[98] but he clearly had his doubts even when using the theory to make a point in his commentary on John:

Behold this sister of Lazarus (if indeed it was she who anointed the Lord's feet with unguent, and dried with her hair what she had washed with her tears) was raised from the dead more truly than her brother – she was freed from the weight of her bad habits . . . And of her it has been said, 'For she was a famous sinner.'[99]

He did not, however, associate Mary Magdalen with Luke's sinner. For him Mary Magdalen stood out above all the other women, and in the *Harmony of the Gospels* he witnessed her great love:

Then came Mary Magdalene, who unquestionably was surpassingly more ardent in her love than these other women who had administered to the Lord . . . so that it was not unreasonable in John to make mention of her alone, leaving these others unnamed who, however, were along with her, as we gather from the reports given by others of the evangelists.[100]

In a lovely play on words, he celebrated her double return to the tomb as described in John 20: 'Then having come away from the body, she thought of what he was not [i.e. dead], and with her courage now returned, she knew who he was.'[101] Augustine also sustains the link first made by Hippolytus between Eve and Mary Magdalen, but creates his own parallels: Adam fell because he believed Eve's words, and the disciples disbelieved Mary Magdalen's words. Mary Magdalen's arrival at the tomb before the apostles was prefigured by Eve's role as protagonist in the Fall; Eve's action had led her to be the first to lose her relationship with God while Mary Magdalen was the first to find the risen Christ. Because she belongs to the weaker sex, woman, reasons Augustine, is the first to find the Lord as she seeks more ardently, being of a more emotional nature than the apostles who are of the stronger sex. Above all, Mary Magdalen represented to Augustine the Church which had believed in Christ when he had ascended to his Father.[102] But nowhere does he unite the three women.

Until the late sixth century there was no fixed tradition concerning the unity or plurality of the women. That their identity intrigued the commentators is undeniable – who they were, what they represented, their importance and their relationship to one another and, above all, to Christ. Some had identified Mary Magdalen with Luke's sinner, others with Mary of Bethany; still others identified the latter two with each

13 The Crucifixion. Below: the Virgin and (presumably) Mary Magdalen at the Tomb; and the resurrected Christ meeting the Virgin and, again presumably, Mary Magdalen. From the Rabbula Codex, dated 586. Florence, Biblioteca Medicea Laurenziana.

other, but not with Mary Magdalen. And there were those like Ambrose, Augustine and Jerome who were unable to decide.[103] But with Gregory the Great's homily on Luke's gospel, delivered at the basilica of S. Clemente in Rome on the Friday after Holy Cross day (14 September) probably in 591, the identity of Mary Magdalen was finally settled, *pace* some dissenting voices later,[104] for nearly fourteen hundred years:

She whom Luke calls the sinful woman, whom John calls Mary,
we believe to be the Mary from whom seven devils were ejected
according to Mark. And what did these seven devils signify, if not
all the vices? . . . It is clear, brothers, that the woman previously
used the unguent to perfume her flesh in forbidden acts. What she
therefore displayed more scandalously, she was now offering to
God in a more praiseworthy manner. She had coveted with earthly
eyes, but now through penitence these are consumed with tears.
She displayed her hair to set off her face, but now her hair dries
her tears. She had spoken proud things with her mouth, but in
kissing the Lord's feet, she now planted her mouth on the
Redeemer's feet. For every delight, therefore, she had had in herself, she now immolated herself. She turned the mass of her crimes
to virtues, in order to serve God entirely in penance, for as much
as she had wrongly held God in contempt.

Hom. XXXIII[105]

Gregory (*c.*540–604), under whose pontificate England was converted
to Christianity, and who gave his name to the music composed for the
liturgy known as 'Gregorian chant', was a profoundly holy man and
popular preacher upon whose words, historians related, huge crowds
hung, and among whose favourite themes were the coming of the Last
Judgement and repentance. Mary Magdalen he now offered as an
example of conversion to the people of Rome, beset by famine, plague
and war, for each individual to reflect upon his own sins and seek his
salvation. In his twenty-fifth homily, on John 20:11–18, given in Rome
at S. Giovanni Laterano on the Thursday of Easter week, Gregory
declared that 'Mary Magdalen, who had been in the city a sinner, came
to the sepulchre'.[106] Gregory's sermons on Mary Magdalen established
her fame as they were assimilated into the liturgies of Holy Week and
the resurrection;[107] his homily collection was highly popular during the
eighth and ninth centuries, more in demand than even that of
St Augustine, and his formulation of the composite Magdalen thus
passed into homiletic literature to become stock-in-trade during the
Middle Ages.[108]

And so the transformation of Mary Magdalen was complete. From
the gospel figure, with her active role as herald of the New Life –
the Apostle to the Apostles – she became the redeemed whore and
Christianity's model of repentance, a manageable, controllable figure,

and effective weapon and instrument of propaganda against her own sex. As the Catholic theologian Peter Ketter was to write in 1935, it is clear that Gregory's identification of the three figures was 'exegetically untenable',[109] in the light of which the process can only be seen as one of wilful misinterpretation, to suit the purposes of an ascetic Church. As the model of conversion and repentance Mary Magdalen becomes absorbed into the ancient biblical imagery of sin, taking to herself the symbolism of the Old Testament harlots like Gomer, the unfaithful spouse of Hosea the prophet, who prefigured Israel's infidelity to God.[110] In terms of the New Covenant, she represented the pagan and Gentile world converted to the Christian faith, and as a moral paradigm she represented the soul, or all sinners, turning to reunite with God. But while the image of biblical harlotry is allegorical of the people's unfaithfulness to Yahweh, Mary Magdalen's sin – fornication – actually bodies forth, representing, in her role as second Eve and symbol of repentance, and together with the Virgin Mary, the rejection of what the Church most feared and abhorred, incarnated in the flesh of the woman, her sexuality.

CHAPTER IV

THE *GRANDES HEURES* OF VÉZELAY[1]

apud Vizeliacum qui est locus celeberrimus

(at Vézelay which is a very famous place)

HENRY II, king of England (1133–89)[2]

THE ABBEY CHURCH of Ste Marie-Madeleine at Vézelay stretches back along its hill, overlooking the valleys of the Cure and Yonne in the lush Burgundian countryside, surrounded by vineyards, with the blue hills of the Morvan in the distance. The present building was begun in 1096 and finally completed by the mid-twelfth century (see Plate 14). The greatest surviving Romanesque church in France, it lies above the tightly packed houses lining the steep, narrow streets of the little town which in the Middle Ages it by turns protected and punished, while the original four Gothic towers of the vast west front menaced the surrounding area. To Walter Pater, that eminently pagan and aesthetic writer of the nineteenth century, the abbey was the 'completest outcome of a religion of threats', and he revelled in its imperious but half-barbaric splendours, in what he saw as the epitome of the 'richest form of the Romanesque'.[3] From the mid-eleventh century, Vézelay became the most important pilgrimage centre in France, and fourth in popularity in Christendom after Rome, Jerusalem and Compostela, this last being the shrine on whose route Vézelay lay. The owner of land and possessions in abundance, all over France, it derived its wealth from its claimed ownership of the relics of Mary Magdalen.[4] Yet, within only two centuries, the fervour which had created those riches had abated drastically, and in 1265 it

14 The west front of the
abbey church of Ste
Marie-Madeleine, Vézelay.
Photographed in *c.*1900.

became the centre, and the Magdalen's relics the object, of an elaborate
piece of chicanery which ultimately led to the abbey's downfall.

Little trace now remains at Vézelay of the saint who gave her name
to the abbey. During the sixteenth-century wars of religion in France,
Catholics and Protestants fought for its possession; in 1567 it was taken
over by the Huguenots who sacked it, mutilated the statues, and burned
the relics. It was further ravaged during the French revolution. In 1840,
in his report to the Commission on Historic Monuments, the architect
and restorer Eugène Viollet-le-Duc suggested that the ruined figures in
the lintel of the great west tympanum had probably once represented
scenes from the life of Mary Magdalen, and he accordingly set to work
to recreate what he imagined had been there.[5] After his labours, however, few of the original stones of the outer western portal survive. In
the gable above the lintel, the large figure of Christ is flanked by that
of the Virgin Mary on his right, and on his left, much mutilated, that

of Mary Magdalen. (A similar disposition of the same figures, but better preserved, is to be found on the west front of the church of St Père-sous-Vézelay, the fourteenth-century church built at the foot of the hill on which the abbey stands.) In the massive, unusually high nave of the abbey church, with its beautiful pink and grey arches, the capitals with their somewhat crudely carved figures bear no reference to her. It has been suggested that the original Romanesque choir and ambulatory, which were burned down in 1165 and replaced by the present Gothic construction, may once have contained some sculptural image of her; a recently discovered thirteenth-century boss from the last bay of the nave bears the scene of Christ appearing to Mary Magdalen.[6] And yet, twice a year, on 19 March, the day which commemorates the 'translation' of her relics from Provence to Burgundy, and 22 July, the feast-day which came to the west from Byzantium, her existence here is celebrated still. In the dank crypt below the transept, in the most ancient part of the church, is the ninth-century 'confession' where, behind a grille, two reliquaries said to contain some of Mary Magdalen's bones are kept. Two smaller reliquaries are set into the pedestal supporting a nineteenth-century statue of the saint in the south aisle by the door giving out onto the cloisters. One was donated by the church of La Madeleine in Paris and the other by the church at St Maximin in Provence. How Mary Magdalen's relics came to Burgundy, how she became a heroine of the Church, and one of the most loved saints of the Middle Ages, is one of the great romances of the age of chivalry, embodying a particular phenomenon – the cult of relics – which was an integral part of medieval civilisation.

Christians had been collecting relics, bones and objects which were believed to have been in contact with the saints, since the second century, treasuring at first the remains of those who had died as martyrs for their beliefs, and later those of the holy personages whom they came to regard as saints. For the faithful, these remains were tangible evidence of the existence of saints on earth, whose souls, having already gone up to heaven, awaited the last day when they would be reunited with their bodies. Even more important for the earthbound mortal was the belief that those who had died martyrs' deaths were in close contact with their Maker and could therefore act as powerful intercessors and protectors. As a result their relics became much sought after and, as in the case of Mary Magdalen, their lives were often embellished by fantastic tales;

these ranged from missionary stories, of bringing Christianity to pagan lands, and of miracle-working, to the return to heaven, the ultimate aim of the Christian.

The earliest known example of the veneration of relics appears in the story of the martyrdom of Polycarp, the aged bishop of Smyrna (trad.*c.*69–*c.*155). A lifelong defender of orthodoxy, particularly against the Gnostic Marcionites and Valentinians, he was burned to death in Rome in his late eighties for refusing to recant his faith. Within a year of his martyrdom, in a letter to the church of Philomelium, the citizens of Smyrna declared before the whole Church their devotion to their bishop's relics, and their intention to commemorate his death annually. It was said in his biography that a sweet smell had arisen from the charred remains, and, as a result, fragrant aromas issuing from saintly tombs became one of the characteristic features of discoveries of holy relics. The Romans, who venerated the bodies of their dead heroes, but only in celebration of their fame when alive, scorned the Christians for what they saw, not surprisingly, as a gruesome practice. The Christians were equally criticised by the pagan Eunapius of Sardis in Egypt for collecting the 'bones and skulls of criminals who had been put to death for numerous crimes', and for claiming that they were gods, thinking that they became better by defiling themselves at their graves.[7] Christian writers were in fact careful to distinguish between the cult of *latria* (worship) which was reserved for God alone, and *dulia* (veneration) which was accorded to saints. In his battle against Vigilantius (*fl.c.*400), the presbyter of Aquitaine who dared to criticise such practices, St Jerome justified the Christian cult of relics with an appeal to scripture and ecclesiastical tradition, and pointed to miracles worked by God through saints' relics. The Jews had also venerated their holy figures and martyrs, so the Christian cult can be seen as continuing late Judaic ritual, but whereas both the Jewish practice and the Roman cult of heroes celebrated those who were dead forever, the early Christians cherished saints and martyrs whom they believed would literally rise again from the dead, as they understood Christ to have promised them. What were heaps of common dust to pagans, in the words of St Jerome, were 'venerable bones' to Christians, highly treasured; as the citizens of Smyrna had written of Polycarp's bones, a saint's relics were of a 'greater value than precious stones and a higher price than gold'.[8]

Relics were customarily 'discovered', the technical expression being 'invention', which usefully covers both the medieval and modern significances of the word. One of the most famous of these 'inventions', and the one whose details were to become common features of later accounts, was credited to St Helena, the mother of the Emperor Constantine, who in the mid-fourth century 'discovered' the relics of the Holy Cross on which Christ had been crucified. According to tradition, Helena had been superintending the building of Constantine's basilica on Mount Calvary, and had dreamt of the place where the cross had been buried, and there, of course, the next day it was found. Another famous invention was that of the bodies of the protomartyrs Gervasius and Protasius, which were discovered in the shrine of Sts Felix and Nabor in Milan in 385 by St Ambrose who, in the paradigmatic way of such occasions, also obeyed a presentiment, dug in search of the remains, and found two skeletons which were henceforth recognised as those of the martyrs and speedily transferred to the basilica which he had just built for himself.[9] A series of miraculous healings ensued, the faithful came in their thousands, and Ambrose's basilica prospered. Relics proliferated rapidly: in 390 two monks claimed to have found the head of John the Baptist in the ruins of Herod's palace in Jerusalem; the body of St Stephen was discovered in 415; and several churches claimed to have the holy foreskin.[10] And of course relics of the Virgin Mary were legion; since she was held to have been taken bodily into heaven, none of these were bones, but consisted of some of her hair, her virginal milk, her girdle – given to Thomas the apostle – her grave-clothes, and dress.[11] A list of famous relics, made in 1839, included two heads of John the Baptist, 'the hem of Jacob's coat of many colours, and a lock of hair with which Mary Magdalene wiped the Saviour's feet'.[12] By the end of the thirteenth century Mary Magdalen had, it seemed, left behind at least five corpses, in addition to many whole arms and smaller pieces which could not be accounted for. In Paris, for example, the church of La Madeleine on the Ile-de-la-Cité claimed to have a bit of Mary Magdalen's forehead supposedly touched by Christ when he said to her in the garden, 'Noli me tangere';[13] and Arnold von Harff (1471–1505), a nobleman visiting Venice on pilgrimage, saw a 'large bone of the breast of St Mary Magdalen' in one of the crucifixes in the church of S. Elena.[14] Of the five corpses, two were to become the subjects of much discussion in the second half of the thirteenth century.

As Ambrose had astutely been aware, relics had not only spiritual significance, but one which was far more mundane: their possession gave both to the churches and to those in charge of them enormous

status and power; status because of the veneration of the relics themselves, and power because of their ability to attract the faithful in large
numbers, and thus quite literally to transform the economy of the church
or monastery and of the surrounding area.[15] It is not surprising therefore
that there was a considerable demand for relics, which a thriving industry grew up to satisfy, becoming in fact one of the 'busiest occupations'
of the Middle Ages.[16]

Relics came to assume such an important part in Christian life that
the Second Council of Nicaea of 787 fulminated against those who
despised them, and ruled that churches could not be consecrated without
them.[17] The *Decretum* (*c.* 1140) of Gratian, the great jurist from Bologna,
ruled that every altar should have one or more.[18] Relics also took on
roles outside purely ecclesiastical spheres as they were required for oath-
taking in courts of law, were carried as agencies to victory in battle, and
as necessary adjuncts to daily life to heal and protect their possessors
against all evils. In the eighth and ninth centuries, hoards of relics were
everywhere unearthed and enshrined. Their collection evolved into an
international business as they were carried north from Italy and Spain,
and from the east by entrepreneurs, who might be commissioned by
'clients', or simply sell to the highest bidders. The trade in relics was to
have an extraordinary influence on the economic and social development
of the western world, and only increased on the return of the crusaders,
especially after the Fourth Crusade, who brought with them relics as
numerous as they were spurious. (In the fifteenth century, Margery
Kempe, an English mystic renowned in her lifetime for her tiresome
weeping and screaming, who identified herself with Mary Magdalen,
went to Palestine and brought back with her as a souvenir what she was
told and firmly believed was a staff made from a piece of Moses' rod.[19])

To the faithful, the dried and somewhat gruesome remains or dust so
repugnant to pagans and sceptics were the saints themselves, to be
revered, touched, passionately kissed. They warded off evil spirits,
brought health to their owners, and wielded extraordinary powers. In
the popular imagination, the saints were real and close familiars, characters with whom they could identify, who worked wonders for them,
who even dressed and talked as they did.[20] Reverence did not however
prevent the pious from mishandling these treasured things: in the eastern
Church, the bodies of saints and martyrs had been exhumed, dis-
membered and transported all over the Empire. By the fifth century,
dismemberment had become an accepted practice since eastern philos-

ophy held that the soul was present in every part of the body, and all
parts of every member were therefore believed to be thaumaturgically
efficacious: a finger of Mary Magdalen was as miraculous as her whole
body. The Byzantine emperors were the first to collect relics and within
five centuries had amassed the largest collection in the world, to be
dispersed when the crusaders took Constantinople in 1204. (A phial
containing a mixture of Christ's blood and some of Mary Magdalen's
spikenard from the collection found its way to the sacristy of the church
of the Frari in Venice where it was kept until the eighteenth century.[21])
Whilst the Latin Church at first disapproved of dismemberment, by the
Middle Ages it was not unusual to hear of holy bodies being torn apart
so that all could partake of their talismanic properties. In the thirteenth
century, Thomas Aquinas' body was decapitated, boiled, and preserved
so that the monks of the monastery of Fossanuova, where he had died,
did not lose the relic;[22] Hugh of Lincoln (d. 1200), an avid collector of
bones, who carried a silver casket containing countless fragments of
saints of both sexes when consecrating churches, visited the monastery
of Fécamp in northern France, which owned an arm of Mary Magdalen.
Desiring a bit for himself, he took the arm, with a knife unwrapped it
from the cloths of silk and linen which were tightly bound round it,
and which the monks had never dared open, and tried to break off a
piece with his fingers. Finding it too hard, he then, to the shock and
anger of the monks present, bit it first with his incisors, and finally
attacked it with his molars. With charming logic, he justified his somewhat rude treatment of the holy remains with the following words: 'If
a little while ago I handled the most sacred body of the Lord of all the
saints with my fingers, in spite of my unworthiness, and when I partook
of it [during Communion], touched it with my lips and teeth, why
should I not venture to treat in the same way the bones of the saints
. . . and without profanity acquire them when I have the opportunity?'[23]

One of the most extraordinary features of the cult of saints were the
furta sacra, or holy thefts, a phenomenon by which Vézelay was to profit
supremely. Here, stories were told of monks or clerics who, hearing by
chance of the holiness and miracle-working powers of a saint of another
parish, were so stirred that they vowed to steal the relics for their own
communities. The theft invariably took place at night, sometimes not
only with the saint's supposed 'permission' but also with his or her
outright encouragement. The thief then forced open the tomb, out of
which often issued the sweet fragrances already mentioned, gathered

up the bones, and returned home to the applause and joy of his own community. Paradoxically, rather than earning universal opprobrium for what were otherwise sinful acts carried out against other Christians, the perpetrators were treated as heroes, and praised for their virtuous labours, while the thefts themselves were often much vaunted by the communities which had profited by them. It was in fact quite usual for a monastery to claim that its patrons' relics had been stolen even when they had either been bought or had been an 'invention' – possibly in both senses of the word. No disgrace was attached to the 'holy' theft as its purpose had been to glorify the local church and bring faith to the people. And profit by them the churches often did for, as in the case of Vézelay, the 'thefts' seem to have been undertaken as a means of extricating themselves from periods of decline. In fact, relics were so frequently stolen that in 1215 the Lateran Council forbade them to be exhibited except on feast-days and then only in reliquaries.[24] But in reducing the visual component, always an important factor in beliefs based on the incredible, or supernatural, the churches did themselves a disfavour, as the pilgrims' faith often diminished. It was in response to such a reaction that Vézelay was to embark on its bizarre 'invention' in the thirteenth century.

As Louis Duchesne pointed out in the late nineteenth century in his wittily sceptical study of Mary Magdalen's legend in Provence, saints' cults began locally, either in the places where some memory of them still lingered, or where their relics had been found; it was only later, during the early Middle Ages when their bodies were translated and dismantled, that they came to be celebrated outside their original locus.[25] So it is natural to find the sisters Mary and Martha being celebrated first in Bethany from the fourth century. The fascinating account of Etheria, a noble lady from Galicia, who made a pilgrimage to the holy places in Palestine in the late fourth century, tells of her visit to the church which marked the place where Christ had met Mary of Bethany. This stood only 'five hundred steps' from another religious building, called the *Lazarium*, whose memory is preserved in the Arab name for Bethany,

el Aïzirièh, and over which Christians in the time of the Crusades had
built a church to contain the tomb of Lazarus.[26] Only a few years later,
at the beginning of the fifth century, St Jerome was to write a letter of
condolence to Eustochium, on the death of her mother Paula, an intrepid
traveller and supporter of Jerome, reminding her of their visit together
to the Holy Land, in c.385–6, where having gone into Lazarus' sepulchre, Paula then visited the house of Mary and Martha.[27] The monk
Bernard, who visited Bethany in c.870, noted the church built on Lazarus' tomb, and wrote of the saint, 'Later, it is said, Lazarus was bishop
of Ephesus for forty years.' He must have assumed that, as Gregory the
Great had conflated Mary Magdalen, Luke's sinner and Mary of Bethany
in the late sixth century, Lazarus had followed his sister to Ephesus (see
below).[28] Pilgrims were still being shown this house, now called the
'castle' of Lazarus, Mary Magdalen and Martha, 'at a distance of three
miles from Jerusalem', in the fifteenth century. In the account of his
journey in 1480 to the Holy Land, the Milanese Santo Brasca described
his visits to Pilate's house, a large stone which marked the place where
Christ had forgiven Mary Magdalen (as Luke's sinner) for her sins, the
spot near 'David's castle' where Christ appeared to the three Marys, and
a great circle in the ground where Christ appeared as the gardener to
Mary Magdalen, a visit to which gained a plenary indulgence for the
pilgrim; three steps from this was another circle where Mary Magdalen
had 'turned and thrown herself at Christ's feet'. Here an altar had been
erected, and a further plenary indulgence was granted to those who
visited this holy place.[29] There was also a chapel dedicated to the Magdalen in the square of the church of the Holy Sepulchre.[30] In c.1421, one
John Poloner was shown 'six bowshots from Bethany, and a stone's
throw from the stone where the Lord was sitting when Martha met
him, the ruins of Martha's house. One bowshot from thence . . . was
the Magdalen's house, on whose site stands a ruined church, now made
into a goat byre.'[31] Such visible and tangible souvenirs of favourite
characters from the New Testament could only whet the pilgrims'
fervour.

Mary Magdalen's first port of call on quitting Palestine, it seems, according to the account of Gregory of Tours (c.538–94), the historian of the
Franks, was in fact Ephesus, the city of Artemis, or Diana, where Paul
had laboured so hard against Gnosticism, and where it was believed
St John the Evangelist had ended his days. The Virgin too had appar-

ently lived there, and today visitors can see the little house, reconstructed over the first-century remains found in the nineteenth century prompted by the dreams of the German mystic Anna Katharina Emmerich (d.1824), where the Virgin stayed with St John, into whose keeping Christ had placed her at the crucifixion. (Sister Anna Katharina was also to have vivid visions of Mary Magdalen.[32]) Mary Magdalen's tomb had also been one of the holy places of Ephesus from the sixth century. Modestus, patriarch of Jerusalem (d.634), explained her arrival there thus:

> after the death of Our Lord, the mother of God and Mary Mag-
> dalen joined John, the well-beloved disciple, at Ephesus. It is there
> that the myrrhophore ended her apostolic career through her mar-
> tyrdom, not wishing to the very end to be separated from John
> the apostle and the Virgin.[33]

Apart from furnishing posterity with the story that Mary Magdalen had died a martyr, Modestus also claimed that she had remained a virgin always and become a teacher of other holy women; to her executioners she had appeared 'a pure crystal' because of her 'very great virginity and purity'.[34] Her sepulchre had apparently been placed near the entrance of the grotto at Ephesus known as the Cave of the Seven Sleepers, after the young Christian men who, legend told, had been walled up in a cave during the persecution of the Roman emperor Decian (c.250), and had awakened, Rip van Winkle-like, two hundred years later in the reign of the Christian emperor Theodosius II (d.450). The link with the Seven Sleepers was Mary Magdalen's entrée into the realm of relics and the miraculous, and her tomb soon accumulated the reputation to be expected of the final resting place of such a saint. When Gregory of Tours came to write of the legend, his rather cryptic reference to her tomb read: 'It is in this town that Mary Magdalen rests, with nothing to cover her', a description which has befuddled interpreters ever since.[35] Another rusting sign, this time at Ephesus (the first being at Magdala), points the way up a mountain to the Cave of the Seven Sleepers, where after scrambling through brambles and undergrowth, the twentieth-century traveller finds an early Christian mausoleum, but no longer any reference to the saint.

Thus began the mythical life of Mary Magdalen. The legend itself was born between 449, when that of the Seven Sleepers was first known, and 590, when Gregory referred to it in his work.[36] Her visit to Ephesus was noted by several Byzantine historians in the tenth century,[37] and pilgrims were still visiting the city in the twelfth century to see her sepulchre. Numerous miracles were said to have taken place there. In the time of Charles Martel, the leader of the Franks who reigned from 737 to 741, it was visited by the Anglo-Saxon monk Willibald, and in 1106 the Russian pilgrim, Daniel, noted that he had seen the tomb and the Magdalen's head, despite the fact that by then the tomb was empty.[38] By the end of the ninth century, Emperor Leo VI, the Philosopher (886–912), had 'translated' or transferred the body to Constantinople, where it was buried alongside that of Lazarus in a new and sumptuously decorated monastery built by the Bosporus, below the ancient imperial palace, and dedicated to the Magdalen's 'brother'.[39] The double translation was commemorated in Byzantine liturgical books on 4 May.[40] Part of Mary Magdalen's remains buried at Constantinople may have been among the trophies brought back in 1205, after the sack of Constantinople, by Conrad de Krosik, bishop of Halberstadt between 1201 and 1209; a notice in the *Gesta episcoporum Halberstadensium* refers to a fragment 'De craneo Marie Magdalene'. This, as Monsignor Saxer has pointed out, is one of the first references to Magdalen relics not linked to Vézelay or Provence, and which could have come from Byzantium, Palestine or Rome, as all were on the bishop's route as he returned home. Saxer has also noted that from the thirteenth century the church of S. Giovanni Laterano in Rome had an altar dedicated to Mary Magdalen which housed 'the body of the saint, minus the head', a skeleton which was also not associated with the claims of Vézelay or St Maximin, and the existence of which they were of course entirely unaware. The fragment from the Magdalen's cranium, he suggests, may have been once part of the headless body in Rome, brought back from Constantinople or the Crusades.[41]

From Ephesus also came Mary Magdalen's feast-day of 22 July, mentioned first in the west in the martyrology of the venerable Bede (*c.*673–735) of about 720, whose source appears to have been an earlier Greek or Byzantine calendar.[42] It was to pass thence into all subsequent liturgical books. (The same date appears in Greek calendars at the beginning of the tenth century, and it also appears in Byzantine synaxaries and menologies, Coptic calendars, Jacobite, Arabic, Marionite and Syriac manuscripts in the eleventh and twelfth centuries.[43]) The earliest Magdalenian cult, at Ephesus, therefore precedes that of Vézelay by nearly five hundred years.

Mary Magdalen's image also reached the foggy British damps of wild, ancient Northumbria where, on one of the two central panels of the Ruthwell Cross of the seventh or early eighth century, Luke's sinner wipes Christ's feet with her hair (see Plate 15). In the corresponding panel on the other side, Christ stands above two beasts in the desert; above him is John the Baptist, and below, the hermits Paul and Anthony. The great stone cross may have belonged to a double monastery, of which there were several in England in this period, and the iconography of asceticism, with John the Baptist, the model of Christian ascetic life who lived in the desert on locusts and wild honey, would have been entirely apt for such an institution in this outpost of the British Church; Mary Magdalen as Luke's sinner had now taken on her new role as the Christian figure of the contemplative life, which Origen had first ascribed to Mary of Bethany in the third century.[44] This is borne out by her second appearance on the cross in the pairing above where Martha and Mary, the types of the active and contemplative lives, embrace. They are identified by an inscription below which reads, 'martha/ maria mr/ dominnae', which has been translated as 'Martha [and] Mary, meritorious ladies'.[45] The iconographic source has been traced to Bede, abbot of Jarrow, a monastery on the eastern side of England from Ruthwell, who between 709 and 715 wrote a commentary on Luke's gospel.[45] The gloss on Chapter 7, in which the feast in the house of the Pharisee is described, opens with the words: 'Sanctissima Maria poenitentis historia' (The most blessed Mary, the story of her repentance). Bede subscribes to the unity theory, as Mary Magdalen is here both Luke's sinner and Mary of Bethany, united in their anointing of Christ, who in the first instance 'running with humility and tears merits the remission of her sins', and in the second, at Bethany, is 'no longer a sinner but with Christ a chaste holy and devoted woman'. As part of his peroration, and to show his erudition, Bede enthusiastically devotes several lines to the origins of alabaster:

> It is a kind of gleaming white marble, veined with various colours, which they are accustomed to hollow out to make unguent jars because it is dedicated to best preserving [things] from corruption. It came from near Thebes in Egypt and Damascus in Syria, [and] of the rest, the most pleasing in truth, from India.[46]

Another feature which would assume extraordinary significance in Mary Magdalen's legend also seems to have been known in Northumbria

15 The Ruthwell Cross, showing
Luke's sinner drying Christ's feet with
her hair in the third panel. At top: Mary
and Martha greeting one another.
Seventh or early eighth century.
Dumfriesshire, Ruthwell Parish Church.

before it made its way to Vézelay. This appears in a mid- to late ninth-
century Anglo-Saxon martyrology which describes how, after the ascension, Mary Magdalen had such great longing for Christ that she could 'no
longer look on any man', but went into the desert and lived there
'unknown to all men'. Here she fasted, but every day at prayertime angels
came to lift her to heaven for spiritual sustenance, and then returned her
to her cave in the rocks; in this way, she lived for thirty years, and when

she died a 'holy mass priest' gave her the last sacrament and buried her, and 'great miracles' took place at her grave.[47] The ninth-century scribe is thought by one authority to have copied a native Latin manuscript of *c*.750,[48] so it seems that the idea that Mary Magdalen had spent her last years contemplating in the desert may have taken on its medieval form as early as the eighth century in England.

As a hermit, yet another character had accrued to her, that of Egyptian Mary, the fifth-century harlot who, after seventeen years of infamy in Alexandria, earned her way across the sea to Palestine according to her *métier*, and spent the last forty-seven years of her life repenting in the deserts of the Holy Land. Naked, clad only in her hair, she too had been fed by angels. On her death she was buried by the bishop Zosimus.[49] But in the ninth century, Mary Magdalen's story differed from that of Mary of Egypt: she was neither naked nor clothed in her hair, she lived in a cave and it was out of sorrow, contemplation and love, rather than penitence, that she had hidden herself away. That her love was reciprocated is earlier made clear by the compiler of the martyrology: 'And since she was so dear to Christ . . . after his resurrection he appeared to her first of all people, and she announced his resurrection to the apostles.'[50] It was no doubt the similarity of their names, and their early lives of sin which led hagiographers to assume that the expiation of their dissoluteness would also be analogous. It was only later that her seclusion, now penitential, and exploited by Vézelay, which may even have localised the cave in the twelfth century, came to be the best known aspect of Mary Magdalen's *vita* in the Middle Ages. In the eighth and ninth centuries, the idea of a feminine model of asceticism would have been particularly attractive and pertinent to the very large number of female ascetics in the north of England at the time. Indeed, the existence of such large double monasteries as that at Whitby, ruled by the redoubtable Hilda (614–80), might well have been the catalyst for the inclusion on the Ruthwell Cross of Mary Magdalen, the female model of repentance and contemplation.[51]

Devotion to Mary Magdalen had been accelerating in the west during the ninth and tenth centuries: prayers were addressed to her in sacramentaries, and in the tenth century she first appeared as one of the myrrhophores in the trope *Quem quaeritis*, or 'Whom do you seek?', enacted during the Easter ceremonies probably for the first time at the monastery at St Gall in what is now Switzerland.[52] The first prayers proper to the mass of her feast-day on 22 July had appeared in a ninth-century sacramentary at St Martin at Tours, and in Essen and Modena in the tenth century, and in England, the German Empire and Spain in the eleventh century.[53] The complete mass was to manifest itself by the twelfth century. At the same time, hymns addressed to her as a beneficiary of divine clemency and penitential model for all sinners, stressing her sinful life and reflecting the growth of a new penitential climate within the Church, had begun to appear by the second half of the tenth century.[54] The stage was set for Vézelay's entry into the field.

Vézelay was not, however, the first sanctuary in France to be dedicated to Mary Magdalen. In 1024 a church at Verdun built under the aegis of the deacon Ermenfroi was put under her patronage. Other notices followed, from Bayeux, c.1027, Bellevault, 1034, Le Mans, c.1040, Reims, c.1043, and Besançon in 1049.[55] Nor was Vézelay the first place in Burgundy to show devotion to the Magdalen: nearby at Auxerre, the feast-day of Mary and Martha, 19 January, seems to have been introduced into the hieronymian martyrology in the late sixth century.[56] Nor indeed was Vézelay the first to claim possession of some of her relics: in the west, the earliest references to Magdalen cults were both outside France, one in Germany, where on 5 November 974 an altar was dedicated to some holy virgins, among whom were Martha and Mary Magdalen, in a crypt of the monastery of St Stephen at Halberstadt in Lower Saxony,[57] and the other at Exeter in England in the second half of the tenth century when King Athelstan, a noted collector of relics, placed a finger of the saint in the keeping of the cathedral. The cathedral clearly prized its treasure, putting it at the head of its list which was compiled in the tenth century:

> First, a finger of St Mary Magdalen, who living washed our Lord's feet with her tears, whom our Lord truly loved and honoured, and to whom he appeared first when he was raised from the dead.[58]

At Echternach, the parish church or monastery of St Willibrord claimed to have relics of Mary Magdalen in 1039.[59] In Spain, at Oviedo, an eleventh-century catalogue of relics claimed to have some hair with which Mary Magdalen had dried Christ's feet.[60] The earliest sanctuary in England dedicated to Mary Magdalen was at Barnstaple in Devon, dating from the time of William the Conqueror,[61] and there may even have been another, pre-Conquest church at Beckery, near Glastonbury.[62]

The cult of Mary Magdalen at Vézelay, also first known of in the eleventh century, in fact bears all the hallmarks of a classic *furtum sacrum*. In 1265 the saint's body was found at the abbey in the most dramatic circumstances. It had been 'known' to be there, indeed the abbey had claimed it to have been so from the mid-eleventh century, but there were elements in the situation which brought about its 'discovery' which were, to say the least, dubious. By 1265 the vast edifice, built to contain the thousands of pilgrims who flocked there to venerate the relics around which it had been constructed, had long been completed. The abbey had grown from humble beginnings as a small monastery founded in c.860 by the famous and pious Count Girart de Roussillon and his wife Berthe, under the patronage of the Virgin Mary. In March 863, they donated it to the Holy See, an arrangement which endowed the monastery with fiscal and judiciary immunity from the local landowners, the counts of Nevers, and from the bishops of Autun in whose diocese Vézelay lay, whilst the monks paid Rome symbolic annual dues in recognition of papal protection.[63] The history of the abbey is well documented between the ninth and fourteenth centuries by virtue of its special relationship with Rome which yielded a large volume of correspondence detailing Vézelay's squabbles with these various authorities from its earliest days. Its autonomous position, relying for spiritual authority only on a distant pope, was to be the cause of frequent struggles with the monarchy, which from the twelfth century was trying to establish a centralist government, and with the townspeople of Vézelay itself, jealous of the abbey's accumulated wealth.

Some time between 1030 and 1040, according to the chronicles, the abbey had fallen into disrepute. In 1026 it had been placed under the rule of the Benedictines at Cluny whose abbot, on hearing of the monks' misbehaviour, sent an expedition against Vézelay. The following year came the first of the many confrontations between the counts of Nevers and Vézelay's abbots – the first intrusion of a lay power into the monastery which denied any feudal overlord or that it answered to any temporal authority, even that of the monarch.[64] A period of decline appeared to have set in, but the abbey's fortunes took a turn for the better when in 1037 Geoffrey, a Cluniac, was elected abbot. Described by his hagiographer as a 'wise reformer, as careful with regard to his personal piety as he was to the progress of his monks', Geoffrey was also attentive to the needs of his abbey, and to this end, to the revival of the flagging devotions of the faithful.[65] Before Geoffrey's abbacy there seems to have been neither any trace of a special Magdalen cult at Vézelay, nor indeed of her relics, and until the mid-eleventh century its patrons had been the Virgin Mary, Sts Peter and Paul, and the holy martyrs Andeux and Pontian, whose relics had been transferred to Vézelay in 863. The first reference to Mary Magdalen came in a bull from Leo IX dated 27 April 1050 where she was included at the head of the abbey's patrons; eight years later, on 6 March 1058, Pope Stephen IX confirmed her as sole patron – thus dislodging Vézelay's earlier protectors – and also ratified the abbey's possession of her relics.[66]

The new abbot of Vézelay, Geoffrey, would certainly have been aware from his time at Cluny of the sermon 'In veneratione Sanctae Mariae Magdalenae' attributed to the abbot Odo (d.942), written during the first half of the tenth century, and read at least annually for several centuries thereafter. Here Mary Magdalen was described, after a life of 'sensual pleasures' – no doubt derived from Gregory the Great's homily – as a 'model of zealous devotion' who carried out the 'ministration of holy familiarity', that is, attending to his daily needs, in Christ's lifetime, and who in contrast to the apostles who ran away, despite the fragility of her sex – 'indeed the feminine sex is usually fearful to walk in the dark' – followed the Lord because she loved him with all her heart. Through having been the herald of the resurrection, she had removed the dishonour of the female sex created by Eve.[67] Odo's panegyric also showed its debts to Hippolytus in its celebration of Mary Magdalen as the Church and as the Bride, but is particularly interesting for its emphasis on her role as apostle to the apostles, and on the virtues of poverty, obedience, chastity and servitude, which would have particularly struck a chord with its monkish audience.

Extraordinary coincidences seem to have been integral to the origins of the Magdalen cult at Vézelay. Apart from his Cluniac beginnings, Geoffrey had also been present at the Council of Reims in 1049, where he had met the bishops of Verdun and Besançon, in both of whose dioceses sanctuaries in Mary Magdalen's honour had been built, and consecrated by Pope Leo IX (under whose aegis the council took place) in the same year.[68] Geoffrey had also attended the Council of Rome at the Lateran on 29 April 1050, two days after Leo's bull confirming the Magdalen's patronage at Vézelay, supplanting even the Virgin Mary. It seems that the abbot had been determined to establish her patronage, and was to persevere until the happy outcome. Geoffrey had been in the pope's entourage for six months prior to the issue of the bull, during which he would have had ample time to persuade Leo that the saint's bones were at Vézelay. He had sought to develop a suitable cult to renew the spiritual life of his brethren, as had Ermenfroi at Verdun, as well as the waning fortunes of his abbey, but had, it appeared, few illusions concerning the truth.[69]

In the Middle Ages, holiness was inextricably bound up with miracle-making. In this, Vézelay was no exception. Pilgrimages to sanctified places had been taking place since the first centuries of Christianity, as Etheria's account demonstrates. In the twelfth and thirteenth centuries, huge pilgrimages grew around the more famous shrines, with vast crowds arriving in the hope of cures, deliverances from demons, and other such manifestations of divine intervention. These were not the only purposes, however, of such festivities, for dissoluteness and debauchery were often companions to the relics being processed. Indeed they were so much so that the knight of La Tour-Landry, lumping them together with profane pleasures, entitled a chapter of his book 'Of ladies who go to jousts and pilgrimages',[70] a feature corroborated by the Wife of Bath, who saw much entertainment afforded by going to 'visitaciouns/ To vigilies and to processions/ To prechyng eek, and to thise pilgrimages,/ To pleyes of myracles, and to mariages'.[71] Seduction, it seems, was rife, and procuresses plying their trade were often much in evidence. But as an alderman of one town told Denys the Carthusian, the local town council would have been extremely loath to abolish its pilgrimage since such processions brought the town large profits as all the pilgrims had to be fed and lodged, and anyway, it seemed, such decadence was all part of the occasion.[72]

Pilgrims flocked from all over France to touch the tomb of Mary Magdalen at Vézelay; some even came from as far as England to be healed, forgiven, and dispossessed of their devils at the holy site. And with these faithful came the merchants too, ever ready to profit from the pious. Precious gifts were offered to merit the Magdalen's intercession, foreign visitors had to pay taxes, and on feast and fair days merchants' stalls were rented at exorbitant prices, all yielding vast revenues to the abbey and townspeople. Hagiographical material issued by the abbey told how the saint worked miracles to support Geoffrey: prisoners, now freed, whose fetters and iron collars she had broken, came to the sanctuary to deposit their chains before her tomb, so many of them that Geoffrey was able to obtain enough metal to surround the high altar with railings (see Plate 16).[73] Through Mary Magdalen's intercession also, peace had been established in Burgundy, within three years of Geoffrey's abbacy, in 1040.[74] And in the Middle Ages, the Church's growing gloomy view of humanity, and its morbid obsession with its sins, which often seemed to be the main topic of medieval sermons, brought visitors in droves in the fond hope that they would be forgiven. Such were the intercessory powers imagined to be within a saint's domain that it was commonly believed that sinners could receive automatic remission of their sins by visiting particular shrines, as did the woman who visited Vézelay early in the twelfth century, and who by laying a schedule of her sins on the altar had them immediately erased.[75] The Magdalen's own intercessory powers were so extraordinary that pilgrims at Vézelay heard from the friend of a certain knight who witnessed there his friend's resuscitation after apparent death in battle. And another knight, from Aquitaine, who in the mid-twelfth century had also been miraculously raised from the dead by Vézelay's saint, even went on annual pilgrimage to her shrine to give thanks.[76]

Vézelay's possession of Mary Magdalen's body was confirmed by the papal bulls of Lucius III, Urban III, and Clement III, and was also supported by the French monarchy.[77] As a result of Geoffrey's labours, Mary Magdalen's feast-day became one of the most popular in Latin Christendom, and the pilgrimage the most celebrated in France, as the meeting-point for the route to Santiago di Compostela, where the body of St James the Apostle lay. Pilgrims came from far and wide to the shrine of the holy sinner, eager to touch the Magdalen's tomb, drawn by the feminine cult of beauty and grace, by the image of Luke's sinner's long hair drying Christ's feet, and her tears of repentance. To them, she was 'Christi dilecta' or 'Christi dilectrix', 'Christ's beloved' or 'lover of Christ', and also particularly, as a result of the Church's growing asceticism during the twelfth century, *peccatrix* or sinner, or *meretrix*, prostitute.

16 Mary Magdalen freeing a prisoner. From a page illustrating her miracles in an Italian, possibly Venetian, manuscript of the first half of the fourteenth century. Vatican City, Biblioteca Apostolica Vaticana.

There was always, however, the awkward question of how Mary Magdalen's body had come to its resting place in Burgundy, so far away from her birthplace in Judaea. Reverence was paid to a tomb, but although the body of the 'blessed Magdalen' was said to rest in the monastery's church, it had never been seen, and nor had adequate account been given of its arrival from Palestine after the ascension. In the eleventh century, the simple answer given to tiresome questions could be 'summed up in a few words', as a document issued by Vézelay rather testily pointed out. 'All is possible to God who does what he pleases. Nothing is difficult for him when he has decided to do it for the well-being of men.' When this reply proved unsatisfactory, the narrator told of how Mary Magdalen had appeared to him standing outside her tomb, saying, 'It is me, whom many people believe to be here.'[78] Warnings of the divine chastisement which had befallen previous doubters were given to those who queried the existence of the Magdalen's body. An excuse for not exposing the remains appears in a late twelfth-century manuscript which told of the occasion when Geoffrey himself had decided to

remove the Magdalen's relics from the little crypt where they had been
found to put them in a precious reliquary. The church had suddenly
been plunged into thick darkness, and the people assisting had fled
terrified, and all those present had suffered; it had henceforth been
decided to relinquish all ideas of opening the holy tomb as such acts
clearly provoked wrath from above.[79] Faith was all that was required,
the monks at Vézelay told their faint-hearted pilgrims.

Documents issued by the abbey in the thirteenth century to justify its
claims to possess Mary Magdalen's relics relate how the pilgrims' faith
had so dwindled that it was clear to the monks that they had to engineer
some way of making their claim credible. A flood of hagiographical
material henceforth issued from the abbey in which a new element
in the Magdalen story emerged (see Plate 17). Tales, often entirely
contradictory, were told of how the body had arrived, not directly from
Palestine, but from somewhere in Provence where she had been buried
between the years 882 and 884, and how a 'holy theft' by one Aléaume
had been perpetrated to bring the precious remains to their final resting
place.[80] A second version described how, during the reign of King
Carloman, Adalgar, the bishop of Autun, had come to Vézelay with his
knight Adelelme, and informed the abbot, Odo, of the whereabouts of
the tomb of the abbey's patroness. Adelelme was then sent off with an
escort to Arles – the entire area having been overtaken by the Saracens
– to find the church in which the saint was buried, and then took the
bodies (that of St Maximinus was also included for good measure),
and returned to Vézelay.[81] Yet another account, apparently the final,
perfected redaction, tells of how, in the eighth century, the monk Badilon was sent to Provence by the abbey's founder, Count Girart de
Roussillon, and its abbot Odo, to retrieve the glorious remains from
near Aix – 'public rumour' had bruited it that she had been buried there
– to prevent them from being ravaged by the Saracens. Aix has been
destroyed, and some old men show him the ruined tomb, which still
contains the sweetly smelling uncorrupted body of Mary Magdalen.
During the night he dreams that Mary Magdalen appears to him,
swathed in a shining white garment, telling him not to fear, and that
she is to be taken to a place pre-ordained by God. The relics thus arrive
at Vézelay.[82] But how and why, it might quite logically have been
asked, had Mary Magdalen come to be in Gaul, so far away from her
birthplace in Judaea?

17 The opening page of the so-called 'Dossier' of 1360–82, containing the history of the arrival of Mary Magdalen's body at Vézelay and her miracles, showing the *Noli me tangere* in an illuminated initial, with the arms of Louis I of Anjou and Marie of Blois. Vatican City, Biblioteca Apostolica Vaticana.

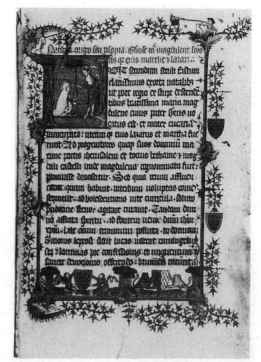

To this question also, Vézelay provided the answer. Somehow, a new mythical element of Mary Magdalen's life which had been slowly evolving over the previous two hundred years or so, and gathering different elements and resonances as time and exigencies required, seems to have arrived at the abbey in Burgundy at the time of Geoffrey's abbacy. This was the legend of the eremitical life of Mary Magdalen, possibly, as we have seen, known in England as early as 750, but given a south Italian origin of the late ninth century by Saxer, who names it the *Vita eremitica beatae Mariae Magdalenae*. It had spread in different versions through Italy, England and the German Empire, but had apparently remained unknown in France until the latter half of the eleventh century.[83] A different strain from that recounted in the Anglo-Saxon martyrology, the *Vita eremitica* tells of Mary Magdalen's retreat into the desert but describes her as naked and repentant – she asks the priest to lend her some clothes as she wishes to see him 'without shame'. This he does, and he leads her 'half-alive' to his church, and buries her when she dies. In this account, she relates her sinful past, and emphasises her terrible penance.

As we have seen, certain aspects of the legend of St Mary of Egypt had already accrued to the composite character of Mary Magdalen. Now, in the eleventh century, further details such as her nakedness, and the long golden hair which grew to cover it, were added. This part of the story derived from the fifth-century legend of St Agnes, a young Roman virgin who, on refusing a suitor, was denounced to the local prefect as a Christian. Nothing could induce the young girl to desist from her intention to preserve her chastity as the bride of Christ. When she was thrown naked into a brothel, her hair grew miraculously to cover her shame. A fire failed to burn her. Undaunted, she was beheaded. The hair of Mary Magdalen and Mary of Egypt also grew to cover the nakedness which, as penitents in the desert, having thrown away all worldly trappings, they had adopted.

The *Vita eremitica*, believed in the Middle Ages to have been written by the Jewish historian Flavius Josephus (*c.*37–*c.*100), became widespread in the eleventh century, and was well known in monastic circles where it was read during the night office or at meals.[84] Until the twelfth century, the precise location of her thirty years of solitude, the purpose of which over a period of time changed from contemplation to penance, was at first unspecified by Vézelay, but it is identified in a late twelfth-century manuscript at Berne where the retreat was said ('dicitur') to have been in a large cavern east of Marseille, not far from Montrieux. Here high up in the *massif* of Provence, four leagues distant from St Maximin, was a grotto which until about 1170 had known only one patron, the Virgin Mary.[85]

In Vézelay's version, Mary Magdalen spent her last days at the grotto of Ste Baume (Holy Balm), but was to die and be buried by bishop Maximinus at Aix. Having established this burial place, from which the monk Badilon had retrieved the glorious bones, it only remained to unearth an explanation of her arrival in Gaul. According to the mid-eleventh century *Gesta episcoporum Cameracensum*, the chronicles of the bishops of Cambrai, Mary Magdalen had been buried in Jerusalem; her body had been brought to Vézelay by 'the man of God', Badilon, who was himself buried in the monastery at Leuze in Hainault.[86] An early account in the *chanson de geste* of Girart, possibly composed at Vézelay when St Bernard came there to preach or, at least, inspired by Vézelay, contains a reference to the transfer of the Magdalen's body, and tells of monks crossing the sea, and bringing the body back from the Holy Land ('del regne paianor').[87] However, the most widely believed story was that she had arrived by boat, like other saints and apostles who made their way to France, and had been accompanied by Maximinus – in the first account – one of the seventy-two disciples (for, as Duchesne wryly remarked, 'a woman could not have come alone as she always has need of support'[88]). They had disembarked at Marseille and there preached the gospel. In this account, our saint had once more become the *apostola apostolorum* who, having been the first apostle of the gospels, now, through her arrival in France, and her preaching, continued her apostolic career, and in the process had converted the pagan prince of Marseille. (A later monkish narrator, however, clearly felt it his duty to explain discreetly how a woman could have taken part in these apostolic and by definition masculine activities, remembering that ecclesiastical discipline was disinclined to favour female apostolacy, and told instead of how, having arrived on French soil, Mary Magdalen had not preached but retired in solitude.[89]) According to this same legend, Maximinus had subsequently become the first bishop of Aix. Mary Magdalen had predeceased her companion who buried her and was then himself buried near her. A special altar at the church of St Sauveur at Aix was dedicated to Maximinus and Mary Magdalen as first founders of the city, which also claimed the honour of having been evangelised in the first century. A false charter purporting to be dated 7 August 1103 refers to this consecration, written by the archbishop and canons of the church in support of their claims at the end of the twelfth century that the bones of its illustrious founders were still in the tomb from which Vézelay had fabricated its *furtum sacrum*.[90]

A later version, recalling the Magdalen's relationship to Lazarus and Martha, recounted the family from Bethany's flight from Palestine during the Jewish persecution – where, as close friends of Christ, they would have been prime targets – their journey across the sea, and arrival at Aix. In this, Lazarus had become first bishop of Marseille, Martha had lived at Tarascon, and overcome the wicked dragon, and they had all died; the bones of Lazarus and Mary Magdalen had been taken to Burgundy, but those of Martha had remained in Provence, where they were 'discovered' in 1187.[91]

By the thirteenth century, an alarmingly confusing array of versions existed of Mary Magdalen's voyage, sometimes featuring Maximinus, sometimes Lazarus and Martha, sometimes including Sidonius (see below) and Marcellina, Martha's servant, and sometimes apostolising Marseille and lower Gaul. But the results were uniform: the relics were now at Vézelay, brought by Badilon in an heroic 'holy' theft. The accounts of how it happened, engendered at Vézelay to establish credibility in its claims, were to have the most extraordinary repercussions, and unfortunate effect on their propagators, in the latter part of the century.

One of the most important reasons for all this effort, apart from the particular needs of Vézelay, was to establish a direct link between the apostles chosen by Christ and France. The process seems to have started with St Dionysius, believed in the Middle Ages to have been the disciple of St Paul, who was sent to convert Gaul, died as bishop of Paris, and was buried in the abbey church named after him, St Denis, near Paris. Mary Magdalen would offer an even more direct link with Christ, and as apostle to Gaul and penitent, accorded better with the aspirations of the age than did the now redundant Roman saints Andeux and Pontian, more so even than Vézelay's other three previous guardians. Such a patron would even allow the abbey to rival Compostela, which boasted the body of James the Apostle.

At Easter 1146, Vézelay lived one of its finest hours when Pope Eugenius III chose the abbey as the departure-point for the Second Crusade. Bernard of Clairvaux, the pope's former teacher and the most influential religious power in Europe, was to preach the Crusade, which had been brought about by the fall of Edessa, the capital of a small crusader outpost in Syria. The building of the abbey church was nearly completed; during the course of 1140–50 it had been enlarged by a narthex, but since the church itself was thought to be too small to hold the hordes of pilgrims and crusaders who would come to see Mary Magdalen's tomb and hear St Bernard's preaching, an open-air ceremony was prepared and a platform erected on the northern slopes of Vézelay's hill to accommodate the most eminent personages. These were to include the king of France, Louis VII, and his wife Eleanor of Aquitaine and their vast entourage. In the event, the crowd was so great that after the abbot of Clairvaux had called for help for the holy places in Palestine and was in the process of distributing crosses, the platform gave way. That nobody was hurt was later deemed to be yet another of Mary Magdalen's miracles.[92]

Vézelay's fame was unrivalled until the end of the twelfth century. New sanctuaries sprang up all over France, the idea of the eremitical Magdalen inspiring monks and recluses to put their retreats both in cloisters and in the forests and wastes of the west and north of France under her protection. Vézelay's own political and symbolic importance had been highlighted in 1118 when the abbot Suger (*c.*1080–1151), Louis VI's brilliant adviser, had suggested the abbey as the meeting-place for his king and Pope Gelasius II.[93] In 1166, the exiled archbishop of Canterbury, Thomas à Becket, came to the abbey to declare his king, Henry II, excommunicate; three years later on Mary Magdalen's feast-day, Alexander III's legates announced the conditions under which the Holy See would accept the peace between the king and his turbulent priest.[94] In July 1190, Philip Augustus and the king of England, Richard Coeur de Lion, met at the abbey for the Third Crusade, reiterating Vézelay's importance.[95]

The abbey's fame and prosperity did not however prevent, and were rather the cause of, a communal insurrection which began in 1151. The local townspeople and priests, jealous of Vézelay's riches, and possibly of its independence, joined forces with the count of Nevers and the bishop of Autun (in whose diocese Vézelay lay), both of whom had the secret backing of Cluny against the abbey. Only threats from Rome persuaded the bishop to yield in 1154, and royal intervention forged peace with the count and the bourgeois in 1156. In the latter year, the chronicler Hugues le Poitevin indignantly described the abbey as having been a 'theatre of great scandal' during Innocent II's pontificate (1130–43),[96] while in 1162, the abbot, Pons de Montboissier, requested that Vézelay be placed once again under the direct protection of the Holy See. This move seemed to have little effect for the new count of Nevers found allies within the monastery, and with their support overthrew the abbot Guillaume de Mello, who had to be reinstated by Louis VII in 1166.[97] In the first half of the thirteenth century, continuing squabbles marked Vézelay's decline as control of the abbey was fought over by the counts of Nevers, the abbots, the monks themselves and the crown. Internal troubles also plagued the abbey; the community itself was divided, abbots were manifestly no longer in charge of their brethren – some were not even resident; monks, like 'a conscript army'[98] without their leader, were in disorder, prey to discontent, and were expelled for bad behaviour. In 1207, Innocent III deposed the abbot Girart d'Arcy for squandering the church's possessions, for spending the money on the sumptuous wedding clothes and feasts of his own children – born during his time as abbot, for having bought his own election, and similarly professing monks, and for distributing benefices simoniacally.[99] Fifty years later, the monks revolted against their legitimate abbot, Jean d'Auxerre, who in turn appealed for support from the count of Nevers, the abbey's traditional enemy, and with his help overcame his unruly monks.[100]

The papacy's concern is evidenced by the two legates sent within six years of each other. In 1259, possibly as the result of the revolt of the previous year, Alexander IV sent an emissary to look into the abbey's affairs, whose conclusions, if ever reported, are unknown. In 1265 Clement IV sent another legate to enquire into the situation.[101] According to the monks, revenues had declined because of their failure to exhibit the relics which had naturally led to 'certain hesitations and scruples as to the authenticity of the said relics'.[102] Whether or not this was the case, it was clear that Vézelay's constant battles with the lay powers had also been instrumental in diminishing the pilgrims' fervour, and with this came a concomitant reduction of the abbey's revenues as the merchants departed, no longer able to find pious visitors to exploit. Vézelay's redemption from total decadence was only possible by imposing rigorous monastic reform which might also dispel doubts concerning the relics' authenticity. This in turn would revitalise the pilgrimage and, as its natural sequel, would also bring back the merchants. It was a temporal solution to a spiritual malaise which would involve king, pope and legates, as well as the abbot and his monks.

Before Simon de Brion, Clement's legate, was able to reach the abbey, however, two other delegates from the Holy See, the bishop of Auxerre, Gui de Mello – of the same family as Guillaume de Mello, an earlier abbot of Vézelay – and Pierre, bishop of Panéade, arrived at Vézelay, at the request of the abbot Jean. On the night of 4–5 October, at matins – the customary hour of 'inventions' – and in the presence of these latter dignatories and the monastic community, the body of the 'glorious' sinner which had, according to a contemporary document, 'long been' placed under the high altar of the crypt, was newly 'discovered'. The official report made by the delegates describes how the witnesses were brought to the place where the body was said to have been buried, and there they found a rectangular bronze metal coffer containing relics wrapped up 'with every sign of veneration' in silk material, together with 'an extraordinary abundance of female hair'.[103]

It was the copious amounts of feminine hair which confirmed to the two bishops that this was indeed the body of Mary Magdalen. The witnesses were equally convinced by a charter purporting to have been written by the 'once-most illustrious king' Charles which, as intended, lent regal confirmation to the authenticity of the relics. In an atmosphere charged with great emotion ('much piety and joy, which showed in a profusion of tears'[104]), the remains were inspected and then wrapped in new silk, sealed, returned to the reliquary, which in its turn was sealed and placed in the coffer, which was put back in its place under the high altar. The following morning, the official document intended to make it all appear credible was sealed by the bishops and also put in the coffer.

While there is no doubt about the authenticity of the witnesses' document, and their own integrity, there has been much scepticism concerning the objects they were required to verify, and the intentions of the abbot himself. The charter of 'king Charles' has been shown to be a forgery based on a true document of Charles the Bald dated 31 August 842 in Vézelay's collection.[105] It seems that the monks, fearing the visit of the legate from the Holy See, decided to take matters into their own hands, and organised the 'invention' – in the process contriving to obtain a head of female hair – thus pre-empting any action on the part of Simon de Brion, the pope's emissary, as well as requesting the assistance of Gui de Mello who could be relied upon to be sympathetic to Vézelay's interests. Having taken the decision to verify and transfer the relics, the monks, it seemed, had written up official records concerning the events, adding falsified earlier documents, and pieces which had been in circulation over the past two hundred years referring to the transfer of the body from Provence by Badilon.

Matters did not rest there, however. Possibly because they had doubts as to whether the official report itself would create the impact they so desired, despite the importance of Gui de Mello and the other church dignatories, and possibly because misgivings about the remains of the holy sinner still lingered, the monks decided to enlist the services of the supreme arbiter, the 'most Christian king' of France, Louis IX. Accordingly, Louis was invited to a solemn exposition and translation of the relics, so that his participation both complemented and guaranteed the testimony of the papal legate. In issuing their invitation, the monks knew they had the right man, one who was deeply religious (he is believed to have been a Franciscan tertiary), and one who had a great affection for Vézelay. He had been there on pilgrimage twice before, in

1244 and 1248, and was to visit it again in 1270 before going on Crusade for the last time.[106] He had a particular fondness for Mary Magdalen, was fascinated by John's account of the *Noli me tangere*, and by Luke's sinner, and knew the legend of the saint's eremitical life; in 1254 he had travelled to Provence to venerate at the shrine of the 'friend of Christ'.[107] He was also naïve and credulous, he loved relics, of which he had a huge collection, and he was, besides, very fond of attending translations of saints' remains.[108]

On 24 April 1267, the octave of Easter, a solemn celebration took place in the presence of Louis, his brother, brother-in-law and three sons, and a vast retinue. Amid huge pomp, which had the added intention of creating a lasting impression on the faithful spectators, the relics were solemnly shown and transferred from their old coffer into a new silver one. The king received a considerable portion and, desirous of sharing with his contemporaries concrete reminders of the object of his devotion, in front of the huge crowd in the basilica, he gave bits to members of the illustrious throng, and to the abbey an arm, the jawbone and three teeth, keeping the major part for himself.[109]

The following August, the abbot received a parcel from Louis containing two precious reliquaries made of gold or silver gilt, encrusted with precious stones, emeralds and diamonds.[110] The king wished to house the relics – the arm, jaw and three teeth – and to this end had commissioned a reliquary in the shape of an arm held out with the hand open; the jaw and teeth were put in another piece, carried by a silver-gilt angel. In gratitude to the monks for his generous share of the remains, the king gave them several relics from his own collection, a substantial part of which consisted of items from the treasure store of the Byzantine emperors looted by the Latin army in 1204, and which he had bought in 1238 from his financially pressed cousin Baldwin, emperor of Constantinople.[111] Amongst these were a piece from the Holy Cross, thorns from the crown of thorns, fragments of the Lord's clothes, from his childhood to the Passion, and of the apron worn at the washing of the disciples' feet, all of which were put into the open hand. For as Louis said, 'It seemed to us fitting that some relics of the Saviour be thus placed close to some relics of this most holy woman who cherished him with such a love that she merited in exchange the great pardon for her sins which she received from him, of that same woman whom he accepted with such familiarity that she touched him.'[112] Louis' sentiments perfectly encapsulate the medieval concept of Mary Magdalen –

Luke's sinner who was forgiven for she loved greatly, allowed to touch him, when she dried his feet with her hair in the house of Simon the Pharisee, a theme much stressed in medieval writings, painting and sculpture, and Mary Magdalen whose love for and intimate relationship with the Lord led her to seek to touch him in the recognition scene in the garden.

A letter dated 9 August 1267 from Simon de Brion (who received a rib of the saint for his part in the affair) contains a precise inventory of the jewel-studded reliquaries and, in the second half, injunctions to keep the relics and their containers intact: 'intactum permanere volentes . . . integraliter conservari'. They were to be neither sold, diminished, altered, given away, nor mortgaged on pain of excommunication. So that no-one could remain ignorant of this fact, de Brion's letter was to be read annually at a general assembly of the monastery.[113] A second letter, of 11 August, gave details of the indulgences obtainable by the faithful who fulfilled the requirements: 100 days' indulgence was to be granted to pilgrims who came to Vézelay on the four major feast-days of Mary Magdalen.[114]

In 1279, however, came the unexpected news that the body of Mary Magdalen had been found in the crypt of the monastery church at St Maximin in Provence. There had been no previous intimation that the Provençal monks might wish to claim possession of relics which their brothers in the north had claimed to have retrieved from Gaul four centuries earlier. One Vézelien text even suggested that the bones had been taken from St Maximin itself. It seems that the Benedictine monks, resentful of the capital Vézelay had made out of relics supposedly taken from their church, may have been seeking to turn the legend to their own profit.

Because of the story encouraged by the monks at Vézelay, the Provençals believed that Mary Magdalen and Martha had lived in their region. It seemed plausible and important that those who had been with the Lord had continued their lives and become illustrious through evangelising in pagan lands. It was thought that after her arrival in Gaul, Mary Magdalen had set about converting the pagan prince of Marseille, bringing Christianity to France, and had then retired as a hermit to the wilds of Ste Baume. Martha had gone to Tarascon, in the diocese of Avignon, and since the remains of her siblings had once been in Provence, it was entirely possible that hers might still be there too. In 1187, her bones were duly 'discovered', and in 1197 the church in

Tarascon was dedicated to her.[115] From the first half of the twelfth century, Lazarus' relics were believed to be at Autun, where one of the most moving sculptures of his 'sister' Mary Magdalen is to be found in the cathedral.[116] In the same century also, the people of Marseille believed that Lazarus had been martyred in their town, that he had been their first bishop and that they possessed his relics. In *c.*1190 an Englishman, Richard of Devizes, on the way to the Crusades in Richard Coeur de Lion's fleet, reported that the inhabitants of Marseille, where the royal fleet put in, claimed to have the relics of Lazarus, 'brother of St Mary Magdalen and St Martha', who had been bishop of the town for seven years;[117] and some years later, Richard de Hoveden noted the abbey of St Victor's claim to possess his jaw.[118] In 1252, the high altar of the charterhouse of Montrieux, in the diocese of Marseille, was dedicated to Lazarus, some of whose relics were stored away, along with some of Mary Magdalen's bones, some hair and her apostolic staff.[119]

Until the mid-thirteenth century, the only Provençal sanctuary to be associated with Mary Magdalen had been a grotto a few miles away from the church of St Maximin, high up in the *massif* at Ste Baume, where the saint was believed to have hidden herself away from the world to do a long and terrible penance. Louis himself had known of it, and had been there on pilgrimage on his return from the Holy Land in July 1254. The chronicler Joinville described his monarch's visit:

> The King crossed the county of Provence to a city called Aix-en-Provence, where it was said that the body of Mary Magdalen lay. We went into a very high rock cavern, in which it is said that Mary Magdalen lived as a hermit for seventeen years.[120]

Ste Baume had already been visited in 1248 by the Dominican friar, Fra Salimbene de Adam, who gave what is probably the first account of the grotto:

> The cave where Mary Magdalen did her penance for thirty years, they say, is fifteen miles from Marseille. I slept there one night, the eve of her feast-day. It is in a very high rock, and to my mind, it is large enough to contain 1,000 people. There are three altars and a spring equal to the fountain of Siloe. A very beautiful path leads up to it. Outside near the grotto is a church served by a priest. Above, the mountain is even higher than the baptistery at

Parma, and the grotto itself is of such a height in the rock that the three towers of the Asinelli in Bologna could not reach it.[121]

The friar's description holds well for the grotto today, despite his enthusiastic exaggeration concerning its capacity. From his account, we learn that a pilgrimage had already been established by the time of his visit, although it is not clear for how long, and possibly not much earlier than 1248,[122] and that 'the women and noble ladies of Marseille' who made the arduous climb up to the grotto took with them donkeys loaded with bread, wine, fish and other provisions which they might need as the area was wild and uninhabited.[123] It was here, it was said, that the saint had hidden herself away and contemplated, but not died. Her burial place had been variously reported to be in the region of Arles, and subsequently either the town or county of Aix, and now finally the abbey of St Maximin. Until 1279 the only St Maximin mentioned in connection with Mary Magdalen was the bishop Maximinus who had given her the last rites according to legend. It seems that Vézelay had laid a trail which was only too tempting and too easy for the monks at St Maximin to follow. From Joinville's memoirs, written in 1304–9, it is not entirely clear whether he was indicating that Provence was claiming from 1254 not only the grotto but also the relics, or simply adhering to the story that Mary Magdalen had been buried at Aix before her removal to Vézelay. If the first explanation is correct, it is hard to understand why Louis attended the translation of the relics at Vézelay in 1267, or indeed why he had not visited St Maximin also during his visit to Ste Baume in 1254. It can only be assumed that the second explanation is correct, and that at that date the monks of St Maximin had not been claiming possession of the relics. This would seem to be corroborated by Salimbene's silence with regard to St Maximin when he went to Ste Baume in 1248: he would surely have visited the church had the monks already been claiming ownership of Mary Magdalen's body. He had also visited Vézelay in 1248, but failed, in writing up his account in c. 1279, to mention Mary Magdalen's presence, presumably in order not to contradict what he had to say about St Maximin.[124]

On 9 December 1279, the body of Mary Magdalen was 'found' by monks in a sarcophagus in the crypt of the church of St Maximin. According to Salimbene, who mistakenly dated the event to 1283 when he wrote up the events several years later, it was discovered complete ('integraliter totum') except for a leg, and with an inscription so ancient that it could scarcely be deciphered 'even with help of a crystal'.[125] Bernard Gui, the Dominican who subsequently became the grand inquisitor of France, and Philippe de Cabassole, bishop of Cavaillon and a friend of Petrarch, later described the oratory where four sarcophagi were found, lining the walls; one of these, made of alabaster, was elaborately sculpted and historiated. Another, of marble and apparently containing the saint's body, was placed along the wall to the right of the entrance. Today, the sculpted sarcophagus, now known to be Gallo-Roman and of the fifth or sixth century, and supposed to have been that of Mary Magdalen, serves as an altar and faces the entrance into the oratory, but in the Middle Ages its placing was clearly different. In December 1279 Mary Magdalen's body was found in the marble tomb, said to be that of St Sidonius. According to Bernard Gui, a 'fragrant scent' issued forth from the tomb which immediately marked it out, and a green plant was growing out of the skeleton's mouth, which he identified as fennel;[126] Philippe de Cabassole, on the other hand, identified the plant as a palm, symbolising her role as apostle and preacher to the people.[127] Further 'evidence' was also found in the tomb, in the form of a piece of parchment purporting to be the official report of an eighth-century transfer of Mary Magdalen's body from its alabaster tomb to the marble sarcophagus in which it had been found on the night of 6 December 710, during the time of the 'infestationis gentis perfidae Sarracenorum', thirty-five years before the supposed *furtum sacrum* by Vézelay.[128] This ruse, apparently designed to trick the infidels, had, it seemed, also had the happy effect of tricking poor Badilon and the early monks of Vézelay. The body they had taken had therefore not been the Magdalen's but, as the Provençals explained, 'de aliquo alio corpore, vel de aliqua forsitan ejus parte' (another body or, at best, a small portion [of the saint's]), that of Sidonius.[129] The document itself had been kept in a wooden box, to prevent it from disintegrating, but had conveniently dissolved into dust the moment it was touched.[130]

Five months later, on 5 May 1280, the solemn exhumation of the Magdalen's relics took place at St Maximin, presided over by Louis IX's nephew, Charles of Salerno, the count of Provence and son of the king of Sicily, in the presence of local ecclesiastical and civil dignatories. It seemed that divine inspiration had come to Charles, revealing to him that her body had never left St Maximin; this had sparked off the monks' search for her tomb, under his instruction. Charles had apparently shown great devotion to Mary Magdalen, and had put extraordinary personal effort into helping to find the relics, even digging with his hands and sweating profusely.[131] As Victor Saxer has quizzically noted, 'On aimerait savoir où le prince avait puisé cette dévotion' (It would be nice to know what had inspired the prince's devotion).[132] According to Gui, on the occasion of the solemn exhumation a second document was found which had not been discovered in 1279; wrapped in wax, it bore the words, in scarcely legible Latin, 'Here lies the body of the blessed Mary Magdalen.'[133] The relics were shown to the faithful, and the following year were transferred to a gold and silver reliquary. On 11 December 1283 Mary Magdalen's head was put into a golden reliquary in the shape of a head surmounted by a royal crown which had been sent by the king of Naples, as Charles of Salerno had now become.

The origins of the cult at St Maximin may never be known, but in 1279 it appeared that the monks of St Maximin believed, or wished to establish a belief, that they possessed the relics of Mary Magdalen. They may therefore have set up, with or without Charles's connivance, or possibly even at his behest, a marvellous hoax, the second to concern the Magdalen's bones. Saxer has shown the 'eighth-century' document to be a forgery, and Duchesne that the fraudsters were unaware that the dating system used today – *ab incarnatione* – was unheard of in France, particularly in the south, in the eighth century. Added to this was the fact that in 710 the Arabs or 'Saracens' were still in Africa, and had not yet reached France.[134] The document must therefore have been put into the box just before the official opening. Nevertheless, the trick had had its desired effect: those pilgrims who had flocked in their thousands to Vézelay, ever desirous of climbing great heights, both spiritual and physical, climbed even higher ones to the grotto in the *massif* of Ste Baume. Although Simon de Brion, witness to the events of 1265 at Vézelay, and now Pope Martin IV, attempted to combat the new situation, his successors were drawn inexorably by the tide: in 1295 Pope Boniface VIII declared himself in favour of St Maximin, authorised the Dominicans to establish themselves near the tomb of Mary Magdalen, and granted indulgences to pilgrims who came there.[135] Two years later, the second Dominican prior at St Maximin decreed that Mary Magdalen's feast-day be solemnly celebrated throughout the entire order; the saint has been a patroness of the order ever since. The cult spread throughout Provence; Vézelay, the first to claim possession of the relics of the holy sinner and apostle to the apostles, was taken under the wing of Philippe le Hardi, son of Louis IX, and was subsequently trounced, eclipsed, and fell into decline. Some years after the events of 1279, Fra Salimbene wrote:

> Henceforth, all these discussions regarding the body of the Magdalen must cease. The people of Sinigaglia have already claimed it for themselves. The monks at Vézelay, a populous town in Burgundy, also claimed to possess it. They even drew up a legend about it. However, it is quite clear that the body of the same person cannot be in three different places.[136]

One wonders what he might have said had he known about the bodies believed to have been at Ephesus and S. Giovanni Laterano.[137]

To the faithful, Mary Magdalen's bones had come to rest at St Maximin, and to this day Provençals commemorate their saint in the week of 21–8 July.[138] Midnight mass is celebrated on the night of 21–2 July in the cold, dank grotto hundreds of feet up in the heights of the

18 Reliquary containing Mary Magdalen's head in a procession celebrating her feast-day, 22 July, at St Maximin, Provence.

massif, lit by hundreds of candles, and damp from the *sources* Salimbene noted in the thirteenth century. In the following days, the townspeople carry about Mary Magdalen's head, a blackened skull said to be that of a woman of the first century, encased in a golden reliquary, a replica of the original, while locals dressed in costume sing of the saint in medieval Provençal as they enter the church filled with gilded statues of her flying into the air (see Plate 18). To them the myth is theirs, honouring the great sinner and lover of Christ, and model of fallen and redeemed humanity.

Without the monastic rivalries of the Middle Ages, and the pilgrimage to Vézelay, Mary Magdalen might never have become as popular as she did. Without the claim of the monks of St Maximin, and her consequent adoption by the Dominicans, the concept of the penitent Magdalen, who had spent thirty years in the desert, might never have been taken to Italy, where it appeared in liturgica and in frescoes painted in churches and monasteries all over the peninsula from the thirteenth century. Through Charles of Anjou, king of Naples and Sicily, the idea of Mary Magdalen was taken to Naples, and through marriage alliances between his own royal house and that of Spain, she also reached the Iberian peninsula. And the movement founded in her name in Germany in 1225 for the moral relief of prostitutes and fallen women, which grew to enormous proportions throughout the Middle Ages, and lasted in various forms until early in the twentieth century, might never have existed had it not been for Vézelay's claims to have in its possession the relics of Christianity's most loved and illustrious penitent.

CHAPTER V

BEATA PECCATRIX

Maidenhood is that treasure that, if it once be lost, will
never again be found . . . Tis a virtue above all virtues, and
to Christ the most acceptable of all. Whence thou oughtest,
maiden, so preciously to guard it, for it is so high a thing,
and so very dear to God, and so acceptable. Hence it is a
loss that is beyond recovery.

*Hali Meidenhad. An Alliterative Homily of
the Thirteenth Century*[1]

MARY MAGDALEN BECAME the favourite female
saint of the Middle Ages, and her *vita*, or 'life', a
veritable medieval best-seller.[2] Until the twelfth century she had only appeared in art in scenes from
Christ's life, at the crucifixion and resurrection, and
also of course in the guise of Luke's sinner or Mary
of Bethany. But from the thirteenth century she
began to emerge in her own right, as the heroine of her own story
which was depicted in stained-glass windows and frescoes, altarpieces,
panel paintings and sculpture, and in miniatures and goldsmiths' work,
in lively, brightly coloured scenes. Her popularity was such that
Humbert de Romans, the thirteenth-century vicar-general of the Dominican order, was able to declare in his sermon addressed to prostitutes,
'Ad mulieres malas corpore sive meretrices' ('To women evil in body,
or prostitutes', in which he referred to Mary Magdalen as having been
'one such'), that after the Virgin Mary, 'no other woman in the world
[than the Magdalen] was shown greater reverence, or believed to have
greater glory in heaven'.[3] She was listed in the litany of saints before all
the virgin saints apart from the Virgin Mary, and on her major feast-day,
22 July, because of her role as 'apostola apostolorum', the Creed was
said during mass, an honour reserved for particularly important Church

festivals, and one which, again apart from the Virgin, she was the only female saint to be accorded.[4] From the thirteenth to the fifteenth century, her feast-day ranked as one of the great feasts of the year, and was usually shown in liturgical books as a *double*.[5] Terrible punishments could be meted out on those who failed to honour the feast appropriately: at Viviers, in northern France, lightning burned a peasant's legs and killed his oxen when, despite admonition from his priest, he laboured in his field on 22 July. But Mary Magdalen cured his burns; and a few days later, the Virgin Mary, on the feast-day of her Assumption (15 August), got him to his feet.[6] In 1450, two women who confessed to having washed linen on the feast-day were sentenced to 'two fustigations [blows] with a hank of linen yarn'.[7] In 1209 there was retribution, unspecified, for the townspeople of Béziers when they killed their viscount in the church dedicated to Mary Magdalen on her feast-day, and were in turn punished on the same day by the crusaders for repeating the Albigensian heresy that she was Christ's concubine. It was, contemporaries said, marvelling, a doubly miraculous occasion.[8]

Of the many trades and institutions which adopted Mary Magdalen as patron, some had obvious reasons for doing so. Because of the scene in the garden at Gethsemane, she became the guardian of gardeners.[9] Her most typical attribute, the jar of precious ointment, made her particularly attractive to ointment-mixers, scent-makers and apothecaries, and her legendary worldly life, and the fine clothes in which she was often depicted, may also have been the source of her appeal to the glove-makers, coiffeurs, seamstresses, shoemakers, whittawers and wool-weavers she protected.[10] She was also the patron of drapers at Bologna, at Chartres of the water-sellers, shown seated below the stained-glass scenes from her *vita*, and, near Bolzano, of wine-producers.[11] Hospitals, leprosaria, prisoners and refuges for repentant prostitutes also boasted her guardianship; and two colleges, one at Oxford, and the other at Cambridge, were named after her.[12] Daughters were given the name Magdalen for the first time in the late eleventh century.[13] With her help as intercessor, St Anselm of Canterbury wrote, 'it will not be difficult for you to attain whatever you wish from your dear and beloved master and friend'.[14]

Her popularity, as we have seen, had arisen from two things: the focus on Christ's Passion and the central role she played in it; and the Church's emphasis on sin and repentance and the individual's responsibility. Stress on penitence had been gathering momentum from the late eleventh century, with the Gregorian reforms, and emphasised at the Fourth Lateran Council of 1215 which made it mandatory for every individual to make his annual confession to a priest. Both strains were to affect Mary Magdalen's image, bringing her to the fore as both the close and faithful follower of Christ, and the redeemed whore. (The same council made the receiving of communion obligatory at least annually at Easter, and the legend of Mary Magdalen's fasting and taking of heavenly communion in the 'wilds' of Provence made her, as we shall see, an appropriate model for this sacrament also.) Her process from prostitute to penitent was an edifying and beautiful story which gathered embellishments as it was told and retold. By the twelfth century, she had acquired an entire pedigree and persona, one which bore little relation to the scant information provided by the gospels. According to some, as the sister of Martha and Lazarus, she had an aristocratic and rich background, which led her to live her life 'in leccherye'; according to others, she had been married to St John the Evangelist at the marriage feast of Cana, and when Christ called John, the 'beloved disciple', to follow him, Mary Magdalen, enraged, determined to live a profligate life. It was after her conversion in the house of Simon the Pharisee that she was able to join the group of Christ's followers, and was designated the 'apostle to the apostles' because of her presence and role at the resurrection. It was also believed that she spent her last years as a hermit and penitent in a grotto in Provence. As Mary of Bethany, she and her sister Martha received Christ in their house, and for this reason became the symbols of the active and contemplative lives, so important in the Church's teaching, and to medieval female mystics.

The general consensus of medieval commentators was that she was the composite character established by Gregory the Great: the 'beata dilectrix Christi' and 'sponsa Christi' was known to the Middle Ages above all as the repentant sinner, the paradoxical 'beata peccatrix' (blessed sinner) and 'castissima meretrix' (most chaste prostitute) who, as the prostitute in Luke 7, had been converted through her great love for Christ, and rose from the depths of carnal sin to the heights of spiritual love. As such her figure was the expression of current ecclesiastical ideals: it signalled the Church's outlook on the world and its teachings concerning salvation, and it also reflected an aspect of the Church's attitude towards that other half of God's creation, woman. For the medieval Church could never forget that it had been Eve who had tempted Adam and had led him and his progeny, the *massa damnata*, into everlasting sorrow and travail. Ever since Gregory the Great's homilies, the sin of Mary Magdalen, symbol of the converted Church of the Gentiles, was that of fornication, the sin regarded by the Church as the most evil and pervasive, and the primal deed of Eve. A period which saw anything and everything as a symbol of a yet greater truth saw Mary Magdalen, without naming her as such, as Everywoman.

From the beginning of the eleventh century, her allegorical role as Ecclesia, which had been pre-eminent in commentaries until the time of Gregory the Great, had almost entirely given way to that of penitent, a model for each and every sinner. Despite Augustine's redefinition of the Fall, attributing it to the sin of pride, the popular idea prevailed that the first sin had been sexual in nature – a residue from Gnostic thinking – and was to be reiterated time and again from the pulpit, particularly during periods of reform within the Church. Mankind was damned from its very conception, declared Gratian, the great jurist from Bologna, in his *Decretum* concerning the Immaculate Conception of about 1140, and he reminded his reader further to: 'hold most firmly and do not doubt on any account that every human being who is conceived by coition of a man with a woman is born with original sin, subject to impiety and death, and therefore a child of wrath'.[15] Such words explain the significance of Mary Magdalen's symbolic presence in the Christian pantheon of saints. To understand why she should have taken on this new importance, we should first examine the Church's views of sin, sexuality and woman.

The idea of redemption, and the consequent emphasis on the virgin birth of Christ, arose out of the ponderings of the early Church Fathers on the nature of sin. Its logical corollary, the theology of redemption, whereby Eve's poor banished children would be delivered of their mortal coil through the incarnation and death of Christ, the Word made flesh, was worked out by the Latin Fathers in direct connection with the doctrine of Original Sin. To expiate man's sins through his sacrificial death, Christ, the Second Adam, had necessarily been born without the stain of that original sin which had been inherited by the rest of mankind. It had followed therefore that the vehicle of his incarnation should also be pure, and, as innocence was always primarily seen in terms of sexuality, a virgin.

The cult of the Virgin Mary, at its peak between the eleventh and thirteenth centuries, had its roots in the fourth-century eastern Church

in Syria, the cradle of Christian asceticism. There, from the very inception of Christianity, much attention had been focused on the gospel
accounts of the birth of Christ, those brief narratives written some
eighty years after the events they describe were believed to have taken
place. And it was there in the eastern Church that ideas about Mary's
sexual purity, her virginity, were both formed and fostered. The infancy
narratives occur only in Matthew and Luke, and contain the essential
elements of the story which was to form the core of Christian belief.
Matthew reports that when Mary 'was espoused to Joseph, before they
came together, she was found with child of the Holy Ghost' (Matt.
1:18). He further relates that Joseph, 'being a just man and not willing
to make her a publick example', intended to hide away his betrothed
for fear of scandal. He then has a dream in which an angel informs him
that Mary has conceived through the Holy Ghost, and that this is in
fulfilment of the Old Testament prophecy in Isaiah 7:14 where it had
been foretold that a virgin would conceive and bear a child called
Emmanuel. Matthew, intent upon stressing Mary's virginity, emphasises in the last verse of his first chapter that Joseph 'knew her not till
she had brought forth her firstborn son: and he called his name Jesus'
(v.25), thus setting in motion a debate concerning the physical relationship between the Virgin and her spouse – who in Nativity scenes was
usually depicted as an elderly dejected figure – as to whether indeed
Mary had had other children later, Christ's 'brothers and sisters' being
mentioned in the gospels in, for example, Mark 6:3. The Catholic
Church has always maintained that Mary remained a virgin forever;
Protestants that after Christ's miraculous birth she took up normal
physical relations with her husband, and had a traditional large Jewish
family. However, in establishing the divine foundations upon which the
Christian story was to be erected, Matthew would have had recourse
to the Septuagint translation of the Old Testament. Here the original
Hebrew word *'almah*, used to describe the young girl in Isaiah's prophecy, and signifying a nubile, *ergo* marriageable, young girl, is translated
into the Greek as *parthenos*, which connotes rather the physical nature
of intact virginity. (The word *neanis*, girl, would otherwise have
probably been used.)[16] With this misinterpretation of a single word
was established and reinforced Christianity's focus and stress on
Mary's sexual purity as prime qualification for her role as *theotokos*, or
God-bearer, the title she would receive at the Council of Ephesus
in 431.

Luke, writing a generation later than Matthew, also emphasised the virginal state of the mother of God which the second evangelist had been so desirous to establish: in his account the angel Gabriel is sent from God 'to a virgin espoused to a man whose name was Joseph, of the house of David; and the virgin's name was Mary' (1:26–7). The angel tells Mary that she is to conceive and bring forth a son, Jesus, who will be called the 'Son of the Highest'. To her startled question, 'How shall this be, seeing I know not a man?' (v.34), the angel replies, 'The Holy Ghost shall come upon thee, and the power of the Highest shall overshadow thee.' Mary then says, 'Behold the handmaid of the Lord; be it unto me according to thy word.' In Chapter 2 Luke tells us that Mary 'brought forth her firstborn son' (v.7), a description which could be taken to suggest that Mary may indeed have gone on to have normal conjugal relations with Joseph.

The idea of the miraculous and virginal birth of the Christian deity – which had its classical and pre-Christian prototypes in the births of Greek gods and also of Buddha – was taken up and expanded in the second-century apocryphal *Book of James*, which lavishly embellished the nativity events in Luke's account, and was also the *locus classicus* of Mary's perpetual virginity, attested to by a midwife who apparently happened to be present and who, having plunged her hand into the Virgin, withdrew it, aflame. (Clement of Alexandria also knew the story of the midwife: 'for after she had brought forth, some say that she was attended by a midwife, and was found to be a virgin'.[17]) Mary's perpetual virginity became official Church teaching during the Fifth Ecumenical Council in 553 and was reaffirmed at the First Lateran Council in 649. The dogmatic assertion of Mary's virginity grew out of the Church's conflicts in the fourth and fifth centuries with the heretical sects, among them the Gnostics, Arians and Docetists. At the Council of Nicaea in 325, set up precisely to combat Arianism, Mary's pre-eminent role as the human mother of God was asserted. To these heresies, the Church replied by asserting Christ's truly human and divine nature, and Mary's status as both virgin and mother of God came to play an ever-increasing part in his deification.

The doctrine of the Immaculate Conception, which referred to the Virgin's conception in the womb of her mother Anne, and not as it is so often believed – particularly by non-Catholics – to Christ's own conception, also originated as a teaching of the eastern Church. The topic was much disputed during the Middle Ages when many leading churchmen, including the Virgin Mary's most fervent champion, Bernard of Clairvaux, were unable to agree that Joachim and Anne had not coupled naturally, and that the Virgin herself had not been conceived in angelic *apatheia* rather than in human 'mire'; the theory was to become dogma in the Roman Catholic Church only as late as 1854. The Virgin's assumption, first references to which appeared in apocryphal writings from the fourth century, derived from the belief that 'having completed her earthly life, [Mary] was in body and soul assumed into heavenly glory', was a popular theme in the Middle Ages, and for many centuries celebrated as a Church festival before becoming an article of faith in 1950. The ultimate accolade, her apotheosis within the celestial hierarchy, her coronation by her son as Queen of Heaven, also a popular medieval image, in which Mary humbly and gracefully inclines her head to receive her final triumph, was officially proclaimed by Pope Pius XII in 1954. (Today, Catholics believe the Virgin Mary, together with her son, to be the only beings bodily present in heaven, the concept of Mary's body, undefiled by sexuality and procreation, intact *post partum*, and forever uncorrupted, stemming from the Christian correlation between sin, sexuality and death, and showing Gnostic principles to be still at work within orthodox Christian thinking.)

As a male construct, in that all ideas concerning her had their origins in monastic and ecclesiastical circles, the Virgin Mary was the ideal of perfect womanhood: she was very feminine, and in the Middle Ages very much the *noble dame*; she was also meek – the antithesis of Augustine's 'Pride' – and above all, she was sexless. As the mother of God, Mary had conceived 'without sin', the very phrase referring to Augustine's equation of concupiscence with libido, and hence the procreative act with man's fallen nature; and, according to the commentaries, she had given birth to her son without travail, and had remained inviolate, *virgo intacta in partu*. She therefore conformed to the medieval monastic tradition which identified virginity with innocence, the ontological state of mankind. Thus had Mary reversed the deadly deed of Eve: the idea was neatly encapsulated in the happy coincidence of the angel Gabriel's greeting to Mary at the Annunciation, *Ave*, with the name Eva, a play on words which appealed to the medieval imagination. The exclamation 'Here this name, *Eva*, is turnyd *Ave*', from the *Mary Play* from the N-Town manuscript, gives dramatic emphasis to a concept which goes back to at least the seventh-century antiphon, the *Ave maris stella*.[18] But in the Virgin Mary, the mother-goddess, symbol of fecundity and nature, becomes transformed into an instrument of asceticism and female subjection. The Virgin's passive attributes, as the woman without sin, the woman without sexuality, and anti-Eve, created and celebrated in monastic circles, had its natural concomitant in the celibates' view of ordinary women. A theory of salvation predicated upon the absolute, virginity, could not but have a deleterious effect upon the status of real women in its essential incompatibility with human sexuality and relations. Real woman, the sexuate feminine, was always equated with Eve; and, seen through the Church's eyes against an ideal of virginity, naturally to her detriment. Mary's apotheosis in the celestial hierarchy, her final triumph as Queen of Heaven, effectively removed her from the sphere of ordinary women.

It was into this niche that the medieval Magdalen now fitted, a figure who could play the part which the Virgin, because of her sinlessness, could not, as a model for mere mortals who could sin and sin again, and yet through repentance still hope to reach heaven. The mythical Magdalen was the perfect vehicle. Her twofold role in salvation as herald of the New Life and paradigmatic penitent sinner allowed her to share with the Virgin the title of New or Second Eve. With the intensified emphasis on her role as repentant sinner in the Middle Ages, she represented the sexuate feminine redeemed, and therefore rendered sexless. In this way, she stood for Eve redeemed, not, like the Virgin, as Eve's antithesis, but rather as her more fully developed counterpart, the beloved and favourite figure whose dramatic story of love and conversion appealed to the popular imagination, and was set before them as a model to follow. Whilst Mary Magdalen was seen predominantly as the penitent, figures like St Peter and St Thomas, guilty of sins regarded as still more serious in the hierarchy of spiritual transgressions – such as denial and doubt – neither achieved the same degree of exposure, nor entered into the affections of the faithful in quite the same way. Peter might equally be posited as a penitent, but his failing was not weighted with the human and physical resonances of Mary Magdalen's 'crimes'. It is as Luke's sinner, the putative prostitute, embodying sexuality, sin, and womankind, incarnate and redeemed, that she achieved her overriding importance within the Church's teaching.

Fornication, Mary Magdalen's sin as Luke's sinner, was the sin of her sexuality. Signifying any sexual relationship outside marriage, fornication, or *porneia* (Greek, unchastity, desire), was seen by the Church as the archetypal sexual misdemeanour, and the root of all evil, as it was akin to other deadly sins, especially pride and gluttony. As the sin against chastity, it was the antithesis to the virginal life lauded by the Church. In the late eleventh century, the ideal of virginity spread from the cloister, where it had been developed and nurtured, to capture the secular Church also. In 1073, under Pope Gregory VII (c.1021–85), a decree forbidding marriage among the clergy was issued in a comprehensive attempt to purify the Church by curbing immorality among the secular clergy, and thus imposing the ideal of monastic virginity upon the whole Church. Until this point, marriage among the clergy had been a frequent, if not normal, occurrence, and even when they were not married, priests often maintained concubines and 'squalling brats' who prevented them, according to their critics, from carrying out their clerical duties. The prohibition, although unable entirely to suppress concubinage, had the desired effect of bringing its sons into line, at least in theory, following the deemed pattern of the apostles.[19] Any sexual misdemeanour on the part of the clergy was henceforth regarded as fornication.

The Church, as we have seen, created and codified norms of sexual behaviour from the earliest centuries, even within marriage. Clement of Alexandria, whilst in favour of marriage itself, had sternly reprimanded those who made love for any purpose other than procreation, adding that when done for pleasure, it was in fact sinful, an outlook which was to colour Roman Catholic thinking even in the twentieth century. Variations in coital positions, for instance, were condemned for this would bring married couples down to the level of animals. Caesarius of Arles (c.470–542) had stated that sexual relations between married couples were forbidden during Lent and on the vigils of major feast-days; also during menstruation and pregnancy, and on Sundays.[20] From the late sixth century, Catholic sexual behaviour had been further regulated by the new Christian literary flowering, the penitentials, written to assist priests giving confession and in which by far the largest category of sins were sexual. Periods of abstention from sexual intercourse were extended even further: Sundays of course were excluded (although some penitentials allowed intercourse after sunset), and in some manuals Wednesdays and Fridays, traditionally days of penance, were also to be days of abstinence. The Lenten prohibition was now extended to include Advent and Pentecost, and abstention was sometimes required for three days preceding communion, sometimes for seven days before and after. Just how much even married sexual relations were deemed as sinful, or at least as a pollutant, may be gleaned from the proscriptions against indulging immediately after the marriage ceremony. Having ultimately consummated the union, bridal couples were forbidden to enter a church for thirty days, and were further demanded to undergo forty days' penance before returning to the church. The rules imposed by celibate monks upon their normally sexed fellow beings are often extraordinarily detailed: intercourse was to take place only at night, and only when the participants were partially dressed, which served to stress the shamefulness of the act; penetration was never to take place from the rear, either anally or vaginally (sodomy, particularly homosexual sodomy, was seen as the the most heinous sexual act, and likened to bestiality) – as deviant positions were sinful both because of the pleasure they gave and as methods of contraception – and never orally, since this was equally unnatural.[21] The sexual act itself, these penitentials imply, reiterating the teaching of the early Church Fathers, was sinful, and marriage was merely a concession to relieve the itch of lust.

In the twelfth century, most of these prohibitions and controls in marriage were restated by Gratian in his *Decretum*. He endorsed the official view, as did other writers of the period: marriage was for procreation only, and must not involve 'extraordinary voluptuousness' or 'whorish pleasures'. It was precisely these whorish pleasures of which Mary Magdalen stood accused, deemed to have committed the 'deadly synne' of lechery, the brutal epithet often applied to the sexual act. Here sexuality is seen in negative terms, and marriage as an inferior choice. This is forcibly exemplified in *Hali Meidenhad*, the most virulent of the many English devotional works written for women in the twelfth and thirteenth centuries, wherein human marriage is denigrated in favour of a spiritual marriage in which Christ is the bridegroom. Echoing St Paul, the writer explains to a young nun how 'Wedlock is for the weak'; '[it was] legalised in holy church, as a bed for the sick, to catch [in their fall] the unstrong'. Marriage itself is described as 'carnal lusts . . . [and] suchlike servitude for fleshly filthinesses', the 'flaming itch of carnal lust . . . that loathesome act, that beastly copulation, that shameless coition, that fullness of stinking ordure and uncomely deed' and, since its purpose is to bring children into the world, the woman will have to suffer the ripping and tearing of her body when giving birth. To the suggestion that the wedded state might bring happiness, the writer retorts, ''tis rarely seen . . . many things shall separate and divide them'. Addressed to nuns, the 'brides of Christ', to deter them from worldly, and fleshly, desires, the treatise reiterates that 'all widows and wedded women' are inferior to the 'elevated state of virginity'; if she succumbs to the flesh, against her will, the virgin will be subject to that of her husband, and 'all his foulnesses and his indecent playings'. The sexual act is equated with spiritual death; its consequence – the birth of yet more children – is the perpetuation of mankind's sinful existence, and the writer graphically and alliteratively describes it as the 'dreary deed which at the last gives the dint of death'. Virginity, physical rather than spiritual maidenhood, is the 'queen of heaven, and the redemption of the world' by which mankind is saved.[22]

Such views of sexuality and marriage, born out of the dualistic ideal of virginity to which the medieval monk was espoused, and in his relentless battle to preserve his own vow of chastity, went hand in hand with a particularly unpleasant vision of woman herself. Eve was the original cause of all evil and, to the men of the Church, all women were her daughters, and therefore inheritors of her disgrace. The Virgin's human counterpart was the nun, herself a bride of Christ, and her antithesis, Eve, a temptress or the woman who led a normal sexual life, and a creature who was almost always associated with luxury and superstition. Just how much woman was seen as a concept rather than a social entity is demonstrated by the classifications into which she was put in the sermons addressed specifically to her, based on the value of chastity, in which the subordinate ranks of married woman and widow were set against that of virginal perfection in the first known collection of sermons *ad status*, addressed to specific categories, written by the Cistercian Jacques de Vitry (*c.*1180–1240), early in the thirteenth century.[23] These categories were expanded by Gilbert de Tournai (d. 1284), again based on virginal perfection, to include young girls, nuns and religious at the superior end of the scale.[24] A sociological rather than moral framework is provided in Humbert de Romans' categorisation of womankind, but the same theological concepts apply despite the inclusion of the classes 'all women', 'noble women', 'rich towns-women', 'young girls or young laywomen', 'maidservants', 'poor women in villages', and prostitutes (where, as we have seen, Mary Magdalen is the paradigm *par excellence*).[25] But in general, woman for the Church was forever Eve, and just as the ideal Christian woman, the Virgin Mary, was an artificial construct, so too was the woman who appeared in the sermons, as far from the historical creature as the Virgin herself.

By imposing such an ideal, the Church set up a tension between itself and real women which could never be resolved, and where the natural sexuate female could only assume the aspect of Eve. Vowed to chastity, the celibate feared his great natural desires, suppressed so that he might devote himself entirely to God. Transferring his fear, woman, the embodiment of the flesh, became a threat, committing sexual sins to satisfy her own gargantuan appetite, the protagonist invariably of any fleshly encounter, the eternal seductress of holy men who tempted them to fall in order to fulfil her own raging sexual desires, thus becoming the embodiment of unchastity, or Luxury.

With Vézelay's help and spreading influence, Magdalenian fervour had been growing steadily since the eleventh century; it was further accelerated when annual confession and communion were made compulsory. Penance had been demanded by the Church from as early as the third century, and in Italy the practice developed after 1260 to the point where penitents publicly scourged themselves, or joined sodalities of flagellants to make public recompense for their sins. Chroniclers described how columns of penitents wended their way through the countryside, and through the cities, whipping themselves into frenzies of grief and sorrow for their sins which had put Christ on the cross. As she rose to the fore as the model of repentance, Mary Magdalen became patroness of several of these penitential associations and lay confraternities founded in northern and central Italy. Spinello Aretino's late fourteenth-century banner painted for the Flagellants of Borgo San Sepolcro shows her enthroned holding a crucifix, with members of the confraternity, in their white cloaks and peaked hoods with eye slits so terrifyingly reminiscent of the Ku Klux Klan, kneeling below (see Plate 19). The verso shows an extremely realistic scene of Christ's flagellation.[26] The rulebook of the confraternity of the Disciplinati di S. Maria Maddalena in Bergamo ordered in 1335 that each *scuola*, or confraternity, had a banner upon which was depicted the figure of Mary Magdalen; when a member died, that banner was to be draped above his door and left there until the body was carried to its burial.[27] In Florence, condemned prisoners said their last prayers in the so-called chapel of Mary Magdalen in the Palazzo del Bargello, which was decorated with, amongst others, scenes of her repentance at Ste Baume, last communion and death. (In the seventeenth

century, the bell which tolled at hangings was nicknamed 'la Maddalena', while the somewhat colloquial expression 'may you be hanged'
was given as 'ti dia la Maddalena'.[28])

The penitential mood which pervaded Europe from the eleventh century was further heightened by the advent of the mendicant orders
(from the Latin *mendicare*, to beg), the best known of whom were the
Franciscan and Dominican friars. Both orders came into being as a
reaction to the religious and economic conditions of the latter part of
the twelfth century, and in particular to a Church they found more
concerned with exerting its temporal power than with spiritual matters.
Francis of Assisi rejected his wealthy background to become a hermit
and devoted his life to caring for the poor and lepers, and to preaching
the word of Christ. After gaining Innocent III's approval of their Rule
in 1210, and espousing poverty, chastity and obedience, the brotherhood
continued to preach penance throughout central Italy. As a young priest,

19 Banner of the
Flagellants of Borgo San
Sepolcro of the late
fourteenth century.
Spinello Aretino. New
York, Metropolitan
Museum of Art.

Dominic had previously persecuted the Albigensian heretics in southern France. Carrying his crusading spirit to the ordinary people, he determined to return the lost sheep to the fold, preaching penitence as the prerequisite of salvation. Through their call to repentance, the Dominicans were instrumental in spreading the Magdalen cult; as patroness of the order from 1295, she appeared in votive images with Dominic himself and other important Dominican personages such as St Thomas Aquinas and St Catherine of Siena. She was a particular favourite of the Dominican Trasmondo Monaldeschi, bishop of Savona, who, when he commissioned a polyptych from Simone Martini in *c.* 1320, had himself depicted being presented by Mary Magdalen to the Virgin and Child (see Plate 20). And it was Thomas who gave the reasons for the colours in which she is usually depicted: as she had passed through humility, which was the blue water of compunction, and charity, which was the red fire of love, the Magdalen would have merited being numbered among the elect.[29] In a sermon given on 22 July 1305 at the church of Mary Magdalen in Florence, another Dominican, Giordano da Rivalto, noted that although Christ and the Virgin offered themselves as examples of perfection in all things, something neither could be because of that perfection was an example of penitence. Christ therefore offered examples in his saints, and particularly in Mary Magdalen, 'more highly and perfectly than in any other saint. For it was read of St Mary of Egypt and Paul the hermit . . . that they ate grass and such things, but she [Mary Magdalen] neither ate nor drank for thirty-two years, except for heavenly victuals.'[30]

The purpose of the zealous friar – described by the Franciscan John Pecham as 'a wheel of God's chariot' – was to bring the word of God to his spiritually ailing flock.[31] This he did, the hermit Robert Rolle (*c.* 1290–1349) observed, having rejected the life of a preacher for a more sedentary one in his cell, by 'run[ning] hither and thither',[32] around the countryside, setting up his *pulpitum* or *scaffaldus* at crossroads and in market-places in towns and villages, in order to harangue, denounce and terrorise his audience, threatening them with the fires of hell, to bring them to repentance. On the importance of preaching, Humbert de Romans wrote, 'Christ only once heard mass, there is no evidence of His having confessed; but He laid great stress on prayer and preaching, especially preaching.'[33] Apart from preaching, the mendicants were granted permission to hear confessions, a fact which drew much hostility from their secular brethren who saw the friars as encroaching upon their territory. But the mendicants had arrived on the scene partly because of the secular clergy's failure to fulfil its tasks, and justified their position on the basis that, in the words of the 'seraphic doctor', the Franciscan St Bonaventure, 'some priests are so vicious that honest women are in fear of losing their reputations if they secretly seek advice and counsel from them'.[34] Bonaventure's criticisms of his secular brethren might just as well have been extended to his own *confrères*, to judge by the minimal sympathy which seems to have been shown by them towards the feminine sex, as manifested in the great literary outpourings from the quills of thirteenth-century friars.

To assist their wandering brethren, the friars produced a wealth of encyclopaedias, confession manuals, sermon collections and preaching handbooks, providing them with anecdotes, *exempla* and fantastical tales with which to enliven their sermons and to keep their audiences' attentions. The texts yield a comprehensive panorama of the world as viewed from the celibate's cell. Here, sexuality and fleshly sin loom large, and here also Mary Magdalen appears as a prime model: 'Contrition is sorrow for sins assumed by free will . . .', says the author of the late thirteenth-century *Speculum Laicorum*, 'take for example Mary Magdalen',[35] echoing the sentiments of a twelfth-century English homilist who had written, 'She is an example of penitence, that is of cleansing, that is what maketh the filthy clean.'[36] Sexuality as ever is the besetting sin, and woman's sexuality in particular the object in the way of man's salvation. Rarely mentioned in sermons other than to illustrate some vice such as lust or superstition, Woman, rather than women, became the subject of the many anti-female diatribes written by Cistercians, Franciscans and Dominicans, all competitors for the Virgin Mary's favours, who rivalled each other in the litany of misogyny. It is to these writings that Mary Magdalen as Everywoman owes her medieval stereotype, imagined and created by monk and friar; and, invariably, she is the figure upon whom the holy man dwells at most length, the redeemed sinner in Luke 7 who rejects her moral vulnerability and sexual nature, as Eve's true descendant.

The feminine images which emerge from the texts and sermons as they waxed eloquently and vituperatively against the other half of God's creation leave no doubt as to the contempt in which women were held by medieval clerics. Woman, according to St Albert the Great (1193–1280), the Dominican luminary and master of St Thomas Aquinas, 'is

20 Mary Magdalen presenting the Dominican Bishop Trasmondo Monaldeschi to the Virgin and Child (detail of a polyptych; *c.*1320). Simone Martini. Orvieto, Museo dell'Opera del Duomo.

a misbegotten man and it is said inferior'.[37] In this he was merely reiterating the thoughts of Aristotle whose works were being translated into Latin in western Europe during the twelfth century, and were to have a profound effect on the status of women in Christianity when reinterpreted by Aquinas. In his treatise *The Generation of Animals*, Aristotle had written, 'the female is as it were a deformed male', a judgement he had arrived at through his somewhat biased grasp of biology and physiology.[38] Woman's inferiority, he believed, derived from her cold-ness, as against the heat of the male. The woman's role was merely progenitive, and even in this she was inferior: because of her coldness, she was unable to concoct semen; she was, however, the possessor of the 'menstrual discharge' which is 'semen, though in an impure condition', which required the 'one constituent, and one only, the principle of Soul', which was provided for by the male.[39] She was the passive receptacle into which the active male emptied his sperm, while she herself func-tioned as a kind of incubator.[40] Her biological inferiority was equalled by her mental shortcomings: her 'deliberative faculty . . . without auth-ority', and like that of a child.[41] Aristotle's theories, or variants of them, were incorporated into the philosophical-theological systems of Albert, and subsequently those of Aquinas, and used, particularly by the latter, to justify the subordinate place of women in society as a whole and, within the Church, their exclusion from the priesthood, and even from preaching. Further, Albert wrote, woman's 'defective nature' renders her untrustworthy, and she obtains 'everything by lying and devilish deception'. Thus, he warns his reader to beware all women 'in the way you would a venomous serpent and horned devil'.[42] In a chapter devoted to the subject of women, with the parenthetical subtitle 'cohabitacione fugienda', or 'the cohabiting with whom is to be avoided', the author of the *Speculum Laicorum* quotes 'Secundus Philosopher' (again Aristotle) as his authority to add to Albert's list of feminine attributes: 'Woman . . . is the confusion of man, an insatiable beast, a continuous worry, an incessant warfare, daily ruin, a house of tempests, a hindrance to devotion, her society to be avoided for three reasons: she ensnares men, pollutes them, and she robs them of their property and strength.'[43] A contemporary miniature shows the anatomically rather odd Adam and Eve tempted by a serpent with a female torso wearing a wimple, who hands the apple to Eve, who then passes it to Adam, the whole illustra-tive of the medieval concept of the Fall as being the fault of Eve, and of woman being the devil's instrument.[44] (A similar motif of Eve with a female-headed serpent, coiled round the tree of knowledge, sculpted in boxwood in the late fifteenth century, has been interpreted as Lilith, the legendary first wife of Adam, who out of jealousy tempted Eve with the forbidden fruit.[45])

The texts also offer a glimpse, equally prejudiced, of medieval church-going where, then as now, by far the major constituent of the preacher's congregation were women, his Eves. The sexes were probably separated, with the women 'sitten all a rewe', as described by the poet John Gower (*c.*1330–1403), possibly to avoid temptation since strange things seem to have taken place in churches: 'lecherye and glotenye beth ofte tyme ydo in holy places'; in Italy too the sexes seem to have been segregated, judging from contemporary paintings by Florentine and Sienese artists, with low canvas screens set up between them in the piazzas.[46] The noise and general disorder, the 'singen, rownyn [and] jangelen', which seem, along with the 'sleepen', to have prevailed in church, were a frequent target of the preacher's tongue, and an opportunity to offer the ubiquitous Magdalen as example: 'Some never stop moving,' he railed, 'sometimes they stand, then they sit, or they leave and re-enter . . . Others while listening to the word of God show no sign of devotion. How different from Mary [that is, Mary Magdalen as Mary of Bethany] who also seated herself at the Lord's feet and listened to his word.'[47] Husbands must have hugely enjoyed the chastisement of their spouses, and the constant reiteration of Eve's secondary place in the order of creation, and the Church's generally low opinion of her daughters, must certainly have helped to reinforce the subordinate role which was the acknowledged lot of the medieval woman. Time and again, she was castigated for her frivolity, light-mindedness, and preoccupation with fashion, 'her vanity exceeding all fancy'. It was, after all, Mary Magdalen's vanity which had led to her fall.

As a literary image, Luxury (from the Latin, *luxuria*), Lust or Lechery had always been personified by a woman. It had been so as early as the fifth century: in the Spanish poet Prudentius' *Psychomachia*, or *Battle for the Soul*, an allegorical struggle between the virtues and vices, all the virtues are portrayed as female, as indeed are some of the vices. Luxury was depicted in the guise of Venus, accompanied by Cupid and Jest, to emphasise the folly of fleshly indulgence.[48] Invariably a feminine figure in Christian art, Luxury is often shown suffering eternally in hell, a feminine model of libidinous desire, ubiquitous in medieval churches. A twelfth-century sculpture on the portal at Moissac, for example, shows her as a scrawny, naked female figure, her breasts and vulva attacked by serpents, her mouth by toads. In the abbey museum, a female devil squats, her knees wide apart, her vagina a deep and hideous hole. Carved on a capital from the cloister, the twelfth-century image was originally intended for the gaze of the cenobite only, doubtless to remind him of what lay in wait for him in the outside world. In Taddeo di Bartolo's fresco of Hell at San Gimignano (1396), the golden tresses of 'Lussuria' are coiled up in the serpent-headed tail of a devil, while another devil blows flames over her, and while yet another stokes her sex, his serpent-headed tail suggestively licking her genitals. (In hell, the Church explained, sinners were punished through the bodily organs with which they had offended.) Such images, whilst ostensibly illuminating philosophical or theological arguments, can be added to the armoury of anti-feminine representations to be found in medieval churches and artefacts, such as the gossips, and women associating with fantastical beasts, depicted in sculptures, wall paintings and manuscript illuminations, the whole illustrative of the conventional medieval, and particularly ecclesiastical, contempt for women.

It was out of such sentiments that the fully fleshed figure of Mary Magdalen emerged. In the *Summa Praedicantium*, the vast preaching anthology amassed by the English Dominican John Bromyard (*fl.* 1390), she appears as Luxury converted, in 'Luxuria', the longest section of the treatise, which abounds in the figures of lustful and false women like Delilah, Jezebel and Herodias, who had procured men's deaths. According to Bromyard, lechery was all filth relating to sensual desire and forbidden pleasure; to Humbert de Romans, all sin was 'filth', but lust the 'greatest filth', for which reason a whore was to be compared to dung as she was the greatest filth.[49] Fornication was a particularly female vice, it was deemed, for woman was more carnal than man, as well as being imperfect from creation. (The archetypal masculine vice, according to the celebrated Dominican Hugh de St Cher [d. 1263], was avarice.[50]) Fornication, in Gratian's view, was the most common sexual crime, equal to perjury and some forms of homicide.[51] The crimes of Eve, Bathsheba and other notorious women of the Old Testament were a constant theme, and the punishments meted out on Lot and Potiphar's wives, and on Jezebel and Herodias, were warnings which all women should heed. Even in the case of good women, however, their virtue was not enough to protect their reputations from later calumniators. In the story of Susanna and the Elders, the original biblical account of Jewish married virtue under siege from male predatoriness became through various medieval commentators that of a temptress, whose bathing lured the Elders from the paths of righteousness. This was illustrated in numerous images of her in fifteenth- and early sixteenth-century psalters, displaying her entirely naked body to the old men, and it was as the temptress or *vanitas*, rather than victim, that later artists like Tintoretto and Rubens chose to depict her.[52] In the *Summa Praedicantium* she even appears as a model of contrition, together with Mary Magdalen, St Peter and Mary of Egypt. Delilah also suffered from this kind of character assassination, becoming a deceiver and destroyer; originally Samson's death was the result of his own weakness.

If, to the homilists, fornication was the prototypical feminine crime, the weapon with which the female lured the male was her beauty. Earthly beauty seduces the eye, and is seen as superficial and transitory, a 'withered flower, a fleshly joy, and human concupiscence', a perilous thing, deceptive, and a divine malediction. 'A beautiful woman is a temple built over a sewer', pronounced Bromyard, in the item 'Pulchritudo' (beauty), quoting as his authority St Bernard.[53] The friar is warned that to look at women is unsafe, and to overcome thoughts of them he should close his eyes and occupy his mind with holy thoughts, and have faith in Christ. Beauty, the devil's instrument, which assails through the female glories, her mouth, eyes and hair, the wherewithal to tempt the unsuspecting male, is a constant refrain in these medieval writings. If the eye sins, look away, says the Dominican Thomas Cantimpré, one among many, in the section 'De oculo impudice'.[54] He who lusts with his eye lusts with his heart is a frequent refrain. The friar inveighing against women who spend an inordinate amount of time tending their hair, washing, combing, colouring and scenting it, in order to 'consume and madden with their manes', added the gruesome, but no doubt sometimes true, reflection that these coiffures and ridiculous headdresses were the haven of worms and lice, and their eggs.[55] It is through these organs, so abhorred by the men of the Church, that Mary Magdalen alternately seduces and repents: as Gregory the Great had declared, and other writers had echoed it ever since, the eyes which had been used to lure men now wept, that glorious hair which she had bedecked with gold to entice young men she now used in humility to dry Christ's feet, the mouth which had so delighted her seducers now in sorrow kissed the soles of his feet, and the body which had lain prostrate with many men now lay at Christ's feet. In the late fourteenth-century *Livre de la Passion*, Mary Magdalen is shown cutting off one of these offending

21 Mary Magdalen cutting off her hair. From the late fourteenth-century French *Livre de la Passion*. Vatican City, Biblioteca Apostolica Vaticana.

weapons, and the caption 'Marie Magdaleine coppe ses cheveux et offrit contrition' reinforces the link (see Plate 21).[56] Her sin as the woman in Luke's gospel was that of her feminine nature, as a lively fourteenth-century homily pointed out:

> Than at the first beginne we,
> That mai ye se aperteli,
> Wit man en sampel witerly,
> Namly bi Mari Maudelayn,
> that lang havid in sin lain . . .
> Werldes welthe gert Marie wede,
> Quil scho was yong in her fairhede,
> Scho fag her hert til sinful play,
> And kest hir maidenhed away.[57]

(And so we begin at the beginning, so that you can see quite clearly that man was given an example, namely Mary Magdalen, who had lain in sin for a long time . . . She was surrounded in worldly wealth, and she was youthful and fair, and she filled her heart with sinful games, and kissed her maidenhood away.)

To the medieval churchman women, like Eve, were weak, easily flattered, had insatiable sexual appetites and were chatterers. (It was a common ecclesiastical accusation against Eve that her garrulity in saying 'yes' to the serpent had led to the Fall and eternal damnation.) However, a tart refutation of this latter criticism is to be found in Christine de Pisan's *Book of the City of Ladies*. She uses Mary Magdalen to make the point:

> if women's language had been so blameworthy and of such small authority, as some men argue, our Lord Jesus Christ would never have deigned to wish that so worthy a mystery as His most gracious resurrection be first announced by a woman, just as He commanded the blessed Magdalene, to whom He first appeared on Easter day, to report and announce it to His apostles and Peter.

'I smile at the folly which some men have expressed,' Christine continues, 'and I even remember that I heard some foolish preachers teach that God first appeared to a woman because He knew well that she did not know how to keep quiet so that this was the way the news of His resurrection would be spread more rapidly.'[58]

Christine (1364–1430) had turned to writing, becoming perhaps the first woman to earn a living in this manner, on the death of her husband, Estienne de Castel, having herself and three children to support. She wrote the official biography of Charles V of France, poetry, several treatises about the status of women and entered the 'quarrel' of the *Romance of the Rose*, attacking this famous piece of French literature for its misogynistical attitudes and immorality.

Chaucer's vociferous Wife of Bath, who delighted in finery and being seen in fashionable places, and boasted of her sexuality and the five husbands she had buried, had astutely commented that no scholar could speak well of women, and that her fifth husband had had the daily habit of reading Jerome and Tertullian, the two Church Fathers most quoted in these medieval texts.[59] Christine, just over a hundred years later, wondered too why so many different men – 'and learned men among them' – had uttered 'so many wicked insults about women and their behavior . . . They all concur in one conclusion: that the behavior of woman is inclined to and full of every vice.' The men, Lady Reason dryly adds, have 'all the while appealed to God for the right to do so'.[60]

Christine was not alone in her positive vision of womanhood, and of Mary Magdalen as its representative. Despite the constant stress upon her secondary place in creation, woman was seen to be privileged in three ways: she had been 'created as a helpmeet for man, not to be his servant', wrote Humbert, referring to the account in Genesis 1; Eve had been created from Adam's rib (Genesis 2), and 'not from his foot as might have been the case'; and, of course, the resurrection had been announced by a woman.[61] Women had three further benefits: the Lord could have had himself incarnated in a man, but had chosen not to; it had been a woman who had tried to prevent the Passion; and, even more, a woman had seen the risen Christ.[62] Woman, apparently, according to another writer, even had some advantages over man:

> Woman is to be preferred to man, to wit, in material: Adam was made from clay and Eve from the side of man; in place: Adam was made outside paradise and Eve within; in conception: a woman conceived God which a man did not do; in apparition: Christ appeared to a woman after the Resurrection, to wit the Magdalene; in exaltation: a woman is exalted above the choirs of angels, to wit the Blessed Mary. St Bernardine even declares thus: 'It is a great grace to be a woman: more women are saved than men.'[63]

In his 'Defence of Women', the Dominican author of the *Southern Passion* sought to redress the damage done to the reputation of women by his brother friars, referring to Mary Magdalen in unusual guise as exemplar. Having explained Christ's appearance to Mary Magdalen first as being on account of her great sinfulness, and that as a consequence no-one need ever despair of forgiveness, he goes on to ask:

> And how hit is thanne of wymmen that we blameth ham so/ In songes and in rymes; and in bokes eke thereto/ To segge that they false be and vuele to leove, ffykel and . . . untrue? . . . More mildness and goodness is not many creature on earth/ as we may see by Mary Maudelyn.[64]

It must have been gratifying also to the real woman in the congregation, constantly harangued and ridiculed for her flightiness, vanity and lustfulness, to hear that her sex could be more faithful than the male, as exemplified by the women at the crucifixion: 'Women in time of cristes deth . . . were nought so flyttynge in the beleve as were the aposteles.' And women were more loving than men too, as in the case of Mary Magdalen who had remained at the sepulchre alone and weeping, loving Christ as much as she had loved the devil before – 'no man', adds the English Dominican, 'is so true in love as is a woman who turns to good'.[65]

But despite these few examples of positive womanhood, the cleric's view of woman was all but unanimous: woman was Eve, wanton, lustful and a temptation from his pursuit of perfection. And it was thus that the sinful Mary Magdalen was portrayed, her association with Luke's sinner everywhere paramount. Sermons opened with references to it as, for example, in the anonymous twelfth-century homily, 'The woman who was in the city named Mary now penitent came to the house of Simon', where the text from Luke 7 was combined with Gregory the Great's interpolation 'nomine Maria'.[66] To Master Robert Rypon, prior of Finchale from 1397, all women were embodied in Luke's sinner, and he crisply summed up celibate sentiments concerning the feminine sex: 'But what am I to say of modern woman? Assuredly, not a "woman that was in the city a sinner", but a woman that *is* in the city a sinner.'[67]

In the Middle Ages, two major reasons were given for Mary Magdalen's lapse into sin, both of which reflected ecclesiastical preoccupations.[68] The first was to have been born the beautiful daughter of a rich and illustrious father. To monks and friars, vowed to corporate poverty and living from begging, riches and worldly possessions were anathema, evil and corrupting in every way, and at the opposite end of the spectrum from those who followed the way of life of Christ and his apostles. The medieval love of narrative details could not allow that those who had seen and known Christ had remained in obscurity: thus, according to the *Golden Legend* of 1276, Mary Magdalen is born of 'right noble lineage', her parents, Cyrus and Eucharia, descended from a line of kings, and her abundance in riches and beauty had led her to yield herself to carnal delights. This gave the homilists a perfect opportunity to condemn the world and its vanities. In the *vita* believed to have been

written by Rabanus Maurus, but now believed to have been penned by a
mid-twelfth-century Cistercian, the description of her physical beauties
when she becomes of marriageable age ('resplendent in the marvellous
beauty of her body, excessively lovely . . . her charming visage, her
marvellous hair, her most gracious air, her sweet spirit . . .') is followed
by the dark aside, 'but a shining beauty is rarely joined to chastity',
reflecting the clerical equation of physical beauty with evil, its speciousness and its dangers, particularly to the beholder.[69] In the eponymous
early sixteenth-century English morality play, Mary Magdalen is the
proud possessor of the castle of Magdala; Lazarus is the owner of a large
part of Jerusalem, and Martha is the proprietress of Bethany. Profligacy
is the natural outcome of Mary Magdalen's inherited wealth, and Martha
is left at home to look after her siblings' properties while Lazarus is in
the army, and the Magdalen is in the stews at Jerusalem.[70]

The second reason for Mary Magdalen's moral decline was related in
the popular medieval legend, already referred to, of her marriage to
St John the Evangelist which had supposedly been celebrated at the feast
at Cana, the story told in the second chapter of John's gospel.[71] Here,
Christ and his mother are the guests at a wedding feast. When the wine
runs out, the Virgin tells her son, 'They have no wine.' Christ's brusque
reply has taxed many a commentator: 'Woman,' he says, 'What have I
to do with thee? My time is not yet come.' He then tells the servants to
fill six water pots with water and to pour them. The governor of the
feast praises the bridegroom – who is unnamed – as the usual practice
is to keep the bad wine until last, but he has instead saved the good
wine.

The idea that John the Evangelist was the bridegroom at Cana is
found first in a preface to St Augustine's writings, but his bride's name
was not divulged.[72] In the seventh century Bede made the same identification, as did Walfried Strabo who added that it was at the wedding
that Christ had commended his mother to John.[73] In his homily for the
feast-day of the Assumption of St John the Evangelist, which is otherwise a celebration of chastity, Ælfric, the Anglo-Saxon, described the
wedding of 'Christ's darling', 'who was so overcome by the miracle [of
the water being changed to wine] . . . that he went forth and left his
bride in maidenhood', but forbore also to identify the bride.[74] The
anonymity of the bride was echoed in Honorius Augustodunensis' commentary on the feast of Cana, where John appears again as the bridegroom, but elsewhere, in his sermon on Mary Magdalen, Honorius

described her as that 'Mary of Magdala castle' who 'betrayed by her husband, fled to Jerusalem' to become a 'filthy and common prostitute', and who 'regardless of her birth, and of her own free will, founded a brothel of sin, a temple of demons, and seven devils entered her'; the fact that he failed to name her husband may have been because the legend was too widely known by the mid-twelfth century to need any further adumbration.[75] In the fourteenth-century Franciscan *Meditations on the Life of Christ*, in a long sequence on the marriage feast of Cana, John is again identified as the bridegroom, and Mary Salome, as the Virgin Mary's sister and mother of John, invites the Virgin to the wedding. The writer, long thought to be St Bonaventure, reveals a delightful *naïveté* when he voices the general doubt as to whose wedding it was: 'Although there exists a doubt as to whose wedding was celebrated at Cana in Galilee, we may meditate that it was John the Evangelist's, for thus it is said in the Prologue on John by Jerome, who seems to affirm it.' The bride is unnamed, but she is only relevant to the story insofar as she illustrates John's decision to reject fleshly union for that of the spirit. The friar consoles his addressee, a Poor Clare, when he tells her that although by his presence at the wedding Christ was blessing carnal marriage as instituted by God, in calling John away from his wife, 'you must clearly understand that spiritual marriage is much more meritorious than carnal', a sentiment which reflects those in *Hali Meidenhad* and other contemporary writings.[76] In John Myrc's fifteenth-century 'Sermo de Nupcijs', the wedding is that of 'Iohn Euangeliste and Mary Mawdelyne'; elsewhere Myrc describes Mary Magdalen 'of Mawdelen-Castell [who] was once engaged to John Evangelist before Christ called him to his service and the Devil entered her'.[77]

Jacopo de Voragine's flat denial in the *Golden Legend* that the feast at Cana celebrated the nuptials of John the Evangelist and Mary Magdalen is the first firm evidence of the currency of the legend. It was a 'false and frivolous tale', he wrote, particularly since John's deserted betrothed 'remained a virgin all her life', and in the company of the Virgin Mary, and could therefore never have been the woman described in the Magdalen's *vita* whose wealth had led her to submit herself to all carnal delights. (According to Jacopo, the evangelist's rejected bride went later to live in the company of the Virgin Mary, but he seems to have been unaware of the story that Mary Magdalen did so too, after the crucifixion.)[78] The fourteenth-century Franciscan writer of the *Life of Mary Magdalen* looked back to a nostalgic past: 'Now, therefore, I like to think that Magdalen was the spouse of John, not affirming it, but finding pleasure in the thought that the world used to be thus.' Social considerations also enter into the argument – Mary Magdalen's aristocratic lineage is contrasted with John's humble origins as merely the son of a fisherman, but nobility of spirit wins out: 'And I say that at the time the crafts and trades did not debase the gentle nature and nobility of a family. Despite the Magdalen's riches, John had been nobler in spirit for he came from a higher race, was a youth of much virtue, and the beautiful nephew of the Blessed Virgin Mary.'[79]

The wedding of Mary Magdalen and John the Evangelist is given a prominent place in the Middle German poem, *Der Saelden Hort* (1298), where Jesus and the Virgin Mary appear as guests. John is named explicitly as the bridegroom ('der brutgom'), and of the bride it is noted, 'Even though no-one said her name in a loud voice, still a master told me this was a true statement, that the bride was Mary Magdalen, as yet free from sin, a child of a noble worthy prince.'[80] The scene of the feast is illustrated in two manuscripts of the fourteenth and fifteenth centuries. In the one at Karlsruhe, although it is not clear which of the two women in the scene is Mary Magdalen, she is more likely to be the young woman on the left; Christ is to the right, and the figure leaving the table is John, called away to become a disciple. She is similarly the bare-headed girl in the Vienna manuscript (see Plate 22). Another miniature, from a manuscript of St Anselm's *Prayers and Meditations* of the late twelfth century, illustrating his 'Prayer to St John the Evangelist', shows John leaving behind a disconsolate bride.[81] The idea of linking the figures of John and Mary Magdalen presumably derived from the gospel accounts, particularly in John, of the crucifixion where they are described standing with the Virgin by the cross, and, as we have seen, it occurs in the *Pistis Sophia*. It is further developed in the early fifteenth-century Towneley play, *Fflagellacio,* where John and the Magdalen comfort the Virgin Mary.[82] Iconographically, their association occasionally appears in fourteenth-century devotional images such as the *imago pietatis*, or Man of Sorrows, and in the large terracotta and stone *pietàs*, or *mises-au-tombeau* or entombments, common in the fifteenth and sixteenth centuries in Italy and France (see Chapter Six).

Whether as a result of her wealthy background or out of understandable pique, Mary Magdalen indisputably became a *vanitas* figure. The exact nature of her profligacy was a subject also much debated: the fourteenth-

22 The marriage of Mary Magdalen and St John the Evangelist from two manuscripts of *Der Saelden Hort* (1298). Left: Codex Vindobonensis 2841, of 1390 (Vienna); and, right: Codex St Georgen 66, *c.*1420 (Karlsruhe).

century Franciscan was convinced that her sinfulness was 'aggravated', or exaggerated. It had probably been no more than 'unseemly merriment', and she had been no more sinful than any modern woman: 'Certain I am that the Magdalen did not uncover her bosom as they do,' he added.[83] A thirteenth-century sermon describes her as the 'pucelle Ste Madeleine', the 'maid', who could thus be represented as she was not a virgin but could be said to be a girl .[84] But to others she had dwelt in carnal filth. A late fourteenth-century fresco in the tiny, mountain-top church dedicated to Mary Magdalen near Bolzano shows her, in a unique image, being chastised for her sins by Martha and Lazarus, while her paramour, clad in parti-coloured hose, a veritable popinjay, places a hand, proprietorially, on her hip, as she stands defiantly, her back to the spectator, showing off her clothes (see Plate 23).[85] The link between the Magdalen/Everywoman and the figure of vanity is vehemently underlined in one of Rypon's sermons on her which is prefaced by a

long disquisition on the history of dress, its development from primitive
skin to wool, and then to linen and silk, contrasting it with life before
the Fall where 'the naked body was without natural shame, [and]
immediately after sin was committed, the whole naked body was
encompassed with the shame of its nakedness'. Men and women
adorned themselves to arouse lust, and were 'without a doubt in the
eyes of God more shameful and foul than the foulest corpses or dung-
hills'. This was shown, Rypon continued tartly, in the way 'some men
wear garments so short that they scarcely hide their private parts and
thus provoke lust'.[86] 'Dowteles muche pepull is stered oft, yea, and
assenteth to lecherye by the nyse aray of women,' declared another
preacher, warning of women's alluring garments.[87] Quite as outraged,
under the item 'Passio Christi', Bromyard drew the most graphic
analogy when he railed against the sideless gown, one of the prevailing
fashions of the day: 'Christ opened his side for the redemption and
salvation of many. And these others open their side for lascivious and
carnal provocation, and for the perdition of those who behold them.'[88]

23 Mary Magdalen with her paramour being chastised by Martha and Lazarus for her
profligate life. Late fourteenth century. Bolzano, S. Maria Maddalena.

(Whether it is just by chance or no, Mary Magdalen's skirt in the Bolzano fresco illustrates the point neatly: it is slit to the hip.)

The accusation of vanity levelled at women (and also sometimes at men) had a greater significance than it might at first be imagined. Vanity was one of the forms of the sin of pride, the sin which according to Augustine had led to the Fall, and its consequences were therefore enormous. It was also a form of presumption, in that when women, even those old and ugly, donned their finery, and wore cosmetics – in the process appearing as 'idols and masks' – they were taking it upon themselves to question and alter the image and likeness of God. This idea was by no means original to the thirteenth-century friar. The *De Cultu Feminarum* of Tertullian had reminded the Christian woman of the introduction of sin through her ancestress, Eve: as Eve's daughter, her only rightful garment should be the garb of penitence. Those who presumed to alter the work of the Creator – the body – with paints and the dyeing of hair were in fact criticising their Maker, and subverting Nature, which had been created by God, the 'artificer of all things'.[89] Tertullian saw modesty as the true Christian virtue (the Virgin Mary was the arch exemplar). In the *Psychomachia* Modesty and Lust (Pudicitia and Libido) form one of the seven conflicting pairs of virtues and vices, as do Humility and Pride. Their holy counterparts, the Virgin Mary and Mary Magdalen, reflected the medieval Church's polarised vision of woman herself.

When Mary Magdalen first set foot on the stage, she emerged there as a worldly character, one who vaunted her sexuality, and adopted the language and fashions of her time to represent in her life the figure of Everywoman. She gained a personality and a past history, which imbued her figure with interest and excitement. Her earliest appearances had been in Easter liturgical drama as one of the three Marys, and later, as these plays developed, as Mary Magdalen herself in the scene where she meets Christ in the garden. But by the thirteenth century, she had become a character in her own right, possibly as a result of the growing emphasis on the repentant sinner, which had prompted the development of religious drama beyond its purely scriptural origins.[90] She becomes a *vanitas* whose *Weltleben* in the thirteenth-century Benediktbeuern Passion *ludus* becomes an instrument of moral and religious didacticism representing the snares of the world embodied in Woman. In the syncopated rhythms of the *Carmina Burana* Mary Magdalen is introduced:

> *Mundi sunt delicie, quibus estuare*
> *Volo, nec lasciviam eius devitare*
> *Pro mundano gaudio vitam terminabo;*
> *Bonus temporalibus ego militabo.*
> *Nil curans de ceteris corpus procurabo*
> *Variis coloribus illud perornabo.*[91]

(In worldly joy, I shall end my life; I shall serve under the banner of temporal well-being. Caring nothing for all else, I shall take care of my body and with different colours I shall adorn it.)

She then goes off to Mercator, the vendor of unguents, to buy the most expensive scent, and rouge for her cheeks ('Chramer, gip die varwe mier, div min wengel roete'), in order that she may attract young men into seducing her. She then rather abruptly falls asleep and Angel enters, to tell her of Christ's presence at the house of Simon. The Magdalen defiantly sings her song, 'Mundi delectatio', and joyfully greets her lover, Amator, who arrives in time to hear her sing, with her two maids, of the cosmetics which will render them beautiful and pleasing, and the three women go off to buy even more. Angel returns with his message, to which she replies for a third time by singing her song. Then in the typical way of medieval changes of heart, she suddenly converts, apostrophising herself, 'Fluxus turpitudinis, fons exsicialis. Heu! quid agam misera, plena peccatorum, Que polluta polleo sorde viciorum' (River of wickedness, source of death. Oh! what shall I do, full of sin, poor creature, I who pollutes others, with the filth of my vices?), and dramatically throwing off her jewels and glittering clothes, she dons a black cloak, the garb of the penitent. Amator and Diabolus, the forces of evil, leave the stage and the Magdalen returns to the merchant, this time to buy 'ungentum' [*sic*] (l.109) in place of the 'odoramentorum' (l.52) she has previously bought, the substitution of names for the ointment signifying her altered moral status. She is no longer a *vanitas* or Venus, but a penitent and holy woman.[92]

In the English morality play *Mary Magdalene* the Magdalen's father Cyrus is a medieval plutocrat, as is Herod, who is surrounded by henchmen who are counts, squires and pages more at home in a medieval castle than in Roman Jerusalem. Cyrus introduces his daughter, 'Mary, ful fayr and ful of femynyte', thus setting the scene for the audience. He then expires, having bequeathed to the Magdalen the castle of Magdala, to Lazarus the city of Bethlehem, and to Martha the town of Bethany. The siblings lament, and the Magdalen is then beset by the World, the Flesh, and the Devil in a concerted attack upon her virtue, while the Seven Dedly Synnys besiege her castle.[93] She is rapidly won over by Lady Luxurya who persuades her to assuage her grief in Jerusalem. In a tavern more redolent of a rustic hostelry in East Anglia, she is 'pursewed' by a gallant called Corysote, or Curiosity, whom she at first rejects. Seduction is only momentarily delayed, however, for within an extremely short space of time she has capitulated, and dances with him (one of the feminine pastimes so frowned upon by the friar), and sups some wine (see Plate 24).[94] She has fallen through the agency of 'Pryde, called Curiosity', the Bad Angel remarks with satisfaction, and thus begins the doctrinal polemic of the play, with its emphasis on human frailty, particularly the vanity of women, and its redemption through penance, contrition and grace. The Magdalen is seen next lying back in her bower, yearning for her lovers. Clearly, she has now also been unfaithful:

> A! God be wyth my valentynys,/ My byrd swetyng, my lovys so dere!/ For they be bote for a blossum of blysse; . . . but I woll restyn in this erbyre/ Amons thes bamys precyus of prysse,/ Tyll some lover wol apere, that me is wont to halse and kysse.[95]

She has taken the road to ruin from which only Christ can redeem her. The Good Angel a little later warns her to seek healing for her soul in terms which reflect the age-old male notion of women when he asks her, 'Woman, woman, why art thou so onstabyll? . . . and veryabyll . . . Fleschly lust is to thee full delectabyll; . . . Remember, woman, for thy pore pryde,/ How thi sowle xal lyn in helle fyre!' (The stage directions to the play imply that a contraption with what has been taken to be seven cut-out devils seems to have been attached to the actor's back so that little figures representing the Seven Deadly Sins could leap out of his body, as though emerging from it, visually emphasising the

24 The Dance of Mary Magdalen. In the middle ground she is seen hunting on horse-back, while in the background, she is lifted to heaven. Lucas van Leyden. Dated 1519. London, British Museum.

Magdalen's sinful state, and linking her in the audience's eyes with the Magdalen out of whom Christ had driven seven devils.[96])

In the *Passion* of Arras, of *c.*1430, Mary Magdalen's *vie mondaine* is summed up in her boast: 'Les mammelotteles poignans,/ La belle vermeillette cotte, Qui me fait mon bel corps parans' (My proud little breasts, my beautiful vermilion petticoat which shows off my body), and she offers her body shamelessly: 'J'ay la char endre que rousée/ et aussi blanche qu'une fée,/ Je suis en drit point et en fleur,/ A tous je suis abandonnée' (My flesh is rosy and as white as a fairy's. I am upright and flourishing, and I am available to all).[97] So bad is her behaviour that Simon the Leper invites Lazarus and Martha to feast with Christ, but does not extend his invitation to their younger sister.

Jean Michel's *Mystère de la Passion*, which was enacted in Angers in 1486, concentrates on the Magdalen's noble origins ('vostre hault estat de princesse'), and her worldly preoccupations:

Je vueil estre toujours jolye,
maintenir estat hault et fier,
avoir train, suyvr compagnie,
encore huy meilleure que hyers.
Je ne quièrs que magnïfier
ma pompe mondaine et ma gloire.[98]

(I always want to be pretty, to keep my high and proud estate, to have a good life and company, today even more than yesterday. I desire only to magnify my worldly pomp and glory.)

She is the *châtelaine* of her *château* of Magdalon, whence her name is derived. The unbreached castle is one of the many attributes of the Virgin Mary, symbolising her unbroken virginity, and in medieval romances chaste and noble ladies were besieged in the castle of love, and from lofty towers they rained down roses upon their knights. In the case of Mary Magdalen, the same symbolism applies, in the Digby play, as the vices besiege the castle of her chastity; in the *Mystère* however, it is also the symbol of her wealth, part of her upper-class worldliness which the playwright is criticising. The Magdalen is surrounded by beautiful jewels and enveloped in the exotic scents of flowers and perfumes 'pour inciter tous cueurs a joye'. The 'spicenard' she orders from her *damoyselle*, Pasiphée, is contained in her ointment jar, or *alabastrum*. And she has all the seven vices:

Je suis en orgueil si hantaine
que je ne vueil point qu'on me passe; et suis si charnelle et si vaine,
qu'en oysiveté le temps passe; d'autre part, je tence et ménasse,
après que en viandes habonde;
et si m'es jouys quant j'amasse
les grandes richesses du monde.[99]

(I am so haughty in my pride that I wish for no-one to be superior to me; and I am so carnal and so vain that I spend the time in laziness; on the other hand, I fight and threaten, after which I abound in possessions; and I am happy when I hoard the great riches of the world.)

The stage directions tell us that Mary Magdalen is fashionably dressed; she is a fifteenth-century coquette, in whose *mondanité* she is aided and abetted by her two maids Pérusine and Pasiphée. (In fifteenth-century northern art, particularly from France, Flanders and Germany, she appears more often than not with elaborate coiffures and richly embroidered gowns.) This character sings about women's noisy ways of attracting lovers, of whom she has several (Comte Rodigon, in Herod's entourage, is currently in favour), as it seems is the custom. A dramatic point is made in the next brief scene when Jesus appears on the stage 'transfigured', before we again see Mary Magdalen, this time the true vanity figure with her accoutrements about her, her scent, jewels, and above all mirror, that symbol of the transience of all earthly things. (Venus is often shown holding a mirror. Later artists like Caravaggio, Rubens and Artemisia Gentileschi [see Plates 53 and 54] painted Mary Magdalen with her worldly attributes strewn around her at the moment of her conversion.) She is out to cut a dash with the men and is only too flattered to be informed that she looks very *à la mode*.

Mary Magdalen's conversion in these *ludi* is brought about in several different ways: through a sudden change of heart, as in the Benediktbeuern play; through the agency of Martha and Lazarus who are concerned for their sister's reputation as she has become the talk of Jerusalem; or by having the example of Martha being cured (as the woman with the issue of blood) before her, and being persuaded by Martha to come and listen to Christ in the market-place. In Jean Michel's *Mystère*, the Magdalen hears by chance from three Jews, Tubal, Gedeon and Abachut, of the 'holy prophet', and on discovering that Jesus is the 'most handsome man in the world', is thirty-two, has long goldenish and slightly curly hair, and eyes as 'clear as moonlight' she sets out to seduce him also, making sure her body is well corseted 'derrière et devant', only to find that she is herself seduced by his words. *Bouleversée*, she weeps for her sins, and covering her hair with a kerchief, goes to the house of Simon the Pharisee.[100] (An illustration from the fourteenth-century *Meditations* shows her, her hair caught up in a snood, demurely making her way to the Pharisee's house.[101]) She washes Christ's feet with her tears, and dries them with her hair, and then anoints his head with an exotic unguent called 'l'eau de Damas'. (The *Golden Legend* gives the reason for her having such an ointment as, 'For the inhabitants of that region used baths and ointments for the overgreat burning and heat of the sun.'[102]) The Pharisee complains and is reprimanded by

25 Mary Magdalen, as Luke's sinner, wiping Christ's feet with her hair. Late twelfth century. St Gilles-en-Gard, west front.

Christ, who forgives the Magdalen her sins. 'J'en quicte la mondanité', she says as she casts away her sumptuous gown, and goes off in a simple garment to tell her sister of her conversion, the figure of vanity vanquished, and in her place, the beloved saint.

Mary Magdalen's conversion is achieved. Weeping at Christ's feet, she rejects terrestrial love for spiritual love, and becomes the symbol of the contemplative life. Luke's sinner, whose sin was rooted in her sexuality, indeed *was* her sexuality, returns to the state of asexuality which the Church regarded as mankind's original state. As Luke's sinner, she resembles the image of woman held by the man of the cloister, constructed from his fears, perceptions and expectations; as an image, she reflects not only religious but also political and social concerns, the role and nature of ordinary women. Her conversion was the most popular motif in medieval hymns, most of which were connected with her feast-day.[103] Ironically, her repentance is one of the most appealing icons of Mary Magdalen because of its pathos, grace and tenderness, particularly in stone. All-pervasive in the twelfth and thirteenth centuries, it appeared first in sculpture, in French Romanesque churches and cloisters, such as the twelfth-century frieze at St Gilles-en-Gard (see Plate 25), and capitals at St Trophîme at Arles, and Mont-Majour (Bouches-du-Rhône) where the marvellously evocative figure of the weeping penitent cast down at Christ's feet curves round the column, her hair following the line of her arm in long, deeply carved curving striations. In a unique instance, she is sculpted in granite on the exterior

of the east end of a fifteenth-century church dedicated to her at Launceston in Cornwall.[104] The scene also featured prominently in the great
stained-glass cycles of thirteenth-century France, where her story,
taking on a life and logic of its own, was depicted in rich mosaics of
velvety deep blues, dark reds, yellows and greens, alongside images of
the other saints and heroes of the Catholic Church – even more popular
in the thirteenth century than Christ himself – such as Charlemagne at
Chartres, St Nicholas anonymously providing dowries for the poor
man's three daughters, and John the Baptist with his cartwheeling
Salome in her dance of the seven veils.[105]

Mary Magdalen served not only as a model for all penitents, but as
prime exemplar for two very different kinds of women in particular,
the female mystic of the Middle Ages, and the whore, the prostitute
who, like the mythical repentant Magdalen, rejected her former life of
sin, and was taken under the protection of the Church, often under the
patronage of Mary Magdalen herself in the convents established by the
Order of the Penitents of St Mary Magdalen. Although of course very
different, the two groups of women were united by having both
emerged from the new urban society – partly as a reaction against it, in
the case of the mystics, many of whom came from wealthy, aristocratic
or bourgeois backgrounds; or, as in the case of the prostitutes, whose
numbers grew with the urban development which began in Europe in
the twelfth century, as a result of it. The history of prostitution is not
within the scope of this book, but it is important to establish an outline
at least so that its relationship to Mary Magdalen can be properly highlighted.

In the mid-thirteenth century, Humbert de Romans remarked upon
the ubiquity of prostitutes: they were *passim*, everywhere.[106] And in this
judgement he seems to have been correct as recent studies have shown
that almost every city, town or village by this time now boasted a
brothel; even the public bathhouse had the function of both bathing-
place and place of prostitution, as illustrations in medieval manuscripts
bear witness. A few years earlier, Cardinal Jacques de Vitry had com-

plained of the strumpets to be seen everywhere in Paris, soliciting passing holy men to enter their establishments, and shouting 'Sodomite!'
after those who had rejected them.[107] But from the twelfth century, the
prostitute who had been beneath contempt became another soul to save.
Humbert was aware of this fact as he allotted them a special category
in his *Sermones ad diversos status*, the first instance of their being singled
out thus as a sociological entity. It was particularly necessary to preach
to women, he had written, and the prostitute was to be included; the
model and incentive put before her was naturally Mary Magdalen, who
having been a *fovea*, or pit, of fleshly iniquity, the very worst of women,
had repented and become the most important saint in heaven after the
Virgin Mary. The prostitute's salvation was for her own sake, but as
the title of his sermon 'Ad mulieres malas corpore' (To women evil in
body) makes clear, the words 'malas corpores' referred not only to the
sinful state of the prostitute's body, but also to that body's power to
corrupt others' bodies and, even worse, their souls. It was not merely
that she might corrupt only men either: there was concern too that
children would be set bad examples, and that other 'honest' women,
weak and fickle as they were, their constitutions more carnal than those
of men, might be tempted to follow suit.[108]

Poverty drove the prostitute into the city and town, where with
neither education nor indeed any marketable skills, nor any other form
of economic support, her body alone was hers to sell. Hunger and
destitution, and sometimes inclination, led her to her *métier*, and she
was prey to the pimps and panders who exploited her, to whom she
paid a large part of her income, and by whom she was often maltreated;
she was also often the object of the violence which is a concomitant of
organised prostitution. Prostitution became institutionalised between
the mid-fourteenth and mid-fifteenth centuries, in that officially organised brothels were established, often as municipal institutions, the *prosti-
bulum publicum*, set up with public funds, and supported by urban
authorities or local aristocracy.[109] The prostitute and her trade were
subject to regulations concerning her place of work: in Avignon for
example, a married whore was prohibited from practising within the
city;[110] in Venice, a prostitute plied her commodity in specially designated areas (the *lupanar*, or red-light district), at Rialto, and later in the
Ca' Rampani.[111] Sumptuary laws regulated what she wore, to mark her
out from respectable women and to this end, for example, there was a
widespread prohibition against her wearing the coif or a veil, the mark

of chaste women; contrasting coloured arm-bands (as in Toulouse),[112] or a yellow cloak in Venice, distinguished her from her honest sister.[113] (In Arles, an *aiguillette*, or knotted cord of a different colour from her dress, fell from her shoulder, marking her out like the Jew's *rouelle*, his round felt patch, or the leper's rattle.[114]) In the towns and cities, her way of life became a trade, organised and with regulations, and as such formed part of the economic system, while in the country it remained a casual and unorganised commodity. She sustained her pander, who in turn sustained the landlords of the rooms or houses which were rented on her behalf, thus creating a network of industry which revolved around her body. In the Middle Ages she was called the *meretrix*, 'she who earns' (derived from the Latin *merere*, to earn), one of Mary Magdalen's sobriquets. It has been suggested, but there appears to be little evidence, that prostitutes set up their own guilds, with their own regulations, decrees and judges; and it was even said that the prostitutes of Paris organised a guild under Mary Magdalen's patronage.[115] In the fourteenth and fifteenth centuries, prostitutes as a body, probably no more corrupt than any other civic organism, took part in civic festivities; and a prostitutes' race was run on Mary Magdalen's feast-day, 22 July, late in the fifteenth century, as part of an annual fair at Beaucaire, in Languedoc.[116]

As a social phenomenon, prostitution fell within the jurisdiction of secular authorities, whether seigneurial, royal or municipal. It was for these authorities to regulate and punish the prostitute or her pimp. Christianity, however, had cast an ambivalent eye over the prostitute and her status and role in society. In the third century, Hippolytus of Rome recorded that practitioners of some professions and trades were denied entry into the Church: amongst these were astrologers, magicians, pagan priests, gladiators, soldiers and prostitutes.[117] In the fourth century, she was regarded as contemptible, since her life was wholly given to lechery, or fornication, the gravest of sins according to the early Church Fathers, and yet, on the other hand, her services were regarded as indispensable – 'a necessary evil' – if rampant and unbridled lust were not to ensue. The classic Christian rationale for toleration of prostitution, which prevailed in the Middle Ages, was based on St Augustine's lapidary pronouncement in *De Ordine*: 'If you eliminate prostitutes from society, you will disrupt everything through lust'; he further justified this position with the argument that by removing prostitution men's lustful attentions would be directed at respectable and other virtuous women; the services offered by the prostitute were prophylactics against any disruption of society, to prevent licentiousness, and even worse sins such as adultery and fornication.[118]

St Thomas Aquinas, who regarded sexual offences as worse than theft, confirmed Augustine's stance: prostitution had the function of a sewer within a palace which, if it were removed, would leave the palace filled with pollution. Similarly, if it were eliminated, the world would be filled with sodomy, which would be infinitely more heinous.[119] Thomas of Chobham (c. 1158–c. 1233), canon of Notre-Dame and author of the *Summa Confessorum* (c. 1216), of which four chapters were devoted to a discussion of the prostitute and her rights, declared that toleration was necessary as the people of his generation were particularly prone to sexual excess. But while the prostitute's working life was the purlieu of canon law and local jurisdiction, her spiritual welfare was that of the Church: while she had practised her trade in the early centuries, she had been forbidden to enter a church, but on her repentance, its doors would be open to her, as they were to all who asked forgiveness.[120]

From a socio-economic point of view too, her situation remained an anomaly. During the Roman Empire, taxes levied on prostitutes' earnings had been a source of government revenue (as they were later in the case of the Venetian state). Thomas of Chobham, who was of the opinion that the majority of prostitutes sold themselves out of necessity, suggested that they be counted among wage-earners since they 'rented their bodies' and 'furnished work'. 'It is shameful for a woman to be a prostitute,' he added, 'but if she is one, she may keep what she receives for such work. If, however, she prostitutes herself for pleasure, and sells her body for this purpose, then the wage is as shameful as the act itself.'[121] This argument had arisen from the question as to whether the Church could legitimately accept alms from prostitutes, that is, from immoral earnings. The answer, it seems, was that if the prostitute took no pleasure in her trade, the Church did not regard her earnings as immoral. Some churchmen believed that the Church should not take alms from such women, but Thomas justified it, for contribution to pious causes was part of penance and conversion, and had not Christ accepted the ointment which Mary Magdalen had given him, which she had bought through her life of sin?[122]

The prostitute's only access to salvation lay in renouncing her profession and repenting: to this end she was offered the edifying stories of the penitent whores – Pelagia, Mary the Harlot, Afra and Thaïs and, of course, above all, Mary Magdalen – to demonstrate that even those so degraded by fleshly lusts could find their way to heaven. Compassion had been shown to them from early on: the Byzantine emperor Justinian had been the first to provide refuge for those who wished to give up their lives of sin. (This may have been because his empress Theodora [c.497–548], a former actress, was believed to have been a prostitute herself before their marriage.) Justinian also set up laws to prevent women from being forced into prostitution and to suppress brothels.[123]

In twelfth-century urban Europe, prostitution flourished, as it was often the only way out of poverty and destitution for women with no other means of survival. In the latter part of the century, the Church recognised the plight of these poor females as it had never done before, and set to work to rescue them. As part of its general programme of moral reform, and with its renewed emphasis on penitence in general, a drive was made to rehabilitate prostitutes in religious houses which offered them asylum from a predatory world. In 1198 Pope Innocent III urged all Christians to make every effort to reclaim them, encouraging the prostitutes themselves to marry, and offering a remission of sins to men who married them. Those who did so were performing a pious work, he pronounced, one which was 'not the least among the works of charity', and which would contribute towards the remission of their own sins. There were drawbacks, however, to carrying out such pious works: those who married prostitutes, apart from being warned that their wives might not change their ways, found themselves prohibited from being ordained, as were their offspring, since they were tainted by their wives' former occupation.[124]

Sympathy for the prostitute had earlier been shown by Robert of Arbrissel (d.1116), a wandering preacher who, in 1100, established the first foundation for women within a double monastery at Fontevrault, which accommodated the women who had gathered around him during his travels, among them, according to his biographer and contemporary, 'rich and poor, widows and virgins, old and young, prostitutes and man-haters alike'.[125] Virgins and widows were housed under the patronage of the Virgin Mary, and penitents in a house dedicated to Mary Magdalen. (Eleanor of Aquitaine was to retire to this latter institution.)[126] St Norbert of Xanten (c.1080–1134), founder of the Premonstratensians, also admitted repentant women in his community.[127] Prostitution seems to have been a frequent topic of discussion in Parisian ecclesiastical circles, as we have already seen in the case of Thomas of

Chobham. In about 1197, Fulques de Neuilly, another member of the group in Paris, founded a religious community to persuade the prostitutes of the city to reform.[128] The real catalyst in the institutionalisation of reforming and reclaiming prostitutes, however, came in c. 1225, when Rudolph of Worms, a preacher and chaplain of the papal legate Conrad of Zähringen, founded the special Order of the Penitents of St Mary Magdalen, which was approved by Pope Gregory IX in 1227.[129] The order set up houses in towns and cities all over the Rhineland, Germany, the Empire, France, Italy and Spain, often under the Augustinian rule, to provide refuge for those who wished to reject their lives of sin, as well as other women of blameless lives who wished to join. Clad in white robes, they were called the *Weissfrauen*, *Dames Blanches*, or 'White Ladies'. In the thirteenth century, there were more than forty such convents in Germany alone.[130] (The title-page of a rule book of c. 1500 for the *filles repenties* of Paris shows Mary Magdalen, jar in hand, with those in her care kneeling around her.[131] See Plate 26.) The likelihood of many inmates of these establishments having religious vocations being remote, these havens were to act as temporary measures, and it was hoped, and the prostitutes were encouraged in this direction, that they would marry. The monasteries therefore functioned as a kind of halfway house during the transition period, providing many of these women with a means to escape their degrading lives.

Under the patronage of the patron saint of prostitutes, the Order of the Penitents of St Mary Magdalen spread rapidly through central Germany and the Holy Roman Empire, thus accelerating the spread of Mary Magdalen's cult particularly between 1200 and 1278, when, out of fifty-one new foundations, thirty-two belonged to the new order.[132] Convents built to house repentant prostitutes not affiliated to the order were also given the patronage of the saint. In Florence, the long narrow street lined with Renaissance palaces known as the Borgo Pinti was named after the penitent women for whom a convent, S. Maria Maddalena la Penitente, was established in 1257. In 1321 it passed to Cistercian nuns, and was rededicated after her canonisation in 1669 to Sta Maria Maddalena de' Pazzi (1566–1607), the Carmelite mystic. Perugino's 1496 fresco of the Crucifixion with the Virgin, John the Evangelist, Bernard, Benedict and Mary Magdalen is still extant in the chapterhouse.[133] In another Florentine monastery founded for fallen women in the fourteenth century, the Convertite di S. Maria Elisabetta, Botticelli painted in c. 1495 an altarpiece of the *Holy Trinity with Mary Magdalen and John the Baptist, with Tobias and the Angel*, the Magdalen an elderly and gaunt hermit, with four predellas, showing her conversion, the scene in the house of the Pharisee, her ecstasy, and last communion, as an inspiration for the 'irregular' women who wished to change their lives.[134] Mary Magdalen's association with the prostitute in the popular mind began therefore in the Middle Ages, and was to stay with her until our own century. Although it was not until the end of the seventeenth century that repentant prostitutes became known as 'magdalens' in England, and not until the nineteenth century as 'maddalene' in Italy, and 'madeleines' or 'madelonnettes' in France, from the Middle Ages refuges for prostitutes often bore her name, so that for eight hundred years or so the name of Mary Magdalen has gone hand in hand with that of the 'fallen' woman.

26 Mary Magdalen surrounded by repentant prostitutes on the title-page of a rule book for a refuge in Paris, printed *c.* 1500.

At the opposite end of the moral spectrum emerges the second group of women who in another way either modelled themselves on or were somehow influenced by the medieval image of Mary Magdalen. These were the female mystics, those penitents, ascetics, contemplatives, visionaries, ecstatics, and hysterics who were an extraordinary phenomenon of the late Middle Ages. Donald Weinstein and Rudolph Bell, in their survey of medieval sanctity, note the unparalleled expansion of women's piety during the period from 1100 to 1400, particularly in the thirteenth century.[135] Most notable were women such as Hildegard of Bingen (c. 1098–1179) and Catherine of Siena (1347–80) who were celebrated for their piety and asceticism in their lifetime, and gained such power and prestige that they even became advisers to kings and popes. Others were like Julian, the recluse of Norwich (1343–1416), who became known for her mystical writings and exercised great spiritual influence from her anchorite's cell. Birgitta of Sweden (c. 1303–73), whose *Revelations* were highly regarded during the Middle Ages, founded an order of nuns (known as the Brigittines), as did Francesca da Romana (1384–1440) who established the Oblates Regular of St Benedict. There were others such as Angela of Foligno (c. 1248–1309), Margaret of Cortona (1247–97), and Dorothy of Montau (1347–94), who were renowned for their great piety and charitable works, their extreme fasting and eucharistic devotions, and their visionary experiences. The fifteenth-century English laywoman Margery Kempe is included in this group because of her pietistical behaviour and because she identified herself with Mary Magdalen. Some of these women became saints, and some were beatified, but all were part of the great wave of religious sensibility which swept through Europe between the late eleventh and fifteenth centuries, a period in which the female ascetic and penitent stood out, a figure whose holiness, austerity, and often neurosis distinguished her from her male counterpart, and whose unique and sometimes grotesque acts of humility and self-abasement, in ever-greater feats of self-denial and extreme fasting – the 'holy anorexia'[136] of the Middle Ages – have been seen as being particularly female. It was a period too when there were not only more female saints, but more women instigating new forms of piety, and creating opportunities for self-expression in a religious context. Recent studies have suggested that the medieval concept of Mary Magdalen may have profoundly affected, directly or indirectly, the form which some of these women's piety took.[137] Before we look at individual cases to see how the lives of these holy women were influenced by Mary Magdalen, as recorded in their *vitae*, we should first look at the growth of the phenomenon itself.

From the fourth century, women had effectively been excluded by the Church from any administrative capacity or positions of spiritual leadership. But from the seventh century, when under the Merovingian and Anglo-Saxon kings they had great power as queens and princesses, royal and noble women were equally able to have such authority as abbesses and nuns. They founded monasteries and convents for lay women and men, and often joined them as abbesses, wielding the power and influence normally reserved to male bishops, abbots and clergy, though never with the full sacerdotal role. They also often presided over the double monasteries, having both spiritual and moral jurisdiction over the male members of the communities also. From the eleventh century, however, their power and status within the ecclesiastical hierarchy were whittled away. The double monasteries were abolished by the Gregorian reforms; and in general abbesses were prohibited from professing novices, hearing confession, and preaching, except to other women and not within the hearing of a male.[138] Gratian's *Decretum* precluded the possibility of female ordination on the basis of gender: only a baptised male could validly receive the sacrament.[139] In the thirteenth century St Thomas Aquinas (*c.* 1225–74) gave further justification for women's ineligibility for ordination, falling back on Scholastic logic: in addition to Gratian's conditions, other impediments were lack of the use of reason, and grave bodily defects. Her lack of reasoning power, again borrowed from Aristotle's *Politics*, put her in the same category as children and mental deficients, and also prohibited her from giving witness in court cases. As an imperfect man (Aristotle's *mas occasionatus*) her physical deficiency also ruled her out: her creation from Adam's rib, and status as dependant and helpmeet in the procreative role, underscored her subordinate position, which also necessarily excluded her.[140]

Using the example of Mary Magdalen and the other women at the crucifixion to justify women's preclusion from preaching, Thomas Aquinas carefully explains that although the women had seen the risen Christ first because of their great love, their subordinate position prevented them from announcing publicly that they had seen him. They had indeed been the first witnesses but did not preach the good news. Instead they had told the apostles who had themselves become witnesses to the people: it was preaching which made witness public, and preaching was not a woman's function.[141] Thomas allows that their witness anticipates the glory which will be theirs when they rise above the state of subjection proper to their sex on earth but this is not, conveniently enough, to be achieved before entering heaven. Thomas further argues that because Mary Magdalen did not actually see Christ rise, her witness to the resurrection was in some way diminished. Indeed a gentle reproof seems implied in his words: 'It seems therefore that there was a certain unfittingness in the fact that Christ appeared after his resurrection first to women, and then to others.' Proscription against public witness is, according to Thomas, the reason for Christ's saying 'Noli me tangere' to Mary Magdalen, as against his allowing Thomas the Apostle to touch his side, since Thomas as a male would become a witness to the people, and his reliability as a preacher would not be questioned. The juxtaposition of the two episodes in John, which are not infrequently depicted during the Middle Ages, serves to underscore the two different types of witness: Mary Magdalen reaches out to Christ who apparently avoids her touch, whilst he often places Thomas's fingers in the wound in his side (see Plate 27).[142]

By the end of the thirteenth century, women within the Church led cloistered lives, unable to leave their convents and having no contact with the outside world. They were, according to Boniface VIII's *Bull Periculoso* of 1293, to remain 'altogether withdrawn from public and mundane sights'.[143]

Like her sisters in prostitution, the medieval female mystic was often a product of the newly urbanised society, for it was the same urban wealth, which created the ever-increasing demand for prostitutes, which led the mystic (and her male equivalent) to retreat from the world. Women were among the first and most devoted followers of the mendicant friars, who, by bringing the religious life out of the cloisters and into the highways and byways of medieval Europe, offered them a role which fulfilled their spiritual needs. Inspired by their calls to repent, to renounce the world, and more importantly, by the emphasis on the pursuit of individual perfection, women from all classes, including the poor and uneducated, but particularly from the urban bourgeoisie or lesser nobility, flocked to the friars in great numbers. (Of the women who were influenced by the idea of Mary Magdalen, Catherine of Siena and Margaret of Cortona had identical urban backgrounds in Tuscany, as had Angela of Foligno in Umbria, and the earlier English mystic, Christina of Markyate; Margery Kempe of Lynne in Norfolk and Dorothy of Montau in Germany had much the same origins; Elizabeth

27 The *Noli me tangere* paired
with Doubting Thomas. Middle
register: Resurrection and Three
Marys at the Tomb; top register:
Crucifixion and Deposition.
From the thirteenth-century
Cherdon Psalter. New York,
Pierpont Morgan Library.

of Hungary, Birgitta of Sweden and Francesca da Romana conformed
to that other pattern of sanctity, the royal or noble female saint.) The
contemplative life, accompanied by, in the case of women particularly,
extreme fasting preparatory to receiving the eucharist, as well as other
forms of self-denial, seems often to have been resorted to in reaction to,
and out of guilt for, the wealth of past lives. It was Mary Magdalen, in
the character of Mary of Bethany, who provided the model for the
contemplative life – this aspect features in Birgitta's *Revelations*, and in
many other devotional works of the period such as the English mystic
Walter Hilton's *Ladder of Perfection*. Hilton (d.c.1395) states that the
contemplative life will bring some measure of the dignity and happiness lost through Adam's sin, in preparation for its full restoration in
heaven. This 'Our Lord promised . . . to Mary Magdalene, who was a
contemplative . . . [who] has chosen the best part – that is, the love of

God in contemplation – for it shall never be taken away from her.'[144]

It was Mary Magdalen again, in her character as penitent ascetic in the cave at Ste Baume, who was the model for fasting, particularly for women. This is made clear in the *Ancrene Riwle*, the manual written for three noble sisters who became recluses during the second half of the fourteenth century, where Mary Magdalen's feast-day is specified as one of the fifteen days on which the anchorites are to receive communion. Fasting is to encourage contemplation, and anchorites who ate with their guests were particularly criticised: 'Men han ofte herd that the ded spak with the quyk. And that they eten with them have men nought herd of.' To do so would distract them from heavenly thoughts, for 'they have chosen 'Maries dele [part] the Maudeleyn and therefore they owen to give their hertes to nothing but to God'.[145] The three noble recluses for whom the *Ancrene Riwle* was written were ceremonially immured into the wall of a church, and followed services through a small window, an existence not dissimilar to that of the occupant of the cell found on the north side of the chancel of the Norman church of St Mary Magdalen, East Ham, in London. The choice of a church with such a dedication is unlikely to have been accidental.[146] Two other solitaries are also known to have placed themselves under Mary Magdalen's protection: one, the 'hermit Joan', one of a number of Norfolk recluses, lived in the early thirteenth century in the 'cemetery of Mary Magdalene of Wiggenhall', a church built in a 'desert place . . . all wild, and far around on every side no human habitation'; and a pious Gertrude who, in 1206, was noted as living in Liège under Mary Magdalen's patronage, having spent seven years in Jerusalem as a recluse.[147]

It has often been argued that medieval women entered the religious life for demographic reasons, because of the shortage of suitable husbands. In a society where women were generally married at thirteen or fourteen, and in which widows were encouraged to remarry to ensure the inheritance of property, single women were seen as an anomaly. This it was believed had been the reason for the establishment of the large numbers of monasteries for women in the seventh and eighth centuries. But judging from the *vitae* of some of the women already mentioned (for example, Catherine of Siena, Dorothy of Montau, Christina of Markyate and Birgitta of Sweden), it seems that it might well have been the presence rather than absence of potential spouses which made them turn to the religious life.[148] It may also have been that these women actively sought a spiritual life, rejecting its alternatives –

marriage and motherhood – the horrors and dangers of which were constantly reiterated in medieval writings such as *Hali Meidenhad*. (Catherine of Siena's desire to become a contemplative was, according to her first biographer, Raymond of Capua, reinforced by her sister Bonaventura's death in childbed.) It has also been suggested that the mystical element, a more striking feature of thirteenth-century women's religiosity than of men's, may be seen as an alternative and complement to, rather than a contradiction of, the male priest's function. Women, who were excluded from a sacerdotal role because of their gender, and whose salvation was supervised by a male, as was their life in the world, as can often be deduced from their *vitae*, took to the new forms of religious life as a form of rebellion against the roles imposed upon them as wives and mothers, regaining their autonomy, and becoming mistresses of their own destinies.[149]

The women included here had several stereotypical tendencies, or characteristics in common: in their pursuit of holiness, some rebelled against parental wishes, some made vows of chastity and adopted penitential practices at an early age, and had a hatred and fear of sexuality which is clearly voiced in their *vitae*; they all practised extreme forms of penitential asceticism, fasting, carrying out extraordinary and sometimes disgusting feats of self-abasement, had ecstasies and visions, diabolical visitations, and many suffered debilitating illnesses. Penitence is an integral part of the lives of most saints, but the emphasis on humility – the supreme and particularly feminine virtue as expounded in contemporary writings, and exemplified in the figure of the Virgin Mary – and the expiation of guilt over vanity and lust by acts of self-mortification seem to have been traits particularly female.[150] Catherine of Siena, perhaps the most illustrious of the women to have been influenced by the idea of Mary Magdalen, received her first vision of Christ at the age of six; having, according to Raymond of Capua, vowed her chastity to the Virgin Mary at the tender age of seven, and having also secretly practised flagellation rites with a group of friends, also from an early age, she resolutely stood her ground when at twelve her parents began to pressure her to marry. Bonaventura, her elder and married sister, was called upon to try to persuade the 'holy maid' to yield, but according to Raymond, died giving birth as a punishment for trying to divert Catherine from her true vocation. It was at this point, on Bonaventura's death, that Catherine, full of remorse, 'casting her selfe downe at the feet of our Lord with Marie Magdalen', wept, begging his mercy and hoping to hear the words addressed to Mary Magdalen herself (as Luke's sinner), 'Thy sinnes are forgiven thee'; she became particularly devoted to Mary Magdalen, 'doing everything she could to imitate her to obtain forgiveness'.[151] The loss of their elder daughter spurred Jacopo Benincasa and his wife Lapa to attempt to keep the family fortunes intact by marrying Catherine off to Bonaventura's relict, and to this end they enlisted the help of a Dominican friar who, noting Catherine's stead-fastness, offered her some practical help: 'I would advise you to cut off your haire; For in so doing, it is like, yee shall both cut of [sic] all hope of mariage in your parentes, and withal redeme a great deale of tyme and labour, which otherwise must needes be spent about the trymmyng of the same.'[152] After a further period of yet worse familial persecution, but ultimately with her father's sympathetic support (he had seen her at prayer, with a dove upon her head), she was allowed to join the Domini-cans as a tertiary.

Much the same treatment had been meted out on Christina of Markyate, the twelfth-century mystic, who had been forced by her family, after a year of close custody, to marry a loutish man despite her refusal; on her wedding night, she escaped and became a recluse. Under the protection of the archbishop of York, she lived to become the first prioress of Markyate in Cambridgeshire (after 1145), and was renowned for her piety as far away as France.[153] (The calendar of an illuminated psalter, probably executed for her, fascinatingly includes an unusually long list of female saints' feast-days, three of which refer to women who were relevant to Christina's situation, who had either suffered or, like Christina, run away from, enforced marriages. It is perhaps significant that the first known depiction of Mary Magdalen announcing Christ's resurrection to the apostles also appears in the psalter;[154] see Frontispiece.) It was in fact to a miraculous appearance of Mary Mag-dalen that, on one occasion, Christina owed the preservation of her chastity from the attentions of a young priest in whose charge she had been placed.[155]

The ascetical life was characterised above all by the renunciation of the flesh, which was represented in real terms by the value of chastity. To the many married women who became ascetics, the model of married chastity, or continence, was St Cecilia, a second- or third-century Roman martyr who, according to her legend, a favourite story in the Middle Ages, on the night of her wedding, begged her husband Valerian to live in continence as she had already become a bride of Christ. To reinforce her request, she informed him that an angel was keeping guard over her, and that if he attempted to consummate the marriage, heavenly wrath would be meted out on him by the avenging angel. Valerian, quite naturally, demanded to see the angel before committing himself to this life of deprivation. Cecilia replied that in order to receive this vision he had to be baptised, and she therefore sent him off to Pope Urban. On his return from his initiation into Christianity, Valerian saw the angel with Cecilia. Having converted her husband, and also her brother-in-law Tiburtius, Cecilia set about preaching to pagans. When she refused to worship Roman idols, she was sentenced by the prefect Almachius, who had already beheaded Valerian and Tiburtius, and was martyred in a cauldron of boiling oil, and buried in the catacomb of St Callistus in Rome.[156] Such was the example of married continence put before unsuspecting medieval husbands to cool their ardour. Christina of Markyate related the tale to Burthred, her betrothed, to no avail; she had to flee.[157] In Birgitta of Sweden's case, it had some effect, but only after she had borne her husband eight children. Margery Kempe, Dorothy of Montau and Birgitta each made pacts of abstinence with their husbands, the first two after producing large families; the last, having allowed carnal knowledge to be undertaken strictly without pleasure for the purpose of begetting heirs, then entered into a pact of total chastity with hers, went on pilgrimages, and ended her life in Rome as the founder of the Brigittines.[158]

The primary qualification for sanctity for women was their sexual condition, the criterion being whether they were virgins or widows. Wives could rarely hope to be considered eligible. In the case of male saints, however, holiness was related to their functions, such as bishops, or confessors. During the thirteenth century, increasing numbers of women became 'honorary' virgins, like the mythical Magdalen, whose inclusion in the list of virgin saints was explained to Margaret of Cortona. The fact that she herself was no longer a virgin, having lived with her lover, disturbed Margaret, for how, in this sinful condition, could she ever hope to enter heaven? One day, after communion (a stereotypical time for mystics to receive visions or to hear heavenly voices), she heard Christ's voice telling her, 'your contrition and sorrow will restore you to your virgin purity'. Instead of being comforted, however, her terror only increased, and she then asked whether he had placed Mary Magdalen in the rank of virgins in heaven. Came the reply, which can only have given her hope: 'After the Virgin Mary and Catherine, the Martyr [of Alexandria], there is none above Magdalen in the choir of virgins.'[159]

The desire to become a virgin was a source of great pain to Margery Kempe. After entering into her pact of chastity with her husband, under rather extraordinary circumstances, she wore white, as 'commanded by our Lord in her mind'. When she inquired, 'Ah, dear Lord, if I go around dressed differently from how other chaste women dress, I fear people will slander me. They will say I am a hypocrite and ridicule me', the Lord replied, 'Yes, daughter, the more ridicule that you have for love of me, the more you please me.' Margery's fears were well founded; her fellow pilgrims, particularly those among them who were English, on the journey to Jerusalem, irritated by her crying and strange dietary habits, criticised and ostracised her, and an English priest stirred up many people against her precisely because she wore white clothing 'more than did others better than her'. From her account, it is not quite clear why she wore white, a colour usually symbolic of purity, and therefore chastity, but her desire to be a virgin, sadly an impossible aim after twenty years of marriage and the birth of fourteen children, was always present for, she said, 'Because I am no virgin, lack of virginity is now great sorrow to me.' As he had consoled Margaret of Cortona, our Lord had comforted Margery also, explaining that although virginity was superior to widowhood, he 'love[d] wives also, and specially those wives who would live chaste if they might have their will . . . yet I love you daughter, as much as any maiden in the world'. He then pointed to the fact that both Mary Magdalen and Mary of Egypt, those fallen women, and other sinners, had found places in heaven.[160] Margery's wearing of white was to draw a somewhat irascible query from Henry Bowet, the archbishop of York (1407–23), when she came to be accused of Lollardy and heresy: ' "Why do you go about in white clothes? Are you a virgin?" She, kneeling before him, said, "No, sir, I am no virgin; I am a married woman," ' a truth which caused her the greatest sorrow.[161]

To Margaret of Cortona (1247–97), whose biographer described her as the 'new' or 'second' Magdalen, Mary Magdalen was a direct model. On the mysterious murder of her lover Arsenio, with whom she had lived for nine years and with whom she had had a child, she suddenly and dramatically converted, resolving to imitate the saint's life to follow Christ. Margaret, born to a tenant farmer and his wife at Laviano near

Lake Trasimeno, had been only eight when her mother died, and her father soon remarried. Her stepmother, jealous of Margaret, maltreated her, to the point where she was driven to begging. At the age of eighteen, she caught the eye of Arsenio, a young nobleman of Montepulciano, and went to live with him in his castle. (They were unable to marry because of her inferior social status, and his family's disapproval.) In the years she lived with him, according to the same biographer, she led a worldly life, was much admired by the local inhabitants, wore make-up and beautiful clothes, had golden ringlets, and rode fine horses; and she also bore his child. Then one day, Arsenio's dog returned home alone, and led her to the woods where his master's blood-spattered body lay under an oak tree. The shock was the catalyst for Margaret's conversion. Taking her child, she attempted to return to her father's house, and was driven away, as it seemed her stepmother still resented her. In her despair, the devil tempted her to take up prostitution, but rejecting him, she went to Cortona, where she was taken in by two pious ladies who worked with the Franciscans, and she devoted her life to penance and charitable activities. Her past life now seemed to her to have been spent in sin: it was the fact that she had known the flesh, rather than that she was an unmarried mother, which led her to a life of penitential asceticism. Her desire to become a Franciscan tertiary herself was at first thwarted – she was too young and beautiful, it was argued – but after three years, the order relented, and she entered, also making her son a *frate minore*. She devoted herself to caring for the sick, and founded the Casa S. Maria della Misericordia, still extant today, which served to look after poor mothers and children. According to Fra Giunta Bevegnati, her confessor and biographer, she inflicted horrific punishments on her body, which she now saw as having been the source of pleasure in her past. She constantly sought new penances and means of mortification, shaving her head one Good Friday, spending her nights in prayer and tears, sleeping on trellises woven with osiers, or hard boards, or sometimes on the bare ground, wearing a hairshirt, flagellating herself with a knotted rope, and punching and slapping herself. Once she even attempted to cut her nose and upper lip to destroy 'the beauty of my face [with which she had brought] harm to many souls' before she was prevented from so doing by Fra Giunta. Her sense of sin was so great that she believed that she had offended God even 'before she came into the world'.[162]

Her self-identification with Mary Magdalen seems to have affected her visionary experiences, most of which coincided with the saint's feast-day. One night, before the saint's feast, when too weak from her fasting and weeping to get up from her bed, and as she was singing the holy canticles, she was seen to arise, much to the astonishment of those around her, and then proceed to have a vision of the Magdalen, 'the blessed apostle of Jesus Christ', surrounded by angels and dressed in a robe of silver, with a crown of precious jewels upon her head. Then she heard Christ's voice telling her, 'You wonder at the brilliant robe that Magdalen is wearing; know that she earned it in the desert cave. There also did she acquire the crown of precious stones by her victories over temptation, and by the penance which she imposed upon herself.'[163] The glory which the Magdalen received in heaven was clearly the reward for her life of self-denial and penance on earth, and represented to Margaret the goal to which she herself aspired. Fra Giunta also related how she was able spiritually to enter the Passion, following the events of Easter, feeling the desolation of both the Virgin and Mary Magdalen at Christ's burial, and only at dawn on Easter Day was she able to rejoice.[164]

Levitation was one of the paramystical manifestations of divine grace and especial holiness. As the souls of these holy people soared heavenward, so it seemed sometimes did their bodies whilst they contemplated or received the eucharist. Margaret of Cortona was said by her biographer to have been 'constantly seen by many witnesses raised in the air, in ecstasy often while praying in the church'. It was during one of these levitations that she was overwhelmed by that supreme mystical experience, the sublime union with God, the so-called mystic marriage. Surrounded by angels and saints, Christ came to the centre of her soul, uniting himself with her. With the ring placed on her finger, and crown upon her head, she heard his voice commanding angels to give her the spirit of contemplation which Mary Magdalen had received. But it was with Mary Magdalen's penitential guise that Margaret of Cortona truly identified herself, as she wept and prayed in her cell, asking God for his pardon.[165]

Weeping was an integral feature of medieval women's piety, and important to the medieval cult of tears. It was all part of what is called 'affective' piety – in which the believer gave full emotional expression to his or her spiritual experiences – and evolved out of devotion to Christ's Passion. Tears were seen as efficacious, and necessary for the expiation of sins, tears of contrition like those of St Peter on hearing the cock crow after his denial of Christ, and those of the contrite Magdalen when she had used them to bathe Christ's feet. Weeping indeed often seemed to form the major constituent of the pious and penitential acts of the female mystic, weeping for her own personal sins, and for those of the world. But there were also the tears of the weeping lover, the models for whom were the Virgin and Mary Magdalen; and at least two mystics, Dorothy of Montau and Margery Kempe, referred to the Magdalen particularly as their lachrymose exemplar. Dorothy (1347–94), a lay-woman influenced by the Dominicans, wept up to ten hours at a time, referring to Mary Magdalen's tears as her models.[166] Catherine of Siena, as we have seen, wept like the Magdalen at Christ's feet after the death of her sister. Margery Kempe, another copious, or perhaps infamous, weeper, was influenced by writing such as that of Anselm of Canterbury, as well as by the accounts of other female mystics, particularly Birgitta of Sweden. In her *Book*, the earliest surviving English autobiographical writing,[167] which she, as a self-confessed illiterate, dictated to a priest, Margery recorded the bouts of weeping and loud sobbing which afflicted her throughout her life after the birth of her first child. The book in fact begins with an account of her first pregnancy, and the sickness from which she suffered, and then the terrible birth which was followed by puerperal fever. When, as she wrote, she returned to her 'right mind', she resumed her former life, dressing fashionably so that she would be 'all the more stared at, and all the more esteemed', despite her husband's attempt to dissuade her. Her subsequent business venture, in brewing, having initially been extremely profitable, failed, as did a further venture. All these, to Margery, were divine 'signs' that she was straying from God's path, and she accordingly asked him for mercy, did 'great bodily penance', and entered the 'way of everlasting life'. It was a very thorny way, however, not least because of Margery's own character, and how she deemed her life should be. In her marvellously frank and down-to-earth manner, we hear how it was after this that 'she never had any desire to have sexual intercourse with her husband, for paying the debt of matrimony was so abominable to her that she would rather,' she thought, 'have eaten and drunk the ooze and muck in the gutter than consent to intercourse, except out of obedience.' The 'inordinate love' and 'great delight that each of them had in using the other's body' had, she now believed, 'often displeased God', and should now cease, she said, but her husband still 'would have his will with her', to which she submitted with 'much weeping and sorrowing'.[168] (In fact, it did not cease for some time, as she subsequently bore him another thirteen children.) She fasted frequently, spent many hours in church, wore a hairshirt, and went to confession sometimes two or three times a day. 'Plentiful tears and much loud and violent sobbing for her sins' became a fixed feature of her life and lasted until her death. It caused her to be accused of being a 'false hypocrite', and she lost many friends. At the church of the Holy Sepulchre in Jerusalem, 'this creature', as she called herself, 'wept and sobbed as plenteously as though she had seen our Lord with her bodily eyes suffering his passion', falling at the Mount of Calvary, 'writhing and wrestling with her body . . . [and] cried with a loud voice as though her heart would have burst apart'. She imagined the mourning of the Virgin, St John and Mary Magdalen, which merely provoked her to weep all the more. But it was whilst she was in these holy places, once even standing in the place where 'Mary Magdalene stood when Christ said to her, "Mary, why are you weeping?" ', that the Virgin comforted her, telling her she should not be ashamed for her weeping, for nor 'was Mary Magdalene ashamed to cry and weep for [her] son's love'.[169]

Margery's eccentric behaviour, which brought her charges of charlatanry, 'sickness' and possession by the devil whilst she was alive, has in the twentieth century been seen as 'religious hysteria', 'hysterical personality organisation' and 'distorted sexuality', but perhaps should be seen against the social and religious climate in which she lived.[170] Her hearing of voices, total self-involvement with Christ's Passion and, above all, her desire to remain chaste – the spouse of Christ rather than of man – together with the external manifestations, roaring and weeping, faintings and ecstasies, are no more than a somewhat extreme example of the behavioural patterns of late medieval female piety, itself a phenomenon which has only recently been regarded as a movement through which pious females may have sought to assert, and to some extent achieved, control over their own religious lives.

Margery Kempe saw Mary Magdalen as a sister, and as such a competitor with her for God's love: ' "Ah, blissful Lord," said she, "I wish I were as worthy to be assured of your love as Mary Magdalene was." Then our Lord said, "Truly, daughter, I love you as well, and the same peace that I gave to her, the same peace I give to you. For, daughter, no saint in heaven is displeased, though I love a creature on earth as much as I do them." ' As she meditated on the Passion, visualising the

scene as Christ's body was lowered from the cross, and laid before the
Virgin, Margery imagined Mary Magdalen saying to the Virgin, 'I pray
you, Lady, give me leave to handle and kiss his feet, for at these I get
grace', and having received permission 'Mary Magdalen soon took our
Lord's feet, and our Lady's sisters took his hands . . . and wept very
bitterly in kissing those hands and those precious feet.' In her envy of
Mary Magdalen's having actually touched Christ, Margery imagined
herself running 'to and fro, as if she were a woman without reason,
greatly desiring to have had the precious body by herself alone, so that
she might have wept enough in the presence of that precious body, for
she thought she would have died with weeping and mourning for his
death, for love that she had for him.'[171]

Whereas Margery had a sisterly relationship, with some sibling
rivalry, with Mary Magdalen, Catherine of Siena had been given the
saint as a second mother in a vision she had once received of Christ.
Christ, who used 'to visite her both verie often . . . sometimes with the
Virgin, Dominick, Marie Magdalen, John the Evangelist and St Paul',
on this particular occasion came with only 'our blessed Ladie and
St Marie Magdalen', and asked Catherine what particular favour she
would like. Reading her mind, he told her that henceforth Mary
Magdalen was now her mother and, noted Catherine's biographer, the
Magdalen 'acknowledged the holie maid for her daughter'.[172]

Catherine, according to Raymond of Capua, had also taken Mary
Magdalen as her penitential model, and he emphasised the great fasting
feats carried out by his subject: 'Her fasting is even greater than that of
the auncient Fathers, for example, S. Antoine, Macarius, Hilarion and
Serapion' because 'they did eate somewhat', whereas Catherine was
closer to the example of the Magdalen who, as he knew from the legend
of Ste Baume, had 'lived in a rocke of the sea for the space of thirtie
yeares together, and,' he added, marvelling, 'never eate nor drancke in
all that tyme'.[173] Whether in fact it was Dominican apologetics which
led Raymond to assert Catherine's extreme fasting as being influenced
by the Magdalen's example (Catherine had also been much impressed
by the accounts of the lives of the Desert Fathers, and as a child had
imitated them, making for herself a cave in which she spent much of
her time), she would doubtless have known of the legends of Mary
Magdalen, and of Mary of Egypt, fasting in the desert.

An important feature of the *vitae* of both saints was their receiving
communion, an act made particularly significant by the proclamation at

the Fourth Lateran Council in 1215 of the doctrine of transubstantiation, which was concisely summarised by Thomas Aquinas:

> The whole substance of the bread is changed into the whole substance of Christ's body, and the whole substance of the wine, into the whole substance of Christ's blood.[174]

With this emphasis on the real presence, the eucharist became the focal point of the female mystic's relationship with Christ: as a bride of Christ, she was actually able to touch him and contain him, like the Virgin Mary before her. And like Mary Magdalen, who from the thirteenth century was depicted on tabernacles, and frescoed in niches made to contain the chalice, receiving communion from Bishop Maximinus, the female mystic could also reach through the eucharist divine communion with Christ.[175]

Raymond of Capua suggested that Mary Magdalen had been Catherine's model in her fasting, but Catherine herself wrote that it was the saint's figure under the cross, inundated with Christ's blood, which was particularly important to her, and with which she identified. In a letter, she advised Monna Franceschina of Lucca to follow that 'sweet and loving Magdalen' who will 'never leave the tree of the most holy cross'. Persevering, she 'became drunk and bathed in the blood of the Son of God'.[176] In another letter, to Monna Agnesa, she offers the Magdalen again as model, the 'loving disciple' who humbles herself at the cross, not fearing the Jews, 'ma, come spasimata, corre ed abbraccia la croce. Non è dubbio che per vedere il maestro suo, ella allaga di sangue' (but, wracked with love, she runs and embraces the cross. There is no doubt that to see her master, she becomes inundated with blood).[177]

Catherine's dramatic image of Mary Magdalen was the most characteristic one of the Middle Ages. The sorrowing Magdalen, repenting of her sins, red-cloaked, and with long loose hair, clasping the cross, represented all those sinners who had brought Christ to his Passion and, as the weeping lover, was the model for those who wished to repent.

CHAPTER VI

DULCIS AMICA DEI

Dulcis amica dei, lacrymis inflectere nostris:
Atque meas intende preces, nostraeque saluti
Consule, namque potes:

(Sweet friend of God, bend to our tears:
And direct my prayers, and upon our salvation
Reflect, for you are able to do so:)

Petrarch (1304–73)[1]

 DURING ONE of his several visits to Ste Baume between the late 1330s and 1353, Petrarch eloquently wrote of Mary Magdalen as the 'sweet friend of God', the woman who had repented and been forgiven her sins in the house of the Pharisee. This was inscribed on a tablet which hung in her grotto. He further celebrated her as a mediatrix between himself and God, a benefactress who bent to his tears, heard his prayers, and safeguarded his salvation. As the poet observed, the close relationship which now existed between Mary Magdalen and Christ allowed her to take up her gospel character as witness to the crucifixion and resurrection. In the medieval mind, she joined the inner sanctum of Christ's intimates and followers, becoming one, if not the most important, of his female disciples. The marvel of it was, as the twelfth-century Pierre de Celle so succinctly put it, that 'Out of a prostitute, Christ ha[d] made an apostle'.[2]

From the twelfth century the crusaders' fervour to recapture the Holy Sepulchre from the hands of the infidels had kindled an ardent interest in Christ's Passion, and Mary Magdalen, her legendary conversion now complete, was to be one of the central figures in the dramatic scenes which illustrated it. (In Jerusalem itself a convent had been founded in her honour for female pilgrims before the Crusades, and the first church to be dedicated to her was built in the Jewish quarter of the city at the beginning of the twelfth century.[3]) She appeared as a myrrhophore in the drama of the resurrection performed at Easter from the tenth century onwards in churches and monasteries in western Europe, and her figure was further elaborated by the new religious climate which from the thirteenth century focused on Christ's redemptive death. The characters who had surrounded Christ in his last days, who had suffered with him under the cross, fired the imaginations of the faithful. Vivid and edifying though images of Mary Magdalen as Luke's sinner might be, it was in the depiction of the events surrounding the crucifixion and resurrection that the true gospel figure was brought to life for it is here that she appeared conspicuously as lover, mourner and weeper. In devotional literature of the thirteenth century, writers revisualised the gospel narrative, filling out the bare bones in colloquial language, describing the 'things that might have taken place'; such realism of detail was translated by artists of the same period, and a wealth of new images was invented where her scarlet-clad figure became a conspicuous element. We are perhaps more used to thinking of the Virgin Mary as the dominant figure at this time, but in Franciscan writings such as the *Meditations on the Life of Christ* by Pseudo-Bonaventure, and the visual images which they influenced in particular, Mary Magdalen's place is no less prominent than the Virgin's, and often even takes precedence over it, the intensity of her grief and love drawing the spectator's eye to her. She is given a new emotive role, to heighten the drama and act as a conduit for the spectator's emotions; 'weep with the Magdalen' was a constant refrain to the faithful. As Petrarch's designation shows, she was perceived as the 'sweet friend of God', and described elsewhere as the 'beloved discipless', the 'apostless of the apostles' and, above all, the woman who loved Christ most, and whom he loved most, the 'beata dilectrix Christi', the blessed lover of Christ. These epithets were reflected in the numerous images inspired by both the gospel narratives of the Passion and the apocryphal stories which burgeoned from the twelfth century. They bear witness to the extraordinary importance with which her figure was endowed, and the affection in which she was held throughout the Middle Ages. As John Myrc was to say in the fifteenth century in his justification of imagery and its purposes, reiterating Gregory the Great's widely repeated pronouncement: 'I say boldly that there are many thousands of people that could not imagine in their hearts how Christ was crucified if they did not learn it by looking at sculpture and painting.'[4] As well as portraying her gospel role as disciple and witness of the resurrection, Mary Magdalen's presence in such images, wringing her hands, her body twisted in grief as in Rogier van der Weyden's *Descent from the Cross*, was to drive into those hearts the pathos of Christ's Passion and death (see Plate 28).[5]

Medieval writers stressed the closeness of the relationship between Christ and Mary Magdalen after her conversion, an intimacy upon which they dwelt in detail. It was perhaps most expressively captured in the passionate and lyrical prayer addressed to her by St Anselm of Canterbury (1033–1109), one of the earliest and greatest exponents of the kind of literature which came to be known as 'affective' from its purpose to stir the emotions (Latin, *affectus*) of its readers. Anselm's prayer was written in 1081 for Adelaide, the younger daughter of William the Conqueror. As she sought Christ in the garden, Mary Magdalen was once again the Bride seeking the Bridegroom in the *Canticle of Canticles*, the ardent lover, and the writer's marvellously striking images conjure up the scene through a series of elaborate antitheses:

> Saint Mary Magdalen, you who came with a fount of tears to Christ, the fount of mercy; from whom you, burning with thirst, are plentifully revived; through whom you, a sinner, are redeemed; by whom you, grieving most bitterly, are consoled most sweetly.

Her passionate tears of sorrow for her sins are also tears for the loss of her love as she stands outside the tomb weeping, and it is those tears which Anselm himself and the meditator reading the prayer wish to share:

> What finally, what then should I tell, or rather how should I tell, of how you, burning with love of him, wept for him in seeking him at the tomb and sought him while weeping? How kindly, and in what a friendly way, he inflamed you, whom he came to console, still more; how he was hiding himself from you when you were seeing him and revealed himself to you when you were not seeing him; until he himself whom you were seeking, asked you whom you were seeking and why you were weeping.

28 Mary Magdalen in Rogier van der Weyden's *Descent from the Cross* (detail). Madrid, Prado. *c.* 1443.

Christ is then addressed:

O wonderful devotion! O fearful treason! While you hang thus, stretched on the wood and pinioned by iron nails, just like a thief for the scorn of the impious: and you say: *Woman, why do you weep?* Because she was not able to help to prevent them from killing you; and she wished to preserve your body with unguents for a long time, lest it should decay: in order that she could at least lament over you now dead, since she could no longer weep over you alive.

All hope of you has now fled because she was not even able to retain your mortal remains as a memorial to you.[6]

The Passion was also the focus of the Franciscans, whose gentle founder himself, through his own devotion to Christ's sacrificial death, received the marks of the crucifixion – the stigmata – on his own body, in his side, hands and feet. The friars were instrumental in spreading the idea of the suffering, broken and human Christ who had died for the sins of mankind; the great Italian crucifixes of the late twelfth and thirteenth centuries painted for their churches show the tragic Christ, no longer the Byzantine *Christus triumphans*, alive in his victory over death, but *Christus patiens*, dead and bleeding, slumped on his cross. Sometimes the tiny red-cloaked figure of Mary Magdalen crouches beneath, catching the blood from his feet, below her Golgotha with the skull and bones standing for Adam's sin and mortality (see Plate 29).[7] To the beholder who gazed upwards at this mournful vision, she was the tearful figure at the foot of the cross, her cloak blazing as 'the fire of love', not only the Church's symbol of faith and witness to the Passion, her hair loose and often entwined round Christ's feet alluding to her past as Luke's penitent sinner, and thus representing all humanity who had contributed to Christ's suffering and death, but also, in her human and feminine sorrow for her loss, the weeping lover.

The closeness between Mary Magdalen and Christ, and the stature this gave Mary Magdalen in the eyes of the faithful, was seen to be so important that where the gospels failed to supply sufficient detail, the imagination was called upon to make good this deficiency. The *Golden Legend*, therefore, relates that after her conversion Mary Magdalen became 'right familiar with' Christ, who 'embraced her in all his life', and desired that 'she should be his hostess and his procuress on his journey', thus considerably enlarging the role she was traditionally thought to have shared with the other women of the gospels, who had 'ministered unto the Lord of their own substance'.[8] In the twelfth century Honorius Augustodunensis had mentioned her ministerial tasks when he described how, 'Fired with zealous devotion, she panted to go about the province with him and his followers, ministering to him according to her ability.' Noting the anomaly with regard to the position of women in the Church in his own day, he added, 'For among the Jews, it was permitted to women to go about with religious men and minister to them their necessity from their resources.' And to a late thirteenth-century writer, she not only administered, but converted, cared for the sick, and even 'turned great numbers from lechery', an entirely appropriate activity for a redeemed prostitute.[9]

Much of the emphasis on the close relationship between Christ and Mary Magdalen arose from the absorption of the character of Mary of Bethany into that of Mary Magdalen. The gospel episodes yielded both the dissolute mistress of the castle of Magdala, sibling of Martha and Lazarus, and the post-conversion hostess of Christ's favourite place of refuge just prior to the crucifixion where, we are told, he came often, 'generally unbidden to that place rather than any other to take his bodily food, and that specially, as I believe, on account of the great love and

29 Mary Magdalen at the foot of the Cross. Detail from a mid-thirteenth-century painted crucifix. Florence, Galleria dell'Accademia.

30 Mary Magdalen, as Luke's sinner, anointing Christ's feet, while seven devils fly through the roof. From Giovanni da Milano's fresco cycle (c.1360–5) of Mary Magdalen's life, in the sacristy of the Rinuccini Chapel, in S. Croce, Florence.

affection that he had to Mary after her conversion'.[10] Although it was the episode in Luke 10 (vv.38–42) which established Mary Magdalen as the patron and symbol of the contemplative life, and although there was constant reference to this aspect of her in devotional literature of the period, it was rarely illustrated until the sixteenth century except in cycles of her life. Thus it appears in Giovanni da Milano's series of frescoes in the sacristy of the Rinuccini chapel in S. Croce, in Florence, with her sitting at Christ's feet, listening to his words, whilst Martha complains to him about her idleness, to which Christ replies that Mary has chosen the better part. (Women are forever tattle-tales, comments the author of the *Mirror of the Blessed Life of Jesu Christ*, as Martha tells tales to the Lord rather than reproving her sister, 'after the manner that women are used to'.[11]) This scene follows that of the feast in the house of the Pharisee, Luke's sinner at Christ's feet, while seven devils dance out of the roof, there to remind the faithful that Luke's sinner, Mary Magdalen and Mary of Bethany are all one and the same (see Plate 30). Rogier van der Weyden shows Mary Magdalen seated, reading, a perfect embodiment of the contemplative life (see Plate 31).[12]

It is again of course as Mary of Bethany that Mary Magdalen appears in the more ubiquitous image of her as the sister of Lazarus; here it was

her tears which moved Christ to weep himself and to raise Lazarus from
the dead: a Purbeck limestone panel in Chichester Cathedral (*c.* 1125–
50) shows Mary and Martha greeting Christ at the gates of Bethany,
and in a fresco at S. Zeno in Verona, the sisters watch the shrouded
Lazarus being helped out of his tomb, whilst onlookers hold their noses
to keep out the stench of death.[13] It had been Martha who warned Christ
that as the body had been buried for four days, 'Lord, by this time he
stinketh' (John 11:39). Mary of Bethany's anointing of Christ in thanksgiving for her brother's life, and in foreknowledge of Christ's death
(John 12:1–9), was frescoed before 1100, together with other scenes
from the life and miracles of Christ, on the north wall of the church of
S. Angelo in Formis in Campania in southern Italy where, dressed in
a diaphanous ochre yellow cloak over a pale blue undergarment, she
bends over, drying Christ's feet with her hair, while he speaks with
Simon, and Judas points to her, scandalised.[14] (cf. Plate 3) (According
to the *Meditations*, Simon the Pharisee was 'perhaps' a relative, or 'very
close' to the family at Bethany, in another instance of imaginative rendering of 'what might have been'; the same author was to 'christen' the

31 Mary Magdalen, as
Mary of Bethany, reading,
the symbol of the
contemplative life. Rogier
van der Weyden.
Mid-fifteenth century.
London, National Gallery.

unnamed Samaritan woman at the well with the ladylike appellation 'Lucy' in his process of familiarising his audience, originally a nun of the Poor Clare order, with the biblical characters. [15])

Mary Magdalen's important role in the hours before Christ's death is stressed in the *Meditations* when she becomes spokeswoman for the disciples in the entirely apocryphal attempt to dissuade Christ from going to Jerusalem, and to persuade him to spend the Passover with his mother and the other disciples, described quaintly as his 'barons, counts, pages and grooms'. [16] When Christ refuses both her and the Virgin's requests, the temperaments of the two are contrasted, the Virgin weeping 'moderately and softly' and the Magdalen 'frantic about her Master, and crying with deep sobs'. This latter description, it was hoped, would act as an example to the reader. It also influenced thirteenth-century images of the saint, particularly by Tuscan and Umbrian painters.

Mary Magdalen becomes the Virgin's female support in one of the earliest hymns in the Italian language, written by the Franciscan Jacopone da Todi (*c.*1230–1306). Jacopone had dramatically converted when on the death of his young wife he discovered that under her gown she wore a hairshirt. A writer of *laude*, religious poetry or dramas enacted by confraternities, he applied dramatic form to his hymn on the Passion, the lovely 'Donna del Paradiso'. Here, a messenger tells the Virgin of her son's arrest by the Jews:

> *Donna del Paradiso*
> *Il tuo figliuolo è priso*
> *Jesu Cristo beato*

(Lady of Paradise, your little son, the blessed Jesus Christ, has been taken.)

The Virgin laments:

> *Come essere potria,*
> *Che ne fe' mai follia, Cristo, la spene mia,*
> *L'avesse omo pigliato*

(How could it be, for Christ, my hope, never did wrong that they have taken him.)

She turns to Mary Magdalen:

> *Soccorri, Maddalena*
> *Gionta·m'è adosso piena:*
> *Cristo figlio si mena*
> *Come m'è annuntiato*[17]

(Help me, Magdalen; misfortune has submerged me; Christ my son is being led away as has been told me.)

The sorrowing Virgin, knees bent and body curved over, appears on a contemporary crucifix with Mary Magdalen, in brilliant scarlet, bending over her protectively from behind, her body following the curve formed by that of the Virgin (see Plate 32).[18]

The *Meditations* tell us that it was to Mary Magdalen's house that the Virgin and her companions repaired during Christ's flagellation and mocking, 'where there is unspeakable grief, lamentation and crying'.[19] According to some medieval writers, Mary Magdalen even attended Christ's trial as well as his crucifixion.[20]

Luke mentions the women who followed Christ on the way to Calvary; in the Middle Ages the scene provided the occasion for artists to add vivid local colour, such as the cruel faces of the soldiers whipping Christ's bleeding body as he staggered beneath the weight of the cross, to depict the soldiers' rough treatment of the Virgin and the other women, and St Veronica wiping his face on her veil, upon which was left the imprint of his face. On Master Guglielmo's beautiful cross at Sarzana, near Lucca, Christ turns a tragic and loving gaze to the women, looking back to where Mary Magdalen stands slightly in advance of her two companions.[21]

The familiar image of the crucifixion with its dying or dead Christ on the cross, sometimes between the two robbers, and with the cluster of figures of his mother and followers below was one which was impressed upon the faithful time and again. The holy women were shown standing 'afar off' (as in Matt. 26:55, Mark 9:40, Luke 23:49), and sometimes grouped by the cross, behind the Virgin, Mary Magdalen more often than not in her customary place at the foot of the cross. In the words of the Franciscan friar, 'with the Lady, there were also John and the Magdalen, and the Lady's two sisters . . . all of whom, especially the Magdalen, the beloved disciple of Jesus, wept vehemently'.[22] It was

on occasion through the Magdalen's weeping that the faithful were
enjoined to feel remorse for Christ's suffering: 'Behold with thy gostly
eyze, his piteous passion . . . the teers of the Maudelyn [and] thou
shalt have compu[n]ccioun, and plente of teerys',[23] and in an interlude
performed on Good Friday, she weeps, to induce her audience to imitate
her:

> *E io, Madalena trista*
> *me gettai su ne' suoi piei,*
> *a' quali feci grande acquista*
> *che purgö i peccati mei:*
> *Su en issi me chiavate*
> *e giammaio non men levate.*[24]

(And I, sinful Magdalen, threw myself at his feet where I
gained greatly through purging my sins; nail me to his feet
and never detach me.)

In Giotto's scene at Padua, she tentatively touches Christ's feet with her
hair, and even the angels reflect the tragedy, one rending its clothes, in
imitation of antique tragic gestures. The up-flung arms of Masaccio's
little red figure beneath the cross (1426) express her passionate grief in
another traditional pose of ritualised mourning, a movement she adopts
in countless other scenes of lamentation (see Plate 33).[25] In Mathias
Grünewald's crucifixion scene of nearly a hundred years later, Mary
Magdalen's distraught figure is at the foot of the cross, while St John
supports the Virgin and John the Baptist points to Christ's slumped
body, its fingers splayed in expressionistic agony (see Plate 34).[26] And
Mary Magdalen sometimes supports the Virgin Mary as she faints,
although this was a controversial theme, criticised for its injustice to the
Virgin who, according to St Ambrose, had in fact not wept over her
son for theological reasons – she had been a party to, and was therefore
privy to, God's salvific plan, and knew that her son would rise again –
as well as out of her moral nature.[27] To other writers like Pseudo-
Bonaventure, the Virgin did weep, but quietly, and with none of the
gestures of grief of late antiquity which had been strongly condemned
by the Church Fathers.[28] Wailing women particularly had been anathema to St John Chrysostom who deeply distrusted their motives, convinced that by shrieking and moaning, and showing their bare arms

32 In the apron to the left of Christ's body, Mary Magdalen, as one of the Two Marys, supports the fainting Virgin. Painted Crucifix by the Master of S. Francesco, active c.1260–c.1272. London, National Gallery.

when they raised them, they were trying to attract new lovers.[29] But from the late thirteenth century, influenced by the emotionalism of Franciscan and other devotional writings, the Virgin herself was allowed to emote, discreetly, while Mary Magdalen was in the forefront of heart-rending images, as the inciter to grief, often almost appearing as chief mourner herself. In the *Lamentatyone of Mary Magdaleyne*, Christ says goodbye to the Magdalen at the crucifixion:

> And ever, me thought he, beyng in that payne,
> Loked on me with dedly countenaunce.
> As he had sayd in his special remembrance,
> 'Farwel, Magdalen, departe must I nedes hens,
> My herte is Tanquam cera liquiscens.'[30]

It was as the first woman mourner, apart from the Virgin, that Benedetto Antelami portrayed Mary Magdalen in his mid-eleventh century stone relief of the *Deposition* in Parma Cathedral,[31] in a procession filing from either side of the crucifix, an evocation of monumental and silent grief, like people at a funeral queuing to pay their respects to the bereaved. Nicodemus stands on the ladder while Joseph clasps the body, and Christ's outstretched hand is taken by his mother and pressed to her cheek; behind her is St Peter. To the right stand the centurions, with the soldiers haggling over Christ's cloak in the foreground. At the end of the thirteenth century, this sorrowful and dignified image had been transformed into one of extreme drama, with figures whose passionate involvement with the events was intended to create those self-same sentiments in the spectator, influenced by the gory and graphic accounts in the *Meditations* and in similar writings, of the deposition, and of the lowering of the body into the lap of his mother, and Mary Magdalen's taking of his feet. In Simone Martini's panel of *c.*1340, the body is lowered, and the Virgin reaches up agonisingly to receive it. To the right, Mary Magdalen flings up her arms in a gesture of grief borrowed from the sarcophagi of the ancient Greeks and Romans where in scenes of battles, and pain and death, women tear their hair, beat their breasts and, like Dido on the departure of Aeneas, throw their arms up in despair.[32]

'And in carrying the body of Jesus to the sepulchre, Mary supported the head, Mary Magdalene, the feet, and the others, the body, weeping tenderly', wrote a fourteenth-century monk, fondly imagining that it

would only be natural for this to have taken place, and despite the fact
that it went entirely against the gospel accounts which merely described
Christ's burial by Joseph of Arimathaea with, according to John, Nicodemus' help.[33] In early images, the body was shown being carried by
Joseph and Nicodemus, and by about the year 1000, the Virgin Mary
was included, and the episode was sometimes combined with the scene
of the two women sitting by the grave who 'beheld where he was laid'

33 Left: Mary Magdalen at the foot of the
Cross. Detail of Masaccio's *Crucifixion*
(1426). Naples, Museo Nazionale di
Capodimonte. 34 Right: Mary Magdalen
weeping below the Cross, from Mathias
Grünewald's Isenheim Altarpiece (1515).
Colmar, Unterlinden Museum.

(Mark 15:47). Although from a much later date, between 1505 and 1507, Raphael's studies for his *Carrying of the Body of Christ*, painted for Atalanta Baglioni, are interesting not only for showing his working method but also important for the evolution of Mary Magdalen's figure within the composition. The artist seems to have originally thought of the painting as a traditional *pietà* with Christ lying across his mother's knees and his thighs and lower legs across Mary Magdalen's legs (Oxford, Ashmolean Museum), and then in an entirely different conceptualisation, a standing Magdalen becomes the central figure, lifting Christ's lifeless hand as he is carried by Nicodemus and Joseph, with the Virgin and John the Evangelist standing to the right of the drawing (London, British Museum). In a later drawing which is closest to the finished painting, Mary Magdalen is again the central figure, clasping Christ's left hand in hers, and leaning over the body, gazing into his face (Florence, Galleria degli Uffizi; see Plate 35).[34]

The *Meditations* describe a touching little vignette in which Joseph of Arimathaea begs the Virgin to allow them to shroud her son's body. In terms of time, it was during an imaginary halt while the body was being carried to the tomb, a scene which had no scriptural source but derived from the liturgy and meditative practices of the Middle Ages, and became a popular devotional image in itself, with the Virgin as the focal point of grief. She asks John and Nicodemus not to take away her son so soon, but finally wishing to 'look still longer' upon his wounds, allows them to prepare the body for interment. The *Meditations* go on to relate how 'the Lady always held His head on her lap . . . and the Magdalen held His feet':

> When they came to the legs, near the feet, the Magdalen said, 'I pray you to permit me to prepare the feet at which I obtained mercy.' This was permitted and she held the feet. She seemed faint with sorrow . . . She wished to wash, anoint, and prepare His whole body well; but there was neither time nor place. At least, she could wash His feet with tears, and at length devotedly wipe, embrace, kiss, wrap and faithfully prepare them as best she knew and could.[35]

In Giotto's *Lamentation* in the Scrovegni chapel of 1304–6, the Virgin cradles the upper part of Christ's body, and Mary Magdalen holds his feet, the position allotted to her in the *Meditations* – 'the feet at which

35 Preliminary study for the *Carrying of the Body of Christ* (1505–7). Raphael. Florence, Galleria degli Uffizi, Gabinetto dei Disegni e Stampe.

she found so much grace' – and traditionally hers, derived from her role as Luke's sinner (see Plate 36). The mourning group around these three figures shows a whole gamut of gestures which might have been seen during medieval mourning rites, such as the veiled female figures squatting to the left and in the centre of the scene, and John with his arms flung back, and a woman with hands raised and another with hands clasped to her face, to the left of the scene.[36] In the tragic Dijon *Pietà* (1440–60), Mary Magdalen wipes her eyes with a corner of her mantle in another formula of grief, whilst St John removes the crown of thorns.[37] This occasion of sorrow and lamentation, however, also provoked a kind of rivalry, with the Virgin and Mary Magdalen vying for first place as chief mourner, as the *Meditations* entertainingly explain – also no doubt for fear of the Virgin's being upstaged – as when 'out of the abundance of her [the Virgin's] tears, she washed the face of her son much more than the Magdalen did His feet'.[38] In a possibly unique piece of iconography, by the early sixteenth-century Master of Delft, Mary

36 *Lamentation* (1304–6). Giotto. Padua, Scrovegni Chapel.

Magdalen's figure occupies and dominates centre-stage as, kneeling by
the dead Christ, she anoints his forehead with ointment from her pot,
while the Virgin and St John watch. In the distance, depicted on a hill
directly above this group, and beyond soldiers in the crucifixion scene
and Joseph of Arimathaea and Nicodemus carrying the body, is the *Noli
me tangere*, the other Passion scene of which she is a major protagonist.[39]
In Luca Signorelli's fresco (1502) at Orvieto, Mary Magdalen is the
central figure of the *Pietà* group, kneeling behind Christ's body, in ochre
with a pink mantle, and kissing his right hand, while his head rests on
his mother's knees. St John the Evangelist and a donor stand to each
side.[40] Another lamentation which stresses Mary Magdalen's relationship with Christ is Botticelli's Munich painting of *c*.1490–2, where
Christ lies across the fainting Virgin's knees while Mary Magdalen,

kneeling at her side, cradles his head in her arms, her face pressed against his, her hair falling around him, an image both intimate and tender (see Plate 37).[41]

Mary Magdalen appeared in another kind of devotional image which also focused on Christ's dead body. This was the mourning group, or *Beweinung* in German, in Italian *compianto*, which consisted of figures placed around the displayed body of Christ. Although of a later date than the devotional literature and religious drama discussed, Guido Mazzoni's brilliantly coloured life-size terracotta group of the 1480s belongs to the same genre of popular piety (see Plate 38).[42] The figures, like characters out of a sculpted mystery play, or *sacra rappresentazione*, gather round the body, their faces and bodies emanating extraordinary grief, above all that of Mary Magdalen, who, together with St John, flanks the weeping Virgin. If the Tours play of the late twelfth century could influence the art of Provence in that century (see below), it is more than likely that art such as Mazzoni's was inspired by the plays performed by religious communities and members of penitential confraternities, or the *disciplinati*. Like the devotional images of the earlier Middle Ages, the purpose of groups such as Mazzoni's was to move the spectator to grief and repentance, and with the eschatalogical preoccupations of his

37 Mary Magdalen cradling Christ's head. Detail from Sandro Botticelli's *Lamentation* (*c*.1490–2). Munich, Alte Pinakothek.

own times also to make a good death. Mary Magdalen leans over the Virgin comfortingly, her mouth open in the violence of her emotions, her hair flowing down in long heavy ribbons, and eyes bulging from weeping, a sculptural embodiment of the description of her in a medieval manuscript where she tears and scratches her face and pulls her golden hair ('la Magdalena tuta se desface'; 'il viso se sgraffa et i biundi cavilli').[43] Her wild grief is depicted again in another terracotta group, created by Niccolò dell'Arca (1463), where she rushes forward, maenad-like, her drapery streaming behind her as she seems stopped in mid-flight, her mouth opened to shriek at the sight of her dead Lord (see Plate 39).[44]

From earliest Christian times, the resurrection had been represented by the procession of the two or three Marys to the sepulchre and their discovery of the empty tomb and meeting with one or two angels. Similarly, it was through these two scenes that the event was first portrayed in the dramatic non-biblical interludes which from the first half of the tenth century were performed during the Easter matins ceremonies which preceded mass on Easter morning in the cathedrals and monasteries of Europe. And it is in these dialogues, called the *Visitatio sepulchri*, that Mary Magdalen, at first just one of the myrrhophores, but later gaining prominence by being given, for instance, a solo lament, became one of the first characters in western drama. It has been suggested that the development of her role in the ceremony may have been a result of the sudden expansion of her popularity in the early eleventh century, and may be seen as one of the manifestations of her cult.[45] The dialogues also inspired some of the most marvellously moving images of her.

In its simplest form, three monks representing the three Marys, dressed in long cloaks and swinging censers, slowly and hesitantly approached either the altar or a coffer representing Christ's tomb ('quaedam assimilatio sepulchri'), in which his body in its winding sheet, represented by a cross wrapped in a veil, had been placed on Good Friday. Another of the monastic community dressed in a white alb as the angel at the tomb, chanting, asked them whom they sought, 'Quem quaeritis?' 'Jesus of Nazareth,' they chanted back. The angel then showed them the empty tomb (the cross having been removed the night before 'with mystery'), the shroud being the only evidence of its former occupant. The Marys took it, and showed it to the faithful, singing joyfully, 'The Lord is risen.' At this, the congregation intoned

38 Left: Mary Magdalen in Guido Mazzoni's *Mourning Group* of the 1480s. Modena, S. Giovanni. 39 Right: as she appears in a *Mourning Group* by Niccolò dell'Arca of 1463. Bologna, Pinacoteca Nazionale.

a triumphal shout, and the bells rang out to proclaim the good news on Easter morning.[46]

In the eleventh century, a new and apocryphal scene, the *Victimae paschali*, was added to the *Visitatio sepulchri*, which gave Mary Magdalen even greater prominence. It was probably written by the monk Wipo of Burgundy who died in 1048. Here monks, probably impersonating the disciples, asked, 'Dic nobis, Maria, quid vidisti in via?' (Tell us, Mary, what did you see on the way?) 'Mary' – it is not clear whether the three monks being addressed here as Mary represented Mary Magdalen or, collectively, the three Marys – replied, 'Sepulchrum Christi viventis,/ et gloriam vidi resurgentis;/ Angelicos testes,/ sudarium et vestes./ Surrexit Christus, spes mea;/ praecedet suos in Galilaea.' (I saw the sepulchre of the living Christ and the glory of the risen one; the witness of the angels, the sudarium and clothes. Christ is risen, my hope; he goes before his brethren into Galilee.) In the earliest plays, male clerics played the parts of the three Marys, and the rubrics give fascinating details about the way they were to appear. In the office of Rouen Cathedral, written in the twelfth century, if not earlier, three *dyaconi canonici*, or deacons, carrying vessels, wore dalmatics and amices over their heads in imitation of women, 'ad similitudinem mulierum'.[47] At Tours, two boys (*duo pueri*) took on the roles of the angels, and three chaplains with white dalmatics and covered heads, the Marys.[48] Nuns took appropriately female parts in the thirteenth-century *Ludus Paschalis* from the female monastery at Origny-Ste-Benoîte: 'Chascune des Maries doit auoir en se main un cierge alumeit, et Marie Magdelainne doit auoir vnne boiste en se main, et les autres deus nient, dusques adout quellez dient acate au Marchant.'[49] (Each of the Marys should have in her hand a lit candle, and Mary Magdalen should have a box in her hand, the other two nothing, since they are going to buy at the merchant's.) In the fourteenth-century play from the nunnery at Barking, the Marys were also impersonated by nuns, and costumed by Katharine of Sutton, abbess from 1363 to 1376, in the chapel of Mary Magdalen, and holding silver ampullae, had their confessions heard and were absolved, before the one representing Mary Magdalen began her lament.[50]

The stage direction from Origny-Ste-Benoîte leads us neatly into a scene which, although as far as the drama is concerned took place before the Marys went to the tomb, was a later addition to the Easter play, inserted into the mass during the eleventh century. The merchant (Mercator) is not, of course, a character taken from the gospels but was added to the episode related in Mark 16:1 to give a human, and even comical, touch to the otherwise dramatic scenes of the Passion. It is to him that the three Marys go to buy the spice with which they intend to anoint Christ's body. In the late twelfth-century Easter play from the diocese of Tours, a young merchant, 'Mercator juvenis', offers to sell the Marys balm which will prevent the holy body from 'being eaten by worms or decomposing'. He overcharges them, and they go to a second merchant who offers them the correct price, so that even in a setting so sorrowful – it is an occasion for the Marys to lament, which is one of the functions of their, and more importantly Mary Magdalen's, role – time is given to reflect upon the foibles of human nature.[51] The dialogue between the Marys and Mercator was enacted in churches in Provence, and the scene seems to have struck a chord with local sculptors as it appears on two churches near Nîmes. (A different version appears on a relief in the cloister of St Trophîme at Arles.) In one, at Beaucaire, a carved frieze showing the events of the Passion has been reset, high on the south side of the rebuilt church, but at St Gilles-en-Gard, in the Camargue, the scene, much defaced, appears on the lintel over the southern door of the great west front as part of a sequence of Mary Magdalen's *vita* which runs below a tympanum displaying a large crucifixion.[52] A further example, more striking as it is undamaged, is to be found at Modena, where the identical scene is carved on a capital and the older bearded merchant weighs out the ointment (see Plate 40).[53]

In a chronological sequence of events, of course, the next scene would be that of the three Marys bearing their ointment jars or *alabastrons*, wending their way to the sepulchre, one of the best-known images in Christian art. In the late eleventh-century benedictional of St Æthelwold, they are greeted by an angel with highly coloured wings, while the soldiers, piled on top of each other, sleep on.[54]

In the Merchant scene from the Tours *ludus*, Mary Salome and Mary Jacoby have singing parts, but when the women come to the tomb, Mary Magdalen becomes the central figure, lamenting and swooning

40 The Three Marys at the Spice Merchant's (*c.* 1170). Modena, Museo Civico Medievale e Moderno.

from sorrow when she discovers the tomb is empty, as the stage instructions given in the rubric make explicit:

> Mary Magdalen, who should be on the left side of the church, rises and goes to the sepulchre, claps her hands, and weeping says: 'I am so sad, oh sorrow, oh unhappiness! Jesus Christ, glory of the world, it is you who have redeemed me, it is through you that I will enjoy eternal life, and the Jews have hung you on the cross and you have died for us . . .

She laments further, and is so overcome that she faints away:

> Then Mary Jacoby comes who takes her right arm and Mary Salome takes her left and they lift her from the ground, saying to her, 'Dear sister, there is too much sorrow in your soul.'[55]

The scene was uniquely and beautifully translated into stone on the other side of the capital at Modena and shows the fainting figure of the Magdalen lying over the empty tomb, out of which hangs the winding sheet left behind by the risen Christ, while the two other Marys lean protectively and comfortingly over her (see Plate 41).[56]

In John 20 Mary Magdalen alone finds the stone moved away. This scene was depicted in a twelfth-century Byzantine gospel book which shows her looking into the sepulchre.[57] A book of hours made in about 1500 for Anne of Brittany, widow of Charles VIII and, by this date, wife of Louis XII, also includes an unusual image showing Mary Magdalen walking alone in a wattle enclosure, carrying her ointment jar, a depiction which perhaps indicates the importance of her solitary witness of the resurrected Christ to the female owner of the book. The two other Marys look on from a distance.[58] Mary Magdalen's visit to the tomb prompted St Bonaventure to exclaim, 'of the women, [she] was so carried away by the burning love of her heart, so affected by the sweetness of her deep devotion, so drawn by the strong bonds of love, that forgetful of her woman's weakness, she braved the darkness of the shadows and cruelty of the persecutors to visit the sepulchre.'[59] She returns to the tomb with Peter and the 'other disciple', whose 'race' was enacted during the Easter liturgical celebrations, particularly in Germany. Peter then enters the sepulchre, followed by the 'other disciple',

41 Mary Magdalen fainting at the Tomb (*c.*1170). Modena, Museo Civico Medievale e Moderno.

to see the discarded grave-clothes. In a thirteenth-century window in the cathedral of Notre-Dame at Laon, Mary Magdalen, holding a book, her attribute as the symbol of the contemplative life, points to Peter who now holds the shroud, in a clear indication that the discovery has been imputed to the male founder of the Church.[60] The disciples then return home.

John's account of Mary Magdalen's bewilderment, sorrow and final joy inspired sculptors and painters from the ninth century to give visual expression to the scene called the *Noli me tangere*. The scene was incorporated into the *Visitatio sepulchri* ceremony by the late twelfth century where it was accompanied by particularly emotive melodies in several versions, among them the Tours play.[61] In the same century, it was given plastic form in Romanesque churches and monasteries of France where, for example, at Saulieu and Autun, carved capitals were decorated with the scene of the three Marys with the angel on one side, and Christ and Mary Magdalen on the adjacent face. At Autun, set among curving graceful foliage, Ghislebertus' lovely crouching figure of Mary Magdalen of 1125–35, carrying her ointment jar, bends forward to

42 The *Noli me tangere*, and the Three Marys going to the Sepulchre,
sculpted by Ghislebertus, *c.*1125–35. Autun, St Lazare.

touch Christ's feet as he lightly moves away, the deep striations in
their transparent-seeming garments following the contours of their
bodies. The tender relationship, almost a visual pendant to Anselm's
poetic meditation, is described in the arc formed by Christ's body as
he leans away at the same time as he looks down towards her (see
Plate 42).[62]

As we have seen, some writers clearly believed that the fact that Christ
first appeared to Mary Magdalen showed a certain lack of decorum, and
sought to rectify the situation. In the *Meditations*, in a chapter entitled
'Of the Resurrection of the Lord and How He First appeared to His
Mother on the Sunday', we hear that the Virgin is suddenly startled by
the appearance of her son 'in the whitest garments, with serene face . . .
[who] said to her, as if beside her, "Hail, saintly parent".' Christ,
feeling remorseful about Mary Magdalen's sorrow as she seeks and does
not find him, dutifully asks his mother if he may take his leave of her,
to console the Magdalen. Much in the way of a mother whose son has
put her before his wife, and therefore her daughter-in-law, the Virgin
approves, 'very much', provided her son returns to her afterwards. The

account then returns to the gospel story, describing how Christ finds
Mary Magdalen 'like an inebriate' in her grief, hoping still, in terms
reminiscent of the *Canticle of Canticles*, 'to hear something new about
her Beloved'.[63] In *The Mirror of the Blessed Life of Jesu Christ*, the writer
adds delightful alterations to the gospels aimed at giving greater prominence to the Virgin, 'as it may reasonably be believed – you should know,
however, that nothing is mentioned in the gospel about the appearance
to the Lady'. He then elaborates upon the scene of the *Noli me tangere*
in a way which must have pleased his female readers, 'And so those two
true lovers stood and spake together with great comfort and joy'; his
later description of Mary Magdalen, as the 'beloved discipless and apostless of the apostles', can have given them no less delight.[64]

Odo of Cluny saw the scene in the garden as a mark of God's compassion and love towards womankind, and in it also the elimination by
woman of death from the world, as it was through the feminine sex
that the Lord had chosen to announce to man the joy of his resurrection. The joyful rhythms of his hymn to Mary Magdalen, written for
the monks at Cluny to chant on her feast-day, evoke her visit to the
sepulchre:

> *Post fluxae carnis scandala/ fit ex lebete phiala;*
> *in vas translata gloriae/ de vase contumeliae.*
>
> *Aegra currit at Medicum/ vas ferens aromaticum:*
> *et a morbo multiplici/ Verbo curatur Medici . . .*
>
> *Surgentem cum victoria/ Jesum videt ab inferis;*
> *prima meretur gaudia/ quae plus ardebat caeteris.*[65]

(After the scandal of fleshly weakness, she made a shallow
cup from a cauldron; the vessel of glory was transformed
from the vessel of contumely. Sick, she ran to the Doctor,
carrying the vessel of spices; and was cured from many ail-
ments, by the Doctor's word. She saw Jesus rise victoriously
from below; she was the first to merit joy because she loved
more than the others.)

The vase, or *alabastron*, becomes from the Middle Ages Mary Magdalen's most common attribute, symbol in ancient and modern times

of the Eternal Feminine, as container of both life and death.[66] As Pseudo-Rabanus Maurus' devoted 'perfumer of Christ',[67] she carries the expensive balm to anoint Christ in death as it was believed she had in his lifetime. The unguent symbolises the 'deep enticements and secrets of the heart', and the vase represents 'the innermost sanctuary of the heart full of faith and charity'; it is the receptacle of the spiritual life.[68] In a genre which became popular in the late fifteenth and early sixteenth centuries, Mary Magdalen appears half-length in a kind of 'holy portrait', holding her pot of ointment, as in Rogier van der Weyden's marvellous panel from the Braque triptych (c.1450, Paris, Louvre) which shows tears trickling down her cheeks.[69] In other images, particularly from sixteenth-century northern Europe, she opens the lid, thus allowing the 'odour of sanctity' to steal forth, and conversely allows the heavenly influences to enter.[70] (The vase itself was said to be preserved in the church of St Victor, Marseille, where the Dominican Silvestro de Prierio said he saw it in 1497; the monastery of St Sever in Les Landes even claimed to possess some of the ointment, too, as 'Mary Magdalen had not emptied all of it on Christ's feet'.[71])

The jar of ointment also links her to the five wise and five foolish virgins who, in the parable in Matthew 25, await the arrival of the bridegroom. The foolish virgins run out of oil, and while they are gone in search of more, the bridegroom arrives, and then goes to the wedding feast with the five wise virgins who had been well prepared, and 'took oil in their vessels with their lamps' (v.4). The foolish virgins knock on the door, but the bridegroom refuses their entry: they were not prepared for his coming. Mary Magdalen, prepared with her jar to anoint Christ, contrasts and acts as a model for the foolish virgins who failed to have enough oil in their lamps, and therefore failed to meet the bridegroom. She is depicted as one of the wise virgins in a predella scene in Lucas Moser's altarpiece of Mary Magdalen (1431, Tiefenbronn).[72]

The metaphor of Christ as the gardener sowing his seed within Mary Magdalen's mind appears in the Easter hymn by Philippe de Grève, the early thirteenth-century chancellor of Paris:

> O Maria, noli flere,/ Iam non quaeras alium;/ Hortulanus hic est vere/ Et colonus mentium,/ Intra mentis hortum quaere/ Mentis operarium.
>
> Unde planctus et lamentum?/ Quid mentem non erigis?/ Quid revolvis monumentem?/ Tecum est, quem diligis,/ Jesum quaeris, et inventum/ Habes nec intelligis.

Unde gemis, unde ploras?/ Verum habes gaudium;/ Latet in te, quod ignoras,/ Doloris solacium;/ Intus habes, quaeris foras/ Languoris remedium.

Iam non miror, si nescisti/ Magistrum, dum seminat;/ Semen, quod est verbum Christi/ Te magis illuminat,/ Et Rabboni *respondisti,/ Dum* Mariam *nominat.*

Pedes Christi, quae lavisti/ Fonte lota gratiae,/ Quem ab ipso recepisti,/ Funde rorem veniae,/ Resurgentis quem vidisti/ Fac consortes gloriae.

Gloria et honor Deo/ Cuius praefert gratia?/ Invitanti pharisaeo; Mariae suspiria,/ Cenam vitae qui dat reo/ Gratiae post prandia.[73]

(O Mary, do not weep, look no further. The true Gardener is here and the cultivator of minds; seek in the garden of the mind the worker of the mind. Why do you weep and lament? Why do you not raise your mind? Why do you turn to the monument? He is with you, he whom you love. You sought Jesus and found him. You do not understand. Why do you moan and cry? You have true joy; the relief of your pain is hidden within you, and you do not know; you have it inside, and you look outside for the remedy to your languor. I would not marvel if you did not know the Master while he is sowing; the seed, which is the word of Christ, enlightens you more, and you replied 'Rabboni', while he is calling you 'Mary'. The feet of Christ, which you washed, are the washed source of that grace which you received from him. Pour the balsam of pardon, make the sharer of your glory she whom you saw when you were resurrecting. Whose grace is more important than glory and honour to God? To the Pharisee's guest who offers the sinner the food of life, Mary's sighs are thanks, the grace after the meal.)

In the fresco of the *Noli me tangere* in the Magdalen chapel at Assisi, Mary Magdalen yearningly leans after Christ, as he moves away, carrying his gardener's spade; in an altogether more brusque depiction of the scene than Ghislebertus', watched by two angels perched on a tomb made of pink Verona marble.[74] And in the lyrical version painted by Fra Bartolommeo (1475–1517) for the tiny garden chapel of the convent of Mary Magdalen near Fiesole, outside Florence, the stone on which the Magdalen's jar rests is inscribed with the words of the Shulamite, 'I found him whom my soul loves', thus recalling the ancient link with the Bride, and at the same time referring to Mary Magdalen as the symbol of the Christian soul who, having sought, was now united with God.[75]

The varying gospel interpretations of how many and which holy women were witnesses to the resurrection resulted in an equally varied iconography. But Mark's account particularly, in the postscript to the resurrection scene where Mary Magdalen alone tells the disciples who 'believed her not', contributed to the marvellous image of Mary Magdalen, as the *apostola apostolorum*, announcing the resurrection to the apostles, described as that '*rarissima* of christological subjects' which first appeared in a twelfth-century psalter probably written in England at St Albans for Christina of Markyate.[76] This shows Mary Magdalen telling the news to a somewhat dumbfounded-looking group of eleven male disciples (see Frontispiece). Another illustration of the same scene appears in the gospel book of Henry the Lion, duke of Saxony and Bavaria, and founder of Munich, and his wife Matilda, of about 1180, where the apostles hold up a scroll, with the words, 'Dic nobis, Maria, quid vidisti in via', the opening words from Wipo's *Victimae paschali* sequence, to which her scroll as she lightly floats towards them replies, 'Sepulchrum Christi viventis, et gloriam vidi resurgentis.'[77] The idea of Mary Magdalen as the 'apostle to the apostles', which may have been revived by the legend of her apostolic career in Provence, seems to have appealed to women in particular, as in the case of the noble lady, Jutta Tersina of Liechtenfels, who in c. 1200 commissioned a psalter, her donor page showing her at Mary Magdalen's feet with the clumsily written words 'apostolorum apostola' above the saint's head (see Plate 43).[78] The scene of Mary Magdalen telling the apostles is also included in at least two other psalters commissioned or made for noble women: the so-called Queen Mary Psalter of c. 1310–20, now in the British Library and believed to have been made for Isabella, wife of Richard II of England (it also contains an exquisite *Noli me tangere*), and the Ingeborg Psalter at Chantilly, written and illuminated for Ingeborg, wife of Philip Augustus (d. 1223), whom she married in 1193.[79] That Mary Magdalen inspired devotion amongst women is manifest in such images as the mid-thirteenth century statue of her holding her *alabastron* in Münster Cathedral, where the diminutive donor figure is a kneeling nun, her arms raised up in supplication.[80] A devotional work, commissioned by Eleanor de Quincy, and made possibly between 1264 and 1267, shows Mary Magdalen wearing a wimple similar to that of Lady de Quincy, in the scene of the *Noli me tangere* placed at the beginning of a series of saints. Some self-identification may have been intended in a book whose predominant theme was one of penitence, and the scene's placing probably reflected some personal devotion to Mary Magdalen.[81] In an antiphoner written in 1290 for the Cistercian abbey of Beaupré, near Grammont in Belgium, a kneeling female figure identified as 'Domicella de Viana', who gave the manuscript to the abbey, is depicted beside the scene of the three Marys at the tomb, below a miniature of the resurrection.[82] The proximity of the donor figure to the three Marys, and the way in which she looks directly at them rather than at the resurrected Christ above, indicates how strongly women might have

43 Mary Magdalen as 'Apostola Apostolorum' with Jutta Tersina of Liechtenfels. Early thirteenth century. Zwettl, Stiftsbibliothek.

identified with the active role of the female disciples as witnesses. It has been suggested that such extraordinary titles as 'apostle to the apostles' and 'beloved disciple', as important as those given to the male disciples Peter and John, might have inspired medieval women to emulate Mary Magdalen.[83] In these rare images of Mary Magdalen giving the news to the disciples, she appears, in the words of Peter Abelard, the controversial philosopher and theologian, as the 'apostle to the apostles', or 'ambassadress of ambassadors'.[84]

Although there is no mention of the presence of women at the Last Supper, traditionally held to have been an all-male event, a fourteenth-century manuscript illumination may show Mary Magdalen seated among the disciples. And in a late thirteenth-century English psalter, Mary Magdalen as Luke's sinner wipes Christ's feet with her hair as he is seated at the Last Supper.[85] She may also have been at the ascension – Honorius Augustodunensis says that after announcing the resurrection, she was present with the disciples when the Lord ascended. She may be one of the women included in the illustration of the scene in the Hunterian Psalter of *c.* 1160.[86]

Mary Magdalen's post-ascension life was the subject, as we have seen, of an enormous number and perplexing variety of legends which proliferated from the eleventh century onwards. Many of them of course were spawned by the supposed arrival of her relics in Burgundy, although the origins of the earliest recorded one, in the Anglo-Saxon martyrology, are unknown. Her travels took her to Asia Minor, Rome, and southern France; or she died in Palestine, Ephesus and at Aix-en-Provence. The legends relating to her arrival in France yielded an equally varied assortment of illustrations, depicted in glass cycles, frescoes, panel paintings and manuscripts from the thirteenth century. The first images of her arrival at Marseille appear in the glass cycles at the cathedrals of Chartres (*c.* 1200) and Auxerre (1230), and at Notre-Dame at Semur-en-Auxois (early thirteenth century).[87] The story itself appears most fully in the *Golden Legend*. The most famous account is that of Mary Magdalen crossing the sea in a rudderless boat with Martha and Lazarus, and the three Marys, and disembarking at Marseille. She is also variously accompanied by her servant Sarah the Egyptian, and Trophimus, Maximinus, Martial, Saturninus, Sidonius, Eutropius, Marcella, Cleon and Joseph of Arimathaea, all figures important in the history of Christianity in France, and in the case of Joseph of Arimathaea, England.

44 Mary Magdalen and her companions being set adrift by heathens; and arriving at Marseille where she preaches to the pagan prince and his people. Late fourteenth century. Bolzano, S. Maria Maddalena.

In the *Golden Legend* we are told the purpose of the journey: of how, after Christ's death and the martyrdom of St Stephen, the disciples 'went into the divers countries, and preached the word of God'. However, the 'heathens' had set Mary Magdalen and her companions, including Maximinus and 'many other Christian men', adrift on the perilous sea of life, prey to storms and the tossing of the waves, in a boat 'without any tackle or rudder . . . for to be drowned' (see Plate 44). Divine providence is to hand – 'by the purveyance of Almighty God' the ship arrives at Marseille, bearing its precious cargo of the Christian faith. The allegory of the Church as a ship captained by St Peter came from Hippolytus in the third century, and by the Middle Ages it was well known, its most famous depiction being probably Giotto's vast mosaic of the *Navicella* which was on the façade of the original basilica of St Peter in Rome, before it was taken down in the seventeenth century.[88] Mary Magdalen's sea-journey is not merely an adventure, and this is underscored by the lack of 'rudder', which renders them helpless except for the guiding hand of God.

Once on land, they seek refuge under a 'porch' of a 'temple of the people of that country'. On seeing those people, pagans all, sacrificing, Mary Magdalen preaches the word of Christ (see Plate 46). (Geoffrey of Vendôme [d. 1132] marvelled at the way that, having been 'previously a famous sinner, she later became a glorious preacher'.) When the hitherto barren prince of Marseille and his wife, rulers of that pagan land, make sacrifices to idols to have a child, she forbids them. She then appears in visions to the princess and her husband, asking why they persecute Christians. They strike a bargain: they will cease their unChristian activities if she asks her god to give them a child. This unlikely arrangement, with its wonderfully naïve concept of the ways of the divine, results in Mary Magdalen's first miracle, the conception of that child. (It has also been seen to associate her with fertility powers, linking her back to the ancient figures of Ishtar and Cybele, and may be the reason why she was named as patron saint of a vineyard in southern France, and of the one near Bolzano.[89]) She is also, by extension, a restorer to life, for when the couple go on pilgrimage to Rome to ascertain from St Peter the veracity of what the Magdalen has told them about Christ, the princess is drowned in one of those enormous storms at sea which happen so frequently in hagiographical literature. Here, the sea-journey becomes symbolic of spiritual renewal, for as the neophytes of early Christianity entirely immersed themselves during the baptism ritual, to cleanse themselves of sin in the waters of redemption, and re-emerged purified, so those who allegorically underwent the dangers of sea-voyages, sometimes drowning, and miraculously restored to life, represented souls passing through their travails and arriving ultimately at their spiritual rebirth, their metaphorical baptism to life.[90] This idea is found in the next part of the narrative. The prince leaves his wife's body on a rock with the child at her breast, covered with a mantle, for the ground is too hard to bury her. He then continues his pilgrimage, spending two years in the company of St Peter who instructs him, and then voyages home to Gaul. Passing the rock where he had left his spouse, he finds the child by the seaside who, 'like small children, took small stones and threw them into the sea'. Frightened, the child runs to its mother's breast, which is still miraculously giving milk. The prince's thanks to Mary Magdalen for keeping his child alive have the effect of restoring the princess to life. The couple return to Marseille where they are baptised, and the Christianisation of Gaul is achieved. (According to a late fifteenth-century manuscript giving a brief history of the rulers of Burgundy, and probably written and illuminated for the instruction of the infant Philip the Fair, the princely couple converted by Mary Magdalen's preaching at Marseille are the king and queen of Burgundy; in this version, the child too is resuscitated, together with his mother, to become the second legendary king of Burgundy, whose true ducal rulers seem to have appropriated the Provençal legend

45 Mary Magdalen carried by Angels to Heaven at the canonical hours. School of Giotto (post-1313). Assisi, Magdalen Chapel.

to their own purposes, to add lustre to the house of Burgundy, within whose territories of course Vézelay lay.[91]) Lazarus becomes bishop of Marseille, and Mary Magdalen watches while idols are destroyed; with Martha and Maximin, she converts the pagans at Aix, by preaching and example, and Maximinus is elected bishop.

Exhausted by all her pastoral activity, Mary Magdalen retires for her last thirty years to a mountain cave 'unknown to anyone' and where there is 'neither water, nor herb, nor tree'. Instead, angels come down from heaven at the canonical hours and transport her in ecstasy to heaven for a celestial repast (see Plate 45). Here in her retreat, clad only in her hair, which has become a long golden mantle which entirely covers her, for she has rejected all worldly things, she prays and fasts, atoning for her past crimes. One day a hermit, who has also hidden himself away from the world, astonished to see her levitating in the sky several miles away, pays her a visit, and hears her life story. She asks him to tell Maximinus that he will find her in his oratory, and shortly afterwards appears there, through the agency of angels, to take her last communion and to die. At Assisi, in the chapel dedicated to her in the lower church, painters of Giotto's school portrayed her kneeling in her cave, being given a cloak by an angel and receiving her last communion, surrounded by priests. Her soul floating up to heaven is a beautiful little figure seated in an orange boat assisted by four angels, on her *peregrinatio ad Dominum*, an image which has as its classical forebears the souls of the dead ferried by Charon across the Styx to Hades. Maximinus then buries her body, next to which he arranges to have his own body interred, and miracles abound from the holy tomb.

A visual counterpart to the story in the *Golden Legend*, and almost contemporary, is a panel painted by a Tuscan artist, the Magdalen Master, in the last decades of the thirteenth century (see Plate 46). This shows the Magdalen as a hermit, with scenes from her life, from her incarnation as Luke's sinner to her burial, depicted around her, blessing and carrying her scroll with the words, 'Ne desperetis vos qui peccare soletis, exemploque meo vos reparate deo', urging all those who have sinned not to despair, and to follow her example by returning to God.[92] It is a lasting image of her, created in the Middle Ages, for from the late fifteenth century the hermit in her grotto becomes the most prevalent representation of Mary Magdalen.

In his etymological preface to his life of Mary Magdalen, Jacopo de Voragine sums up her significance in three ways: firstly, in a play of words on her name, Mary is interpreted as 'amarum mare' or 'bitter sea'; secondly, she is the 'illuminatrix', or 'light-giver', and thirdly, the 'illuminata', or 'enlightened one'. By these three parts, Jacopo goes on to explain, are to be understood penitence, contemplation and heavenly glory. Mary Magdalen, described in terms curiously reminiscent of Gnostic ideas about her, is the receiver of light, or spiritual illumination, and in turn becomes the vessel through which that light is brought to others. Jacopo's emphasis on her as 'illuminatrix' can be seen as preparing the reader for her apostolic mission to Gaul, the story of which takes up by far the greater part of her *vita*. The first stage in her enlightenment was necessarily that of penitence and her life ends in solitary contemplation in her Provençal grotto in preparation for her celestial reward.[93]

Thus we have turned full circle, for it was Vézelay's latching onto the early legend of the eremitical Magdalen which contributed to the efflorescence of the medieval myth. From now on, to serve doctrinal purposes, her penitential end would take precedence over the other, gospel, elements of her story. Mary Magdalen's progress from the state

46 Mary Magdalen as a hermit with eight scenes from her life, by the Magdalen Master (c.1280). Florence, Galleria dell'Accademia.

of sin to sanctity mirrors the way in which, through the personae she assumed, she represented and reflected not only the medieval Church's notions about women, sin and redemption, but also the social concerns of the Middle Ages. Petrarch's 'dulcis amica Dei', in her grotto at Ste Baume, was an appealing image of contrite femininity, demonstrating that even the greatest of sinners could reach heaven.

CHAPTER VII

THE WEEPER

Loe where a Wounded Heart with Bleeding Eyes conspire.
Is she a Flaming Fountain, or a Weeping fire?

RICHARD CRASHAW (1612–49)[1]

 IN 1599 A WORKMAN at the Fabriano paper mill in northern Italy was crushed in the papermaking presses. Calling upon Mary Magdalen for help, he was released unhurt. The local church had been dedicated to the saint since its foundation in the last decade of the thirteenth century as the chapel-church of a hospital and, now, because of this miracle, the Magdalen was adopted as the patron saint of the mill. Painting a picture of her for the high altar of the church a few years later in c.1605, possibly to commemorate this miracle, Orazio Gentileschi depicted her as a voluptuous, beautiful woman, emphasising her sculptural form (see Plate 47).[2] Her hair is loose, her breasts are almost bare, and she holds a crucifix in her hands; a skull and book lie on the stone block before her. She has been a worldly creature, a *vanitas*, the source of whose pain is palpably in her former pleasure. A miraculous intercessor, she is also the true embodiment of the Counter-Reformation spirit, meditating upon death, and weeping for her sins. Her semi-nudity, symbolic of her conversion to God, assimilates her to the figure of Truth in philosophical terms, the 'naked Truth' of which the poet Horace had written.[3] The penitent in her grotto, the most pervasive image of Mary Magdalen during the sixteenth and seventeenth centuries, was, as we have seen, not new; what was novel was the visual language used to describe her, and which gave the image new meaning.

Hermits, ascetics and penitents usually appear in Christian art naked, or clad in animal skins or gracefully draped loincloths. Saints like John the

Baptist and Jerome, gaunt, bearded and long-haired, weep and pray in the desert, their eyes raised to heaven in anguish, having discarded their clothes to divest themselves of the world's vanities. Naked or semi-naked, they return to the primal state, to nature, their innocence redeemed. In Genesis, that first innocence is also represented as nakedness, and yet in the Old Testament nakedness had ambiguous connotations: Adam and Eve frolic naked and sinless until the Fall when knowledge opens their eyes, and they cover their genitals to hide their shame. In Genesis 9, having built the Ark, and saved a male and female of each of the species, Noah replenishes the world, planting a vineyard (v.20). He then drinks of the wine, becomes drunk and uncovers himself in his tent. Averting their eyes, Noah's sons Shem, Ham and Japheth cover their father's shame.

In the story of Adam and Eve the fall from innocence is represented by the protagonists' covering of their genitalia, an image which left its legacy in the Christian tradition where the first sin has always been associated with sexuality. From the earliest centuries, therefore, the body was regarded as the source of sin and, in Christian iconography, its various states of dress and undress signify some kind of moral judgement. In the fourteenth century, body symbolisms, or, more precisely, the appearance of the naked body, were codified by the Benedictine Pierre Bercheur in his dictionary of moral theology. Nakedness, he wrote, was nothing other than the lack of clothes, and since clothes signified many things in the scriptures, it was possible to distinguish several kinds of nakedness, and their symbolic meanings. These he defined as *nuditas naturalis*, the nakedness in which man was both born and died, and which was conducive to humility; *nuditas temporalis*, which connoted the lack of worldly possessions, which might be either by choice, as had been shown by Christ and the apostles, or through poverty; *nuditas virtualis*, the nakedness of Adam and Eve before the Fall, which symbolised innocence, but could also represent innocence regained through confession; and *nuditas criminalis*, which signified the lack of all virtues, and was exemplified in the Benedictine's vocabulary of things sinful by the vanity of the 'men of Ethiopia' who went around naked, glorifying that impious state.[4]

In the cases of Saints John the Baptist and Jerome, and of Anthony and Paul, the Egyptian hermits, their nakedness in the desert refers to *nuditas naturalis*, their return to the natural first habitat, akin to the animals. They are joined in this state by the fourth-century anchorites

47 The repentant Mary
Magdalen in her grotto
(c.1605). Orazio
Gentileschi. Fabriano, S.
Maria Maddalena.

Macarius of Alexandria and Onuphrius who led their lives of expiation
in the Thebaid, long shaggy hair covering their emaciated bodies, their
beards hanging below their knees, and, in the case of Macarius, forked.
It is into this iconography of hirsute penitence and asceticism that Mary
Magdalen and Mary of Egypt are absorbed, the only female saints to be
represented naked in medieval art. Feminine nakedness also made an
appearance in Christian imagery in scenes of the birth of the Virgin
where she is occasionally shown naked, death scenes in which the soul
is shown leaving the body as a naked baby or diminutive naked adult
figure, and in the Last Judgement; and in such Old Testament scenes as
Susanna and the Elders and David and Bathsheba; and of course the
prelapsarian Eve appears unclad. But whereas the nakedness of St Jerome
or St John the Baptist infers nothing other than their repentance and
rejection of the world, that of Mary Magdalen and Mary of Egypt

always relates to their femaleness and to their sexuality. They can be seen as possessing *nuditas temporalis* in their repudiation of the world's vanities, or *nuditas virtualis* in redeemed chastity, but powerful overtones of *nuditas criminalis*, the sin of lust for which they have both been pardoned, are always present. The contrite Mary Magdalen becomes the symbol of reconquered purity, but her very nakedness is a negative comment upon her feminine and sexual nature.

The earliest images of the naked Mary Magdalen appeared in the second decade of the thirteenth century – naked, that is, by implication, for, with few exceptions, her body is generally covered from head to foot by hair. The first known image of the hairclad penitent, signed by the Umbrian artist Bonamicus, and dated 1225, is frescoed onto a wall in a chapel of the church of S. Prospero in Perugia.[5] The eremitical element of Mary Magdalen's life derived from Mary of Egypt's legend, first painted in the tenth century in the rock churches of Cappodocia where that saint's cult was widespread.[6] From the thirteenth century, the penitent Magdalen became the most popular image of the saint in Italy, painted in churches, monasteries and hospitals, in fresco and on panel, particularly in Tuscany and Umbria where, under the aegis of the mendicant orders, and especially promoted by the Dominican preaching of public penitence, she became the patron of several lay associations and confraternities. As patron saint of the guild of drapers, the Arte de' Drappieri, in Bologna, she is portrayed in a miniature in the register and statutes of the guild dated 1339, enveloped in her hair. Six such hairy visions appear in one church alone, in S. Zeno at Verona, and two in S. Maria Maggiore in Florence.[7]

By the fifteenth century, however, in Germany at least, that veil of hair had been drawn back to reveal most, if not all, of Mary Magdalen's body. The altarpiece of the Apocalypse, in the Victoria and Albert Museum, probably executed for the Franciscan Magdalen cloister in Hamburg in about 1400, shows her entirely naked except for a strategically placed frond, the personification of innocence. Here she is paired with St Aegidius, or Giles, the patron saint of cripples, beggars and blacksmiths, who had probably been a sixth- or seventh-century anchorite, who had lived in the wilds of the Rhône valley near Nîmes, fed by a tamed doe. It is also in Germany that she becomes associated with that mythical creature, the 'wild man', the *uomo selvatico* or *wilde Mann* who became popular particularly in the alpine regions of central Europe, and was believed to inhabit mountainous and wooded regions, hiding from humanity and abducting children. Like the satyrs and fauns of classical literature, and the hairy men of pagan myth such as Enkidu, Polyphemus, Sylvanus and Silenus, the wild man was covered from head to foot in a thick coat of hair, with only the face, hands and feet left bare, and in the case of his feminine counterpart, the 'wild woman', the breasts.[8] Animal-like in his uncouthness and violence, he too sometimes appeared depicted on all fours. Still the focus of folkloric festivals in various mountainous regions of Europe today, the wild man grew out of medieval society's preoccupation with a world which it saw as steeped in sin, chaos and insanity; he embodied those fears, being himself the very antithesis of culture and order. Through the traditional association of mental and physical disorder with sin in Christian thought, he became linked with the holy hermits and penitent saints who in medieval art came to be depicted in hairy garb and even, in the case of the golden-mouthed St John Chrysostom, on all fours, caught by the hunter and his hounds. (Before his election to the see of Constantinople, John had spent years as a hermit in the desert atoning for his sin: in German Renaissance and baroque art, particularly, he is depicted creeping ape-like with the source of that sin portrayed above him – the woman he had seduced, naked also, suckling her child.[9]) St John's lustful sin couples him with Mary Magdalen and, like him, she becomes affected by the imagery of the wild man in German art for, from the mid-fifteenth century, she is often shown covered, except for her face, breasts, feet and hands, in a kind of fur which seems to grow from every pore. Tilman Riemenschneider's limewood carving of her *Ecstasy* of 1492 (Munich, Bayerisches Nationalmuseum) portrays her in this way, the 'wild woman' now tamed, as she is joyfully lifted to heaven by putti, some of whom themselves have been endowed with scaly skins under their swirling cloaks.[10] That nakedness could indeed signify innocence is borne out in one of two panels by Quentin Metsys (1466–1530) where she kneels facing Mary of Egypt, both entirely naked and at the same time appearing innocent and sexless (see Plate 48). But such a theme as the Ecstasy allowed both Dürer and his follower Hans Baldung Grien (1484/5–1545), whose favourite theme was the female nude, to dwell in their woodcuts on the saint's ample curves. In Grien's version, she is down-covered and a bit worn at the knees, as she is raised aloft by dimpled *putti*. Dürer's print may have influenced Gregor Erhardt's polychrome wooden statue of her (now in the Louvre) of about 1510, until recently known as 'La Belle Allemande' (see Plate 90).

48 The penitent Mary Magdalen. Quentin Metsys. Philadelphia, Museum of Art, John G. Johnson collection.

Tall for a woman of her time – she stands five feet nine inches – naked and penitent, she is shaped to the tastes of northern beauty with her slender arms and legs and fashionably bulging belly; her red-gold hair falls over one shoulder, parting to reveal one rounded breast – the other is bare – and drapes below to establish her modesty.[11]

In fifteenth-century Italy the range of images of the penitent and hirsute Mary Magdalen was enormous, but perhaps the most striking for both its execution and emotional content is Donatello's gaunt, ascetic figure, whose ravaged and elderly features speak of her thirty years' retreat, clad in her hair and wearing an animal skin to emphasise her neglect of worldly possessions (see Plate 49). Donatello's scrawny creature bears little resemblance to her beautiful and well-endowed sisters, and adheres to the story

of her harsh life of penitence in the *Vita eremitica*. Dated by scholars variously to the end of the sculptor's career, *c.*1455–6 or from the late 1430s
to the 1450s, the statue is painted: Mary Magdalen's hair is red with gold
streaks, her skin browned and toughened by the sun. Her sunken eyes
stare unfocused, her mind on heavenly things.[12]

Very different are the figures which follow her in the early sixteenth
century. The entirely naked *Mary Magdalen* painted by Leonardo's disciple Giampetrino (active in the first half of the century), seated reading
in a landscape, turns to look suggestively rather than penitently at the

49 The penitent Mary Magdalen.
Mid-fifteenth century. Donatello.
Florence, Museo dell'Opera del Duomo.

spectator (Vonwiller collection, Milan). Her jar, skull and keys are theological adornments rather than ciphers. The artist's half-length depictions of Mary Magdalen are similarly images of naked women with a
veneer of sanctity, gazing up to heaven, with hair draped carefully to
expose the breasts.[13] But the Renaissance penitent in her grotto is at
her most appealing in a painting, now lost, by Antonio Correggio,
that 'great poet of the body' (see Plate 72).[14] Painted in c. 1522, it showed
a curvaceous little form lying on her stomach in her grotto, her head
propped upon her hand, two little breasts, the nipples of which rest
upon her book, and two tiny feet peeping out, so absorbed in her pious
reading as to be unaware of the spectator. It is not far removed in
spirit from the series of paintings treating of the 'Loves of Jupiter'
commissioned from Correggio in about 1530 by Federico II Gonzaga,
duke of Mantua, as a gift for the Emperor Charles V, showing amongst
others the nymph Danaë ecstatically receiving her shower of gold from
the ever-generous god. (Correggio's penitent in her grotto had an extraordinary career which took her into the realms of eighteenth- and nineteenth-century erotica, ending only when the painting disappeared from
Dresden after the Second World War.) The combination of delicate
eroticism and religious sensibility in the Dresden *Mary Magdalen* is found
again in another painting of the saint by Correggio in the National
Gallery in London wherein she stands, resting her right elbow on her
book, holding her jar in her left hand, gazing mournfully at the spectator. Her blatant sensuousness, curves, bare nipple and plump leg
beckon the spectator's scrutiny, betokening a Venus-Magdalen in whose
form and content the line between holy and profane is drawn very
finely indeed. Correggio's Magdalens, like his nymphs, were painted
for a courtly clientele with a taste for decorative, beautiful art on a small
scale to adorn private chapels, bedchambers and *studioli* in ducal palaces
and apartments, for private devotion.[15] It was within these aristocratic
confines that the iconography of the repentant Magdalen developed
from the sixteenth century onwards.

The transmutation of Mary Magdalen into a Venus-figure took place in
Italy during the first decades of the sixteenth century. It arose against a
background to which it is only superficially and aesthetically related –
the theories about love and beauty discussed by the group of learned
men which formed around the gentle humanist philosopher Marsilio
Ficino (1433–99) at the villa at Careggi, outside Florence, given to him

by Cosimo de' Medici in 1462. Their purpose was to translate into Latin the works of Plato and the Neoplatonists and to make commentaries on them, and to synthesise pagan philosophy with the Christian religion into a coherent system which could serve for their own day. Ficino, who described himself as 'Philosophus Platonicus, Theologus et Medicus', and who coined the term 'Platonic love' (*amore platonico*), was the first to formulate the doctrine of Platonic love in his commentary on the *Symposium*, the *Commentarium in Convivium Platonis de Amore* of 1469, which was printed in 1484. His translation of it into the vernacular, called the *Convito*, was to influence poets, artists and thinkers for over a century. Love, the cornerstone of his philosophy, was the spiritual or intellectual love between friends which, in another guise, was the love of the soul for God; it was also the basis of morality. Love, he wrote, was the link between the divine and the terrestrial, in a continuous chain reaction, the *circuitus spiritualis*, or spiritual circuit, which led from and back to God; as the agent through which God poured his essence into the world, it was also the force which drove man to seek reunion with him. And it was beauty which generated love, 'calling the soul to God'. Ficino wrote of the *circuitus spiritualis*: 'The one and self-same circle may be called beauty insofar as it begins in God and attracts to Him; love, insofar as it passes into the world and ravishes it; and beatitude insofar as it reverts to the Creator.'[16] As the 'reflection of divine splendour', beauty was symbolised by the two Venuses, the celestial Venus who represented the primary and universal splendour of divinity, and mediated between the human mind and God, and the earthly Venus, the generative force, who represented the image of beauty made manifest in the corporeal world. When divine goodness which revealed itself as beauty was the goal of desire, love was defined as the 'desire for the fruition of beauty'.[17]

The ideas of love and beauty taken from the labours of Ficino and his 'Platonic Academy' in lesser hands became the subjects of innumerable treatises on the subject of love, *trattati d'amore*, which became the great literary vogue of the sixteenth century. By extension, women's beauty was discoursed upon at length in the many Renaissance works devoted to ideal beauty. Excoriated in the Middle Ages as an instrument of the devil and of man's perdition, it now became a quality to be celebrated, and not merely celebrated but eulogised and glorified: for in the translation of Platonic love to more mundane spheres, it was said that by praising feminine beauty Supreme Beauty was extolled. To Plato and the Greeks, beauty resided in the harmony and order of the parts; it created delight in the beholder, and led the mind to desire for heavenly things. Feminine beauty was said in the Renaissance to engender rapture in the lover, which in turn fostered in him the desire for God. (The love of course was always platonic.) Women were the source of love, according to Cardinal Pietro Bembo, in *Gli Asolani* (1505).[18] The perfect lady is the subject of much of the third and fourth books of Baldassare Castiglione's *Book of the Courtier*, a dialogue concerning comportment at court, published in Venice in 1528. Messer Cesare (Gonzaga) tells the assembled group that 'women alone take from our hearts all vile and base thoughts, woes, miseries and those troubled humors that so often attend such things . . . women do not distract but rather awaken our minds, and in war they make men fearless and daring beyond measure'.[19] The *Courtier*'s popularity all over Europe made it one of the most influential works of its kind, spawning numerous derivatives in its wake. Regarded as a 'divine being', and sometimes as an 'imperfect animal' (some treatises retained a strongly misogynistic character), woman became the subject of treatise upon treatise, of a superficially philosophical rather than empirical nature – characterised by Erwin Panofsky as a 'mixture of Petrarch and Emily Post couched in Neoplatonic language'.[20] In them her beauty and virtue were described and extolled, and her comportment and relationship to man defined. What once had been a learned topic now became a courtly pastime where discussions, or *dialoghi*, took place in the palaces of duchesses (as in *The Courtier*, at the palace of Urbino), in the idyllic gardens of illustrious women like Caterina Cornaro, the former queen of Cyprus, at Asolo, in *Gli Asolani*, and in the boudoirs of erudite courtesans. And in the fusion of Neoplatonism with Christianity, couched in elegant prose and poetic flourishes influenced by the supreme poet of love, Petrarch, Venus could be invoked together with the Virgin Mary, who in turn could be apostrophised as the 'goddess of goddesses'.[21] Madonnas and Magdalens consequently resembled Venuses and vice versa: sixteenth-century art and literature were replete with images of beautiful women, naked and draped, celestial and terrestrial Venuses, depicted and described in conformity with the ideals of feminine beauty propounded by male writers of the period. (The seventeenth-century Dutch Catholic writer Jan Vos [c.1615–67], commenting on a canvas by Govert Flink who altered a Venus to a Mary Magdalen, was to praise artists who could 'convert the unchaste by means of their brush'.[22])

It was thus that Mary Magdalen became the 'goddess of Love' or 'Venus of Divine Love' so often described in the wealth of literature devoted to her in the sixteenth and seventeenth centuries. Similarly Correggio uses the dual vocabulary of Eros and of Christian love to create his images of her. Pre-eminently regarded as Luke's sinner in this period, forgiven for she had loved greatly, she ascends from the excesses of sensual love to the heights of spiritual love: she is the 'amante Donna' (loving woman), 'l'innamorata' (the enamoured one), who is inflamed by her love. In the same vein, in a heated debate about Neoplatonic love in the fourth book Castiglione refers to her as an example of love which can aspire to heavenly love. When Signor Gasparo, who takes the role of the traditional misogynist among the assembled group, denies that women, constrained as they are by their less spiritual natures, can achieve divine love in the way men are able to ('I think that for men it will be hard to travel, but for women impossible,' he states), the Magnifico Giuliano de' Medici retorts that the great Socrates himself, in the *Symposium*, had confessed to having been instructed in the mysteries of love by a woman, the wise Diotima. A further example of feminine love, this time Christian, is Mary Magdalen for, the Magnifico says, 'You must remember also that [she] was forgiven many sins because she loved much, and that she, perhaps in no less grace than St Paul, was many times rapt to the third heaven by angelic love.'[23]

It was in the climate of Christian humanism also that Titian painted the first of his many Mary Magdalens, one of which, now in the Pitti Palace in Florence, became perhaps the most famous of all Magdalen pictures, and was the progenitor of a long line of weeping penitents (see Plate 50). In 1531 the artist was commissioned by Federico II Gonzaga to paint a Mary Magdalen as a gift for the marchese del Vasto, although in fact the picture appears to have been destined for the marchese's mother Vittoria Colonna (1490–1547), the poetess and religious reformer.[24]

In the Pitti painting, Titian dwells on the plumply voluptuous body of his saint in her grotto, silhouetted against the dramatic sky behind her which serves as a foil to her warm flesh tints and the magnificent red-gold tresses which she gathers to her. Her hair is no longer a mantle but an adornment which not only does not cover her but in fact half reveals and describes her body. By placing her arms diagonally across her body, one hand clasping her hair above her breasts, the other holding her hair across her stomach, the painter enhances her physicality, and

50 The penitent Mary
Magdalen (c.1531–5).
Titian. Florence, Palazzo
Pitti, Galleria Palatina.

thus emphasises her sensuousness. In his adaptation of the pose of an
antique statue, the classical Venus Pudica, or 'Venus of Modesty', which
was described as expressing the 'dual nature of love both sensuous and
chaste', Titian may well have intended to recreate the erotic overtones
of the Venus-model within his figure.[25] It was the Magdalen's hair
which struck the baroque poet Giambattista Marino: in his celebration
of the painting (1620), he waxed hyperbolically over the 'flowing mane
[which] makes a golden necklace around the naked alabaster [breasts]'
('e fanno inculte le cadente chiome/ agl'ignudi alabastri aureo monile').[26]
The hair also caught the eye of Giorgio Vasari when he saw the painting
in 1548 – together with one of a young and 'charming' (vaga) Venus,
gracing the dressing-room of the duke of Urbino – which he described
as of Mary Magdalen 'con i capegli sparsi che è cosa rara' (with her hair
spread about, which is a rare thing).[27]

Titian's Magdalen seems to have been enthusiastically received by his
contemporaries and near-contemporaries; indeed so popular was it that
the painting was copied frequently by other artists. Titian himself

returned to the theme several times, particularly during the 1560s when as a result of Counter-Reformation strictures concerning decorum, he modified his earlier treatment, giving Mary Magdalen a loose chemise and shawl to cover her nakedness, and a skull and book, both Tridentine attributes. The first of these later paintings was commissioned in 1561 by the king of Spain, Philip II; another (1567) was for Cardinal Alessandro Farnese. Vasari is once again our interpreter (although in fact he confused a similar painting he saw in Titian's studio – now in St Petersburg – with that painted for the king, and now lost):

Dopo fece Tiziano, per mandare al re Cattolico, una figura da mezza coscia in su d'una Santa Maria Maddalena scapigliata, cioè con i capelli che le cascano sopra le spalle, intorno alla gola e sopra il petto; mentre ella, alzando la testa con gli occhi fissi al cielo, mostra compunzione nel rossore degli occhi, e nelle lacrime dogliezza de' peccati: onde muove questa pittura, chiunche la guarda, estremamente; e, che è più, ancorchè sia bellissima, non muove a lascivia, ma a comiserazione.[28]

(Titian then made a picture to send to the Catholic king from the mid-thigh upwards, of a dishevelled St Mary Magdalen, that is, with hair which falls over her shoulders, round her throat and over her breast; while she, lifting her head with her eyes fastened on heaven, shows compunction in the redness of her eyes, and in her tears sorrow for her sins. This picture, therefore, greatly moves anyone who looks at it; and, moreover, even though it is very beautiful, it moves not to lust, but to pity.)

(According to Vasari, the painting he had seen so delighted a gentleman of Venice, one Silvio, that he bought it for one hundred *scudi*. Titian had therefore to paint another one for Philip 'che non fu men bella', which was no less beautiful. It was later sold to a Flemish merchant working in Venice, and was then sent to Flanders.[29])

Although to modern eyes little of the repentant Magdalen might be distinguishable in Titian's first known painting of Mary Magdalen, it would seem that, like Vasari, other contemporaries regarded her as a penitent. In 1624 Cardinal Federico Borromeo admired the way the painter had been able to depict the 'Maddalena penitente' naked, but within the bounds of decorum ('nel nudo l'onestà'), referring to a copy in the Ambrosiana in Milan.[30] This would imply that he found nothing improper in the depiction of a naked Magdalen whose nudity might have signified Truth, and her return to the state of innocence as *nuditas naturalis*. And the cardinal of course would have known the story of Mary Magdalen's retreat and repentance at Ste Baume. To later commentators, the 'upturned face and eyes, or tears which drop down the cheeks, are emblems of a penitent which the forms belie. It is clear that Titian had no other purpose in view than to represent a handsome girl.'[31] The historian Jakob Burckhardt wrote: 'the repentant sinner is meant to be represented, but in the wonderful woman, whose hair streams like golden waves around her beautiful form, this is clearly only an accessory'.[32] In the second volume of *Modern Painters*, Ruskin showed his horror of the painting, describing it as 'the disgusting Magdalen of the Pitti Palace'. The image of beauty that he preferred was a fifteenth-century one, not of the Magdalen at all, but of one whose 'hair falls like that of the Magdalene, its undulation just felt as it touches the cheek, and no more', he wrote of the tendrils of hair around the delicate Gothic face of Ilaria de' Caretto, sculpted by Jacopo della Quercia in Lucca. Ilaria's chaste marble figure had become 'at once, and has ever since remained my ideal of Christian sculpture'. In the fifth volume, he modified his earlier comment, demonstrating his aesthetic response and world view. It was not merely the sensuousness of Titian's Magdalen but the artist's type of beauty which offended his sensibilities:

> Truly she is so, as compared with the received types of the Magdalen. A stout, red-faced woman, dull, and coarse of feature, with much of the animal in even her expression of repentance – her eyes strained, and inflamed with weeping. I ought, however, to have remembered another picture of the Magdalen by Titian . . . in which she is just as refined, as in the Pitti Palace she is gross; and had I done so, I should have seen Titian's meaning. It had been the fashion before his time to make the Magdalen always young and beautiful; her, if no-one else, even the rudest painters flattered; her repentance was not thought perfect unless she had lustrous hair and lovely lips. Titian first dared to doubt the romantic fable, and reject the narrowness of sentimental faith. He saw that it was possible for plain women to love no less vividly than beautiful ones; and for stout persons to repent, as well as those more delicately made. It seemed to him that the Magdalen would have received her pardon not the less quickly because her wit was none

of the readiest; and would not have been regarded with less compassion by her Master because her eyes were swollen, or her dress disordered. It is just because he has set himself sternly to enforce this lesson that the picture is so painful: the only instance, so far as I can remember, of Titian's painting a woman markedly and entirely belonging to the lowest class.[33]

A recent interpretation of Titian's *Mary Magdalen* sees her as the embodiment of sixteenth-century theories concerning sacred and profane love, setting her as a sacred prostitute within the context of Renaissance ideals of beauty and the contemporary celebration of courtesanry; by emphasising both her sensuality and the sanctity of the celestial Venus, it is suggested that the artist created an image which embodies terrestrial love, erotic appeal and divine love.[34] This interpretation disregards an important factor: Mary Magdalen stands, her ointment jar at her side, raising tearful eyes towards the light, the source of divine love, regretting her fleshly sins, and thus rejects the role of terrestrial Venus. The heavenly Venus and her earthly sister are not opposites, but gradations of the same principle, equal and coterminous. Mary Magdalen's nudity, and the fact that her eyes are raised to heaven, and lips are slightly apart, might also have been understood allegorically, alluding to contemporary representations of both Truth and Penitence. In his treatise on painting (1436), the architect and humanist Leone Battista Alberti exhorted artists of his day to imitate the *Calumny*, a celebrated painting by Apelles, the fourth-century BC painter. The painting itself had been lost, but had been described by the poet Lucian in the second century AD. In rendering it from a Greek translation, however, Alberti had perpetrated an error which was first noticed by Panofsky.[35] Commenting upon the figure of Truth, which appeared with Repentance in the *Calumny*, Alberti transferred to her Lucian's description of Repentance as 'pudica' or 'pudibunda' (modest or shamefaced), portraying her as a 'young girl, shamefaced and bashful' ('una fanciulletta vergogniosa et pudica, chiamata la Verità'), which suggests that he may have visualised Truth as a naked figure of the Venus Pudica type, and implying that Truth's nakedness rendered her shamefaced or shy. Lucian himself had made no comment upon Truth's appearance.[36] The representation of Truth as a naked figure, Horace's *nuda Veritas*, had long been known, and became one of the most popular personifications of the Renaissance and baroque periods. (A Venus Pudica had appeared once before in a

Christian context, sculpted by Giovanni Pisano as one of the cardinal virtues, Chastity or Temperance, in his pulpit in Pisa of 1300–10, and described by Kenneth Clark in his study of *The Nude* (1956) as 'one of the most surprising false alarms in art history'.[37]) When Botticelli came to re-create Apelles' painting in *c.*1495 (Florence, Uffizi), he depicted Repentance in her grey gown and torn black rags, turning towards Truth, *nuda Veritas*, a beautiful naked golden-haired woman, modestly draping her hair across her abdomen in an adaptation of the Venus Pudica, her face raised and right hand pointing to heaven.

Mary Magdalen's penitence, once symbolised by nakedness cloaked in hair, coincides with the Renaissance rebirth of the classical female nude of which the Venus Pudica was one of her guises. Clark observed that while the Greeks had sculpted the male nude, the female body because of ancient traditions of ritual and taboo, until the fourth century, was always draped. Apollo's nakedness was an aspect of his divinity, but when the Venus of the Ludovisi throne (early fifth century BC) rises between her maidens, the pleats of her wet garment, her *draperie mouillée*, follow the contours of her rounded shape: she is naked but clothed. Pliny the Elder relates the story of how for ritualistic reasons the people of Cos rejected Praxiteles' sculpture (*c.*350 BC) of an entirely nude Venus; the Cnidians instead accepted her, standing naked, holding her drapery in her left hand, her right held slightly away from her pelvis. But her Capitoline version is in the pose of the Venus Pudica, or Venus of Modesty; her right arm crosses her body, her hand just below her full left breast, while her left hand is placed modestly over her pelvis. No longer required by religion, and as a decorative motif *démodé* – there is no known statue of a female nude after the second century AD – Venus vanishes to rise again in the late fifteenth century, heralded, as we have seen, by Clark's 'false alarm', and again in her 'Pudica' pose, transformed into paint by Botticelli, as she is blown across the waves in the *Birth of Venus* (*c.*1484–6, Florence, Uffizi), and through Alberti's misinterpretation of Lucian, as the figure of Truth. Although nakedness in the female nude might signify an abstract concept, it is never, however idealised, entirely devoid of its erotic charge. The exposed breast alone is a complex symbol, at the same time source of both maternal nurture and sexual pleasure; its accidental unveiling can denote innocence whilst simultaneously eliciting a voyeuristic response. Whilst fourteenth-century images of the Virgin giving suck to the infant Jesus are images of the mother of God offering succour through her son to mankind, the significance of the naked breast changes in the late fifteenth century. It becomes attached to nymphs, graces and goddesses, perceived at first through graceful diaphanous draperies and then in the full exposure of the female nude. Mary Magdalen's naked breasts might represent 'naked Truth', or penitence and vulnerability, but inevitably they retain their connotations of sexuality, encompassing a whole range of human experience, from unconscious echoes of maternal comfort to the blunter pleasures of male desire.[38]

The extent to which Alberti's misidentification of Truth and Repentance could have influenced Titian's painting is open to question. Titian was not an artist to allow abstract theories to dominate his creativity, and it is unlikely that, in his *Mary Magdalen*, he was depicting anything more esoteric than a beautiful repentant woman, and using current artistic and literary tropes to do so. That his aims were aesthetic rather than pietistic would seem to be confirmed by a recently published anecdote from the *ricordi* of a Florentine nobleman, Baccio Valori (1535–1606), who as a young man visited Venice:

Conobbe qui Tiziano, quasi fermo in casa per l'età, e come che fusse stimato per ritrarre al naturale, mi mostrò una Maddalena nel deserto da piacere; anche mi ricordo hora che dicendoli che era da piacer troppo, come fresca e rugiadosa in quella penitenza. Conosciuto che io voleo dire che devesse con scarna del digiuno, mi rispose ghignando avvertisce [?] che l'è ritratta pel primo dì che rientra, innanzi che cominciasse a digiunare, per rappresentar la pittura penitente sì, ma piacevole quanto poteva, e per certo era tale.[39]

(There I met Titian, almost immobilised by age who, despite the fact that he was appreciated for painting from the life, showed me a very attractive Magdalen in the desert. Also I remember now that I told him she was too attractive, so fresh and dewy, for such penitence. Having understood that I meant that she should be gaunt through fasting, he answered laughing that he had painted her on the first day she had entered [her repentant state], before she began fasting, in order to be able to paint her as a penitent indeed, but also as lovely as he could, and that she certainly was.)

Whilst the beauty of Titian's *Mary Magdalen* might be disputed by modern commentators, it did conform to contemporary canons of femi-

nine pulchritude. A woman, according to the Florentine Agnolo Firenzuola (1493–1548/9), was very beautiful if she was very fat, and the
'new Helen' of Federico Luigini da Udine had 'plump arms and legs,
chubby hands and buxom flanks', as well as buttocks. Breasts were to
be *picciole* (small), firm and like 'two round and sweet apples'. Thighs
were to be soft, wanton and quivering.[40] The essayist Montaigne, who
visited Italy in 1580–1, when writing of the multiplicity of feminine
forms and of national predilections, described how 'the Italians fashion
beauty gross and massive', while the Spaniards preferred the gaunt and
slender, and his fellow Frenchmen delighted in an infinite variety.[41] In
this sense, the abundant flesh of Titian's figure merely reflects the
national tastes of his time. (A woman could equally be slender, graceful
and long-necked, and even dark-haired, and still be beautiful, according
to some treatises.) Marino had celebrated the saint's personal attributes
– her eyes which had broken thousands of hearts, and which now wept
– her mouth, her snow-white hand, and the clear alabaster of her skin;
but it is her golden *chiome*, the mane of hair, which enthused him most,
unfastened in a precious shower over her shoulders, which he compared
with that of Berenice, the aristocratic courtesan who ensnared Herod
Antipas.[42]

Marino's apophthegms were not original, and are important in showing how images of Mary Magdalen conformed to contemporary standards of beauty. While the hair of the beloved was a common object of
praise, long hair in the Renaissance served as an erotic cipher. It could
stand as a symbol, or as the vital surrogate for a person, as in Marino's
poem where it evokes the sensuous character of his penitent courtesan.
Biblically, as in the case of Samson, it could represent physical strength
as well as strength of soul; when Samson is shorn he loses his miraculous
strength. The ideal colour of a woman's hair shows a remarkable consist-
ency down through the ages: the crowning glories of Aphrodite/Venus
and the heroines of medieval epic romances and the troubadour poets
have always been blonde or golden. And Petrarch, from whose poetry
much of the ideal Renaissance beauty derived, often dwelt on Laura's
various perfections, her eyes, lips and her amber-like fair hair.

Loose hair had been a moral indicator in the Middle Ages, symbolising the innocence of the virgin girl who, on attaining maturity, or on
her marriage, put it up, a tradition which was emphasised again in
Victorian times; in an adult woman, however, it alluded to moral laxity.
According to the sixteenth-century physiognomist Giovanni Battista

della Porta, the thickness of a woman's hair also implied her degree of wantonness, and although he agreed that fair hair was a symbol of purity – one only has to think of the many female saints depicted with fair or red-gold hair – he added darkly that 'all are not maidens that wear fair hair'.[43] In the most comprehensive treatise on beauty, first published in 1542, and dedicated flatteringly to the 'noble and beautiful women of Prato', Firenzuola defined as one of the most important aspects of a woman's beauty her perfect hair. This was to be 'fine and blonde, similar to gold or honey or to the rays of brilliant sunshine'; to be 'wavy, thick, and long'.[44] 'Man was adorned with two beauties – one of the soul, the other of the body,' wrote Luigini in his *Libro della bella Donna* (1554), another *trattato* devoted to the perfect woman in which physical perfection, however, predominates. The most important part of a woman is her hair for, he continues,

> how can a field be without flowers or a ring be without gems, the night without stars or day without sun? If the goddess Venus had come down from heaven, been born in the sea, raised in the waves, surrounded by the Graces . . . without her mane . . . she would scarcely have been loved by Vulcan.[45]

(This allusion to Vulcan's somewhat limiting criterion for placing his affections had come from the second-century *Golden Ass* by Apuleius which Firenzuola had translated and which was well known in the Renaissance.) The best colour is 'puro e ben fin oro' (pure and very fine gold); and tracing the source of ideal beauty to the 'Ancients' as well as the poets Petrarch, Boccaccio, Sannazaro, Bembo and Ariosto, who had written of women's hair as 'aurea chiome' and 'crini d'oro' (golden manes), Luigini stresses that the most beautiful colour of all is that of the clearest metal which is gold.[46]

In sixteenth-century Venice the passion for golden hair, or the *arte biondeggiante*, the art of being blonde or auburn-haired, was carried to absurd extremes. In his 'Observations of Venice' (1608), Thomas Coryate describes at first hand (he happened to be staying with an English friend whose wife was a Venetian, 'a favour not affoorded [*sic*] to every stranger') the process by which the required colour was obtained:

> Every Saturday in the afternoons [the Venetian women] do use to annoint their haire with oyle, or some other drugs, to the end to

make it looke faire, that is whitish. For that colour is most affected of the Venetian Dames and Lasses. And in this manner they do it: first they put on a readen hat [called 'la solana'], without any crown at all, but brimmes of exceeding breadth and largenesse: then they sit in some sun-shining place in a chamber, or some other secret roome, where having a looking glasse before them they sophisticate and dye their haire with the foresaid drugs, and after cast it back round the brimmes of the hat till it be thoroughly dried with the heate of the sunne.[47]

It is not surprising, therefore, that Mary Magdalen from the fourteenth century was depicted in both painting and literature with red – particularly in fifteenth-century Florentine art – or golden hair, conforming to the contemporary ideal of feminine beauty.

When Cardinal Federico Borromeo referred to the 'decorum', or appropriateness, of the nakedness of Titian's *Mary Magdalen*, he was writing within a specific context, that of the function and nature of religious art. In his treatise *De Pictura sacra* (1624) he had explicitly rejected the inclusion of nude figures, unless strictly demanded by the subject of the painting, as they might either offend the sensibilities of viewers or diminish the devotion of believers.[48] Decorum in art had been a subject much discussed during the sixteenth century; and Protestant criticism of what they regarded as the Church of Rome's idolatrous use of images had prompted a further need to define propriety in religious art. The final session of the Council of Trent in December 1563 re-established and reinforced the role of religious images as fundamental supports to the dissemination of orthodoxy.

The penitent in her grotto became the most popular image of Mary Magdalen in the sixteenth and seventeenth centuries. As the 'favourite saint of the Counter-Reformation',[49] her popularity arose out of the desire of the Catholic Church to consolidate its power both at home and abroad. In 1517, over eighty years before Orazio Gentileschi painted his *Mary Magdalen*, and a decade before Titian painted his, Martin

Luther (1483–1546) nailed his Ninety-Five Theses upon Indulgences to the door of Wittenberg Cathedral – perhaps appropriately on All Saints' Eve, 31 October – and called for an end to the abuses of the Church, and to its clergy's corruption and ignorance. From his reading of St Paul's Epistle to the Romans, he had formulated his own doctrine of justification, by faith alone, for had not Paul written: 'the just shall live by faith'? It was through faith, without good works, that divine grace would come into the soul of man. It was only a matter of time, therefore, before Luther came to deny the necessity of the Church's mediating function, and by extension the priesthood, together with its preoccupation with externals such as ritual, and its practice of accruing income through the sale of indulgences, by which the faithful believed their penitential period in purgatory would be shortened.

The sacraments, seen by the Church as the means to salvation, also came under Protestant attack. On the basis of his understanding of the New Testament, Luther admitted of baptism and the eucharist only, while the Church of Rome held that there were seven, which included also confirmation, penance, extreme unction, holy orders and matrimony. He denied the necessity of confession since baptism removed the stain of original sin and was itself therefore the true sacrament of penance; he regarded the sacrament of the eucharist as being merely symbolic, a commemoration of the Last Supper. Mary Magdalen's role as exemplar and intercessor brought her into the argument as a prime propaganda weapon against Lutheran tenets, and to uphold the Tridentine doctrine of merit. In this role too, she was once again running counter to Protestant ideology. To the Protestants, who banned images and proscribed religious art, the intercession of the saints had little scriptural authority, and the use of images consequently reeked of idolatry. Zwingli, the iconoclastic Swiss reformer, cited Mary Magdalen particularly as an example of the speciousness of saintly intercession, and demanded that the cult be abolished, and that images of her be destroyed.[50] Calvin, in addition, criticised the ignorance of Catholic clergy for believing that Mary of Bethany and Luke's sinner (and therefore Mary Magdalen) were one and the same: 'Under the papacy, monks and other hypocrites have exhibited too great ignorance in imagining that Mary the sister of Lazarus was the sinner whom St Luke mentions,' he wrote, and elsewhere he poured scorn on the Provençal legend, and the claim by three places to be in possession of Mary Magdalen's body.[51]

The heretics were not alone in their criticism of Catholic insistence upon the composite figure of Mary Magdalen. In the year in which Luther nailed up his theses, Jacques Lefèvre d'Etaples, the leading French Christian humanist, stirred up theological controversy when his letter *De Maria Magdalena et triduo Christi disceptatio* was published in Paris. This had been written in reply to a former pupil, François Moulins de Rochefort, who had been requested by the queen mother, Louise of Savoy, after a visit to Ste Baume the year before, to write a biography of Mary Magdalen, for whom she had a great affection. A humanist scholar, de Rochefort had naturally gone back to the primary sources, the gospels, seen their conflicting evidence, and turned to Lefèvre for assistance. The result was the tract in which Lefèvre declared himself in favour of distinguishing the three women, basing his authority on Origen and John Chrysostom, and claiming further that Ambrose and Jerome were of this opinion. In a second edition, he was supported by another humanist and former pupil, Josse Clichtoue, who published his own *Défense de la disceptation sur sainte Madeleine*. Lefèvre was, of course, flying in the face of Catholic tradition; it was not surprising therefore that orthodox quarters defended their position with a stream of tracts from the Augustinian Marc de Grandval in 1518, from the chancellor of Cambridge and bishop of Rochester, John Fisher, and from the Franciscans and Dominicans, to which latter order Lefèvre himself belonged.[52] Willibald Pirckheimer (1470–1530), the German humanist, writing to Erasmus of Rotterdam in 1520, criticised Lefèvre's attackers, for 'snatch[ing] St Mary Magdalen from her deliverer Lefèvre, and thrust[ing] her with most disgraceful harlots into a stinking brothel when it would rather be more becoming in such a doubtful matter to follow the opinion which approaches closer to piety'.[53] Fisher fought from the standpoint of Church tradition: the unicity of Mary Magdalen was the common opinion of the whole Church; it was confirmed by the Roman martyrology, and was incontrovertibly the case according to his reading of the gospels and commentaries. Mary Magdalen's retreat to the desert, he added, was attested to by all the hagiographers, a fact to be accepted as it was adopted by the common consent of the Church, and neither refuted by the Fathers, nor in the Scriptures.[54] (Erasmus wrote wittily that it was a pity that Fisher's first work had not treated of a more suitable theme, and also penned a burlesque poem about the composite Magdalen.[55]) In 1520 the furore faded away, and de Grandval died. The following year Lefèvre was reprimanded by the

Faculty of Theology at Paris University, and accused of heresy. Clichtoue testified before the faculty that both he and Lefèvre had rejected
their earlier opinions but they stood condemned. Lefèvre fled to Strasbourg in 1525, but was recalled to France a year later by François I,
and was appointed tutor to the king's children and librarian at Blois.

Lefèvre's theory of distinction challenged an ecclesiastical tradition
in a debate which could have had enormous religious implications had
he won. In a letter to the bishop of Rochester, Stephen Poncher, the
ambassador to England, bishop of Paris (1503–9) and archbishop of
Sens (1519–25), wrote of the 'great peril [which] lay hidden and what
great confusion and disgrace could arise for the whole Church of Christ
from this difference of opinions'.[56] By admitting to having held such
erroneous beliefs, as accused by both humanists and Protestants, Rome
would not only have laid itself open to further doctrinal questions but,
by distinguishing the three women, would also have lost one of its
most valuable theological and moral exemplars. Any re-evaluation of
Mary Magdalen would have deprived the Church, preachers and playwrights of their *exemplum*. The Lefèvre controversy arose in a period
in which the image of Mary Magdalen promoted in Jean Michel's *Mystère* (1486) was still current. That religious drama had focused on her
inherited wealth which had led her into debauchery. Sermons by Olivier
Maillard, published in the 1470s, and Michel Menot, of *c*.1500, show
the same moral outlook. Maillard dwelt on her life abandoned to fleshly
sins as a courtesan, and Menot on her raucous life, and the banquets,
gaming and dancing she enjoyed.[57] Had Lefèvre won, in his attempt
to bring scholarly and humanistic integrity to the reading of the gospels,
the moralists would have been expropriated of much of the weaponry
in their armoury. As it was, in the second half of the sixteenth century,
the repentant sinner, voluptuous and weeping, came into her own.

Demands for reform within the Catholic Church came not only from
the Protestants. In the Church itself, particularly among the group of
humanist reformers which had formed around Paul III, and included
Vittoria Colonna and Michelangelo, there was a desire for spiritual

revival, for a more adequate, educated clergy, both uncorrupted and incorruptible, for the renewed practice of faith and the reorganisation of internal Church government. In 1542 Protestant and Catholic theologians met at Ratisbon, and under Gasparo Contarini, the papal legate, a humanist and reformer, the Church of Rome came close to agreement over the doctrine of justification by faith. The Protestants, however, refused to accept the Catholic position on transubstantiation. Negotiations broke down and it was not until 1545 that the next council took place, this time at Trent. Schism between Rome and Protestantism was virtually irrevocable from 1545, and all hope of reconciliation was gone by the third meeting of the council, in 1562–3. The effect of Trent on the figure of Mary Magdalen was twofold and far-reaching, both in its pronouncements on the sacraments and, closely allied with those, in its directives concerning religious art. It is perhaps not too much to suggest that Mary Magdalen might stand as the symbol of the Church Triumphant, of the true faith, as it emerged from the deliberations of the Council of Trent.

By the end of the council, eighteen years later, art had not only been preserved for religion but had become one of its major vehicles for the dissemination of orthodoxy. The calls for reform from north of the Alps had ironically been the stimulus to Catholic art. Setting aside its earlier conciliatory policy, Rome retrenched itself in its traditional stance on the sacraments, and, in the last session, restated its teaching on the use of images as incitements to piety and as a means of salvation. It stressed, however, that the subjects of such images were to be 'honoured' and 'venerated', and not worshipped. The purpose of religious art, the 'Bible of the illiterate', to quote the well-worn phrase of Gregory the Great, was to teach the faithful through images which were clear, simple and realistic, so that they might be reminded constantly of the articles of the faith, imitate the saints and cultivate piety. A massive programme of church building had begun in Rome in the mid-century, partly as a result of the exigencies of the new reforming orders, such as the Oratorians and Jesuits; and existing churches were either rebuilt or restored. Consequently, there were vast wall-spaces to adorn and churches, as the image of heaven on earth, were decorated with frescoes, paintings and statues in brilliant colours, marbles, gilt- and stucco-work. Saints, as *exempla*, were often depicted at climactic moments of their lives, as was Gentileschi's *Mary Magdalen*, in dark, dramatic settings, where the light falling on their faces might betoken their inward experience, at their moment of conversion, or in the full intensity of their sufferings – praying, performing miracles and receiving the sacraments.

St Ignatius Loyola (1491/5–1556), the founder of the Jesuits, had himself described paintings as icons for meditation, and his *Spiritual Exercises*, published in 1548 but written twenty years earlier, and aimed at leading the participant through various stages of meditation to ecstasy and union with God, stressed the imaginative pictorial realisation of the subject being meditated upon through the use of all the senses. The exercitant, when meditating on the Passion, was to *see* Christ in all his suffering, *feel* his wounds, *hear* his cries. Loyola's recommendations concerning realism and tangibility had a profound effect on the works of such artists as the Umbrian Federico Barocci (c.1535–1612), whose

51 The penitent Mary Magdalen (1663). Gian Lorenzo Bernini. Siena, Duomo, Chigi Chapel.

Christ appearing to Mary Magdalen of 1590 (Munich, Alte Pinakothek, and Florence, Uffizi) shows the saint, startled by the sight of her divine Lover, with her hand raised to her cheek in bewilderment, and the draperies fluttering around her mirror her inner turmoil. Bernini, who practised the *Exercises*, sculpted the beautiful weeping Magdalen in her niche in the Chigi chapel in Siena (1663), her body writhing in her sorrow, and the draperies swirling around her, stressing her torment (see Plate 51).

At the end of the *Spiritual Exercises*, in the meditation entitled 'The Mysteries of the Life of Christ our Lord', the exercitant is to concentrate upon the events in Christ's life, among them the conversion of Mary Magdalen, together with the raising of Lazarus, supper at Bethany and the appearance of the resurrected Christ to Mary Magdalen.[58] Mary Magdalen's importance to sixteenth-century religious reformers as a symbol of penitence, salvation and mystical love is borne out by the numerous references to her in devotional writings of the period. In her *Vida*, St Teresa of Avila (1515–82), the Spanish Carmelite and mystic, wrote of her 'great devotion to the glorious Magdalen' of whose conversion she was often reminded, particularly when she took communion. It was to Mary Magdalen that she turned as her intercessor so that she might gain pardon for her sins. In her yearning after union with God, Teresa compares her love to its detriment with that of St Paul and of Mary Magdalen in 'whom this fire of the love of God burned so vehemently' that their sufferings must have been 'one continuous martyrdom'.[59] In the *Introduction to the Devout Life*, François de Sales (1567–1622), a prominent leader of the Counter-Reformation, again stresses Mary Magdalen's role as model of conversion and love. Dating his preface 'Annecy, the Feast of St Magdalen, 1609', he encourages his readers to follow the Prodigal Son and Mary Magdalen in begging God's pardon.[60] The association between the Prodigal Son – the parable told in Luke 15:11–32 – and Mary Magdalen as repentant sinners appears in two paintings by van Dyck, *David, the Prodigal Son and Mary Magdalen before the Virgin* (Paris, Louvre) and *The Good Thief, the Prodigal Son, Peter and Mary Magdalen before the Resurrected Christ* (Augsburg), both of which are based on Rubens' painting, *Christ and the Penitent Sinners* (*c.*1616, Munich, Alte Pinakothek), which gives Mary Magdalen the prominent position as she kneels, half-naked, before the resurrected Christ, whilst the Good Thief, David and Peter look on (see Plate 52). In de Sales' treatise *Of the Love of God* (1616), she is again a model of

52 Mary Magdalen with the Good Thief, King David and St Peter before Christ (*c.*1616). Peter Paul Rubens. Munich, Alte Pinakothek.

conversion: 'Remember the sorrowing Magdalene: "They have taken away my Lord, and I know not where they have laid Him"; but when she had found Him amid her tears she held Him fast in love. Imperfect love longs for Him; penitence seeks and finds Him; perfect love clasps Him tight . . .'[61]

From the second half of the sixteenth century, the cults of saints who had won their way to heaven through repentance were particularly sanctioned and promoted by the Church. Mary Magdalen was the sinner *par excellence*, surpassing even St Peter and St Jerome in the plethora of images produced in the century following the Council of Trent. Tears of penitence were an important issue in the Church's defence of the sacrament of penance: to Cardinal Roberto Bellarmino, it was the fact that St Peter had wept for his sins which constituted his confession to

Christ, for tears, the cardinal said, were in themselves an image of confession. (Bellarmino, theologian to Clement VIII from 1597, composed a hymn on the three stages of Mary Magdalen's conversion entitled 'Pater superni luminis', which was inserted into the Roman Breviary as part of the office for her feast-day.)[62] St Jerome, often depicted emaciated and weeping in the desert, who had believed he would earn his salvation by spending a contemplative life as a hermit, is also associated with Heraclitus, the weeping philosopher, who withdrew from the world to explore the nature of knowledge. The parallel with the weeping Magdalen in her grotto is manifest, and gave rise to such depictions of the two saints together as the frontispiece to the *Christian Heraclitus* by Pierre de Besse of 1612, and Bernini's portrayal of them facing each other across the Chigi chapel in Siena.[63]

Having admitted religious imagery and stated its dogmatic purpose, Catholic propagandists were concerned to ensure that only the right kinds of religious art were permitted, that theological inaccuracies were expunged, and that nothing might be depicted which could mislead the ignorant, or give the Protestants cause for complaint. For these reasons, paintings containing new imagery were to be submitted for the approval of bishops. Obscenity was proscribed and incidents not related in the scriptures were discouraged; and artists were also specifically instructed not to read texts such as the *Golden Legend* (where Mary Magdalen's Provençal sojourn is related), or hagiographical compilations like that of Pietro de Natalibus, as the stories contained in them were legend rather than fact.[64] Despite this kind of injunction, it was the wholly legendary aspect of Mary Magdalen which stood out in this period, constituting by far the major element of the Magdalenian *oeuvre*. The range of images was enormous. She might appear in her gospel guise under the cross, as she often did (as in Guido Reni's *Crucifixion* [1617–18], Bologna, Pinacoteca), or in the scenes of the Deposition (Caravaggio [1602–4], Rome, Pinacoteca Vaticana), or in the *Noli me tangere* (Eustache Le Sueur [1640s], Paris, Louvre); but she also appeared as Mary of Bethany, as the representative of the contemplative life (Vermeer [1655], Edinburgh, National Gallery), and in the numerous depictions of the Raising of Lazarus (Federico Zuccaro [1563], Venice, S. Francesco della Vigna). The Feast in the House of the Pharisee was also popular in the sixteenth century, depicted in both sacrament chapels (Girolamo Romanino [1524], Brescia, S. Giovanni Evangelista) and monastic and conventual refectories, as an image of repentance, as well as being a suitable subject for dining-halls.[65]

A new artistic subject, the Conversion of Mary Magdalen, was created to accompany her newly emphasised role as converted sinner. This consisted of scenes of her renouncing her worldly life and throwing her jewellery away, such as in Veronese's painting in the National Gallery in London (c.1550), or Rubens' treatment in Vienna (c.1620), where she is watched by Martha who, according to the *Golden Legend*, was instrumental in her conversion. Martha's role is evident in Caravaggio's marvellous painting in Detroit (Institute of Arts) of c.1600 which shows her advising Mary Magdalen of the error of her ways (see Plate 53).[66] The Magdalen, clad in a magnificent gown of purple and white with red sleeves, her hair pinned up, unadorned except for a delicate golden circlet on her left hand, and clasping an orange blossom to her heart, addresses Martha with her eyes. Her arm rests on a large convex Venetian mirror which reflects her hand pointing to the light coming from a window fictively behind the spectator. On the table before her

53 *The Conversion of Mary Magdalen* (c.1600). Caravaggio. Detroit Institute of Arts.

are a slightly damaged ivory comb and cosmetic dish with a sponge. At one level the mirror and such objects signify their feminine owner as a creature of vanity, but the double meaning contained within the mirror reveals Mary Magdalen at the moment of her conversion. Because a mirror cannot lie, it is a symbol of truth, and the light it reflects and to which Mary Magdalen points represents her spiritual illumination, which is reinforced by the light in which she is bathed. Through her conversion, she has come to wisdom – the mirror is also symbolic of prudence – and Mary Magdalen becomes therefore the symbol of the contemplative life, contemplation being the 'vray exercice de Magdelaine', according to François de Sales[67] – as the counterpart of the active life represented by Martha, stressing the Tridentine doctrine of faith and good works.

The wonderful *Magdalen* by Artemisia Gentileschi, Orazio's daughter, was probably commissioned in 1620 by Grand Duke Cosimo of Tuscany as a gift for his wife, the Archduchess Maria Magdalena of Austria, Grand Duchess of Tuscany (see Plate 54). She too is caught at the moment of conversion as she puts her hand out to reject the jewels – attributes of the *vanitas* – as is the mirror in which her profile and pearl earring are reflected which doubles, as in Caravaggio's painting, as the vehicle of truth. She wears a sumptuous, low-cut gold damask gown over a chemise. The words inscribed on the mirror frame, 'Optimam partem elegit', and the fact that she has her hand on her heart point to her conversion. (The gold of the Magdalen's gown may relate to the liturgical colours for her feast-day which were white and/or gold, the latter referring to the Contemplatives. She also wears gold in Barocci's *Christ appearing to Mary Magdalen* and gold and green in Domenichino's *Ecstasy* [St Petersburg].)[68]

Such powerful images, however, served as a backdrop against which the figure of the semi-naked penitent was always pre-eminent. Although criticism had been levelled earlier against the effect of naked figures in Church art, the Church itself had made no specific rulings prohibiting such images. Now, in its justification of religious art, decency, or decorum, became as important as orthodoxy, and the council declared that 'all lasciviousness must be avoided; so that figures shall not be painted or adorned with a beauty exciting to lust'.[69] (In Florence, a little over sixty years earlier, the fiery Dominican prior Girolamo Savonarola had instructed that voluptuous paintings be burned; and he had also specifically objected to the use of beautiful contemporaries as models in

54 *The Conversion of Mary Magdalen* (1620). Artemisia Gentileschi. Florence, Palazzo Pitti, Galleria Palatina.

devotional art, since 'people in the streets of Florence would say "there goes the Magdalen" '.[70]) A stream of treatises on art and compilations of images was published after the council, mostly written by churchmen and reformers with the aim of helping artists to orientate themselves in the intricacies of allegory and symbolism, and to correct iconography which did not conform to ecclesiastical ideology. Nudity was often discussed, and generally condemned: painters who showed naked saints were criticised for removing 'a great part of the reverence due to their subjects'.[71] Johannes Molanus, the Fleming, and most prominent Catholic reformer of iconography, warned in his treatise *De Historia SS. Imaginum et Picturarum pro vero earum usu contra abusus* (1570) against the representation of subjects which might lead to concupiscence.[72] Naked figures in Michelangelo's *Last Judgement* had already been draped on the orders of Pope Paul IV, and in a letter of 1582, the Florentine sculptor Bartolommeo Amannati repudiated the statues of naked men and women he had made earlier, and since he was unable to destroy them, wished to make public repentance.[73] The wings of artistic imagination were henceforth clipped; and, as a consequence, south of the Alps naked figures in general appeared less often in sacred art, and figures of ecstatic saints such as Mary Magdalen were swathed in billowing drapery.

Specific instructions regarding the depiction of saints and holy personages were also given in these manuals. Mary Magdalen's appearance was mentioned often and precisely: her maturity was cited when painters were censured for depicting the three Marys as young girls, ignoring the fact that at the time of the crucifixion 'one had four children, the other two, and they were all apostles of the Lord'.[74] Artists who depicted her 'tutta pulita' (very smart), scented, bejewelled, and in velvet gowns, forgot that she was no longer a sinner, but a disciple. The pious Molanus, who had vehemently criticised artists for depicting her as the bride and John the Evangelist as the bridegroom at the feast of Cana, admitted that although the evangelists had not actually described her as being dressed as a penitent, there was no doubt that Mary Magdalen was the 'example of perfect penitence' ('perfectae poenitentiae exemplar'). He too insisted that artists depicted her improperly (*indecenter*) when clothing her sumptuously in her penitence or under the cross. Although she was a sinner, she was not to be painted immodestly, as, it was noted, was often the case.[75] Many sinners, on seeing images of Mary Magdalen and Mary of Egypt, according to the painter and critic Gian Paolo Lomazzo, were inspired to leave the delights of the world and to follow the 'harshness of solitude'. And in this solitude Mary Magdalen, instead of being shown entirely naked, was to be portrayed most skilfully with 'modest gestures', so that her arms raised in prayer covered 'as much of her nakedness as possible', and her hair was spread beautifully over her shoulders, chest and breasts.[77] It was precisely concerning decency that Gabriele Paleotti, bishop of Bologna and a distinguished reforming churchman, complained in his unpublished treatise of 1582 of those artists who, instead of depicting Christ, created an Apollo, and when painting saints such as Mary Magdalen or St John the Evangelist adorned them in a manner 'worse than prostitutes and ham actors'. He might have been referring to images of Mary Magdalen when he attacked artists who 'in the guise of saints depicted portraits of concubines', thereby steering souls 'in inciting them to damnation for the glory of God'.[78]

Despite Tridentine instructions concerning the pictorial illustration of apocrypha, the Church of Rome continued to use and even to emphasise the 'past life' and entirely non-scriptural aspects of Mary Magdalen. The *Golden Legend* had described her as naked and cloaked in her hair; and Renaissance symbolism and allegory underscored that nakedness when she was taken to represent Truth and Repentance. And justification for her nudity is perhaps found in the long disquisition on Mary Magdalen by the Jesuit Pierre Sautel who quaintly explains: 'this woman burns so with the love of God that she cannot bear to wear clothes'.[79] The naked and penitent Magdalen, in her Provençal grotto, was too far rooted in the popular imagination, and in Catholic dogma, to be discarded for the sake of veracity and decorum, and duly became an object of legitimised voyeurism.

Titian's *Mary Magdalen* was the prototype of images of the Magdalen of the latter half of the sixteenth and seventeenth centuries. In the hands of lesser artists such as the Venetians Palma il Giovane, Giovanni Contarini and Domenico Tintoretto, the saint became little more than a beautiful woman, an idealised feminine body rather than a repentant sinner, similar to the many paintings of courtesans of the period, her attributes – the jar or skull – often being the only means by which she might be distinguished. She became, to use Mario Praz's words, the 'great amorous penitent' or 'Venus in sackcloth',[80] in a period when contrition and forgiveness were the hallmarks of the Catholic faith, and eroticism the means to express pietistical emotionalism.

Towards the end of the sixteenth century, Rome took over Venice's role as the artistic centre of Italy, after the deaths of the great Venetian painters, Titian, Tintoretto and Veronese. The city of the Church Triumphant, it sought to display itself as such in visual terms, in the building of beautiful baroque churches and palaces, decorated with frescoes, paintings and sculptures, executed by artists from all over Italy. One of these, a Bolognese called Annibale Carracci, was summoned to Rome in 1595 to paint in the Palazzo Farnese, and he brought with him a new style of painting which was to affect the course of art for the next 150 years, and which at the same time was to have a profound effect on the image of Mary Magdalen.

In 1585 Annibale, together with his brother and cousin, founded the Accademia delle Belle Arti in Bologna which became one of the most famous schools of fine art of its kind, with pupils such as Guido Reni, Giovanni Lanfranco, Francesco Albani, Domenico Zampieri, or Domenichino, and Francesco Barbieri, nicknamed 'Guercino' or 'Squint-eyed', in the first years of its inception. All these artists contributed to the seventeenth-century image of Mary Magdalen. Bologna was also the new artistic 'school' of the Tridentine revival. One of the most important tenets in the Carracci teaching was the emphasis laid on naturalistic drawing from the model, partly in reaction to the prevailing Mannerist style with its elongated, emotional forms and unnatural colouring (in which the recent Venetians had excelled). Here the Bolognese painters produced an art which conformed to the Tridentine demands for painting that was realistic, clear and didactic. The ideas of Gabriele Paleotti, the bishop of Bologna, on the nature and role of art, and the value of the artistic object as an incitement to piety, may also have influenced them. Visible representations, he wrote, appealed more vividly to the minds of many than the spoken word.[81] Figures now became heroic in stature, monumental and sculptural, and saints became heroes, in settings where light and shadow, or *chiaroscuro*, played dramatically on those large forms.

Annibale's best pupils soon followed him to Rome, and the new style evolved in what had become the creative capital of Europe. Patronage was often on a grand scale, with popes, cardinals and princes fashioning artistic taste. Much in demand among this ecclesiastical and aristocratic clientele was the subject of the weeping Magdalen – an image which was both essentially of the Counter-Reformation, as it treated of the sinner's return to God, and erotic, a kind of penitential pin-up, to be hung in private apartments. Most pictures of Mary Magdalen during this period were privately commissioned, small-scale works, often on copper, and intended for personal rather than public devotion. It is perhaps not surprising, therefore, that some of the most powerful portrayals of the saint, where her sorrow and ecstasy are depicted with a strong sense of realism, are also some of the most erotic. The figure is often close up to the picture plane, filling the whole picture area. Realism allows the artist to render the human body graphically, and the spectator cannot be entirely sure whether it is the depiction of the saint's piety, or her physical attributes, which fascinated the artist or his patron most. Annibale's two well-known paintings of the half-naked penitent (*c.* 1600, Cambridge, Fitzwilliam Museum, see Plate 55; and Rome, Galleria Doria Pamphilj) set her as a smaller figure within a landscape, grief-stricken, red-eyed, head on hand, bare-breasted and draped in blue, whilst his sketch of her shows a beautiful, semi-naked woman gazing up to heaven (Royal collection, Windsor Castle). In Francesco Albani's painting of *c.* 1610, she is on her knees, being shown by the angel the whip used to scourge Christ, the exiguous drapery contributing little to disguise. Orazio Gentileschi painted at least four other variations of his penitent between 1621 and *c.* 1630, derived from Correggio's recumbent figure of over a hundred years earlier. In the version painted for Charles I, she lies back gazing up to heaven, swathed in ochre drapery, resting her elbow on a book, the book of nature, and source of knowledge necessary for salvation; she is also, in conformity with the iconography of the day, naked from the waist up (see Plate 73).[82]

55 *The Penitent Mary Magdalen* (*c.* 1600). Annibale Carracci. Cambridge, Fitzwilliam Museum.

56 *Mary Magdalen scourging herself* (1663). Elisabetta Sirani. Besançon, Musée des Beaux-Arts et d'Archéologie.

The personification of penitence, according to Ripa's *Iconologia* (1603 edition), is an emaciated woman dressed in dark rags or a hairshirt, kneeling while beating herself with a whip with weighted thongs, the emblem of fleshly mortification. She gazes heavenward, with a crucifix and a book at her side.[83] Although the penitent rarely appears emaciated during this period, she often conforms to the penitential figure recommended by Ripa. Guercino's Magdalen in her grotto scourges herself before a crucifix, on a dark tempestuous night (London, Sir Denis Mahon collection); the painting was probably the one recorded as 'Saint Mary Magdalen who punishes herself', painted in 1649 for Cardinal Fabrizio Savelli, a papal legate of Bologna.[84] A painting of the same subject by the Bolognese artist Elisabetta Sirani (1638–65) shows in the masochistic expression of pleasure in pain, how much an iconography created and refined by male artists of the period had made its impression equally on a woman painter (see Plate 56). (The same painter's penitent in the grotto [Bologna, Pinacoteca] lies bare-breasted before the spectator.)[85] Mary Magdalen is the bereaved lover and penitent in another painting by Guercino where she contemplates the instruments of the Passion (1640s, Rome, Vatican). All these paintings were intended to inspire the spectator to feelings of remorse and contrition, but the visual language of many of them, such as Francesco Furini's blatant figure of 1633 – the very year in which the artist was ordained – would probably have inspired less creditable emotions (see Plate 57).[86] These Magdalen images stand, together with other paintings of holy subjects with erotic undercurrents such as Susanna and the Elders and Bathsheba, as examples of pious pornography which were popular in the period.

In Guido Reni's painting (1633, Rome, Galleria Nazionale d'Arte Antica), Mary Magdalen is seated wearing an unfastened chemise, and draped in a pink mantle, calm and tranquil, meditating, her hand resting on a skull, while two *putti* hover in the sky above her. By her side are radishes, the harsh diet of his fasting saint. Another version of the painting which belonged to Louis XIV moved a seventeenth-century French priest, Pierre Le Moyne, to write a poem, 'La Madeleine nouvellement convertie, de Guide', in which he waxed ecstatic about the 'celebrated and glorious' penitent whose 'rubies [lips] are passionate with the

57 The Penitent Mary Magdalen (1633). Francesco Furini. Vienna, Kunsthistorisches Museum.

new flame [of love]', whose 'beautiful eyes' are the 'sacred channels of a precious flood', and whose love 'burns the sky with [her] tears'.[87] 'Sweet Guido', as Ruskin was to call him, was a prolific painter of images of Mary Magdalen, and his particular combination of pious sentiment and sensuousness rendered his paintings irresistible to many contemporaries. The sieur de Chantelou related the occasion when, on his visit to the French court in 1665, Bernini stopped in front of one of Reni's Magdalens. After some time, the sculptor remarked: 'This painting is not beautiful,' immediately following this up by, 'It is very beautiful; I wish I had not seen it; they are paintings of paradise.' It has been noted that the figure of Justice on Bernini's tomb of Urban VIII in

58 *The Penitent Mary Magdalen*
(1664). Pedro de Meña. Valladolid,
Museo Nacional de Escultura.

St Peter's bears a remarkable resemblance to Reni's *Mary Magdalen*.[88] Le Moyne's application of erotic terminology to describe Mary Magdalen's love for Christ echoes contemporary artists' use of erotic visual language to depict that same sacred love. (Like Gentileschi's recumbent Magdalen, Reni's image became a prototype for portraits *à la* Magdalen in the second half of the seventeenth and well into the eighteenth century.[89])

In Spain, where religious art was also used as an effective propaganda weapon in promoting the ideals of the Counter-Reformation, the image of the penitent in the grotto is less erotic than ascetic and pietistical. El Greco, whose passionate and ecstatic style was much influenced by Loyola's *Spiritual Exercises*, depicts the tormented spirituality of his *Magdalen*, of *c.*1580 (Budapest, Szépmüvészeti Múzeum), emphasised by the cold, bluish colouring and silver-grey tones.[90] The *Magdalen* of José Ribera (1560s, Madrid, Prado), whose naturalistic style derives from Roman painting, and whose strong feeling for individual humanity is evident in his portrayal, weeps in her grotto, wearing a hairshirt under which her red drapery swirls round her, with the light from heaven falling on her upturned face. A much more theatrical image is the Magdalen sculpted by Pedro de Meña (1664), a life-like polychrome wood figure, clad in a coarse tunic, her right hand to her breast, and gazing in anguish at the cross she holds in her other hand (see Plate 58). The naturalistic hair clings to her scalp, her forehead is furrowed, and painted tears trickle down her face. She is close in spirit to Donatello's ascetic figure, sculpted two hundred years earlier.[91]

Ecstasy, the spiritual union with God, was the summit of religious experience according to the many treatises on the mystical life, such as Loyola's *Exercises,* written in the sixteenth and seventeenth centuries. Images of saints in ecstasy, *in pieno abbandono*, became even more popular after the canonisation in 1622 of Teresa of Avila who in her *Vida*, published in 1588, wrote of her ecstastic experiences. She described her ecstasy taking hold like a 'powerful eagle, rising and bearing you up with it on its wings', and of being sure neither that 'the soul is in the body, nor that the body is bereft of the soul'. The soul was conscious mainly of 'fainting almost completely away, in a kind of swoon, with an exceeding great and sweet delight'.[92] Bernini captured Teresa's 'fainting away' at the moment of exit of the flaming spear held by the seraph, lifting her up in her ecstasy, in his sculpture in the Cornaro chapel (1645–52, Rome, S. Maria della Vittoria), a marble embodiment of *le petit mort*. Teresa wrote of her vision:

> I did see an angel not farre from me toward my left hand . . . [who] was not great but litle, very beautifull, his face so glorious . . . I did see in his hand a long darte of gold, and at the end of the yron head it seemed to have a little fyre, this he seemed to passe thorough my heart sometimes, and that it pierced to my entrayles, which me thoght he drew from mee, when he pulled it out agayne, & he left me wholy enflamed in great love of God, the payne was so great that it made me complayne greevously, & the sweetenesse was so excess, which this exceeding great payne causeth, that I could not desyre to have it taken away . . .[93]

In Caravaggio's painting (known only in copies by Louis Finson), Mary Magdalen reclines, a deathly pallor in her face, and her eyes rolling back into her head, her body drained of physical strength. Rubens' *Magdalen*, painted for the Franciscans in Ghent in 1630, shows the saint supported by two angels, with the light from heaven falling on her body, and her ointment jar tipped over by her side. The canvas has a greyish tonality, giving an other-worldly quality to its subject. Often given the title, incorrectly, of the 'death' of Mary Magdalen, the painting depicts rather the ecstatic trance into which she regularly fell after her daily elevations into heaven described in the *Golden Legend*.[94]

Mary Magdalen's hair-clad 'Ecstasy', or elevation, had first appeared in the late thirteenth-century altarpiece by the Magdalen Master (see Plate 47). In the late sixteenth-century interpretation of the scene there was a new emphasis: by denying the saint water and nourishment, heavenly food was to be her only sustenance. This divine provender was the eucharist and in the representation of Mary Magdalen being lifted up to heaven lies the Church's visual affirmation of the true presence, and the assertion of the dogma challenged by Protestantism. The flesh represents the state of the soul nourished by heavenly victuals in Giovanni Lanfranco's painting of *c.*1605 (Naples, Galleria Nazionale di

Capodimonte) as a naked Magdalen floats in ecstasy over the silver and blue landscape of the Roman Campagna. It is the apotheosis of a Christianised Venus. Ecstasy, the summit of mystical experience and true end of the *Spiritual Exercises*, is the reunion of the soul with God, and Mary Magdalen, the supreme mystical exemplar, and truly the lover of Christ in this period, is transported in all-giving love to her Lord.[95]

The theme of death had been a medieval preoccupation and, inspired by the Catholic reformers who emphasised the transitoriness of life, it came into prominence once again in the sixteenth and seventeenth centuries. Regarded as a blessed and sweet repose, it was to be prepared for through meditation on the 'four last things' – death itself, judgement, heaven and hell – recommended by Loyola in the *Exercises*. The Jesuits believed that the constant thought of death controlled the passions; and, as an aid to meditation, penitents were urged to close themselves up in darkened rooms, and contemplate with a skull before them. Skulls were readily available from cemeteries and charnel-houses, and on one occasion, a monk was reported being seen in the street carrying his breviary in one hand and a cranium in the other. Two popes, Alexander VII (1599–1667) and Innocent IX (1519–59), were so concerned to make a good death that the former kept his coffin beneath his bed, and the latter had before him a painting of himself as a corpse. With gruesome reality, death's heads appeared ubiquitously to remind the beholder of the familiar *Hodie mihi, cras tibi*, 'My turn today, yours tomorrow'.[96] As examples to the faithful, Counter-Reformation saints such as Francis, Jerome and Mary Magdalen were shown contemplating death: Georges de la Tour's paintings of Mary Magdalen are amongst the best-known images of the theme. In the version in Washington of *c*.1640, she is seated, head supported on her hand, while the sensitively portrayed fingers of her other hand, thrown into relief by the candlelight behind, lightly explore the eye sockets of the skull lying on the book before her (see Plate 59). In the mirror beyond, the eye finds not what it expects – the Magdalen's reflection – but that of the skull. The fine delicate stuff of the Magdalen's chemise reveals the feminine form beneath. The

senses, sight and touch, are united with the emotions and intellect to
meditate upon death and upon what lies beyond.[97] Gentileschi's Fabriano *Magdalen* with her skull and crucifix, pondering on death and her
sins, reminds its spectators of their brief span on this earth, a mere
preparation for eternal repose in heaven.

The last sacraments were an integral part of the good death, and as
the visual support of Catholic dogma, particularly after the Council of
Trent, examples were offered in the form of images of saints taking
their last communion, being given the last rites and dying. Once again,
Mary Magdalen, together with St Jerome and, less often, other saints,
became an instrument of propaganda. Francesco Vanni's *Last Communion of Mary Magdalen*, where Bishop Maximinus administers to the
dying Magdalen (*c.*1600, Genoa, S. Maria di Carignano), is a visual
reaffirmation of the doctrine of the real presence, the triumph of the
eucharist, the victory of the Catholic faith over Protestantism.

Mary Magdalen's tears flowed into the great literary cult of penitential
poetry, the 'cycle of remorse', which sprang up in Italy during the
Counter-Reformation, flooding across Catholic Europe, and even manifested itself amongst Anglican poets in England. Here she was often
paired with St Peter, weeping for his denial of Christ, who was himself
the subject of the most influential example of the *genre*, Luigi Tansillo's
Le Lagrime di S. Pietro. In 1585, this poem was published together with
Erasmo de Valvasone's *Lagrime di S. Maria Maddalena* in one volume in
Venice. Valvasone's poem relates the life of the 'nobil peccatrice' who,
converted, lived in cold solitude in harsh woods among 'horrid wolves'.
Her beauty, her gold chains, necklace, girdle, and gems were the
occasion of her downfall. She seeks Christ clad in her finery, which
allows the poet to dwell at length on lurid *descriptio*. On seeing him, she
is *bouleversée*: henceforth, she will follow only her 'divine lover' whose
'divine rays have caught her'. With her 'beautiful golden mane', she
dries her 'divine hero's' 'holy feet' which she has washed with her tears.
This is merely the beginning of her weeping, which ends only with the
end of the poem. As a 'proud Maenad', she rushes to weep at the foot
of the cross; her tears flow yet again when she finds the empty tomb.
'Piange ella anchora' (Again, she weeps) on recognising the gardener;
and after Christ has risen, in 'loving sadness', the 'amante donna', the
loving woman, follows the 'beloved leader' in her thoughts, alone in a
remote cave. Clothed only in her 'long mane', she makes the rocks and

59 *Mary Magdalen meditating* (*c.*1640). Georges de la Tour. Washington, National Gallery of Art.

trees fall in love with her, and her body is then taken up by angels to heaven where, as the 'holy Hermit', and in her humble ardent faith, she is reunited once more with 'her lover'.[98]

Whilst ostensibly tracing Mary Magdalen's life from sinfulness to sanctity, Valvasone's poem, like the many which followed it in the rest of Catholic Europe, dwells on the externals with gusto, often becoming merely a paean to her beauty. Tears are the outward manifestation of internal anguish, but they are also the occasion for elaborate discourses on the reason for those tears – Mary Magdalen's beauty. She becomes the heroine of a series of 'magdaliades', epic poems in which her tears are the subject as in César de Nostredame's *Les Perles ou Larmes de la Saincte Magdelaine* (1606), a threnody of 752 decasyllables. In England her tears provoked the wit and invention of five major poets of the seventeenth century, two of them Catholic and three Anglican. The Jesuit Robert Southwell, whose poem 'St Peter's Complaint' was influenced by Tansillo, presents Mary Magdalen as the model of the 'perfect lover' in his prose meditation *Marie Magdalens Funerall Teares*, printed in 1594 and so popular that it was followed by seven further editions in England before 1636 and by two continental editions. The meditation explores her grief at the tomb and her meeting with Christ; imagining himself to be with her, the meditator even speaks with her, as well as with the angels and Christ. The Magdalen's love for Christ is described in the language of Elizabethan love poetry: 'the fire of her true affection inflamed her hart', 'her eye was watchful to seek whom her hart most longed to enjoy',

> And as men in extremity of thirst are still dreaming of fountaines, brookes and springes, being never able to have other thought, or to utter other word but of drinke and moisture: so lovers, in the vehemencie of their passion, can neither thinke nor speake but of that they love & if that bee once missing, everie part, is both an eye to watch, and an eare to listen, what hope or newes may be had of it.[99]

Through psychological examination, the meditator attempts to understand Mary Magdalen's great grief. It is the Jesuit art of self-examination in literary guise, visualising the gospel events in detail, in a tightly knit, formal style, using rhetorical devices to analyse the Magdalen's state of mind at the sepulchre:

> But feare not *Marie* for thy teares will obtaine. They are too mightie oratours, to let any suite fall, and though they pleaded at the most rigorous barre, yet have they so perswading a silence, and so conquering a complaint, that by yeelding they overcome, and by intreating they commaunde.[100]

Through it all is the sense of the loss of the beloved, 'so is thy love a continuall hunger, and his absence unto thee an extreme famine'.

Southwell also wrote two lyrics about Mary Magdalen, one, 'Marie Magdalens blush', and the other, one of the most beautiful English love poems of the period, 'Marie Magdalens complaint at Christs death', in which the despairing Magdalen grieves for Christ when she finds the empty tomb, seeing earthly life as death in life, a mere shadow without his presence.

> Sith my life from life is parted:
>   Death come take thy portion.
> Who survives, when life is murdred,
>   Lives by meere extortion.
> All that live, and not in God:
> Couch their life in deaths abod.
>
> Seely starres must needes leave shining,
>   When the sunne is shaddowed.
> Borrowed streames refraine their running,
>   When head springs are hindered.
> One that lives by others breath,
> Dieth also by his death.

The theme is once again the loss of the lover, the language that of love profane. The marvellous imagery (Southwell's use of paradox shows his debt to the Jesuit art of meditation) continues in the last two stanzas, one a passionate self-apostrophe by Mary Magdalen, the other a conventional outburst against the spear which had pierced Christ's side, the

> Spitefull speare, that breakst this prison,
>   Seate of all felicitie, . . .
> Though my life thou drav'st away,
> Maugre thee my love shall stay.[101]

A mid-seventeenth century engraving showing Mary Magdalen seated mourning over the dead body of Christ is an exact visual analogue to the sorrowful, meditative quality of such poetry (see Plate 60). Probably designed for a devotional work, this unusual image, together with more conventional scenes of the grieving Magdalen, illustrates how close the literary and artistic treatments of the subject can be.[102]

Mary Magdalen's tears are also the subject of a poem, 'Marie Magdalene', by the Anglican divine George Herbert (1593–1633). In his 'Life' of Herbert, Izaak Walton endorsed the seventeenth-century image of Mary Magdalen as 'that wonder of Women, and Sinners and

Mourners'.[103] In Herbert's poem, she weeps not for Christ's death but as Luke's sinner. A series of hyperbole, incongruous and extended metaphors, and violent transitions, forges a narrative which moves decisively to its quiet end.

> When blessed Marie wip'd her Saviour's feet,
> (Whose precepts she had trampled on before)
> And wore them for a jewell on her head,
>   Shewing his steps should be the street,
>   Wherein she thenceforth evermore
> With pensive humbleness would live and tread:
>
> She being stain'd her self, why did she strive
> To make him clean, who could not be defil'd?
> Why kept she not her tears for her own faults,
>   And not his feet? Though we could dive
>   In tears like seas, our sinnes are pil'd
> Deeper than they, in words, and works, and thoughts.
>
> Deare soule, she knew who did vouchsafe and deigne
> To bear her filth; and that her sinnes did dash
> Ev'n God himself: wherefore she was not loth,
>   As she had brought wherewith to stain,
>   So to bring in, wherewith to wash:
> And yet in washing one, she washed both.[104]

Richard Crashaw (1612–49), England's only 'baroque' poet, and the son of a noted Puritan divine, converted to Roman Catholicism in the 1640s. In his poem 'The Weeper', he extravagantly throws himself into a litany of conceits about Mary Magdalen's tears: they are both the symbol and the effect of her penitence, and elemental companions to the flames of her love, a concept pointed to in the couplet quoted at the beginning of this chapter, and played with throughout the poem, as in the apostrophe

> O flouds, o fires! o suns ô showres!
> Mixt & made freinds by loue's sweet powres.

Crashaw's exuberant descriptive powers are perhaps best exemplified by the famous lines in which Christ is seen walking among the Galilean mountains, where

60 Mary Magdalen mourning over the dead body of Christ. Anon. Mid-seventeenth century.

> He's follow'd by two faithful fountaines;
> Two walking baths; two weeping motions;
> Portable, & compendious oceans.

Anxious to trace the destination of all these tears, the poet finds in the end that they 'goe to meet/ A worthy object, our lord's FEET'.[105] A similar conceit occurred to Andrew Marvell in the wonderful stanza from 'Eyes and Tears':

> So Magdalen, in tears more wise
> Dissolved those captivating eyes,
> Whose liquid chains could flowing meet
> To fetter her Redeemer's feet.[106]

It was thanks to these tears that the term 'maudlin', meaning lachrymose, mawkishly emotional or tearfully sentimental, came into the English language in the seventeenth century, its pronunciation derived from the French 'Madeleine'; it is a pronunciation which the colleges at Oxford and Cambridge still retain. Less felicitously it could also be applied to that stage of drunkenness which was tearful and effusively affectionate. In *Hudibras* Samuel Butler punningly described the weeping Heraclitus as the 'maudlin Philosopher'.[107]

The penitent Magdalen had been the subject of a long sermon given in Venice in 1539 by the Capuchin Bernardino Ochino (c.1486–c.1564), the most popular Italian preacher of his day, who had himself visited her grotto at Ste Baume. Here she was held up as the model of the Church Militant, interestingly enough some years before the Council of Trent, and as an example of penitence to all, but particularly the ladies of Venice, who were reminded in the course of the sermon of the repentant prostitutes in the nearby city of Padua: 'I strongly recommend to you the convertites of Padua. They will be at the gates [of the city]. I recommend them to you as strongly as I can.' Mary Magdalen's vanity – 'there will never be another woman more sensual than I', Ochino has her say – and her conversion are paradigms. He teases the females of his audience: 'Oh you will say: I do it to please my husband', and turning to the husbands, he adds, 'And you gentleman, if you have your wives who are beautiful and well dressed, why are you not content with them, and not with so many prostitutes: it might be enough if you were in a battalion of soldiers, where there were no women, but each of you is married, and has your companion: you should be content with her.'[108]

Ochino was preaching at the end of the decade which saw the first of Titian's paintings of Mary Magdalen, and the connection between Mary Magdalen and Venice was by no means coincidental since the city already had a long-established tradition of venerating the penitent saint. It is for this reason that the Republic can stand as an example of the way in which the saint was used both as a civic emblem, as the patron of a state institution, and as an object of personal and popular piety. From Venice also came a wide repertoire of images of Mary Magdalen, depicting her in ways which appear to be unique to Venetian art. The significance which Mary Magdalen had for the *Serenissima* and her citizens can only be understood in the context of the history of her cult in that city.

The earliest known Venetian dedication to Mary Magdalen has been dated to 1155 when a small *sacrarium*, or memorial chapel, was erected in her honour as 'S. Maria Maddalena Penitente' in Canaregio by the Baffa or Baffo family; it was later enlarged to become the local parish church. A finger of the saint was believed to have been placed, together with relics of other saints, under the high altar.[109] In the sixteenth century the church was decorated with paintings of a *Conversion* and a *Penitent Magdalen* by Jacopo Tintoretto, who also painted a *Noli me tangere* on the exterior of the two organ shutters. It also contained an *Ecstasy of Mary Magdalen* on the high altar, and altarpieces of *Christ converting Mary Magdalen*, while Tintoretto's son Domenico had painted her soul going up to heaven, and a *Magdalen in Glory* was depicted on the ceiling.[110] The sixteenth-century historian Francesco Sansovino noted that this was the last church to be visited by the people during the civic ceremonies on Good Friday evening,[111] an honour which may have derived from the saint's Paschal role. Venice's pride as a great maritime power was recorded in the many feast-days during the liturgical year when masses and huge processions were held to commemorate her victories.[112] The month of July was particularly full of such commemorations, and in 1356, on Mary Magdalen's feast-day (22 July), the Venetians had celebrated their victory over the Genoese earlier that month; two thousand Genoese prisoners were released from prison (situated where the *pescaria* or fish-market of San Marco now is), and processed in thanksgiving, 'divotamente', each carrying a lit candle, to the church in Canaregio. The Senate decreed that the saint's feast-day henceforth be included among the civic festivals, 'so that the memory of that day should forever remain'.[113] In 1361 a hospice for seven old women ('sette vecchie'), with an oratory dedicated to Mary Magdalen, was set up by two brothers, Gabriele and Luciano Prior, in the parish of the Arcangelo Raffaele[114] – today, one of the last remaining untouched *campi* in Venice – the first of such charitable institutions for which Venice became renowned, to be placed under the patronage of Mary Magdalen. The hospice, now a Casa di Riposo, or rest-home, for women, still exists on the same site.

Mary Magdalen's civic importance is further attested to by her appearance on a fifteenth-century city banner for a public building or institution with Saints John the Baptist, John the Evangelist and Jerome,

flanking the Lion of St Mark.[115] She is also a beautiful figure rushing to
lean over Christ's body, which is held by John the Evangelist and the
Virgin, in the lunette of the *Pietà* (Milan, Brera) painted by Tintoretto
between 1563 and 1567, which was originally in the courtyard of the
Procuratie, the highest representative magistrature after that of the doge
(see Plate 61).[116] In 1374, Verde Scaligera, daughter of the lord of Verona
and wife of Niccolo d'Este, marquis of Ferrara, had died, specifying
in her will that she be buried in a chapel to be dedicated to Mary
Magdalen in the church of S. Maria dei Servi in Venice, and leaving the
money for this. She had, however, to wait 150 years for her wishes to
be fulfilled. In 1524 the altar was erected and a richly attired statue of
the saint by Bartolomeo Bergamasco was erected, following instructions
from the Procurators of San Marco to have her dressed *all'antica*, with
'chavelli legadi et non zo per spalla', gracefully drawn-back hair.[117] This
statue is now placed on an altar in the second apsidal chapel right of the
high altar of the vast Dominican church of SS. Giovanni e Paolo, where
it was taken after the demolition of the Servite convent. (Its original
altar serves as a backdrop to a statue of St Jerome by Alessandro Vittoria
in a chapel on the left of the same church.) Mary Magdalen appears once
again in SS. Giovanni e Paolo, on the sculptural monument to Andrea
Vendramin, together with St Margaret, both figures dressed in classicising draperies, and transferred from the high altar of S. Marina, and now
occupying the space left by those of two warriors which in turn replaced
the original figures of Adam and Eve.[118]

In the sacristy of the Franciscan church, the Frari, is a touching memorial to the close relationship between Mary Magdalen and Christ, symbolised in the union of their relics, and reminiscent of Louis IX's
veneration of their remains at St Maximin. Housed in Tommaso Lombardo's late fifteenth-century marble tabernacle, whose bronze door is
decorated with a penitent Magdalen on her knees, is a drop of Christ's
blood mixed with some of Mary Magdalen's unguent. These, which
had been greatly cherished in Constantinople whence they had been
brought, were donated to the church in 1479 by Melchiore Trevisan, the
generalissimo da mar, or commander-in-chief, of the *Serenissima*'s navy.[119]

As might be expected in a city with so many links with Byzantium
and the east, the earliest image of Mary Magdalen in the basilica of San
Marco is a twelfth-century mosaic, on the north wall of the central aisle
of the nave, where she appears as one of the two Marys meeting Christ
on their return from the tomb, a scene which is in conformity with the

61 *Pietà* (1563–7). Jacopo Tintoretto. Milan, Pinacoteca Brera.

eastern Church's emphasis on Mark's gospel. On the underside of the easternmost arch of the south arcade is an early thirteenth-century Byzantine mosaic icon of her, veiled, dressed in dark blue, hidden away in the dark, and lit only occasionally by flickering candlelight. In the eighteenth century the treasury of S. Marco listed amongst its possessions part of the stone upon which Mary Magdalen had been seated when Christ appeared to her, and where she had said 'el nostro Signor'.[120]

A very youthful and virginal Mary Magdalen emerges from the shadows of Giovanni Bellini's *Madonna and Child with Saints Catherine and Mary Magdalen* of *c.*1490 (Venice, Accademia), her red-gold hair falling to her shoulders and hands crossed over her breast, gazing pensively into the distance past the Christ child (see Plate 62). An entirely different, but equally beautiful, image is Sebastiano del Piombo's statuesque figure, mature and sensual, which appears in his painting (1510) on the high altar of the church of S. Giovanni Crisostomo where Mary Magdalen is the most prominent of the 'three figures of Venetian ladies' which so struck Henry James (see Plate 63):

The picture represents the patron-saint of the church, accompanied by other saints . . . These ladies stand together on the left, holding in their hands little white caskets; two of them are in profile, but the foremost turns her face to the spectator. This face and figure are almost unique among the beautiful things of Venice, and they leave the susceptible observer with the impression of having made, or rather having missed, a strange, a dangerous, but a most valuable, aquaintance. The lady, who is superbly handsome, is the typical Venetian of the sixteenth century, and she remains for the mind the perfect flower of that society. Never was there a greater air of breeding, a deeper expression of tranquil superiority. She walks a goddess – as if she trod without sinking the waves of the Adriatic. It is impossible to conceive a more perfect expression of the aristocratic spirit either in its pride or in its benignity. This magnificent creature is so strong and secure that she is gentle, and so quiet that in comparison all minor assumptions of calmness suggest only a vulgar alarm. But for all this there are depths of possible disorder in her light-coloured eye.[121]

Today, the painting's discolouration and poor condition prevent the spectator from making any moral judgement about the 'lady's' eye; perhaps one is to infer from that last sentence, and from the word 'disorder', that without naming her, or indeed any other saint shown with the enthroned St John Chrysostom, James was alluding to Mary Magdalen.

Girolamo Savoldo's powerful and arresting half-length 'portrait' of Mary Magdalen with a view of the Venetian lagoon behind her has been a source of interest and misunderstanding over the centuries, as she stands outside the sepulchre on Easter morning, swathed in her silvery cloak, her ointment jar to the left, behind her on a stone ledge (see Plate 64). The painter, a Brescian, worked mainly in Venice, where he was influenced by Giorgione and Titian; his Magdalen is in fact contemporary with Titian's Pitti painting. Mary Magdalen is in the process of turning, in *contrapposto*, her veiled hand, in a mourning gesture, held up to her mouth, and she has been weeping. She looks at the spectator, apparently caught momentarily. A cursory glance might lead one to assume that she was on her way to the sepulchre, as in the gospel of John, with the dawn rising ahead of her. But this would be to ignore the position of the jar on the ledge, which would imply that Mary

62 Mary Magdalen. Detail from *Madonna and Child with Saints Catherine and Mary Magdalen*, (*c.*1490). Giovanni Bellini. Gallerie dell'Venice, Accademia.

Magdalen has already been to the sepulchre. The picture, described in the seventeenth century as 'a famous painting from which many copies have been made', has been given many interpretations since it was painted sometime around 1530 by critics who have suggested its setting as being at any time between sunset and midnight, and its subject as 'a romantically veiled beauty' but for the 'diminutive ointment jar', enticing, mysterious, and Mary Magdalen in the guise of a Venetian courtesan. The latest and most persuasive argument suggests[122] that the Magdalen's *contrapposto* reflects the passage in John 20:11–16 which tells of her return to the sepulchre, after she has told Peter and John of the removal of Christ's body, and in particular verses 14–16 when she turns back and sees Christ standing and 'knew not that it was Jesus'. When Christ addresses her by name, she 'turning, saith to him, Rabboni'. She

63 Mary Magdalen with
Saints Catherine and Agnes.
Detail from the S. Giovanni
Crisostomo Altarpiece
(1510). Sebastiano del
Piombo. Venice, S. Giovanni
Crisostomo.

64 Mary Magdalen turning towards the risen Christ (*c.*1530).
Girolamo Savoldo. London, National Gallery.

recognises him in turning; and it is this moment in the gospel narrative
which Savoldo has chosen to illustrate. The light falls from the right,
showing strongest on the Magdalen's hood and jutting left arm, and her
startled, mournful glance, fictively caught by the spectator first, comes
out of the shadows, reflecting her process of conversion, her growing
'enlightenment'. With the light falling on the left side of her nose, she
swings round to her left to see, and understand, the source of the light,
Christ.

Titian's own epitaph to himself, his *Pietà*, and his last altarpiece (1576),
can serve fittingly as a final example of the ways in which some Venetian
painters envisioned Mary Magdalen (see Plate 65). The figures of the
Virgin with the dead Christ lying across her knees are set within a
classicising niche, to the left of which is a statue of Moses, to the right,

65 *Pietà* (1576). Titian. Venice, Gallerie dell'Accademia.

of the Hellespontine Sibyl; on his knees in the garb of a penitent is a
supplicating St Jerome, to whom Titian gave his own facial features.
The Magdalen rushes in, a maenad figure, again half submerged in the
shadows, her right arm up announcing Christ's death to the world, and
the other thrown back to the Virgin and Christ. Her gesture, taken from
an Aphrodite figure grieving for the death of her lover Adonis sculpted
on a sarcophagus in the Palazzo Ducale at Mantua, expresses her own
great sorrow, as her mantle swirls around her, created out of the broad
strokes from a heavily loaded paintbrush, and she is here *par excellence*
the herald of the New Life, and witness to Titian's own Christian
humanism.[123]

Mary Magdalen's name had already been associated from the fourteenth
century with charitable activities in Venice involving women. In the
mid-sixteenth century, she once again became a protectress of women,

this time the repentant prostitute. Her supposed suitability for this kind of patronage was the subject of an old popular Venetian song (*ninna nanna*) which describes her living in a splendid palace from a window of which she sees Christ passing by,

> *Maria Madalena, istoria bela*
> *Quando fu morto Lazaro e so sorella*
> *e quando scominzio morir so pare*
> *un bel palazzo avea Madalena.*
>
> *El giera pien de'oro e pien de argento,*
> *La se fa al finestrin per guardare*
> *La se fa al finestrin per guardare*
> *la vede Gesù Christo a ripassare.*

(Here is the fine story of Mary Magdalen. When Lazarus died, and his sister, and when her father began to die, Magdalen had a beautiful palace which was full of gold and full of silver. There she sat at the window to watch, there she sat at the window to watch, and saw Jesus Christ pass by.)

Overcome, she goes to the house of Simon:

> *Simeon, Simeon! – Chi bate a questa porta?*
> *La xe la Madalena pecatrice.*
> *Tire 'l spaghetto che la vegna in casa*
> *Soto la tola la se inzenociava.*[124]

(Simon, Simon! – Who knocks at this door? It's Magdalen the sinner . . . Lift the catch so that she can enter the house [and] under the table, she knelt down.)

Having been forgiven in this somewhat telescoped account for her life of vanity, she goes off to live in a grotto ('Trentatre anni me ne vogio stare'). A Venetian list of saints' names, giving their roles as protectors from specific illness and as patrons of particular circumstances in life, records: 'Santa Maria Maddalena xe sora le done del mondo' (Mary Magdalen looks after the women of the world).[125] And in the *Ragionamenti* (by Titian's friend, Pietro Aretino, a bawdy dialogue about the three states of women, nuns, married women and whores), the *ruffiana* or procuress Nanna tells Antonia, a candidate for the meretricious profession, that Mary Magdalen is 'nostra avocata' (our patroness), and that they do not work on her feast-day.[126]

In sixteenth-century Venice, the name of the Magdalen became synonymous with the feminine sex at two distinct social levels of purchased sex: at the superior stratum, that of the courtesan 'famoused over all Christendom', her link was a literary one in a period when, as we have seen, women's beauty, love and sexuality were lauded. But at the lower level, that of the common prostitute, she represented, as she had since the Middle Ages, the model of repentance and conversion. And nowhere was her example more appropriate than in Venice which from the fourteenth century, after the Fourth Crusade and the fall of Constantinople, became the most important port on the eastern Mediterranean between western Europe and Byzantium and the east, a position which she held unrivalled for the next three centuries. A departure-point for pilgrims bound for the Holy Land, with mercantile traffic to and from the Levant, bearing cargoes of spices and rich textiles, Venice as an exotic centre naturally provoked an enormous trade in sexual commodities, typical of cities and ports with a large itinerant male population. From 1360 the government had declared the prostitutes as 'omnino necessarie in terra ista', entirely necessary to the state.[127] (As Coryate ironically noted later, the tax levied on them enabled the Senate to maintain a dozen galleys.[128]) In the mid-fourteenth century the Council of Ten opened a public house called the Castelletto, justifying the act thus: 'It is necessary, because of the multitude of men who continually enter and leave our city, to find in Venice a place adapted to the habitation of sinners.'[129] The Rialto, the commercial centre of the city, was the site chosen for the municipal brothel, so that prostitution was sanctioned and even encouraged by catering to the needs of local male inhabitants as well as to merchants and visitors. The prostitutes were strictly regulated, and kept within the confines of Rialto, and in particular sections of that area, in order not to offend those respectable people ('congrue et honeste persone') who used the taverns and inns. Allowed to wander about during the day, 'when the first [night] bells of San Marco began to chime' they had to return to the *lupanar*.[130] Despite Council legislation, by the fifteenth century they had spread to a *contrada* called the Carampane, and later on into the San Marco area. In 1416 a law obliged them and their *ruffiane* to wear a yellow scarf over their clothes when going into the city, so they could be recognised for what they were and avoided by decent persons. If found without this garment, they could be punished by flogging. The law was confirmed in 1486, and again in 1490, but fell into desuetude soon thereafter.[131]

It was when syphilis broke out in the wake of Charles VIII's invasion of Italy in 1494 that the Venetian authorities were spurred into action, if only to prevent the disease from swelling to epidemic proportions. This, it was hoped, could be achieved by containing and controlling the means of transmission, sexual activity, and the commodity itself, the prostitute. Venetian charity was already involved in the welfare of its female citizens: to prevent impoverished young women from straying from the straight and narrow, the *scuole*, or devotional and charitable lay organisations, set up dowries to enable them to marry or if this were not possible to enter nunneries. But such charities benefited only those who were termed *poveri vergognosi*, or 'shamefaced poor', particularly amongst them young women from gently-born backgrounds.[132] It was not until about 1525 that prostitutes were able to benefit from philanthropic activity, although in 1353 a hospice had been set up for those who wished to abandon their way of life. But in the sixteenth century, as part of a campaign to save souls and to improve moral standards, the Compagnia del Divino Amore founded the first general hospital in Venice, the Ospedale degli Incurabili, to house syphilitics. In 1525 a wing was given over to accommodate women who wished to leave their lives of prostitution (described as 'sinful women converted to God'), in a revival of the kind of institution already established in Florence, Siena, Bologna and Rome, as well as Brescia and Paris, all under the patronage of Mary Magdalen. In the 1540s, the women were moved to the island of the Giudecca where houses had already been bought, and in 1551 into a purpose-built monastery with a chapel dedicated to Mary Magdalen.[133] (The building is now, ironically, or perhaps appropriately, the local women's state penitentiary, the only sign of its hospitality of such feminine inmates within its crumbling walls being the pots of geraniums and herbs which now decorate the barred windows to what were once nuns' cells.) Fynes Moryson wrote of the prostitutes that 'when they are past gayning much, they are turned out to begg or turne bauds or servants. And for releife of this miserye, they have Nonneryes where many of them are admitted, and called the converted sisters.'[134] Married women were turned away, as were young girls (*donzelle*), and escaped nuns, pregnant women, or those with incurable or contagious diseases, and those over forty years of age. Francesco Sansovino attested to their beauty:

così le peccatrici pentite, habbiano parimente, dove salvarsi in tutto da i peccati. Quivi dimorando assai gran numero di donne, & tutte bellissime (percioche non vi si accettano se non quelle, che hanno somma beltà; acciochè pentendosi, non ricaggino ne' peccati per la forma loro, attrativa de gli altrui desideriij) si essercitano con ordine mirabile in diversi artificiij.[135]

(Thus even penitent prostitutes could have a place where they could be saved from and kept away from sin. Here live quite a large number of women, and all very beautiful because only those who are very beautiful are accepted; so as not, after repenting, to fall back into sin through their beauty, which attracts the desires of others, they devote themselves with marvellous order to diverse occupations.)

Before them always was the model of Mary Magdalen: the title-page to the monastery's statutes refers to the saint as the 'Mirror of Repentance', the patron saint of the 'donne illuminate', or 'enlightened women' who, like their model, had been 'taken from the hands of the devil . . . and from the filth of the flesh ['dalla spurcitia della carne'] . . . to the chaste life of the spirit' (see Plate 66).[136] On the high altar of the church attached to the monastery was a *Noli me tangere* by Luigi Benfatto, and on the ceiling, an ecstatic Magdalen being lifted by angels, by Palma Giovane.[137] Sexual scandal, however, soon followed. Pietro Leon da Valcamonica, the first rector and governor of the Convertites, confessed to having carnal relations ('commercio carnale') with twenty of the inmates in his charge; he was beheaded and burned in Piazza San Marco, between the columns, according to the custom, on 10 November 1561. (The abbess ended her days in prison in 1564, despite Valcamonica's gentlemanly attestation to her innocence.)[138] The dramatic change of existence from a sexual to ascetic life must have been, as Veronica Franco (1554–99), the most famous Venetian courtesan, *la cortigiana onorata*, put it, 'extremely difficult' ('oltreche difficilmente si possino indurre a passare in un momento da una tanta licentia, ad una cosi stretta et austera sorte di vita, come quelle delle Convertite').[139]

Veronica herself was a highly cultivated woman who wrote poetry and gave her favours to the French king, Henri III. She also sent a copy of her works to Montaigne on his travels. In later life and like other 'fallen' women, she retired to a convent after having – according to

66 Title-page of the
statutes of the Convento
delle Convertite, Venice
(1695). Venice, Biblioteca
Correr.

CONVERTITE

Nel nome della SS:ᵐᵃ Trinità, Pⁿᵉ, Figliolo, et
Spᵒ Sᵗᵒ, e della Gloriosa V. MARIA, mⁿᵉ del
nᵗᵒ clementissᵒ Sigᵗᵉ et Redentore m. Iesù Xᵖᵗᵒ,
et della sua diletta Discepola Sᵗᵃ MARIA MAD:
DALENA Specchio di Penitenza. Incominciano
li ordeni che si hanno à tenir circa il gouerno, et Re:
gola delle Donne illuminate, et conuerse à penitenza
del Monasterio di Sᵗᵃ Maria Maddalena
della Città di Venetia nella Zuecca,
tratte fuora dalle man del Demonio
al santo seruitio di esso m Iesù
Xᵖᵗᵒ et dalla spurcitia
della carne alla monda
et castissima uita dello Spirito.

Venetian tradition – founded a refuge for repentant prostitutes in 1577.[140]
That some prostitutes did indeed find reclusion difficult is shown in the
story of an Englishman, John Brown (Giovanni Bren or Brin), attached
to the ambassador, who in 1643 took a gondola to help an escaped nun
whom he hid under the cabin. Other nuns gave the alarm, and Bren/
Brin was caught and imprisoned for six months; he was later absolved
because of his youth and because he had been duped by an old madam
who was condemned to four years' imprisonment.[141] Large numbers of
prostitutes were, however, drawn to the Convertite as it provided them
with a safe haven, respectability of a sort, useful employment such as
making lace and printing books, and for those with true vocations, a
spiritual life.[142]

In 1561 Giovanni Grimani, cardinal patriarch of Aquileia and the greatest
connoisseur of antique and modern art in his family, commissioned
Battista Franco to fresco his family chapel in the Venetian church of S.
Francesco della Vigna, where he was also to be buried. Battista, how-

ever, died and the Roman Mannerist painter Federico Zuccaro was called in to replace him. The two frescoes, *laterali*, flanking the main altar were of the *Conversion of Mary Magdalen* and the *Raising of Lazarus*, an iconographical scheme pairing spiritual awakening of the living with the triumph of spiritual life over death, both subjects central to Counter-Reformation precepts. (The subject of the Raising of Lazarus was also popular in Venice because of the plague.) The *Conversion* had been lost by the early eighteenth century, but the sketch owned by Vasari, now in the Uffizi, shows how Zuccaro imagined the worldly Magdalen, richly clad, and with all men's eyes upon her.[143]

Mary Magdalen appears in another Tridentine guise in the Scuola Grande di S. Rocco, in the chapter-room of the great Venetian guild named after the patron saint of the plague, St Roch. Between 1582 and 1587, Tintoretto painted the *sala inferiore* with scenes from the Virgin's life. On either side of the altar, he painted vertical panels of Mary Magdalen and Mary of Egypt, sitting tranquilly in moonlit landscapes, in a spirit of contemplation, a theme which, as we have seen, had been revitalised by the Counter-Reformation. To the north of the altar, Mary Magdalen, lost in her own world, is shown reading a book, close to a tree and some water, the shimmering light falling on her and on the tree, and picking out details of foliage.[144]

As the model of repentance, Mary Magdalen gave occasion to several pieces of edifying literature, sacred dramas, motets and oratorios from the mid-sixteenth century, many of which were published in Venice. The dramas, or *rappresentazioni*, were mostly written by members of religious orders, of doubtful literary merit, and bear such titles as *Rappresentazione d'un stupendo miracolo di S. Maria Maddalena*, and the *Devotissima Rappresentazione di S. Maria Maddalena: Specchio di Penitenza*.[145] In almost all, Mary Magdalen is to be found weeping in her grotto, repenting of her 'bestial, worldly' life, which had been 'full of carnal filth'. As in Marino's poem, she is described as a 'Berenice', whose 'beautiful face, gestures and voice' have, Helen-like, led a thousand lovers to war, and as a woman who 'could be confused with Venus'. Usually depicted as a courtesan, she is also the 'noble sinner', of a royal house, 'with a beautiful body', with maid-servants, gold, jewels and splendid palaces. Although the details may vary in each tale, Mary Magdalen becomes a mouthpiece for Catholic tenets such as the Virgin Birth, the Trinity, justification by faith and good works, and the virtues of the active and contemplative lives. One of these *rappresentazioni*, which were in essence mystery or morality plays set to music, was *La Maddalena*, performed at Mantua in 1617, the prologue to which was composed by Claudio Monteverdi to a libretto by Giovan Battista Andreini.[146] Andrea Gabrieli (*c*.1510–86), an organist at San Marco, and another of Venice's most famous composers, wrote four- and six-part motets entitled 'Maria Magdalena' in 1576 and 1587, and a seven-part motet 'Maria stabat ad monumentum' in 1587. His nephew Giovanni (1557–1612), who also became organist at San Marco, wrote two Magdalen motets in the 1580s,[147] while Lorenzo Giustiniani (1570–1620), later a member of the Dieci, the Venetian oligarchy, recited his *Laudatio Mariae Magdalenae* in 1588 at the College of Rome.[148]

As a city, Venice gathered to her aspects of the cult of Mary Magdalen which are found severally elsewhere. As in other cities, she was the model for and patroness of penitent prostitutes and other *donne 'irregolari'*, 'irregular' or marginalised women.[149] (In Florence, the Magdalen prayer said at the Duomo during Lent in 1579 in fact gave occasion to the conversion of several prostitutes.[150]) Other Venetian charities with which she was associated included a hospice for old women, and the guild of the *finestrieri*, or window-makers.[151] The city shows how pervasive the idea of Mary Magdalen could be, and how it could be adapted to serve both social and religious ends. But it is through the artistic expression of Venetian humanism – in its revival of classical forms – that Mary Magdalen's figure becomes imbued with the opulence and maturity given it by such artists as Titian and Sebastiano del Piombo, and the sculptors Bartolomeo Bergamasco and Lorenzo Bregno. The Venetian Magdalen, richly attired in paintings in Venetian *colore*, in greens, golds, russets and dark reds, is very much a creature of her city; it is through Titian in particular that this image broke its Venetian confines and became celebrated throughout Europe.

Whilst Italy could lay claim to the greatest riches in terms of painting and sculptures of the holy hermit, France could lay claim to one inalienable treasure, possession of the site of her retreat. The ubiquity of her penitent image may well have acted as a stimulus to the pilgrimage which continued to draw illustrious devotees from all over Catholic Europe, its popularity seemingly little affected by the controversy provoked in 1641. In that year, Jean de Launoy, a scholar from the Sorbonne, published a treatise with the provocative title of *Dissertatio de Commentitio Lazari et Maximini, Magdalenae et Marthae in Provinciam appulsu*, or 'Dissertation on the false arrival in Provence of Lazarus, Maximinus, Magdalen and Martha'. Such a thesis was not unnaturally attacked vigorously by the Provençals with refutations entitled, for example, *Disquisitio theologico-historica* and *Preuves de la foi et piété de Provence* which give some hint as to their contents. The battle raged until 1646 when both sides retired, feeling that they had acquitted themselves with honour.[152]

From the thirteenth century, the French kings had been patrons of the church at St Maximin where Mary Magdalen's relics were kept, and had also endowed the royal convent which was in the care of Dominican monks. Her importance to the French monarchy is manifested in such objects as a book of hours belonging to Charles VIII (1470–98), first husband of Anne of Brittany, which contains a miniature of the king kneeling while Mary Magdalen presents him to Christ in an unusual rendering of the *Noli me tangere* (New York, Pierpont Morgan Library).[153] Such was her significance to the Valois that after the battle of Marignano in 1515 in which he took the duchy of Milan, François I went to give thanks at St Maximin, taking with him a large entourage. As women were excluded from the crypt, the king brought the head and reliquary into the church so that the female members of the group might see and marvel at the saint's relics. As a result of this royal visit, large sums of money were donated for church works, altars and statues.[154] The church built by 1529 is the church which stands today; and out of his 'singulier dévotion' for the saint, François also paid for the reconstruction of the monastic buildings at Ste Baume. In 1517 Isabella d'Este, marchioness of Mantua, had visited St Maximin, and in 1536, the Emperor Charles V, at the head of an army of sixty thousand men on their way to besiege Marseille, reached the town to discover that the relics had vanished. The monks, fearful that his devotion to this 'great lover of God' might lead him to remove them entirely, had hidden them in a well. Having failed to discover their whereabouts, Charles then also failed to take Marseille, and returned to Germany with his army diminished by half.[155]

François' grandson, Henri III, was the last of the Valois kings before the disastrous wars of religion arrived to wreak havoc on France in the seventeenth century. A pious man, he attempted to lead the Counter-Reformation in France, setting up orders, *confrèries* and other religious institutions. In a period when splendid entertainments were part of the courtly way of life, Henri filled the streets of Paris with religious processions to display his own piety. In one such procession in 1583, the king, his courtiers and members of the *confrèries* progressed down the *quais* of Paris, costumed as the various emblems and allegories they represented. A series of drawings illustrated the occasion: behind three Knights of the Holy Spirit, an order founded by Henri in 1579, come Mary Magdalen with her alabaster pot and Mary of Egypt, carrying her three loaves, followed by penitent women. In another part of the procession, again behind Knights of the Holy Spirit, come the three Marys with their jars of ointment and the angels, followed by the Wise Virgins with lighted lamps, the whole representing the theme of 'Les bonnes oeuvres des femmes pénitentes'. Such manifestations of his devotion were much disapproved of, and drew accusations of hypocrisy from the Catholic League. In 1585 war broke out; Henri was driven out of Paris and, in 1589, assassinated.[156]

In 1622 Louis XIII overcame the Calvinists of Languedoc, and ended the war with the siege of Montpellier. He went to St Maximin to give thanks for the Magdalen's intercession. Five years later, he dealt the last blow against Calvinism in France at La Rochelle where on 22 July, Mary Magdalen's feast-day, his forces defeated the English army under the duke of Buckingham which had come to the heretics' assistance. As François I had done before him, Louis gave thanks at the grotto of Ste Baume, celebrating Mary Magdalen as the 'apostle to the apostles' and as protectress of the Catholic faith.[157] A painting by Blé Ronjoi in the cathedral at Beauvais, dated 1637, of Mary Magdalen at the foot of the cross flanked by the figures of Louis XIII and his father Henri IV also stresses her importance in the eyes of the French kings. This was to bear fruit the following year when Louis' queen, Anne of Austria, gave birth to a dauphin, after several childless years. Fearful that the crown might fall into the hands of another branch of the family, Anne and her mother-in-law Marie de Médicis, unable to go in person to St Maximin and Ste Baume, had begged the king for a relic which they could pray before in their private oratory. Despite the fact that an earlier request on behalf of Pope Urban VIII for a portion of Mary Magdalen's bones had fallen on deaf ears, and that a second request with letters patent had met with a physical attack on the civic officers charged with the undertaking,

Veüe au naturel de la Saincte Baume en Prouence.

67 *Veüe au naturel de la Saincte Baume en Provence.* Israel Sylvestre. Late seventeenth century.

Louis wrote again to the convent at St Maximin. This time his orders were complied with: a bone from one of the Magdalen's hands, together with four hairs, were sent to the queen, whilst a finger was conveyed to the pope.[158] In thanksgiving for the birth of an heir in 1638, Anne of Austria resolved to rebuild the convent of Val-de-Grâce, work on which was begun in 1645, and to commemorate the saint's intercession, the queen commissioned the royal painter Philippe de Champaigne to execute a series of paintings of the *Miracles of the Penitent Magdalen.* (His painting of Mary Magdalen in her grotto [Rennes, Musée des Beaux-Arts] was one of the more austere images of the saint in her grotto of the period, reflecting his Jansenist beliefs.)[159]

Not surprisingly, literary effusions concerning the penitent in her grotto continued to be written unabated, spurred on by pilgrimages to the Provençal cave. Antoine Godeau, bishop of Vence, wrote of 'cette grande sainte dans la Fontaine des Larmes d'une sincere, & amoureux pénitence' in his 'Ste Madeleine dans son rocher vulgairement appellé La Sainte Baume', while J. Balin's 'Poème héroique de Saincte Magdelaine' described the saint's odyssey – 'sa vie, sa navigation en Provence, & le lieu de sa pénitence' – in manner truly Homeric.[160] Although the representation of the cave had largely been a product of the artistic imagination, from the sixteenth century, and particularly in northern art, knowledge of its precise geographical location became widespread.[161] In an altarpiece of the Magdalen (Brussels, Musée des Beaux-

Arts), by the Master of 1518 and probably from the abbey of Dilighem, Mary Magdalen floats in ecstasy above a fairly accurately delineated portion of Les Baux of Provence, and in Israel Sylvestre's late seventeenth-century etching, she whirrs away, assisted by two angels, above her cave in a landscape to which, whilst generally resembling that of Ste Baume, a touch of artistic licence is added (see Plate 67).[162]

At St Maximin, the relics of Mary Magdalen rest in a porphyry urn, on top of which lies Alessandro Algardi's beautiful gilt-bronze figure (see Plate 68). In 1632 the general of the Dominican order had been shocked to find the copper urn containing the saint's body in a mean wooden casket, while her head, hair, one of her arms, and the relics of many other saints were kept carefully locked away. On his return to Rome, he commissioned a new reliquary which was blessed by Urban VIII on the saint's feast-day in 1634. Urban, who had written a sonnet to Mary

68 *Mary Magdalen in Ecstasy* (c. 1634). Alessandro Algardi. St Maximin, basilica.

Magdalen, further showed his affection for her by asking for the old wooden casket which had originally contained the remains. These were sent to him by ship. Louis XIII gave his permission for the translation of the relics on 10 July 1635, but the event did not take place until 1660, when it was presided over by his son, Louis XIV.[163] Algardi's *Mary Magdalen* reclines, protecting the remains believed to be hers, ecstatic and sensuous, the embodiment of Counter-Reformation piety.

CHAPTER VIII

VANITAS

Fallax gratia et vana est pulchritudo
Mulier timens dominum ipsa laudabitur.

Favour is deceitful, and beauty is vain:
but a woman that feareth the Lord, she
shall be praised.

Proverbs 31:30[1]

THE 'PENITENT IN HER GROTTO', emblematic of all human frailty, particularly that of her own sex, during the late seventeenth and eighteenth centuries became the very thing her image had been set up to do away with, a *vanitas*. She reappeared in a new genre of painting, the 'saintly' portrait, known primarily in England and France, created by and for courtly circles. Indeed, from this period, her image and significance became entirely secularised, adhering, firstly, to the tastes of monarchs, princelings and minor aristocrats and, secondly, to the context of the establishment in mid-eighteenth-century England of reformatories for women called 'Magdalen-houses'. In the 'saintly' portraits, her penitential guise now adorned the flesh of kings' mistresses, duchesses, other aristocrats, and the 'lighter ladies' of the court, as well as artists' wives, mistresses and daughters. Few of these sitters were penitents, and for the Restoration court of Charles II particularly, the saint's image was adopted merely as an irreverent joke or as yet another fancy dress, alongside the shepherdesses, goddesses, virtues and other allegorical figures as whom these predominantly upper-class women chose to have themselves portrayed. The paintings of Mary Magdalen by Guido Reni, Annibale Carracci and Orazio Gentileschi, in turn based on prototypes by Correggio and Titian, provided the basic formulae for many of the 'saintly' portraits of the seventeenth and eighteenth centuries.[2] From the mid-seventeenth century, Italian art, once the purlieu of Catholic patronage, both ecclesiastical and lay, became much sought after by monarchs and aristocrats in Protestant northern Europe, and the image of the penitent Mary Magdalen accordingly began to make its mark in a secular context. Paintings of her, semi-naked in her repentance, joined the canvases of other nude and semi-nude females which carried such biblical, mythological, historical and allegorical titles as 'Susanna and the Elders', 'Judith', 'Bathsheba', 'Minerva', 'Danaë', 'Cleopatra' and 'Lucretia', commissioned and bought to decorate palaces, stately homes and *boudoirs*.[3] Italian art, and particularly paintings of female nudes, was especially popular among the rich German princelings: two *Mary Magdalens* found their way into one such collection. One, Correggio's small figure reading in her grotto, painted on copper, known for two hundred years through countless copies and variations, was rediscovered in Dresden in the mid-eighteenth century, to *grand éclat*, and became one of the most famous paintings of the time, celebrated by such Romantic aesthetes as the playwright Schiller and the critic Friedrich von Schlegel, and men of letters and sensibility like Horace Walpole (see Plate 72).

This of course was not the first time women had been painted as Mary Magdalen: in the late fifteenth and early sixteenth centuries, artists such as the Fleming Jan Gossaert had depicted noble women in this guise, as in the portrait believed to be of Isabella of Portugal (1503–39), wife of the Holy Roman emperor, Charles V, and that of Louise de Brabant.[4] Piero di Cosimo painted an unknown sitter as Mary Magdalen (c. 1510, Rome, Galleria Nazionale di Palazzo Barberini), as did Domenico Puligo (1525, Florence, Palazzo Pitti) and Il Poppi (c. 1580, Florence, private collection), the latter two coldly erotic Mannerist images rather than saintly portraits.[5] At least three women whose names were Mary Magdalen were depicted as, or with, their name saint: in Hugo van der Goes' 1475–6 Portinari triptych, Mary Magdalen stands behind Maria Maddalena Baroncelli, wife of the donor Tommaso Portinari;[6] Lucas Cranach painted Magdalena Reidinger thus[7] and, between 1625 and 1630, Justus Sustermans, court painter to Cosimo II de' Medici, painted a portrait of the Archduchess Maria Magdalena of Austria, grand duchess of Tuscany and Cosimo's widow, as the prayerful-Magdalen, Hapsburgian in her mien (see Plate 69).[8] Maria Magdalena's fondness for the saint with whom she shared her name led her in 1625 to commission

frescoes of Mary Magdalen's life in the chapel of the Medici villa at
Poggio Imperiale.[9] In the first of his two collections of *Arie musicali* of
1630, dedicated to the archduchess's son, Grand Duke Ferdinand II,
the composer Girolamo Frescobaldi included a setting of a sonnet, 'La
Maddalena alla Croce', for soprano voice, which may have been
intended as a compliment to his patron's widowed mother whose piety
was renowned.[10]

Of the four mistresses of Charles II who had themselves depicted as
Mary Magdalen, for Barbara Villiers (1641–1709), duchess of Cleveland, it was yet another pose in which she could appear. She had been
painted as her namesake, St Barbara, playfully holding the symbolic

69 *Archduchess Maria Magdalena of
Austria, Grand Duchess of Tuscany,
as Mary Magdalen* (1625–30).
Justus Sustermans. Florence,
Palazzo Pitti, Galleria Palatina.

tower of chastity in her left hand, and as St Catherine of Alexandria. Lely's portrait depicting her, with her son, as the Virgin and Child, was particularly audacious. In 1662–3, Peter Lely (1618–82), principal painter to Charles II from 1661, portrayed the notorious duchess as the penitent Magdalen in a painting which is known from the copy attributed to Remigius van Leemput in the Royal collection. Lely also painted Nell Gwynn as the saint, and he was to portray yet another of Charles's mistresses, Louise de Kéroualle, duchess of Portsmouth (1649–1734), as the penitent reclining in her grotto: la Kéroualle lies in a tranquil landscape setting, naked to the waist, draped in a deep blue cloak, her hair trailing over her shoulder, and tendrils, as in Titian's *Penitent Magdalen*, curling around her breasts, proudly thrust up at the spectator, symbols of truth transformed into the sensuous forms of the *vanitas* (see Plate 70). No Magdalen this, nor penitent either, as the sitter gazes coolly out of the picture, inviting the viewer's scrutiny.[11]

Godfrey Kneller (1646/9–1723), Lely's successor as principal painter to Charles II, also painted several court beauties as Mary Magdalen, including Henrietta, duchess of Marlborough, Martha Blount, Lady

70 *Louise de Kéroualle, Duchess of Portsmouth, as Mary Magdalen* (c.1670). Sir Peter Lely.

71 *Miss Catherine Voss as Mary Magdalen*. Mezzotint after Sir Godfrey Kneller. 1705.

Wyndham and Elizabeth Villiers, countess of Orkney. Around 1705, he painted his own illegitimate daughter Catherine Voss as Mary Magdalen, a painting which was issued as a mezzotint by John Raphael Smith, a conventionally demure and pious image, whose contemporary dress belies the judgement of the compiler of the Kneller catalogue, 'She may have been the model, but there is no reason to suppose that [this is] not primarily [an image] of the saint.'[12] (See Plate 71.) Kneller's only serious rival, the Swedish painter Michael Dahl (1656/9–1743), portrayed Lady Anne Sussex (*c.*1707) in the pose of the repentant Magdalen, her hair flowing, head resting on one hand, the other placed on an open Bible. The artist's soft and warm style produced in his earlier *Magdalen* (*c.*1695) – bare-breasted, a blue-grey cloak draped around her, reading her book – an image of a sleepily voluptuous woman rather than a penitent.[13]

Across the Channel in Catholic France, it also became the vogue to be painted *à la Madeleine* in courtly circles. Pierre Mignard (1612–95), the leading French portraitist of his day, painted several of Louis XIV's mistresses in this way. In Rome from 1636–57, he had formed his style by studying the Carracci, Domenichino and Poussin. His painting of Hortense Mancini, duchesse de Mazarin, and mistress of Charles II, derives from Reni's seated *Magdalen*.[14] He also painted Louise de la Vallière as Mary Magdalen, the only one of Louis XIV's mistresses to have taken her paradigm to heart, and truly repented of her past life. Born Françoise-Louise de la Balme le Blanc in 1644, she became one of the king's mistresses at the age of seventeen, and soon his *maîtresse en titre*, bearing him four children. She was later ennobled as *duchesse*. In 1668, she was ousted from the king's affections by Mme de Montespan who, it seems, had had designs upon the king for some time; the two mistresses were given adjoining rooms, and lived in this *ménage à trois* for several years. In February 1671 la Vallière fled from the court to the convent at Chaillot, only to return within twelve hours at the king's request. Recovering in May from a grave illness, she turned her mind to religion, and wrote her *Réflexions sur la Miséricorde de Dieu*, the third of these *pensées* having as a title, 'Sur les vertus necessaires pour s'approcher de Jésus-Christ, à l'exemple de la Cananée, de la Samaritaine, et de Madelaine'. That she modelled herself on Mary Magdalen is palpable from a sentence a few pages on: 'Surtout regardez-moi sans cesse comme Madelaine, et faîtes que, comme cette sainte Pénitente, j'arrose vos pieds de mes larmes, et qu'en tâchant de vous aimer beaucoup, j'essaie d'éffacer la multitude de mes crimes.'[15] (Above all, look upon me ceaselessly as Magdalen, and only allow me, like that holy Penitent, to wash your feet with my tears and, in seeking to love you greatly, to try to wipe away the multitude of my crimes.) Torn between her love for Louis and her yearnings for the religious life, she lived austerely, eating little, wearing a hairshirt, and sleeping on the floor, until 1674, when she asked the king's permission to retire to the Carmelite convent in the rue St Jacques, taking the name Sister Louise de la Miséricorde; there she died in 1710. Sometime before her departure, she was painted by Mignard as Mary Magdalen, seated in her grotto, head propped on her right hand, with the saint's attributes of book and ointment jar, fully clad, and somewhat pensive.[16] A string of the Sun King's usurped mistresses followed La Vallière's example in having themselves painted *à la Madeleine*: Béatrice de Cusance, Isabelle de Ludre, Mlle de Fontanges, and even Mme de Montespan herself.[17] As Françoise Athénaïs de Mortemart (1641–1707), La Vallière's successor came from a great family, was beautiful, cultivated and extravagant, and exerted enormous influence over Louis, but resorted to love potions, spells and black masses when her powers began to fail. In 1691 she left the court, and devoted herself to good works and a pious life. Her youngest sister, Gabrielle de Rochechouart de Mortemart, whom she had asked Louis to appoint abbess of Fontevrault, was painted (c. 1675) reclining à la Madeleine in her grotto with her Bible, in her religious habit, a suitable pose for the abbess of an institution one of whose patrons was Mary Magdalen. Isabelle ('Belle') de Ludre, who supplanted Béatrice de Cusance, who apparently died of sorrow, was shown seated three-quarter length, bare-breasted, but otherwise draped in blue, her hand on an enamel vase, and her eyes swivelled heavenward. A penitent whose end was illustrious, Isabelle became 'chanoinesse de Poussey', a chapter of noble women, as the inscription which runs along the top of the painting indicates.[18]

The fashion for being painted as Mary Magdalen continued in France during the 1740s and 1750s when Rococo artists like Jean-Marc Nattier, who painted Louis XV's favourite, Mme de Mailly, in this way, depicted other courtly ladies thus, but the vogue became rare.[19] In England, Thomas Hudson painted his wife Mary Richardson à la Madeleine (c. 1727–9) and, possibly, also the duchess of Marlborough.[20]

Of the works by artists who painted wives or mistresses as Mary Magdalen, Simon Vouet's portrait of his wife, the painter Virginia del Vesto, stands out for its dramatic pose.[21] George Romney's portrait (c. 1792) of his own and Nelson's former mistress, Lady Emma Hamilton, as the penitent saint, soulfully gazing up to heaven, in a grey muslin dress, her head propped up on her right arm, an hour-glass and book by her side, is yet another artistic pose to strike, along with the shepherdesses, Venuses and various virtues Emma assumed.[22] Perhaps the oddest 'repentant Magdalen' image is Robert Walker's 1648 painting of John Evelyn, the seventeenth-century English diarist, who, in a witty parody, seems to have had himself depicted as the penitent. In an otherwise conventional image, in the typically English allegorical and Melancholic vein, and close in style to the Lothian portrait of John Donne, Evelyn sits, his head resting on his right arm, hand placed on a skull, a black satin cloak thrown carelessly over his undone chemise. Above his head are words in Greek which translated read, 'Repentance is the beginning of wisdom'. The words on the piece of paper under the skull, the *memento mori*, come from a letter, *Epistle XXX*, written by Seneca to

72 *Mary Magdalen reading in a Landscape* (*c*.1522). Correggio. Dresden, Gemäldegalerie, formerly.

Lucilius, and have been deciphered to mean, 'but when death comes to meet him, no one welcomes it cheerfully except the man who has long since composed himself in death'. The portrait was sent together with a treatise on the ethics of marriage to Evelyn's new bride, Mary Browne, daughter of the British ambassador to Paris, whom he had married the previous year, but left with her parents because of her extreme youth. (She was apparently as young as eleven.)[23] One wonders how a bride of such tender years might have responded to this example of seventeenth-century wit.

Although the vogue for saintly portraits in general declined in the eighteenth century, the taste for images of Mary Magdalen did not. Indeed at probably no other time was one painting of her in particular, Correggio's Dresden *Magdalen reading in a Landscape*, quite so famous, or more commented, or waxed lyrical, upon (see Plate 72). It had been the prototype for paintings of the saint by the Bolognese artists, Guido Reni and Annibale Carracci, and Orazio Gentileschi, who had compiled the iconographical vocabularies later used by northern painters such as Lely,

Kneller, Le Brun and Mignard, the last three of whom all went to
Italy during the earlier part of their careers. Correggio's one image had
spawned a host of variations.

Italian art had become much sought after outside Italy by the mid-
seventeenth century. In England, Charles I was an avid collector, as
were the first duke of Buckingham and the earl of Arundel, the second
of whom was described as '[leaving] no stone unturned in his efforts to
strip Italy of her precious treasures'.[24] In France, Cardinal Richelieu,
minister of Marie de Médicis, sent agents scouring for Italian art; his
successor Mazarin, an Italian, an even greater *amateur*, brought Italian
painters and paintings back to France. In 1625, one of Orazio Gentileschi's *Mary Magdalen*s had been bought from the artist by George
Villiers, duke of Buckingham (1592–1628), on a trip to Paris; Gentileschi
himself was brought to England by Charles I the following year where
he became court painter, and painted another version for the king (see
Plate 73).[25] Mary Magdalen's reclining pose formed, as we have seen,
yet another prototype, ultimately derived from Correggio, for English
painters to exploit in their saintly portraits. (Gentileschi's first Magdalen

73 *The Penitent Magdalen* (c. 1625–8). Orazio Gentileschi. New York, Richard L. Feigen
collection.

painting, of *c.*1621, for Giovan Antonio Sauli, had been commissioned together with paintings of *Danaë* and *Lot and his Daughters*, those subjects much favoured by collectors.[26]) Buckingham's *Mary Magdalen*, together with its pendant *The Rest on the Flight into Egypt*, was sold to the Archduke Leopold Wilhelm by his son, the second duke who, in exile, was forced to part with the collection he had inherited; the paintings were sent to the castle at Prague, and thence to Vienna where they still are.[27]

Much Italian art made its way north of the Alps, accommodating the particular predilection for sixteenth- and early seventeenth-century paintings of female nudes manifested by many northern princelings, which Italian artists hastened to supply. Artistic discrimination does not seem to have entered the considerations of such collectors, judging by one letter:

> *Une Souzanne et la Pudiphar seroit assez à mon gout; quant à la nudité je ne m'en scandalise pas trop dans les peintures, pourvue quelles ne soit obscène, et qu'il n'y ayet pas des actions ou gesticulations infames, et comme j'ay observé que le plus fort de Strudel consiste in dem nakenden, allso muss man ihn davon nich abhallten outre qu'un beau corps et visage de femme orne bien un tableau.*[28]

(A Susanna or Potiphar's wife would please me well enough; with regard to nudity, I am not too shocked by it in paintings provided that they are not obscene, and there are not too many scandalous movements or gesticulations and, as I have noticed that Strudel's strong point consists in nakedness, one must not deny, besides, that a beautiful body and face of a woman embellish a picture well.)

Some painters were summoned north: Guido Cagnacci (1601–63), who worked in Reni's workshop, went to Vienna in *c.*1657 to work for the Emperor Leopold, providing his patron with sensuous and sinuous nudes ostensibly as allegorical conceits. His *Mary Magdalen carried to Heaven by an Angel* (Munich, Alte Pinakothek) of *c.*1640 is typical of his semi-pornographic female figures, her ecstasy rendered earthly rather than spiritual through the artist's attention to her physical attributes. The painting was engraved in the eighteenth century (see Plate 74).[29]

However, it was Correggio's curvaceous figure which was to provoke such ecstasy in the eighteenth century. By 1745–6, it too had made its

74 *Mary Magdalen carried to Heaven by an Angel.* Eighteenth-century engraving after Guido Cagnacci.

way north, to Dresden. The painting was identified as probably that mentioned by Filippo Baldinucci as having been in the collection of 'il Cavaliere Gaddi' in the time of Grand Duke Francesco de' Medici (1541–87); it was in the Este collection at Modena in 1682 and was included in the assortment of 100 pictures sold in 1745–6 by Francesco III d'Este to Augustus III, elector of Saxony and king of Poland.[30] It had been widely copied and adapted by painters both adequate and mediocre before its departure from Italy, and copies were made of copies, particularly by painters catering to erotico-pornographic markets. On its rediscovery in 1746, it was the Dresden *Magdalen* which above all 'struck an ecstatic chord in the man of feeling of the eighteenth century. [Its] combination of sentimental religiosity and sensuality proved irresistible and gave rise to extraordinary panegyrics.'[31] Commenting upon another painting entirely – *The Chastity of Joseph* by Deshays – Denis Diderot wrote to Baron Grimm of the figure of Potiphar's wife, 'I have never seen so voluptuous a figure, not even Correggio's Mary Magdalen in Dresden, whose print you keep with such care for the mortification of your senses';[32] in 1767, Diderot argued that it was possible to paint beautiful compositions on themes of the lives of saints and martyrdom, quoting as an example Correggio's 'Magdalen . . . so voluptuously stretched out on the ground in her cave'.[33] The painter Anton Raphael Mengs (1728–79), whose father, a court painter at Dresden, had had him named after both Correggio (Antonio) and Raphael, wrote ecstatically: 'This sole image contains all the beauty which can be imagined in painting'; his own two paintings of Mary Magdalen (1752 and 1772–3) show their debt to Correggio.[34]

Correggio's *Mary Magdalen* became even more widely known through Pompeo Batoni's version, painted in *c*.1742 for the Merenda family of Forlì, which by 1754 had also found its way into Augustus III's collection, and seems to have suffered the same fate as Correggio's painting in 1945 (see Plate 75).[35] Batoni, who may never have seen the original, secularised further Correggio's image by bringing his figure closer to the spectator, and making her rest on both elbows, her hands clasped loosely together, exposing one breast, while she looks down to her left at her Bible whose distanced position emphasises the divorce from pious depiction, and stresses instead the sensuousness of his saint, her *dégagée* appearance due to the slipped-off shoulder of her chemise. Batoni's *Magdalen*, his most popular painting outside Italy – even put on a par with Raphael's Sistine *Madonna* by A. W. von Schlegel – was also widely copied and engraved until the nineteenth century, and is another essay in eroticism in the guise of sanctity. In fact, a detail comprising the Magdalen's head and the upper part of her torso was copied onto the oval-shaped china plaques of painted erotica manufactured by a Berlin company in the late nineteenth century. Such objects, including Batoni's *Magdalen*, are apparently still much sought after, particularly by Japanese collectors, in the late twentieth century.[36]

The pose of Correggio's *Magdalen* was so engraved on the minds of eighteenth-century men of *sensibilité* that one of them, Horace Walpole, describing a performance by adults and children of Nicholas Rowe's play *Jane Shore* at Holland House, wrote to his friend George Montague, 'I was infinitely more struck with the last scene between the two women than ever I was when I have seen it on the stage. When Lady Sarah [Lennox] was in white with her hair about her ears and on the ground, no Magdalen by Correggio was half so lovely or expressive.'[37] Walpole would also, no doubt, have enjoyed the Magdalenkapelle (1725–8) built for the Bavarian elector Max Emanuel to ornament his park at the castle

75 *The Penitent Magdalen reading in her Grotto.* Nineteenth-century chromolithograph after Pompeo Batoni's painting of *c*.1742.

of Nymphenburg. Here, in a mock-ruined chapel, Mary Magdalen repents prettily in elegant seclusion, in a grotto of rock and shell-work, a hermitage where aristocrats might play at retiring from the world – in the way they also disported themselves as peasants – and a precursor of the taste for Gothick and the Picturesque which Walpole himself was to champion in England.[38]

Walpole's is the first description we have of an institution founded in London in 1758 which had as its patron Mary Magdalen and was given the name of the 'Magdalen-house'. His account of a visit made there, as one of his 'entertainments', was given in another letter to Montague of 1760, when it seems he was one of an aristocratic party which travelled in four coaches to see for themselves the home for repentant prostitutes. Walpole was an acquaintance of Jonas Hanway (1712–86), a philanthropist, friend of Joshua Reynolds, and one of a group of London merchants who had formed a committee to set up a charitable institution or reformatory for the benefit of these 'fallen' women. Hanway was otherwise renowned for being the first man in London to sport an umbrella, a habit which brought him both ridicule and threats against his person from sedan-chair carriers and cabbies who saw their livelihoods at risk. His pity for the plight of the prostitute is eloquently expressed in his introduction to the rulebook for the newly established Magdalen-house in London:

> There cannot be greater Objects of Compassion, than poor, young thoughtless Females, plunged into ruin by those Temptations to which their very youth, and personal advantages expose them, no less than those passions implanted by Nature for wise, good, and great ends; surrounded by snares, the most artfully and industriously laid; snares laid by those endowed with superior faculties and all the advantages of Education, and Fortune; what virtue can be proof against such formidable Seducers, who offer too commonly, and too profusely promise, to transport the thoughtless Girls, from Want, Confinement, and Restraint of Passions, to Luxury, Liberty, Gaiety, Joy? and once seduced, how soon their golden dreams vanish! abandoned by the Seducer, deserted by Friends, contemned by the World, they are left to struggle with Want, Despair, and Scorn, and even in their own defence to plunge deeper and deeper in sin, till Disease and Death conclude a human Being.[39]

Hanway was aware that charitable institutions had been set up in London for other such poverty-stricken sections of society as orphans and widows, and that the prostitute had been overlooked: 'Unfortunate Females seem the only Objects that have not yet catched the attention of public benevolence.' He had also heard of the institutions which had been set up for such women on the Continent, including the earliest convents dedicated to Mary Magdalen, and it was considerations like these, he wrote, which 'induced a set of Gentlemen to enter into a private Subscription, making themselves at the same time accountable for such Benefactions as should flow from the Public'.[40] A letter suggesting that a home for repentant prostitutes be set up had appeared in the *Rambler* in March 1751, followed a month later by another in the *Gentleman's Magazine*. Short stories and a novel, *The Sisters* (1754) by William Dodd, on the subject kept it in the public eye, until Robert Dingley, a London silk merchant, and author of the *Rambler* letter, having collected over £3,500 in subscriptions, together with Hanway and other members of the committee, set up the Magdalen-house.[41]

In his *Thoughts on the Plan for a Magdalen-House for Repentant Prostitutes* of 1759, however, Hanway cavilled at the plan put forward to adopt Mary Magdalen as patroness of the institution on the basis of her reputed fallenness:

> First, give me leave to take notice of the name of your charity. It does not appear to me that Mary Magdalen was deficient in point of chastity, as is vulgarly understood. I rather imagine she was not. It is certain she was a lady of distinction, and of a great and noble mind. Her gratitude for the miraculous cure performed upon her, was so remarkable, that her story is related with the greatest honor, and she will ever stand fair in the records of fame.[42]

In her true character, however, he considered her a perfect model for the reformatory: 'Your charity requires a zeal like hers: you are her *disciples*, and the dedication of your institution to her *memory*, is entirely consistent with the honor due to her *character*; and in this light, no name more proper could be given it.' He further noted that although St Luke's Hospital had been founded to house madmen, 'that would not occasion our posterity to consider this Evangelist as a madman'.[43]

The first premises of the 'new convent' which Walpole and his friends visited were 'beyond Goodman's Fields', in premises vacated by the London Hospital in Whitechapel, and were such, as Walpole wrote, 'I assure you, would content any Catholic alive!' The quaintness of it all much appealed to him: 'we were received by – oh! first a vast mob, for princes are not so common at that end of town as this . . .'. It was his little joke to write of the inmates as 'the sisterhood', of whom he saw 'above an hundred and thirty' enclosed at the west end of the church. They were clad in the uniforms given them on entering, 'all in greyish brown stuffs, broad handkerchiefs, and flat straw hats, with a blue ribband, pulled quite over their faces . . .'. To the accompaniment of an organ, he wrote, 'the Magdalens sung a hymn in parts; you cannot imagine how well . . . and there wanted nothing but a little incense to drive away the devil – or to invite him!'[44] The *Second Collection of Psalms and Hymns Used at the Magdalen Chapel* shows such eminent personages as Dryden to have written hymns, and Dr Thomas Arne, the leading English composer of his day, to have written the 'Musick', set for 'Organ, Harpsichord, Voice, Violin, German Flute and Guittar'.

Prayers, similar in theme to the one produced for the repentant prostitutes of Venice, stress the former carnality of the inhabitants, beseeching
the Lord to 'renew in us whatsoever hath been decayed by the fraud
and malice of the Devil, or by our carnal Will and Frailness. Preserve us,
after escaping the Pollutions of the World, from being again entangled
therein; and keep us in a State of constant Watchfulness and Humility.'[45]

The print of a 'Magdalen in her Uniform', which serves as the frontispiece to the hymn collection, shows her standing with her music sheet
outside the palisaded precinct of the penitents' home (see Plate 76). The
buildings were described as 'formed out of several contiguous messuages
or tenements, with a wall and small area before it: and to prevent the
prying curiosity of the public, there is not only a close gate and a porter,
but the windows next the street are concealed by wooden blinds sloping
from the bottom of each, so as to admit light only at the top'.[46] Here,
some of the girls, and again Walpole is our informant, 'were handsome,

A MAGDALEN in her UNIFORM.

76 *A Magdalen in her Uniform*
(*c.*1760). Etching.

many . . . seemed to have no title to their profession, and [there were] two or three of twelve years old; but all recovered, and looking healthy'; he seems to have been surprised to find one inmate the niece of an acquaintance: 'one of these is a niece of Sir Clement Cotterel!'[47] In his Anniversary Sermon of 1759, Mr Dodd, now chaplain to the Magdalen-house, who ended his life at Tyburn for fraud, also reflected on the extreme youth of some of the hospital's inhabitants: 'Out of an hundred girls now in the Magdalen-house, above a seventh part have not seen their fifteenth year; several are under fourteen; and one third of the whole have been betrayed before that age.'[48]

A year after its foundation, the charity noted that the number of prostitutes reported to have applied to date had been 344. It was soon necessary to remove to larger premises, purpose-built at St George's Fields, the foundations of which lie under the Peabody Buildings in Blackfriars Road. Here, Dodd's sermons, maudlin and mawkish, drew, as intended, congregations in their droves to see the magdalens in their home, to dispense of their charity towards these poor unfortunates. Services were attended by the fashionable, the *bon ton*, like Walpole, while the inmates remained discreetly behind a latticed grid in the west end of the church. So affecting were Dodd's sermons that, according to Walpole, when he 'apostrophised the lost sheep, [they] sobbed and cried from their very souls – so did my Lady Hertford and Fanny Pelham, til I believe the City dames took them both for Jane Shores'.[49]

Intended as a halfway house for those driven to seek asylum through penitence rather than penury – and excluding those who might be infected with venereal diseases – the Magdalen-house gave its inmates a harsh regime of moral education, and feminine employment such as making and mending linen, lace, artificial flowers, millinery, children's toys and gloves and weaving hair for wigs to earn their keep until, at the end of their time, they were sent off to suitable situations as domestics, or as seamstresses. Those who were able to read could choose from such titles of improving literature as Hanway's own *Instruction for the Conduct of Women* and *Virtue in the Humble Life*, Bishop Wilson's *Knowledge and Practice of Christianity – An Essay towards the Instruction for the Indians*, and the anonymous *Exhortation to Chastity*.[50]

Some idea, albeit fanciful, of the kinds of young women who were lodged at the Magdalen-house can be gleaned from Edward Jerningham's *The Magdalens: an Elegy*. A friend of Walpole, Jerningham (1727–1812) seems to have had a curious interest in the cloistered woman as evinced by two further literary pieces, *The Nunnery* and another elegy, *The Nun*. He dedicated *The Magdalens* to Lady Mary Lepel, Baroness Dowager Hervey of Ickworth (1700–68), a wit and beauty, whose praises had been sung by Pope and Gay, and who was another of Walpole's large number of correspondents.

> Lo! kneeling at yon Rail with pensive air.
> A num'rous Train of suppliant Nymphs I spy:
> Their youthful Cheek is pal'd with early Care,
> and sorrow dwells in their dejected Eye.
>
> Are These the Fair who wont with conscious Grace
> Proud Ranelagh's resplendent Round to tread?
> Shine in the studied Luxury of Dress?
> and vie in Beauty with the high-born Maid? . . . .
>
> For sober needs they change their bright Attire,
> Of the Pearl Bracelet strip the graceful Arm,
> Veil the white Breast that lately heav'd Desire,
> and thrilled with tender exquisite Alarm.[51]

The Magdalen-house also served as a refuge for countless fictional characters which appeared in the stream of short stories, novels and articles concerned with the plight of the prodigal daughter, written to tug at the heart-strings of potential benefactors, some claiming to have been written by repentant prostitutes such as *The Histories of some Penitents in the Magdalen-house, as supposed to be related by themselves* (1760), *The Magdalen, or Dying Penitent, exemplified in the Death of F.S.* (1759), and Hugh Kelly's *Memoirs of a Magdalen* (1767). In most of these, the heroine, of a genteel background, is the victim of some vile seducer, and very different from the creature of city backstreets. She has fallen, like Sir Clement Cottril's niece, and 'F.S.', the daughter of a general in the army, through 'various stratagems', poverty, or 'still oftener vanity'. In *F.S.*, a typical story of seduction, the heroine had had 'a genteel and liberal education', but was reduced to great poverty by various circumstances, and had been taken advantage of by someone she had known in her more prosperous days. Believing some false promises, she had been 'directed into criminal intimacy with him', borne his child, and then been deserted. Her mother had not been able to afford to look after her.

F.S.'s next move was to go upon the stage – in the little theatre in the Haymarket. Her genteel person, good voice and lively genius made it a suitable employment for her. She then joined some strolling players, but left as she had not found the life congenial. Her next employment, as a seamstress, proved to be a failure, and she irrevocably 'went upon the town and turned prostitute'. Her repentance was almost immediate; 'many tears flowed from her eyes' and she resolved to take shelter in the Magdalen-house, but 'something' made her leave after three months, although its exact nature the writer of the missive did not disclose. She then became a haymaker near Canterbury; when harvesting was over, she went to a tradesman's house where she caught a violent cold which ended in consumption 'which in about four months brought her to her grave'. Reduced to beggary, she was found weeping at prayers at the cathedral, and offered food every day at his house by a kind clergyman. Knowing she was dying, she returned to London, where she found shabby lodgings, and lying in her sickbed, sent for her mother. After a tearful reunion, she returned home. On her deathbed, she praised and blessed God. As she drew her last breaths, her mother heard her whisper, 'Holy, holy, holy, Lord god of Sabaoth, into thy hands I commend my spirit.' She then fetched a short sigh or two, and died without the least sign of pain.[52]

Mary Magdalen became protectress of repentant lower- and middle-class prostitutes in an establishment whose major criterion for their acceptance was true repentance. Here they were offered a framework of middle-class and Christian values, imposed upon them with the aim of making them acceptable once more in the outside world. Similarly their portrayal as sexual victims in much of the polemic and moral literature of the period derived from that middle-class perspective, and thus objectified them. Despite criticism of the seducer, manifest in Hanway, as well as in other publications, the period was *par excellence* one in which the double standard prevailed: male sexual experimentation was licit and normal, and virginity before marriage was required in genteel girls. And although such girls as Laetitia, heroine of the first serial addressed to women (1789), and other literary prodigal daughters, might be reformed and their return welcomed by their parents, society in general did not accept them back into its midst. With younger sons often remaining single and marriage in males tending not to take place before the age of twenty-six, male passions had to have outlets which the growing numbers of prostitutes in the eighteenth century supplied.

Domestic servants were the easy victims of their masters, seduced, abandoned and often pregnant, whose next step was to enter the disease-ridden profession of prostitution. The number of prostitutes swelled during the eighteenth century, due to under-employment and low wages for women. As the radical reformer Francis Place wrote, 'chastity and poverty [were] incompatible'.[53] And in the mid-nineteenth century, because of the perceived threat of disease and decadence to middle-class England from the prostitute, charity – once again in the name of Mary Magdalen – was to cast its benevolent eye over her.

CHAPTER IX

MAGDALENS

Who can tell the pestiferous influence exercised on society
by the single fallen woman? Who can calculate the evils
of such a system? Woman, waylaid, tempted, deceived,
becomes in turn the terrible avenger of her sex. Armed
with a power which is all but irresistible, and stript of all
which can alone restrain and purify her influence, she steps
upon the arena of life qualified to act her part in the
reorganization of society. The *lex talionis* – law of retaliation
is hers. View it in the dissolution of domestic ties, in the
sacrifice of family peace, in the cold desolation of promising
homes; but above all, in the growth of practical Atheism,
and in the downward trend of all that is pure, and holy in
life.

The Magdalen's Friend and Female Homes' Intelligencer (1861)[1]

The Monthly Address: 'Woman, why weepest thou?' Dear
Reader, you may think this a strange question. But it is
one that concerns you. Consider a moment who uttered
these words, and to whom they were addressed. They were
spoken by Jesus, the son of God, after His resurrection, to
Mary Magdalen, a poor sinner, whom He found weeping
beside His tomb. What He said to her, He says to you,
'Woman, why weepest thou?' Her sins which had been
many, were forgiven, and Jesus, her Saviour, condescends
now to notice and inquire into the cause of her grief. He
whom she had pierced by her sins is now concerned at the
sight of her sorrow. Oh, what boundless compassion, what
love and tenderness, are revealed in these words, 'Why
weepest thou?' And has not Jesus seen you too weeping
over the loss of all that can make you happy and respected?
Are there not moments in your life when you have wept,
as if your heart would break, at the thought of what *you
once were, and of what you are now, and of what you might have
been*? . . . I know that even now, lost as you may be to
every sense of womanly shame and purity, there are times

when you feel *an agony of remorse* at your past life, and when
you look forward with fear and trembling to the future
. . . Will you not, like Mary of old, fall upon your knees
before Him, and seek but to touch the hem of His garment,
that you may be whole? and will you not, like her, learn
to love much, because you have had much forgiven. Will
you not give the last years of your misspent life to Him
who has given Himself for you? . . . hear Him ask,
'Woman, why weepest thou?' and then in the anguish of
your spirit, and the consciousness of your sin, turn to him
and cry, 'Lord, if Thou wilt, Thou canst make me clean.'
But, dear Reader 'what thou doest, do quickly.'

> *The Magdalen's Friend and Female Homes' Intelligencer* (1860)[2]

THE *Magdalen's Friend and Female Homes' Intelligencer*
appeared monthly from 1860 to 1864 and carried on
its cover the words 'edited by a clergyman, and
devoted to the cause of the Fallen'. Like several other
periodicals which appeared in mid-nineteenth century
England in a spirit of Christian philanthropy, it was
concerned with reclaiming the prostitute or 'fallen'
woman. Its title, and the monthly address, show how Mary Magdalen
had once again become inextricably linked to the 'sinning' woman, to
the point where the euphemistic term for the latter, in medical and legal
writings of Victorian England, was now 'magdalen'.[3] (Mary Magdalen
even lent her name to an 'ism' when the survey of prostitution, *Mag-
dalenism: An Inquiry into the Extent, Causes and Consequences of Prostitution*,
by the Evangelical physician William Tait, was published in Edinburgh
in 1840.[4]) The hopeful words 'Thy sins are forgiven!' were emblazoned
across the top of the cover of the journal itself, whose purpose was to
encourage lay rescue-workers in their labours; on one issue there
appeared an image of Luke's sinner in the house of the Pharisee, emphasising the traditional association between Mary Magdalen and the fallen
woman. It contained reports on the activities of workers, edited sermons, and edifying articles with such ringing titles as 'Death-splash
heard from London-Bridge', 'The Outcast', 'The Crushed Daisy', 'The
Recovered Wreck', 'Woman's Weakness Her Chief Danger', 'An
Awfully Sudden Death', all painting an image of the fall, degradation

and, sometimes, suicide of the magdalen, to remind its readers of the fate which all too often befell her.

In nineteenth-century England, Mary Magdalen's name was synonymous with what the Victorian middle classes regarded as the 'Great Social Evil', prostitution. From the mid-eighteenth century, philanthropy had come to look upon the fallen woman as a suffering object of pity; charitable institutions had been set up to reclaim her from the street and from the brothel, the victim of her own weakness or vanity, or of some vile traducer. In the mid-nineteenth century, Mary Magdalen became the representative of the 'single fallen woman' whom Victorian society had come to see as a moral disease which posed a very real threat to its most cherished values – the family, domesticity, and Christian purity. She was the antithesis of the figure which now became central to Victorian domestic ideology, the virtuous wife and mother, borne out of the bourgeois, and masculine, concept of woman, encapsulated once again in the dichotomy between the Madonna and the Magdalen. It was only natural that Mary Magdalen herself should return to her role as paradigm for the repentant fallen woman, but that she should become, perhaps paradoxically, a model for those rescue-workers too, as Joseph Hanway had suggested a century before,[5] and in the process be restored to her gospel character, was attributable to the basically Protestant ethic which recreated the old duality of madonna and magdalen.

The view that sexuality was not repressed during the Victorian period – or at least not in the way that we have hitherto imagined – was demonstrated by Michel Foucault in the opening pages of his *History of Sexuality*. Nineteenth-century sexuality has usually been assumed to have been a covert thing, secreted away in the innermost sanctum – the bourgeois bedroom – or relegated to the brothel or boudoir, the subject of silence and prudery in respectable society. But, in fact, said Foucault, rather than the massive silence which was once ascribed to it, there 'was a regulated and polymorphous incitement to discourse'.[6] From the mid-eighteenth century, sexuality had come under the scrutiny of science as part of the process of categorising, organising, and regulating society. Those mechanisms in charge – state, medicine and law – had annexed what had been the Church's preserve since the Middle Ages, namely the examination of the sexual conscience through the confessional, and had relocated it to the secular sphere, to the realm of 'public interest'. Sexuality became a central focus in the emergence of 'population' as an economic or political problem, and was expanded in the nineteenth century into a subject of enquiry in the areas of demography, medicine, biology, psychiatry and education. This vast gathering of knowledge was a 'carefully analytical discourse . . . meant to yield multiple effects of displacement, intensification, reorientation and modification of desire itself'. Rather than a law of prohibition or censorship of sex, the effect was in fact to establish 'an apparatus for producing an ever greater quantity of discourse about sex, capable of functioning, and taking effect in its very economy'.[7]

Through these interrelated sets of ideas, these mechanisms of power, sexuality itself was analysed, categorised and codified, and thereby controlled, regulated, and above all constructed; criteria were established for what was licit and illicit, normal and deviant, respectable and not respectable in a continuous process of definition and redefinition of sexuality and sexual mores. And although sexuality had been transposed from the purely ecclesiastical sphere of control and influence, its symbiotic relationship with penance, or sin, was never entirely lost: Catholic dogma was simply replaced by the Puritan or Protestant ethic which continued to exert its influence over and to colour the image of madonna and magdalen.

Foucault's argument deals with sexuality in absolute terms, and with the concepts and power mechanisms which he sees as controlling and constructing it. It does not, however, extend to gender, which of course was equally defined, controlled and regulated by those very same mechanisms. Gender established the parameters of womanhood through the re-emerged notions of madonna and magdalen, the two images of femininity which owed their existence to the nineteenth-century 'discourses' on sexuality. A further, brief, examination of the ideology will show how once again Mary Magdalen represented, now in secular terms, the fallen, outcast woman, and the significance of the term 'magdalen' for bourgeois society.

The moral indignation and rhetoric of the first passage quoted at the beginning of this chapter illustrates the view of the respectable Victorian. Prostitution, it seems, had become a contagion which threatened the very fulcrum of middle-class society, the domestic felicity which was ideologically propounded as a microcosm of society and stability, the fount of morality, and stood as a metaphor for social order. What domesticity, or the home, represented to Victorian thinking was expressed most clearly by John Ruskin in a lecture which he delivered at the Town Hall, Manchester, in 1864, which went under the title 'On Queens' Gardens'. He said:

> This is the true nature of home – it is the place of Peace; the shelter, not only from all injury, but from all terror, doubt, and division. In so far as it is not this, it is not home. But so far as it is a sacred place, a vestal temple, a temple of the hearth watched over by Household Gods, before whose faces none may come but those whom they can receive with love, so far as it is this . . . so far it vindicates the name, and fulfils the praise, of Home.[8]

Home was the haven to which the Victorian man repaired from his day's work, to tranquillity and repose away from the hubbub of urban life. From the late eighteenth century onwards, home and work had become two separate spheres as middle-class families increasingly set up their homes away from the business and commerce of the *paterfamilias* which had formerly been part of the establishment, thus creating a clear demarcation between place, and a correspondingly defined separation of roles and functions, based on gender: 'The woman's place was within the Home.' Within the hallowed portals of this 'vestal temple', the man of affairs, eminently, according to Ruskin, 'the doer, creator, the discoverer, and defender', found a 'noble' woman, who was to be 'enduringly, incorruptibly good; instinctively, infallibly wise'. But, added Ruskin, this wisdom was not for her own self-improvement: it was to show her how to put herself aside in the interests of her husband, as his support, and not to seek to be his superior. Invested with quasi-religious imagery, this stereotypically patriarchal view of the Victorian home and woman's role within it as the 'Angel in the House' was not unique to Ruskin. To William Acton, author of several books on prostitution and venereal diseases, the 'perfect ideal of an English wife and mother [was one who was] kind, considerate, self-sacrificing, and sensible, so pure-hearted as to be utterly ignorant of and averse to any sensual indulgence, but so unselfishly attached to the man she loves, as to be willing to give up her own wishes and feelings for his sake'.[9] This virtuous creature, dependent upon her man, but supportive of him too, to whom sexual desire was an unknown quantity according to most male scientific deductions, was the chaste mother to the patriarch's progeny, his heirs and descendants, the madonna in a conscious parody of her prototype, the Virgin Mary. The need for her purity was stressed time and again, even by women writers of the period.[10] It was in this guise that she often appeared in domestic genre scenes, the didactic High art of the Victorian period, painted to confirm and reiterate bourgeois values to the middle-class exhibition-goer and picture-buyer, saccharine images which bore such titles as 'Maternity', to emblazon forth and set upon a pedestal the function assigned to woman by nature, and man. George Henry Lewes, companion of George Eliot, who was neither particularly conventional nor of a religious bent, wrote:

> The grand function of woman, it must always be recollected, is, and ever must be, *Maternity*: and this we regard not only as her distinctive characteristic, and most endearing charm, but as a high and holy office – the prolific source, not only of the best affections and virtues of which our nature is capable, but also of the wisest thoughtfulness, and most useful habits of observation, by which that nature can be elevated and adorned.[11]

It was this icon of middle-class respectability, the pure, loving and self-sacrificial Victorian wife and mother, engenderer and nurturer of the heirs to capitalism, which appeared to its creators to be menaced by the magdalen, whose ever-increasing visibility in the great urban centres of England made her a potential source of both moral and physical contagion. Already in the 1820s the German Prince Pückler-Muskau had noted with shock the ubiquity of prostitutes in England:

> It is most strange that in no country on earth is this afflicting and humiliating spectacle so openly exhibited as in the religious and decorous England. The evil goes to such an extent, that in the theatres it is often difficult to keep off these repulsive beings, especially if they are drunk, which is not seldom the case.[12]

By the mid-century, it seemed to some that morality had vanished, that the very Empire itself was under the sword of Damocles: 'The page of universal history is filled with the rise and fall of empires,' wrote E. W. Thomas, secretary to the London Female Preventive and Reformatory Institution, in 1862. All that had been great, 'the glory of Babylon', 'proud Nineveh', the greatness of Egypt, and the 'glory of the cities of Greece', had been destroyed, through yielding to luxury ('then effeminacy stole upon them gradually and fatally invading all classes . . . till destruction came upon them'), and this was manifested above all in the statistics for the magdalen's trade in London: '40,000 poor unfortunates, 4,000 houses of bad repute'. In the United Kingdom, 250,000 outcast females lived by the wages of iniquity: '8,000,000 [pounds] per annum is spent upon this vice', he continued. Who was to blame but the married man? asked Mr Thomas, in a manner which was not merely rhetorical, but at the same time accepted the double standard as the norm.[13] (He also failed to include the unmarried man in his calculations, a serious omission at a time when late marriages for men were common and when it was expected that young men would sow their wild oats before marriage.)

From 1850 interest in the 'Great Social Evil' had been fanned by the publication of a long article on prostitution by W. R. Greg which appeared in the *Westminster Review*. Here the economic causes of prostitution were stressed forcefully: 'poverty is the chief determining cause which drives women into prostitution in England as in France'. A very different picture of the magdalen from the one commonly conceived of her, as shameless, 'revelling in the *enjoyment* of licentious pleasures . . . wallowing in mire because she loves it', was emphasised. In all but the most exceptional cases, Greg wrote, she suffered from 'cold, hunger, disease, often absolute starvation', and could only operate when ginsodden. She had fallen in some cases through vanity, venality, or through deception; but by far the greater number were victims of circumstances, 'grinding poverty' in towns and cities, 'want of work and low earnings'. Further, society was culpable:

> Forgetting our Master's precepts – forgetting our human frailty – forgetting our own heavy portion in the common guilt – we turn contemptuously aside from the kneeling and weeping Magdalen, coldly bid her to despair, and leave her alone with the irreparable. Instead of helping her up, we thrust her down when endeavouring to rise. Every door is shut upon her . . . She is driven to prostitution by the weight of all society pressing upon her.[14]

Such voices were unfortunately few in number. Fear that her contagion, particularly venereal disease, might spread to respectable society led to the Contagious Diseases Acts of the 1860s, by which any woman deemed to be a 'common prostitute' was registered by the police and made to undergo periodic, and sometimes extremely brutal, medical examinations. (In fact the Acts themselves were designed to protect the physical and moral health of soldiers and sailors at the barracks and ports of England and Ireland, and to ensure their military efficiency; they were yet another manifestation of the 'double standard', in which the prostitute was punished and her equally culpable customer left free to consort with other prostitutes. The outrage which greeted this iniquitous legislation was instrumental in setting in motion the feminist movement in England.)[15] But in the mid-nineteenth century, it was Christian philanthropy, in England, Germany and the United States, which mounted concerted campaigns to rescue the magdalen from her life of moral depravity.

Ruskin's lecture, in its mawkish and sentimental glorification of woman's nature and mission, couched in chivalric terms as he apostrophised her, 'Oh – you queens – you queens!', did no more than endorse the *status quo*. It was a metaphor for maintaining, albeit flatteringly, her subservient position, as queen of her own domain, the home, and sustainer and supporter of her knight, a role which Ruskin saw as being reconcilable with 'true wifely subjection'. While neither sex was superior to the other, they were very different, he agreed, their total dissimilarity rendering them impossible to compare with each other. This very differentness naturally assigned them very different roles: the husband was to be active, his 'duties' public; his spouse, 'the lily' of the title *Sesame & Lilies*, was 'for sweet ordering', her duties private.[16] Yet, Ruskin allowed her to purposefully make a foray into active and public life: carrying his botanical metaphor further, but this time to 'rougher ground among the moorlands and rocks', he finds his magdalen, the euphemistic 'feeble floret', 'far in the darkness of the terrible streets': it is the queen's duty to retrieve, rescue and set a good example to these frail plants, with 'their fresh leaves torn and their stems broken'. 'Will you never go down to them,' he beseeches the 'queen', 'nor set them in order in their fragrant

little beds, nor fence them in their shuddering from the fierce wind?'
Another poetic flight of fantasy which concerns Mary Magdalen herself
occurs at the end of the lecture. Sustaining the garden theme, and no
doubt reminded of her by the reference to the 'feeble florets', he compares to its detriment the garden of the Fall with the garden of Gethsemane where Mary Magdalen had met the risen Christ:

> Did you ever hear, not of a Maud, but a Madeleine, who went
> down into her garden in the dawn, and found One waiting at the
> gate, whom she supposed to be the gardener? Have you not sought
> Him often; – sought Him in vain, all through the night; – sought
> Him in vain at the gate of that old garden where the fiery sword
> is set? He is never there; but at the gate of *this* garden He is waiting
> always – waiting to take your hand . . .[17]

It is perhaps illustrative of his sentimental view of woman's nature as
pure that Ruskin's own visual conception of Mary Magdalen, coloured
by his preference for what he regarded as the purity of medieval and
early Renaissance art, was, as we have seen, a creature similar to Jacopo
della Quercia's chaste cool marble of Ilaria de' Caretto.[18]

When Ruskin, almost as an afterthought, permitted his queen to
extend her domestic role, where care for husband, children, sick and
elderly were paramount, to philanthropic works outside the home – in
this case rescuing the magdalen – he was in fact offering her no more
than what she had been doing for centuries. Women, particularly those
from the upper classes, had been involved in charitable deeds, sometimes
under the auspices of religious organisations, from the early centuries
of Christianity. From the mid-nineteenth century there was a massive
expansion in philanthropic activity, much of it undertaken by upper-
and middle-class women, many of them Evangelicals, and much of it
rescue work, often assisted by new help in the form of working-class
Bible women and home missionaries. With ever greater leisure at their
disposal by virtue both of the increasing wealth of the nation as a whole,
and of the inactivity, except in the domestic environment, forced on
them by society, women could now take the opportunity afforded them
to extend their usefulness to the outside, male, world, and use their
talents in organising and carrying out such tasks. Philanthropy was
regarded as an amplification of the female role; it was something a
woman could do without exceeding the bounds of propriety, and it was

also seen as part of that religious bent which from early childhood, as she sewed her sampler and read her Bible, was deemed to be particularly hers. And in that Bible, had not Christ stressed charity as the most important virtue? And had not the New Testament particularly, in the figures of Dorcas and Phoebe, and more especially Mary Magdalen, sanctioned women as charitable workers?[19] Woman's mission could now reach out to embrace those fallen among her own sex, and her suitability for this role was stressed in articles and books of the period. As Mrs Emma Sheppard wrote, 'a woman's hand in its gentle tenderness can alone reach those whom *men* have taught to distrust them'.[20]

In the nineteenth-century crusade against immorality and impurity, the recovery of the fallen woman was seen in some mid-century texts as the highest form of love, and the kind of love which most closely resembled Christ's in its self-sacrifice and endurance. Charity in the form of almsgiving was not sufficient: 'Upon the whole, then, mere almsgiving is not the highest development, nor the finest outgrowth of the charitable woman. Charity of judgement ranks far before it. And where is this so nobly shown as in loving pity for the fallen?' It was for the woman rescue-worker to go out and 'lift them tenderly from the dust where they lie, to wipe from them those foul – disfiguring stains which have marred their comeliness and hidden the beauty of their faces, to lead them carefully across the gulf lying between them and the world of their unspotted past, and help them back to virtue and self-respect . . . to be to them friend, physician, guide and mother.'[21] The model *par excellence* of Christian charity, of course, was Christ himself whose active charity in the form of seeking out the poor unfortunates as he had in the cases of the adulteress and Mary Magdalen was to be emulated. In a sermon preached before the Church Penitentiary Association in 1862, and entitled 'The Accepted Penitent', the Revd H. Drury emphasised the tenderness and compassion extended by Christ even to prostitutes, just as he had accorded them to Mary Magdalen:

No woman is so entirely lost that she cannot be redeemed . . . Who knows but if their sin may drive them at last to some door of repentance? Some door that shall open wider as they approach it? Some avenue through which they may catch sight of the skirts of a Saviour's robe; . . . may throw themselves at His feet; kiss His feet, and anoint them with the ointment? and stand behind

Him weeping; and weep, and weep, until . . . He shall mercifully accept their repentance and bid them 'go in peace'.[22]

Rescue-workers were encouraged to show the same loving mercy as Christ had done, and the happy and consoling example was held up of 'one sacred Mary sitting at the foot of the Divine, with the Magdalen's soiled hand in hers, and the publicans and the sinners bidden to her pure companionship'.[23]

It was in some Evangelical writings of the period, however, that the restoration of Mary Magdalen's biblical character took place and where she became the paradigm of charity, fidelity and love. To John Angell James (1785–1859), author of *Female Piety: or the Young Woman's Friend and Guide through Life to Immortality*, Christ had tended to exalt the dignity of the female sex during his sojourn on earth and it was upon Mary Magdalen, in reward for her love and fidelity at the crucifixion, that the 'honor of the first manifestation of our Saviour' had been bestowed.[24] Furthermore, Christianity had been a liberating process for woman: not only had it further exalted the female sex through Christ's elevation of her from the 'degradation of Mohammedanism and Paganism', but it had also given her an important role in the establishment of Christianity:

But the finishing stroke which Christianity gives in elevating the condition of women, is, by inviting and employing their energies and influence in promoting the spread of religion in the world . . . The honor so liberally bestowed upon the pious women of antiquity, in ministering to the personal wants of the Saviour, and in being so constantly about his person . . . was the least of those distinctions designed for them by our holy religion.[25]

These 'pious women of antiquity' were the model for those nineteenth-century women who wished to find a practical outlet for their energies within a patriarchally organised society. But how different the day when such illustrious females as Phoebe and Priscilla (Rom. 16) were employed in the office of deaconesses in 'the setting up of Christ's kingdom', was pointed out by the same author:

The primitive age of Christianity was in advance of ours in the respect thus paid to the feminine sex, by officially employing them

in the services of the church. It has been said that the usages of
society have somewhat changed since that time, so as to render the
service of women less necessary now than they were then . . .
some truth, no doubt, there is in these assertions; but perhaps not
so much as is by some imagined.[26]

The emphasis on Mary Magdalen as the woman by the cross in Evangelical writings was a clear refutation of the traditional view of her, still
upheld by the Roman Catholic Church and some elements of the Anglican community, as primarily the repentant prostitute. This in spite of
Dom Augustin Calmet's attempt to rescue the authentic Magdalen in
his 'Dissertation sur les trois Maries' of 1737, in which he remarked
caustically that since the qualities of possession (Mary Magdalen's) and
debauchery (Luke's sinner's) were incompatible, 'it was scarcely likely
that one possessed would be a prostitute'.[27] It was as the fallen woman
that Mary Magdalen appeared in the visions of the ecstatic and stigmatist
Anna Katherina Emmerich (d. 1824), the German peasant woman who
became an Augustinian nun. Here the conventional idea of Mary Magdalen, no doubt influenced by images and devotional works, was
reinforced with a liberal dose of imagination:

> The youngest child, Magdalen, was very beautiful and, even in
> her early years, tall and well-developed, like a girl of more
> advanced age . . . full of frivolity and seductive art . . . Even as a
> child she was vain beyond expression, given to petty thefts, proud,
> self-willed, and a lover of pleasure.
>
> I saw her at the window and on the terraces of the house upon
> a magnificent seat of carpets and cushions, where she could be seen
> in all her splendour from the streets . . . Even in her ninth year,
> she was engaged in love affairs . . .[28]

In France, Louis XVIII, in the process of revitalising Catholicism after
the vicissitudes of the revolutionary period, rededicated the great church
of La Madeleine in Paris, founded by Charles VIII in the sixteenth
century, rebuilt by Louis XV, and entirely reconstructed in 1807 by
Napoleon as the Temple of Glory immortalising his memory. In 1816
it was declared by Louis XVIII 'l'église royale de la Madeleine' and
consecrated to the memory of Louis XVI, Marie-Antoinette and other
members of the royal family executed during the revolution.[29] It has

been suggested that the figure of Mary Magdalen kneeling before Christ at the Last Judgement in the pediment represents France herself begging for forgiveness for the royal murders.[30] It was six years later, in 1822, 'before 40,000 people', that the cult of Mary Magdalen at Ste Baume, which had been ravaged during the revolutionary years, was re-established.[31] The royal sanction of France's favoured saint and her wide-spread popularity may well account for the flood of images of her produced in France throughout the rest of the nineteenth century, a large proportion depicting her in her grotto at Ste Baume. Another product of the revived interest in Mary Magdalen's legendary career in the south of France was the Saint-Sulpicien E.-M. Faillon's monumental two-volume compilation of the records relating to her supposed apostol-acy in Provence, first published in Paris in 1848.[32] It was a reflection of a recurrent desire to establish a direct apostolic link between Christ and Gaul, using Mary Magdalen as the vehicle, much as the monks of Vézelay had done some eight centuries earlier. In 1871 Vrain-Denis Lucas was sent to prison for palming off as many as 27,320 forged letters, which he had forged himself, to a M. Chasles, a geometrican and astronomer. Among the missives from, for example, Louis XIV, Pascal, Shakespeare, Rabelais, Roman emperors, Cleopatra, Plato, Pliny and the apostles which the credulous scientist had bought, there was one from Mary Magdalen to Lazarus, and another to the king of Bur-gundy, in which she referred to herself as the sister of Martha and Lazarus, and sent him a casket:

> In it you will find the letter I spoke of to you which was sent me by Jesus Christ a few days before His passion. It is accompanied by two sentences which constitute the basis of the religion of Christ. Take good care therefore of these precious objects: so you will be happy and live in peace, which is the wish . . .[33]

The fact that the letters were written both on paper and in French did not appear to trouble M. Chasles. The appeal of the Provençal legend is still so strong that not even Louis Duchesne's thorough refutation of the entire story in 1894 has failed to eradicate the cults at St Maximin and Ste Baume.[34]

Thus was her image fixed and reinforced in the popular mind, in a heady mixture of nationalist and religious fervour. However, within a decade of the celebrations at Ste Baume, a German Protestant theologian was to question the very divinity of Christ, and by extension the sanity of Mary Magdalen herself. In an attempt begun during the Enlightenment to discover the historical Jesus, scholars and theologians, basing their methods of enquiry on reason and scientific observation, came to deny both his divinity and the supernatural constituents of the gospel accounts such as the theophanous events of the resurrection. This was the approach of David Friedrich Strauss, whose famous *Leben Jesu kritisch bearbeitet* (1835–6), which was first translated into English by George Eliot, claimed that the miraculous, mythic elements had accrued to the gospels during their composition in the second century.[35] Not surprisingly, his views earned him his dismissal from his post at Tübingen University. By denying the objective reality of the resurrection, the testimony of its witnesses was obviously called into question. Strauss mocked the fact that Christianity had been founded on the 'ravings of a demented and love-lorn woman'; Mary Magdalen's 'impetuous temperament' accounted for her return to the tomb, 'she having been formerly a demoniac'.[36] (But despite his extreme views, Strauss believed Christianity had not been destroyed in essence by the myths since all religion was based on ideas rather than facts.)

A similar fate was to overtake Ernest Renan (1823–92), the French philosopher, theologian and orientalist who, in his opening lecture at the Collège de France in 1862, referred to Jesus merely as an 'incomparable and itinerant preacher'. This opinion lost him his professorship in Hebrew the following year, and he was only reinstated in 1870. Fascinated by the new science of the nineteenth century and higher criticism of the Bible, he had become a rationalist and sceptic. Of the resurrection, he wrote in the *Vie de Jésus* (1863), the first volume of his history of the origins of Christianity:

> the strangest rumours were spread in the Christian community.
> The cry 'He is risen!' spread amongst the disciples like lightning.
> Love caused it to find ready credence everywhere . . . For the
> historian, the life of Jesus finishes with his last sigh. But such was
> the impression he had left in the hearts of his disciples and of a few
> devoted females, that during some weeks more it was as if he were
> living and consoling them. Had his body been taken away? Or
> did enthusiasm, always credulous, in certain circumstances, create
> afterwards the group of narratives by which it was sought to estab-
> lish faith in the resurrection? . . . Let us say, however, that the

strong imagination of Mary Magdalene played in this circumstance
an important part. Divine power of love! Sacred moments in which
the passion of one possessed gave to the world a resuscitated God![37]

Mary Magdalen, Renan saw as Jesus' 'most faithful friend'. He further
described her in the measured tones of his age as a 'very excitable person'
afflicted with 'nervous and apparently inexplicable maladies'. Jesus
soothes 'that excitable organism'; she is thereafter ever faithful to him,
and subsequently plays 'a most important part, for . . . she was the
principal medium through which was established faith in the resurrection'.[38] Elsewhere, somewhat in the vein of Strauss, he gives her a
curiously, and unexpectedly, important role as inventor of the Christian
religion: 'The glory of the resurrection belongs, then, to Mary Magdalene. After Jesus, it is Mary who has done the most in the founding
of Christianity.'[39]

Faced with a world which could countenance such heresies, the
Church of Rome had found itself in urgent need of a new rallying point
for the faithful. The chosen figure-head was the Virgin Mary; mariolatry
became the mark of the revitalised Catholicism as it recovered from the
assaults of eighteenth- and nineteenth-century rationalist thinking. On
8 December 1854, Pius IX (1846–78), hoisting the banner of religion
against reason and enlightenment, proclaimed in his bull *Ineffabilis Deus*
the dogma of the Immaculate Conception, effectively bringing to an
end a debate which had raged for seven centuries within the Catholic
Church. To hold the Virgin to be the sole human creature kept free
from all stain of original sin, and thus apart from all other humans, was
another strike for dualism, and also a blow against modernism. The
Virgin Mary, meek and mild, pure and passive, acting as an intercessor
for her son, appeared in 1858 at Lourdes, telling the peasant-girl Berna-
dette Soubirous, '*Que soy era Immaculata Counception*' (I am the Immaculate Conception), as if to corroborate the dogmatic assertion of four
years earlier. The retreat into absolutism was confirmed in 1870 when
Pius declared the dogma of papal infallibility.

However important she might have been in nineteenth-century
mariolatry, the image of the Virgin Mary provided by the Catholic
Church was still not a practical model for women, a fact pointed out
by Protestant writers. In an outright attack on Catholicism's cult of the
Virgin – and in reaction to its adoption by the High Church revival in
England led by the Oxford Movement (1835–45) – John Angell James

blasted forth: Christ's sojourn on earth, his manner of arriving, and his incarnation had also exalted the dignity of the female sex. This honour had not been made to the Virgin Mary alone, however; it included all her sex. Strongly objecting to Mary's treatment by the 'apostate' church, 'wherein she has become an object of idolatrous homage', he continued, 'Woman is not the mother of God as the Papists absurdly, and as I think, almost blasphemously, say; but the mother of that humanity only which was mysteriously united with divinity.' To the staunch Protestant, the Virgin Mary was wife, mother and saint, only:

> In an age when Popery is lifting up its head in triumph and with hope, no fair opportunity should be lost to expose its pretensions and refute its errors. There is no part of this dreadful system more contrary to Scripture, or more insulting to God, than its Mariolatry, or worship of the Virgin Mary. She is styled 'mother of God': 'Queen of Seraphim, Saints and Prophets': 'Advocate of Sinners': 'Refuge of Sinners': 'Gate of Heaven': 'Queen of Heaven'.[40]

The same author further criticised Catholics for worshipping the Virgin as they did Christ, with no biblical justification whatsoever: 'The Acts of the Apostles make mention of her name but once, and that without any mark of eulogy; and in the Epistles she is not mentioned at all.'[41]

James had offered Mary Magdalen and other 'pious women of antiquity' as models for Victorian women, and in 1847 Clara Lucas Balfour presented them with another list of female scriptural characters whom they could emulate. Amongst these were Hannah as a model of maternal piety, Esther of patriotism, Dorcas and Lydia of Christian belief, and Priscilla and Phoebe, of Christian intelligence. The Virgin Mary appeared in her usual role as the model of humility, while Mary Magdalen, 'heroine of the Cross', was model of fidelity. Mrs Balfour determined to put history to rights, strongly defending Mary Magdalen's purity, and lauding her fidelity:

> A popular error has confounded the name of Mary Magdalene with that of the penitent named in the previous chapter. Hence, public institutions for penitent women have been very erroneously called by the name of one, whose life, so far as the gospel narrative unfolds it, was pure and spotless . . . It appears she was miraculously cured of one of those grievous and mysterious maladies

known in the gospel as demoniacal possession. . . . But the most glorious record of women's faith is connected with the name of Mary Magdalene . . . That little knot of weeping women . . . at the foot of the cross, faithful among the faithless . . . The last mention of Mary Magdalene is the record of her having assembled with the disciples, – with Mary, the mother of Jesus, and the other faithful women, when they gathered together for prayer before the day of Pentecost. No subsequent event of her life is recorded.[42]

Mrs Balfour saw Mary Magdalen's announcement of the resurrection as the supreme point of favour to women, who had been highly honoured 'throughout the whole gospel history'. And it was for her intense faith and devotion at the crucifixion that it was to a woman to whom the Redeemer had appeared.[43] Mid-nineteenth century Evangelicals turned to the New Testament as a source of truth, in an attempt to bring reality into religion and to put the gospels into practice in missionary work and social reform. Mrs Balfour's reassessment of Mary Magdalen was part of this process.

Despite Mrs Balfour's protests concerning the propriety of naming homes for repentant prostitutes after Mary Magdalen, echoing those of Joseph Hanway almost exactly a century earlier, Magdalen-homes continued to be thus called, and their numbers to swell: in 1856 there were 60 such homes in England, and 308 fifty years later, having taken in 12,500 prostitutes.[44] The Magdalen Society of New York had been founded in 1830, to provide 'An Asylum for Females who have deviated from the paths of virtue', and the largest *Magdalenenstift* in Germany had been established in 1833 in Kaiserswerth, Berlin.[45] From the mid-nineteenth century on, faced with the growing number of prostitutes and the increased threat to the very basis of society which they were seen as representing, philanthropic females from all walks of life, middle and upper-class Evangelicals, Catholic sisters and Anglican deaconesses, working-class biblical women, volunteers and the paid, armed with, and inspired by, Mary Magdalen and other examples of ministering, faithful and charitable women of the New Testament, took to the streets and brothels in search of these lost souls, those other magdalens, to alleviate the lot of their fallen sisters in the spirit of Christian charity.[46]

The duality of madonna and magdalen is neatly encapsulated in the touching and tragic tale of a young woman recounted by Samuel Warren in his *Passages from the Diary of a late Physician* of 1838.[47] No doubt much embellished by its narrator, 'The Magdalen' tells of a doctor who one Sunday evening, sitting by his hearth, is bidden by his servant to receive a lady who bears a message from a certain Miss Edwards. Loath as he is when he understands the significance of the location of the lady he is to visit, he nevertheless accompanies the old woman, to find the lady in question upon her sick bed in an advanced stage of consumption. He recognises her as the daughter of a widowed boarding-house keeper to whose establishment in a fashionable seaside resort he had taken his wife several years previously. The young girl's beauty had been so great that all around her had given her the sobriquet 'Madonna'. But 'Madonna' it seemed had not lived up to her chaste name. Pride – her mother's reduced circumstances had forced her to become a landlady – had led her into a relationship with a young officer who, under the pretence of a promised clandestine marriage, had taken her to France; 'Madonna' had then taken up with an aristocrat; thence it had been the usual tale of the harlot's progress, and now lying sick unto death in a brothel, she had remembered the address of the doctor. After several visits to the den of iniquity, where indeed the doctor himself is accosted by a pimp, he deems the lady to have recovered from her consumption; as she has been left some money in a legacy, most of which she intends to leave to a charity (' "You can guess the charity I mean," she asked the doctor. "The Magdalen hospital?" said [he] in a low tone'), with the doctor's assistance she hires a cottage, 'covered in jessamine and honeysuckle'. ' "Doctor," she whispered to him, "if you ever write to me, call this, *Magdalen* cottage!" ' From this new home, she carries out little offices of 'an unassuming charity', is believed to be a good widow as she wears half-mourning, and teaches catechism to 'neighbouring peasants'. Three years later, however, returning from church, she catches a severe cold. The doctor hastens to her side, but too late. From her 'insensible grasp', he takes a sampler, 'not finished'. Upon it, he sees her tragic life recapitulated: 'And let the reader imagine my feeling, on seeing nothing but the letters "Mary Magdalen" and "E" below it. The other letter of her initials "B", the finger of death had prevented her from doing. I shall never part with that sampler till I die – Oh poor Mary Magdalen! I will not forget thee!'

And so, strange as it may seem, as model to the repentant prostitute, and as charitable and faithful ministrix to the rescue-worker, the paradigmatic Magdalen moved with the times, embodying all things to all men and, it seems, to many women. Society's preoccupation with the fallen woman had brought her back into focus as the most famous sinner, the most beautiful feminine, human and apparently eminently fallible creature, in whom artists and writers of the second half of the nineteenth century found once more a source of inspiration. She became the subject of novels, plays and poetry: Frances Arnold-Forster noted in her *Dedications of English Churches* that while the name Magdalen was a 'great favourite' in nineteenth-century France and Germany, it was not quite so popular in England.[48] Nevertheless, it lent itself to several novels from the 1840s, some of which explored the position of fallen or otherwise marginalised women, and some of which did not, but merely reflected the popularity of the name. Prostitutes had appeared in such novels of the 1840s as Mrs Gaskell's *Mary Barton* (Esther) and Dickens' *Dombey & Son* (Alice Marwood) as pathetic, hungry, cold and wet creatures, drenched in Victorian sentimentality, shabby garments and self-disgust, who came out of the storm in order to die, surrounded by loving, charitable women.[49] Gertrude Maes, the mother of Henry Esmond, hero of Thackeray's eponymous novel (1852), ruined by Captain Thomas Esmond, entered a convent, and took the name Soeur Marie-Madeleine.[50] Wilkie Collins, author of – amongst several other novels – the 'first thriller', *The Moonstone*, wrote of the fall and redemption of two women, giving the name Magdalen (Vanstone) to his heroine in *No Name* (1862; see Plate 77), and using it in the title of another book, *The New Magdalen* (1873). He explored the madonna–magdalen polarity in two later novels, *Armadale* and *Basil*.

In *No Name*, Collins deals with the moral and social stigma associated with illegitimacy, which not only barred offspring from inheriting, but also prevented them from taking their father's name; the absence of a name signified non-personhood and non-existence, both morally and legally. He uses the name Magdalen explicitly to designate the outcast woman for whom there was no place in society for this very reason . Magdalen is the lively, passionate and younger of the two daughters of a Mr and Mrs Vanstone. By a carefully contrived twist in their parents' marital history, Magdalen and her sister Norah find themselves on their parents' sudden deaths not only illegitimate but cast out of the society of which they had previously been members. Penniless and nameless,

ALONE ON A STRANGE SHORE.—No Name, Vol. XII., page 194.

77 Magdalen Vanstone plots her
return to society. From *No Name*
by William Wilkie Collins (1862).

Magdalen and Norah are thrown upon their own resources. Norah, the
more conventional of the two, takes the classic course of becoming a
governess – the only employment for genteel ladies fallen on hard times
– but Magdalen takes her fate into her own hands with a courage and
determination typical of Collins' heroines.[51]

Collins may well have been aware of the medieval tradition of giving
the name Magdalen to daughters born out of wedlock, but he also uses
it symbolically for Magdalen's lack of status.[52] Determined that she is
going to overcome Fate's nasty trick, Magdalen makes use of her dramatic abilities by taking to the stage, another classic action in Victorian
melodrama, and a metaphor also for linking her with a whore. When
opportunity presents itself, she uses her feminine wiles to charm Mr
Noel Vanstone, her sickly and miserly cousin and inheritor of her
father's fortune, into falling in love with her: so great is her desire to

regain what she sees as rightfully hers that she is able to overcome her loathing for him sufficiently to lure him into marriage – tricking his housekeeper and guardian who recognises her beneath her disguise – and flees to Scotland with her prize. Her revenge too is classic, as she marries for money, which she regards as rightfully hers, a man whom she hates, and degrades herself in her own estimation: she has fallen.

Fate, however, deals her another nasty blow: Noel Vanstone dramatically dies but not before altering his will in favour of yet another male cousin, with a pay-off to his guardian rather than his wife. Magdalen is again made destitute, only to be rescued in the end from either the hospital or the workhouse by the Merchant Navy captain who had fallen in love with her instantly, on the promenade in Suffolk. Much concerned that she was at least half his own age – forty – and therefore far too young, he had sailed away to China, but never forgotten her. Magdalen falls in love with him also, realising that in order to redeem herself, she must tell him all, the whole shameful story.

Collins' first Magdalen story points to the dependent position of the women of his day, dependent that is on the husbands, fathers, or male relations whom they might have, and the lack of status they enjoyed in middle- and upper middle-class society without them. As Magdalen points out bitterly in a letter to Miss Garth, her former governess, her marriage takes her from being 'Nobody's child' to becoming 'Somebody's wife'. She again becomes a non-person when Noel Vanstone dies, and only resumes her identity and status when she finds Captain Kirke, whose own name has a strong ring of the Protestant Church about it. Her re-encounter with the honourable captain and her redemption through his agency, from destitution of body and soul to physical and spiritual renewal, seems a conscious literary parallel with Luke's sinner saved by Christ. Collins' suspense-ridden story is not merely a marvellous tale with plots and counter-plots which constantly overlap. Like many of his heroines, Magdalen Vanstone is a lively, strong, courageous and independent-minded female, given to fairly unconventional behaviour: the changes in her emotional state mirror her growth from girlhood to womanhood, from being outcast to acceptance and self-realisation, from being a non-person to becoming someone with status in the eyes of law and society.

Much the same happy ending is allotted to Mercy Merrick, Collins' heroine of *The New Magdalen*, a former prostitute who disguises herself as a woman she believes to be dead, in order to regain her status in society. Through various vicissitudes – she appears first as a nurse at the front, an Angel of Mercy – including betrothal to the scion of an ancient upper-middle class family (but only at his insistence as she is not without moral scruples, and does not wish to deceive him), she too winds up redeemed through her remorse for her deception, and through the auspices of a good man, this time a radical Evangelical preacher. Collins takes the opportunity afforded by the novel's subject-matter to give Mercy Merrick two forceful outbursts against what she sees as the inadequacies of contemporary philanthropic work to help prostitutes of the type described at the beginning of this chapter. It was all very well to have benevolent schemes, but to what avail were they if the people for whom they were organised remained ignorant of them? They 'ought to be posted at the corner of every street':

> What do *we* know of public dinners, and eloquent sermons and neatly printed circulars? Every now and then news of some forlorn creature (generally of a woman), who has committed suicide, within five minutes' walk perhaps of an institution which would have opened its doors to her, appears in the newspapers, shocks you dreadfully, and is then forgotten again. Take as much pains to make charities and asylums known among the people *without* money, as are taken to make a new play, a new journal, or a new medicine known among the people *with* money, and you will save many a lost creature who is perishing now.[53]

And as, at the beginning of the novel, she points out to Grace Roseberry – the woman whose identity she adopts – in a moving plea on behalf of the prostitute (for '*I* was once of those women'):

> have you ever read of your unhappy fellow creatures (the starving outcasts of the population) whom Want has betrayed to sin? . . . Have you heard . . . of Refuges established to protect and reclaim them? . . . Society can subscribe to reclaim me – but Society can't take me back.[54]

Collins thus underscores the marginalised status of the nineteenth-century magdalen, who could never be readmitted into society. In both novels, however, the social outcast who is forced, either by her own action or by someone else's, to leave the narrow and constricting path of respectability is helped back to society by the Good Man, the Christ-figure whose function is to seek and save their fallen heroine, the magdalen.

The traditional conception of Mary Magdalen also inspired Emile Zola to explore the nature of love and sexuality in one of his earliest major novels, *Madeleine Férat* (1868), the heroine of which, halfway through the story, identifies herself with Mary Magdalen because of her own 'fallenness'.[55] The novel's theme is fallen sexuality and religious bigotry in the form of Protestantism which rears its head with the promise of hellfire and damnation to those who have transgressed. Madeleine has stereotypically 'a magnificent mane of auburn hair' – she might almost be a Pre-Raphaelite woman – full lips, which are vividly scarlet ('indeed they were too red in so white a face'), strong features, large grey-green eyes, and she is also tall and lissom. Her physiognomy is integral to her fallenness. When she meets Guillaume, she has been intending to retire to a nunnery, having been seduced and abandoned by her first lover, Jacques. She marries Guillaume, having confessed to her previous liaison, but the ghost of Jacques is constantly present. Old Geneviève, the maidservant, knows a whore when she sees one (Madeleine's beauty, her red hair and red lips reek of things carnal, things sinful; she has the luscious hair of a whore), and reads the Old Testament to her, brandishing the Protestant ogre of sin and retribution. Madeleine is only stirred, however, when she hears the story of Mary Magdalen – as Luke's sinner – and identifies with the forgiven prostitute: the Bible seems to be speaking of her own shame, her tears, and Guillaume who, Christ-like, has forgiven and absolved her; even the 'very name was really hers'.

The ghost of Jacques then takes over: indeed it even turns out that Jacques is the best friend, 'brother' of Guillaume, so that when the latter discovers the true identity of Madeleine's first lover, even his own and Madeleine's child Lucie, in an extraordinary understanding of biological and psychological processes and heredity, bears the imprint of Jacques, whose blood is 'largely responsible' for Madeleine's pregnancy. Although she now loves Guillaume only, at night she has orgasmic dreams of her first lover, witnessed by her shocked husband, as he lies in bed beside her twitching form. And Jacques, hitherto believed to be dead, returns, to make their lives even more unbearable: the only way out is for Madeleine to commit suicide, her child having died, and for Guillaume to go mad. Zola's *Madeleine Férat*, characterised by its remarkable sexual explicitness, demonstrates the hypocrisy with which women were treated, and the workings of the perennial double standard. Guillaume is willing to accept Madeleine, though fallen, as his own mistress and wife until he discovers that her seducer has been his best friend; he sees her as sinful, but nevertheless forgives them both. He is shocked and disgusted by Madeleine – she is now 'a mere courtesan, her mien the hard mien of a woman who has had all the sex she wants'. 'Impregnated' by that first lover, a woman is forever marked by her first sexual encounter, with either husband or otherwise, and equally forever tainted by her fall. And a beautiful woman – many of these Magdalenian heroines have auburn hair, large grey or grey-green eyes, with the white skin which accompanies Titian-hair – is always suspect, as the old maidservant knows, in the age-old equation of beauty and sinfulness which had given birth to the idea of Mary Magdalen.

In Georg Büchner's *Woyzeck* (1837), the first wholly successful tragic representation of the common man, Marie the prostitute and lover of the anti-hero Woyzeck, like Zola's Madeleine, suffers pangs of conscience whilst reading the Bible to her child. Her infidelity with the Drum Major is brought into stark reality when she reads the words, 'And stood at his feet weeping, and began to wash his feet with tears, and did wipe them with the hairs of her head, and anointed them with ointment.' She cannot be forgiven, and is not forgiven, as Woyzeck murders her, in this play about the sufferings of man in an absurd world. In the same scene in Alban Berg's marvellous opera, based on Büchner's play, Marie leafs through the Bible while her child sleeps, and having read Luke's account, looks up, stressing her self-identification with Mary Magdalen, with the cry 'Maria Magdalena'.[56]

Eugène Fromentin (1820–76) used the name Madeleine for the heroine of his autobiographical novel *Dominique* (1862), about the sanctity of love and of the marriage vow. In Germany, Friedrich Hebbel's play of 1844, *Maria Magdalena*, dealt with the shame brought on her family by the seduction and pregnancy of Klara, and more particularly its effect on her father, to whom its subtitle, 'A Bourgeois Tragedy', refers.[57] The name Madalena is given to the mother in Almeida Garrett's *Pilgrim* (1840), one of Portugal's most celebrated plays, in which the heroine Maria, her daughter, is a child of sin, the product of the inadvertently bigamous union between Dona Madalena and the man she marries under the impression that her first husband has died in battle. Set in the seventeenth century, the only options left to the parents are a nunnery and monastery, while for poor Maria there is no alternative but death.[58] Novels and plays using the name Mary Magdalen are part of a wider trend of the literary examination of the status of nineteenth-century woman. They make explicit the sexual 'fallenness' of their heroines, and fit into the category of such works as Hawthorne's *Scarlet Letter* (1850), Flaubert's *Madame Bovary* (1857), Tolstoy's *Anna Karenina* (1877) and Fontane's later *Effi Briest* (1895), all novels which deal in some way with the theme of the fallen woman. While the pious woman-as-redemptive-agent to wicked or misguided men is something of a Victorian *cliché*, it is less common for the fallen woman to become a saviour: the redeeming nature of Mary Magdalen herself is reflected in the figures of two prostitutes, Maslova and Sonya, in respectively Tolstoy's *Resurrection* (1899) and Dostoevsky's *Crime and Punishment* (1866). Both Maslova – seduced by the hero and rejected by her family, she becomes a prostitute – and Sonya, a prostitute whom Raskolnikov meets, bring the anti-heroes to spiritual regeneration. Sonya's reading of the gospel episode of Lazarus' resurrection leads Raskolnikov to admit to the murder of old Alyona Ivanovna, the money-lender, and her sister Elisaveta, and therefore to his own redemption.

What is common to all these works is their use of the non-gospel character of Mary Magdalen which, paradoxically, whilst it offered a metaphorical vehicle through which women's 'nature' and sexuality could be explored, at the same time helped to ensure that Mary Magdalen herself remained locked in her mythical persona. The same process was at work in the visual arts where, although the gospel figure appears frequently, depictions of the penitent Magdalen were predominant. In England, for example, of 147 recorded paintings and sculptures featuring Mary Magdalen, executed between 1800 and 1896, 91 were of the mythical Magdalen as against 44 showing the gospel character.[59] Artists and sculptors were no more able to resist the appeal of the penitent than were the novelists, though the moral purposes to which she was put differ sharply.

Perhaps the most pervasive image of Mary Magdalen in the nineteenth century was one not executed in that century, but which, like Correggio's figure, exerted its influence over a later period. This was the sculpture by the Venetian Antonio Canova, of 1796 (Genoa, Palazzo Bianco), much admired in the early nineteenth century, and copied throughout the century by artists and sculptors to whom its neo-Classical form and

combination of penitence and eroticism appealed (see Plate 78). She
kneels with a crucifix in her hands, a skull by her side, a piece of cloth
draped partly over her breasts, stomach and upper thighs, and tied under
her breasts, her beautiful back and buttocks bare. In its demonstration
of the female body, vulnerable in repentance, and at the same time
sensual, Canova's figure presented a formula which was at once erotic
and appealing to mawkish Victorian sentimentality. It had a *succès de fou*
in Paris where it was taken by the conte Giambattista Sommariva, and
the sculptor was commissioned by Napoleon's brother-in-law Eugène
Beauharnais to repeat his earlier achievement. Stendhal enthused over
the Sommariva sculpture, claiming that it proved that Canova, who
was to execute two further sculptures of Mary Magdalen, was 'the
supreme artist of *expression*'. The public, the critic Quatremère de
Quincy noted, saw 'a piteous decency in its nudity' and, 'above all, an
undefined religious sorrow' in the Magdalen's face.[60]

Canova's sculpture of the penitent Magdalen prompted a series of
imitations of and variations on the theme, both in stone and on canvas.
These readily conformed to the genre of the idealised nude of
'smoothed-out form and waxen surface' described by Kenneth Clark, a
genre which won official favour in the Salons from the 1850s.[61] Nude
females graced Turkish baths, were chained to rocks, sold as slaves, or
lay in dark landscapes, offering their bodies to the spectator's gaze,
compliant objects of the image. A painting by Ferdinando Cavalleri
(1816) was a direct copy of Canova's figure; and amongst the earliest
directly influenced by it was Francesco Hayez' painting (1825), showing
Mary Magdalen seated entirely naked on the ground, gazing wistfully
to heaven, her plump flank catching the spectator's eye.[62] A crouching
Magdalen, naked apart from a piece of cloth draped gracefully over her
loins, was sculpted by H. de Triqueti in 1840.[63] The kneeling pose of
Canova's figure was used by Jean-Jacques Henner in his painting of
*c.*1880, one of a long series which he exhibited in the Salons from 1861
to 1885, the result of an apparent obsession with the subject. Shown
with her face turned away from the spectator, she offers a view of her
naked torso in profile and, as nearly always in Henner's depictions,
without any attribute to identify her as the saint.[64]

Contemporary concern about the 'Great Social Evil' and the mid-
century religious revivals in England and France have been suggested as
reasons for the great proliferation of images of Mary Magdalen.[65] In
France, in addition, there was also a pressing need to restore the artistic

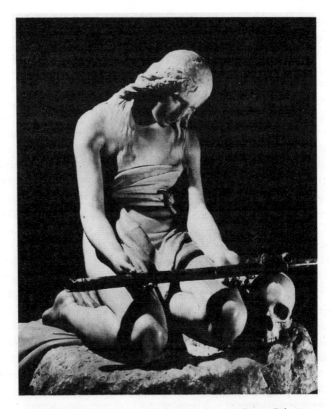

78 *The Penitent Magdalen* (1796). Antonio Canova. Genoa, Palazzo Bianco.

patrimony of the Church which had been destroyed during the years of revolution. After the Bourbon reinstatement, religious paintings were largely executed for both state and Salon: in the Salon of 1837, 100 paintings of religious subjects were shown, rising to 232 in 1844.[66] In the same year a writer in the *Athenæum* remarked upon the boom in paintings of religious subjects exhibited at the Royal Academy: 'The taste for scriptural compositions among our artists would seem to be reviving, if we are to judge.'[67] Paintings of episodes from the life of Christ were extremely popular, and another favourite biblical subject of the time was the Woman taken in Adultery, whose own popularity has been linked to the furore surrounding the Matrimonial Causes Act of

1857.[68] The majority of the British paintings on the theme of Mary Magdalen were executed in the 1840s and 1850s, during the first burst of enthusiasm to reclaim prostitutes, and, significantly, most of them depicted her as the penitent.

An English painter who showed a particular affection for this subject was William Etty, the most prolific painter of the nude in nineteenth-century England, whose lubricious images were aimed at a disparate but generally middle-class clientele. A pious Methodist who in later years became a Roman Catholic, Etty justified his choice of subject-matter in the autobiography he wrote in 1849, the year of his death, having fulfilled his intentions with a stream of paintings of 'Toilets of Venus', 'Andromedas', 'Sleeping Nymphs' and several nubile Magdalens (see Plate 79), all essays on the female nude. (It should perhaps be added that Etty also painted several male nudes.) He wrote:

> Finding God's most glorious work to be WOMAN, that all human beauty had been concentrated in her, I resolved to dedicate myself to painting – not the Draper's or Milliner's work – but God's most glorious work, more finely than ever had been done.[69]

To those who criticised his peculiar treatment and choice of subject, and accused him of deliberate pornography, he replied, 'People may think me lascivious but I have never painted with a lascivious motive. If I had, I might have made great wealth . . . If in any of my pictures an immoral sentiment has been aimed at, I consent it should be burned.' Thackeray, who admired him as a great and original colourist, 'as luscious as Rubens and rich almost as Titian', commented in 1844 how every year the Royal Academy exhibition 'sparkle[d] with magnificent little canvases, the works of this indefatigably strenuous admirer of rude Beauty', in whose art 'the feminine figure is often rather too expansively treated'.[70] Etty sometimes scandalised his buyers, and on more than one occasion was asked to repaint a nude for fear of shocking purchasers' relatives and friends. One wonders how the Victorian clergyman, the Revd Isaac Spencer, who commissioned the little nude figure exhibited at the Royal Academy in 1842 received his painting of the Magdalen. The remark of the reviewer in *Blackwood's Magazine* is perhaps apt: 'There is not here the deep feeling of penitence of a Magdalen. Was the title an afterthought?'[71]

This very same question might have been asked of at least three further images of Mary Magdalen painted in France in the second half of the century. Paul Baudry's *Penitent Magdalen* (Nantes, Musée des Beaux-Arts) was exhibited with great success at the Salon of 1859, and owes much to Italian seventeenth-century painting with its subject's smoothly rounded breasts and arms. It has a suggestive quality, scarcely diminished by the crucifix which lies by the Magdalen's hands. Jules-Joseph Lefèbvre's *Mary Magdalen* (Salon of 1876, St Petersburg, Hermitage) was actually bought as the 'séduisante Madeleine' by Alexandre Dumas *fils*, to hang as a pendant to the *Femme couchée* by the same artist already in his possession. In this almost photographic image, the Magdalen writhes in her anguish, while simultaneously offering her entirely naked body to the spectator's delectation. Her raised left leg ostensibly conceals her pubic triangle but in so doing invites erotic speculation. The pubic hair of Marius Vasselon's *Penitent Magdalen* (Salon of 1887) is cast in shadow, or entirely omitted, as she lies stretched out across the picture plane, in conformity with the conventions of academic art by which the physical reality of the body is glossed over, rendering acceptable what would otherwise have scandalised Victorian prudery (see Plate 80). Nude, Mary Magdalen becomes yet another passive sexual commodity, made safe and sanitised to feed male fantasies, without the threat of differentiated personality. With scarcely any pretence at religious imagery, the picture is nothing more than another

79 *A Magdalen* (1840s).
William Etty. London,
Victoria & Albert
Museum.

80 *The Penitent Magdalen* (1887). Marius Vasselon. Tours, Musée des Beaux-Arts.

example of the pornographic studies of women posing as art which were a regular feature of the Salons.[72]

In the 1870s in England raids were made on photographers' studios for images made to sustain the trade in pornography. In the mid- to late nineteenth century a lower-class girl might earn a few meagre pence, or some gin, in return for sitting in various poses usually negotiated by photographer and sitter. In 1864 Hannah Cullwick, a domestic servant of the middle-class Arthur Munby, posed as Mary Magdalen for a photographer James Stodart in Margate. She had already posed in her 'dirt' at the instigation of her master, 'Massa' as she wrote of him in her diaries, who was also her lover in a clandestine relationship (because of their different social stations), and later her husband. Stodart had asked if he could photograph her again in 'other ways', with 'one to be done as *Magdalene*, & I shd want nothing to wear but a white skirt' (see Plate 81). Her diary also records:

> Well, I went again & was done. I had to strip off my servant's things – to my shift, what I hardly liked, but still I knew there was no harm in that, & Mr S. was a serious sort o' man & and we neither of us laugh'd or smil'd over it. He took me in a kneeling position as if praying with my hair down my back & looking up. The side face was good for it, but the *hands* was too big & coarse he said, so it wouldn't do as a picture. And so it's best for me to be done as a drudge what I am, for my hands & arms are tho' chief

to *me*, to get my living with, & I don't care about my face if Massa likes it . . .[73]

She further noted her embarrassment at removing her clothes:

When I was stripp'd for the Magdalene I was a little confused, having my steel chain & padlock around my neck, for Mr S. said, 'Oh take that chain off.' I said, 'I canna sir.' He said, 'Is it lock'd?' I blush'd a bit as I said, 'Yes, & I've not got the key'. 'Ah, there's some mystery about that,' he said. And so it was done wi' the chain on . . .[74]

Stodart does not seem to have paid Hannah for posing, but gave her 'one or two of the Magdelenes on cards', though the purposes to which other prints were put were not recorded. But in her partial nudity, a representation of the real, as opposed to the fictive human naked body,

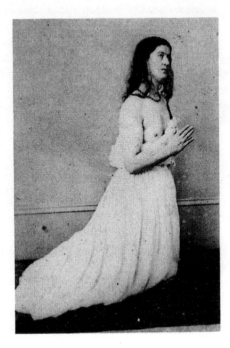

81 Hannah Cullwick photographed as Mary Magdalen by James Stodart in 1864. The portrait is endorsed by Munby: 'Hannah, 1864. This is the Magdalen portrait mentioned in my diary & hers 1864.' Cambridge, Trinity College Library.

she was not dissimilar to other photographic or other images which were traded under the appellation of art.

Of the paintings of Mary Magdalen by members of the Pre-Raphaelite Brotherhood, some are as much a part of their cult of feminine beauty as the other images of women which populate their art, whilst others, like Holman Hunt's *Christ and the Two Maries* of 1847 (Adelaide, Art Gallery of South Australia), sprang from the artist's intention to paint a 'new kind of religious art'.[75] Rossetti, who was an agnostic, but whose mother and sisters were both High Anglicans, saw religious art as a means of earning a living rather than a mission, despite his fascination with the cult of the Virgin Mary. His Mary Magdalen is a beautiful creature, of the new kind of beauty which Rossetti himself created, unconventionally striking rather than pretty, remote and at the same time mysteriously enticing. Like others of the female phantoms who flit through Pre-Raphaelite art, she is endowed with the extraordinarily abundant mane which emphasises her sexuality and her erotic allure, whilst simultaneously acting as drapery, the female hair so often lauded in Romantic poetry.[76]

A highly elaborate drawing of Mary Magdalen by Rossetti (1858), the design of which he had been working on since 1853, had a powerful effect on Ruskin who wished to exchange it for the St Catherine which he had already commissioned (see Plate 82). 'That "Magdalene" ', Ruskin wrote to the artist, 'is magnificent to my mind, in every possible way: it stays by me.' In a second letter, he qualified the latter phrase: by 'stays by me', he had meant that the image 'stay[ed] in [his] eyes and head'. 'But I do wish you could get the "Magdalene" for me,' he continued. 'I would give that oil picture [the St Catherine] for it willingly, at 50 guineas.'[77] But his desire, it seems, was not to be fulfilled. Rossetti himself described the picture to Mrs Clabburn, the wife of a Norwich manufacturer who commissioned an oil replica in 1863. The scene showed Mary Magdalen (as Luke's sinner) as one of a group of revellers and musicians who, passing the house of Simon the Pharisee, catches a glimpse of Christ within, seated at a table. She is arrested by

82 *Mary Magdalen at the Door of Simon the Pharisee* (1858). Dante
Gabriel Rossetti. Cambridge, Fitzwilliam Museum.

the sight, her bare arms raised up to pull the roses from her hair. Her
lover puts his hand on her foot to prevent her from entering, and the
young girl places her arm across the door. The image is suffused with
the usual Pre-Raphaelite symbolism, but also includes further significances. In Rossetti's sonnet written to accompany the painting, the first
stanza is in the words of the lover: 'Why wilt thou cast the roses from
thine hair?' – but the Magdalen cannot be stayed; it is her Bridegroom's
face which draws her.[78] Rossetti thus returns to the theme first
expounded by Hippolytus of Rome in the third century: his Magdalen,
although Luke's sinner, is the Bride of the *Canticles*. The dramatic
encounter is heightened by the way the artist chose to depict the protagonists, contrasting the dynamic, strikingly beautiful woman with a

gentle Christ. His sitters were Edward Burne-Jones, and Ruth Herbert, an actress, of whose beauty and eminent suitability to sit for Mary Magdalen Rossetti wrote enthusiastically:

> I am in the stunning position this morning of expecting the actual visit at ½ past 11, of a model whom I have been longing to paint for years – Miss Herbert of the Olympic Theatre – who has the most varied and highest expression I ever saw in a woman's face, besides abundant beauty, golden hair, etc. Did you ever see her? O my eye! she has sat to me now and will sit to me for Mary Magdalene in the picture I am beginning. Such luck![79]

Rossetti seems to have seen his *Mary Magdalen* as a counterpart to *Found*, the painting he began in 1854, of a young girl, seduced and abandoned, found by her rescuer after a life of prostitution. His second image of Mary Magdalen, an oil painted in 1877 (Wilmington, Delaware, Bancroft collection), shows the sitter, possibly May, the daughter of William and Jane Morris, holding a pomander, but for all the world resembling an Eve or a Pandora rather than a Magdalen. Burne-Jones, who painted a *Mary Magdalen's Face on Resurrection Morning* in 1856 (London, Courtauld Institute, Witt Library), also executed a typological counterpart to Rossetti's *Magdalen* in a highly detailed pen and ink drawing of the *Wise and Foolish Virgins* at about the time he was sitting for Rossetti's study, both images thematically representing the soul seeking after God.[80]

The fallen woman herself also exerted a particular fascination on the Pre-Raphaelites and their associates, not the least on Rossetti who also wrote poems in addition to depicting her visually, and whose sympathy for the prostitute was noted by Thomas Hall Caine: 'For the poor women themselves, who after one false step, find themselves in a blind alley in which the way back is forbidden to them, he had nothing but the greatness of his compassion. The pitiless cruelty of their position often affected him to tears.'[81] Rossetti's *Found* is one of many paintings which focused on the contemporary magdalen whose plight was traced to her tragic end: the popular illustrator George Cruickshank's *Drowned, Drowned* (1850), G. F. Watts' *Found Drowned* (1848–50), and paintings by other members of the Pre-Raphaelite Brotherhood and their followers such as J. R. Spencer Stanhope's *Thoughts of the Past* (1859), Richard Redgrave's *Outcast* and, possibly most famous of all, Holman Hunt's *Awakening Conscience* (1848), are all variations on the same theme. In this last painting (London, Tate Gallery), the kept woman rises from the gentleman's knee – her fingers are conspicuously beringed except for the third on her left hand – dawning recognition of the enormity of her deed reflected in her expression, and heavenly illumination falling on her face. Her seduction, interrupted by the memory of her innocent youth evoked by the vision of spring seen through the open window, takes place in an ornately and tastelessly over-furnished room hired for such dalliances, and certainly not 'home', as Ruskin pointed out in his appreciation of Hunt's painting. The painting is furnished with symbols which point to the young woman's situation, including, perhaps most obvious of all, the painting of *Christ and the Woman taken in Adultery* on the wall. Given the lofty aspirations of the Pre-Raphaelites, of whom Hunt was a founding member (he was also an Evangelical, as was Ruskin), the modern magdalen was an entirely suitable subject for their art which aimed at social realism, and had a high moral purpose and seriousness.[82]

Although there had been a 'slight revival' in England of dedicating churches to Mary Magdalen during the first half of the century, this was followed by a much greater number of new dedications to the saint in the second half of the century, encouraged both by the demand for new churches in the expanding towns and cities and the High Church movement's enthusiasm for saints.[83] As a result, a large quantity of nineteenth-century painted glass is to be found in churches all over England, in new churches, such as George Street's magnificent neo-Gothic church of St Mary Magdalen in Paddington, London (1868–78), or those with old dedications, restored in the nineteenth century, such as the large early fourteenth-century Norfolk church of Pulham Market refurbished in 1873, with its beautiful windows depicting the life of Mary Magdalen. Influenced by Burne-Jones's stained glass designs, Henry Holiday (1839–1927), who also designed windows at St Mary Magdalen, Paddington, provided designs for three windows of a small medieval church dedicated to the saint at Madehurst, in West Sussex. His is a beautiful Pre-Raphaelite patron saint with golden tresses, in the north chancel (see Plate 83).[84] William Morris's *Mary Magdalen* for All Saints, Langton Green, Kent, is another example, and a strong female image, her abundant blonde hair streaming over her shoulders. (Similarly in France, large medieval churches such as the church of Ste Marie-Madeleine at Montargis, outside Paris, were also refurbished during the nineteenth century. Here, from 1860 to 1873, stained-glass windows by

83 *Mary Magdalen* (1890).
Stained-glass window
designed by Henry
Holiday and executed by
Messrs Powell & Sons.
Madehurst, West Sussex,
St Mary Magdalen.

Lobin de Tours depicting Mary Magdalen's life from the episode in
Luke to penitence in the grotto were installed.) For all the splendour of
many of the images, however, the iconography is conventional. Within
it, the Pre-Raphaelites had created an image of a strong, confident and
sexually powerful woman, in stark contrast to the passive pornography
found in the Paris Salons. Liberated from the restraints of these conventions, the Mary Magdalen of the Orientalists, Decadents and other *fin
de-siècle* writers and artists took on an exotic, mystical and, sometimes
even sinister persona, in which the nature of the relationship between
her and Christ was explored with a freedom characteristic of the age.

European travellers to the Orient in the nineteenth century were overwhelmed by the boundless vistas of desert lands, the incredible antiquity, the ruins of palaces and temples, the broken columns, all evoking the splendours of vanished dynasties, of pagan gods, and of biblical poetry. The Orient also set before them a haunting and exotic beauty: it was a land in which sphinxes might emerge, only, in the European imagination, to shed their masks to become *femmes fatales*, another incarnation of the Eternal Feminine.[85] Cleopatra, Isis, Salome and Lilith, those sexually voracious creatures, arose from this mysterious environment, and came to embody the erotic fantasies and fears of the late nineteenth-century artists and poets who re-created them. In the Orient the European sensibility seems to have found the eroticism it had been deprived of in strait-laced Victorian society – a dangerous sexuality and a seemingly perverse morality which encouraged writers and painters to cast their own inhibitions to the wind. The oriental woman – of whom Mary Magdalen became an example in the hands of Romantic writers and artists – the courtesan, slave, or *houri*, became an ineluctable source of erotic mystery, and the subject of innumerable paintings, poems, and novels like Flaubert's *Salammbô*, and his *Temptation of St Anthony*. Gérard de Nerval who, along with Flaubert, was one of the writers most inspired by his visits to the Orient, traced the fascination for such exotic creatures to their essential unknowability, the result of their alien languages and customs. Nerval himself wrote of the slave Zetnaybia:

> There is something extremely captivating and irresistible in a woman from a faraway country: her costumes and habits are already singular enough to strike you, she speaks an unknown language and has, in short, none of those vulgar shortcomings to which we have become only too accustomed among the women of our own country . . . I had the impression . . . that I owned a magnificent bird in a cage.[86]

To these writers and artists, Mary Magdalen also became a magnificent bird in a cage, an exotic bejewelled oriental, appropriately in her eastern setting, as Théophile Gautier described her in his poem 'Magdalena', 'Au milieu des parfums, dans les bras du palmier,/ Le chant du rossignol et le nid du ramier'[87] (Amid the perfumes, in the branches of the palm tree, the song of the nightingale and the ring-dove's nest). Her long hair flows on her neck in waves of ebony, like the 'ebony sea' lauded in 'La Chevelure', Baudelaire's reverie on women's hair; her beautiful face is drowned in it. For Gautier, she is the Ideal Woman, 'sainte prostituée', and lover of his favourite dreams, 'ô femme vraiment femme', 'most loving among women', and 'divine courtesan', clad in diaphanous gown. She is even more beautiful than the Virgin, so that the kneeling priest, 'sighing and praying in his pious ecstasy' before the picture the poet is describing, hesitates between the two. Gautier's lyrical effusions have her more scented than the 'lys de Sharon'; the Magdalen's perfumed oriental surroundings are transposed to the incense-drenched church in which the painting which has so inspired the poet hangs. This leads to the climax of the poem: 'Quand d'un brouillard d'encens la nef est toute pleine,/ Regardez le Jésus et puis la Madeleine.' (When the nave is filled with a fog of incense, look at Jesus and then at the Magdalen.) He now alludes to the 'mystère', the mystery which he would simultaneously like both to reveal and yet also remain silent about, the 'ineffable secret' which will be 'yielded in a long sigh by the organ': the inexpressible enigma hinted at but never stated being the human and physical relationship between Christ and Mary Magdalen.

When Massenet came to write his lyrical and lachrymose *Marie-Magdeleine* (1873), the first of his operas about women of doubtful virtue, his eponymous heroine was a sultry oriental courtesan, such as was depicted by Henrik Siemiradzki in his painting of *The Penitent Magdalen or First Meeting between Christ and the Magdalen* (1872, Florence, private collection). Unlike Massenet's other female characters such as Manon, Salomé or Herodias, Mary Magdalen neither succumbs to a fatal illness, commits suicide nor arrives at some other unfortunate end; her physical death is transformed into eternal life. Massenet's oratorio, which was first performed at the Théâtre de l'Odéon in Paris, with the celebrated mezzo-soprano Pauline Viardot (1821–1910) in the title role, was instrumental in establishing the reputation of its composer. Massenet had jumped on the bandwagon of the taste for figures of reformed courtesans which had been popular in France since Victor Hugo's *Marion Délorme* and Dumas' *La Dame aux Camélias*. His *Marie-Magdeleine* was also one of the first of a long line of operas written during the late nineteenth and early twentieth centuries about feminine sexual psychology, which became a hallmark of works by Massenet himself, Puccini, Richard Strauss and Janáček.[88] In *Marie-Magdeleine*, Massenet combined eroticism with religious overtones which were much in line with various devotional currents in contemporary French Catholicism; it proved an irresistible mixture, especially to the opera-going Parisienne. Subjects of such 'discreet and pseudo-religious eroticism' (*bondieuseries*), as they were described by the composer Vincent d'Indy, were extremely popular with the public. Massenet profited by the tastes of the bourgeoisie, and was entirely cynical about his own part in pandering to them: 'I don't believe in all that creeping-Jesus stuff', he wrote to d'Indy. 'But the public likes it, and we must always agree with the public.'[89] *Marie-Magdeleine* was followed by the equally successful *Eve* in 1875, *La Vièrge* (which was a failure), and *Thaïs*, the last of his operas on sacred themes, in 1894; and a host of heroines such as Salome in *Hérodiade* (1881), *Manon* (1884), *Sappho* (1897), Charlotte in *Werther* (1892) and *Thérèse* (1907). D'Indy himself composed a cantata to Mary Magdalen in 1889, to the accompaniment of piano and harmonium.[90]

The fallen woman was also an extremely popular figure in late nineteenth-century operas by Verdi, Puccini and Bellini, doomed to die because she had transgressed society's boundaries of respectable sexual mores, with Toscas throwing themselves off battlements, and Mimis, Normas and Violettas expiring, but no other composer explored the figure of the Magdalen. She did however appear in two other operatic disguises: as Maddalena, the woman of easy virtue in Verdi's *Rigoletto* of 1851, the sister of Sparafucile, a bravo, who is set to lure men to be robbed and murdered. Maddalena is the bait used to entice the duke of Mantua, a licentiate, to his death, in a plan of revenge concocted by Rigoletto who is to the duke what Leporello is to Don Giovanni, his aider and abetter in amatory affairs. However, Maddalena becomes fascinated by the duke, who gallantly courts her as 'Bella figlia d'amore' (Beautiful daughter of love), and persuades her brother to spare his life. Rigoletto's revenge turns into personal tragedy as the whole plot goes awry, his daughter dies, and the duke's voice is heard singing offstage, 'La donna è mobile'. In *Tosca* (1900), it is a picture of Mary Magdalen with large blue eyes and golden hair, in fact a portrait of the marchesa Attavanti, which Cavaradossi is in the process of painting, which provokes the jealousy of his beloved Floria Tosca, and leads to the tragic *dénouement*.[91]

The whore Maddalena is given her name in memory of Christianity's most famous repentant prostitute. Her siren-like role in *Rigoletto*, leading men to their destruction, is similar to that of Kundry, the wild and fatal woman of Wagner's opera *Parsifal* (1882). Kundry is used by the magician Klingsor to lure virtuous Christian knights from their true mission as guardians of the Holy Grail. In Wagner's opera, however, the link with Mary Magdalen is not confined merely to sexual licence as it is in Maddalena's case, but is made explicit by the parallel drawn between Parsifal, the 'pure' or 'holy fool', and Christ. Parsifal has to experience and reject sexual temptation in order to reclaim the Sacred Spear, lost to Klingsor by Amfortas, ruler of the Kingdom of the Grail. Parsifal's innocence and his redemption of humanity in the guise of Amfortas make the identification with Christ quite clear. Sometime in her past, Kundry has sinned and has been cursed by Klingsor to tempt men until she is rejected, and it is her rejection which will release her. Out of guilt for her sins, she also has a somewhat contradictory role as a faithful messenger to the Grail Knights, and first appears, like the wild horseback messengers of Valhalla, her hair streaming behind her, bringing a small crystal flask containing 'Balsam for the King', to soothe Amfortas' wounds, like Luke's sinner, Mary of Bethany and Mary Magdalen herself, bearing their ointment jars to anoint Christ. But through her main role, as temptress – to be rejected and thus saved by the Christ/Parsifal figure – she subsequently performs the characteristically Magdalenian task of washing Christ/Parsifal's feet and drying them with her long hair, to be forgiven and redeemed through her love. Parsifal then baptises her, and she dies a forgiven sinner. What Wagner establishes is the reciprocal connection between the *femme fatale* – Kundry's function up until the appearance of Parsifal – and Mary Magdalen. If it is to be assumed – as it always has been – that Mary Magdalen was beautiful because physical beauty was a necessary weapon in the armoury of the successful temptress or prostitute – then the seductive beauty and long hair of Kundry can also fit her for the role of Mary Magdalen. (In the 1987 production at Covent Garden, Kundry was given long red hair, thus identifying her explicitly with the stereotypical Magdalen.) Where beauty is the lure to sin, as it is when Kundry seduces the knights of the Holy Grail, then its rejection, by Parsifal in this instance, can lead to redemption and salvation. Wagner employs the characteristic Christian equation of feminine beauty and evil, and the equally characteristic Christian notion that salvation is only for those who are pure, seen in terms of sexual continence. His Kundry/Magdalen is ever the victim to Christian ideology.[92]

What Gautier had merely so delicately, even coyly, hinted at, namely the idea of a physical relationship between Christ and Mary Magdalen,

84 *Mary Magdalen in the House of the Pharisee* (1891). Jean Béraud. Paris, Musée d'Orsay.

was seized upon by several late nineteenth-century artists and writers. It even became the explicit subject of a play, *L'Amante du Christ*, which was performed at the Théâtre Libre in Paris in October 1888. 'It is one of the most daring pieces of realism ever achieved on the French stage', ran the report in the *New York Herald Tribune* of the day. A 'mystery' in one act, it vividly represented the story of 'Mary Magdalen throwing herself at Christ's feet and washing him during the meal with Simon the Pharisee'. The piece was assured of a *succès de curiosité*, with the protagonists shown as loving each other in an 'ultra Parisian way', and with all the realism that a 'Zola could throw into such a situation'.[93] Three years later, Jean Béraud created a similar sensation with his painting *La Madeleine chez le Pharisien* (Paris, Musée d'Orsay) in which he set the scene of Luke's sinner in a Parisian dining-room of the 1880s (see Plate 84). The artist stunned his public by using famous contemporaries as his models, among them Ernest Renan as the Pharisee, Alexandre

Dumas *fils* as one of the guests, the duc de Quercy as Christ, and the beautiful courtesan Liane de Pougy as Mary Magdalen herself. Its realistic treatment and contemporary *mise-en-scène* naturally provoked violent reactions, in both praise and condemnation.[94]

By having Christ alone in biblical costume, Béraud's painting may be read as a social critique rather than as a strictly biblical image, and it clearly makes no reference to any physical relationship between Christ and Mary Magdalen. This aspect is, however, made the explicit subject of a series of erotic crucifixions by different artists at the end of the nineteenth century: in Lovis Corinth's *Deposition* (1895, Cologne; see Plate 85), a forceful mother looks on from behind, while Mary Magdalen, leaning against him, hand to her face and bare-breasted, with her other arm brings up her red drapery to clasp round him. In 1885, the Belgian Decadent Félicien Rops executed a soft-ground etching of the Magdalen masturbating below a cross upon which is nailed, not the body of Christ, but a large and haloed penis. The arch-exponent of the kind of art which Mario Praz described as 'at the same time sexless and lascivious', Rops often portrayed woman as incarnate evil, the *femme fatale*, in sadistic phallocentric images; the Magdalen is but a variant of his women with voracious sexual appetites, as in for example *Les Sataniques*, where a woman carried off to hell has sexual intercourse with an ithyphallic statue of Satan, in the perennial equation of Eros and Death. These are images which combine sadism and misogyny to repellent effect. (Another soft-ground etching shows a post-coital scene, Mary Magdalen lying back and the phallus detumescent, all desire sated.)[95]

In an even more subjective and personal vein, in that he depicted himself as Christ, and his wife Fanny Grenfell as Mary Magdalen, Charles Kingsley, the Anglican clergyman, moralist and controversialist, and author of children's books such as *The Water Babies*, sketched his vision of their relationship in two drawings done before their marriage in 1844, which he gave to his wife, neither of which seems to have offended her for she kept them in her journal. Again, there are as in Rops strong overtones of blasphemy and sadism: his wife/Magdalen appears as the repentant sinner, kneeling in subjection at her Christ/ husband's feet in a coarse penitent's shift, a rope around her neck, the words 'Thy sins are forgiven' written below; in the other, the figures, both naked, are each tied to the cross and to each other, floating on a wave in the lassitudinous aftermath of love. Despite his strong anti-

Catholic sentiments, Kingsley appears to have used themes from the mysticism usually attributed to that religion to illustrate his sado-erotic union with his bride.[96]

Mary Magdalen as the human and physical lover of Christ is the image which Auguste Rodin (1840–1914) created in two plaster studies of c.1892 and 1894 (see Plate 86). The interpretation is both tender and erotic: the drooping, sagging figure of Christ which fuses with the roughly textured cross, which seems to both bear and be borne by him, is complemented by the swaying, keening shape of the Magdalen, her left arm, on which his head rests, raised up protectively, her body bent across him, and right arm around him, and hair flowing over her arm. She has, oddly, two left feet.[97] Rainer Maria Rilke, who had come to know the sculptor well – he had also married Clara Westhoff, one of Rodin's students – in 1902 was commissioned to write a monograph on Rodin. Of the *Christ and the Magdalen* he wrote:

85 *Deposition* (1895). Lovis Corinth. Cologne, Wallraf-Richartz Museum, on loan.

Christ, in the gesture of the Crucifixion, his outstretched arms resembling a signpost at the crossroads of all pain, dies under the burden of his destiny which, like this stone (a heavy and petrified Cross), towers above him.

And she, who once came to anoint his indefatigable feet, approaches, now that the sacrifice is accomplished, to surround this abandoned, bloodless body with the belated and meaningless tenderness of her own. In a fit of despair she has thrown herself down on her knees before him. With her left arm she supports his abused head, whose expression she could not bear. And this face drifts along on her trembling arm, like a floating object, while she, bent over to the right, like a flame tormented by the wind, tries to embed and hide the ineffable suffering of this so greatly loved body in her own broken love. She surrounds him with a disconso-

86 *Christ and the Magdalen* c.1892. Auguste Rodin. Paris, Musée Rodin.

late and entreating movement, and with a gesture of hopelessness she looses her hair in order to bury Christ's tormented heart in it.[98]

Rilke himself seems to have been inspired by the character of Mary Magdalen and her love for Christ. But it was his explicit belief that Christ was not divine, was entirely human, and deified only on Calvary, expressed in an unpublished poem of 1893, and referred to in other poems of the same period, which allowed him to portray Christ's love for Mary Magdalen, though remarkable, as entirely human. In 'Visions of Christ', seven poems of 1897, Christ is even the father of a child born to Mary Magdalen,[99] an idea expounded by the curious secret association of Rosicrucians, one of whose founders claimed to be a direct descendant of that child.[100] In 1910 Rilke translated an anonymous French sermon, 'L'Amour de Madeleine', attributed to the great seventeenth-century French theologian and preacher Bossuet, which had recently been discovered in St Petersburg. This rather extraordinary document, although depicting a traditional biblical image of the relationship between Christ and Mary Magdalen, contained ambiguities which were reflected in Rilke's own poetry. In the sermon, Christ is a tantaliser, provoking love and in turn withdrawing from the lover: 'What do you mean', Christ is apostrophised, 'when you pull so strongly at the hearts and draw them so firmly to you, and then go away when they do not in the least expect it? How cruel you are! What a strange game you play with the hearts that love you.' Having allowed Mary Magdalen to kiss his feet and anoint his head despite both the Pharisee's demurral and Judas' disapproval, Christ is described as praising her; then, when he has formed this union, he vanishes, only to arise from the dead, and to tell her, 'Noli me tangere.'[101]

Rilke may have seen himself as a kind of Don Juan, or as the cavalier Christ of the sermon, in his own relationships with women. When the translation was in final proof, he apparently asked his publisher Anton Kippenberg to produce it as cheaply as possible: 'how many women need this, how many will it support and comfort . . . This is where women's suffering is transformed into greatness . . . Let us make sure this vademecum comes into many, many hands (hands of women and girls, it's no concern of man, *cet animal*).'[102] The book was published in 1912, bound in humble sackcloth, entirely suitable to its subject, a format with which Rilke was entirely satisfied.

The idea that Christ 'flirted' with women's emotions is to be found in 'Der Auferstandene', or 'The Arisen'. Here Mary Magdalen comes to the sepulchre, 'Aber da sie dann, um ihm zu salben,/ an das Grab kam, Tränen im Gesicht' (But when she came to the sepulchre to anoint him, tears on her face), to where Christ has risen for her sake, 'merely to tell her joyfully, "Do not –" '. It is only in her cave, having become stronger through his death, that she comes to understand his rejection of her touch and, in the last stanza, that her earthly passion for him has to become spiritual:

> um aus ihr die Liebende zu formen,
> die sich nicht mehr zum Geliebten neigt,
> weil sie, hingerissen von enormen
> Stürmen, seine Stimme übersteigt.[103]

(So that to form from her the lover who no longer inclines upon the beloved, since she, carried away by vast storms, goes far beyond his voice.)

The first two lines of the last stanza which describe the lover she must now become might be another graceful and lyrical complement to Rodin's tender figure. In 'Pietà', a poem written eighteen months earlier in Paris in 1906, the human relationship is described:

> So seh ich, Jesus, deine Füsse wieder
> die damals eines Jünglings Füsse waren,
> da ich sie bang entkleidete und wusch;
> wie standen sie verwirrt in meinen Haaren
> und wie ein weisses Wild im Dornenbusch.
>
> So seh ich deine niegeliebten Glieder
> zum erstenmal in dieser Liebesnacht.
> Wir legten uns noch nie zusammen nieder,
> und nun wird nur bewundert und gewacht.
>
> Doch, siehe, deine Hände sind zerrissen –:
> Geliebter, nicht von mir, von meinen Bissen.
> Dein Herz steht offen und man kann hinein:
> das hätte dürfen nur mein Eingang sein.

Nun bist du müde, und dein müder Mund
hat keine Lust zu meinem wehen Munde –
O Jesus, Jesus, wann war unsre Stunde?
Wie gehn wir beide wunderlich zugrund.[104]

(So, Jesus, I see your feet again which were once those of a young man and which I anxiously uncovered and washed; how tangled they were in my hair; like a white deer in a thornbush.

So for the first time in this night of love, I see your limbs which have never been loved. Nor have we ever lain together, and now one can only wonder and watch.

Yet, look, your hands are torn—: Beloved, not by me, by my bites. Your heart is open and all can enter there: which should have been for me only to enter.

Now you are tired, and your tired mouth has no desire for my sad mouth – oh Jesus, Jesus, when was our hour? How strange that we both die together.)

At the foot of the cross, Mary Magdalen looks back to the moment when as Luke's sinner in the house of the Pharisee, she first touched his feet, and meditates on the body which has never loved, not even loved hers. Her yearning for physical contact with Christ is mixed with bitterness that his love is not for her alone, but for all mankind. Events have overtaken them, and she can only mourn, in a lyrical elegy for lost love which again has affinities with Rodin's figure.

Rilke was much impressed by the gossamer-like dramas of the psyche of Maurice Maeterlinck (1862–1949), the Belgian Symbolist poet, dramatist and essayist. In Maeterlinck's allegories, the heroines, and a few of the heroes, are sensitive souls seeking after a higher spiritual reality beyond their earthly existence. Mélisande, married to Golaud whom she does not love, falls in love with Pelléas, and sees love transcendental. In *Mary Magdalen*, his three-act play, first performed in 1910, his eponymous heroine is also seeking spiritual truth, and at first mistakes its physical semblance for it.[105] She tells Silanus and Verus, two Romans, that until lately, she has 'lived among falsehoods by which others profited'; for the past six months, she has lived among truths by which she herself profits: she is a courtesan, well known to the local

Jews who despise her for having sold herself to Romans. 'Roman woman!' they shout at her, 'Adulteress!' She is a soul struggling, but one finding, and ultimately transcending, itself in a process which is Platonic in concept. The Magdalen is also that exotic-erotic creature of the Romantic imagination, the oriental *femme fatale*, heralded before her first appearance by a double flute, 'clad in a raiment that seemed woven of pearls and dew, in a cloak of Tyrian purple with sapphire ornaments, and decked with jewels that rendered a little heavier this eastern pomp'. She is no vulgar courtesan, as Verus who has long desired her remarks. She has slaves too, whom she dismisses 'harshly', and tortures when she suspects them of having stolen her 'Carthaginian rubies', pearls, and 'Babylonian peacock'. To Silanus, she is the Shulamite perfumed with myrrh and frankincense, drenched with the orientalisms which the Romantics and Symbolists found so artistically alluring. (Somewhat incongruously for a *houri*, she also has golden hair.) However, when she hears the voice of the Nazarene, the name by which Christ is referred to throughout the play, she is 'irresistibly drawn by [it]', and, when threatened with stoning by the crowd as an adulteress, the 'divine voice' saves her with the words, 'He that is without sin among you, let him throw the first stone.'

The play then develops into a struggle on the part of Mary Magdalen, between her love for Verus and the teaching of the Nazarene. Like the creatures in Plato's cave, she takes the shadow, Verus (are we perhaps intended to see an irony in his name?), for reality, or real love, but he is merely the semblance of that reality. At the climax of the play, Verus, who has arrested the Nazarene, gives to Mary Magdalen the choice: to yield to him and save the Nazarene, or to refuse him and see the Nazarene die. Her immediate reaction is to save the Nazarene, as he had saved her, but prompted by Joseph of Arimathaea, she realises that although her refusal to sell her body will mean the Nazarene's death, it will allow the redemption to take place, and she has now understood the plan. Her recognition of her destiny comes slowly: 'I only begin to understand . . . For one sees only little by little.' As the Nazarene is led away, Verus leaves; looking back, he sees Mary Magdalen motionless 'as though in ecstasy' and 'illumined with the light of the departing torches'. The enlightened soul, in the form of Mary Magdalen, has transcended, has seen the shadows for what they are, illusory, and 'guided by the light', has come to know itself in the human psyche, and has become aware of its divine potentialities. Maeterlinck's Mary Magdalen, always the focus in this allegory – the Nazarene is never seen, interacting in her life three times from offstage – is a strong figure, a character in search of her true role; Maeterlinck gives her the extraordinary power of holding the Nazarene's fate in her hands. In her rejection of terrestrial or fleshly love in the form of false Verus, she delivers the Nazarene to his death, and finds spiritual or real love, or the absolute Good, the ultimate *agathon*, becoming once more the Gnostic Mariham.

The nineteenth-century Mary Magdalen was used as a vehicle to explore ideas about sexuality, love, sin, and the position of women in middle-class society. Her age-old association with fallen women made her a central figure in the examination of feminine sexuality with its connotations of sin and moral inferiority, particularly as societies struggled with the major social problem of prostitution. It was the battle for women's rights, including those of the prostitute, which led to women's emancipation in the twentieth century. Romanticism and Symbolism equated Mary Magdalen with Eros, and the connection was to be further explored by writers such as Lawrence and Kazantzakis in the twentieth century. But her re-evaluation in non-Catholic churches was perhaps the most important development of all. The woman by the cross represented the more positive aspects of woman in Christianity: her ministering role, strength, courage and faith are in sharp contradistinction to traditional 'feminine' meekness and passivity, traits which had long served only to subordinate women.

CHAPTER X

MUCH MALIGN'D MAGDALEN

> How much scriptural interpretation and legitimization
> served political functions for the Church can be illustrated
> by the example of Mary Magdalen.
>
> ELISABETH SCHÜSSLER FIORENZA, *In Memory of Her*[1]

 IN APRIL 1990 five Roman Catholic extremists were jailed for bombing Paris cinemas which had shown *The Last Temptation of Christ* in 1988. Their fire-bombs, thrown in anger at the film's dream sequence during which Jesus makes love to a naked Mary Magdalen, injured thirteen people. The bombers were jailed for up to three years, and three were to compensate a British couple injured in one blaze. Iconoclasm and religious bigotry had raised their heads once again. During the summer of 1988, thirty-one thousand Protestant pastors in the United States had threatened to boycott the film, some radical members amongst them claiming that the film's production company, MCA, was engaged in a vile Jewish plot to debase Jesus' image, and had staged mock crucifixions outside its chairman's estate. Fundamentalists like the Revd Jerry Falwell of the Moral Majority urged Christians to shun all MCA products, and the Catholic Church declared the film immoral. And feminists, both Christian and otherwise, were up in arms as in the film the temptation which tore 'the son of Mary' from his divine mission is symbolised by an entirely feminine world, exemplified in particular by Mary Magdalen. Late in the 1980s, she had re-emerged into the spotlight once again.[2]

The uproar engendered by the film was a testament to the latent violence which can still be aroused by threats to dogmatic belief – *vide* the reaction within the Muslim world to Salman Rushdie's novel *Satanic*

Verses in 1989 – and which arguments over the figure of Christ and the interpretation of his ministry can still provoke. The film's director, Martin Scorsese, was even accused of blasphemy. The film exhibited the renewed interest in the figure of Mary Magdalen, which has spawned in recent years a plethora of novels written in an attempt to reassert Eros and the Feminine within Christianity. Feminist reactions to the film's treatment of Mary Magdalen were in part conditioned by the re-evaluation of her identity and of her role within Christ's ministry, itself the fruit of recent scholarly study of the early Church and of women's position within it. This research has been carried out princi-pally in the United States; it has most recently also rendered Mary Magdalen a figure-head in the argument over women's ministry.

Martin Scorsese faced the furore, and answered the barrage of ques-tions. As a lapsed Catholic and ex-seminarian, he affirmed that Christ still exerted a hold over him. Barbara Hershey, the actress who played Mary Magdalen, had fifteen years previously given Scorsese a copy of *The Last Temptation* by Nikos Kazantzakis (1885–1957), with a request that should he ever make a film of it she might be cast as Mary Mag-dalen. Scorsese replied in interview after interview that he regards Chris-tianity as poetry, and Christ as a symbol: 'It's the struggle to get to God which is interesting. I'm a believer, but I'm struggling. It's always been part of my life. The premise [of the book] is that Jesus is God. Whether you believe it or not, that's another issue . . . But I didn't want the Christ of Catholic iconography, glowing in the dark.'[3]

The director must have felt vindicated when, at the press conference which followed the film's showing at the Venice Biennale in Sep-tember 1988, an elderly, grey-suited man stood up to say in Italian how greatly moved he had been by the film, and how important it was to him. It was only when he turned to sit down that people in the packed auditorium were able to see that the speaker was a Roman Catholic priest.

Kazantzakis' Jesus, who is Scorsese's too, is also a struggler: he fights against his natural human desires in order to assume his identity as the Messiah, in the landscape of the Christian *psychomachia* where the spirit wages eternal war with the things of the flesh.[4] In the knowledge that he is the Chosen One, he inherits his father Joseph's *métier* as carpenter; as a prophylactic, he hopes, against having to take on his divine role as saviour, he becomes the 'cross-maker', reviled by his acquaintances for the job he does, never going to the synagogue, and working on the

Sabbath. He is constantly assailed by his humanity, the symbol for which is naturally his procreative urge. The flesh itself is embodied by Mary Magdalen, and to a lesser extent by Mary and Martha. Kazantzakis' Magdalen, following the age-old tradition, is the local whore when we see her first, and it's all Jesus' fault. On his mother's advice he looks for a wife in Cana. Like all mothers, and Jewish mothers, according to Kazantzakis, in particular, she longs for her boy to marry and give her grandchildren, unaware that he has a higher destiny. He chooses the beautiful Mary Magdalen, his cousin, for whom since childhood he has had sensual yearnings. As a three year-old, he had taken her by the hand, and they had undressed and lain on the ground, pressing the soles of their feet together; 'from that time on Magdalene was lost – she could no longer live without a man'. He is instantly attacked by his conscience, in the form of ten claws nailing themselves into his head and two frenzied wings flapping above him: he knows he is consecrated to God, and he therefore rejects her. He flagellates and scourges himself to relieve himself of his lust.

Mary Magdalen is first described as 'cackling' with laughter, in her red sandals, unplaited hair and 'complete armour of ankle bands, bracelets and earrings'. She is the only daughter of his uncle, the rabbi, and, like Milton's Delilah, 'decorated bow to stern like a frigate sailing with the wind', sexual temptation personified. She is described further on in the book as 'proud-gaited, high-rumped Magdalene, her breasts exposed, lips and cheeks covered with make-up'. Distraught because he has denied her sexuality – sexuality is a woman's soul, she later tells him – she goes off to become a whore, setting up shop at Magdala, 'at the crossroads, where the caravans pass by'. To forget him, she becomes a 'liberated woman' – as a prostitute she emancipates herself from all men, and in so doing becomes mistress of herself. On his way to a monastery to devote himself to things of the spirit, the 'son of Mary', Kazantzakis' poetic title for his protagonist, knows that he must save Magdalene because he has destroyed her, even though going to her house will be the 'greatest degradation'. The house itself is festooned with all the symbolic paraphernalia: a door with two intertwined snakes, an immense pomegranate, a male and female cypress on either side (the male's trunk appropriately 'straight as a sword' and the female's 'wide open spreading branches') and a caged partridge.[5] He queues up behind bedouins, foreign princes and rich merchants, watching voyeuristically as she services her clients. When it is his turn, he finds her 'stark-naked, drenched in sweat, raven-black hair spread out over the pillow', smelling of all the men she has been with. Her rage on seeing him is predictable, as is Kazantzakis' characterisation of one who has become a whore: she is crude and coarse, she 'titters' and 'hisses', and into her mouth Kazantzakis puts truisms about the feminine: 'Woman is a wounded doe'; 'in order to forget one man . . . I've surrendered my body to all men'. She rejects his help, but he nevertheless sleeps in her room, and as he dreams he sees him as a child at the breast, and 'looks over him as a mother'. He is tempted again as he leaves in the morning, seeing the 'woman [lie] on her back, motionless, her hair veiling her naked breasts. She watche[s] him through her eyelashes, and her whole body tremble[s].' Hearing his own voice utter her name, he takes fright at his own desire and departs. Dramatically sitting up, Mary Magdalen begins to weep, degraded in her own eyes, and rejected by the man she loves.

Kazantzakis' Mary Magdalen is a composite creature: she is both Luke's sinner and the woman taken in adultery, about to be stoned by the Pharisees (John 8:3–11). In Kazantzakis' story, she is thrown into a pit and is on the verge of being stoned by Barabbas the Zealot for selling her wares on the Sabbath. The 'man in white', as Jesus has now become, saves her, and she in turn becomes Luke's sinner redeemed, 'fallen at Jesus' feet' which she 'secretly kisses', and which are 'buried in her hair'. She is now his 'sister', he her 'brother'. She becomes 'born again with a virgin body', her task every evening to wash his travel-sore feet, let down her hair and wipe them dry. When at the marriage feast of Cana other guests shun her, Jesus tells them the parable of the Wise and Foolish Virgins. He and Mary Magdalen become Bridegroom and Soul/ Bride, and she gives to him of the fruit of the pomegranate tree. This gives Kazantzakis occasion to put further words of feminine wisdom into Mary Magdalen's mouth: 'I must look at you, because woman issued from the body of man and still cannot detach her body from his. But you must look at heaven, because you are a man, and man was created by God. Allow me to look at you therefore, my child.' She becomes a follower. More poetic profundities follow:

> she was not a man, she had no need for words. Once she had said to him, 'Rabbi, why do you talk to me about the future life? We are not men, to have need of another, an eternal life; we are women, and for us one moment with the man we love is ever-

lasting Paradise, one moment far from the man we love is everlasting hell. It is here on this earth that we women live out eternity.[6]

A little later, not daring to speak to a Jesus absorbed in sorrow, she muses: 'At times a woman's speech gladdens a man, at times it makes him furious.'

The now notorious dream sequence at the end of Scorsese's film has its source in Kazantzakis' book. It was this which offended Christians most. It was heretical to suggest that not only did Jesus have to make a choice on the cross between his divine and human natures, but also that he made love with Mary Magdalen. In the book, the Devil in the form of a male angel, rather than the golden-haired girl with the oddly English accent of the film, persuades Jesus to descend from the cross where he is preparing to die, and leads him to Mary Magdalen, whose 'eyes frolic seductively and cunningly'. In a scene which is both beautifully and tastefully executed in the film, they make love, and Mary Magdalen says, 'We shall have a son.' She then wanders off. (In the book, she meets her death through stoning, by the as-yet unconverted Saul of Damascus, persecutor of Christians until he turns coat and persecutes those who do not, like him, become followers of the new faith; in the film, she dies, it is assumed, in pregnancy.) Jesus' progenitive urges are not left to lie there: the angel next offers him Mary and Martha, the sisters of Lazarus, by whom earlier in the book he has been tempted. ('When he thought of Magdalene, his eyes grew misty; and just last night, as he secretly gazed at Lazarus' sister Mary.') He is momentarily disconcerted, what about Mary Magdalen? But the angel tells him of her death, and assures him: 'There's only one woman, but she has many faces.' Mary Magdalen was merely a symbol of womankind, so forget her, he further advises. Jesus settles into a *ménage à trois*, and fathers a horde of blond children, becoming a patriarch; he has conquered death through procreation; taken the easier option. The scene switches, and the taste of vinegar on his lips brings Jesus back to the fact that he is on the cross. Relieved that it has all been a dream, that he had in fact rejected this vision of terrestrial bliss, he gives up the ghost.

Scorsese argued on Kazantzakis' behalf that woman *per se* was not Jesus' temptation, but merely symbolised the daily temptations that man is prey to and in which she is protagonist. This may seem a nice distinction but is of course an old argument which reiterates the dualistic polarities of divinity and mundanity, spirit and flesh, male and female, good and evil, and is endorsed by Kazantzakis' celebration and emphasis of Jesus as 'the young man' and 'the youth', in all his male vigour. The world and its temptations are represented by the feminine. Even the devil who tempts Jesus in the desert is female, bare-breasted, and, in the film, speaks with Barbara Hershey's voice. Mary Magdalen's crude, stereotypical characterisation, with its accumulated symbolism and metaphors, derives from the author's own spiritual 'odyssey' which led him through Marxism to orthodoxy, and, for a certain period, asceticism. Scorsese's adaptation is so true to Kazantzakis' novel that he uses the author's epigraph as his own:

> The dual substance of Christ – the yearning, so human, so super-human, of man to attain to God, or more exactly, to return to God, and identify himself with him – has always been a deep inscrutable mystery to me. This nostalgia for God, at once so mysterious and so real, has opened in me large wounds and also large flowing springs.[7]

By contrast, Kazantzakis' Mary Magdalen is Woman, flesh – the universal, timeless symbol of man's temptation to stray from God.

By making his hero choose to reject his humanity in favour of his divinity, Kazantzakis was accused by the Church of docetism, the heresy which denied that Christ was both fully man and fully God, and out of which evolved what is now called 'Incarnation theology', the teaching which proclaims that the son of God took human flesh from his human mother, and which was promulgated at the Council of Chalcedon in 451. The debate did not, however, rest there. In his provocative and on the whole persuasive essay *The Sexuality of Christ in Renaissance Art and in Modern Oblivion*,[8] Leo Steinberg suggested that certain devotional images of the Christ child or dead Christ, painted between the late fourteenth and mid-sixteenth centuries, actually embody incarnation theology of the period. Various iconographic devices were used to represent Jesus as both God and man, as icons for the literal display of his carnality, the *ostentatio genitalium*, a figuration of 'God's descent into manhood'. Steinberg also suggests that such images – in which the Virgin touches, points to, protects or draws the child's drapery aside to reveal his sex – would have had a profound significance for the late medieval and Renaissance spectator, whereas they have either eluded the notice of modern viewers, perhaps at least slightly perplexed some, or been tactfully overlooked. Other saints may also witness the doctrine, guiding the viewer's gaze: in Cavaliere d'Arpino's painting (1592–3), Mary Magdalen points in the direction of the Christ child's genitalia, as do the Virgin and St Anne.[9] As a naked figure, both as child and man, Christ also becomes *nuda Veritas*, a symbol of truth and purity. In what he has styled the 'enhanced loincloth' of Christ on the cross which appears in northern art of the mid-fifteenth century, Steinberg sees a synecdochic device – it draws attention to the thing it ostensibly seeks to conceal – which acts as a metaphor for the resurrected Christ: great swags and sweeps of gauzy material which disguise Christ's erect penis, the 'body's best show of power'. As a symbol of revivified puissance, the imagery of the erect penis derives from the myth of Osiris, the Egyptian god of the afterlife who is 'represented with his restored member out like a leveled lance', and in mythic terms prefigured Christ in his resurrection.[10]

In his last novella, the marvellously crafted 'Man who Died', D. H. Lawrence returned to the equation of erection and resurrection in the Osiris myth with the happy outcome of his two-part story.[11] In the first half, he uses the Mary Magdalen–Christ relationship to explore his central theme, the Platonic dichotomy between body and soul. The story involves an unnamed protagonist, clearly Christ himself, who wakes up in the sepulchre, having been taken down from the cross 'too soon', having not, in fact, died at all. Overcome by a deep sense of disillusion at having made the wrong choice – 'his virginity had been an excess, a kind of greed', and later, 'He had misunderstood love' – at dawn in the garden, he meets Madeleine whom he identifies as the repentant prostitute, who now represents the self-denying (and thus life-denying) chaste virtues of conventional Christian thought. Madeleine had taken more from her lovers than she gave while he, on the other hand, had given more than he had taken. Unable to bear the thought of rejoining his previous existence, he rejects Madeleine who, needing to be saved from the 'old wilful Eve', clutches for 'the man in him who had died and was dead'. The first part of the story ends with his wandering off alone. The second half tells of his regeneration through woman (and specifically through sexual union with that woman), here identified as a priestess of Isis who has been awaiting the return of her lost god Osiris. The mythic links between Christ and Mary Magdalen and Osiris and Isis are confirmed by the scene in which the priestess anoints the unnamed man's wounds, fulfilling the role which Mary Magdalen had been unable to because of Christ's resurrection. The fact that both women wear yellow further indicates that a parallel was intended, which allows the Magdalen-figure finally to achieve physical union with the Christ-figure, and where Christ/Osiris becomes fully man, body and spirit integrated into a harmonious whole. The priestess conceives: 'I shall be big with Osiris,' she tells him. The man sails away. Like all Lawrence's protagonists, he will go alone to his destiny, but like Osiris and other nature gods who are reborn with the seasons, and like the Christian god, he will return 'sure as the spring'.

Lawrence's story abounds with images borrowed from the gospels but which are now imbued with his own oft-repeated ideas about the supremacy of sexuality, and his consecration of the 'mystery of the phallus', *par excellence* figured in the cock which opens the story – which of course had crowed thrice when Peter denied Christ – and functions now as a metaphor for what the Christ-figure is not. The young cock – the story was originally entitled 'The Escaped Cock' – is seen with his three 'shabby' hens, a life-affirming relationship which contrasts with the life-denying relationship of Christ and his three women, Madeleine, 'the woman who had been his mother and Joan'. (Joan is Lawrence's deprecatory translation of the name Joanna, wife of Chuza, one of Christ's female followers, just as his omission of the Virgin's name relegates his mother to an entirely subservient function.) The cock is also associated with the idea of the 'risen' body (the Christ-figure punningly exclaims 'I am risen!' on finally achieving an erection). Lawrence's ingenious use of the *Noli me tangere* as a leitmotif links the two parts of the story – it is the automatic reaction to physical approaches which the Christ-figure must overcome to achieve his fulfilment, and it is through touch, of the woman, that he becomes fully man. 'Do not touch me yet! I am not yet healed or in touch with men,' he says to Madeleine. Instead of the anguished cry of 'Why hast thou forsaken me?' at the moment of his death, we hear the exclamation, 'Father why did you hide this from me?' as he touches the priestess's breasts. He finds his salvation in the full use of his sexuality.

Whilst Lawrence, writing in 1929, could use the concept of the two natures in Christ to criticise and condemn Christian ideas about love and sexuality in fiction, Christ's genuine humanity, and therefore his sexuality, have also been the subject of several serious studies over the past three decades. Unlike the Renaissance images which drew attention to his genitalia in order to stress his humanity, recently the problem has been how to deal with his sexuality in the context of his human exist-ence. The suggestion that he may have been married, as a rabbi of his age would probably have been, has led one writer, as we have seen, to conjecture that he might even have been married to Mary Magdalen. This was argued by the Protestant theologian William E. Phipps in his book *Was Jesus Married? The Distortion of Sexuality in the Christian Tra-dition*, first published in 1970, and reissued in 1989.[12] Marriage to Mary Magdalen, he suggests, might have taken place during the second decade of Christ's life; she may even, in a further extension of the hypothesis, have been unfaithful, and Christ, out of unwavering love, may well have duly forgiven her. This experience, according to Phipps, rendered Christ far more understanding about the nature of adultery and love, *agape*, and convinced him to reject all notion of divorce. Phipps' 'intriguing conjecture' could therefore be taken to accord to Mary Mag-dalen the power to influence to some extent Christ's views of human relationships, a theme which has been resumed recently, and with rather less authority, by other more populist writers. A book published in 1992, Dr Barbara Thiering's *Jesus the Man*, goes so far as to claim that Mary Magdalen was not only married to Jesus, but left him after the crucifixion (which he survived for thirty years), having borne him a girl and two boys. Christ, it seems, then married again. The author, a lecturer in the school of divinity at Sydney University, bases her claims on a new reading of the Dead Sea Scrolls.

The idea that Mary Magdalen might have been married to Christ, and the bearer of his children, receives an airing in *Holy Blood, Holy Grail*, one of the more bizarre manifestations of the late twentieth-century popular interest both in the story of Christ and in conspiracy theory.[13] Following a staged crucifixion, in which Jesus is either taken down from the cross in a drugged state, or replaced by Simon of Cyrene, his family is obliged to flee from those, headed by St Peter, who were not part of the plot and are bent on preserving the reputation of Christ the Messiah. Mary Magdalen, together with brother Lazarus and others, arrive in the south of France, she bearing the *Sang Raal*, or Holy Grail, which the authors interpret as the holy blood of Christ in the form of his child or children. Once established within the Jewish community in the south of France, the family intermarries with the Merovingian kings and so on down through Godfroi de Bouillon (who almost becomes king of Jerusalem), the house of Lorraine, the Hapsburgs and the ever shadowy, but ever present, Prieuré de Sion, who hold the secret of it all, whatever it may be (and are also poised to create a unified state of Europe with a descendant of Christ, and of course Mary Magdalen, on its throne), which is rumoured to be hidden near the town of Rennes-le-Château, whose curé Saunière discovered coded documents in the church, and constructed the mysterious Tour de Magdala to house his library. The authors breathlessly bend to their purpose whatever information comes their way, and the book offers no new insights into the historical figure of Mary Magdalen, but concentrates on trying to assemble proof for some of the more far-fetched of the legends which have accumulated around her over the centuries, using as their guiding principle the idea that there is no smoke without a fire.

Kazantzakis' novel achieved wider notoriety through its translation into film; in the last decade a parable based on another gospel story which features Mary Magdalen in a major role and a film which discusses the nature of love through a character given the name of Maria Magdalena have both appeared on the cinema screens. The success of these two films, Denys Arcand's marvellous *Jesus of Montreal* (1989), and Krzysztof Kieślowski's *A Short Film about Love* (1989), shows the continuing relevance of using Mary Magdalen's composite figure to illustrate sexual mores within a contemporary setting. Whilst in neither is she actually depicted as a prostitute, in one she is seen as a model who uses her body as her source of income, and, in the other, as a sexually liberated woman whose lifestyle would inevitably fall foul of Roman Catholic, and specifically Polish Catholic, morality.

Mary Magdalen is a thoroughly modern Magdalen in *Jesus of Montreal*, an allegory on several levels about society, the media, the organised Church, modern Montreal and the Passion of Christ. The parallel between Mary Magdalen and the character of Mireille is established when we first see the latter selling her body in a commercial for a scent. She joins the band of actors led by Daniel Coulombe who has been commissioned to bring the annual Passion play up to date, and whose name itself may be a play on words and therefore a metaphor for

Christ.[14] From that moment on, their own activities parallel the story of the Passion play in a complex interrelationship which allows subtle and biting criticism of both the modern Church and the business world which the Church so often appears to emulate. Mireille naturally takes the part of Mary Magdalen, who, at the end of the Passion play, runs down from the shrine, her cloak fluttering behind her, to announce to the disbelieving disciples, 'I saw him!' In the course of rehearsals, continuing references to the gospel story crop up as she falls under the spell of Daniel/Jesus, who rescues her from her meretricious career; indeed when it looks as though the play will not go on – the ecclesiastical authorities object strongly to its new ideas about the historical Jesus and early and Gnostic Christianity: their play is not traditional enough – she says to the group, 'You have saved me, you can't let me down', and the show goes on. In another scene, with Constance/Martha, she appears as a *vanitas* figure, looking at herself in a mirror, incapable of going out without her make-up, and further parallels are involved when she washes Daniel while he takes a bath, and supports his dead body in her lap in a surreal *pietà* scene glimpsed through a train in the Montreal underground. When Daniel/Jesus is tempted at the top of a modern temple of commerce – a skyscraper – by a lawyer/Devil, he is offered riches, fame, sex and Montreal, and, in the rooftop restaurant, a 'Virgin Mary' to drink and a 'Magdalen lobster' to eat. When, after Daniel's death, that same lawyer tempts the actors/disciples to set up a theatre, ostensibly to commemorate Daniel, the faithful Magdalen walks away from them, divorcing herself from the rest of the group.

The anti-hero of Kieślowski's film is the nineteen year-old peeping Tomek, a virgin, the object of whose obsession is an unnamed liberated older woman artist who lives in the Stalinist housing block opposite his own, whose sexual activities he watches through his telescope from his bedroom.[15] Tomek works at the post office, and he intercepts and detains her mail so as to engineer their meeting face-to-face. His awkwardness somehow conveys his genuine love for her, and she offers herself to him as is her custom. For she believes that love does not exist, that it is merely a physiological condition known as lust; he cannot bear the burden of such an interpretation, and tries to commit suicide. Her despair at her own existence he has already witnessed as she weeps after a telephone call from a lover who, when he rings, gives her her name, 'Maria Magdalena'. She is left, having destroyed the one who loved her, to reflect upon her degraded image of herself as one who used her body for erotic pleasures, but was devoid of love. The revelation that her name is Maria Magdalena comes late in the film, suddenly crystallising the inherent immorality of her life, and Kieślowski uses the name, just as the nineteenth-century novelists did, to confirm hints about the character's past (there has already been reference to the sinfulness of sex outside marriage). It also clarifies her need for redemption through the virgin Tomek, whose attempted death and 'resurrection' – his mysterious recovery – further echo the gospel story, as does her appearance at his bedside reflecting Mary Magdalen's visit to the sepulchre. The image of her alone with nothing but the awareness of the errors of her past can be seen as a modern interpretation of Mary Magdalen weeping in her grotto. It is also a testament to the enduring power of the Magdalen-as-fallen-woman myth from which it sometimes seems that the gospel figure will never escape.

Mary Magdalen's first appearances on celluloid were in such silent religious epics as *La Vie et la Passion de Jésus-Christ* (1902), *La Vie de Jésus* (1905–14) and *Satana; overro, il Dramma dell'Umanità* (1912), in which she is usually depicted as one of the three Marys, but with no reference to her past sinful life. In *La Vie et la Passion de Jésus-Christ*, she has a central role in the Passion scenes, helping to raise Christ as he carries the cross, touching him as he is nailed onto it, lying across the rock of Golgotha, and supporting the Virgin as Christ is put into a coffin, the scenes showing their debt to earlier religious iconography.[16] It is not until much later, in films such as Franco Zeffirelli's *Jesus of Nazareth* (with a screenplay by Anthony Burgess), that Mary Magdalen, played in this instance by Anne Bancroft, appears as a prostitute – she is first shown getting out of bed with a client – and as the Virgin Mary's support at the crucifixion.[17] Similarly she is the redeemed prostitute in Tim Rice and Andrew Lloyd Webber's rock opera, *Jesus Christ Superstar* (1970), who bathes and anoints a travel-weary Jesus but, accustomed to sexual love, sings, 'I don't know how to love him.'[18] But when Judas criticises Jesus ('What does a man like you want with a woman like her?'), Jesus replies that Mary Magdalen alone is trying to give him what he needs 'right here and now'.

In a century which has produced less religious art than any other, the Church having ceased to function as a great patron of the arts, it may come as no surprise to find that comparatively few artists have chosen to portray Mary Magdalen. The idea of Mary Magdalen, ancient symbol of the Church and Bride of Christ, attracted the English typographer and social reformer Eric Gill (1882–1940). In his engraving *The Nuptials of God* she is clearly the curving female form which presses up against a crucified Christ, reminiscent of Rodin's group, her figure consisting merely of waves of hair down to the ground (see Plate 87).[19] In this heavily charged image, Gill seems to combine his ideas about sexual liberation and the Roman Catholicism to which he converted in 1913. Not surprisingly, such an overtly erotic image shocked the artist's Catholic supporters. In a secular society, crucifixions and depositions have also been used to express the theme of the horror of war and human suffering, as in Graham Sutherland's Buchenwald-inspired *Deposition* (1946) where Mary Magdalen is only identifiable from the simple 'O' shape for a breast, and the skull-like grimace which represents the universal scream (see Plate 88).[20] Picasso's drawings of her show a convulsed body, arching backwards in torment and despair. David Wynne's strikingly stark bronze interpretation of the *Noli me tangere*, his *Christ meeting Mary Magdalen* (see Plate 89), with its tall, gaunt figures redolent of Giacometti's emaciated forms, shows a Christ returned from a terrible death, the horror in his eyes, whilst Mary Magdalen, in a

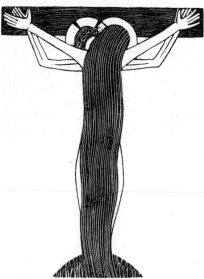

87 *The Nuptials of God* (1922). Eric Gill. London, Victoria & Albert Museum.

88 *Deposition* (1946). Graham Sutherland. Cambridge, Fitzwilliam Museum.

brief, figure-hugging dress, raises her arm to shield her eyes from his gaze.[21]

Despite the paucity of contemporary images of Mary Magdalen, the wider interest in her has prompted one major, and two smaller, exhi-

89 *Christ meeting Mary Magdalen* (1963). David Wynne. Ely Cathedral, south transept.

bitions devoted wholly or in part to her appearance in art. The larger exhibition, *La Maddalena tra Sacro e Profano*, mounted by the Pitti Palace in Florence in 1986, surveyed a huge variety of images of Mary Magdalen from the Middle Ages to modern times. Whilst it did not specifically distinguish Mary Magdalen from the characters with which she has been associated (this issue was addressed in an article in the catalogue), the exhibition was able to gather together images illustrating the various themes surrounding the composite character, divided into seven sections, described as 'seven like the sins of the Magdalen'.[22] The exhibits demonstrated not only the important place she has held in the Christian imagination but also, and perhaps more significantly, the rapid growth in recent years of interest in the idea and image of the feminine, and its relationship to the divine. A much smaller show, *Marie-*

Madeleine. Figure inspiratrice dans la mystique, les arts et les lettres, was held in 1988 at Fontaine-la-Vaucluse.[23] Here, too, there seemed little attempt to separate Mary Magdalen from her past, and constant reference to her 'sin', her position as 'temptress' and as 'object of desire', 'affirming in woman's body the power of her femininity', would seem to relate more to Luke's sinner than to Mary of Magdala. More recently, she featured in the exhibition *Les Vanités dans la peinture au XVIIe siècle* which was mounted in Caen and at the Petit-Palais in Paris (1990); this demonstrated her links with Venus, Pandora and Eve.[24]

In the winter of 1991–2 the streets of Paris were filled with images of Mary Magdalen, gazing down from hoardings advertising two exhibitions. Gregor Erhardt's naked figure was used to attract visitors to *Sculptures allemandes de la fin du Moyen-Age* at the Louvre, where the sculpture itself, newly conserved, was the centrepiece provoking some surprised and puzzled reactions (see Plate 90).[25] Similarly a huge poster

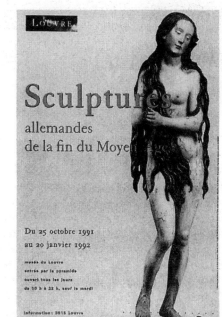

90 Mary Magdalen by Gregor Erhardt. Poster advertising the exhibition *Sculptures allemandes de la fin du Moyen Age* (1991–2). Paris, Musée du Louvre.

91 *Noli me tangere*. Poster advertising the exhibition *Martin Schongauer: maître de la gravure rhénane (vers 1450–91)* (1991–2). Paris, Musée du Petit Palais.

showing Martin Schongauer's delicate engraving of the *Noli me tangere* was used to announce an exhibition of the artist's prints (see Plate 91).[26]

It might be thought that the women who have written about Mary Magdalen, of whom there have been several in the last decade or so, would have offered a different perspective on her than that presented by the male writers, film-makers, and artists referred to above. And indeed they do, inasmuch as they celebrate Mary Magdalen for her sexuality, often in ecstatic terms, rather than condemn her, and in so doing perpetuate the man-made myth. Happily, this is not the only modern view of Mary Magdalen, as hand-in-hand with the recent flurry of novels about her as the quintessence of female sexuality is the much more hard-headed re-examination, undertaken by scholars and theologians, of the biblical texts and early Christian history. This has naturally led to a re-evaluation of the group around Christ, and of the role of the women within it. This new focus is concomitant with the renewed emphasis on feminine values in what can be regarded as an entirely patriarchal religion, an emphasis central to the discussion of the part played by women in the Church today, and crucial in the move towards female ordination. The lawyer in *Jesus of Montreal* tells the protagonist Daniel Coulombe, 'Jesus is "in" '; he might have added that the women around Jesus are also 'in'. Along with books on the subject of women, goddesses and whores, the feminine bias in religion is ever more strongly represented on the shelves of bookshops across the western world. In 1987 Monica Furlong was able to observe that

Feminist, and indeed anti-feminist, books are now fairly streaming off the pious printing presses. It seems only yesterday that Christian publishers used to groan if you offered them a book about women; now they apparently cannot get enough of the subject and we are bombarded with the sensible and the loony, the original and the stale, the orthodox and the heretical.[27]

Over the last decade or so, Mary Magdalen has also become the heroine of a steady stream of semi-mystical novels and short stories which has flowed from the fountain pens of feminists, Christian and non-Christian alike, in a form which were it not for the feminist element might be dismissed as romantic fiction. Most exploit the legendary aspects of her life – Luke's sinner, the Gnostic writings, apocrypha, and the *Golden Legend* – repeating the same formulae but with different emphases, to explore areas of female experience which have little or nothing to do with the gospel character. Some have caused a *frisson* because of their unorthodoxy, or their daringly sexually explicit or even blasphemous content. Mary Magdalen, with her famous, or infamous, sexuality has come to represent the liberated woman of the late twentieth century, and her myth has been recreated in that light: she is a rebel, a traveller, an independent woman; she might even have had a child by Christ. The imagination that fills in the missing details of her life is matched only by the ingenuity of the medieval hagiographers. Most of the novels are written in the first person, in a poetic, ruminative tone. Aurélia Briac's

Evangile selon Marie-Madeleine opens with the laconic: 'J'ai rencontré un drôle de type. Il s'appelle Jésus. C'est le seul qui n'ait pas essayé de faire l'amour avec moi . . . Pourtant, c'est tout à fait mon genre.' (I met this odd bloke. He's called Jesus. He's the only one who hasn't tried to make love to me. Still he's just my type.)[28] Her Magdalen is a business woman, a scent-maker, and her tale unfolds in some fairly heady prose. Her expertise in unguents and perfumes accounts for the wonderful condition of her hair – which she is careful not to use in wiping Jesus' feet, drying them with her veil instead. Having rejected the advances of nearly all the apostles, including the future St Paul, she yields to Jesus halfway through the book. Very contemptuous of the other disciples, she regards the Virgin as *petite-bourgeoise* and not very intelligent, and after the crucifixion sails off with Martha and Lazarus to France.

Carolyn Slaughter, working from the premise that 'there is no reason to suppose she is Luke's sinner', gives her *Magdalene* an extraordinary identity and biography; she is the creation of an imagination given full rein.[29] 'Today is my birthday, I am thirty-seven', the story lugubriously opens. And instead of a life spent in luxurious sin, her heroine enjoys not only one but two marriages. Firstly, she marries her brother's tutor to escape a parentally arranged union, but he is castrated by her brothers in revenge; secondly, she marries Samuel, a gentle woodcarver; she has two miscarriages, is deemed by the villagers to be cursed and, when Samuel dies, they burn her home and kill her child. She is then taken under the wing of the very odd and rich old Boaz, apparently a sadomasochist with peculiar and sinister sexual inclinations. Christ is unnamed, and although the recipient of these stream-of-consciousness outpourings, his part in the story is minimal, except that he is the object of her love. She does, however, see him die on the cross and at the resurrection, her account of which earns Peter's scorn, and he tells the others to ignore her as an hysteric. 'Later, though, he chose not to ignore what I had said, he put it to good effect,' she adds dourly. She is highly educated too, in Greek literature and philosophy: her first husband tells her she can write, and she therefore does, in an unrelievedly monotonous, consciously poetic voice. Christ seems to have spurned her physically, and it is only after his death, when she is reading the *Symposium*, that she understands his love as a 'controlled and heavenly love', but she cannot care for all that 'philosophy, religion and politics'. The Hellenistic connections which appear in Slaughter's novel, and in *The Wild Girl* by Michèle Roberts (see below), are reminiscent of the Neoplatonic study *Marie-Madeleine* (1952), described by its author, the Dominican Raymond Léopold Bruckberger, as a 'detective story'.[30] It places Mary Magdalen in the Greek ambience of early Christianity, where she becomes a Phryne or Berenice in the licentious court of Herod at Tiberias, reads the *Symposium* when bored with dancing, and becomes the Christian Antigone at the resurrection, in her progress from *eros* to *agape*. The Mary Magdalen of Bruckberger's novel in turn bears more than a passing resemblance to the mature, sensual, cultivated woman who features in the Jewish writer Sholem Asch's novel *The Nazarene*.[31]

Michèle Roberts' *Wild Girl* (1984) is the story of the liberated woman Mary Magdalen became in the Eighties. She too is a product of the imagination, a myth of the author's own making, arrived at whilst dissecting the various components of earlier stories. Written as a fifth gospel, according to Mary Magdalen, it is an account of love for Christ which seems to veer too often too close to the autobiographical for comfort. The Magdalen is 'stubby-nosed', 'long-backed' and lean, as we are often told, while Jesus is 'quite ugly, with a lined face and big nose'; he is also 'very feminine'. But to begin with the story. Our heroine was tomboyish when young and sang songs, running away 'angry' and 'wild' on her mother's death; a gang-bang is her initiation into womanhood. 'Brutalised' but 'free' (as no man will want to marry her), she travels across the sea, paying her way with her body to Alexandria. Here she is gently guided into the art of woman-love by Sybilla, the ultra-civilised *hetaira* from Rhodes who presents her with the alabaster jar, the ancient symbol of Woman, which becomes her emblem. She returns home a delinquent like brother Lazarus, but then meets Jesus. They become lovers. Union with the divine is described as 'tickl[ing] and caress[ing] and rid[ing] each other to our hearts' content', in a manner which is not so much mystical as mundane. But this is an unorthodox Magdalen, for, as the author points out, she has used in great part the Gnostic gospels to conjure up a very personal alternative Christianity in which human and physical love are part of divine love, are the resurrection and the life. Jesus says, in words hardly original, 'I am the new Adam, Mary, and you are the new Eve . . . Between us, and inside each other, we bear witness to the fullness of God.' Roberts has also used the Gnostic gospels to posit a tract for a Christian feminist religion: Jesus teaches the equality of male and female, giving the women a special role in his group – Mary Magdalen has endless dreams and mystical revelations which she discusses with him, and she does a lot of prophesying, too – declaring that knowing God is only possible when the male and female of each person are integrated. The antagonism between Peter and Mary Magdalen shown in the *Gospel of Thomas* and *Gospel of Philip* is used here to demonstrate how the misogynist and flesh-hater Peter becomes the head of the orthodox Church. The feminine element, all loving and sexuate, represented by Mary Magdalen, is cast forth, proscribed from performing as preachers, prophets and priests, as they had in Christ's lifetime. The Eternal Feminine retreats to Provence with her female cohort, gives birth to her daughter by Jesus, and then vanishes without trace, to proclaim the Word. Her gospel is found by the 'daughter of the daughter of she who wrote it'. The studied simplicity of the Magdalen's prose style is equalled only by the simplicity of the ideas of equality and love, and the what-might-have-been if patriarchy hadn't taken over. In the end, Michèle Roberts' interesting use of much Christian feminist thinking and research into the figure of the Gnostic Mariham is overwhelmed by the romantic elements of the novel which do much to defuse its argumentative power.

Similarly, the sacred prostitute who, perfumed and burning with passion, explodes out of Jacqueline Kelen's *Amour infini: Marie-Madeleine, Prostituée sacrée* (1982) is another re-creation of an ancient myth embodying the Eternal Feminine.[32] 'Je suis la femme de Magdala,' she declares; she gives herself to all because she is as beautiful as life. Men have eaten her body, bitten her shoulders and thighs, drunk from her stomach. They 'had thought to consume her, but left empty'. An entire history of prostitution in antiquity (earth mothers included) issues forth in this paean to feminine sexuality. On her conversion, she proclaims to the world, 'j'étais exubérante, je montrais, je hurlais mon amour', and at the crucifixion she boasts, 'la courtisane était la seule femme qui pût se tenir près de la croix, hurler ce scandale à la face des hommes' (I was exuberant, I showed, I yelled my love . . . the prostitute was the only woman who could stand by the cross, yell this scandal in the sight of men).

Such literary effusions surely do Mary Magdalen a disservice, as their creators fall into the trap that the earlier male writers have created for them: by portraying Mary Magdalen as a prostitute or courtesan, or gang-banged rebellious teenager who has a sexual relationship with Christ, they merely reinterpret her as a primarily sexual being, using as the central component of their fictions the character of Luke's sinner,

even if they do so in a more celebratory and less censorious manner
than do their male counterparts. By doing so, they deny her a dignity
in which her sexuality could be an integral part of her humanity, a
dignity which accords the gospel figure her proper prominence. This is
to a great extent precisely what Luise Rinser's novel *Mirjam* (1983) has
achieved.[33]

Mirjam (Mary Magdalen), rejects the tale that she was a harlot as pure
myth: she is a virgin and has resolved to remain so, deterred from
marriage by her father's treatment of her mother as a chattel. She is
beautiful – she rejects suitors – independent and rebellious; she does
not conform to what is expected of her, she disdains marriage and
motherhood. She is also rational and critical of the various ideologies –
Judaism, Hellenism and that of the Essenes – with which she comes
into contact on her odyssey, having left home on becoming orphaned.
Following Jeschua (Christ), she continues her search for truth by questioning him about his teachings, religious matters in general, and his
being the possible Messiah; he is always able to convince her. After the
crucifixion, she is the faithful, strong-minded follower who has to console and encourage the male disciples. She apparently flees to a less
hostile refuge by escaping on a boat. Luise Rinser uses the gospel character as an allegory of the soul seeking after spiritual truth, and in doing
so recreates a credible and courageous figure by extending rather than
embellishing the hints to be found in the New Testament.

The mythical Magdalen is naturally interpreted according to her authors'
biases – for male writers she has in the main been seen as the temptress,
while for women she has become the symbol of the complete woman
beside Christ. A very different interpretation is that of Marguérite Yourcenar in 'Mary Magdalene, or Salvation', 'the product of a love crisis',
published in 1936.[34] Here Mary Magdalen is portrayed as disappointed
in her self-sacrificial love for Christ, a variation on the Christ-figure in
Lawrence's 'Man who Died'. In the place of the overwrought romantic
emotionalism of the Magdalen novels already discussed is a note of sour
reality. Mary Magdalen looks back on a life ruined by her salvation in
which 'God' not only deprives her of her husband (John the Evangelist)
on her wedding night, but also by saving her in the house of Simon the
Pharisee – where she has gone as a prostitute to revenge herself on John
by seducing his God – also deprives her of a natural life. As a redeemed
sinner, she is denied the pleasures of physical love, motherhood and

growing old with children, all for a God 'who loved my tears only', and who, in an echo of Rilke, 'saved [her] from happiness' as, in the end, he 'escapes to the sky'. Yourcenar in this story uses the legendary aspects of Mary Magdalen's life in an entirely original way: she gives the Magdalen a wholly credible persona and also gives to her a role within 'God's ministry' – as not only a disciple but one who also recruited other disciples, healed the blind and sick, and did the dishes at the Last Supper.

Marguerite Yourcenar wrote her short story before changes in the Roman Calendar of 1969 were promulgated as part of which, as the result of scholarly re-evaluation of her biblical persona, Mary Magdalen's character was officially relieved of its sinful imputation.[35] She was no longer Luke's sinner, nor even Mary of Bethany, but Mary of Magdala who, cured of her seven devils, became the devoted follower and witness of the resurrected Christ. This view had already been propounded in 1935 by Peter Ketter, professor of theology at Trier University,[36] echoing the work of the distinguished eighteenth-century Benedictine exegete and historian Dom Augustin Calmet, which had indignantly demolished the arguments in favour of the composite Mary Magdalen.[37] Both, of course, were only rehearsing the thesis, on precisely the same terms, textual study of the gospels, of Jacques Lefèvre d'Etaples in the sixteenth century. (It is perhaps worth noting also that other female saints like Catherine of Alexandria and Margaret of Antioch, long celebrated as virgins and martyrs, held up as models of chastity to Christian women, and frequently depicted as companions to Mary Magdalen in medieval art, were also removed from the General Calendar of Saints as historical research had proved that they had never actually existed.) In 1978 the epithets 'Maria poenitens' (penitent Mary) and 'magna peccatrix' (great sinner) were also deleted from the entry for Mary Magdalen in the Roman Breviary, thus officially removing the stigma which had been attached to her name for nearly two thousand years. How long it will be before the impact of the penitent, so often written about and depicted, can be erased from popular memory, and before artists and writers will no longer find it a creatively fertile subject, will depend on the strength of its grip on the Christian imagination. That most of these novels were written since the changes to the Roman Calendar, and that the great part of their narratives is still woven around the prostitute myth, shows how very persistently embedded in our cultural consciousness it is.

Probably in recognition of those changes, however, it is to Mary of Magdala rather than the composite figure that a Jungian gloss has recently been applied. In *Gesù e le Donne* by Marco Garzonio,[38] she appears as one of the women Jesus meets during his mission, who helps him to become the 'integrated', adult man, the 'animus' reconciled with his 'anima' – the feminine archetype of the unconscious – in his process of 'individuation', or 'wholeness'. The author's intention is to show the important role women (among them Jesus' mother, the Samaritan woman, Mary of Bethany and Mary Magdalen) played both in the gospel events and, more specifically, in the spiritual journey undertaken by Jesus, which helped to bring about transformations in his personality, enriching his perceptions and behaviour. Garzonio points out that, unlike the twelve disciples, the women close to Jesus 'were not chosen or called': they came to him and met him on his travels. Some had grave sicknesses, among them Mary of Magdala, who 'probably suffered' from some form of 'psychotic' illness. She is a 'particularly sensitive and attentive type of the Anima', her illness 'probably such to render her emotional makeup more acute, subtle and delicate'. She is moreover 'an introverted intuitive type who has feeling as a secondary function'. Mary Magdalen's role in the resurrection is as second mother in Christ's second birth, to spiritual life, as the necessary feminine creative element, and she thus forms a counterpart to the Virgin Mary. When Jesus tells her not to cling to him, he is telling her that a phase in her life is accomplished: he is on his inner journey, and she too must travel on hers, and thereby become transformed. Which of course she does as she has seen him, and now her own spiritual journey can begin. The function of child-bearer/mother with which, together with her capacity to absorb and understand, the author endows Mary Magdalen is the supreme feminine trait amongst those ascribed to the feminine archetype by Jung, and not one with which she is usually credited.

It would seem that the women in the gospels in general, and Mary Magdalen in particular, are all there to serve as midwives to the emerging adult integrated male Jesus by nurturing his 'feminine' side. The book's purpose is to show the role of the feminine in Christ's inner life, but within the gospel narratives the female figures are apparently quite able to stand on their own, without imposing a Jungian interpretation on the events. And one has to ask whether it is really useful to project twentieth-century theories of the unconscious and archetypes on a subject so remote in time, particularly when the historical aspect is not taken into consideration. If by 'integration' is meant that incorporated into Jesus' psyche are what are regarded by Jungians as qualities accorded to the 'anima', such as receptivity, understanding and empathy, it would appear from the gospel accounts that Jesus is already a 'fully integrated' male in that he accepts all comers, does not discriminate on the basis of sexuality or taboo and regards women as equals with men. Each encounter with women demonstrates his so-called 'integratedness' which is there proffered to these 'real women' – Garzonio's phrase, distinguishing them from the goddesses of other Mediterranean religions – without their prompting. It is difficult to see what if anything such an approach adds to our understanding of Jesus' relationship with women, or vice versa; and difficult also to regard this book as anything other than yet another on women in Christianity, this time written by a male 'feminist' to show his sympathy with and understanding of women, and to patronise them with the unusual idea that women, and particularly Mary Magdalen, were integral to the formation of Jesus' psyche. It could be argued that the overall effect of such an approach is rather to disempower Mary Magdalen than to enhance her significance.

In a similarly psychoanalytic vein, Mary Magdalen becomes the principal 'hidden gospel hero' as the ideal disciple and 'inner successor of Jesus' in Joseph A. Grassi's *Hidden Heroes of the Gospels: Female Counterparts of Jesus* (1989).[39] A 'special relation between her and Jesus' allows her to be witness of the resurrection; her relationship as counterpart to the Beloved Disciple allows her to become 'inner successor' within the Johannine community, and model of the true believer. Grassi's allusive style and hazy use of symbolism can itself be seen as a kind of complement to Elisabeth Moltmann-Wendel's unveiling of the women in Christ's life in *The Women around Jesus* (1982).[40] Here, Grassi's 'special relationship', vague as it is but doubtless of spiritual significance only, is made more concrete in the suggestion that the 'tender and friendly' man, Jesus, might have had sexual relations with Mary Magdalen. Mary Magdalen is the 'mature leader of the group'; her evil spirits – the biblical description for mental illness – are identified as 'manic depression or epilepsy'. The claim that she 'had the qualities of a leader' and 'like Joanna helped to bring an urban element to the middle-class Jesus movement' has the ring of socially conscious commentary, but seems to ignore the status of the fishermen who belonged to the community. It is presumably her reading of the Gnostic gospels that leads the author to assert: 'The Jewish women were submissive to her. She was eloquent and persuasive. She could speak.' Mary Magdalen's attempts to persuade the disciples of what she has seen, however, seem to have met with signal failure. It is, naturally, the Johannine Easter encounter which has prompted conjectures about a 'particularly intimate relationship': John's 'inference' itself has, apparently, 'undergone spiritual sublimation'. She speculates on the argument of Phipps and others that rabbis of Christ's age were generally married, and that he may even have been a widower. (Luther had also apparently assumed that a sexual relationship had existed between Christ and Mary Magdalen.)[41] Some of these conclusions may ring a bell, but whereas Moltmann-Wendel's propositions derive from intuition and imagination, Phipps' hypotheses, if a trifle far-fetched, are based on historical research. It is to Moltmann-Wendel's credit that she can say, 'Anyone who loves the biblical Mary Magdalen and compares her with the Christian Mary Magdalen must get very angry', and thereby distinguish Mary Magdalen from Luke's sinner. Her claim, however, that the 'portrait of Mary Magdalen, constructed by men, served to kindle male fantasies' might with some justification be turned back on herself, her own portrait of Mary Magdalen serving to kindle female fantasies.

Fantasy has played a large part in the career of Mary Magdalen through the ages, and no less so in the twentieth century. Her chimera-like existence has reflected the exigencies of the periods in which she has flourished; each era has modelled her according to its own preoccupations, fears and aspirations. Once chief woman disciple and apostle to the apostles, she came to represent sexuate woman and sinful carnality redeemed. Refashioned for the present time, she once again embodies the sexuate female, but where once her carnality was sinful, it now becomes the mark of the complete, experienced woman of the late twentieth century. Her relationship to Christ, long a subject of speculation, loses both its metaphorical function as the soul seeking after the divine, and also the only reality it has – as closest woman follower – and becomes explicitly eroticised, in the 'humanisation' of Christ to discover his 'historical' figure. Mary Magdalen is archetypal Christian temptress, liberated woman, sexual partner of Jesus, feminine counterpart, 'anima' and 'inner successor to Christ', mirroring the period through which she has travelled so far in this century. Whilst placing her within the psychoanalytical confines of 'archetype' or 'anima' may have its use within those spheres, the dictates of the twentieth-century *Zeitgeist* have, despite bringing Mary Magdalen up to date, shed little light on her historical, or gospel, character and its significance. Modern biblical scholarship, on the other hand, has done so, and in turning full circle, it is to the biblical figure that we should now revert, to understand its validity in the last decade of the twentieth century.

Early Christianity has proved over the past two decades to be highly fertile ground for biblical scholars, historians and theologians, particularly those of a feminist persuasion, among them Elisabeth Schüssler Fiorenza, Susanne Heine, Elaine Pagels, Rosemary Radford Ruether, Leonard Swidler, Ben Witherington III and, most recently, Carla Ricci.[42] In the radical revision of much of what until now had been accepted interpretations of the early Church and women's participation in it, Mary Magdalen's figure has emerged in bold relief, restored to her New Testament role as chief female disciple, apostle to the apostles, and first witness of the resurrection. The significance of this re-evaluation has so far gone mostly unacknowledged by the Church of Rome, whilst it is only partially conceded by other churches, because of the residual patriarchalism of those institutions. If the 'victimisation' of Mary Magdalen can stand as a metaphor for the historically subordinate position of women in Christianity, now that the woman so long regarded as a penitent sinner has been shown in her true light, then it may be that Christianity's view of woman in history itself requires some kind of radical revision.

Christianity has offered, one could say imposed, two alternative feminine symbols, Mary the Virgin and Mary Magdalen, the whore, encapsulating in these two figures a moral code, based on the virginal ideal, which has obtained for nearly two thousand years. Even though Mary Magdalen may now be seen in her rightful role, this in itself has done little to re-establish the importance of that role. But as awareness of her role increases, so too does our awareness of her importance; she has become a touchstone in relation to such contentious issues as the wrangle within the churches over that last bastion of patriarchy, the ministry and ordination of women. From the early centuries of the Christian era, Mary Magdalen has, like the women she represents, been the scapegoat of the ecclesiastical institution, manipulated, controlled and, above all, misrepresented. Whilst the defences have been stormed in other areas like education, the right to vote, control of personal property and in the professions, all hitherto male preserves, no breach has been made in the palisades of the Church of Rome, although gradual inroads have been made into the Protestant churches. The resistance to the idea of women priests derives from deeply entrenched responses, conditioned by centuries of dogma which have fashioned the image of the Virgin Mary. It is perhaps time to recognise the true feminine model, one which, according to the gospels, embodies strength, courage and independence, all feminine qualities which the Church has attempted to suppress by subordinating women to the model it has created, the passive virgin and mother.

Mariolatry seems to raise its head whenever the Church finds itself in crisis, as it did in the nineteenth century under Pius IX. In the twentieth century, under the perceived onslaught of communism, the Virgin appeared again, and again to peasants, at Fatima in Portugal after the First World War. As late as 1950 came the article of faith which proclaimed her bodily integrity, its incorruptibility even in death, her assumption into heaven, an honour given to no other human being, to be celebrated on 15 August. In the 1950s and 1960s, Catholic girlhood was offered this vision of purity as a model, her motherhood in virginity an awesome miracle to be believed in and, later, sometimes an obstacle to be overcome; they became 'Marians', 'little children of Mary'. (Some, but only a few, however, had the ingenuity and imagination to choose Mary Magdalen, because she had not only sinned but also been forgiven, as their model.) The cult of the Virgin suffered a setback at the end of the Second Vatican Council in 1965, when, during the ecumenical period inspired by the council, worship of Mary was played down in response to Protestant criticism, and it was emphasised that the Virgin's importance derived only from her son and that the Vatican did 'not hesitate to profess [Mary's] subordinate role'. In her important, perceptive and above all critical study of the cult of the Virgin Mary, Marina Warner wrote:

> But the reality her myth describes is over; the moral code she affirms has been exhausted. The Catholic Church might succeed, with its natural resilience and craft, in accommodating her to the new circumstances of sexual equality, but it is more likely that, like Ishtar, the Virgin will recede into legend . . . As an acknowledged

creation of Christian mythology, the Virgin's legend . . . will be
emptied of moral significance, and thus lose its present real powers
to heal and to harm.[43]

She spoke too soon: the past two decades have seen an extraordinary
revival in mariolatry, this time outside the Roman Catholic Church, in
the Anglican and in some of the Free churches. It has also flourished
again with renewed vigour in the eastern Orthodox Churches, and in
the Church of Rome, with the advent of the Polish pope, Papa Wojtyla,
whose particular devotion is to the Virgin. In June 1987 John Paul II,
determined to strengthen Mary's standing in Catholic piety, declared a
Marian Year: devotion to the Virgin accelerated rapidly, in the form of
pilgrimages to shrines, images, books and reinterpretations. To appeal
to the faithful of today, she is presented as the model of Christian
spiritual life, and as the spiritual mother of mankind, not just the remote
and unattainably perfect mother of God. Even the radical Catholic feminist Rosemary Radford Ruether has written of her as the 'patroness of
reproductive choice' because she can be seen, presumably from the gospel infancy narratives, to have made her own choices about her body
and sexuality.[44] It is a view in line with the orthodox Catholic interpretation of Mary's 'free consent', her *fiat*, divinely to conceive Jesus, but
tailored to the concerns of the late twentieth century. Debate about the
virgin birth still rages on, as in an article in *The Times* in 1986 which
referred to the tradition that its historical veracity had been attested to
by the holy family itself: St Joseph had told Matthew, and Mary had
told Luke.[45] The Virgin has even been described by a Christian feminist
as working in the fields – in an agrarian, peasant society – when not
suckling her child, and as 'fun' and 'partying'.[46] However, a more
'realistic' image of her as natural mother, with Joseph as natural father,
and a whole host of natural siblings, the 'brothers and sisters' of Jesus
mentioned in the gospels, has been presented as the more positive model
of Christian womanhood.[47] What these different conjectures have in
common is a desire to make the Virgin Mary more acceptable to contemporary tastes.

At the end of the Marian Year, John Paul II issued a second encyclical,
Mulieris Dignitatem, or 'On the Dignity and Vocation of Women',[48] the
title of which gave hope of some enlightened thinking, as did such
opening statements as: 'A woman [the Virgin Mary] is to be found at
the centre of this salvific event'; woman is the 'representative and arche-

type of the whole, human race'; both men and women are 'human beings to an equal degree, both are created in God's image'. But these remarks are rapidly succeeded by such old red herrings as 'In Genesis are to be found the models of marriage which serve as the basis for later definitions of truth concerning motherhood and virginity as the two particular dimensions of women's vocation in the light of divine revelation.' The Creation story speaks of God's 'instituting marriage as an indispensable condition for the transmission of life'. (Of the word 'helper' used to describe Adam's mate, we are to understand 'mutual help'.) Women are not to seek to overcome the biblical message, 'He shall rule over you', through 'masculine characteristics', but through 'feminine personal resources which are no less than male ones'; otherwise, their essential feminine potential will become corrupted and lost.

Pope John Paul declared Christ to be a promoter of women's true dignity and the vocation consonant with this dignity, which he further acknowledged was in stark contrast to contemporary Judaic customs. Sick women and those 'labelled sinners, public sinners and adulteresses' came to him; others supported him like Joanna and Susanna. And then, at the crucifixion, women proved to be more faithful than the male disciples, demonstrating a 'special sensitivity characteristic of their feminity'. The first to see the empty tomb, they were first to see Christ, and to tell the apostles. Mary Magdalen's special role had been stressed by John: in his gospel, 'she is the first to meet the risen Christ . . . Hence she came to be called the apostle to the apostles . . . This event, in a sense, crowns all that has been said previously about Christ entrusting truths to women as well as men.' It is further reiterated that motherhood and virginity are the two dimensions of women's vocation – with the aside that 'for the sake of the kingdom' virginity has value for both men and women. This celebration of Christian womanhood is followed by the inevitable sting in the tail: that 'in calling only men as his apostles, Christ acted in a completely free and sovereign manner'. At the Last Supper had taken place the 'calling of the Twelve'; these and these 'alone receive[d] the sacramental charge, "do this in remembrance of me"'.

Thus is stated, only too clearly, the Roman Catholic Church's stance on the ordination of women, a hornets' nest in which the Anglican churches found themselves until 11 November 1992, when the General Synod of the Church of England voted to ordain women as priests. 'Civil war' and 'schism' were words used to describe their predicament.[49] The arguments against women's ordination are rooted in a patriarchy which predates the time of Christ. In Leviticus, the taboos against menstruating women prohibited them from entering the holy of holies. In I Corinthians 11 is to be found St Paul's oddly phrased argument concerning the wearing of veils whence Christianity has found its justification for male authority, and female subordination, whereas in reality the directives applied to the particular circumstances at Corinth, and referred to contemporary secular practice. In the traditional reading of the gospels are found grounds for the assumption that as Christ's male followers are described as 'disciples' (followers), and the women are described as 'following and ministering', the roles are different, that of the male disciples, the chosen 'Twelve', necessarily superior, by virtue of their sex.

In December 1988 Pope John Paul II wrote to the then archbishop of Canterbury, Dr Robert Runcie, stating unequivocally that

> The Catholic Church, like the Orthodox Church and the ancient Oriental Churches, is firmly opposed to this development, viewing it as a break with tradition of a kind we have no competence to authorise.[50]

The tradition here referred to is surely a cultural rather than theological one, for if the argument for tradition is held, then should not the Church revert to the early Christian *praxis* referred to by St Paul within only a generation after Christ's death whereby women such as Phoebe were deacons, that is to say, in positions of ecclesiastical power similar to the role of today's bishops, administering to a community? Even Atto, the tenth-century bishop of Vercelli, was happy to admit that women had shared in the ceremonies of divine worship in the early Church.[51] Indeed the epistle of Pope Gelasius I (492–6) to three episcopates in southern Italy in which he refers disapprovingly to the fact that 'women are encouraged to officiate at the sacred altars, and to take part in all matters imputed to the offices of the male sex, to which they do not belong' suggests that the tradition of women at the altar survived in some regions at least as late as the end of the fifth century.[52] The repeated prohibitions against the practice in the canons of the councils of Nicaea (325), Laodicea (second half of the fourth century), Nîmes (394 or 396) and Orange (441) indicate that Gelasius was not referring to an isolated instance of women being admitted to the priesthood. There are even indications of the participation of women in liturgical service in Gaul in the early sixth century.[53] If the churches today regard the ordination of women as a break with tradition, it would appear either that they have not explored fully the origins of that tradition, or perhaps have been somewhat selective in defining it.

In his encyclical, John Paul II referred somewhat lamely to the 'active and important part' played by women after Christ's death; but had he forgotten about the 'active and important part' they played during Christ's lifetime, as disciples, equals with their male counterparts in ministering?[54] The ecclesiastical commotion in both the United States and Britain caused by the election in America of the first woman bishop, Barbara Harris, in 1989 was again based on male symbolism, and an interesting letter on the subject in the London *Times* pointed up the inadequacy of such symbolism, citing Mary Magdalen as evidence:

> Dear Sir,
> The election of the Revd Barbara Harris to the episcopate is very shocking, almost as shocking as the admission of Mary Magdalene to the inner circle of Christ's disciples.[55]

Mary Magdalen has become a figure-head for many women in the Church today. In 1986, the German Catholic women's organisation, the Gruppe Maria von Magdala, was formed, its goal the achievement of equal rights for women in the Church, including the right to be ordained.[56] Mary Magdalen continues to travel with the times, once again a prototype for women, but this time in her own guise, and as the symbol of women's right to resume their place and role in the Church.

The ideas of taboo and pollution derived from ancient anthropological beliefs found in Judaism and Hellenistic philosophy, though rejected by Christ, re-emerged after his death and were reabsorbed into Christian thinking in the succeeding centuries. Woman is still associated in the Christian imagination with the carnal, which in turn is still associated with sin, underscoring the persistent influence of Gnostic Manicheaism. Symbolism has been and is still used to perpetuate patriarchal systems: when the symbol of good and purity is seen as a virgin woman, and her moral counterpart, of evil and luxury, as a sexuate woman, power politics come to mind. And we should perhaps ask ourselves who created these symbols. The surviving major religions have also been the creations of men, and have therefore naturally incorporated male world-views. As Mary Midgley has pointed out, 'A very ancient patriarchal ideology really has distorted our tradition . . . First, women have been seen, typically in the story of Eve, as a main source of evil. Second, and more generally, the whole way in which evil as such is conceived has been fatally deformed by patriarchal thinking.'[57] Within the sphere of religion, women are seen as inferior and secondary creatures – as daughters of Eve, without moral strength and rectitude, or under the cloak of Mary as subordinate and submissive – as until recently they were in society. By insisting on male symbolism at the altar, as in 'do this in remembrance of me', and being what can only be seen as selective about tradition, male authority and pre-eminence is maintained in an attempt to cling to power within existing and as yet unchanging structures.

Despite the fact that the repentant prostitute is no longer a symbol, it would seem that the ideology behind her creation is one which has not retreated but remains ever-potent. One has to ask whether she has been entirely replaced by her true figure. It would seem not: as late as September 1989, a daring piece suggesting that the Virgin Mary was out of date, *démodée*, too perfect, to be a model for modern woman, appeared in the *Guardian* newspaper. Two alternatives were suggested, one Julian of Norwich, the other Mary Magdalen. Julian of Norwich qualified as she was 'potentially an ordinary married woman', thus making her more accessible than the 'host of female saints who achieved their status by chastity and purity'. Mary Magdalen qualified as the 'full-blooded and emotional woman' who saw Christ after the resurrection. She was 'very human':

> She cried a lot, for a start. And she was given to the grand gesture. She is widely acknowledged as the woman who washed [*sic*] Jesus' feet with her hair . . . her humanity has a deeper relevance. Most important is her sinfulness. She was, after all, a member of the oldest profession, yet Christ chose to pick her out and bestow extraordinary privileges on her. His love for her, his willingness to accept her human weakness is surely the blueprint of his attitude towards all believers.[58]

Apart from the fact that the image propounded is both anachronistic and erroneous, it is in effect another example of patronising male 'feminism'; Christianity's preoccupation with sin still, it would seem, requires a scapegoat. Much more encouraging is the sermon given in New York by a Lutheran minister on Mary Magdalen's feast-day, 22 July 1990:

> But there certainly is no biblical basis for identifying her as the reformed prostitute or that she had long red hair. The sole characteristic that stands out about Mary is the fact that she is not identified as the mother or the wife of some man. She has the audacity . . . to stand completely on her own as a person. For as long as this parody of Mary Magdalene stands, the church provides a continued obstacle to its own and the world's understanding of female social equality.
>
> This feast which honors Mary of Magdala for what she really is could be a key to a new level of Christian sexual consciousness. All we need do is proclaim honestly the true role this woman had in the story of our redemption. Recognize her as a full member of the revolutionary community created by the One who considered men and women equal . . . Jesus valued her as a unique person in whom the life and power of God flowed with the same degree of intensity as it did in Peter, James or John.[59]

The sermon ends with Paul's exhortation that men and women be free and equal to emphasise the 'co-equal role of women' both within the Church and outside it. Mary Magdalen, the 'first preacher of good news', stands before us as a 'key that helps unlock the door to a new age of sexual equality and liberation'.[60]

So long as the Church chooses to disregard the new scholarship which has reinterpreted the women in the gospels – so easily dismissed by calling it feminist – it will continue to subordinate the 'real' Mary Magdalen in favour of 'mother Mary'. That is, it will deny her her active role in the ministry of the Church at a time when her modern counterparts are seeking their own role in the institution. It may be that historical reappraisals of Mary Magdalen have revealed a figure which appears lacklustre and unromantic beside the mythical golden-haired whore; but the more accurate picture will have greater relevance and resonance for the majority of women looking for active roles both within and outside the Church. The true Mary Magdalen has much to offer when freed from the restrictions which gender bias has imposed upon her. Symbolism has done her an injustice; modern scholarship has made restitution possible. If there is still need for symbolism, would not the true Mary Magdalen, the disciple by the cross and herald of the New Life, no less beautiful than her mythical persona, and far more edifying as a figure of independence, courage, action, faith and love, serve women better as a symbol for today? Nietzsche wrote that every culture needed myth and was impoverished when it lost or lacked myth.[61] In losing the myth of Mary Magdalen, however, has not our culture not only nothing to lose, but also everything to gain?

Reference Notes

The references given below are not necessarily to the first appearance of the works in print, but generally to easily accessible editions. References to works available in many editions usually cite chapter or section numbers, to allow easier location of references in editions other than those cited here. The following abbreviations have been used throughout the references:

Bibl. Sanct.	*Bibliotheca Sanctorum*, Rome, 1967, vol. VIII.
CE	*Catholic Encyclopedia, The*, ed. C. G. Heibermann et al, 15 vols, London and New York, 1907–14.
Dict. Spir.	*Dictionnaire de Spiritualité, Ascétique et Mystique, Doctrine et Histoire*, ed. M. Viller et al, Paris, (1932) 1978, fascs LXVI–LXVII.
EETS	Early English Text Society, London, 1864ff.
Encyc. Relig.	*Encyclopedia of Religion*, ed. Mircea Eliade, 15 vols, New York, 1987.
La Maddalena	*La Maddalena tra Sacro e Profano*, ed. Marilena Mosco, exhibition catalogue, Milan-Florence, 1986.
MEFRM	*Mélanges de l'Ecole française de Rome. Moyen Age. La Madeleine (VIIIe–XIIIe siècle)*, tome 104–1–1992.
NCE	*New Catholic Encyclopedia, The*, Editorial Staff of the Catholic University of America, Washington, DC, 15 vols, New York and London, 1967.
NHL	*Nag Hammadi Library in English, The*, ed. James M. Robinson, 2nd edn, Leiden, 1984.
NTA	E. Hennecke, *New Testament Apocrypha*, ed. W. Schneemelcher, Eng. edn. ed. R. McL. Wilson, 2 vols, London, 1963 and 1965.
PG	J.-P. Migne, *Patrologiae cursus completus. Series graeca*, 162 vols, Paris, 1857–66.
PL	J.-P. Migne, *Patrologiae cursus completus. Series latina*, 221 vols, Paris, 1844–64.
Réau	Louis Réau, *Iconographie de l'art chrétien*, 3 vols, Paris, 1958.
Schiller	Gertrud Schiller, *Ikonographie der christlichen Kunst*, 5 vols, Gütersloh, 1966–91.

CHAPTER I

1. The chapter title is taken from that of the tract of John Fisher, bishop of Rochester, one of several concerning the identity of Mary Magdalen in the controversy provoked by the French humanist Jacques Lefèvre d'Etaples in 1517. This is discussed more fully in Chapter Seven. Although Fisher's title, translated as 'The Single Magdalen,' refers to his standpoint, in defence of the Latin Church, that Mary Magdalen was the composite figure incorporating both Mary of Bethany and the sinner in Luke 7, I have used it punningly to signify Mary Magdalen's unicity.

2. John Donne's witty sonnet, 'To the Lady Magdalen Herbert: of St Mary Magdalen', was sent to Lady Herbert, mother of the Anglican divine, George Herbert (see Chapter Seven), on Mary Magdalen's feast-day in 1607. The lines quoted would seem to resume the present argument. From *The Poems of John Donne*, ed. Sir Herbert Grierson, London, 1912, vol. I, pp. 317–18, and notes, vol. II, pp. 228, 229–30.

3. Easter was the traditional time when neophytes were baptised. *NCE*, vol. V, p. 7. See also John F. Baldovin SJ, 'Easter', *Encyc. Relig.*, vol. IV, pp. 557–8.

4. Herbert Thurston, 'Easter', *CE*, vol. V. p. 224.

5. Easter is celebrated on Sundays between 22 March and 25 April, its moveable character deriving from the Jewish method of fixing the date of Passover, the fourteenth day of Nisan, which depended on a lunar calendar which did not restrict it to a particular day. From early on Christians celebrated Easter on the Sunday after the Jewish feast, after the first full moon following the spring equinox, when the first full moon of the spring occurs. Passover itself was once a nomadic moon myth (W. O. E. Oesterley, 'Early Hebrew Festival Rituals' in *Myth and Ritual, Essays on the Myth and Ritual of the Hebrews in Relation to the Culture Pattern of the Ancient East*, ed. S. H. Hooke, London and Oxford, 1933, pp. 111 and 117). See also T. H. Robinson, 'Hebrew Myths' in Hooke, op. cit., pp. 190–5, for the 'ancient moon myth' theory, that Israel adopts the general pattern of myth and ritual from her predecessors in Palestine. The rite took place at the full moon. In 325, the Council of Nicaea prescribed the celebration of Easter on the first Sunday after the first full moon following the spring equinox.

6. R. M. Grant, *Formation of the New Testament*, London, 1965, p. 24.

7. See Chapter Five.

8. See 'Mark, Gospel of', in *Concise Oxford Dictionary of the Christian Church*, ed. Elizabeth A. Livingstone, Oxford, 1980.

9. The Sanhedrin was the supreme

Jewish council and highest court of justice at Jerusalem at the time of Christ. It collected taxes, dealt with religious problems, and acted as a civil court for Jerusalem. It pronounced the death sentence on Christ.

10. D. E. Nineham, *The Gospel of St Mark*, Harmondsworth, 1963, p. 435.

11. The verses which end Mark's gospel, 16:9–20, called the Marcan Appendix or Longer Ending of Mark, are not the original ending of the gospel but were probably added in the second century, according to most scholars, to replace a lost further narrative. Some scholars, Raymond E. Brown amongst them, believe that the gospel ends at v.8. See *The Gospel according to John (xiii–xxi)* (The Anchor Bible), introd., trs. and notes by Raymond E. Brown SS, London, 1971, pp. 967–9. I am grateful to Professor Elaine Pagels for referring me to this work.

12. Matt. 27:56 and Mark 15:40. See 'Relatives of Jesus', in *NTA*, vol. I, pp. 426–8, where the 'other Mary' is denoted as the mother of James the Less and Joses, and the possible identification with 'Mary of Clopas' in John is noted.

13. According to a thirteenth-century legend, however, Joseph continued to have an illustrious career, taking the Holy Grail to England, where he built the country's first church at Glastonbury, in Somerset.

14. For a discussion of how many and which women are described in John's account of the crucifixion, see Brown, op. cit., pp. 904–6. Brown (p. 904) refers to scholars who reject the historicity of John's account, such as C. K. Barrett, *The Gospel according to St John*, London, 1955, p. 98, who doubts that the Romans would

have allowed Christ's friends and relations to approach the crucifixion; however, E. Stauffer, in *Jesus and His Story*, London, 1960, pp. 111 and 179, cites evidence that crucifixions were often surrounded by friends, family and enemies.``

15. The sudarium, or *soudarion*, a loan word in Greek, was a cloth used to wipe off sweat (from the Latin, *sudor*, sweat). The meaning of the words 'saw, and believed' is ambiguous: some commentators see them as referring to the 'other' disciple's being the first to believe in the risen Jesus, as the verb *pisteuein*, 'to believe', can also connote 'to be convinced'. St Augustine, amongst others, argued that it referred to the disciple's belief in the veracity of Mary Magdalen's report of the disappearance of the body rather than his credence in the resurrection. Brown, however, argues that the disciple is the first to believe in the risen Christ. See Brown, op. cit., p. 987. Brown sees here an editorial joining of what were once independent episodes: if the 'other disciple' had seen and believed, it is odd that he had not communicated to Mary Magdalen his understanding of what had taken place; also, there is the question as to why she sees angels rather than the grave-clothes seen by the disciples. He also adds that she weeps because she thinks Jesus' body has been stolen, rather than lamenting after his death. There is also an earlier ambiguity in v.2 where she announces to the disciples, 'they have taken away the Lord out of the sepulchre, and *we* know not where they have laid him' (the italics are mine). See Brown, p. 984, for a discussion of the word 'we'.

16. John Marsh, *The Gospel of St John*, Harmondsworth, 1985, p. 63. Mary Magdalen's use of the word *rabboni* is close to Thomas's profession of faith in v.28 (*New Jerusalem Bible*, London, 1985, p. 1789, note e). Brown (p. 992), however, argues that by translating *rabboni*, or *rabbuni*, into Greek as 'teacher', the writer is not deliberately using a form primarily addressed to God, and that therefore Mary Magdalen is not making a statement of her faith. See Brown (p. 990) for Hebrew and Aramaic renderings of 'Mary' and *rabbuni*.

17. *The RSV Interlinear Greek-English New Testament*, The Nestle Greek Text with a Literal English Translation by Revd Dr Alfred Marshall, 1968, London, p. 455.

18. See Brown, op. cit., pp. 979–1017 for 'The Risen Christ'.

19. *RSV Interlinear Greek-English New Testament*, p. 456.

20. See Barrett, op. cit., p. 466.

21. Elisabeth Schüssler Fiorenza, *In Memory of Her. A Feminist Theological Reconstruction of Christian Origins*, London, 1983, p. 139. Susanne Heine, *Women and Early Christianity. Are the feminist scholars right?*, London, 1987, p. 129 suggests that from the text of Luke 8:1–3 emerges the fact that Mary Magdalen was the 'closest woman companion of Jesus'.

22. See Schüssler Fiorenza, op. cit., pp. 320–1, where she discusses the use of 'follow', 'minister', 'came up' in Mark 8:34 and 10:8, and also Heine, op. cit., p. 61.

23. S. W. Baron, *A Social and Religious History of the Jews*, New York, 1958, vol. II, pp. 237–8, which notes that a woman was also required to wash her husband's face, hands and feet. In return she received food, lodging, clothing, cosmetics and funeral services, the cosmetics bought by her husband to enhance and maintain her attractions for his delectation.

24. G. M. Caird, *The Gospel of St Luke*, Harmondsworth, 1963, p. 116; and Ben Witherington III, *Women in the Ministry of Jesus*, Cambridge, 1984, pp. 118 and 196, note 239.

25. Baron, op. cit., p. 240.

26. Mishnah Sotah 3, 4, quoted in Leonard Swidler, *Biblical Affirmations of Woman*, Philadelphia, 1979, p. 163.

27. Shaye Cohen, however ('Menstruants and the Sacred in Judaism and Christianity' in Sarah Pomeroy, ed., *Women's History of Ancient History*, Chapel Hill, 1991, pp. 287–8 and note 53), argues that there is no evidence of such segregation at this early date. For restrictions in worship see Baron, op. cit., vol. II, pp. 240–1. For 'Impure Menstruous Women', see Leonard Swidler, *Women in Judaism. The Status of Women in Formative Judaism*, Metuchen, 1976, pp. 130–9, and Witherington, op. cit., p. 8. According to Philo, 'a woman should not show herself off like a vagrant in the streets for the eyes of other men except when she has to go to the temple and even then she should take pains to go, not when the market is full but when most people have gone home' (Baron, op. cit., p. 241).

28. Heine, op. cit., p. 61.

29. In Judaism, women could not become disciples unless their husbands or masters were rabbis willing to teach them (Witherington, op. cit., p. 117 and note 232).

30. For the distinction between *niddâ* (menstruant) and *zābâ* (woman with discharge) see Cohen,

p. 274 ff. See Ewa Kuryluk, *Veronica and her Cloth. History, Symbolism, and Structure of a 'True' Image*, Oxford and New York, 1991, where the woman with the issue of blood is associated with St Veronica, and a possible link between Mary Magdalen and the 'Haemorrhissa' is explored.

31. Witherington, op. cit., p. 117.

32. Although in John 8:46−9 direct comparison is made between being a sinner and having a devil.

33. Clara Lucas Balfour, *Women of the Scriptures*, London, 1847, p. 321, where Mary Magdalen is 'miraculously cured of one of those grievous and mysterious maladies known in the gospel as demoniacal possession'; see also J. E. Fallon, 'Mary Magdalen', *NCE*, vol. IX, p. 387.

34. Fallon, ibid. See now Carla Ricci, *Maria di Magdala e le molte altre. Donne sul cammino di Gesù*, Naples, 1991, pp. 141−7, for a discussion of the seven devils. I am extremely grateful to Professor Mary Grey for bringing this book to my attention.

35. The Second Temple was begun in 520 BC and was still standing in Christ's time. It was destroyed by the Roman armies under Titus during the sack of Jerusalem in AD 70. I should like to thank Rita Adam for going to el Mejdel and for providing me with photographs of both site and signpost.

36. *RSV Interlinear Greek-English New Testament*, p. 258, and Caird, op. cit., p. 114.

37. Witherington, op. cit., p. 55, and note 14.

38. Paul Fréart de Chantelou (1609−94) was a highly cultivated man and had an important collection of paintings. Poussin's painting is in Edinburgh, National Gallery of Scotland, on loan. An earlier image of the scene which shows Christ reclining to eat is to be found in Hieronymus Mercurialis, *De arte gymnastica*, Venice, 1601, p. 64, illustrating a discussion of the Roman practice of lying down to eat. I am grateful to Adele Airoldi for providing me with a copy of the woodcut.

39. Caird, op. cit., p. 114.

40. *Theological Dictionary of the New Testament*, ed. Gerhard Kittel, trs. and ed. Geoffrey W. Bromiley, Grand Rapids (Mich.), 1964, vol. I, p. 327.

41. As in Numbers 5:18. See Witherington, op. cit., p. 163, note 20.

42. Swidler, *Biblical Affirmations*, p. 187, and see the same author's *Women in Judaism*, pp. 121−3 ('Women's Head and Face Covering').

43. This was the punishment which the Pharisees, supported by the strong arm of Mosaic law, intended to mete out on the woman taken in adultery in John 8:7 (see below pp. 28−9).

44. As Marina Warner (*Alone of All Her Sex*, London, 1976, p. 226) has already pointed out, neither the Greek *agapo*, to love, nor the Latin *diligere*, used by Christ, has any erotic significance. Christianity's obsession with sexual love and its analogy with sin has led to confusion here as elsewhere. In the fifteenth century, Dionysius the Carthusian (1402−71) called the episode of Luke's sinner 'the Institution of the Sacrament of Penance' (*In Evangelium Lucae*, Paris, 1542, f.149v).

45. Fallon, op. cit., p. 393.

46. ibid.; and Witherington, op. cit., p. 101.

47. In the Book of Jonah, the prophet is called by the Lord to go to

Nineveh and preach repentance. He attempts to escape by sea, is thrown overboard and swallowed by a whale. After three days he is delivered, his mission a success. In Matthew 12:39ff, the 'sign of Jonah' is seen as a prophecy of Christ's resurrection.

48. Schiller, vol. I, p. 190.

49. See Marsh, op. cit., pp. 452–4. My thanks to Professor Mary Grey for her help in elucidating this passage for me.

50. Marsh, op. cit., p. 454.

51. ibid., p. 455.

52. Ben Witherington III, *Women and the Genesis of Christianity*, Cambridge, 1990, pp. 108–9.

53. Marsh, op. cit., p. 454.

54. See Chapter Seven. The tradition was again questioned in 1636, with further correspondence in 1699; these attempts to clear the slur from Mary Magdalen's name are summarised in Augustin Calmet, 'Dissertation sur Les Trois Maries', in *La Sainte Bible en latin et en français, avec des notes littérales, critiques et historiques, des préfaces et des dissertations, tirées du Commentaire du Dom A. Calmet*, Paris, 1773, vol. XIII, pp. 331–49. See also Chapter Nine, p. 328.

55. In the Orthodox Church, Mary Magdalen is seen above all as the witness of the resurrection, and is given the titles 'Myrrhbearer', and 'Equal to the Apostles', which occur in the *Menaion* and the *Synaxarion*. From the end of the fourth century, the Greek Church celebrated the second Sunday after Easter as the 'Sunday of the Myrrhophores'; Mary of Bethany was celebrated on 4 June and Mary Magdalen variously on 30 June, 22 July and 4 August (see Victor Saxer, 'Les saintes Marie Madeleine et Marie de Béthanie dans la tradition liturgique et homilétique orientale', *Revue des sciences religieuses*, vol. XXXII, 1958, pp. 1–37). In the Orthodox observance of Holy Week, the Wednesday is devoted particularly to the woman in Luke 7 (see *The Lenten Triodion*, trs. from original Greek by Mother Mary and Archimandrite Kallistos Ware, London and Boston, 1978). In the Russian Orthodox church of Mary Magdalen at Gethsemane, Mary Magdalen appears in a large nineteenth-century wall painting presenting the Emperor Tiberius with a red egg and greeting him with the words, 'Christ is Risen'. The iconography derives from a well-known legend in Orthodoxy which tells of her journey to Rome. I am extremely grateful to Bishop Kallistos Ware for information about Mary Magdalen in Orthodoxy.

56. See Chapter Three.

57. The Jews hated the Samaritans and regarded them as Gentiles who were still loyal to the pagan gods. Samaritan women were regarded by Jewish law as 'menstruants from their cradle'; drinking from the same vessel meant that a Jew would be made unclean. Marsh, op. cit., p. 210, who quotes D. Daube in *Journal of Biblical Literature*, LXIX, 1950, pp. 137–47.

58. See Raymond E. Brown SS, *The Community of the Beloved Disciple*, London, 1979, pp. 188–9. I am grateful to Father Robert Murray SJ for bringing this book to my attention.

59. See also Swidler, *Women in Judaism*, pp. 123–5 ('Conversations with Women').

60. Although the episode of the woman taken in adultery is included in John's gospel, scholars agree that it was not written by

the author of the fourth gospel. It does not appear in the earliest Greek manuscripts, and comes into the canonical writings through manuscripts of the western Latin Church, although references to the story appear in the *Didiscalia*, of third-century Syrian origin. It has often been suggested that its exclusion was due to Christ's forgiveness of adultery, and his compassion towards a 'sinful' woman. Swidler, *Biblical Affirmations*, pp. 185–6. Nikos Kazantzakis in his novel *The Last Temptation* (see Chapter Ten, p. 369), for example, conflates the woman taken in adultery, as well as Luke's sinner, with the Magdalen when he has Mary Magdalen stoned by the Pharisees for selling her wares on the Sabbath.

61. C. G. Montefiore, *The Synoptic Gospels*, London, 1927, vol. I, p. 389, quoted in Nineham, op. cit., p. 431.

62. See Grant, op. cit., p. 56. Swidler, *Biblical Affirmations*, p. 203, suggests that, as a Pharisee, Paul's omission of any reference to an appearance to Mary Magdalen or other women disciples may reflect the Jewish custom of disallowing the testimony of women. See also Swidler, *Women in Judaism*, pp. 115–16 ('Bearing Witness'). According to Josephus, 'The testimony of women is not accepted as valid because of the lightheadedness and brashness of the female sex' (*Antiquities* IV, 219); they were also apparently given to lying (Swidler, p. 115, and note 11). In the Hellenistic world, however, women were allowed to bear witness in Graeco-Egyptian law (Swidler, p. 116, and note 16).

CHAPTER II

1. Both the chapter title and quote come from the *Gospel of Philip*, written in the second half of the third century. Philip himself is mentioned once, and does not appear as a transmitter of revelation. *NHL*, pp. 135–6 and 138.

2. James M. Robinson, introd., *NHL*, p. 10.

3. ibid., p. 21.

4. R. M. Grant, *Gnosticism and Early Christianity*, revised edition, New York, 1966, p. 7.

5. ibid., pp. 6–7.

6. Irenaeus, *Adversus Haereses* I, 18.1 (quoted in Hans Jonas, *The Gnostic Religion*, Boston, 1958, p. 42). According to Jonas, non-conformism was 'almost a principle of the gnostic mind and was closely connected with the doctrine of the sovereign "spirit" as a source of direct knowledge and spiritual illumination'.

7. Constance F. Parvey, 'The Theology and Leadership of Women in the New Testament', in Rosemary Radford Ruether, ed., *Religion and Sexism*, New York, 1974, p. 122.

8. 'Spirituals' were saved by their nature; 'psychics' had a latent capacity for *gnosis* but required to be instructed in the intricacies of the Gnostic gospel. There was no salvation, however, for 'earthly' or material men. R. M. Grant, *Gnosticism: An Anthology*, London, 1961, introduction, p. 16.

9. Jonas, op. cit., pp. 9–10.

10. Grant, *Gnosticism: An Anthology*, p. 18.

11. Irenaeus, 'On the Detection and Refutation of Gnosis falsely so-called' (Grant, *Gnosticism: An Anthology*, p. 14).

12. See John Bugge, *Virginitas: An*

Essay in the History of a Medieval Ideal, The Hague, 1975.

13. It was published in 1892.

14. The Coptic manuscript is now in the British Library, Codex Askewianus, MS Add. 5114. Askew had bought it in a London bookshop in 1773.

15. An incomplete fifth-century Coptic manuscript of the *Gospel of Mary* is in Berlin, Papyrus Berolinensis 8502, probably from an original of the second century. Another, early third-century, fragment in Greek is in the John Rylands Library, Manchester, Papyrus no. 463. Three more Coptic versions were found at Nag Hammadi. The gospel is translated in *NHL*, pp. 471–4.

16. M. R. James, *The Apocryphal New Testament*, Oxford, 1924, p. xiii.

17. The idea of the Demiurge had already appeared in Plato's *Timaeus* as the creator of a beautiful, harmonious cosmos. According to a 'psalm' by Valentinus, quoted by Hippolytus of Rome, Sophia's fall led to the creation of the Demiurge, which in turn was the creator or 'artificer' of the world and matter. See Jonas, op. cit., pp. 190–9.

18. Robert Murray SJ, *Symbols of Church and Kingdom*, Cambridge, 1975, p. 332. The ubiquity of the name, Mary-Mariam, and its variant forms led to confusion as to whether it referred to Mary the mother of Christ or Mary Magdalen: '. . . in the Babylonian Talmud there are many garbled references to Jesus and his mother, in which the most coherent features are the name Miriam, the profession of "meᵍaddᵉlâ nāṣâyâ", "women's hairdresser", and her unfaithfulness.' This tradition confused Christ's mother and Mary Magdalen 'whose name is

betrayed in "meᵍaddᵉlâ"', and shows that both Jews and Christians were perplexed by the subject. Murray includes with these Marys 'the Mariamme or Mariamne of the Naassenes' in Hippolytus' *Philosophoumena*, supposed to have been an intermediary for secret revelations by James, the 'brother' of the Lord. He suggests that 'Mary' may be a mystery with several modes of existence, corresponding first to the cosmic Sophia, then to the 'sought one' reunited to Christ, and prototype of all who through asceticism seek final union with him in the heavenly wedding chamber (pp. 332–3).

19. This is the view of most commentators on the Mary-figure who appears in the Gnostic gospels. See also Marvin W. Meyer, 'Making Mary Male: The Categories "Male" and "Female" in the Gospel of Thomas', *New Testament Studies*, vol. XXXI, 1985, pp. 554–70. 'A definite identification of this Mary is impossible; the possibilities include (in descending order of likelihood) Mary Magdalene, certainly the best single choice . . .' (p. 562).

20. The *Gospel of Peter* was written sometime between the end of the first century and middle of the second. It was known to Origen, Eusebius and Theodoret, who were all writing at the end of the second century. M. R. James, op. cit., p. 90, dates it to *c.*150. Criticised for its unorthodox, docetic, character, as it cast doubt on Christ's sufferings, it is also very anti-Semitic. It uses the four canonical gospels, but with characteristics of its own. It clearly states Mary Magdalen's reason for going to the sepulchre: 'Now very

early on the Lord's day, Mary
Magdalene, a disciple of the Lord –
which, being afraid because of the
Jews, for they were inflamed with
anger, had not performed at the
sepulchre of the Lord those things
which women are accustomed to
do unto them that die and are
beloved of them – took with her
the women her friends and came
unto the tomb where he was laid.
And they feared lest the Jews
would see them, and said: Even if
we were not able to weep and
lament him on that day whereon
he was crucified, yet let us now do
so at his tomb' (p. 93).

21. *Dialogue of the Saviour, NHL*, pp.
235 and 236.

22. *Pistis Sophia*, trs. George Horner,
introd. F. Legge, London, 1924.

23. P.-M. Guillaume, 'Marie-
Madeleine', *Dict. Spir.*, fasc.
LXVII, col. 563.

24. *Gospel of Philip*, op. cit., p. 138.

25. Giovanni Filoramo, *A History of
Gnosticism*, trs. Anthony Alcock,
Oxford, 1990, pp. 176 and 242,
note 22. Filoramo also refers to
the Gnostic *Gospel of Mark* as
being directly connected with
Mary Magdalen's revelations: see
p. 242, note 21, quoting P.
Perkins, *The Gnostic Dialogue*, New
York, 1980, pp. 133–7; in the *Acts
of Philip*, she is referred to as
'chosen of women', Filoramo, op.
cit., p. 242, note 20.

26. The dating of the *Gospel of Mary*
can be ascertained as it is
mentioned by Irenaeus
(*c*.130–200).

27. *Gospel of Mary, NHL*, p. 472.

28. ibid.

29. Elaine Pagels, *The Gnostic Gospels*,
Harmondsworth, 1985, p. 43, and
p. 161, note 55.

30. This theme is taken up below,
p. 43.

31. *Gospel of Mary, NHL*, pp. 473–4.

32. See next chapter.

33. *Gospel of Philip, NHL*, pp. 135–6.
It was among those found in
Coptic in the Gnostic library
found near Nag Hammadi. It was
probably written in Syriac during
the second century (Murray, op.
cit., p. 25, and note 4).

34. See R. McL. Wilson, *The Gospel
of Philip*, London, 1962, p. 35, on
the word *koinonōs* as 'consort'.

35. *Gospel of Philip, NHL*, p. 138.
Elaine Pagels refers to Mary
Magdalen in this gospel as 'Jesus'
most intimate companion' and as
the 'symbol of divine Wisdom'
(*Gnostic Gospels*, p. 84); she has
since pointed out to me that she
sees no link between this
symbolic role of Mary Magdalen
and the goddesses.

36. See James A. Montgomery, 'The
Song of Songs in Early and
Medieval Christian Use', in *The
Song of Songs: A Symposium*,
Philadelphia, 1924, pp. 18–26, and
Theophile James Meek, 'The
Song of Songs and the Fertility
Cults', ibid., pp. 49–64.

37. *Gospel of Philip*, quoted in Meyer,
op. cit., p. 560.

38. Wesley W. Isenberg, introd., *Gospel
of Philip, NHL*, p. 131, and Meyer,
op. cit., pp. 557–8. See also Elaine
Pagels, 'Adam and Eve, Christ and
the Church', in *The New Testament
and Gnosis. Essays in honour of
Robert McL. Wilson*, ed. A. H. B.
Logan and A. J. M. Wedderburn,
Edinburgh, 1983 (I am grateful to
Professor Pagels for giving me a
copy of this article). In the
Valentinian paradigm of spiritual
harmony, each essence of syzygy
has its counterpart with which it
has to be reconciled, and each
member with all the others, to
attain fulfilment. Mary Magdalen
and Christ are the Church
reconciled with Christ.

39. Epiphanius (*Panarion*, 26.8, 2–3), quoted in H.-Ch. Puech, 'Gnostic Gospels and Related Documents', in *NTA*, vol. I, pp. 338–9. The procedure described to Jesus was influenced by the account in Genesis 2:21ff, where Eve, the first woman, was produced from Adam's side. According to Epiphanius, such actions served as a model for eucharistic rites in use among the Nicolaitans, Borborians and other licentious Gnostics in Egypt.

40. *Pistis Sophia*, p. 29.

41. ibid., p. 80.

42. Pagels, *Gnostic Gospels*, pp. 84–8.

43. See next chapter.

44. For the story of Pistis Sophia, see below, p. 49ff.

45. *Gospel of Thomas, NHL*, p. 130. Probably written before AD 200, and possibly as early as the second half of the second century, the treatise was found at Nag Hammadi and, like the *Gospel of Philip*, appears to have come from a Syriac milieu. It was believed to have been written by Didymos Judas Thomas, Judas 'the Twin', who was identified in the Syrian Church as the apostle and twin brother of Jesus (Helmut Koester, p. 115, introd. *NHL*, p. 130). See Meyer, op. cit., pp. 560ff for a discussion of the theme. The transformation is to be effected by mutual elimination of sexual characteristics, rather than hermaphroditic manifestation of sexual features similar to Paul in Gal. 3:27–8 (p. 560). Sexual transformation also featured in Ovid, Plato and Egyptian mythology (ibid., p. 563).

46. See Marjorie M. Malvern, *Venus in Sackcloth. The Magdalen's Origins and Metamorphoses*, Carbondale and Edwardsville, 1975, who sees Pistis Sophia as an attempt to 'simultaneously reinstate and dematerialise the goddess of wisdom, Ishtar, or Siduri or Athene, long since dethroned by patriarchal monotheism but preserved in the Bible through vivid personifications of wisdom as a woman who is the male deity's "daily joy"' (p. 42). Mary Magdalen is the 'particular' of the 'universal' Sophia, and Christ's feminine counterpart.

47. Grant, *Gnosticism: An Anthology*, p. 17: 'The figure of the fallen Sophia, who among some Valentinians bore the semi-Hebrew name Achamoth, may be derived from the "daughter of God" or "mother of the universe" . . . but in Gnosticism she became the subject of an elaborate mythology as though a mother-goddess like those found in Mesopotamia and the Mediterranean world.' See also Gilles Quispel, 'Sophia', *Encyc. Relig.*, vol. XIII, p. 416, who regards the theme of Pistis Sophia as the Christianisation by Valentinus of the Hebrew Old Testament *hokhmah* (wisdom), in Greek as *Sophia*, of the great goddess, pre-Greek, and pre-Hebrew, of the Mediterranean area, known as Anat, Athirat or Astarte.

48. T. H. Robinson, 'Hebrew Myths' in *Myth and Ritual*, ed. S. H. Hooke, London, 1933, p. 185.

49. See S. David Sperling, 'God: God in the Hebrew Scriptures', *Encyc. Relig.*, vol. VI, p. 3.

50. Hosea 1–3, where the prophet uses the infidelity of his own wife Gomer as a metaphor for Israel's to Yahweh.

51. It is possible that in this inscription the name Asherah had become a common noun meaning 'consort', Sperling, op. cit., p. 5.

52. Anat Jahu is seen as an androgynous blend of Yahweh and Anat, Sperling, op. cit., p. 5. See also Quispel, op. cit., p. 416; and Moshe Weinfeld, 'Israelite Religion', *Encyc. Relig.*, vol. VII, p. 482, for a reference to a ninth-century BC inscription found at Kuntillet 'Ajrud (in southern Palestine) where YHVH is blessed next to Asherah, suggesting a syncretic religious worship.

53. Susanne Heine, *Christianity and the Goddesses. Systematic criticism of a feminist theology*, trs. John Bowden, London, 1988, pp. 22–5 and 43.

54. Sperling, op. cit., p. 5; Quispel, op. cit., p. 416. In some cases the goddesses took on male features: Isis became Osiris who soon became sole god of the sun and of Egypt, and Ishtar, beloved and great mother-goddess of Babylonia and Assyria, became Ashtar, the king.

55. Edmund Leach, 'Why did Moses have a sister?', in *Structuralist Interpretations of Biblical Myth*, with D. Alan Aycock, Cambridge, 1983, pp. 34–56, especially p. 56.

56. See Chapter Five. The *Biblia Pauperum*, the 'poor man's bible', illustrates New Testament passages with their types alongside. See Avril Henry, *Biblia Pauperum. A Facsimile and Edition*, Aldershot, 1987, p. 74. The scene of Nathan bringing David to repentance appears opposite Miriam and Moses, and completes the trio of types representing repentance (p. 74). I am grateful to Nicholas Hadgraft for providing a photograph of this for me.

57. So-called after the seventy-two translators employed, according to Jewish tradition, by Ptolemy Philadelphus (285–246 BC) to translate the Hebrew Bible into Greek. For *Hokhmah*, see Quispel, op. cit., p. 416.

58. ibid. According to Origen and Irenaeus, the Valentinians gave Sophia the name 'Prunicos', or 'lewd', an epithet which had already been ascribed to Aphrodite, the goddess of fertility; Irenaeus also linked her to the Helen who appears in the story of Simon Magus (the founder of the Gnostic religion, again according to these commentators, and redeemer in some Gnostic writings, replacing Jesus), as his companion and 'Queen' since she is 'all maternal Being and Wisdom', whom he had rescued from a brothel in Tyre. It has also been suggested that Sophia is the Jewish substitute for Ishtar or Isis, and is also associated with Helen of Troy and Athena. Similarly, the prototype for Simon and his marriage to Helen is in the marriage between the prophet Hosea and Gomer, symbolic of Yahweh's relationship with Israel. See Grant, *Gnosticism and Early Christianity*, pp. 11–87.

59. A *suzugos* is a pair of emanations from the Supreme Being or God.

60. *Pistis Sophia*, pp. 7 and 6.

61. The word 'aeon' originally referred to periods of time but was later applied to the spaces controlled by astral spirits or to astral spirits themselves. See R. M. Grant, *Gnosticism: An Anthology*, p. 17, and F. Legge, introd., *Pistis Sophia*, pp. xv–xvi, and xvi, note 3. In the Valentinian cosmos, whose complexities were much criticised by orthodox opponents of Gnosticism, the twelve Aeons or signs of the zodiac lie below the powers of the Five Helpers, Five Marks and Great Light, all eleven of which are governed by the First Law,

and within the space of the First Mystery, or God Manifest, of whom Jesus is the incarnation. The lower part of this 'space' is the *kerasmos* or confusion, where light is mingled with matter, and in the highest is the Treasure House where Light alone dwells (ibid., p. xv).

62. ibid., pp. 13, 14 and 17.

63. ibid., p. 61.

64. ibid., p. 99.

65. ibid., p. 116.

66. 'Psalms of Heracleides', in *A Manichean Psalm-Book*, Pt II, vol. II, ed. C. R. C. Allberry, Stuttgart, 1938, p. 187. According to Murray, op. cit., p. 27, the manuscript was translated from a Syrian original of not later than *c*.340. Manes (*c*.216–76) was the founder of the Manichaean sect, a radical and severely ascetic variant of Gnosticism which established a strong foothold not only in Egypt and Rome, but also in Africa where St Augustine was for a time an ardent adherent.

67. This is an allusion to Satan.

68. Allberry, op. cit., p. 192, l. 21.

69. This in itself was anathema to the Gnostics whose own *gnosis* they saw as infinitely superior to the faith of the Church, and giving them the right to claim spiritual freedom, and at the same time to refuse to acknowledge any form of ecclesiastical authority. Knowledge of the divine came to them as individual revelation and was unchannelled by what they regarded as clerical interference.

70. F. A. Sullivan, 'Apostolic Succession', *NCE*, vol. I, pp. 695–6.

71. See Chapter Three for a fuller discussion.

72. Quoted in Pagels, *Gnostic Gospels*, p. 81. For the passage in I Timothy, see Chapter Three, p. 87.

73. Tertullian, *De Praescriptione* 41, 2–6. See Filoramo, op. cit., p. 173, and Heine, *Women and Early Christianity*, p. 132.

74. ibid., pp. 139–40.

75. Montanus, founder of the second-century apocalyptic movement named after him, began preaching in 156/7 or 172. The extreme asceticism of his sect prohibited second marriages, insisted on rigorous fasting and even forbade flight in the face of persecution.

76. Irenaeus, *Adversus Haereses*, 1.13.1–5, quoted in Pagels, *Gnostic Gospels*, p. 80.

77. *Dialogue of the Saviour, NHL*, p. 237.

78. Peter Brown, *The Body and Society. Men, Women and Sexual Renunciation in Early Christianity*, London and Boston, 1989, p. 113.

79. Sullivan, op. cit., p. 695.

80. Pagels, *Gnostic Gospels*, pp. 38, 39, 40–1. Schüssler Fiorenza, op. cit., p. 304: 'How much scriptural interpretation and legitimization served political functions for the church can be illustrated by the example of Mary Magdalen.'

81. This, of course, as Heine has pointed out, we shall never know unless other texts appear. Heine, *Women and Early Christianity*, p. 173, note 378.

82. See Chapter Ten, p. 392ff.

83. Such as the Ugaritic myth of Anat (*c*.1400 BC) who is described as fighting, 'wading in the blood of her opponents, not sated with her killing; the heads she has cut off reach up to her waist'. See Heine, *Christianity and the Goddesses*, pp. 44–7, and notes 11 and 17.

84. Elisabeth Badinter, *Man/Woman, The One is the Other*, trs. Barbara Wright, London, 1989, suggests that patriarchy evolved from an original situation of equality, or complementarity, which prevailed

in Palaeolithic times, when the roles of hunter (male) and gatherer (female) were interlocked in a survival system, to a period in the agricultural society when because of the link between the fertility of the woman and the earth's own fruitfulness, woman and female sexuality were held in high esteem. Whether or not the statuettes of fecund female forms which date from this period are themselves symbolic of a matriarchal system, but not necessarily a matriarchy, which had existed before the advent of patriarchy, they witness the existence of ancient fertility cults, and where this was the case, it is unlikely that women in the societies which celebrated such mother-goddesses would have been held as inferiors.

85. Legge, *Pistis Sophia*, introd., p. xliii.
86. A Gnostic church, the Holy Order of Mary Magdalen, was established in the 1970s in Palo Alto, in California, and claims 'its Apostolic and Episcopal line of succession from Mary Magdalene herself. According to tradition, she received her hierophantic powers directly from the Christ together with the other apostles at the time of the Last Supper' (*The Gnostic*, newsletter, Summer 1984). I am extremely grateful to Melinda Lesher Parry for obtaining the information for me, and for putting me in touch with the Gnostic church.

CHAPTER III

1. *PL* XXII, col. 1090. (My translation.) St Jerome's letter to the virgin Principia, written in 412, concerns Marcella, a wealthy upper-class woman who had formed a community with her mother Albinia on the Aventine Hill outside Rome where Jerome would meet his female disciples. The letter appears in full in the *Select Letters of St Jerome*, trs. F. A. Wright, London, New York, 1933, pp. 450–1 (Letter CXXVII), where Jerome adds a flattering gloss for the benefit of his female correspondent: 'Those unbelievers who read me may perhaps smile to find me lingering over the praises of weak women. But if they will recall how holy women attended to Our Lord and Saviour and ministered to him of their substance, and how the three Marys stood before the cross . . . they will convict themselves of pride rather than me of folly, who judge of virtue not by the sex but by the mind.' Jerome's attribution to Mary Magdalen of the epithet 'fortified with towers' derived from the fact that the Hebrew word *migdol* or *magdol* means 'tower'.

2. G. Abbott-Smith, *A Manual-Greek Lexicon of the New Testament*, Edinburgh, 1937, p. 54.
3. Walter Bauer, *A Greek-English Lexicon of the New Testament and Other Early Christian Literature*, trs. and ed. F. Wilbur Gingrich and William F. Arndt, Chicago and London, 1979, p. 99.
4. See C. Hopkins, 'The Christian Church', in *The Christian Church at Dura-Europos*, New Haven, 1934, pp. 1–12; Susan B. Matheson, *Dura-Europos. The Ancient City and the Yale Collection*, New Haven, 1982, pp. 28–30; fig. 25a shows a reconstruction of the baptistery. My thanks to Dr Matheson for her help with archival photographs.
5. Henry Chadwick, *The Early Church*, Harmondsworth, 1978, pp. 62 and 279, where it is stated that one of the scenes shows Peter

walking on the water; Matheson, op. cit., p. 28, however, describes the figure as that of Christ.

6. P. V. C. Baur, 'The Paintings in the Christian Chapel', in *The Christian Church at Dura-Europos*, New Haven, 1934, pp. 35 and 38.

7. See also André Grabar, 'La fresque des saintes femmes au tombeau à Doura', *Cahiers Archéologiques*, vol. VIII, 1956, pp. 9–26.

8. According to Schiller, vol. III, p. 19, the two stars on the gable of the sarcophagus signify two angels as in Syrian art stars and angels are signs of the divine epiphany.

9. Robert Murray SJ, *Symbols of Church and Kingdom*, Cambridge, 1975, pp. 146–8 and 329–31.

10. St Augustine, commentary on John (*PL* XXXV, cols 1955–9), quoted from Sister Magdalen LaRow SSJ, 'The Iconography of Mary Magdalen. The Evolution of a Western Tradition until 1300', unpublished PhD thesis, New York University, 1982, p. 32, note 3.

11. Gregory had written to the bishop of Marseille who had been disquieted by those in his congregation who tended to fall before images in church as though they were pagan idols. In Epistle 9:9 he wrote, 'That which the written word is for readers, so are pictures for the uneducated.' It was the bishop's duty to make sure that while images might be retained for dogmatic purposes, the people were not to sin through worshipping them (Epistles 9:105, and 11:13). James Hall, *A History of Ideas and Images in Italian Art*, London, 1983, pp. 4 and 65.

12. *Hippolyts Kommentar zum Hohenlied*, ed. G. Nathanael Bonwetsch, Leipzig, 1902, N.F. VIII, 2, XXIV, p. 60.

13. ibid., p. 60. Hippolytus extends

his allegory: having found the angels, as the Bride found the watchmen, what was the significance of the town they guarded, if it were not the new Jerusalem in the person of Christ's body? (ibid., p. 62).

14. ibid., p. 63.

15. Quoted in P.-M. Guillaume, 'Ste Marie-Madeleine', *Dict. Spir.*, col. 565.

16. Hippolytus' ideas were expanded by others, amongst them Hilary of Poitiers, Optatus of Milevis and Ambrose of Milan. See Guillaume, ibid., col. 566.

17. The parallel between Eve and Mary was introduced, possibly for the first time, by Justin Martyr (died *c*.165) in his *Dialogue with the Jew Trypho* of *c*.95. Justin's parallel was a pendant to Paul's comparison of Adam and Christ in I Cor. 15:45. Hilda Graef, *Mary: A History of Doctrine and Devotion*, London and New York, 1963, vol.I, pp. 37–8. Eve's fault would be cancelled by the Virgin Mary.

18. Eve (Hebrew, *ḥawwâ*), the name given by Adam to the first woman, as she was 'mother of all living', was popularly believed to have been related to the Hebrew word for 'life', *ḥayyâ*.

19. Genesis contains two traditions regarding the origins of mankind, one called the 'Priestly' – Genesis 1:1–24a, and the other 'Yahwist', in Genesis 2:4b–3:24, a division between two texts from two different sources occurring in 2:4. Genesis 1:26–7 relates that God created man 'in his own image, in the image of God created he him; male and female created he them'. The second account, describing Eve's secondary creation, offers a marked contrast to the version which suggests that the primordial

person was androgynous in some way.

20. N. P. Williams, *The Ideas of the Fall and of Original Sin*, London, 1927, p. 57.

21. ibid., p. 20. In the mid-sixth century BC, to the Hebrews returning to their homeland after their ignominious captivity in Babylon, the fault lay in themselves as a nation and as individuals. As believers in a good deity, they were unable to blame Yahweh for the evil which had led to such a catastrophe. The cause was ultimately found in the myth which is recorded in the sixth book of Genesis which tells of the fall of the angels. Their offspring were giants, like the Titans of Greek myth.

22. Williams, op. cit., pp. 64–9. Jung's rather than Freud's as it was not entirely sexual in nature.

23. Williams, op. cit., p. 71.

24. 'I came not to call the righteous, but sinners to repentance', he said in Mark 2:17. He had come to return erring man to the path of righteousness: 'For the Son of man is come to seek and to save that which was lost' (Luke 19:10).

25. Peter Brown, *The Body and Society. Men, Women and Sexual Renunciation in Early Christianity*, London and Boston, 1989, p. 93.

26. See John Bugge, *Virginitas: An Essay in the History of a Medieval Ideal*, The Hague, 1975, pp. 13ff.

27. ibid., pp. 18–19, and notes 44 and 45.

28. Gregory of Nyssa, *De Virginitate*, quoted in Bugge, op. cit., pp. 16–17.

29. See Elaine Pagels, *Adam, Eve, and the Serpent*, London, 1988, p. 27.

30. ibid., pp. 27–8.

31. Clement of Alexandria, *Stromata* III, 15, 94, quoted in Williams, op. cit., p. 204.

32. Quoted in Pagels, op. cit., p. 29.

33. ibid.

34. ibid., p. 35.

35. Williams, op. cit., p. 195.

36. St Augustine, *The City of God*, trs. Henry Bettenson, Harmondsworth, 1986, Book XIII, chap. 14.

37. Williams, op. cit., p. 155, quoting William James, *The Variety of Religious Experience*, 1902, Lecture VIII.

38. St Augustine, *Confessions*, trs. and introd. R. S. Pine-Coffin, Harmondsworth, 1984, Book VI, chap. 15.

39. St Augustine, *de Genesi ad Litteram*, in Williams, op. cit., pp. 360ff.

40. St Augustine, *The City of God*, Book XIV, chaps 22–4.

41. ibid.

42. ibid., chap. 26. In chap. 9, Augustine himself defines *apatheia* as possibly being 'translated in Latin by *impassibilitas* [impassibility] if such a word existed'.

43. ibid., chap. 21; chap. 11. See the extremely useful discussion of Augustine's thinking on Genesis, Eve and the Fall in Kari Elisabeth Børresen, *Subordination and Equivalence. The Nature and Role of Woman in Augustine and Thomas Aquinas*, trs. Charles H. Talbot, Washington, DC, 1981.

44. Williams, op. cit., p. 171. For the 'Wisdom of Ben Sirach' (Eccles. 25:24) of *c*.180 BC, see Williams, p. 54.

45. Tertullian, *On Female Dress (De Cultu Feminarum)* in *The Writings of Tertullian*, vol.I, in The Ante-Nicene Christian Library, ed. Revd Andrew Roberts and James Donaldson, Edinburgh, 1869, vol. XI, pp. 304–5. The caustic question which continues the quotation, 'And do you think about adorning yourself over and

above your tunics of skins',
invokes the penitential garb that is
appropriate to woman as the
daughter of Eve who introduced
sin into the world.

46. Jerome's letter was written in 384.
Letter XXII, in *Select Letters of St
Jerome*, op. cit., p. 93. Earlier in
the letter he had written, 'Some
one may say: "Do you dare to
disparage wedlock, a state which
God has blessed?" It is not
disparaging wedlock to prefer
virginity. No one can make a
comparison between two things, if
one is good and the other evil' (p.
91).

47. St John Chrysostom, *On Virginity
(De Virginitate)*, quoted in Julia
O'Faolain and Lauro Martines,
eds, *Not in God's Image*, London,
1979, pp. 150–1.

48. See Chapter Five (pp. 137–41).

49. Qumran community rule 5,
quoted in Brown, op. cit., p. 37,
and note 13, from *The Dead Sea
Scrolls in English*, trs. Geza Vermes,
Harmondsworth, 1968, p. 85.

50. Pliny the Elder, *Natural History*,
5.15.73, ed. Rackham, Cambridge
(Mass.), 1969, 2:277, quoted in
Brown, op. cit., p. 38, and note
22.

51. Brown, op. cit, p. 38.

52. ibid., p. 40.

53. As, for example William E.
Phipps, *Was Jesus Married? The
Distortion of Sexuality in the
Christian Tradition*, New York,
Evanston and London, 1970, and
Schalom ben Chorin, *Bruder Jesus.
Der Nazarener in jüdischer Sicht*,
Munich, 1967.

54. Christ cures Peter's mother-in-law
in Mark 1:30–1. Brown says that it
was about a century after the
crucifixion before followers
claimed to base their own celibacy
on that of Christ (p. 41, note 36:
Ignatius, *Letter to Polycarp*, 5.2).

55. Quoted in Henry C. Lea, *History
of Sacerdotal Celibacy in the
Christian Church*, London, 1932,
pp. 26–7.

56. Brown, op. cit., p. 33, quoted
from Richard Walzer, *Galen on
Jews and Christians*, Oxford, 1947,
p. 15. Brown, note 1, suggests that
the remark may have been a 'later,
Christian interpolation in the
Arabic tradition'.

57. The expression is Brown's, op.
cit., p. 96.

58. Lea, op. cit., p. 26.

59. ibid.

60. St Jerome, Letter XXII, in *Select
Letters of St Jerome*, p. 95. 'I praise
wedlock, I praise marriage, but it
is because they produce me
virgins.' Ambrose saw marriage as
a bondage, indignity and burden, a
perpetually galling yoke (*Exhort.
Virginitatis*, 21, 24, 31, 34). 'Even a
good marriage is slavery; what
then, must a bad one be?' he
wrote in *De Viduis* 69, quoted in
F. Homes Dudden, *The Life and
Times of St Ambrose*, 2 vols,
Oxford, 1935, vol. I, p. 139, and
notes 8 and 10.

61. Brown, op. cit., p. 158.

62. See Brown, op. cit., pp. 341–5.

63. See Chapter One, p. 404, note 29.

64. Susanne Heine, *Women and Early
Christianity. Are the feminist scholars
right?*, trs. John Bowden, London,
1987, pp. 131 and 173, note 396;
Origen, *Contra Celsus* 2:55,
referred to in William E. Phipps,
*The Sexuality of Jesus. Theological
and literary perspectives*, New York,
1973, p. 65, and note 63.

65. In his Epistle to Philemon, v. 2,
Paul greets 'beloved Apphia' who,
together with Philemon and
Archippus, was leader of the
house-church at Colossae. Priscilla
and Aquila, the tentmakers
converted by Paul at Corinth, also
founded and supported the

'church in their house' (I Cor. 16:19; Rom. 16:5), as did Nympha of Laodicea (Col. 4:15).

66. Heine, op. cit., p. 61, and Elisabeth Schüssler Fiorenza, *In Memory of Her. A Feminist Theological Reconstruction of Christian Origins*, London, 1983, p. 170–1.

67. ibid., p. 170.

68. ibid., p. 181.

69. Lea, op. cit., p. 40.

70. Heine, op. cit., p. 175, and note 423.

71. Cf. 1 Cor. 14, 33b–36 which demands that women 'keep silence in the churches', and learn 'from their husbands at home' as 'it is a shame for [them] to speak in the church', a later interpolation also, often used on Paul's authority to justify women's exclusion from positions of authority in the Church. For Paul's own ambivalence, see 1 Cor. 11, 2–16. See Heine, p. 139.

72. See Raymond E. Brown SS, *The Community of the Beloved Disciple*, London, 1979, p. 189, where Mary Magdalen's seeing the risen Christ and proclaiming him in John, both Pauline requisites for the apostolate, are only almost fulfilled. Hers is 'not a mission to the whole world' although she 'comes close to meeting the basic Pauline requirements of an apostle' (pp. 189–90). I am grateful to Father Robert Murray for drawing my attention to this work.

73. Quoted in Heine, op. cit., p. 42, and note 141. Andronicus and Junia had been fellow prisoners and were Christians before Paul.

74. Lea, op. cit., p. 30.

75. ibid., p. 37.

76. Bonnie S. Anderson and Judith P. Zinsser, *A History of Their Own. Women in Europe from Prehistory to the Present*, Harmondsworth, 1989, vol. I, p. 53. Among the Roman religions, the cult of Diana of Ephesus was popular all over the Mediterranean area; in the state cult of Ceres women under the leadership of priestesses celebrated the Mysteries to ensure fertility. Cybele became popular in the Roman Empire from the third century BC and, two centuries later, the cult of Isis was even more widespread, from north Africa to Germany and Asia Minor to Spain. The priestesses of the goddess cults often had the greatest legitimate power in Greece and Rome, with spiritual power and religious leadership, and in the first century AD the priestess was often also a magistrate, thus possessing both secular and religious power (pp. 53–4).

77. Lea, op. cit., pp. 48–9.

78. ibid., p. 52.

79. R.-L. Bruckberger, *Marie-Madeleine*, trs. H. L. Binsse, London, 1953, p. 232.

80. Ephrem the Syriac, 'Sermo in mulierem peccatricem', in *Opera Omnia Greca*, Rome, 1743, vol. II, pp. 279–306, quoted in Guillaume, op. cit., col. 565.

81. My realisation that different versions of this scene must be connected is supported by August C. Mahr, *The Relationship of Passion Plays to St Ephrem the Syrian's Homily De Peccatrice quae peccato laborabat*, Columbus, 1942. See Chapter Five (p. 164, and note 92) for a more detailed account.

82. Severinus of Gabala, in Guillaume, op. cit., cols 565–6.

83. Amphilocus, in ibid., col. 566.

84. Origen, *The Song of Songs. Commentary and Homilies*, trs. and annot. R. P. Lawson, no. 26 in

Ancient Christian Writers: The Works of the Fathers in Translation, ed. Johannes Quasten STD, Westminster (Md.) and London, 1957, p. 23.

85. ibid., p. 160.

86. Cyril of Alexandria, in Guillaume, op. cit., col. 566.

87. Proclus, in ibid., col. 566.

88. Gregory of Antioch, in ibid., col. 568.

89. Modestus of Jerusalem, in ibid., col. 568. See also Chapter Four, p. 107.

90. Murray, op. cit., pp. 329–30. A similar confusion reigns in the *Twentieth Discourse* of Cyril of Jerusalem of *c.* 315–87, who claimed to derive his information from the Virgin herself, who had apparently told him that she had been born in Magdalia and was also called Mary Magdalene. She belonged to Cleophas and James the son of Joseph the carpenter. After the resurrection she lived for ten years with John in Jerusalem. Warned by Jesus of her approaching end, she summons her virgins to prepare them. 'Mary [then] took hold of the hand of one of them, who had waxed exceedingly old, that is to say Mary Magdalene, out of whom Christ had cast seven devils, and said to the virgins, "behold your mother from this time onwards".' E. A. Wallis Budge, *Miscellaneous Coptic Texts in the Dialect of Upper Egypt*, London, 1915, pp. 626 and 646. M. R. James refers rather testily to the 'reckless identification of the Virgin Mary with all the other Maries of the gospels', which he sees as 'characteristic of these Egyptian rhapsodies' (James, *The Apocryphal New Testament*, Oxford, 1924, p. 88).

91. Murray, op. cit., pp. 147–8.

92. ibid., p. 148.

93. Florence, Biblioteca Medicea Laurenziana, MS Plut.I, 56, fol. 13r.

94. St Ambrose, 'M. Magdalenae an plures personae fuerint?', *PL* XV, cols 1616–17.

95. Quoted in Guillaume, op. cit., col. 567.

96. St Ambrose, *PL* XV, cols 1616–17.

97. In *De Isaac et Anima* (5:43), quoted in Guillaume, op. cit., col. 567.

98. 'My opinion is that there is but one interpretation to be put upon the matter. That is not, however, to suppose that the woman who appears in Matthew was an entirely different person from the woman who approached the feet of Jesus on that occasion in the character of a sinner, and kissed them, and washed them with her tears and wiped them with her hair and anointed them . . . But my theory is that it was the same Mary who did this deed on two separate occasions, the one being that which Luke has put on record, when she approached him first of all in that remarkable humility and with those tears and obtained forgiveness of her sins. For John too . . . has at least mentioned the fact, commending the same Mary to our notice when he has just begun to tell the story of the raising of Lazarus.' (*Harmony of the Gospels*, Book II, trs. Revd S. D. F. Salmond, vol. VIII, *The works of Aurelius Augustine*, ed. Revd Marcus Dods, Edinburgh, 1873, pp. 359–60).

99. St Augustine, *In Joannis Evangelium, PL* XXXV, col. 1748.

100. *Harmony of the Gospels*, Book III, p. 452.

101. *In Joannem* 121, 2, quoted in Guillaume, op. cit., col. 567.

102. *Sermon* 243, 2, and 245, 4, *PL*

XXXVIII, cols 1144 and 1153, referred to in Guillaume, op. cit., col. 567.

103. For a survey of the various exegetes, see Dom Augustin Calmet, 'Dissertation sur Les Trois Maries', in *Sainte Bible en latin et français, avec des notes littérales*, etc., Paris, 1773, vol. XIII, pp. 331–49; see also U. Holzmeister, 'Die Magdalenfrage in der kirchlichen Überlieferung', in *Zeitschrift für katholische Theologie*, vol. XLVI, 1922, pp. 402–22 and 558–84.

104. Victor Saxer gives the dates of Gregory's sermons in 'Les Origines du Culte de Sainte Marie Madeleine en Occident', in *Marie Madeleine dans la mystique, les arts et les lettres*, ed. Eve Duperray, Paris, 1989, p. 41. For the dissenting voices, see Jacques Lefèvre d'Etaples (pp. 250–1), Augustin Calmet (pp. 328 and 388) and Peter Ketter (pp. 97 and 388).

105. Gregory the Great, *Homily XXXIII*, *PL LXXVI*, col. 1239.

106. Gregory the Great, *Homily XXV*, *PL LXXVI*, col. 1180.

107. Victor Saxer, *Le Culte de Marie Madeleine en Occident des origines à la fin du moyen âge*, Paris, 1959, p. 33.

108. Patricia Allwin De Leeuw, 'Gregory the Great's "Homilies on the Gospels" in the early Middle Ages', *Studi Medievali*, vol. XXVI, fasc. II, 1985, pp. 855–69.

109. Peter Ketter, *The Magdalene Question*, trs. Revd Hugo C. Koehler, Milwaukee, 1935, p. 36.

110. See Chapter Two, p. 46.

CHAPTER IV

1. The chapter title comes from J. Calmette and H. David, *Les Grandes Heures de Vézelay*, Paris, 1951.

2. Henry II was referring to Vézelay on the occasion of his excommunication by Thomas à Becket, which had been launched at the abbey. Quoted in Aimé Chérest, *Vézelay. Etude historique*, 3 vols. Auxerre, 1863–8, vol. I, p. 127 and note 2. St Bernard of Clairvaux described Vézelay as the 'illustre monastère' when writing to Pope Innocent II in 1133 (quoted in F. Salet and J. Adhémar, *La Madeleine de Vézelay. Etude iconographique*, Melun, 1948, p. 25 and note 9).

3. Walter Pater, *Some Great Churches in France*, Portland (Me.) 1893, p. 93. Vézelay 'might seem a still active instrument of the iron tyranny of Rome, of its tyranny over the animal spirits' (p. 93). On p. 107, he wrote, 'As a symbol of the resurrection, its choir is a fitting diadem to the Magdalen, whose remains the monks meant it [the church] to cover.' In the narthex he found, in a low-vaulted crypt, 'the relics of the friend of Jesus' (p. 102).

4. Victor Saxer, *Le Culte de Marie Madeleine en Occident des origines à la fin du moyen âge*, Paris, 1959, p. 91. At the beginning of the twelfth century, Vézelay owned forty-one churches. By 1170 it was the head of 100 churches or chapels, as well as owning windmills, hospices, land and tithes (p. 139).

5. Salet and Adhémar, op. cit., pp. 33–4.

6. Joan Evans, *Cluniac Art of the Romanesque Period*, Cambridge, 1950, pp. 99–100. Lydwine Saulnier and Neil Stratford, *La Sculpture oubliée de Vézelay*, Geneva, 1984, cat. no. 155, keystone of vault (fig. 153 and Plan III, 4).

7. Quoted in Peter Brown, *The Cult of Saints*, London, 1981, p. 7 and note 31.

8. St Jerome, *Contra Vigilantium* 8, *PL* XXIII, col. 346, quoted in Brown, op. cit., p. 9, and note 36; A. Fliche and V. Martin, *Histoire de l'Eglise depuis les origines jusqu'à nos jours*, Paris, 1945, vol. III, p. 375.

9. Brown, op. cit., pp. 36–7.

10. Jonathan Sumption, *Pilgrimage: An Image of Medieval Religion*, London, 1975, p. 25; Patrick J. Geary, *Furta Sacra: Thefts of Relics in the Central Middle Ages*, Princeton, 1978, p. 3, and note 1. Both these books, particularly Geary's, give useful résumés of the Magdalen cult at Vézelay. Geary shows how the latter was influenced by the cult of Ste Foy at Conques.

11. A medieval legend told of how, at her assumption, the Virgin let her girdle drop down to the earth to make doubting Thomas believe in her ascent to heaven.

12. 'A list of famous relics, given by John Brady', 1839, p. 263 in *A Dictionary of Miracles. Imitative, Realistic and Dogmatic*, by Revd E. Cobham Brewer, London, 1884. The list, the author adds, is 'given on the authority of John Brady, who must be held responsible. It is a pity he has not given the whereabouts of each relic, that the accuracy of his statements might be verified.'

13. Réau, vol. III, 2, p. 848. In 1183 Philip Augustus expelled the Jews from Paris, turning their synagogue into a sanctuary dedicated to Mary Magdalen. On the rue de Juiverie, on the corner of the rues de la Licorne and des Marmousets, it was enlarged down the centuries until it was demolished in 1794 and the parish, which had been extended to take in the neighbouring parishes of St Symphorien, St Christophe and Ste Geneviève des Ardents, was suppressed. Nothing is now left of it, since the Hôtel-Dieu was built on its site at the beginning of the nineteenth century. The historian Joinville heard mass at the church of the Madeleine on the eve of the day Louis IX took up the Cross for the last time on 25 March 1267 (para. 733, p. 212, *The Life of St Louis* by John of Joinville, trs. René Hague, from the text ed. Natalis de Wailly, London and New York, 1955).

14. *The Pilgrimage of Arnold von Harff, Knight*, ed. Malcolm Letts, Hakluyt Society, London, Second Series no. XCIV, 1946, p. 68. Von Harff made his pilgrimage between 1496 and 1499. His suspicions about relics were raised when at S. Giorgio Maggiore, which he described as 'a fine monastery in the sea'. Having seen the 'head of St George', and 'his left arm with the flesh', he noted the 'head of St James the Less which I saw later at Compostella in Galicia. These muddles of the priests I leave to God's judgement,' he added, somewhat dismissively (p. 67). A late fifteenth-century reliquary monstrance, probably from Florence, and now in the Metropolitan Museum, New York (17.190.504), contains a tooth supposed to have been one of Mary Magdalen's.

15. Brown, op. cit., pp. 39ff; see also Geary, op. cit., pp. 33–4.

16. G. G. Coulton, *Five Centuries of Religion*, Cambridge, 1936, vol. III, p. 106; R. W. Southern, *The Making of the Middle Ages*, London, 1959: 'for most people – and those not the least learned – it is very probable that the resting places and relics of saints were the most conspicuous feature of the landscape' (p. 254).

17. Sumption, op. cit., p. 29.

18. Gratian's *Decretum*, pars II, dist. i, c. 26, in Coulton, op. cit., p. 87.

19. *The Book of Margery Kempe*, trs. B. A. Windeatt, Harmondsworth, 1985, p. 156.

20. J. Huizinga, *The Waning of the Middle Ages*, Harmondsworth, 1975, p. 161.

21. See Chapter Seven (p. 278 and note 119).

22. Huizinga, op. cit., p. 161.

23. *Life of St Hugh of Lincoln*, written by Adam of Eynsham, ed. Decima L. Douie, Dom Hugh Fraser OSB, 2 vols, London, 1962, vol. II, pp. 169–70. St Hugh (*c.*1140–1200) had the reputation of being the most learned man in England of his time, and was unusually accessible to women (introd., vol. I, p. xi). He was also sceptical about supposed miracles. Adam recorded that 'Having attained at last to the desired embraces of the lovely and glowing Rachel, the new aspirant to the eremitical life was like the most holy Mary in his cell alone', using the metaphor of Rachel to show that Hugh had now achieved contemplation, and was now, like the legendary Mary Magdalen (as Mary of Bethany), Rachel's New Testament counterpart, meditating in his cell (vol. I, p. 30). He uses the metaphor of Mary of Bethany again (vol. I, p. 34); and he alludes to the legend of the marriage of John the Evangelist and Mary Magdalen at Cana (vol. II, p. 12; for this legend, see Chapter Five, pp. 136 and 158–60, and Plate 22, p. 161).

24. Sumption, op. cit., p. 35.

25. Louis Duchesne, *Les Origines du culte chrétien*, Paris, 1923, pp. 300–1, referred to in Saxer, 'Les saintes Marie Madeleine et Marie de Béthanie dans la tradition liturgique et homilétique orientale', *Revue des sciences religieuses*, vol. XXXII, 1958, pp. 1–2.

26. Louis Duchesne, *Fastes épiscopaux de l'ancienne Gaule*, Paris, 1907, vol. I, p. 323; and Saxer, 'Les saintes Marie', p. 15. The account of Etheria is in H. Petré, *Ethérie, Journal des Voyages*, Editions du Cerf, Paris, 1948.

27. St Jerome, Letter to Eustochium (*PL* XXIII, col. 887), referred to in Saxer, 'Les saintes Marie', p. 15.

28. ibid., p. 18. Lazarus' tomb was also to be seen at Larnaca, on Cyprus, where an ancient church was dedicated to him.

29. *Viaggio in Terrasanta di Santo Brasco, 1480, con l'Itinerario di Gabriele Capodilista, 1458*, ed. Anna Laura Momigliano Lepschy, Milan, 1966, p. 93, para. 154; p. 92, para. 150; p. 72, paras 71 and 72; p. 90, para. 144; p. 265, note 185. Born in 1444, Santo Brasca became chancellor in the *entrate ordinarie* under Galeazzo Maria Sforza. In 1480 he went to the Holy Land; he died in 1522. He was one of those who subscribed to the theory that the risen Christ first appeared to his mother. I am grateful to Aldo De Poli for referring me to this work.

30. A church was dedicated to Mary Magdalen at the beginning of the twelfth century in Jerusalem in the Jewish quarter of the city, and another church dedicated to her was mentioned 1101–2 at Ascalon (Saxer, *Culte*, p. 122).

31. *John Poloner's Description of the Holy Land* (*c.*1421), ed. Aubrey Stewart, Palestine Pilgrim's Text Society, London, 1894, p. 17.

32. See Chapter Nine, p. 328.

33. Saxer, 'Les saintes Marie', pp. 21–6; Modestus of Jerusalem, *PG* LXXXVI, cols 3273–6.

34. Modestus, of course, was of the eastern Church, which always distinguished Mary Magdalen from Luke's sinner and Mary of Bethany. Quoted in P.-M. Guillaume, 'Ste Marie-Madeleine', *Dict. Spir.*, col. 568, where Modestus also describes her as 'chief of the women disciples'.

35. 'In ea urbe [Ephesus] Maria Magdalena quiescit, nullum super se tegumen habens' (Gregory of Tours, quoted in Duchesne, *Fastes épiscopaux*, p. 325, note 1; Saxer, 'Les saintes Marie', pp. 23–4, suggests that the description refers to an oratory open to the sky so that visitors first visited the tomb before entering the grotto.

36. Saxer, 'Les saintes Marie', p. 36.

37. Duchesne, *Fastes épiscopaux*, p. 326.

38. ibid., p. 325; Saxer, 'Les saintes Marie', p. 28.

39. Duchesne, *Fastes épiscopaux*, p. 326; Saxer, 'Les saintes Marie', p. 29.

40. Duchesne, *Fastes épiscopaux*, p. 326.

41. Saxer, *Culte*, pp. 218–19.

42. ibid., pp. 40–2.

43. Duchesne, op. cit., p. 326; the date of 22 July appears in an Anglo-Saxon martyrology of the monk Oengus as the 'blessed nativity of Mary Magdalen', and 28 March as the 'feast of her conversion to Christ'. Saxer, *Culte*, p. 34, and note 7.

44. Meyer Shapiro, 'The Religious Meaning of the Ruthwell Cross', in *Late Antique, Early Christian and Mediaeval Art. Selected Papers*, vol. III, London, 1980, pp. 150–95. Shapiro dates the cross to the seventh century.

45. D. R. Howlett, 'Two Panels on the Ruthwell Cross', *Journal of the Warburg and Courtauld Institutes*, vol. XXXVII, 1974, p. 334, who gives a possible *terminus a quo* for the cross of 709–15, the date of Bede's commentary (p. 335).

46. For the commentary on Luke 7, see *The Complete Works of Venerable Bede*, ed. Revd J. A. Giles, London, 1844, vol. XI, p. 53. According to J. E. Cross, 'Mary Magdalen in the *Old English Martyrology*: The Earliest Extant "Narrato Josephus" Variant of her Legend', *Speculum*, vol. LIII, 1978, p. 16, Bede's information about alabaster came from Pliny.

47. *An Old English Martyrology*, ed. and introd. George Herzfeld, EETS, no. 116, London, 1900, p. 127. Herzfeld dates it in introd., p. xxxii: 'I should say that the Martyrology cannot possibly [be] later than 900. We might even fix its date as early as 850.' See also Cross, op. cit., pp. 16–25.

48. Shapiro, op. cit., p. 164, and note 52, where it is suggested that material in the martyrology may have originated in liturgical books plundered from Capua in *c*.600–650.

49. Duchesne was the first to recognise this parallel, but assumed that the Mary of Egypt legend was annexed to Mary Magdalen's life in the twelfth century, pp. 346–7. See Jean Misrahi, 'A Vita Sanctae Mariae Magdalenae (*BHL* 5456) in an Eleventh-century Manuscript', *Speculum*, vol. XVIII, 1943, pp. 335–9. For the story of Mary of Egypt, see Benedicta Ward, *Harlots of the Desert. A study of repentance in early monastic sources*, London and Oxford, 1987, pp. 26–56. (The earliest known account of her life is in the mid-sixth century *Life of St Cyriacus* by Cyril of Scythopolis.) Mary Magdalen is also included in Ward, op. cit., pp. 10–25.

50. *An Old English Martyrology*, p. 127.

51. Shapiro, op. cit., p. 164. See now Veronica Ortenberg, 'Le culte de Sainte Marie Madeleine dans

l'Angleterre anglo-saxonne', *MEFRM*, pp. 13–35.

52. Saxer, *Le Dossier vézelien de Marie Madeleine. Invention et translation des reliques en 1265–1267*, Brussels, 1975, p. 182.

53. Saxer, *Culte*, pp. 55–6; ibid., 'Maria Maddalena', *Bibl. Sanct.*, vol. VIII, cols 1091–2.

54. ibid., col. 1092; for the hymns, see J. Szövérffy, 'Peccatrix Quondam Femina. A Survey of the Mary Magdalen Hymns', *Traditio*, vol. XIX, 1963, pp. 79–146, esp. p. 90.

55. Saxer, *Culte*, pp. 60–1; pp. 62, 65 and 63.

56. ibid., pp. 35 and 351. Saxer has shown that the attribution of the feast-day to Mary and Martha was due to confusion with Persian martyrs called Marius and Martha (p. 351).

57. ibid., pp. 54–5, and note 34.

58. ibid., p. 54, and note 32. Athelstan's passion for relics, according to William of Malmesbury, was greater than that of any other ruler of his century (*Gesta Pontificum Anglorum*, Rolls Series, Kraus reprint, 1964, p. 425), Geary, op. cit., p. 59.

59. Saxer, *Culte*, p. 63.

60. ibid., p. 84, and note 127.

61. ibid., and note 125.

62. See David A. Mycoff, *A Critical Edition of the Legend of Mary Magdalena from Caxton's* Golden Legend *of 1483*, Salzburg, 1985, p. 57, note 43. According to the Glastonbury tradition, 'there may be a very early pre-Conquest church at Beckery dedicated to Mary Magdalen'. This was later rededicated to St Bridget (John Morland, 'St Bridget's chapel, Beckery', *Proceeding of the Somerset Archaeological and Natural History Society*, vol. XXXV, 1889, pp. 121–6).

63. Chérest, op. cit., vol. I, pp. 58–9.

64. Salet and Adhémar, op. cit., p. 21.

65. Chérest, op. cit., vol. I, pp. 21–2. See E.-M. Faillon, *Monuments inédits sur l'apostolat de Sainte Marie-Madeleine en Provence*, 2 vols, Paris, 1865, vol. II, col. 735 for the hagiographical account of Geoffrey, and Mary Magdalen's miracles; and Saxer, *Culte*, pp. 71–2.

66. Saxer, *Culte*, pp. 66 and 68–9.

67. Odo, 'In veneratione Sanctae Mariae Magdalenae', *PL* CXXX, cols 713–21. See now Dominique Iogna-Prat, 'La Madeleine du *Sermo in Veneratione Sanctae Mariae Magdalenae* attribué à Odon de Cluny', *MEFRM*, pp. 37–70.

68. Saxer, *Culte*, p. 67.

69. ibid., pp. 67–8, who also suggests that Ermenfroi, who was of German origin, may have imported the cult from Germany (pp. 85–6). On his death, Ermenfroi's sanctuary was one of the richest in the Empire and France.

70. *The Book of the Knight de la Tour-Landry*, ed. Thomas Wright, EETS, no. 33, London, 1868, chapter XXV, p. 35. The knight Geoffrey wrote his treatise between 1371 and 1372, under the pretext of instructing his own daughters, but its purpose was in fact to discuss the education of women. Caxton translated it in 1483, publishing it the following year. The EETS edition is taken from MS Harl. 1764 in the British Museum, supplemented by Caxton's edition of 1483.

71. 'The Wife of Bath's Prologue', in *The Canterbury Tales. The Works of Geoffrey Chaucer*, ed. F. N. Robinson, London and Oxford, 1974, p. 81, lines 555–8.

72. Huizinga, op. cit., p. 155.

73. Duchesne, op. cit., p. 329. The miracle is illustrated in Biblioteca

Apostolica Vaticana, MS Vat. Lat. 8541, f. 104r.

74. Faillon, op. cit., vol. II, col. 735.

75. Sumption, op. cit., p. 103.

76. ibid., pp. 69 and 119.

77. Duchesne, op. cit, pp. 335–6.

78. Faillon, op. cit., vol. II, col. 735.

79. Related in Duchesne, op. cit., p. 330, note 1.

80. Soon after 1297, these documents, called the 'Dossier' by Saxer, were amassed to present to Boniface VIII, who had by this time confirmed St Maximin's possession of Mary Magdalen's bones. They have been found in various versions, the most complete being in the bound volume in the Vatican Library (Archivio S. Pietro, MS E.25), assembled for Louis I of Anjou between 1360 and 1382, who had a particular affection for Mary Magdalen. They have been published in Saxer, *Le Dossier vézelien de Marie Madeleine. Invention et translation des reliques en 1265–1267*, Brussels, 1975. Aleaume's exploit is referred to in Saxer, *Dossier*, p. 78.

81. Faillon, op. cit., vol. II, cols 741–4.

82. ibid., vol. II, cols 745–52.

83. For the different accounts of the origins and diffusion of the legend, see Misrahi, op. cit., p. 337; Hans Hansel, *Die Maria-Magdalena-Legende. Eine Quellen-Untersuchung*, Greifswald, vol. I, esp. p. 128; Saxer, *Culte*, p. 126; and most recently, Mycoff, op. cit., p. 14.

84. Saxer, *Culte*, p. 126.

85. ibid., pp. 129–32, who also suggests (p. 151) that the cult at Ste Baume was entirely independent of Vézelay, and might have been inspired by monks at Marseille before being exploited by the hermits of Montrieux.

86. ibid., pp. 70–1.

87. *Chanson d'Oxford* (lines 9015–20), in René Louis, *De l'histoire à la légende. Girart, comte de Vienne . . . et ses fondations monastiques*, Auxerre, 1946, quoted in Saxer, *Dossier*, p. 204.

88. Duchesne, op. cit., p. 333.

89. Baudouin de Gaiffier, 'Hagiographie bourguignonne', *Analecta Bollandiana*, vol. LXIX, 1951, p. 140.

90. Duchesne, op. cit., pp. 336–7; Saxer, *Culte*, pp. 95–108.

91. Duchesne, op. cit., pp. 340–1.

92. Chérest, op. cit., vol. I, p. 127; Saxer, *Culte*, pp. 93–4.

93. ibid., p. 92. Gelasius had been forced to leave Rome and seek asylum in France, where he was greeted by Suger, and was to meet Louis at Vézelay, but died on the way.

94. Saxer, *Culte*, pp. 138–9.

95. ibid., p. 140.

96. Chérest, op. cit., vol. I, p. 41.

97. Saxer, *Culte*, p. 137.

98. The expression is R. W. Southern's, *The Making of the Middle Ages*, London, (1967) 1987, p. 156.

99. Saxer, *Culte*, p. 186.

100. Chérest, op. cit., vol. II, pp. 130–2.

101. Saxer, *Culte*, p. 187.

102. Faillon, op. cit., vol. II, col. 754.

103. Chérest, op. cit., vol. II, p. 142.

104. ibid., p. 143.

105. Saxer, *Culte*, pp. 191–5.

106. ibid., pp. 185–6.

107. Saxer, *Dossier*, p. 223.

108. Chérest, vol. II, p. 145; Saxer, *Dossier*, pp. 104–5, which refers to L. Carolus-Barré's 'St Louis et la translation des corps saints', in *Etudes d'histoire du droit canonique dédiés à Gabriel le Bras*, Paris, 1965, vol. II, pp. 1087–112.

109. Saxer, *Culte*, pp. 195–6.

110. In the *Dictionnaire de mobilier*, article 'Réliquaire', Viollet-le-Duc

remarked that the most ingenious creations of medieval goldsmiths were due to the necessity of enshrining some sacred bone in crystal or setting it in gold (quoted in E. Mâle, *L'Art religieux du XIIIe siècle en France*, Paris, 1898, p. 405).

111. Chérest, op. cit., vol. II, p. 148. Relics of the Passion represented the earthly Jerusalem which Louis desired to reconquer for Christ. He also built Ste Chapelle to house the relics (pieces of the crown of thorns, the true cross, holy sponge, the lance that pierced Christ's side, purple vestments and of the sepulchre stone). Also included were some bones of Mary Magdalen, the occipital of John the Baptist, the mantle of the Virgin and the sponge used in the washing of the feet (William C. Jordan, *Louis IX and the Challenge of the Crusade*, Princeton, 1979, p. 108, and note 14).

112. Quoted in Saxer, *Dossier*, p. 109.

113. Chérest, op. cit., vol. II, p. 149.

114. ibid. Also in Faillon, op. cit., vol. II, col. 761.

115. Duchesne, op. cit., pp. 340–6.

116. Duchesne, op cit., pp. 338–40. Lazarus had arrived from Cyprus where he had been bishop for thirty years. The cathedral at Autun, built below an earlier cathedral dedicated to a St Nazaire, was built in the first half of the twelfth century, although Lazarus may have been venerated there in the tenth century. The diocese of Autun, not to be outdone by its close neighbour Vézelay, decided that it too would cash in on the fame of its sister abbey, claiming that the bones of its namesake were there. An eyewitness of the translation of the relics in 1147 testified that a bishop's gloves and pastoral staff were found in the sepulchre. There was, however, no reference to the relics' provenance.

117. Saxer, *Culte*, p. 208.

118. ibid.

119. ibid., p. 210.

120. Joinville, quoted in Saxer, *Culte*, p. 211, and note 115. The period of Mary Magdalen's penitence was usually computed as thirty years (according to the *Golden Legend* and Fra Salimbene de Adam), and twenty, according to Vincent de Beauvais – in the *Speculum historiale*, the fourth volume of his compendium the *Speculum maioris*, Venice, 1591.

121. Fra Salimbene de Adam, *Cronica Fratris Salimbene de Adam Ordinis Minorum. A. 1283 in Monumenta Germaniae Historica*, Leipzig, 1889, p. 521. As to the enormous proportions the Fra claimed for the grotto: in Bologna there is one tower of the Asinelli, but he may have meant that the grotto's interior was three times the height of that tower; he merely exaggerated by about fifty per cent the number of people who might be accommodated in the space.

122. Saxer, *Culte*, pp. 206ff.

123. Salimbene, op. cit., p. 521.

124. Saxer, *Culte*, p. 240–1.

125. Duchesne, op. cit., p. 350.

126. Saxer, *Culte*, p. 231.

127. ibid.

128. Duchesne, op. cit., p. 353.

129. Faillon, op. cit., vol. II, col. 780.

130. Saxer, *Culte*, p. 231.

131. ibid., p. 234; Faillon, op. cit., vol. II, cols 791–2.

132. Saxer, *Culte*, p. 235. Charles's descendant, René of Anjou, was to maintain the Angevin dynasty's affection for Mary Magdalen. In 1448 he ordered an invention and discovered the bodies of Mary

Magdalen's companions who, legend told, had arrived with her at Marseille, a destination which changed to the mouth of the Rhône, and then to Notre-Dame-de-la-Mer, which was named in consequence Stes-Maries-de-la-Mer (Saxer, *Culte*, pp. 238–9). René's enthusiasm for Mary Magdalen and St Maximin is outlined in Otto Pächt's article 'Dévotion du roi René pour sainte Marie-Madeleine et le sanctuaire de Saint-Maximin', *Chronique méridionale*, vol. I, 1981, pp. 15–28. I am grateful to Véronique Plesh for making this available to me.

133. Saxer, *Culte*, p. 234.
134. Duchesne, op. cit., pp. 355–6.
135. Saxer, *Culte*, pp. 241–2.
136. Salimbene, op. cit., pp. 520–1.
137. According to J.-A.-S. Collin de Plancy, *Dizionario critico delle reliquie e delle imagini miraculose*, Rome, 1982 (trs. from the French edition, 1821–2), there were six bodies – one in Constantinople, one in Rome divided between S. Giovanni Laterano and S. Maria del Popolo; a further one at Monserrato, and yet another at Naples. He lists other smaller relics such as some drops of blood which Mary Magdalen collected at the foot of the cross, which were boiled up annually on Good Friday at St Maximin immediately after reading the account of the Passion (pp. 160–2).
138. In the Middle Ages the translation of the relics from Provence to Burgundy was celebrated at Vézelay on 19 March and in Provence on 5 May (Saxer, *Culte*, pp. 324–5).

CHAPTER V

1. *Hali Meidenhad. An Alliterative Homily of the Thirteenth Century*, ed. F. J. Furnivall, EETS, OS, no. 18, 1922, pp. 14 and 15. See also the useful introduction and notes to the later edition of *Hali Meidhad* by Bella Millett (EETS, no. 284, London, 1982), who dates the treatise to 1190–1220 (p. xvii), and describes it as 'a letter on virginity for the encouragement of a virgin or virgins' (p. xxii).
2. The description is Monsignor Saxer's ('Santa Maria Maddalena dalla storia evangelica alla legenda e all'arte', in *La Maddalena*, p. 25).
3. Humbert de Romans, 'Ad mulieres malas corpore sive meretrices' in *Sermones ad diversos status*, Hagenau, 1508, *Sermo* C.
4. J. A. Jungmann, *The Mass of the Roman Rite*, New York, 1950, vol. I, p. 470, note 55. 'And therfore in oure litanie we take hure before all virgines except the moder of God, the whiche noght onely is set and prayed afore virgines but also afore alle other seyntis after hire sone', *Speculum Sacerdotale*, ed. E. H. Weatherly, EETS, OS, no. 200, 1936, p. 172, lines 22–5.
5. A double was a feast-day on which antiphons and plainsong were recited in full before and after psalms and canticles. In the Middle Ages, another feast, the 'festum conversionis beatae Mariae Magdalenae', was celebrated on 1 March, 10 April, or as a moveable feast on the Thursday after Judica, contingent upon the date on which Easter was celebrated (see J. Szövérffy, 'Peccatrix Quondam Femina: A Survey of the Mary Magdalen Hymns', *Traditio*, vol. XIX, 1963, p. 91; and Saxer, *Le Culte de Marie Madeleine en Occident des origines à la fin du moyen âge*, Paris, 1959, pp. 324–5).
6. Gilbert of Nogent in *De Laude S. Mariae*, cap. ii, *PL* CLVI, cols

568–70, quoted in Saxer, *Culte*, p. 80, and note 105.

7. Depositions, etc., of Durham (SS 1845), 26ff, quoted in G. G. Coulton, *Medieval Panorama*, Cambridge, 1958, p. 184.

8. The account of the massacre at Béziers is in P. Belperron, *La Croisade contre les Albigeois, et l'Union du Languedoc à la France (1209–49)*, Paris, 1944, p. 163. See also Arno Borst, *Die Kathärer*, Stuttgart, 1953, p. 164, who refers to the heretics' belief that Mary Magdalen was Christ's concubine.

9. Réau, vol. III, 2, p. 846.

10. Marga Anstett-Janssen, 'Maria Magdalena', *Lexikon der christlichen Ikonographie*, ed. E. Kirschbaum SJ and W. Braunfels, Rome, etc., 1974, vol. 7, col. 518.

11. As patron of the drapers' guild, the Arte de' Drappieri, she appears in the *matricole* and statutes of the guild, dated 1339 (Bologna, Museo Civico Medievale, MS 634; illus. in *La Maddalena*, p. 44); at Chartres, the Mary Magdalen window is at the west end of the south aisle of the nave. The winegrowers' church of St Mary Magdalen, situated in vineyards near Bolzano which are first recorded in 1170–4, was dedicated to the saint by 1295 (Helmut Stampfer, *La chiesa di Santa Maddalena presso Bolzano*, Bolzano, 1988, p. 6).

12. Magdalen College, Oxford, was founded by William of Waynflete, bishop of Winchester, who, having already founded a 'hall, or college in honour of his blessed patroness', in 1457 was granted a licence by Henry VI to establish a college 'on a more magnificent scale' to be dedicated to the same 'glorious apostoless'. James Ingram, *Memorials of Oxford*, Oxford and London, 1837, vol. II,

pp. 4–5 and note i. Magdalene College, Cambridge was first founded in 1428 as a hostel for Benedictine monks from Croylands Abbey, and then again in 1542 by Lord Audley of Audley End.

13. Saxer, *Culte*, p. 77. Illegitimate daughters in the Tyrol were also given her name (Réau, vol. III, 2, p. 849).

14. Anselm of Canterbury (*c*.1033–1109), archbishop of Canterbury from 1093, 'Oratio ad Sanctam Mariam Magdalenam', *PL* CLVIII, col. 1010.

15. Gratian, Pars III, dist. IV, cap. iii, quoted in G. G. Coulton, *Five Centuries of Religion*, Cambridge, 1929, vol. I, p. 176.

16. Justin Martyr (died *c*.165) in his *Dialogue with the Jew Trypho* discusses the translation of '*almah*. Trypho says the word should be *neanis* (young girl), and Justin that the Septuagint, the Greek translation of the Old Testament accepted by the Jews, gives *parthenos* (virgin). See Hilda Graef, *Mary: A History of Doctrine and Devotion*, London and New York, 1963, vol. I, pp. 3–6 and 37–8; and Marina Warner, *Alone of All Her Sex*, London, 1976, pp. 19–24.

17. Clement of Alexandria, *Stromata*, vii, 93, quoted in M. R. James, *The Apocryphal New Testament*, Oxford, 1924, p. 38, note 1. The midwife is shown extracting her withered arm in a fresco at Castelseprio, Italy, reproduced in Meyer Shapiro, 'The Frescoes of Castelseprio', in *Late Antique, Early Christian and Medieval Art. Selected Papers*, London, 1980, fig. 16.

18. *The Mary Play. From the N. Town Manuscript*, ed. Peter Meredith, London and New York, 1987, p. 73, I. 1282. I am grateful to Sarah Carpenter for sending me this

reference. 'Ave maris, stella sumens illud Ave? Gabrielis ore, Funda nos in pace/ Mutans nomen Evae', (Anon) in: *The Penguin Book of Latin Verse*, ed. Frederick Brittain, Harmondsworth, 1962, p. 129.

19. John Bugge, *Virginitas: An Essay in the History of a Medieval Ideal*, The Hague, 1975, p. 81.

20. Caesarius of Arles, in: James A. Brundage, *Law, Sex, and Christian Society in Medieval Europe*, Chicago and London, 1988, pp. 91–2, and notes 58 and 59.

21. ibid., pp. 154–63.

22. *Hali Meidenhad*, pp. 28, 12, 37–8, 44 and 22. A 'mild wife and meek widow' are seen to be preferable to a 'proud maiden' who falls into the 'filth of flesh' and laments with bitter weeping like Mary Magdalen (p. 61).

23. See *Prediche alle donne del secolo XIII*, ed. Carla Casagrande, Milan, 1978, pp. vii–xxv. I am grateful to Evelyn Welch for referring me to this selection.

24. For Gilbert de Tournai, see Casagrande, op. cit.

25. Humbert of Romans, op. cit., sermons XLIX, L, LI, LII. He also distinguished between the various classes of female religious: cloistered nuns, those in care of the Dominicans, the *Humiliate*, Augustinian nuns, and girls who were brought up by religious women. (In another volume, Humbert [1193/4–1277] also included a sermon to the Beguines, the groups of lay women who, debarred from a place within the Church, set up religious houses on their own.)

26. Spinello Aretino, banner, New York, Metropolitan Museum, no. 13.175a. I am grateful to the staff of the museum for allowing me to look at the banner while it was in conservation. Mary Magdalen appears on another confraternity banner painted by Perugino (Perugia, Galleria Nazionale dell'Umbria), together with St Jerome.

27. A. G. Roncalli and Pietro Forno, *Gli atti della visita apostolica di S. Carlo Borromeo a Bergamo (1575)*, 2 vols in 5, Florence, 1936–57, vol. I, ii, pp. 189 and 190. Next to the church was a hospital for the sick, particularly beggars and invalids and the mentally ill, one of the first of its kind in Italy (p. 132).

28. The Bargello chapel, now in a much damaged state, has frescoes of Mary Magdalen's penitence, last communion, and miracle of the prince and princess of Marseille; see 'Maddalena' in Carlo Battisti and Giovanni Alessio, *Dizionario etymologico italiano*, Florence, 1952, vol. III, p. 2305.

29. Simone Martini's panel is in Orvieto, Museo dell'Opera del Duomo. While at Orvieto, Monaldeschi paid for a daily mass for Mary Magdalen for fifteen years which he celebrated as often as possible himself. (See Joanna Cannon, 'Dominican Patronage of the Arts in Central Italy: the Provincia Romana, *c.*1220–*c.*1320', unpublished PhD thesis, London, 1980 p. 147.) 'In Festo Sanctae Mariae Magdelenae', *Sermones Aurei*, p. 783, attributed to St Thomas Aquinas, referred to in *La Maddalena*, p. 34, and note 13.

30. *Prediche del Beato Fra Giordano da Rivalta . . . recitate in Firenze dal MCCCIII al MCCCVI*, ed. Domenico Moreni, vol. I, Florence, 1813, pp. 181–2. I am grateful to Salvatore Camporeale for referring me to this work. The church, now demolished, stood on the Costa di S. Giorgio.

31. John Pecham, *Tractatus Pauperis*,

quoted in A. G. Little, *Studies in English Franciscan History*, Manchester, 1917, p. 131, and note 3. Pecham (*c.*1225–92) was made archbishop of Canterbury in 1279. As a Franciscan he opposed the teachings of Thomas Aquinas concerning the nature of man; he also wrote a standard treatise on optics.

32. Richard Rolle was comparing the preacher's role with his own eremitical existence: 'Good it is to be a preacher, to run hither and thither, to move, to be wearied; but it is better, safer, and sweeter to be a contemplator, to have a foretaste of eternal bliss, to sing the delights of the Eternal Love.' Quoted in G. R. Owst, *Preaching in Medieval England*, Cambridge, 1926, pp. 113.

33. Humbert de Romans, *De Eruditione Praedicatorum*, in *Maxima Bibliotheca Veterum Patrum etc.*, xxv, pp. 426–567, quoted in Little, op. cit., p. 132, and note 2.

34. St Bonaventure, *Opera Omnia*, ed. Quaracchi, viii, p. 381, quoted in Little, op. cit., p. 118, and note 3.

35. *Speculum Laicorum*, ed. J. Th. Welter, Paris, 1914, pp. 26–7. See now Nicole Bériou's survey of thirteenth-century French sermons in 'La Madeleine dans les sermons parisiens du XIIIe siècle', in *MEFRM*, pp. 269–340.

36. *Old English Homilies of the Twelfth Century. From the unique MS B.14.52, Trinity College, Cambridge*, ed. R. Morris, EETS, Series 2, no. 53, 1873, XXIV: 'Mary Magdalene', p. 140. Mary Magdalen is the only female saint, apart from the Virgin Mary, in the collection. In the fifteenth-century *Speculum Sacerdotale*, the sermon for her feast-day stresses her sinfulness thus: 'In syche a day ye schull have the feste of Seynt

Marye Magdalene, whiche was the synneful woman and servyd to hure fleschely desires, and to whome God afterward gave siche grace that sche servyd forgeveness of here synnes' (op. cit., cap. xlvii, p. 170).

37. Albertus Magnus, 'De Natura et Origine Animae', in *Opera Omnia*, Monasterium Westfalorum, 1955, vol. XII, *Quaestio* 22, p. 135:53–4.

38. Aristotle, *The Generation of Animals*, trs. A. L. Peck, London and Cambridge (Mass.), Loeb Classical Library, 1943, II.iii, p. 175.

39. ibid., II.iv and II.iii, pp. 181 and 175. In the second century, Galen confirmed Aristotle's views, derived possibly from Hippocrates, on women's coldness and inferiority: 'The female is less perfect than the male for one principal reason, because she is colder' (quoted in Anderson and Zinsser, op. cit., p. 30, and note 25).

40. Aristotle, op. cit., II.iii, pp. 173–5; II.iv, pp. 185 and 199–201, where male and female are described as 'the one active and the other passive'.

41. Aristotle, *Politics*, quoted in Anderson and Zinsser, op. cit., p. 27, and note 3.

42. Albertus Magnus, op. cit., pp. 265:61, and 266:3.

43. *Speculum Laicorum*, op. cit., 'De mulierum [cohabitacione fugienda]', cap. liii, p. 77.

44. Psalter, miniature, *c.*1270–80, St John's College, Cambridge, MS K. 26 (231), f. 23. Illustrated in the catalogue *Age of Chivalry*, London, 1987, no. 353, p. 353. The personification of the serpent as a woman may have ultimately derived from the fact that the gender of the Latin word for 'serpent' is feminine. In a twelfth-

century sermon, the serpent puts into practice what the devil performs spiritually: 'The serpent hath malice and envy, and creeps about secretly and poisoneth all she stingeth'; 'She hath much venom in her, and is hateful to man . . .; she becometh very thirsty and then seeketh a well and drinketh until she bursteth and vomiteth her venom.' XXX: 'Estote fortes in bello, et pugnate cum antiquo serpente', *Old English Homilies of the Twelfth Century*, ed. R. Morris, EETS, Series 2, no. 53, 1873, pp. 190 and 198.

45. Dated 1470–80, New York, Metropolitan Museum, Cloisters, 1955 (55.116.2).

46. John Gower, *Confessio Amantis*, Book V; and MS Harl. 2398, f. 9b, both quoted in Owst, *Preaching*, p. 173, and notes 2 and 3. This kind of segregation can be seen depicted in paintings by the fourteenth-century Sienese artists Sano di Pietro and Vecchietta.

47. Complaints about 'sleepen in church, singen, rownyn, jangelen' are made in *Jacob's Well*, a fifteenth-century English treatise on the cleansing of the conscience, and are quoted in Owst, *Preaching*, p. 175; Humbert de Romans, *Treatise on Preaching*, (chap. XXII: 'Omitting to Preach or Refusing to Listen'), ed. Walter M. Conlon OP, Westminster (Md.), 1951, p. 90.

48. Prudentius' (348–c.405) poem was extremely popular in the Middle Ages and appeared in illustrated editions. See H. Woodruff, *The Illustrated Mss of Prudentius*, Cambridge (Mass.), 1930. See also A. Katzenellenbogen, *Allegories of Virtues and Vices in Medieval Art*, London, 1939. The personification of Virtues and Vices was

formulated in Tertullian's *De Spectaculis*, where they were represented as two armies contending for the soul. It received epic imagery in Prudentius' *Psychomachia*.

49. John Bromyard, 'Luxuria' (L. vii.i), in *Summa Praedicantium*, Venice, 1586, vol. I, p. 457 (Mary Magdalen as an example appears in L. vii.xxxii); Humbert de Romans, *Opera de Vita regulari*, ed. J. J. Berthier, Casali, 1956, p. 272. Bromyard regarded preachers as among the seven classes of good labourers in the world, and was a vigorous opponent of John Wyclif.

50. Greed was represented by a rich man. Absolute poverty was not part of the Dominican rule in the beginning as it had been in the Franciscan order, but from 1220 the Order of Preachers was also bound to absolute poverty. R. F. Bennett, *The Early Dominicans*, Cambridge, 1937, p. 43. Hugonis de Sancto Caro, 'In evangelia secundum Matthaeum, Lucam, Marcam, & Joannem', in *Opera Omnia in Universam*, Venice, 1754, vol. VI, cap. xxi: 'Et quamvis multa peccata sint in utroque sexu: tamen avaritia praecipue abundat in viris, fornicatio in mulieribus.' Hugo was the first cardinal of the Dominican order. The vice of avarice attributed to man, the moral counterpart to woman's abundance in fornication, has been seen as the result of the Church's criticism of the change from feudal society and rise of the bourgeoisie, and in particular the latter's demand for communal rights (Meyer Schapiro, 'From Mozarabic to Romanesque in Silos', *Art Bulletin*, 21, 1939, pp. 313–74, referred to in Henry Kraus, 'Eve and Mary: Conflicting Images of Medieval Woman', in

Feminism and Art History. Questioning the Litany, ed. Norma Broude and Mary D. Garrard, New York, 1982, pp. 79–99, esp. p. 81–2). However, according to John Bromyard, amongst others, women's greed was insatiable: 'Pro quo est sciendam, quod avariciae gula vilior est omni alia gula, sive foeminarum, quia est insatiabilior' ('Avaritia', *Summa Praedicantium*, [A. xxvii, x]).

51. Gratian, quoted in Brundage, op. cit., p. 247.

52. See Mary D. Garrard's illuminating essay 'Artemisia and Susanna' in Broude and Garrard, op. cit., pp. 147–71.

53. 'Mulier pulchra templum est aedificatum super cloacam . . . Et sicut dicit Bernardus,' John Bromyard, 'Pulchritudo', op. cit., vol. II, cap. xiii, p. 280 (p. XIIII.ii).

54. Thomas Cantimpré (1201–70), in Book II of *Bonum Universale de Apibus*, ed. Colvenerius, Douai, 1627, p. 337.

55. Etienne de Bourbon, 'De Vano Ornatu', in *Anecdotes historiques, Légendes et apologues*, ed. A. Lecoy de la Marche, Paris, 1877, p. 240: 'pena laboris quem habent in adquirendo et excolendo, abluendo, pectinando, tingendo, ungendo, vermes et lendes et pediculos ibi sustenendo'. Women who wear make-up are like actors who don make-up to play and mislead men: 'Contra illasque, cum sint vetule, quasi ydola se pingunt et ornant, ut videantur esse larvate [masks], ad similitudinem illorum joculatorum qui ferunt facies depictas, que dicuntur artificia gallice [masques], cum quibus ludunt et homines deludunt.'

56. The illustration Pl. 21 appears in a fourteenth- to fifteenth-century manuscript in the Vatican Library,
MS Reg.Lat. 473, fol.IIIr.

57. *English Metrical Homilies from Mss of the Fourteenth Century*, ed. John Small, Edinburgh, 1862, p. 15.

58. Christine de Pisan, *Book of the City of Ladies*, trs. Earl Jeffrey Richards, London, 1983, pp. 28–9. Christine was born in Venice, the daughter of a municipal counsellor, who shortly after her birth was invited to become court astrologer to Charles V. At the age of fifteen, she married Estienne de Castel, by whom she had three children. Widowed at twenty-five, and left without financial support, she earned her living through writing, which she did very successfully. In the *Book of the City of Ladies* she also reiterated the steadfastness of the women at the crucifixion in contrast to the desertion by the apostles: 'God has never reproached the love of women as weakness, as some men contend, for He placed the spark of fervent love in the hearts to the blessed Magdalene and of other ladies, indeed His approval of this love is clearly to be seen' (p. 219).

59. 'The Wife of Bath's Prologue', *The Works of Geoffrey Chaucer*, ed. F. N. Robinson, London, 1974. 'For trusteth wel, it is an impossible/ That any clerk wol speke good of wyves,/ But if it be of hooly seintes lyves' (lines 688–90 and 669–76).

60. Christine de Pisan, op. cit., pp. 3–4 and 10. Lady Reason further tells Christine in reply to the male criticism of female weeping, taken from a Latin proverb, 'God made women to speak, weep and sew', that 'God placed these qualities in those women who have saved themselves by speaking, weeping and sewing . . . What special favours has God

bestowed on women because of their tears! He did not despise the tears of Mary Magdalene, but accepted them and forgave her sins, and through the merits of those tears she is in glory in heaven' (p. 27). Christine may in this instance have been alluding not only in general to earlier works which had treated of women, but in particular to the *Romance of the Rose*, by Guillaume de Lorris and Jean de Meung, which she had attacked for its immorality and its slandering of women.

61. Humbert de Romans, quoted in R. F. Bennett, *The Early Dominicans*, Cambridge, 1937, p. 123, and note 1.

62. Humbert de Romans, 'Ad Omnes Mulieres', *Sermo* XCIV in *Sermones ad diversos status*.

63. From a manuscript in the Cambridge University Library, cited in E. E. Power, 'The Position of Women', in C. G. Crump and E. F. Jacob, eds, *The Legacy of the Middle Ages*, Oxford, 1926, p. 402; this view, however, contrasted with that of the Dominican preacher Johannes Herolt, who stated categorically that more women than men went to hell (Coulton, *Five Centuries*, vol. I, p. 180).

64. *The Southern Passion, (1275–85), from Pepysian MS 2344 in Magdalene College, Cambridge*, ed. with an introd., notes and glossary by Beatrice Daw Brown, EETS, OS, no. 169, 1927, p. 70 and 72. (A pseudo-etymological derivation for the word 'feminus', showing women to be lacking in faith, 'fe-minus' (faith-minus), is to be found in Jacobus Sprenger, *Malleus Maleficarum*, 'dicitur enim *femina a fe* et *minus*, quia semper *minorem* habet et servat *fidem*' (for it is said

that 'femina' [is made] from fe [faith] and minus [lacking], because she always has and retains less faith). Quoted in Coulton, *Five Centuries*, vol. I, p. 180.

65. British Library, MS Roy. 18.B xxiii, f. 98, quoted in G. R. Owst, *Literature and Pulpit in Medieval England*, Cambridge, 1933, p. 120; *Southern Passion*, op. cit., p. 70.

66. *Old English Homilies of the Twelfth Century*, op. cit., p. 140.

67. Master Robert Rypon, MS Harl. 4894, f. 181, quoted in Owst, *Literature and Pulpit*, p. 385.

68. A third, given in a sermon on her feast-day by the Byzantine Nicephorus Callistus, tells of Satan's hearing Isaiah's prophecy that a virgin would conceive and bear a son. Fearing that the Incarnation might be effected in Mary Magdalen, Satan snatched away her virginity himself. Nicephorus' is the only such account known. 'In Sanctam Mariam Magdalenam', *PG* CXLVII, col. 548, quoted in Helen Meredith Garth, *Saint Mary Magdalene in Mediaeval Literature*, Johns Hopkins University Studies in History and Political Science, series LXVII, no. 3, 1950, p. 370.

69. Pseudo-Rabanus Maurus, probably a twelfth-century Cistercian, relates that Mary Magdalen's mother was the 'most noble Eucharia', of a royal Israelite family. Her father was Theophilus, a Syrian. 'De Vita Beatae Mariae Magdalenae et sororis ejus Sanctae Marthae', *PL* CXII, cols 1431–1508. This *vita* has been translated and annotated by David Mycoff in *The Life of Saint Mary Magdalene and of her Sister Saint Martha*, Cistercian Studies Series 108, Kalamazoo, 1989.

70. 'Mary Magdalene', in *The Digby*

Plays, ed. F. J. Furnivall, EETS, ES, no. 70, London, 1896, and in *The Late Medieval Religious Plays of Bodleian Mss Digby 133 and e Museo 160*, ed. Donald C. Baker, John L. Murphy and Louis B. Hall, Jr, EETS, ES, no. 283, London, 1982. The play, of *c*.1515–25, is of East Anglian origin, probably performed at King's Lynn, Norfolk, where the medieval parish church, to which Margery Kempe often went, was dedicated to St Mary Magdalen, St Margaret, 'and all the Virgins'. See also Sidney E. Berger's extremely useful *Medieval English Drama: An Annotated Bibliography of Recent Criticism*, New York and London, 1990. I am very grateful to Michèle Cloonan for making this material available to me.

71. Gospel of St John, 2:1–10.

72. *Prefatio Incerti Auctoris* to S. Aurelius Augustinus, *In Joannis Evangelium, PL* XXXV, col. 1380, referred to in *Der Saelden Hort, Alemannisches Gedicht vom Leben Jesu, Johannes des Täufers und der Magdalena*, ed. H. Adrian, Deutsche Texte des Mittelalters, vol. XXVI, Berlin, 1927, p. 101, note to line 5632.

73. Emile Mâle (*Religious Art in France in the Thirteenth Century*, trs. D. Nussey, London and New York, 1913, p. 221) suggests that the idea that Mary Magdalen and John the Evangelist were betrothed was known as early as Bede. See also H. Hansel, *Die Maria–Magdalena–Legende. Eine Quellen–Untersuchung*, Greifswald, 1937, pp. 96–9. Walfried Strabo, *PL* CXIV, col. 916.

74. Ælfric, the 'Grammarian' (*c*.955–*c*.1020), was a Benedictine who in 1005 became the first abbot of Eynsham. His greatest claim to fame was the provision of books of literary merit for the rural clergy in the vernacular. *The Homilies of Ælfric*, ed. and trs. Benjamin Thorpe, London, 1843, vol. I, pp. 58–9, homily for 27 December.

75. Honorius Augustodunensis, *Speculum Ecclesiae, PL* CLXXII, cols 834 and 979.

76. *Meditations on the Life of Christ. An Illustrated Manuscript of the Fourteenth Century* (Paris, Bibliothèque Nationale MS Ital. 115), trs. Isa Ragusa, ed. Ragusa and Rosalie B. Green, Princeton, 1961, p. 150. The *Meditations* have been attributed to Giovanni de Caulibus di San Gimignano, a Tuscan Franciscan of the second half of the thirteenth century.

77. John Myrc, 'Sermo de Nupcijs', in *Festial*, ed. Theodor Erbe, EETS, Part I, 1905, p. 292: 'Thus is weddyng holy in begynnyng. And also it is holy in lyving. In tokening therof Cryste and hys modur Mary and his disciplus weren callud to a wedding betwysse Iohn Euangeliste and Mary Mawdelyne; and so be hyr comyng he halowod weddyng, that is now usud as I have sayde before.'

78. Jacobus de Voragine, *Legenda Aurea*, ed. Dr T. Graesse, Dresden and Leipzig, 1846, vol. I, col. 416 (cap. XCVI, 'De Sancta Maria Magdalena').

79. *Life of St Mary Magdalen*, trs. Valentina Hawtrey, from the Italian of an unknown fourteenth-century Franciscan writer, London and New York, 1904, pp. 3 and 2. According to this author, Mary Magdalen was 'scorned and ridiculed' for being jilted, and 'may be somewhat excused in the eyes of worldly people' for her subsequent behaviour (p. 5). Some idea of the medieval imagination

at play can be gleaned from this author's apologetics: 'for the sake of greater impressiveness, I will tell the stories as they occurred or as they might have according to the devout belief of the imagination and the varying interpretation of the mind', ibid., p. 5.

80. *Der Saelden Hort*, op. cit., pp. 101 and 104: 'der brutgom gewesen ist/ Johannes selb ewangelist/ . . . swie daz sie nieman uber lut/ nemmet inder warheit,/ doch hat ain maister mir geseit/ dis fur ain wares mar/ das do du brut da war/ dannoch du sunde vrie/ Magdalene Marie, eins edeln, werden fursten kint'. The translation comes from Garth, op. cit., p. 368, note 17.

81. The marriage of Mary Magdalen in *Der Saelden Hort* is illustrated on f.26v of the Codex St Georgen 66 of *c*.1420, at Karlsruhe, Badischen Landesbibliothek, with twenty-three other illustrations from her *vita*. The Vienna manuscript, the Codex Vindobonensis 2841 of 1390 in the National Library, is the first extant example of illustrations of Mary Magdalen's *Weltleben*. An even earlier example of the scene appears on an enamel reliquary of the first half of the twelfth century (Frankfurt, Museum für Kunsthandwerk, illustrated in Otto von Falke, 'Die Sigmaringer Kunstgewerbe Museum II', in *Pantheon*, I, 1928, p. 117). See Marga Janssen's iconographical thesis, 'Maria Magdalena in der abendländischen Kunst. Ikonographie der Heiligen von den Anfängen bis ins 16. Jahrhundert', unpublished PhD. diss., Freiburg-am-Breisgau, 1961, whence the above references, pp. 217–23. The image of St John leaving his wife appears in MS 289, f. 56 (Admont, Stiftsbibliothek), and is illustrated in Otto Pächt, 'The Illustrations of St Anselm's Prayers and Meditations', *Journal of the Warburg and Courtauld Institutes*, vol XIX, 1956, pp. 68–83, pl. 17(f), where it is suggested that the theme of St John's desertion of his bride was influenced by the new current of spiritualism which was first manifested in the writings of Peter Damian (p. 78). The story of John leaving his bride is apocryphal, and goes back to the *Acts of John* (M. R. James, *Apocryphal New Testament*, Oxford, 1924, p. 269). The scene is also illustrated in Anselm's 'Prayer to St John the Evangelist' in *Orationes sive Meditationes*, *c*.1150, MS. Auct. D.2.6, f. 56v in the Bodleian Library, Oxford, which came from the priory of Benedictine nuns at Littlemore, Oxford. I am grateful to Dorothy Shepard for referring me to this article.

82. For the story of Mary Magdalen's reunion with John at Ephesus, see references in Chapters Four and Six. The early fifteenth-century play 'Fflagellacio' is in the *Towneley Plays*, EETS, ES, no. 71, 1897, ed. George England, introd. Alfred W. Pollard, pp. 252–3. John laments for Jesus, telling the Virgin that her son is not dead, and reminding her of his words about his death and resurrection. Mary Magdalen replies, 'Alas! this day for drede! Good John, neven this no more!/ Speke prevaly I the pray,/ ffor I am ferde, if we hir flay.' The two are portrayed together, for example, in the Neapolitan Roberto d'Oderisio's panel of *c*.1350, in New York, Metropolitan Museum of Art, Lehmann collection, 1975.1.102, and Rogier van der Weyden's

Braque altarpiece (Paris, Musée du Louvre).

83. *Life of St Mary Magdalen*, op. cit., p. 9.

84. Réau, vol. III, 2, p. 846, 'quae non virgo sed puella dici potest'.

85. The scene is on the south wall in the church of S. Maria Maddalena, Bolzano.

86. Master Robert Rypon, 'Et certe ut apparet ad ostendendum mulieribus membra sua ut sic ad luxuriam provocentur', sermon in MS Harl. 4894, f. 176b, quoted in Owst, *Literature and Pulpit*, p. 404.

87. MS Royal 18.B xxiii, ff. 132 b-3, quoted in Owst, *Literature and Pulpit*, p. 118.

88. John Bromyard, quoted in Owst, *Literature and Pulpit*, p. 397, and note 5.

89. Tertullian, *On the Dress of Women (De Cultu Feminarum), Disciplinary Works*, 3, in *Patrology*, vol. II, in Johannes Quasten, ed., *The Ante-Nicene Literature after Irenaeus*, Utrecht and Antwerp, 1953, p. 294. 'Since we are all the temple of God, modesty is the sacristan and priestess of the temple, who is to suffer nothing unclean or profane to be introduced into it, for fear that the God who inhabits it should be offended, and quite forsake the polluted abode.'

90. Eleanor Prosser, *Drama and Religion in the English Mystery Plays*, Stanford, 1961, p. 111.

91. Karl Young, *The Drama of the Medieval Church*, Oxford, 1933, vol. I, p. 520. Young (p. 534) suggests that the scene of Mary Magdalen buying cosmetics may have been suggested by the scenes between the Marys and the *unguentarius* in the Easter plays (see next chapter). (The scene which focuses on Mary Magdalen constitutes one-third of the entire play, and may originally have been

an independent work [p. 534, note 9].)

92. ibid., p. 522. The only reference to Diabolus in the play is his exit from the stage. August C. Mahr (*The Relationship of Passion Plays to St Ephrem the Syrian's Homily De Peccatrice quae peccato laborat*, Columbus, 1942) suggests the scene of Mary Magdalen going to Mercator derives from Ephrem's homily which was widely translated.

93. 'Mary Magdalene', *Digby Mysteries*, op. cit., Part. I, scene 7.

94. For Mary Magdalen's dancing, see also p. 251. Although Lucas van Leyden's engraving shows Mary Magdalen dancing, the scene does not in fact refer to her worldly life. See Chapter 7, n. 57. According to Etienne de Bourbon, dancing was the devil's instrument (*Anecdotes historiques*, op. cit., p. 397). Another sinful amusement was playing ball: this Mary Magdalen does in a German play (*Erlauer Spiel* IV; Marga Janssen, op. cit., p. 41). In the Church's view, Mary Magdalen stood accused and convicted. See also Cornelia Elizabeth Catharina Maria van den Wildenberg-de Kroon, *Das Weltleben und die Bekehrung der Maria Magdalena in deutschen religiösen Dramen und in der Bildenden Kunst des Mittelalters*, Amsterdam, 1979. Mary Magdalen's worldly life also appears in a window of the church of Notre-Dame at Sablé (Sarthe). My thanks to Jacques Lalubie for bringing this image to my notice and for sending me his unpublished article. See my article, 'Political cypher and pietistical pawn: Mary Magdalen and the Burgundian Question', forthcoming.

95. 'Mary Magdalene', *Digby*

Mysteries, op. cit., p. 43, II. 564–71.

96. Mary Loubris Jones, 'How the Seven Deadly Sins "Dewoyde from the woman" in the Digby Mary Magdalene', in *American Notes & Queries*, referred to in *The Year's Work in English Studies*, vol. LIX, London, 1978, p. 104. According to the stage instructions for scene xv (pp. 82–3), all seven devils were beaten on their buttocks on the stage.

97. *Passion of Arras*, quoted in Gustave Cohen, 'Le Personnage de Marie-Madeleine dans le drame religieux français du Moyen Age', *Convivium*, anno 24, 1956, p. 147.

98. Jean Michel, *Le Mystère de la Passion, 1486*, ed. Omer Jodogne, Gembloux, 1959, pp. 114–15.

99. ibid., p. 116.

100. ibid.

101. *Meditations*, op. cit., pl. 154, p. 170.

102. *The Golden Legend or Lives of the Saints as Englished by William Caxton*, London, 1900, vol. IV, p. 74.

103. J. Szövérffy, 'Peccatrix Quondam Femina. A Survey of the Mary Magdalen Hymns', *Traditio*, vol. XIX, 1963, pp. 79–146.

104. At Launceston, a local children's game says that a stone which lands on Mary Magdalen's back will bring good luck. See the Charles Causley poem, 'Mary, Mary Magdalene', in *Collected Poems 1951–1975*, London, 1975, p. 239: 'Mary, Mary Magdalene, lying on the wall/ I threw a pebble on your back./ Will it lie or fall?' I am grateful to the late John Kassman for telling me of this poem. There is also a sculpture of Luke's sinner of *c*.1130 at the church of St Swithun at Leonard Stanley, Wilts., originally the church of a small Augustinian priory. This is described and illustrated in James F. King, 'The Old Sarum Master: a Twelfth-Century Sculptor in South-West England', in *Wiltshire Archaeological and Natural History Magazine*, vol. LXXXIII, 1990, pp. 70–95, illus. p. 93. My thanks to Veronica Sekules for bringing this article to my attention.

105. As for example at Chartres (1205–10) and Bourges (1214–18). The Chartres windows are also where Mary Magdalen's *vita* is first depicted, showing her arrival at Marseille, preaching and her soul going up to heaven. See also Chapter Six, note 87. The Feast in the House of Simon is usually depicted first as the scene of the sinner's conversion. At Chartres, Bourges and Auxerre (1230), the association with Mary of Egypt is sustained, in the pairing of windows at Auxerre, scenes in the same chapel at Bourges and the close proximity of the two windows devoted to them at Chartres. See also Colette Deremble, 'Les premiers cycles d'images consacrés à Marie Madeleine', *MEFRM*, pp. 201–8.

106. Humbert de Romans, op. cit., *Sermo C*.

107. Jacques de Vitry, *Historia Occidentalis* 7, quoted in Brundage, op. cit., pp. 390–1.

108. Humbert de Romans, op. cit. Vern Bullough, 'Prostitution in the Middle Ages', *Studies in Medieval Culture*, vol. X, Western Michigan University, 1977, pp. 9–17, especially p. 12, suggests that the medieval compassion for the prostitute was derived from Mary Magdalen's importance in Christian thought. 'Her equation with prostitution is significant since next to Mary, mother of Jesus, she is the most significant

female figure in early Christianity
. . . Perhaps because of her
influence, Gospel writers were
careful to portray prostitutes as
poor exploited women, more to
be pitied than condemned.' This
view surely derives from the idea
of Luke's sinner and Mary
Magdalen being the same person,
a view not shared by the writers
of the gospels.

109. Jacques Rossiaud, *Medieval
Prostitution*, trs. Lydia G.
Cochrane, Oxford, 1988, p. 59.

110. Leah Lydia Otis, *Prostitution in
Medieval Society. The History of an
Urban Institution in Languedoc*,
Chicago and London, 1985, pp. 18
and 161, note 18.

111. P. Molmenti, *La Storia di Venezia
nella vita privata dalle origini alla
caduta della Repubblica*, Bergamo,
1927, vol. I, p. 478.

112. Otis, op. cit., pp. 80 and 200,
note 29.

113. [G. B. Lorenzi,] *Leggi e Memorie
venete sulla prostituzione fino alla
caduta della Republica*, Venice,
1870–2, p. 35. See Chapter Seven
for further discussion on
prostitution in Venice and its
relationship to Mary Magdalen.

114. Rossiaud, op. cit., p. 57.

115. Shulamith Shahar, *The Fourth
Estate*, London and New York,
1983, pp. 208 and 326, note 159,
where she refers to and refutes B.
Geremek's suggestion in *Les
Marginaux parisiens aux XIVe et
XVe siècles*, Paris, 1976, pp. 260–1.
For the prostitutes' guild in Paris,
see Brundage, op. cit., p. 465, and
note 242, which refers to Vern
Bullough, *The History of
Prostitution*, New York, 1964,
p. 112.

116. See Brundage, op. cit., p. 465 and
note 242 for prostitutes'
involvement in pageants in
fourteenth-century Perugia. I am

grateful to Evelyn Welch for
information concerning prostitutes
participating in civic activities
found in Milanese archives. For
the prostitutes' race in Beaucaire,
see Otis, op. cit., pp. 71 and 192,
note 86.

117. Hippolytus, in Brundage, op. cit.,
p. 73 and note 134.

118. St Augustine, *De Ordine* II, IV:12
(*PL* XXXII, col. 1000), quoted in
Brundage, op. cit., p. 106, and
note 141.

119. St Thomas Aquinas, *Summa
Theologica*, 2:2, Quest. 10, art. 11,
quoted in Otis, op. cit., p. 23, and
note 60.

120. Thomas of Chobham, *Summa
Confessorum*, 7.2.6.2., ed. F.
Broomfield, in *Analecta Mediaevalia
Namurcensia*, Louvain and Paris,
1968, vol. XXV, p. 348. In
Roman law, where she had been
required to register as a prostitute,
the stigma of her profession never
left her. Otis, op. cit., p. 12.

121. Thomas of Chobham, op. cit., p.
296. When a group of prostitutes
wished to pay for a window in
Notre-Dame, their offer was
rejected as it was thought that by
allowing this the Church would
be seen to condone their
profession (ibid., p. 349). The
knight of La Tour-Landry
considered that noblewomen with
incomes who took lovers were far
worse than prostitutes who had
become what they were through
poverty, deprivation, and the
'cunning' of pimps, because they
sinned out of mere lust (*Le Livre
du Chevalier de la Tour-Landry*, ed.
M. A. Montaiglon, Paris, 1854,
127, quoted in Shahar, op. cit., p.
207).

122. Thomas of Chobham, op. cit., p.
352.

123. Brundage, op. cit., pp. 120–1; see
also Bonnie S. Anderson and

Judith P. Zinsser, *A History of their Own. Women in Europe from Prehistory to the Present*, vol I, London, 1989, pp. 47–8 and 365–6.

124. For Innocent III's letter see *PL* CCXIV, col. 102, 29 April 1198 (quoted in Otis, op. cit., p. 193, note 96), also referred to in Brundage, op. cit., pp. 395–6, and note 368.

125. Baudry, *Life of Robert of Arbrissel, PL* CLXII, cols 1052–8, quoted in R. W. Southern, *Western Society and the Church in the Middle Ages*, Harmondsworth, 1970, p. 312. See also Jacqueline Smith, 'Robert of Arbrissel: *Procurator mulierum*', in *Medieval Women*, ed. Derek Baker, Oxford, 1978, pp. 175–84.

126. ibid., p. 180. I am grateful to Canon Nourser for the reference concerning Eleanor of Aquitaine.

127. See also Southern, op. cit., pp. 312–13.

128. See Saxer, *Culte*, p. 222, and Brundage, op. cit., p. 395.

129. Saxer, *Culte*, p. 223.

130. 'Magdalens', *NCE*, vol. IX, pp. 57–8.

131. The constitutions were given in 1497. According to the text, the king, Louis XII, allowed the 'filles repenties' to set themselves up in 'l'hostel qui fut appele de Bochaigne'. Among the conditions for admission: 'item que nulle ne sera receue en vostre dit monastere sinon qu'elle eust peche actuellement du peche de la chair. Et avant qu'elle soit receue sera par aucunes de vous a ce commises et deputees visitee . . . Et de faire vray et loyal rapport tant a scavoir si elles sont corrompues comme si elles ont aucunes maladies secretes.' *Catalogue de Très Beaux Livres Anciens*, Maurice Bridel SA, Lausanne, 1948, no. 16. I am grateful to Nicholas Pickwoad for finding this for me.

132. Saxer, *Culte*, pp. 224. Saxer has noted that the cult itself waned in England and France during this period. For the history of the Order of Penitents, see A. Simon, *L'Ordre des Pénitentes de Ste-Marie-Madeleine en Allemagne au XIII siècle*, Fribourg-en-Suisse, 1918. Most of the new Magdalenian sanctuaries in Languedoc during the fourteenth century (at Narbonne, Toulouse, Carcassone, Gaillac and Montpellier) owed their existence to the attempts to deal with the problem of prostitution and to the relief of prostitutes. Saxer, ibid., pp. 249–50.

133. 'Pinti' is a contraction of the words *penitenti* or *pentite* (penitents). See also Alison Luchs, *Cestello. A Cistercian Church of the Florentine Renaissance*, New York and London, p. 128, note 7. A fourteenth-century altar was dedicated to Mary Magdalen, and the altar of S. Jacopo contained relics of St Luke, Mary Magdalen and Stephen (p. 176, note 4). An altarpiece, now in the Louvre, of the *Madonna in Glory with Mary Magdalen and St Bernard* attributed to Francesco Botticini (1446–97), may have been in the high altar (ibid., p. 77).

134. The main panel of Botticelli's painting is in London, Courtauld Galleries; the predellas are in the John G. Johnson collection, Philadelphia, Museum of Art. Mary Magdalen was the patron saint of the late sixteenth-century Florentine confraternity, the Compagnia di S. Maria Maddalena sopra le Malmaritate, which set up a hospice for women of 'evil lives . . . many of whom would turn to repentance

if they had a place to which they could withdraw', and for those who having husbands, or for other reasons, were unable to become nuns; the house was accordingly called 'that of the Malmaritate', or of the 'unhappily married women'. Sherill Cohen, 'Convertite e Malmaritate: Donne "irregolari" e ordini religiosi nella Firenze rinascimentale', *Memoria. Rivista di storia delle donne*, vol. V, November, 1982, pp. 46–7.

135. Donald Weinstein and Rudolph M. Bell, *Saints and Society. The Two Worlds of Western Christendom, 1000–1700*, Chicago and London, 1982, p. 220. See also Michel Lauwers, '"Noli me tangere": Marie Madeleine, Marie d'Oignies, et les Pénitentes du XIIIe siècle', which discusses Mary Magdalen's importance to semi-religious women and the Beguines in *MEFRM*, pp. 209–68.

136. *Holy Anorexia* is the title of Rudolph M. Bell's book (Chicago, 1985). Weinstein and Bell, op. cit., have pointed to the fact that from the thirteenth to the mid-sixteenth century, most saints were Italian, describing the phenomenon as the 'era of the Italian saints, more specifically the northern Italian urban saint', with the Tuscan hilltowns 'tend[ing] to provide the setting for guilt-ridden conversions of adolescent girls', pp. 168 and 166.

137. As, for example, Caroline Walker Bynum, *Holy Feast and Holy Fast*, Berkeley, 1987, especially pp. 94 and 340, note 134.

138. See David Herlihy, 'Women in Medieval Society', in *The Social History of Italy and Western Europe, 700–1500*, Variorum Reprints, London, 1978, vol. IX, p. 8. The male monastery was subject to the abbess and attached to provide the

male prerogative, the sacraments and temporal administration.

139. Anderson and Zinsser, op. cit., p. 191, and note 25.

140. Thomas Aquinas, *Summa Theologiae*, in Kari Elisabeth Børresen, *Subordination and Equivalence. The Nature and Role of Women in Augustine and Thomas Aquinas*, trs. Charles H. Talbot, Washington, DC, 1981, pp. 236–43.

141. ibid., pp. 245–6.

142. Thomas Aquinas, 'Question 55, The Manifestation of the Resurrection', *Summa Theologiae*, ed. C. Thomas Moore OP, London, 1976, vol. LV, 3, p. 37; and in Børresen, op. cit. p. 246.

143. Anderson and Zinsser, op. cit., pp. 192 and 483, note 28.

144. Walter Hilton, *The Ladder of Perfection*, trs. and introd. Leo Sherley-Price, 1957, Book I, chap, 11, p. 12.

145. *The English Text of the Ancrene Riwle*, ed. A. Zetterstein, EETS, no. 274, 1976, pp. 182 and 183.

146. The church of St Mary Magdalen, East Ham, was built in about 1130.

147. *Victoria County History: Norfolk*, London, 1906, vol. II, p. 408. The hermit Joan is noted in a fourteenth-century manuscript register of Crabhouse Nunnery in the British Museum (MS 4731); Gertrude appears in a *Notice* of 1206, Rénier de Liège (Saxer, *Culte*, p. 219, and note 161).

148. This is suggested in Caroline Walker Bynum, *Jesus as Mother. Studies in the Spirituality of the High Middle Ages*, Berkeley and Los Angeles, 1982, p. 20.

149. Bell, op. cit., p. 54, and p. 200, note 1, who refers to the article by Ida Magli, 'Il problema antropologico-culturale del monachesimo femminile' in

Enciclopedia delle religioni, Florence, 1972, 3: 627–41. Also, Walker Bynum, *Jesus as Mother*, pp. 261–2.

150. See Walker Bynum, ibid., p. 26, and Weinstein and Bell, op. cit., p. 234. Women's mysticism was characterised more than that of men by self-inflicted suffering, more affective writing, containing erotic and nuptial themes, and manifested itself in levitations, visions, stigmata and trances. Walker Bynum, p. 83, suggests that these stereotypes existed more among women than men, possibly because women's lives were less varied, or because they were influenced by what they had heard of each other: Dorothy of Montau was influenced by Birgitta of Sweden, for example, and Margery Kempe was inspired by Angela of Foligno, Catherine of Siena, Birgitta of Sweden and Dorothy of Montau. Walker Bynum refers to Michael Goodich, 'Contours of Female Piety in Later Medieval Hagiography', *Church History*, 50 (1981), pp. 20–32, where it is suggested that religous women tended to be associated in groups, and to come from socially and geographically homogeneous backgrounds. We know of these women's lives from their *vitae*, their biographies either written by them, or dictated by them to their confessors, or written after their deaths in the process of canonisation. They are usually second hand, and so subject to the redactional labours of the biographer. Some of these lives, as in the cases of Elizabeth of Hungary and Catherine of Siena, were written for devotional and instructional purposes, to demonstrate how to follow the contemplative and moral life; and

in the case of Catherine, written by Raymond of Capua, the *libellus* was sponsored by the Dominicans to promulgate their teachings and further the cause of her canonisation. It is necessary when reading the lives of these holy women to take into account their purpose. Emphases on certain aspects of the holiness in question has to do with the order which commissioned the *vita*.

151. Raymundus de Vineis, *The Life of the Blessed Virgin, Sainct Catharine of Siena*, in *English Recusant Literature 1558–1640*, ed. D. M. Rogers, Ilkley, 1978, vol. CCCLXXIII, pp. 34–5.

152. ibid., p. 37.

153. *The Life of Christina of Markyate. A Twelfth Century Recluse*, ed. and trs. C. H. Talbot, Oxford, 1959. Christina was born in *c*.1096–8, and died between 1155 and 1166. Her reputation for holiness spread abroad: she was invited to become abbess of the communities at Marcigny and Fontevrault.

154. See next chapter, p. 220.

155. While she was being looked after by a 'certain cleric' (whose name Christina's biographer was under 'obligation not to divulge'), she became the object of his passion. He was not alone in such feelings: Christina too struggled 'with this wretched passion with long fastings, little food, nights without sleep, [and] harsh scourgings' (*Life*, p. 115); but one night, John the Evangelist, Benedict and Mary Magdalen appeared to the cleric in his sleep. 'Of these, Mary, for whom the priest had particular veneration, glared at him with piercing eyes, and reproached him harshly for his wicked persecution of the chosen spouse of the most high King. And at the same time, she threatened him that if he

troubled her any further, he would not escape the anger of the almighty God and eternal damnation.' Terrified by the vision, the chastened cleric went to Christina, in a 'changed mood', begged her pardon, and changed his life. Her biographer tells us that she too had to cool her passion, and went into the wilderness to pray, weep and lament (*Life*, p. 117).

156. An altarpiece in the Uffizi, no. 449.181, by a follower of Giotto, shows scenes from St Cecilia's life. Illustrated in Richard Fremantle, *Florentine Gothic Painters*, London, 1975, figs. 69–74, pp. 37–9. St Cecilia became the patron saint of music, and as such is shown holding a portable organ, in error. During her wedding, 'while the organ was playing' she 'sang in her heart' to Christ, praying that her maidenhood might be preserved. Confusion over the meaning of the words, implying that she sang to the accompaniment of the organ, led her to become the patroness of music.

157. *The Life of Christina of Markyate*, op. cit., p. 51.

158. Although of a slightly later period, Francesca Romana (1384–1440) was a noblewoman who whilst she was still married founded a society of pious women to help the poor; on her husband's death, she entered the community of the Benedictine Olivetan Oblates, and became its superior. After her death, scenes from her visions, related to her confessor, were painted in the monastery of the Tor de' Specchio in 1468, showing Mary Magdalen, Paul the Apostle and Benedict. See George Kaftal, *Iconography of the Saints in Central and Southern Italian Schools of Painting*, Florence,

1965, figs 505–8, 510, 513 and 526. See also Guy Boanas and Lyndal Roper, 'Feminine piety in fifteenth-century Rome: S. Francesca Romana', in *Disciplines of Faith. Studies in Religion, Politics and Patriarchy*, ed. J. Obelkevich, L. Roper, and R. Samuel, London and New York, 1987, pp. 177–93.

159. *The Life and Revelations of Saint Margaret of Cortona, written in Latin by her confessor, Fra Giunta Bevegnati*, trs. F. M'Donogh Mahony, London and Dublin, 1883, pp. 65–6.

160. *The Book of Margery Kempe*, trs. B. A. Windeatt, Harmondsworth, 1985, chap. 21, pp. 84–5.

161. ibid., chap. 52, p. 162. According to Walker Bynum, *Holy Feast, Holy Fast*, p. 415, note 22, men also took female saints as models, as in the case of John of Alverna, who was seen as another Mary Magdalen.

162. Quoted in Bell, *Holy Anorexia*, p. 99. The destruction of her beauty was a sacrifice which she wished to offer up to Christ (*Life and Revelations of St Margaret of Cortona*, p. 53).

163. ibid. This scene may have been depicted in an altarpiece of the second quarter of the fourteenth century, where Margaret, dressed as a young Franciscan tertiary wearing a chequered tunic, black cloak and white veil, is shown by Christ the throne surrounded by seraphs which she will receive in heaven. He holds by the wrist a female figure dressed in red and blue, with a veil and coronet, who, it has very plausibly been suggested to me by Joanna Cannon, may be Mary Magdalen. I am grateful to Joanna Cannon for sharing her thoughts on the imagery of this painting, which is in the Museo Diocesano,

Cortona. It is reproduced in George Kaftal, *Iconography of the Saints in Tuscan Painting*, Florence, 1952, fig. 670, p. 670.

164. Nesta de Robeck, *Among the Franciscan Tertiaries*, London, 1929, p. 69. At her canonisation, on 16 May 1728, Pope Benedict XIII referred to Margaret as the St Mary Magdalen of the Franciscan order. The choir sang 'Many sins have been forgiven her, for she loved much', the response to which was, 'I am my Beloved's and He has turned towards me. I have found him whom I love.' ibid., p. 69.

165. *The Life and Revelations of St Margaret of Cortona*, pp. 37 and 530. See also Clarissa W. Atkinson, *Mystic and Pilgrim: The Book and World of Margery Kempe*, Ithaca and London, 1983, p. 58.

166. *Vita Dorotheae Montoviensis Magistri Johannis Marienwerder*, ed. Hans Westpfahl, Graz, 1964, cap. xxx, 'De lacrimarum fervencium indigencia, utilitate et causa', 5.30a, p. 260. Born in 1347 of Dutch peasants, Dorothy began secret penances at the age of six. She was married to a rich armourer of Danzig to whom she bore nine children, all of whom except for one died young. Despite her husband's maltreatment, she achieved her vow of chastity. After his death in 1390, she went to Johannes Marienwerder and related her visions to him. In 1393 she became a recluse in the cathedral, rarely sleeping, taking daily communion, and barefooted, apparently not feeling the cold. She died in 1394. Her way of life was much influenced by that of Birgitta of Sweden whose relics had passed through Danzig in 1374.

167. *The Book of Margery Kempe*, introd., p. 9.

168. ibid., chap. 3, p. 46. Margery seems to have been knowledgeable about devotional literature such as Richard Rolle's *Form of Perfect Living*, Walter Hilton's *Ladder of Perfection*, and Julian of Norwich's *Revelations of Divine Love*. She in fact visited Julian. See Clarissa W. Atkinson, *Mystic and Pilgrim: The Book and the World of Margery Kempe*, Ithaca and London, 1983, especially pp. 58–65.

169. *The Book of Margery Kempe*, chap. 30, p. 111, and chap. 29, p. 109.

170. See Roy Porter, 'Margery Kempe and the meaning of madness', *History Today*, February 1988, p. 43. My thanks to Celia Jones for referring me to this article.

171. *The Book of Margery Kempe*, chap. 80, p. 234.

172. See Richard Kieckhefer, *Unquiet Souls. Fourteenth-Century Saints and their Religious Milieu*, Chicago and London, 1984, pp. 133–4; Raymundus de Vineis, *The Life of . . . Sainct Catharine of Siena*, Part II, chap. 18, pp. 187–8.

173. ibid., Part II, chap 13, p. 172.

174. The sacrament of the eucharist was recorded by St Paul in I Cor. 11: 23–5, and in the synoptic gospels. It was a regular part of Christian worship from a very early date as evinced from accounts in Acts. Belief in transubstantiation, i.e. the conversion of the bread and wine into the body and blood of Christ, was defined, *de fide*, at the Lateran Council in 1215. In 1280, Albert the Great advised against women receiving daily communion because of their levity, but the practice of frequent communion was revived in Flanders and Liège in the thirteenth century.

175. Mary Magdalen was often shown

taking communion, e.g. in the fresco by Cenno di Francesco di Ser Cenni (Florence, St Trinità), and in the cycles of her life at Assisi, Bolzano (Museo) and in Florence (Bargello).

176. Catharine of Siena, letter to Monna Franceschina in *Le lettere di S. Caterina da Siena*, foreword and notes by Niccolo Tommaseo, Florence, 1860, vol. I, pp. 264–6.

177. ibid., letter to Monna Agnesa, vol. II, p. 443. Mary Magdalen was associated with Catherine of Siena through the Dominicans' adoption of her as their unofficial patroness, and they are consequently often depicted together in Dominican images. In 1509 Fra Bartolommeo portrayed them as the exponents of divine contemplation, a constant theme of Girolamo Savonarola (1452–98), the Dominican prior and reformer whose denunciations of the Florentines and contemporary clergy led to his excommunication in 1497, and his hanging by the people as a heretic and schismatic. Fra Bartolommeo's painting of the two saints (1508, now in Lucca, Museo Nazionale di Villa Guinigi) has been interpreted as a visual tract of Savonarola's writings: the Magdalen gazing earthward as the contemplative life and Catherine of Siena curving heavenwards as the active life in the Platonic tripartite cyclical concept of giving, receiving and returning. Ronald M. Steinberg, 'Fra Bartolommeo, Savonarola and a Divine Image', *Mitteilungen der Kunstgeschichte im Florenz*, 18, 1974, pp. 319–28. I am grateful to Christ Fischer for bringing this article to my attention. See also Peter Humfrey, *The Venetian Altarpiece in the Renaissance*, London and New Haven, 1993, Appendix

69, for a different, and more likely, interpretation. The painting was done for the Dominican church of S. Pietro Martire, Murano, whose prior was the expert of his day on the life of Catherine of Siena; he died before the painting was finished, and it has remained in Lucca ever since. The two saints also share a chapel in Rome, in the church of S. Silvestro al Quirinale, decorated with frescoes by Polidoro da Caravaggio in *c*.1527.

CHAPTER VI

1. The inscription is quoted in full in E.-M. Faillon, *Monuments inédits sur l'apostolat de Ste Marie-Madeleine en Provence*, Paris, 1865, vol. I, col. 959.

2. 'D'une femme publique, le Christ a fait une apôtre', Pierre de Celle, 'De meretrice apostolam constituit', *PL* CCII, col. 839, quoted in Victor Saxer, *Le Culte de Marie Madeleine en Occident des origines à la fin du moyen âge*, Paris, 1959, p. 344.

3. ibid., p. 122. There was also a Jacobite monastery dedicated to the Magdalen in Jerusalem in the twelfth century, ibid, note 173.

4. John Myrc, *Festial*, ed. Theodor Erbe, EETS, ES, no. 96, 1905, p. 171, quoted in G. R. Owst, *Literature and Pulpit in Medieval England*, Cambridge, 1933, p. 146.

5. The *Deposition* is the centre panel of an altarpiece, the wings of which are lost. It was probably commissioned by the Great Archers' Guild for their chapel. See Lorne Campbell, *Rogier van der Weyden*, London, 1989, p. 6.

6. St Anselm of Canterbury, *Oratio* LXXIV, 'Ad Sanctam Mariam Magdalenam', *PL* CLVIII, cols 1010 and 1011. My thanks to

Nicholas Pickwood and Adele Airoldi for their translation. Anselm became prior and abbot at Bec in Normandy, and archbishop of Canterbury in 1093. He wrote prayers for monks, and also wrote for lay people, particularly highly born pious women, such as Countess Matilda of Tuscany. He sent the prayer to Mary Magdalen, together with five other prayers to saints and a meditation, at her request to Adelaide, who spent her life in seclusion, but did not become a nun. In 1104 he sent a complete collection of the *Orationes sive Meditationes* to the Countess Matilda, also at her request. The prayer to the Magdalen in this collection, now at Admont, Stiftsbibliothek (MS 289), is illustrated by a beautiful miniature of Luke's sinner anointing Christ's feet (f.86). The standing figure to the right, half out of the miniature's frame, is also the Magdalen, referring to the words, 'Her faith has saved her'. Otto Pächt, 'The Illustrations of St Anselm's Prayers and Meditations', *Journal of the Warburg and Courtauld Institutes*, vol. XIX, 1956, p. 79, where he also suggests that the iconography of this miniature influenced the scene of Luke's sinner in the St Albans' Psalter, probably done for Christina of Markyate. Another manuscript of the *Prayers and Meditations*, from the Benedictine nunnery at Littlemore in Oxfordshire, now in Oxford, Bodley, MS Auct.D.2.6, shows Mary Magdalen anointing Christ's head, and the *Noli me tangere*. I am grateful to Dorothy Shepard for referring me to this article.

7. Painted Crucifix, mid-thirteenth century, by an unknown Sienese painter. Florence, Accademia, inv.

1890, no. 3345. It came from the monastery of S. Spirito on the Costa di S. Giorgio, Florence. See also Evelyn Sandberg-Vavalà, *La Croce dipinta italiana*, vol. II, Verona, 1929, p. 785, fig. 489.

8. Jacobus de Voragine, *The Golden Legend or Lives of the Saints as Englished by William Caxton*, London, 1900, vol. IV, p. 75.

9. Honorius Augustodunensis, *PL* CLXXII, cols 980–1: 'Crist hire havede a-boute i-sent: sarmoni and to preche;/ To sunfole men he was ful rad: to wissi and to teche,/ and to sike men heo wa[s] ful glad: to beon heore soule leche;/ Mani on to cristinedom: heo broughte, and out of sunne,/ From lecherie und hore-dom: thoru schrift, to Ioye and alle wunne.' *Early South-English Legendary or Lives of the Saints*, ed. C. Horstmann (EETS, OS, no. 87, London, 1887, p. 466, lines 158–62), quoted in Helen M. Garth, *St Mary Magdalene in Mediaeval Literature*, Johns Hopkins University Studies in History and Political Science, Series LXVII, no. 3, 1950, p. 373.

10. Nicholas Love, *The Mirror of the Blessed Life of Jesu Christ*, London, 1926, chap. 33, p. 153. Love (d.1424) was prior of Mount Grace Charterhouse, Yorkshire, from 1410 to 1421. He presented the *Mirror*, the only extensive Middle English translation of the *Meditations on the Life of Christ*, to Archbishop Arundel in 1410 as a contribution towards the campaign against heresy. Intended for both religious and lay readers, it was the most popular book in fifteenth-century England.

11. ibid., p. 154.

12. Rogier van der Weyden's *Mary Magdalen* is a fragment only of a larger painting.

13. The fresco in Verona, S. Zeno, is of the fourteenth century.

14. The cycle at S. Angelo in Formis includes the Raising of Lazarus, the Crucifixion and Two Marys at the Tomb. The Feast in the House at Bethany may also be seen as the Feast in the House of the Pharisee or in the House of Simon the Leper. They are fully illustrated in Ottavio Morisani, *Gli Affreschi di S. Angelo in Formis*, Naples, 1962. See also Janine Wettstein, *Saint Angelo in Formis et La Peinture médiévale en Campanie*, Geneva, 1960.

15. *Meditations*, chap. 70, p. 304, and chap. 31, p. 190.

16. ibid., chap. 72, p. 308.

17. Jacopone da Todi, 'Donna del Paradiso', in *Oxford Book of Italian Verse. Thirteenth to Nineteenth Centuries*, ed. St John Lucas, Oxford, 1952, pp. 20–5.

18. Painted Crucifix by the Master of S. Francesco (active *c.*1260–*c.*1272), London, National Gallery. See exhibition catalogue, *Italian Painting before 1400*, David Bomford et al, London, 1989, pp. 54–5.

19. *Meditations*, chap. 75, p. 326.

20. Garth, op. cit., p. 373, refers to medieval commentators who mention Mary Magdalen's attendance at Christ's trial, but cites no references.

21. The earliest Italian painted cross of its kind, it was made in 1138. Two mourning women appear with the Virgin and John in the top half of the side panels. Below them are the Kiss of Judas, the Way to Calvary, Flagellation and Deposition, the Women at the Sepulchre and the Entombment. The cross is illustrated in Schiller, vol. II, p. 518, fig. 495. The Way to Calvary is illustrated on p. 422, fig. 287. Another interesting

depiction of the scene is that of Nardo di Cione, whose three women, with the Magdalen clearly defined by her hair, are prevented from approaching Christ by an oriental-looking soldier who bars their way. Fresco, Florence, Badia, dated *c.*1350 or earlier. Illustr. in *Frescoes from Florence*, exhibition catalogue, London, 1969, pp. 80–1.

22. *Meditations*, chap. 78, p. 335.

23. MS Harl. 2398, f.186, quoted in G. R. Owst, *Preaching in Medieval England*, Cambridge, 1926, p. 121.

24. *Lauda del Venerdi Santo* from Assisi and Gubbio. V. De Bartholomeis, *Laude Drammatiche e Rappresentazioni Sacri*, vol. I, Florence (repr. 1943), 1967, p. 325; also pp. 321–33, quoted in Nurith Kenaan-Kedar, 'Emotion, Beauty and Franciscan Piety: A New Reading of the Magdalen Chapel in the Lower Church of Assisi', in *Studi medievali*, 3, vol. XXVI, fasc. II, 1985, pp. 699–710. Mary Magdalen is used again as an inciter to grief in the Digby play, when the Virgin asks her to sing: 'A, A, Mawdleyn! Why devise ye nothinge,/ To this blessid body for to gyfe preysinge?/ Sum dolorose ditee Express now yee,/ In the dew honour of this ymage of pitee' (*The Digby Mysteries*, ed. F. J. Furnivall, London, 1882, p. 197, ll. 793–6). Another example of the Magdalen's emotive role is in the York pageant, 'Jesus appears to Mary Magdalene after the Resurrection', where she laments the loss of her master in the alliterative language of the period:

Allas, in this world was nevere no wight/ Walkand with so mekill woo,
. . . Mi wite is wast nowe in wede,/ I walowe, I walke, nowe woo is me,/ For laide now is that lufsome in

lede,/ The Jewes hym nayled untill a tree./ My doulfull herte is evere in drede,/ To grounde now gone is all my glee.

Quoted in Garth, op. cit., from *The York Plays*, ed. Lucy Toulmin Smith, Oxford, 1885, pp. 421–5. The guild of the 'wynedrawers' was responsible for producing this particular pageant.

25. Padua, Scrovegni chapel, painted between 1304 and 1306. It is on the left wall, first register. Masaccio's *Crucifixion* was painted in 1426, and forms part of the Pisa polyptych, which is dispersed in London, Berlin and Pisa. The *Crucifixion* is now in Naples, Museo di Capodimonte. She is depicted similarly in the scene of the *Lamentation* by a fourteenth-century Umbrian master at Perugia Galleria Nazionale dell'Umbria. See below, note 32.

26. Mathias Grünewald (c.1470–1528), Isenheim Altarpiece, 1515 (Colmar, Unterlinden Museum); in the predella below, Mary Magdalen accompanies the Virgin while St John the Evangelist shows the dead Christ in the Entombment scene.

27. Moshe Barasch, *Gestures of Despair in Medieval and Early and Renaissance Art*, New York, 1976, p. 35. In the fourteenth century the Virgin was allowed to faint as the *Meditations* tell us: 'On the opening of Christ's side . . . the Mother falls into the arms of the Magdalen', p. 341. The Madonna's fainting was first reported in the *Gospel of Nicodemus*, an apocryphal writing popular in the Middle Ages which greatly amplified the stories round the crucifixion (M. R. James, *The Apocryphal New Testament*, Oxford, 1924, p. 116).

28. Although the Virgin is described as 'tearful' (*Meditations*, chap. 83, p. 346), she also weeps 'incontrollable tears' (ibid., chap. 82, p. 242).

29. Barasch, op. cit., p. 36. Chrysostom angrily rejected all violent movements, women's wailing, cries of distress, breast beating, tearing of hair and bloodying of cheeks, rolling on the ground and dashing heads against the floor, ibid., p. 22.

30. *The Lamentatyon of Mary Magdaleyne*, ed. Bertha M. Skeat, Cambridge, 1897, pp. 143–7, is quoted in Garth, op. cit., p. 374. The Latin quote is from Psalm 22:14.

31. Benedetto Antelami, *Deposition*, Parma Cathedral. Illustrated in Schiller, vol. II, p. 547, fig. 555. For an account of the evolution of the scene of the Deposition, see Schiller, pp. 177ff. (Nicodemus does not appear in the synoptic gospels, but is recorded as being present, bringing spices to anoint the body in John 19:39 ff). Early examples of the scene showed Joseph and Nicodemus at the cross, and two of the holy women standing to the side as mourners.

32. Simone Martini's *Descent from the Cross* (Antwerp) is part of his Antwerp polyptych. This scene is illustrated in Schiller, vol. II, p. 550, fig. 560. In the *Way to Calvary* (Paris), she is a long-haired haloed figure in red, hovering over the group of disciples, and throwing up her hands in the same manner, as does the same figure in the *Entombment* (Berlin). This gesture of mourning was one of several, such as women tearing their hair and faces, beating their breasts, and men smiting their foreheads, found on antique sarcophagi of the types known as the Meleager or Hippolytus sarcophagi, and

which provided later artists with a vocabulary of emotional gestures. For a discussion of the depiction of emotion and its origins, see Barasch, op. cit.

33. *Gospel of Nicodemus*, in J. de Q. Donehoo, *The Apocryphal and Legendary Life of Christ*, New York, 1903, p. 370, who suggests it may have been written in Greek as early as the end of the second century. According to M. R. James, op. cit., p. 94, it cannot be earlier than the fourth century.

34. Uffizi 538E. The painting is now in the Galleria Borghese, Rome. Raphael's *Carrying of the Body of Christ*, dated 1507, was commissioned by Atalanta Baglioni to commemorate her sorrow for the death of her son, to hang in the church of S. Francesco in Perugia. Several autograph drawings for the painting exist. See Anna Forlani Tempesti, in *Complete Works of Raphael*, introd. Mario Salmi, Novara, 1969, pp. 346–51. Raphael seems also to have considered the idea of having the Virgin Mary in Mary Magdalen's place (BM 1963.12.16.1). Another study shows a detail of St John and Mary Magdalen, she seated, and her hands clasped in sorrow (BM 1895.9.15.636). There are other detailed studies in the British Museum. A further study of the Magdalen's figure, in pen and brown ink, is in the F. Lugt collection, Paris (F.177).

35. *Meditations*, chap. 82, p. 344.

36. Giotto, *Lamentation*, Padua, Scrovegni chapel, *c*.1305.

37. The Dijon *Pietà* is in the Louvre, Paris.

38. *Meditations*, chap. 84, p. 344. Further competition occurs later in the *Meditations* when it is related that while the Virgin and

her companions remained indoors with John after the crucifixion on the morning of the Sabbath, Peter and the other male disciples arrive, shamefaced and crying, to tell them about Peter's denial and their abandonment of Christ. 'Oh, how attentively the Magdalen listened, and how much more attentively the Lady!' (chap. 84, p. 349).

39. The painting by the Master of Delft is in Oxford, Christ Church Gallery.

40. Luca Signorelli's painting is in the Cappellina dei Corpi Santi in the cathedral at Orvieto.

41. Sandro Botticelli, *Lamentation*, Munich, Alte Pinakothek. It was painted for a chapel in S. Paolino, Florence. I believe the figure cradling Christ's head to be Mary Magdalen, as she is dressed in her traditional colour, red, although the figure at Christ's feet is shown in her customary pose. Both women have long hair. Ronald Lightbown (*Sandro Botticelli: Life and Work*, London, 1989, p. 207), however, sees the Magdalen as the figure behind the group holding three nails (not shown), as she sometimes appears with nails in her hand.

42. Guido Mazzoni (*c*.1450–1516). Mazzoni's group was commissioned by the confraternity of St John of the Good Death which originally installed it in their hospital in the town. It is now in the church of S. Giovanni, in the confraternity's chapel. The *compianto* was a genre which became particularly Emilian in the late fifteenth century. It derived from Italian depositions of the thirteenth century and Franco-Flemish and German entombments, and the type had come through Piedmont into

Lombardy and the Veneto, and into Emilia, 'that part of Italy in which people have a more intense reaction in a dramatic situation' (quoted in Timothy C. Verdon, 'The Art of Guido Mazzoni', Ph.D. dissertation, Yale University, 1975, xerox, University Microfilms, Ann Arbor, p. 20). See also Norberto Gramaccini, 'Guido Mazzonis Beweinungsgruppen' in *Städel Jahrbuch*, Sonderdruck, Neue Folge Band 9, 1983, pp. 7–40, which traces the development of Mazzoni's figure groups from the earlier *Vesperbild*, linking it with contemporary developments of *laude* performances, and setting them in the context of popular piety and courtly patronage. My thanks to Professor Thomas Puttfarken for making this article available to me. Mazzoni executed other mourning groups at Ferrara, S. Gesù , and Naples, S. Anna dei Lombardi. Fragments from another group executed for a Venetian monastery of S. Antonio Abbate or S. Antonio Castello (Verdon, op. cit., p. 65) are in the Museo Civico in Padua, where the Magdalen appears even more violently grief-stricken than at Modena. Mary Magdalen appears in similar groups in France (called *mises-au-tombeau*) as a beautifully dressed young woman with long plaits (e.g. Carennac, St Pierre [fifteenth century] and Rodez, cathedral [sixteenth century]), and in a brilliantly polychromed maiolica group from Faenza of 1487 in the Metropolitan Museum of Art, New York, Rogers Fund 04.26. A *mise-au-tombeau* group from the château de Biron, Périgord, *c.*1515, is in the Metropolitan Museum (16.31.2). See William H. Forsyth, *The Entombment of Christ. French*

sculptures of the fifteenth and sixteenth centuries, Cambridge (Mass.), 1970.

43. Florence, Biblioteca Laurenziana, Ashburnham 368 (300), p. 22v, and Ashburnham 369 (301), p. 34. Quoted in Verdon, op. cit., pp. 52 and 185, note 13.

44. Niccolò dell'Arca's group was originally in the church of S. Maria della Vita, Bologna, and is now, after restoration, in the Pinacoteca Nazionale. It has been dated 1462–3 by James H. Beck, in 'Niccolò dell'Arca: A Re-examination', *Art Bulletin*, vol. XLVII, 3, 1965, p. 337. The head of Niccolò's Magdalen is related to a fresco fragment showing her head (also in Bologna, Pinacoteca) by Ercole de' Roberti, which came from the Garganelli chapel in the church of S. Pietro.

45. Susan K. Rankin, 'The Mary Magdalene Scene in the "Visitatio sepulchri" Ceremonies', *Early Music History*, vol. I, 1981, pp. 227–55. I am grateful to Preman Sotomayor for referring me to this article, and to Iain Fenlon for sending it to me through the auspices of Gillian Malpass.

46. The scene of the women at the tomb often appears on Easter Sepulchres, found in eastern England, and sculpted during the fourteenth and fifteenth centuries. The *Noli me tangere* also appears as a central scene. Most of these were sadly defaced in Cromwellian times. They sometimes flank a central aumbry, or small cupboard in which the chalice was placed, with the resurrected Christ above, and sleeping soldiers below, as at Heckington in Lincolnshire. See Veronica Sekules, 'The Tomb of Christ at Lincoln and the Development of the Sacrament

Shrine: Easter Sepulchres Reconsidered', *Medieval Art and Architecture at Lincoln*, British Archaeological Association, 1986, pp. 118–31, who suggests that rather than 'Easter Sepulchres', which were usually of a temporary nature, to be used during the Easter ceremonies, these structures had a permanent function as a place of safekeeping for the host.

47. An extension of the *Quem quaeritis* trope, the *Victimae paschali* still forms part of the mass for Easter. Wipo of Burgundy was priest and chaplain to the Holy Roman emperors Conrad II and Henry III. See Karl Young, *The Drama of the Medieval Church*, Oxford, 1935, vol. I, pp. 273ff. The dalmatic is the wide-sleeved vestment marked with two stripes worn by deacons and bishops in the western Church, and the amice a hood or hooded cape worn by the clergy.

48. ibid., p. 241.

49. ibid., p. 415.

50. '. . . procedant tres sorores a Domina Abbatissa preelecte, et nigris vestibus in capella Beate Marie Magdalene exute, nitidissimis superpellicijs induantur, niueis velis a Domina Abbatissa capitibus earum superpositis. Sic igitur preparate et in manibus ampullas tenentes argenteas dicant *Confiteor* ad abatissam; et ab ea absolute, in loco statuto cum candelabris consistant. Tunc illa que speciem pretendit Marie Magdalene canat hunc versum: *Quondam Dei*, etc.' (Oxford, University College, MS 169. Ordin. Berkingense saec. xv, pp. 121–4). Quoted in Young, op. cit., p. 381.

51. ibid., pp. 438–50.

52. For the scene of the three Marys

and Mercator, see Emile Mâle, *L'Art religieux du XIIe siècle en France*, Paris, 1922, pp. 133ff, and figs 114 and 113. It has been suggested that the scene may have been included as a reference to the pharmaceutical interests of the Knights Hospitallers, for whom St Gilles was an important centre. The town was a significant pilgrimage centre at the junction of the main routes for Santiago, Rome and Jerusalem. See Carra Ferguson O'Meara, *The Iconography of the Façade of St Gilles-du-Gard*, New York and London, 1977, p. 140. She also quotes Jonathan Riley-Smith, who suggests that the Order of St Mary Magdalen was founded as a sister organisation to that of St John, to care for female pilgrims (p. 141).

53. Three Marys and Mercator, capital, late twelfth century, Modena, Museo Civico Medievale e Moderno. I am grateful to Dottoressa Enrica Pagella for allowing me to see and photograph the capital whilst in storage. It came originally from the church of S. Vitale di Carpineti.

54. The benedictional was produced for St Æthelwold, bishop of Winchester between 963 and 984. It is now in the British Library, Add. MS 49598. The illumination (f.51v) is illustrated as the title-page in G. F. Warner, *The Benedictional of St Æthelwold*, Oxford, 1910.

55. Tours MS 237, quoted in Mâle, op. cit., p. 136.

56. Mary Magdalen fainting at the Tomb, capital, Modena, Museo Civico Medievale e Moderno.

57. Paris, Bibliothèque Nationale, MS gr.74, f.209r. The other scenes on the same folio show the meeting

with Peter and John, and the latter looking at the grave-clothes.

58. The miniature, painted by Jean Bourdichon, is illustrated in *Les Heures d'Anne de Bretagne*, text by Louis Mâle, Paris, 1946, pl. xxvi. It is MS lat.9747 in the Bibliothèque Nationale, Paris. Anne was queen of France twice, from 1491 to 1498, and from 1499 to 1514. In another prayer book made for her (New York, Pierpont Morgan Library, MS 50, f.18v), Mary Magdalen as Luke's sinner is almost entirely beneath the table in the Pharisee's house.

59. St Bonaventure, *Lignum Vitae De Mysterio Glorificationes*, VIII, 80b, quoted in E. Battisti, *Cimabue*, Philadelphia, 1967, p. xi. Mary Magdalen's visit to the sepulchre is compared to a passage in Seneca: 'In Seneca we find the following lines spoken by Andromache:

But I, even though woman,
Will resist
With my unarmed hands.

I will rush among you,
I will fall to the tomb
That I have so strongly defended.'

My thanks to Paul Hills for this reference.

60. Laon, east window. In the previous scene, she peers into the tomb, her hands raised in shock and sorrow.

61. Rankin, op. cit., p. 255.

62. Autun, St Lazare, capital, north side of aisle, third pillar. On the right of the capital the three Marys go to embalm Christ's body. See Denis Grivot and George Zarnecki, *Ghislebertus: Sculpteur d'Autun*, Paris, 1960, p. 64. One of the earliest known depictions of the *Noli me tangere*

appears in the sacramentary of Drogo, Bibliothèque Nationale, MS lat. 9426, f.63v, of *c*.830–40. The scene was also depicted on liturgical vestments, book-covers, in ivory, enamel and leather, and such objects as an Ottonian ivory reliquary of *c*.1000 (British Museum, M & LA 55, 10–31, 1), becoming increasingly popular in the eleventh century. It appears in a fresco of the second half of the eleventh century at Belisirama, in the church of Bahatin Samanligi in the north-east nave. It was also painted on to a late eleventh-century 'Exultet' roll, a lengthy piece of Latin prose chanted by a deacon on Easter Eve, at the blessing of the candle which was lit to symbolise the resurrection. While the deacon read, the image became visible to his audience as the roll gradually slipped over the lectern. An example from Monte Cassino is in the British Museum (Add. MS 30337). The foregoing is by no means an exhaustive list, but is intended to give some idea of the widespread use of the image. See Moshe Barasch's discussion of the iconographical evolution of the *Noli me tangere*, pp. 169–82, in *Giotto and the Language of Gesture*, Cambridge, 1987.

63. *Meditations*, chap. 88, p. 362.

64. *Mirror of the Blessed Life of Jesu Christ*, chap. 52, p. 265; chap. 57, p. 372.

65. Odo of Cluny, quoted in Joan Evans, *Monastic Life at Cluny 910–1157*, Oxford, 1931, pp. 103–4. My thanks to Adele Airoldi for her translation.

66. See Erich Neumann, *The Great Mother. An Analysis of the Archetype*, trs. Ralph Manheim, New York, 1955.

67. Pseudo Rabanus Maurus, *De vita beatae Mariae Magdalenae et sororis*

ejus Sanctae Marthae, cap. XVII, *PL* CXII, col. 1457, where she is described as 'pigmentaria', or perfume-maker.

68. Ludolphus Carthusiensis, *Vita di Giesu Christo*, Venice, 1585, 'La Penitentia di Maria Maddalena', p. 167v.

69. The painting of Mary Magdalen is inscribed with the words from John 12:3: 'Then took Mary a pound of ointment of spikenard, very costly, and anointed the feet of Jesus.' The triptych was probably commissioned by or adapted as a memorial to Jehan Braque of Tournai, who died in 1452.

70. As, for example, in Quentin Metsys' *Mary Magdalen* (Antwerp, Koninklijk Museum voor Schone Kunsten).

71. Quoted in C. Chabaneau, *Ste Marie Madeleine dans la littérature provençale*, Paris, 1887, p. 134, and note 2.

72. See Schiller, vol. I, p. 167. I am grateful to Peter Humfrey for pointing out the connection between Mary Magdalen and the Wise and Foolish Virgins to me.

73. Philippe de Grève, 'De sancta Maria Magdalena: Ad laudes', in *Analecta Hymnica*, Medii Aevi, ed. Clemens Blume and Guido M. Dreves, Leipzig, 1907, 534 (365).

74. Assisi, S. Francesco, lower church, Magdalen chapel. (The scene is close to Giotto's own depiction in the Scrovegni chapel in Padua.) The frescoes, painted probably after 1313, are mostly by the school of Giotto, although it is likely that Giotto himself had a hand in the work. The chapel is now generally agreed to have been built and decorated for Teobaldo Pontano, bishop of Assisi from 1314 to 1329, who, dressed as a friar, is depicted kneeling at the feet of a red-clad statuesque Magdalen, and as a bishop, kneeling before St Rufinus, first bishop and patron saint at Assisi. See Lorraine Schwartz, 'Patronage and Franciscan Iconography in the Magdalen Chapel at Assisi', *Burlington Magazine*, vol. CXXXIII, January 1991, 1054, pp. 32–6, and refs. See also Nurith Kenaan-Kedar, op. cit., pp. 699–710, who sees the cycle as embodying the Franciscan virtues of obedience, chastity, poverty, humility, charity and hope.

75. The convent of Mary Magdalen at Caldine, near Florence, was originally a *spedaletto*, or hospice, belonging to the Cresci family, and rebuilt in *c*.1460 'for the love of God, in honour of St Mary Magdalen, and on account of her sins' ('in isconto di li peccati sua').

76. Otto Pächt, 'The Full-Page Miniatures', in *The St Albans Psalter (Albani Psalter)*, Otto Pächt, C. R. Dodwell, F. Wormald, London. 1960, p. 62. The Albani Psalter is now at Hildesheim; Wormald suggests that the manuscript was completed before 1123 (p. 5). The *apostola apostolorum* scene first appeared in the eleventh century. It was carved on twelfth-century capitals at Geneva, St Pierre, and Pamplona, cathedral cloister. In Florence, Biblioteca Laurenziana, MS Plut. VI, 23, from Constantinople, the Magdalen alone announces the resurrection; and in the twelfth-century manuscript in Paris, Bibliothèque Nationale, MS gr. 74, two Marys announce to a jolly little frieze of eleven male figures. The scene also appears in stained-glass and fresco cycles from the twelfth to the fourteenth centuries. Its infrequency as an image probably

stemmed in part from the incongruity of women preaching in a church which proscribed evangelical roles for women (except within the confines of female nunneries or priories), and the even greater incongruity, in a patriarchally organised society, of a woman preaching to men. This anomaly was noted in the preface to Angela da Foligno's *Book of Visions and Instructions*, where her confessor wrote to his brethren: 'Bear in mind, my dearly beloved, that the apostles, who first preached the life of Christ, learnt from a woman that He had risen from the dead; and so too, as most dear sons of our holy mother Angela, learn along with me the rule . . . Now this is contrary to the order of God's providence, and for the shaming of carnal man, to make a woman a doctor . . . , to whose teaching . . . there is nothing like in all the earth for the shame of men who were doctors of law but transgressors of what it commanded, the gift of prophecy had been translated unto the weaker sex of woman.' Angela (1249–1309) dictated her *Book* to the Franciscan Brother Arnold in 1297. *The Book of Visions and Instructions of Blessed Angela of Foligno*, ed. and trs. A. P. J. Cruickshank, London and New York, 1871, p. 3. See now Kristine E. Haney, 'The Saint Alban's Psalter and the New Spiritual Ideals of the Twelfth Century', *Viator*, 28, 1997, pp. 145–73, which puts the Albani Psalter into its context.

77. Henry's wife Matilda was the daughter of Henry II of England. The manuscript was illuminated by the monk Herimann of Helmarshausen Abbey. It was bought for the German government by a banking consortium at Sotheby's in London, in 1983, for £8,140,000, over ten times more than had been paid for any other illuminated manuscript, and then the most expensive work of art sold at auction. See Christopher de Hamel, *A History of Illuminated Manuscripts*, Oxford, 1986, p. 75. It is now in the Herzog August Bibliothek, Wolfenbüttel, Germany. It is illustrated in Schiller, vol. III, p. 429. The illustration of the Feast in the House of the Pharisee (Plate 1) comes from this manuscript.

78. Zwettl, Stiftsbibliothek, MS 204, f.128v. I am grateful to Dr Jörg Oberhaidacher of the Institut für Kunstgeschichte der Universität Wien for supplying me with photographs. See Paul Buberl, *Die Kunstdenkmäler des Zisterzienser Klosters Zwettl*, Baden-bei-Wien, 1940, pp. 203–6.

79. The Queen Mary Psalter is in the British Library (Roy. 2 BVII); the scene of Mary Magdalen announcing the resurrection is on f.301v; the late twelfth-century Ingeborg Psalter is at Chantilly, Condé 1695; the image is on f.30v. See Florens Deuchler, *Der Ingeborgpsalter*, Berlin, 1967, pl. 26.

80. The over life-size figures are in the so-called 'Paradies' of Münster Cathedral. I am most grateful to Professor Dr René Baumgartner for sending me a photograph of the sculpture.

81. Nigel Morgan, *Early Gothic Manuscripts [II] 1250–1285. A Survey of Manuscripts Illuminated in the British Isles*, London, 1988, p. 103. The Lambeth Apocalypse (Lambeth Palace Library, MS 209) was owned by Eleanor de Quincy, countess of Winchester, before 1267.

82. The miniature appears at the beginning of the service for Easter Day in vol. I, f.3v. The manuscript, which was sold at the Henry Yates Thompson sale (Sotheby, Wilkinson & Hodge, 22 June, 1921, lot no. 67), is dated by its scribe 1290, with the injunction that future possessors should take good care of it – advice which was not heeded by its later owner, John Ruskin, who ripped it apart for distribution to friends and schools. The 'Domicella' who gave the volumes to the convent was Marie de Bornaing, wife of Gérard de Viane.

83. Clarissa W. Atkinson, *Mystic and Pilgrim: The Book and the World of Margery Kempe*, Ithaca and London, 1983, p. 150.

84. Peter Abelard (1079–1142), in an Easter sermon: 'The saint merits to be the first to be consoled by the Saviour's resurrection, as his death had been a cause of sorrow and anguish to her. She is also called the apostle to the apostles, that is ambassadress of the ambassadors, as the Lord sent her to the apostles to announce the joy of the resurrection.' 'Sermo XIII in die Paschae', *PL* CLXXVIII, col. 486, quoted in Saxer, *Culte*, p. 344.

85. *Speculum humanae vitae*, New York, Pierpont Morgan Library, MS M. 766, f.37v; New York, Metropolitan Museum, Acc.22.24. I, f.7, where, in an English psalter of *c*.1270, the Last Supper is conflated with the episode in Luke 7:38. This manuscript is catalogued as no. 152(a) in Morgan, op. cit., p. 140. My thanks to Professor Morgan for giving me this reference. A similar conflation is made in the Palatine Passion (*La Passion du Palatinus,*

Mystère du XIVe siècle, ed. Grace Frank, Paris, 1972). I am grateful to Véronique Plesch for this reference.

86. Honorius Augustodunensis (*PL* CLXXII, col. 981) records that after the Magdalen had announced the resurrection to the apostles she was also present with the disciples when the Lord ascended. This would have referred to the episode described in the first chapter of the Acts of the Apostles, v.13, where, after the resurrection, the disciples gathered together in an upper room, and in v.14, 'all continued with one accord in prayer and supplication, with the women, and Mary the mother of Jesus, and with his brethren'. In Chapter 2 they were 'filled by the Holy Ghost, and began to speak with other tongues, as the Spirit gave them utterance' (v.4). The Virgin Mary is often included in the scenes of both the Ascension and Pentecost, but the Magdalen's presence is not marked. The *Meditations* put it this way: 'For it is possible that the most divine Lord often visited His Mother and the disciples and the Magdalen, the beloved disciple, comforting and cheering . . . He bids the Mother farewell and the disciples and the Magdalen and all the others prostrate themselves and weep' (p. 373). Further, it is related, 'they all gazed after Him into heaven as far as they could' (p. 379). The Hunterian Psalter is in the Glasgow University Library, MS Hunter 229, f.14.

87. See Marga Janssen, 'Maria Magdalena', in *Lexikon der christlichen Ikonographie*, eds E. Kirschbaum SJ and W. Braunfels, Rome, etc., 1974, vol. 7, cols 534–6, for an extensive list of where Mary Magdalen's

missionary life and the legend of the prince of Marseille are depicted. Virginia Chieffo Raguin (*Stained Glass in Thirteenth-Century Burgundy*, Princeton, 1982, p. 89) suggests that the depiction of the entire legend at Semur-en-Auxois might relate to Burgundy's claims to possess Mary Magdalen's relics (p. 156). She discusses the iconography of these windows (pp. 155–7, and figs 136–40), as well as those at Auxerre (pp. 154–5), and illustrates the Mary Magdalen window at Bourges (fig. 43).

88. The edition of the *Golden Legend* quoted is Caxton's, op. cit. For the significance of the rudderless ship in medieval literature, see V. A. Kolve, *Chaucer and the Imagery of Narrative: The First Five Canterbury Tales*, London, 1984, pp. 325ff. I am grateful to Ad Putter for this reference. In the 'General Prologue' to the *Canterbury Tales*, the Shipman's 'barge', or ship, 'ycleped was the Maudelayne', or was called 'The Magdalen' (*The Works of Geoffrey Chaucer*, ed. F. N. Robinson, London, 1974, line 410).

89. In 1499 a doll described as a 'saint Mary Magdalen dressed in red satin and pearls' was included in the trousseau of the wife of the Florentine Giovanni Buongirolamo, possibly as a magical agent of fertility or, more probably, as a devotional aid. See Christiane Klapisch-Zuber, *Women, Family, and Ritual in Renaissance Italy*, trs. Lydia Cochrane, Chicago and London, 1985, pp. 312 and 318. My thanks to Anthony Burton for bringing this to my attention.

90. Kolve, op. cit., p. 319.

91. *A Brief Account of the Rulers of Burgundy* (British Museum, MS

YT 32). It was written and illuminated in Ghent or Bruges, probably between 1482 and 1486; Philip's mother, Mary of Burgundy, died in 1482.

92. Maestro della Maddalena: panel with eight scenes from the life of Mary Magdalen. Florence, Galleria dell'Accademia. It shows the first depiction of her receiving communion from St Maximinus. It was executed in *c*.1280 for the Servites of SS. Annunziata, Florence.

93. Jacobus de Voragine, *Legenda Aurea vulgo historia lombardica dicta*, ed. Dr T. Graesse, Dresden and Leipzig, pp. 407–8.

CHAPTER VII

1. Richard Crashaw, 'Sainte Mary Magdalene or The Weeper', in *The Poems, English, Latin and Greek*, ed. L. C. Martin, Oxford, 1957, p. 307. The couplet serves as an introduction to the poem.

2. See R. Ward Bissell, *Orazio Gentileschi and the Poetic Tradition in Caravaggesque Painting*, University Park and London, 1981, cat. no. 11, p. 143.

3. Horace, *nuda Veritas* (*Carmina* 1,24,7), quoted in Erwin Panofsky, *Studies in Iconology. Humanistic Themes in the Art of the Renaissance*, New York, 1972, p. 155.

4. Petrus Berchorius, *Dictionarii seu Repertorii moralis. Ordinis divi Benedicti. Quae dictiones fere omnes sacrae theologiae*, Venice, 1639, pars prima, p. 588.

5. Marga Janssen, 'Maria Magdalena in der abendländischen Kunst. Ikonographie der Heiligen von den Anfängen bis ins 16. Jahrhundert', unpublished Ph.D. dissertation, Freiburg-am-Breisgau, 1961, p. 125. See also

the note 'Antichi dipinti della cappella di S. Prospero fuor di Perugia' in *L'Arte*, vol. IX, 1906, pp. 306–7.

6. Mary of Egypt's Last Communion was frescoed before 964 in the north apse of the church of Tokali kilise (Göreme 7) (Christopher Walter, *Art and Ritual of the Byzantine Church*, London, 1982, p. 230). See also Nicole and Michel Thierry, *Nouvelles églises rupestres de Cappadoce*, Paris, 1963, p. xvi.

7. For the Arte de' Drappieri, see Chapter Five, note 11. For the images at S. Zeno, Verona, see Evelyn Sandberg-Vavalà, *La Pittura veronese del Trecento e del primo Quattrocento*, Verona, 1926, particularly pp. 76, 77 and 81. Further examples include the late-thirteenth century fresco of Giovanni Bartolomeo Cristiani's *Praying Magdalen*, with a nun donor at her feet, in S. Domenico, Pistoia; the fourteenth-century frescoes in the so-called Magdalen chapel, the Cappella del Podestà, in the Palazzo del Bargello, Florence; a fresco fragment by Lorenzo di Bicci at Scarperia, Propositura; and a recently discovered fresco in S. Agostino, San Gimignano. She also appears hairclad in Naples, S. Domenico, and in a late thirteenth-century miniature from a north Spanish manuscript of the lives of saints (Sotheby's, *Western Manuscripts and Miniatures*, London, 8 June 1991). I am grateful to Evelyn Welch for bringing this last image to my attention.

8. See Timothy Husband, *The Wild Man, Medieval Myth and Symbolism*, New York, 1980, esp. pp. 97 and 100–1. See also Cesare Poppi, 'Il tipo simbolico "Uomo

selvaggio": motivi, funzioni e ideologia', *Mondo Ladino*, vol. X, 1986, pp. 95–118; and Roberto Togni, 'L'uomo selvatico nelle immagini artistiche e letterarie. Europa e arco alpino (secoli XII–XX)', *Annali di S. Michele*, Museo degli Usi e Costumi della Gente Trentina, 1989. My thanks to Cesare Poppi for drawing my attention to the link with Mary Magdalen.

9. See Edgar Wind, 'The Saint as Monster', *Journal of the Warburg and Courtauld Institutes*, vol. I, 1937–8, p. 183. My thanks to Elizabeth McGrath for referring me to this article.

10. Tilman Riemenschneider's *Ecstasy* formed part of a triptych formerly in the choir of the parish church of Münnerstadt. She also appears, unusually in an Italian painting, with golden fur similar to the 'wild man' iconography, entirely naked and pious, as well as anatomically rather odd, holding a cross in one hand and her jar in the other, in a panel painted after 1475, possibly from a triptych, by the Sienese painter and illuminator Giovanni di Paolo (*c.*1400–82). Since she is paired with St Lucy (both panels are in a private collection) and the figures they probably accompanied (in New York, Metropolitan Museum) were the other virgins, Catherine, Barbara, Agatha and Margaret, this can be nothing other than a bona fide representation of nakedness as *nuda naturalis*. John Pope-Hennessy, 'Giovanni di Paolo', *Metropolitan Museum of Art Bulletin*, vol. XLVI, no. 2, Fall 1988, fig. 52, p. 38. I am extremely grateful to Evelyn Welch for making this article available to me.

11. The figure's red-gold hair has only recently reappeared during

conservation work. Her unrestored appearance, with black hair, has been reproduced, in eastern guise, as a mass-produced statuette made in Hong Kong, seen in an oriental art shop in 59th Street in New York in 1991. See also Chapter 10, p. 381.

12. Charles Avery, *Florentine Renaissance Sculpture*, London, 1974, 1970, p. 92, gives the latest date; Frederick Hartt in *Donatello – Prophet of Modern Vision*, London, 1974, dates it to *c*.1455–6; and Bonnie A. Bennett and David G. Wilkins, *Donatello*, Oxford, 1984, p. 35, date it to the late 1430s and 1440s. Deborah Strom suggests that the *Mary Magdalen* might be dated at the same period as Donatello's *John the Baptist*, in Venice, 1438 (ibid., p. 58). The sculpture was in the Baptistery in Florence by 1510, and is now in the Museo dell'Opera del Duomo. Donatello was the first artist to depict Mary Magdalen as a maenad: in the *Lamentation over the Dead Christ*, Victoria & Albert Museum, *c*.1440, and the *Lamentation* on the south pulpit in Florence, S. Lorenzo (1460s), and in the *Entombment*, Padua, S. Antonio (1446–50).

13. The half-lengths are illustrated in *La Maddalena*, pp. 56–7.

14. Kenneth Clark, *The Nude*, Harmondsworth, 1976, p. 125, where he describes Correggio as 'another great poet of the body', contemporary and complementary to Titian. For the reference to Correggio's recumbent Magdalen, see Chapter Eight, pp. 306–8, and notes 30–3. It was extremely popular in the late sixteenth century, copied by Cristofano Allori (1577–1621; Florence, Pitti Palace), and copied in turn by the latter's followers.

15. Correggio seems to have painted another 'Magdalen in the Desert' referred to in a letter of 3 September 1528 from Veronica da Gambara to Isabella d'Este, and described as 'La Madalena nel deserto ricoverata in orrido speco a far penitentia'. It was so beautiful that everyone who saw it marvelled. See Cecil Gould, *The Paintings of Correggio*, London, 1976, p. 280. The Magdalen appears in three other paintings by Correggio, including the *Madonna and Child Enthroned with St Jerome, the Magdalen and John the Baptist as a child* (1527–8, Parma, Galleria Nazionale), in which her beautiful figure, in pink and gold, curves gracefully to kiss the Christ child's foot. A preparatory drawing at Christ Church, Oxford, shows Jerome in the position which the Magdalen now has, with her originally behind him. It has been suggested that since the picture was supposed to have been commissioned by a woman, the Magdalen's original position was not sufficiently prominent (Gould, op. cit., p. 262). The *Madonna di Albinea* of 1517, now lost (copies in Parma, Galleria Nazionale, and Rome, Museo Capitoline), showed the Virgin and Child with Sts Lucy and Mary Magdalen; and she appears in a further devotional picture with Sts Martha, as her 'sister', Peter and Leonard (New York, Metropolitan Museum of Art). Quite a different image is her distraught little form in the *Lamentation* (Parma, Galleria Nazionale, originally for the side walls of a private chapel in S. Giovanni Evangelista), seated to the right of Christ's body. This was to serve as a model for later artists such as Guido Reni in their depictions of Mary Magdalen. The Mary rushing in

on the left shows Correggio's
knowledge of the Marys in flight
in Niccolò dell'Arca's *Lamentation*
group in Bologna. The artist
painted a *Noli me tangere* (Madrid,
Prado), of *c*.1518, which is very
close to Titian's painting of the
same subject in the National
Gallery, London. Gould, p. 93
remarks that it is 'close enough in
arrangement – and in accent on
landscape – to Titian's painting of
the same subject . . . to make one
wonder if he knew it'.

16. Erwin Panofsky, *Renaissance and
    Renascences in Western Art*, New
    York, 1972, p. 185.

17. Erwin Panofsky, *Studies in
    Iconology. Humanistic Themes in the
    Art of the Renaissance*, New York,
    1972, p. 141, and note 44.

18. Cardinal Pietro Bembo's *Gli
    Asolani* was a guide in the form
    of a dialogue to good and bad
    love which was reported to have
    taken place during a wedding-
    feast at the villa at Asolo. It was
    composed between 1497 and
    1502, and was first published in
    Venice in 1505. See Elizabeth
    Cropper, 'On Beautiful Women,
    Parmigianino, *Petrarchismo*, and the
    Vernacular Style', *Art Bulletin*, vol.
    LVIII, 3 September 1976, pp.
    374–94. Bembo's work is
    discussed on p. 390.

19. Baldassare Castiglione, *The Book of
    the Courtier*, ed. and trs. Charles S.
    Singleton, New York, 1959, Book
    III, p. 256.

20. Erwin Panofsky, *Studies in
    Iconology*, p. 148. Emily Post was
    author of *Etiquette in Society, in
    Business, in Politics, and at Home*,
    New York and London, 1922.

21. Panofsky, *Renaissance and
    Renascences*, pp. 186–7. The
    quotation is from an astro-
    mythological poem by a friend of
    Ficino, Lorenzo Buonincontri,

who invokes the Virgin Mary as a
goddess of goddesses ('diva
dearum').

22. Quoted in John B. Knipping,
    *Iconography of the Counter
    Reformation in the Netherlands*,
    Leiden, 1974, vol. II, p. 45.

23. Castiglione, op. cit., Book IV,
    p. 358.

24. The Pitti picture has been
    identified with the one Giorgio
    Vasari saw in 1548 in the
    dressing-room of Duke
    Guidobaldo II at Urbino, which
    was sent to Florence in 1631 with
    the della Rovere inheritance, and
    may have been done a century
    earlier for Federico Gonzaga
    according to various commission
    documents on behalf of Vittoria
    Colonna and the marchese del
    Vasto (*La Maddalena*, cat. no. 68,
    p. 194). Whether the Pitti picture
    is the same as that commissioned
    by Federico or another version, it
    appears to conform to Federico's
    request in a letter of 5 March
    1531 for a Magdalen 'as beautiful
    but as tearful as possible' (quoted
    in J. A. Crowe and G. B.
    Cavalcaselle, *The Life and Times of
    Titian*, London, 1881, vol. I, p.
    348), and Titian's description in a
    later letter of 'la prefata Madalena
    . . . cum le mani al petto',
    referring to a painting, already
    made, of the 'Magdalen . . . with
    her hands to her breast'). Quoted
    in William Hood and Charles
    Hope, 'Titian's Vatican Altarpiece
    and the Pictures Underneath', *Art
    Bulletin*, vol. LIX, 4 December
    1977, p. 540. Hope (*Titian*,
    London, 1980, pp. 75–6) dates the
    Pitti painting to *c*.1535, suggesting
    that it is a later version than that
    commissioned by Federico
    Gonzaga.

25. According to Carlo Ridolfi, the
    pose of Titian's *Magdalen* derived

from an ancient statue in his studio, 'the idea of which was taken from an antique marble of a woman, which can be seen in the studios'. *Le Maraviglie dell'arte ovvero le vite degli illustri pittori veneti e dello stato descritti da Carlo Ridolfi* (1648), ed. D. von Hadeln, 1914, vol. I, p. 189.

26. Giambattista Marino, 'Maddalena di Tiziano', in *Poesie varie*, ed. Benedetto Croce, Bari, 1913, p. 242. Marino's poem comes under the genre of writing known as *ekphrasis*, in which a work of art is verbally recreated or evoked in verse or prose. See Norman E. Land, 'Titian's *Martyrdom of St Peter Martyr* and the "Limitations" of Ekphrastic Art Criticism', *Art History*, vol. XIII, 3, 1990, pp. 293–317, which also discusses the Pitti painting (p. 304). I am grateful to Norman Land for giving me an offprint of his article. Marino's poems, together with works by other seventeenth-century Italian poets on the theme of Mary Magdalen, are discussed in Salvatore Ussia, 'Il tema letterario della Maddalena nell'età della Controriforma', *Rivista di Storia e Letteratura religiosa*, 1988, no. 3, pp. 385–424. I am very grateful to Professor Paolo Prodi for making this article available to me.

27. Giorgio Vasari, *Le vite de' più eccellenti pittori, scultori ed architettori*, ed. G. Milanesi, Florence, 1881, vol. VII, pp. 443–4.

28. ibid., p. 454.

29. ibid., note 3. In fact, the painting Vasari saw was probably the one now in the Hermitage, St Petersburg, of which Titian himself had been particularly fond, keeping it in his studio until his death. Several copies were made of the later penitent

Magdalen both in Titian's workshop and by contemporary and later artists. For the St Petersburg and Naples versions see entries 62 and 63 in *Titian: Prince of Painters*, exhibition catalogue, Venice and Washington, 1990–1.

30. Cardinal Federico Borromeo, *Il Museo del Card. Federico Borromeo* (1625), ed. L. Beltrami, Milan, 1909, p. 64.

31. Crowe and Cavalcaselle, op. cit., vol. I, p. 350.

32. Jakob Burckhardt, *The Cicerone. An Art Guide to Painting in Italy*, trs. Mrs A. H. Clough, revised and corrected by J. A. Crowe, London, 1879, p. 192.

33. John Ruskin, *Modern Painters*, vol. II, in *The Works of John Ruskin*, ed. E. T. Cook and Alexander Wedderburn, vol. IV, London, 1903, p. 195; p. 122, note 1; p. 347; *Modern Painters*, vol. V in *The Works of John Ruskin*, vol. VII, pp. 295–6.

34. See Monika Ingenhoff-Danhäuser, *Maria Magdalena: Heilige und Sünderin in der italienischen Renaissance. Studien zur Ikonographie der Heiligen von Leonardo bis Tizian*, Tübingen, 1984.

35. The allegory of the 'Calumny of Apelles', described by the poet Lucian, told of the conviction and punishment of an innocent victim who was ultimately vindicated by Repentance and Truth. See Panofsky, *Studies in Iconology*, pp. 158–9. See now Jean Michel Massing, *Du Texte à l'Image. La Calomnie d'Apelle et son Iconographie*, Strasbourg, 1990. My thanks to Elizabeth McGrath for bringing this book to my attention.

36. Panofsky, *Studies in Iconology*, p. 158.

37. Clark, op. cit., p. 89.

38. ibid., pp. 64–102. See also Anne

Hollander, *Seeing through Clothes*, New York, 1979, pp. 83–97, 187–98. The Ludovisi throne is in the Museo Nazionale Romano, Rome.

39. The anecdote refers to a conversation which probably took place between 1559 and 1561. I am extremely grateful to Dr Robert Williams for sending me this information from an article, 'The Façade of the Palazzo dei Visacci', to be published in *I Tatti Studies*. I am also grateful to Dr Thomas Frangenberg for first telling me of the anecdote.

40. Agnolo Firenzuola, quoted in A. Rochon, *Histoire mondiale de la Femme*, Paris, 1966, vol. II, p. 221. Federico Luigini da Udine, quoted in Rochon, ibid., p. 221. See also Cropper, op. cit., pp. 38off.

41. Michel de Montaigne, *Essays*, I, lxiii, 'Apology for Raimonde de Sebonde', quoted in Cropper, op. cit., p. 394, note 107.

42. Marino, 'Maddalena di Tiziano' in *Poesie varie*, ed. cit., p. 244: 'Chiome, che, sciolte in preziosa pioggia,/ su le rose ondeggiate e su le brine,/ beate, voi, che, 'n disusata foggia/ incomposte e neglette e sparse e chine,/ quell'altezza appressaste, ove non pioggia/ di Berenice/ il favoloso crine!' Marino may also have been referring to the lock of hair of another Berenice, which becomes a minor constellation known as the Coma Berenices, in a poem by Catullus (*Catullis Carmina*, no. 66), his translation of a poem by Callimachus (see *The Poems of Catullus*, trs. James Michie, introd. and notes by Robert Rowland, London, 1972). I am grateful to Elizabeth McGrath for this reference.

43. Giovanni Battista della Porta,

quoted in Charles Berg, *Unconscious Significance of Hair*, London, 1951, p. 30.

44. Agnolo Firenzuola, *Del Dialogo . . . Della belleza delle Donne, intitolato Celso*, Florence, 1548, f. 91v.

45. Federico Luigini da Udine, *Il Libro della Bella Donna*, Venice, 1554, Book I, pp. 16 and 18.

46. ibid., pp. 18 and 19.

47. Thomas Coryate, 'Observations of Venice', in *Coryate's Crudities* (1611), vol. I, London, 1905, p. 48. The *arte biondeggiante* is also described in Cesare Vecellio, *Habiti antichi et moderni di Diverse Parti del Mondo*, Venice, 1598; the process is illustrated in the 1590 edition, and reproduced in E. Rodocanachi, *La Femme italienne à l'époque de la Renaissance*, Paris, 1907, facing p. 112.

48. Cardinal Federico Borromeo, chapter vi, 'Del nudo', of his *De Pictura sacra* (1624), ed. Carlo Castiglioni, Milan, 1932, p. 65.

49. H. C. J. Grierson, *Cross Currents in English Literature of the XVII Century, or The World, the Flesh and the Spirit, their Actions and Reaction*, London, 1929, p. 181, and note 2.

50. Ulrich Zwingli, 'De vera et falso religione', *Operum D. Huldrychi Zwingli*, tom. 11, f. 240; quoted in E.-M. Faillon, *Monuments inédits sur l'apostolat de Sainte Marie-Madeleine en Provence*, 2 vols, Paris, 1865, vol. I, p. iv.

51. Jean Calvin, *Commentaire sur la concorde des Evangiles*, Geneva, 1563, p. 720, quoted in Faillon, op. cit., p. iv, and 'Admonitio de reliquiis', in *Tractatus theologici*, Geneva, 1612, p. 236, quoted in Faillon, p. v.

52. For an account of this controversy, see Anselm Hufstader, 'Lefèvre d'Etaples and the Magdalen', *Studies in the Renaissance*, vol. XVI, 1969,

pp. 31–60, and Edward Surtz SJ, *The Works and Days of John Fisher*, Cambridge (Mass.), 1967.

53. Quoted in Surtz, op. cit., note 14, pp. 403–4.

54. ibid., pp. 279, 39, 275; p. 33 and note 16; p. 71 and note 98, and pp. 278–9.

55. Hufstader, op. cit., pp. 38 and 41. While agreeing that Lefèvre was correct in his view, but not wishing to rock the ecclesiastical boat, Erasmus was to give the female interlocutor of his colloquy, 'The Abbot and the Learned Woman' (1519), the imaginary name, Magdalia, but one clearly prompted by the Lefèvre controversy. A satire on the clergy's ignorance, the colloquy serves as an example of contemporary understanding of women's education and its purposes, much debated in contemporary treatises concerning women's behaviour (*Collected Works of Erasmus*, vol. 39: *Colloquies*, translated and annotated by Craig R. Thompson, Toronto, 1997, pp. 501–5). Magdalia, a wife, states that her learning in Greek and Latin are necessary for the wisdom required to rear children and run the house. The figure of Magdalia is thought to have been based on Margaret Roper, daughter of Sir Thomas More. To my knowledge, no one has yet linked the name Magdalia to the Lefèvre controversy. See my article, 'Political cypher and pietistical pawn: Mary Magdalen and the Burgundian Question', forthcoming.

56. Surtz, op. cit., p. 5 and note 12.

57. See Jacques Rossiaud, *Medieval Prostitution*, trs. Lydia G. Cochrane, Oxford, 1988, pp. 140–2. Lucas van Leyden's engraving of the so-called 'Dance of Mary Magdalen' (Plate 24) shows Mary Magdalen traipsing the *bassedanse*, the elegant stepping

dance popular between the fourteenth and second half of the sixteenth centuries, to music from a drummer and transverse flautist, while amorous courtly couples sit on the ground around her. In the middle ground, she hunts a stag, while in the background, angels raise her to heaven, above a more or less accurately described *massif* of La Sainte-Baume, where her grotto was said to be. The engraving is not insignificantly dated 1519. Van Leyden was thus supporting Church tradition by emphasising her iconography, and reiterating her missionary activities in Provence. On the engraving and its symbolism, see H. Colin Slim, 'Music and Dancing with Mary Magdalen in a Laura Vestalis', in *The Crannied Wall*, ed. Craig A. Monson, Ann Arbor, Mich., 1992, pp. 139–60; and Liesel Nolan, 'Is she dancing? A new reading of Lucas van Leyden's "*Dance of the Magdalene*" of 1519', in *Equally in God's Image: Women in the Middle Ages*, in eds Holloway, Wright and Bechtold, New York, San Francisco, Berne, Frankfurt, Paris, London, 1990, pp. 233–50; see my article, 'Political cypher and pietistical pawn: Mary Magdalen and the Burgundian Question', forthcoming.

58. St Ignatius Loyola, *Exercitia Spiritualia*, ed. Josephus Calveras SJ, Rome, 1969, § 282, 285, 286 and 300.

59. St Teresa of Avila, *Life*, in *Complete Works of St Teresa of Jesus*, trs. and ed. E. Allison Peers, London, 1946, vol. I, pp. 54 and 133. There are numerous references to Mary Magdalen as model repentant, lover and contemplative throughout Teresa's writings.

60. François de Sales, *Introduction to the Devout Life*, trs. and ed. John K.

Ryan, New York, 1950, p. 20.

61. François de Sales, *Of the Love of God*, trs. H. L. Sidney Lear, London, 1888, pp. 83–4.

62. Cardinal Roberto Bellarmino on tears is quoted in Emile Mâle, *L'Art religieux après le Concile de Trente*, Paris, 1932, pp. 65–6. His hymn is referred to in Frederick Cummings and Luigi Spezzaferro, 'Detroit's "Conversion of the Magdalen" (the Alzaga Caravaggio)', *Burlington Magazine*, vol. CXVI, 859, October 1974, p. 577, and notes 20 and 21.

63. See Ann Tzeutschler Lurie, 'The Weeping Heraclitus by H. Terbruggen in the Cleveland Museum of Art', *Burlington Magazine*, vol. CXXI, 914, May 1979, pp. 279ff, especially pp. 283–6. A study for Bernini's statue of Mary Magdalen in the Chigi chapel, Siena (Leipzig, Museum der bildenden Kunste, 29–68), is illustrated in *Selected Drawings of Gian Lorenzo Bernini*, ed. Ann Sutherland Harris, New York, 1977, pl. 77.

64. Pietro de Natalibus, 'Maria Magdalena' in *Catalogo Sanctorum*, Venice, 1506, cap. xxiiii, p. 140, contains woodcuts of the Feast in the House of the Pharisee, Ecstasy of Mary Magdalen, and of the sea-journey to Marseille.

65. In the sixteenth century, devotion to the real presence, the body and blood of Christ, insisted upon by Rome, increased. Sacrament chapels were set aside to house the reserved host, some belonging to confraternities of the Sacrament. They were often decorated with scenes pertaining to the eucharist, such as the Gathering of Manna, to life after death, such as the Raising of Lazarus, or to confession, as was required of every communicant,

represented by Mary Magdalen as Luke's sinner, in the Feast of the House of the Pharisee.

66. See Cummings and Spezzaferro, op. cit., pp. 563ff.

67. R. P. Louis de la Rivière, *La Vie de l'illustrissime et révérendissime François de Sales*, 1625, pp. 527–8.

68. Artemisia Gentileschi's painting was possibly the one referred to in a letter of 10 February 1620 in which she promises to deliver to Grand Duke Cosimo II a painting for his wife, Maria Magdalena of Austria, for which the artist had already received part-payment. Maria Magdalena had herself painted by Justus Sustermans as Mary Magdalen. (See Pl. 69, and Chapter Eight, pp. 298–9, and notes 8–10). For a discussion of liturgical colours, see Mary Pardo, 'The Subject of Savoldo's *Magdalene*', *Art Bulletin*, March 1989, p. 71, note 10, which also refers to Victor Saxer, *Le Culte de Marie Madeleine en Occident*, Paris, 1959, pp. 320–2, where he discusses the liturgical colours for Mary Magdalen's feast-day in use until at least the late fifteenth century.

69. Session XXV, 'On the Invocation, Veneration, and Relics, of Saints and on Sacred Images', in *The Canons and Decrees of the Sacred and Oecumenical Council of Trent celebrated under the Sovereign Pontiffs, Paul II, Julius III, and Pius IV*, trs. Revd J. Waterworth, London, 1848, pp. 235–6.

70. Ronald M. Steinberg, *Fra Girolamo Savonarola: Florentine Art and Renaissance Historiography*, Athens (Ohio), 1977, p. 51. I am grateful to Chris Fischer for this reference.

71. Giovanni Andrea Gilio da Fabriano, 'Degli errori de' pittori circa l'istorie', in *Trattati d'Arte del*

Cinquecento fra manierismo e controriforma, ed. Paola Barocchi, Bari, 1961, vol. II, p. 80: 'Tenga per fermo il pittore che far si diletta le figure de' santi nudi, che sempre gli leverà gran parte de la riverenza che se li deve.'

72. The title of chap. xlii in Book II warns of the danger of pictures likely to excite lust: 'In picturis cavendum esse quid quid ad libidinem provocat.'

73. Anthony Blunt, *Artistic Theory in Italy 1450–1600*, London, Oxford and New York, 1975, p. 120.

74. Gilio, in Barocchi, op. cit., p. 32.

75. ibid., pp. 32–3.

76. Johannes Molanus, *De Historia SS. Imaginum et Picturarum pro vero earum usu contra abusus*, Louvain, 1771, Book III, chap. xxv, pp. 136v–137r.

77. G. P. Lomazzo, *Trattato dell'arte de la pittura, scultura et architettura* (Milan, 1584), Rome, 1844, vol. I, p. 7, and vol. II, p. 231.

78. Cardinal Gabriele Paleotti, *Discorso intorno alle immagini sacre e profane*, in Barocchi, op. cit., p. 266: 'c però opera che un pittore, in vece di formare uno Cristo, formi uno Apolline . . . Entra fino nei santi, e se la beata Maddalena o san Giovanni evangelista . . . si dipinge, fa che siano ornati et addobati peggio che meretrici o istrioni; overo sotto coperta di una santa fa fare il ritratto della concubina.'

79. R. P. Sautel, *Divae Magdalenae ignes sacri et piae lacrimae*, Cologne, 1684, p. 282, quoted in Knipping, op. cit., vol. I, p. 61.

80. Mario Praz, *Secentismo e Marinismo in Inghilterra. John Donne – Richard Crashaw*, Florence, 1925, quoted in Grierson, op. cit., p. 181, note 2.

81. Paleotti, in Barocchi, op. cit., vol. II, p. 227.

82. Albani's painting was sold at Christie's, 4 May, 1979, lot 88. For Orazio Gentileschi see Chapter 8, pp. 305–6.

83. Cesare Ripa, 'Penitenza', in *Iconologia*, Rome, 1603, p. 387.

84. Carlo Cesare Malvasia, *Felsina pittrice. Vite de' Pittori bolognesi* (1678), 1841, vol. II, p. 376. 'Una S. Maria Maddalena che si disciplina', together with pictures of St Francis in the desert and St Jerome.

85. Elisabetta Sirani, *Mary Magdalen flagellating herself*, Besançon, Musée des Beaux-Arts et d'Archéologie. See Whitney Chadwick, *Women, Art and Society*, Harmondsworth, 1989, pp. 81, 82, 87, 89, 92 and 93, for interesting comments on Sirani's life.

86. Another version of Furini's *Penitent Mary Magdalen* is in Florence, in the collection of Emilio Pucci.

87. The version of Guido Reni's *Mary Magdalen* in Rome was painted for Cardinal Valerio S. Croce, and given him by Cardinal Antonio Barberini by 1641. D. S. Pepper, *Guido Reni. A Complete Catalogue of his Works with an Introductory Text*, Oxford, 1984, cat. no. 137; R. P. Le Moyne's poem is quoted from his *Oeuvres poétiques*, Paris, 1671, p. 432.

88. Chantelou's anecdote is quoted in *Guido Reni 1575–1642*, exhibition catalogue, Bologna, Los Angeles and Fort Worth, 1988, cat. no. 59. The same entry refers to Howard Hibbard's identification of the figure of Justice with that of Reni's *Mary Magdalen*.

89. See next chapter.

90. The most popular writing concerning Mary Magdalen of the Spanish Counter-Reformation is Pedro Malón de Chaide, *La conversión de la Magdalena* (1589), which concentrates on her life as

a sinner, her repentance and reunion with God (ed. with foreword and notes by P. Félix García, Madrid, 1947). It is similar to many contemporary Italian works on the subject of Mary Magdalen. The Dominican friar Luís de Granada also wrote of the Magdalen's conversion in his *Meditationi molto divote, sopra alcuni passi*, trs. R. M. Pietro Buonfanti da Bibbiena, Venice, 1587, pp. 239ff.

91. Ribera executed several paintings of Mary Magdalen, including a *Penitent Magdalen* (Prado) and an *Ecstasy* (New York, Hispanic Society of America). Pedro de Meña (1628–88) also executed a *Magdalen* (1664) for the Visitation convent in Madrid.

92. St Teresa of Avila, op. cit., vol. I, pp. 120 and 108.

93. [St Teresa of Avila,] *The Lyf of the Mother Teresa of Iesus, Foundresse of the Monasteries of the Descalced or Bare-footed Carmelite Nunnes and Fryers, of the First Rule. Written by her self, at the commandement of her ghostly father, and now translated into English, out of Spanish by W. M. of the Society of Iesus*, Antwerp, 1611, chap. xxix, p. 232.

94. Caravaggio's painting is known only through copies by Louis Finson (e.g. Aix-en-Provence, private collection [1613] and Marseille, Musée des Beaux-Arts); the original is believed to be in a private collection in Rome. See cat. no. 59, pp. 163–5, in *La Maddalena*. For Peter Paul Rubens, *Ecstasy of Mary Magdalen* (Lille, Musée des Beaux-Arts), see *Corpus Rubenianum Ludwig Burchard*, ed. Hans Vlieghe, London and New York, 1973, vol. II: *Saints*, cat. no. 131.

95. Illustrated in *La Maddalena*, cat. no. 93, p. 223.

96. Emile Mâle, *L'Art religieux de la fin du XVIe siècle, du XVIIe siècle et du XVIIIe siècle*, Paris, 1951, p. 209.

97. Three other versions of Georges de la Tour's *Penitent Magdalen*, considered autograph, are in New York, Metropolitan Museum of Art; Paris, Louvre; and Los Angeles, County Museum of Art.

98. Erasmo di Valvasone, *Le Lagrime di S. Maria Maddalena*, printed with Luigi Tansillo, *Le Lagrime di S. Pietro*, Venice, 1592.

99. Robert Southwell, *Marie Magdalen's Funerall Teares* (1594), London, 1602, pp. 39–40.

100. ibid., p. 65.

101. Southwell, 'Marie Magdalens complaint at Christs death', in *Poems of Robert Southwell, SJ*, ed. James H. McDonald and Nancy Pollard Brown, Oxford, 1967, stanzas 1, 2 and 7, pp. 45–6. See also Louis Martz, *The Poetry of Meditation*, New Haven, 1962.

102. The style of the engraving suggests the work of Cornelis Bloemaert, who was active in Rome in the mid-seventeenth century. I am grateful to Nicholas Turner for his thoughts concerning this picture. An example of the kind of devotional book for which this engraving might have been made is Carl Stengel's *S. Mariae Magdalenae, Vitae historia, Commentario illustrata*, Augsburg, 1622.

103. Izaak Walton, *The Lives of John Donne, Sir Henry Wotton, Richard Hooker, George Herbert and Robert Sanderson*, introd. G. Saintsbury, London, 1927, p. 258.

104. George Herbert, 'Marie Magdalene', from 'The Church', in *The English Poems of George Herbert*, ed. A. A. Patrides, London and Totowa (NJ), 1974, pp. 178–9.

105. Richard Crashaw, 'Sainte Mary Magdalene or The Weeper', op. cit., p. 312.

106. Andrew Marvell, 'Eyes and Tears', in *The Complete Poems*, ed. Elizabeth Story Donno, Harmondsworth, 1976, p. 53.

107. *Shorter Oxford English Dictionary*, vol. I: 'Magdalen. 2. One whose history resembles that of the Magdalen; *spec.* a reformed prostitute 1693. 3. [Short for *M. hospital*.] A home for the reformation of prostitutes 1766. 4. A kind of peach 1706.' ibid., vol. II: 'Maudlin. 1. Heraclitus the Maudlin Philosopher BUTLER.'

108. Bernardino Ochino, 'Nove Prediche', in *Predicazione dei Cappuccini nel '500 in Italia*, Loreto, 1956, pp. 556, 558, 561. I am grateful to Darius Sikorski for bringing this sermon to my attention, and for providing me with a copy.

109. The earliest reliable date for the title of the church is 1155 (S. Tramontin, A. Niero, G. Musolino, C. Candiani, *Culto dei Santi a Venezia*, Venice, 1965, p. 124), although Flaminio Corner (*Notizie storiche delle Chiese e Monasteri di Venezia*, Padua, 1758, p. 16) gives an earlier one of 1025. Giuseppe Tassini, *Curiosità veneziane, ovvero origini delle denominazioni stradali* (1863), 1933, p. 390, gives a foundation date of 1222 when the church was erected by the Baffo family.

110. Francesco Sansovino, *Venetia città nobilissima et singolare*, Venice, 1663, p. 140r. Marco Boschini, *Le Minere della pittura . . .* , Venice, 1664, pp. 477–9; the church also contained pictures of Mary Magdalen's boat journey, preaching and the Raising of Lazarus. Boschini–Zanetti, *Descrizione di tutte le pubbliche pitture della Città Venezia etc . . .* , Venice, 1733, pp. 413–14; Carlo Ridolfi, *Le Maraviglie dell'Arte*

ovvero le vite degli illustri pittori veneti e dello stato, 2nd edn, Padua, 1837, vol. II, p. 179. The church was renovated in *c.*1760 by the architect Tommaso Temanza (1705–89), a work which is regarded as his masterpiece, when the paintings were probably removed. In 1810 it ceased to be a parish church, was closed, and reopened as a sacramental oratory.

111. Sansovino, op. cit., p. 140r.

112. Edward Muir, *Civic Ritual in Renaissance Venice*, Princeton, 1981, pp. 212–13.

113. 'Onde la memoria di quel giorno rimase perpetua', Sansovino, op. cit., p. 351v.

114. Tassini, op. cit., p. 391.

115. Giovanni Buonconsiglio, il Marescacco, Venice, Accademia, Depositi 826. According to Boschini, op. cit., the picture hung above the *tribunale* in the Magistrato della Messetaria in the *sestiere* of S. Polo (p. 264).

116. Mary Magdalen also appears in the *Paradiso*, Tintoretto's last great work, which decorates the Council Hall of the Ducal Palace, commissioned in 1587 and finished in 1592. For a discussion of the symbolism, see R. Pallucchini and P. Rossi, *Tintoretto. Le Opere sacre e profane*, Milan, 1982, vol. I, pp. 233–4. Mary Magdalen is the last figure on the canvas on the right over the doorway.

117. Franca Zara Boccazzi, *La Basilica dei SS. Giovanni e Paolo in Venezia*, Venice, 1965, pp. 98–9 and 343, note 81. See also Peter Humfrey, *The Altarpiece in Renaissance Venice*, London and New Haven, 1993, Appendix 97.

118. The Vendramin memorial by Tullio Lombardo is on the left of the chancel. The statues of Mary Magdalen and Catherine are by

Lorenzo Bregno. See Boccazzi, op. cit., pp. 131–2.

119. See the account of Louis IX's reunion of their relics at Vézelay, Chapter Four. The tabernacle was originally in the chapel of St Michael which Melchiore Trevisan had endowed in 1480. Sansovino describes the annual procession in honour of the blood: '[At the Frari] every year on Passion Sunday, the Sunday of Lazarus, all the people honour the Blood of Christ, which was brought from Constantinople by Marchio Trevisan, as recorded in an inscription on the stone at his shrine and given to this church, together with some unguent with which the Magdalen bathed the feet of Our Lord' (*Venetia*, 1581, p. 65v). Quoted in Rona Goffen, *Piety and Patronage in Renaissance Venice. Bellini, Titian, and the Franciscans*, New Haven and London, 1986, p. 21, and note 78. Another relic of Mary Magdalen, an arm, was at S. Lazzaro, and in the care of the prior. It was exhibited on Good Friday. Marin Sanudo il Giovane, *De origine, situ et magistratibus urbis Venetae . . . (1493–1530)*, ed. Aricò, Cisalpino, 1980, p. 227.

120. For the treasury, see Tramontin et al, op. cit., p. 191.

121. Sebastiano del Piombo, Altarpiece, 1510, Venice, S. Giovanni Crisostomo. Henry James's description comes from *Italian Hours*, London, 1909, pp. 26–7. Mary Magdalen is shown with Saints Catherine and Agnes; to the right is John the Baptist, whose companion may be Onuphrius; the saint in armour may be Theodore. The painting was commissioned in March 1510, following the wishes recorded in the will of Caterina Contarini,

wife of Niccolò Morosini, of 13 April 1509 (Michael Hirst, *Sebastiano del Piombo*, Oxford, 1981, p. 24). See also Humfrey, op. cit., Appendix 77.

122. Girolamo Savoldo worked in Venice during the 1530s and 1540s, and was known as a painter of *invenzioni*. He painted three versions of this painting, of which the London one is regarded as the best. Others are in Florence and Berlin. In an important article, 'The Subject of Savoldo's Magdalene', *Art Bulletin*, March 1989, pp. 67–91, Mary Pardo places the painting within the narrative and formal developments in half-length devotional images, or dramatic close-ups, and studies its relationship to theories of pictorial illusion, and the link between poetry and painting. I concur with Pardo's rejection of Monika Ingenhoff-Danhäuser's courtesan-Magdalen. The quotations in the previous sentence come from Pardo's article, p. 70. My thanks to Evelyn Welch for directing me to it.

123. Titian may have intended the picture to hang in the Cappella del Cristo at the Frari, in return for the concession to be buried there, but he died before the painting was finished. At his death in 1576, the painting was found in his studio, and subsequently acquired by Jacopo Palma il Giovane, who finished it. It was first referred to in a letter of 1575 from the marquis of Ayamonte, who wrote: '. . . even if where there is the Mother and Son there is no need for additional effects, it is good that there is the Magdalene because she is such a great example of the effect God has on sinners and such a great

lesson of how those who have sinned should put themselves aright, and so she is welcome in the painting of the Mother and the Son . . .' (*Titian, Prince of Painters*, op. cit., cat. no. 77). It now hangs in the Accademia Gallery. On Titian's humanism, see Fritz Saxl, 'Titian and Aretino' in *Lectures*, London, 1957, vol. I, p. 173, who notes, '. . . the figure that dominates this picture, conceived to express Titian's hope for an afterlife, is the figure taken from classical antiquity'. See also the note by 'E.W.', 'The Maenad under the Cross', *Journal of the Warburg and Courtauld Institutes*, 1937, vol. I, pp. 70–1. David Rosand, in *Painting in Cinquecento Venice: Titian, Veronese, Tintoretto*, New Haven and London, 1982, pp. 75–84, refers to this painting. Hope (1980), p. 165, suggests that the painting may actually have been begun for Ayamonte.

124. Quoted in A. Niero, G. Musolino, S. Tramontin, *Santi a Venezia*, Venice, 1972, p. 99.

125. ibid., p. 196. In this list St Jerome looks after thieves and assassins, St Peter the fishermen, Catherine, married women ('le done maridade'), and St Roch, plague victims. Lucy, Mary Magdalen and Martha were especially venerated in Venice; the Magdalen was third most popular female saint after Catherine and the Virgin Mary, in having onomastics or place names called after her. At Canaregio, the Magdalen gave her name to a *campo, calle, fondamenta, rio* and gondola stop (*traghetto*). As the 'sister' of Martha, Mary Magdalen was also given special prominence in the church of the Augustinian nunnery of S. Marta, which boasted relics of the Magdalen (Cicogna, op. cit., vol. V, p. 107)

and ten paintings of her life by Luigi Bonfatti and by Leandro Bassano, a *Christ in the House of Martha and Mary Magdalen* (Boschini, op. cit., p. 269). A monastery was also dedicated to Mary Magdalen on the small island of Gaiada, now half submerged, near Torcello.

126. Pietro Aretino, *Ragionamento della Nanna e della Antonia fatto in Roma sotto un ficaia composto dal divino Aretino per suo capriccio a correzione dei tre stati delle donne*, or *Sei giornate*, ed. Giovanni Aquilecchia, Rome-Bari, 1980, p. 4. Aretino's sacred work, '*La Maddalena*', first published in Venice in 1535 in *I Quattro Libri de la Humanità di Christo di M. Pietro Aretino*, is a conventional image of Mary Magdalen, written in overblown style, to suit the tastes of the time. He describes her as 'unable to restrain herself from lascivious costume; despite Martha's scorn, she lets herself be seen quite naked'. She wears a 'fine linen blouse decorated with gold, and studded with pearls', held in place by a golden circlet full of emeralds above her right elbow, thus allowing those around her to admire the form of her arm. She had the 'same bad habits of lasciviousness which imbue the actions of courtesans' (1539 edn., p. 58). See Christopher Cairns, *Pietro Aretino & The Republic of Venice: Researches on Aretino and his Circle in Venice 1527–1556*, Florence, 1985, esp. pp. 69–97, and 118, note 59. I am grateful to Daria Perocco for referring me to this last work.

127. Coryate, op. cit., p. 401, wrote, 'the name of a Cortezan of Venice is famoused all over Christendom'. For the legislation of 1360, see [G. B. Lorenzi,] *Leggi*

e memorie venete sulla Prostituzione fino alla Caduta della Republica, Venice, 1870–2, p. 32. Legislation of 14 June 1360 established brothels, using the following words: 'de loco habili pro peccatricibus quia omnino sunt necessarie in terra ista'.

128. Coryate, op. cit., p. 402: 'As for the number of these Venetian Cortezans it is very great. It is thought to be 20,000 [here Coryate exaggerated]. A most ungodly thing without doubt that there should be a tolleration of such licentious wantons in so glorious, so potent, so renowned a city! . . . Large dispensations and indulgences granted – Venetians think wives might be assaulted, and therefore they should be "capricornified", (which of all the indignities in the world the Venetian cannot patiently endure) were it not for these places of evacuation and revenues paid to the senate for their tolleration doe maintaine a dozen of their galleys . . . and so save them a great charge.'

129. *Leggi e memorie,* p. 31 (29 June 1358). See also on the subject of prostitution in Venice Elizabeth Pavan, 'Police des moeurs, société et politique à Venise à la fin du Moyen Age', *Revue historique,* Oct.–Dec. 1980, pp. 241–88. I am grateful to Dennis Romano for referring me to this article.

130. *Leggi e memorie,* p. 37 (15 July 1423). Pavan, op. cit., pp. 247–8, lists the greater religious feasts when activity also had to cease.

131. *Leggi e memorie,* p. 35 (23 May 1421), p. 69 (14 March 1486), and p. 73 (7 May 1490); Molmenti, op. cit., p. 478; Pavan, op. cit., p. 261.

132. Brian Pullan, *Rich and Poor in Renaissance Venice,* Oxford, 1971,

pp. 183, 186 and 228. Pullan suggests, however, that these charitable ventures may have been more concerned to prevent 'the gently-born poor from bringing the ruling classes into disrepute by public begging' than with more altruistic motives.

133. Pullan, op. cit., pp. 232 and 257–8.

134. Fynes Moryson, *Shakespeare's Europe,* ed. Charles Hughes, London, 1903, pp. 411–12, who seems to suggest that the Convertite was a home for retired rather than penitent prostitutes. Quoted in Pullan, op. cit., p. 379. Mary Magdalen was also held up as an example to adulteresses in Venice: the high altarpiece of the Chiesa del Soccorso, painted by Benedetto Caliari, shows her as an intermediary between the Virgin and Child and a group of well-dressed women, one of whom is tearing jewels from her hair to the right, while another group of women, already convertites in the institution to which the church belonged, is shown on the left. The Casa del Soccorso, set up in c.1577, provided refuge for women who had 'loosed the reins of modesty and continence in their husbands' absence' and adulteresses. Pullan, op. cit., p. 391, and note 76. Illustrated in Bernard Aikema, 'L'Immagine della Carità veneziana', in Aikema and Dulcia Meijers, eds, *Nel Regno dei Poveri, Arte e Storia dei Grandi Ospedali. Venezia in età moderna 1474–1797,* Venice, 1989, fig. 47, pp. 84–5. The rest of the article also relates Mary Magdalen to charitable institutions in Venice. I am very grateful to Peter Humfrey for bringing this book to my attention.

135. Sansovino, op. cit., p. 192r.

136. Correr Cod. Cic. 3234. I am grateful to the Archivio Fotografico of the Biblioteca Correr for making a photograph of this title-page available to me.

137. Ridolfi, op. cit., vol. II, pp. 339 and 413.

138. Tassini, op. cit., p. 189.

139. Veronica Franco, quoted in E. Cicogna, *Delle iscrizioni veneziane*, 6 vols, Venice, 1834–61, vol. V. p. 414.

140. Arturo Graf, 'Una cortigiana fra mille', in *Attraverso il Cinquecento*, Turin, 1888, p. 343.

141. Tassini, op. cit., p. 189.

142. Correr Cod. Cic. 3234 (unpaginated). Other convents of the Convertite were established in the Venetian territories (Verona, Vicenza, Treviso; in Lombardy, Bergamo, Brescia and Crema [Pullan, op. cit., p. 379]). At Treviso, there is on the external wall of the church of Mary Magdalen (1559) a faded sixteenth-century fresco of the penitent Magdalen. On the high altar is a *Noli me tangere* with two donors by Paolo Veronese, and on the right wall a *Feast in the House of Simon* by Antonio Molinari (1600), amongst images of the saint which decorate the church.

143. See W. R. Rearick, 'Battista Franco and the Grimani Chapel', *Saggi e memorie della Storia dell'Arte*, vol. II, 1959, pp. 107–39.

144. The identification of these figures as Mary Magdalen and Mary of Egypt has been standard in the literature since the early nineteenth century only, and is still a matter of debate. See Tom Nichols, *Tintoretto: Tradition and Identity*, London, 1999, who suggests the figures may be the Virgin Mary and St Elizabeth (pp. 225–6, and n. 79). Upstairs, she appears in the *Raising of*

Lazarus. The Scuola was established during the plague of 1478, and became a Scuola Grande eleven years later (Pullan, op. cit., p. 38). Tintoretto also painted a *Christ in the House of Martha and Mary* (*c.*1567, Munich, Alte Pinakothek), where Martha points down to a seated Mary wearing a beautiful blue gown with white and gold fichu and ochre drapery.

145. A piece of improving literature is the *Devotissima conversione di S. Maria Maddalena*, published in Venice in 1550. Amongst others are the *Rappresentazione d'un stupendo miracolo di S. Maria Maddalena*, Florence, 1554; G. F. Giovanni Maria Ben Assai da Foligno, *Devotissima Rappresentazione di S. Maria Maddalena: Specchio di Penitenza*, Perugia, 1589.

146. Andreini (*c.*1579–1654) was an actor, dramatist and poet. The *sacra rappresentazione* was based on his poem 'La Maddalena' (1610). The prologue, 'Su le penne de' venti', is all that remains. The musical sections were composed jointly by Monteverdi, Salamone Rossi, Muzio Efrem and Alessandro Giunizzoni. A further revised version was *La Maddalena lasciva e penitente*, Milan, 1652.

147. See *The New Grove Dictionary of Music and Musicians*, ed. Stanley Sadie, London, 1980, vol. 7, entries under Andrea and Giovanni Gabrieli.

148. Cicogna, op. cit., vol. VI, p. 835. In 1763, the Venetian composer Baldassare Galluppi wrote an oratorio for six voices, *Maria Magdalena*, for the Casa delle Zitelle, which had been established in 1559–61 to receive and educate imperilled girls (ibid., vol. V, p. 318). In 1694, the Incurabili published an oratorio,

L'Indice della Penitenza, in honour of Mary Magdalen, dedicated to the Dogaressa Elisabetta Querini Valier (ibid., vol. V, p. 325). Benedetto Marcello (1686–1739), another Venetian composer, set music to *Il Sepolcro*, a sacred drama sung for the Emperor Leopold I on Good Friday, 1705. The characters involved were the Virgin Mary, John the Evangelist, a soprano as Mary Magdalen, Simon of Cyrene, Joseph of Arimathaea, Nicodemus and chorus. Eleanor Selfridge-Field, *Music of Benedetto and Alessandro Marcello*, Oxford, Clarendon, 1990, p. 312.

149. See Sherrill Cohen, 'Convertite e Malmaritate. Donne "irregolari" e ordini religiosi nella Firenze rinascimentale', *Memoria. Rivista di storia delle donne*, vol. V, 1982, p. 46–62.

150. ibid., p. 50.

151. The Scuola dei Fenestrieri, or window-makers' guild, had its chapel at the church of Mary Magdalen in Canaregio; from 1619 to 1648, the Scuola della Maddalena had a chapel at S. Francesco di Paola (A. Niero, G. Musolino, S. Tramontin, *Santità a Venezia*, Venice, 1972, pp. 69 and 43).

152. Faillon, op. cit., col. 1342ff. It is interesting to note that in France several ecclesiastical provinces, the churches of Paris, Orléans and Vienne and the Cluniac order reformed the old office which assumed that the three Marys were one, and established a distinction between them during the pontificate of Pius V (1556–72). Clement VIII (1592–1605) had an old hymn removed from the office of Mary Magdalen's feast-day because it marked too strongly that Mary

Magdalen was the sister of Lazarus and had committed social crimes (Dom Augustin Calmet, 'Dissertations sur les Trois Maries' in *Sainte Bible en latin et en français* etc., Paris, 1773, vol. XIII, pp. 344–5).

153. New York, Pierpont Morgan Library, MS 250, f. 14. Mary Magdalen's *Ecstasy* appears on f. 143v.

154. Faillon, op. cit., vol. I, cols 1033–4.

155. ibid., cols 1045–6.

156. Frances A. Yates, *Astraea. The Imperial Theme in the Sixteenth Century*, London and Boston, 1975, pp. 173–86, and pls 24 and 25, *Drawings of Religious Processions in Paris*, 1583–4, illustrating Henri III's Religious Movements (Paris, Bibliothèque Nationale, Cabinet des Estampes, Pd 29 Réserve). I am grateful to David Thomson for directing me to these drawings.

157. Faillon, op. cit., vol. I, cols 1068–70.

158. ibid., cols 1065–8.

159. Philippe de Champaigne's painting of the *Feast in the House of the Pharisee* (Paris, Louvre) was commissioned by Anne of Austria for Val-de-Grâce.

160. Antoine Godeau, *Les Tableaux de la Pénitence*, 3rd ed., 1662, pp. 533–64; J. Balin, *Poème héroïque de Saincte Magdelaine – où est descrite sa vie, sa navigation en Provence, & le lieu de sa pénitence*, Paris, 1607. Antongiulio Brignolle-Salle's *Maria Maddalena, peccatrice e convertita*, Bologna, 1677, is in the same vein.

161. See Robert A. Koch, 'La Sainte-Baume in Flemish Landscape Painting of the Sixteenth Century', *Gazette des Beaux-Arts*, vol. LXVI, 1965, pp. 273–82. See also Myra Dickman Orth, 'The Magdalen shrine of La Ste-Baume in 1516.

A series of miniatures by Godefroy La Batave (BN Ms fr. 24.955)', *Gazette des Beaux-Arts*, ser. 6, tome 98 (1981), pp. 201–14. Her reliance on Faillon's claim that a sculpture of Mary Magdalen had been in the grotto since the fifth century should however be treated with caution (p. 210, n. 3). Martha Mel Edmunds' suggestion ('La Sainte-Baume and the Iconography of Mary Magdalene', *Gazette des Beaux-Arts*, ser. 6, tome 114, 1989, pp. 11–28) that Byzantine nativity scenes showing the Virgin Mary lying on a mat or on the ground may have been the prototype (p. 22) is more persuasive.

162. I am grateful to Nicholas Pickwoad for giving me this engraving.

163. Faillon, op. cit., vol. I, cols 1064–5; Jennifer Montagu, *Alessandro Algardi*, London and New Haven, 1985, cat. no. 94, pp. 389–90. Algardi (1598–1654) was from Bologna. His work combines the classicism of his training with his rival Bernini's more extrovert style, witness his stucco statue of Mary Magdalen (c.1628), in the Cappella Bandini in S. Silvestro al Quirinale, Rome, which is paired with that of John the Evangelist (Montagu, cat. nos 57, 58 and pl. 10). My thanks to Professor Richard Spear for pointing out Faillon's mistaken claim that Urban VIII had visited the grotto.

CHAPTER VIII

1. This proverb appears on the engraving by Arnold de Jode after a painting of Mary Magdalen by Sir Anthony van Dyck (Hollstein 3, first state). I am grateful to Jan Johnson for bringing this image to my attention.

2. See Françoise Bardon, 'Le Thème de la Madeleine pénitente au XVIIième siècle en France', *Journal of the Warburg and Courtauld Institutes*, vol. XXXI, 1968, pp. 274–306.

3. Lucretia and Mary Magdalen had often been associated in painting from the sixteenth century. See Susan Foister, 'Paintings and other works of art in sixteenth-century English Inventories', *Burlington Magazine*, vol. CXXIII, 938, 1981, pp. 273–82. Pictures of Mary Magdalen were not found in English inventories until the second quarter of the sixteenth century. The inventory of Richard Fermour of 1540 shows that he had in his parlour a Lucretia, together with a 'table of Mary Magdalen'; Sir John Cope (1558) also had such a pair (p. 277). It would seem that in such a pairing the religious element of Mary Magdalen's image would not have been the most important aspect in the choice of subject-matter; the pair would more likely have been chosen as pictures of attractive women.

4. Formerly believed to be a portrait of Isabella of Austria, Charles V's sister, the portrait of Isabella of Portugal (Musée royal des Beaux-Arts, Brussels) was painted by an anonymous artist in the circle of Vermeyen or Gossaert in c. 1530. Jan Gossaert's (1478–1532) painting of Louise de Brabant as Mary Magdalen is in Antwerp, Mayer Museum. Contemporary with these were the half-length paintings showing Mary Magdalen reading and playing the lute, painted by artists such as Ambrosius Benson, Adriaan Isenbrandt and anonymous Flemish artists like the Master of the Magdalen Legend and Master of the Female Half-lengths which

became a 'pseudo-genre' in the 1520s. Mary Magdalen appears in architectural settings, not in her grotto, reading her psalter or prayer book at precisely the time when women of the period were exhorted in contemporary treatises on female comportment and education to do just that, and in Juan Luis Vives' *De istitutione foeminae christianiae* (1523), Mary Magdalen was presented as a model – in the guise of Mary of Bethany, the symbol of the contemplative life – of perfect womanhood: one who read the holy Gospels, the Acts, the Old Testament, Sts Jerome and Augustine, a little Latin for her comportment and no French romances, as these led her astray. These paintings were hung in private chambers, and were contemporary with, and from similar workshops as the more famous image of well-dressed young women playing music by the Master of the Female Half-lengths. See H. Colin Slim, 'Music and Dancing with Mary Magdalen in a Laura Vestalis', in *The Crannied Wall*, ed. Craig A. Monson, Ann Arbor, Mich., 1992, pp. 139–60; and Slim, 'Paintings of Lady Concerts and the Transmission of Jouyssance vous donneray', *Imago Musicae*, I, 1984, pp. 54–8. See my article, 'Political cypher and pietistical pawn: Mary Magdalen and the Burgundian Question', forthcoming, which discusses these half-lengths and their relationship to contemporary books on female behaviour.

5. These paintings are illustrated in *La Maddalena*, fig. 6, p. 71, cat. nos 14 and 17, pp. 74 and 77.

6. Hugo van der Goes, Portinari Altarpiece (1475–6), Florence, Uffizi. Mary Magdalen's companion is St Margaret, the name saint of Maria Maddalena's daughter, Margaret. Tommaso Portinari is flanked by Saints Thomas and Anthony (one of his sons was named Antonio). Maria Maddalena Baroncelli's (b. 1456) portrait by Memling is in New York, Metropolitan Museum of Art, 14.40.627.

7. Lucas Cranach's portrait of Magdalena Reidinger as Mary Magdalen is in Cologne, Wallraf-Richartz Museum.

8. Archduchess Maria Magdalena of Austria married Cosimo II, grand duke of Tuscany, in 1608; she died in 1631. See also Chapter Seven, p. 258.

9. The frescoes of scenes from Mary Magdalen's *vita* at Poggio Imperiale were painted by Francesco Curradi (1570–1661). See article 'La cappella della Maddalena nella villa di Poggio Imperiale a Firenze', by Marilena Mosco, in *La Maddalena*, pp. 237–9. Frescoes of scenes from Mary Magdalen's *vita* also appear in another chapel dedicated to her in Florence, in the Palazzo Salviati, in the Corso di San Piero. Executed by Alessandro Allori for Jacopo Salviati between 1578 and 1580, the scenes show her as Luke's sinner, as Mary of Bethany, taking communion, and being lifted to heaven.

10. Girolamo Frescobaldi (1583–1643) was the most important keyboard composer of the first half of the seventeenth century. He seems to have had an affection for the name Magdalen. In February 1613 he married Orsola del Pino, and on 22 July, the Magdalen's feast-day, his daughter was born, receiving the name Maddalena on 28 July. Frederick Hammond, *Girolamo Frescobaldi. A Guide to*

Research, New York and London, 1988, p. 21. In 1621 the Compagnia di S. Antonio performed a play in five acts, *Santa Maria Maddalena* by Jacopo Cicognini, repeating it five times(Angelo Solerti, *Musica, ballo e drammatica alla Corte Medicea dal 1600 al 1637*, Florence, 1905, p. 157). During Holy Week and the feast of the Annunciation, musical sacred performances were enacted in the archduchess's chapel: in 1629, a *Festa di S. Maria Maddalena* by Francesco Bracciolini (1566–1645) was thus performed (Solerti, op. cit., p. 195). I am grateful to Christopher Hogwood for referring me to Professor Hammond's work.

11. Sir Peter Lely, portrait of Louise de Kéroualle as Mary Magdalen (Sotheby's, London, 29 April 1937).

12. Sir Godfrey Kneller, *Portrait of Catherine Voss as Mary Magdalen*, mezzotint engraved by John Smith, 1705 (author's collection). Kneller referred to Titian's *Magdalen* in his seated portrait of Elizabeth Villiers, countess of Orkney (J. Douglas Stewart, *Sir Godfrey Kneller and the English Baroque Portrait*, Oxford, 1983, p. 46, pls. 40a and 40c). See also Ellen G. D'Oench, 'Prodigal Sons and Fair Penitents. Transformations in Eighteenth-Century Popular Prints', *Art History*, vol. XIII, no. 3, 1990, p. 71, and note 55.

13. Michael Dahl, *Portrait of Lady Anne Sussex as Mary Magdalen*, Horsford Manor, Sir R. Barrett Lermard. Dahl's painting of *A Magdalen* is in York City Gallery, no. 852 (*Catalogue of Paintings*, vol. II, *English School 1500–1850*, City of York Art Gallery, 1963, p. 10).

14. Pierre Mignard, *Portrait of Hortense Mancini, duchesse de Mazarin as Mary Magdalen* (Trustees of the Earl of Sandwich's 1943 Settlement).

15. Pierre Mignard, *Portrait of Louise de la Vallière as Mary Magdalen*; Bardon, op. cit., p. 302, and note 107. A miniature of Louise de la Vallière by Mignard, possibly a copy, is in the collection of the Duke of Buccleuch and Queensberry, KT, GCVO, Boughton House, Northamptonshire. The quote from her *Réflections* is in Bardon, op. cit., p. 302.

16. ibid., p. 302.

17. ibid., p. 303.

18. Her portrait as Mary Magdalen is in the Hospice d'Oiron, ibid., p. 303. Gabrielle de Rochechouart de Mortemart's is in the church of Montreuil-Bellay, and Isabelle de Ludre's (attributed to Mignard) is in the Musée, Epinal.

19. Nattier's portrait of Mme de Mailly is in the Louvre, Paris.

20. See Frank Cossa, 'John Evelyn as Penitent Magdalen: "Saints" and "Malcontents" in Seventeenth-Century English Portraiture', *Rutgers Art Review*, vol. I, January 1980, pp. 37–48. Thomas Hudson's *Penitent Magdalen* is thought to be a portrait of the duchess of Marlborough (p. 44, note 31). I am grateful to Ellen D'Oench for sending me this article.

21. Simon Vouet's portrait of his wife Virginia is in the Los Angeles County Museum, and is illustrated in *La Maddalena*, fig. I, p. 231.

22. George Romney, *Portrait of Lady Hamilton as a Magdalen* (Herbert sale, Christie's, 28 July, 1939, no. 9).

23. See Cossa, op. cit. The portrait is on loan to the National Portrait Gallery, London.

24. Quoted in Francis Haskell, *Patrons and Painters*, London, 1963, p. 177.

25. Charles I's painting is believed to be the one formerly in the Elgin and Kincardine collection, and is now in the collection of Richard L. Feigen, New York. The figure was previously endowed with a blouse, probably added for reasons of prudery in the nineteenth century. I am extremely grateful to Mr Feigen for allowing me to see the painting. See R. Ward Bissell, *Orazio Gentileschi and the Poetic Tradition in Caravaggesque Painting*, University Park and London, 1981, cat. no. 55, pp. 181–2, where it is suggested that the painting was executed in Paris, but for whom is not known.

26. Sauli's painting is now in London in the collection of Mrs Thomas P. Grange. See Bissell, op. cit., cat. no. 46 and pl. 97.

27. This is illustrated in Bissell, op. cit., cat. no. 56 and pl. 117, and is in the Vienna Kunsthistorisches Museum.

28. Lothar Franz von Schonborn, letter of 10 October 1708, quoted in Haskell, op. cit., p. 195. Peter von Strudel (1660–1714) was court painter at Vienna in 1689 and the most eminent baroque painter there. A painting of Susanna by Strudel was recorded at Dresden.

29. Another version is in the Palazzo Pitti, Florence. His *Conversion of Mary Magdalen* of *c*.1660 (Pasadena, Norton Simon Art Foundation) shows the Magdalen lying on the ground, naked except for a flimsy loin cloth, in the pose of Correggio's *Magdalen*, her clothes, jewels, a broken strand of pearls, and a very smart pair of brocade shoes beside her, Martha scolding her, her maids weeping, and an angel chasing off the devil from her bed. See Pier Giorgio Pasini, *Guido Cagnacci: Pittore 1601–1663*, trs. Isabella Vichi, Rimini, 1986.

30. Cecil Gould, *The Paintings of Correggio*, London, 1976, pp. 279–80.

31. ibid., p. 93.

32. Denis Diderot, *Salons*, 1763, ed. J. Seznec and J. Adhémar, Oxford, 1957, vol. I, p. 215, quoted in D'Oench, op. cit., pp. 73 and 84, note 66.

33. Diderot, 'la Magdeleine . . . si voluptueusement étendue à terre dans sa caverne par le Corrège' (III, p. 314). Quoted in D'Oench, op. cit, p. 84, note 66.

34. Quoted in A. M. Clark, *Pompeo Batoni*, Oxford, 1985, cat. no. 60, p. 227.

35. ibid., pp. 226–7.

36. See Monika Ingenhoff-Danhäuser, *Maria Magdalena: Heilige und Sünderin in der italienischen Renaissance*, Tübingen, 1984, p. 119, note 10. I am grateful to James Layte for providing me with the information about the plaques with erotic subjects. An example on the market in 1990 fetched £2,000. Oddly enough, the erotic content of Batoni's painting seems to have escaped the notice of Harriet Beecher Stowe (1811–96), author of *Uncle Tom's Cabin*, when she came to write her *Women in Sacred History* (1873). In her essay on Mary Magdalen, she described it as 'one of the most splendid ornaments of the Dresden gallery'. Other artists had chosen to depict the saint's physicality rather than penitence, such as Titian, who seems to 'have felt . . . nothing but the beauty of the woman's hair . . . clothing a very common-place weeping woman'; Correggio's Magdalen

was 'a fat, pretty, comfortable little body lying . . . reading'; but Batoni's is a 'creature so calm, so high, so pure, that we ask voluntarily, How could such a woman ever have fallen? The answer is ready. There is a class of woman who fall through what is highest in them . . . utter self-sacrificing love.' Mrs Stowe was aware of the lack of consensus over Mary Magdalen's identity, but nevertheless adhered to the composite figure and saw the story as 'symbolic of what is too often seen in the fall of woman', a 'noble and beautiful nature wrecked' through deception and betrayal (New York, 1990 edn, pp. 207 and 211, and illus. facing p. 212). I am extremely grateful to JoAnne Robertson and Jeannie Farr for giving me this book.

37. *Horace Walpole's Correspondence with George Montague*, ed. W. S. Lewis and R. S. Brown, Jr, New Haven, 1941, vol. 1, p. 335 (letter dated 21 January 1761), quoted in D'Oench, op. cit., pp. 76 and 84, note 74. Rowe's tragedy of 1714 was based on the life of Jane Shore, who left her husband to become the mistress of Edward IV. She was made to do public penance for her adultery; in his play, Rowe gave her a long drawn-out and affecting death scene. See D'Oench, p. 84, note 75.

38. Karsten Harries, *The Bavarian Rococo Church. Between Faith and Aestheticism*, New Haven and London, 1983, pp. 172–4; my thanks to Celia Jones and Malcolm Wilson for bringing the grotto to my attention.

39. Jonas Hanway, *The Rules, Orders and Regulations of the Magdalen House for the reception of Penitent Prostitutes*, London, 1760, p. 4.

40. ibid., p. 5.

41. Eric Trudgill, *Madonnas and Magdalens. The Origin and Development of Victorian Sexual Attitudes*, London, 1976, p. 277.

42. Jonas Hanway, *Thoughts on the Plan for a Magdalen-house for Repentant Prostitutes*, 2nd ed., London, 1759, p. 23.

43. Jonas Hanway, quoted in Revd S. B. P. Pearce, *An Ideal for the Working – The Story of the Magdalen Hospital 1758–1958*, London, 1958, p. 21.

44. Walpole, quoted in Pearce, op. cit., p. 24.

45. *A Second Collection of Psalms and Hymns Used at the Magdalen Chapel*, London, n.d. I am grateful to Nicholas Pickwoad for this reference.

46. Quoted in Pearce, op. cit., p. 22.

47. ibid., p. 24.

48. ibid., p. 48.

49. *Horace Walpole's Correspondence with George Montague*, vol. I, pp. 273–4, quoted in D'Oench, op. cit., pp. 81 and 84, note 81.

50. Pearce, op. cit., p. 50. Prostitutes with venereal diseases were accommodated in lock hospitals (from the word 'loke', or house of lepers), the first of which was established in London in 1746 (Linda Mahood, *The Magdalenes: Prostitution in the Nineteenth Century*, London and New York, 1990, p. 30).

51. Edward Jerningham, *The Magdalens: an Elegy, by the author of the Nunnery*, 2nd edn, London, 1763, stanzas i, ii and v.

52. Martin Madan, *The Magdalen: or Dying Penitent: exemplified in the Death of F.S., who died April, 1763, aged twenty-six years*, Dublin, 1789.

53. *Laetitia*, London, 1789, published by J. R. Smith after paintings by George Morland. Lawrence Stone, *The Family, Sex and Marriage in*

England 1500–1800, Harmondsworth, 1979, pp. 391 and 404. Francis Place (1771–1854) was a friend of J. S. Mill and Jeremy Bentham; 'Place's Law' is referred to in Stone, op. cit., p. 392.

CHAPTER IX

1. *The Magdalen's Friend and Female Homes Intelligencer*, vol. II, 1861, p. 134.
2. ibid., vol. I, 1860, p. 33.
3. *Magdalena* was also the title of a Dutch Evangelical periodical of the 1850s and 1860s; its title-page bore an engraving of *Mary Magdalen at the Foot of the Cross* by Ary Scheffer, and the 1861 volume carried a translation of Victor Hugo's *Chants du Crépuscule* (XIV) with the quote, 'Oh! n'insultez jamais une femme qui tombe.'
4. I am grateful to Christopher Lloyd for referring me to this study.
5. See last chapter (p. 311).
6. Michel Foucault, *The History of Sexuality. An Introduction*, trs. Robert Hurley, Harmondsworth, 1981, vol. I, p. 34.
7. ibid., p. 23.
8. John Ruskin, *Sesame and Lilies*, London and Glasgow, n.d., p. 18. Much the same sentiments are to be found in Samuel Smiles' *Self-Help* (London, 1859), where home is seen as the foundation of morality and society: 'The Home is the crystal of society – the very nucleus of national character; and from that source, be it pure or tainted, issue the habits, principles, maxims, which govern public as well as private life. The nation comes from the nursery; public opinion itself is for the most part the outgrowth of the home' (p. 294). The phrase 'Angel in the

House', now much better known than the poem whence it derived – Coventry Patmore's eulogy on womanhood – was inspired by his great love for his wife Emily Andrews (1824–62). Some women, however, declined the honour of being angels as, for example, Maria Deraismes who noted: 'Of all woman's enemies, I tell you the worst are those who insist that a woman is an angel.' Quoted in *Victorian Women. A Documentary Account of Women's Lives in Nineteenth-Century England, France, and the United States*, ed. Erna Olafson Hellerstein, Leslie Parker Hume, and Karen M. Offen, Brighton, 1981, p. 140.

9. William Acton, *Functions and Disorders of the Reproductive Organs in Youth, in Adult Age, and in Advanced Life*, 4th edn, London, 1865, p. 114.
10. Clara Lucas Balfour, *The Bible Pattern of a Good Woman*, London, 1867, p. 10. 'My reader may say, "Why is society so severe on women who are not virtuous?" For this reason – on female chastity the purity and legitimacy of families must depend. No homes can be pure and truthful – no notion can be good or great – if the laws of chastity are not rigidly observed by wives, and by all women, and any violation must be sternly dealt with. Much heavier on woman than on man fall both the natural and social. This, perhaps, cannot be avoided in human laws. But a righteous God, who knows the limits of human power, will not let those go unpunished who escape earthly justice . . . Chastity is like truth itself, the basis of all the virtues in the female character, but it is not a substitute for all the others.' A

teetotaller, Mrs Balfour (1808–78) took the pledge at the Bible Christians' Chapel and became a temperance lecturer. Elected president of the British Women's Temperance League the year before her death, she had lectured on the influence of women in society. Among her many writings were the *Wanderings of a Bible* (1862), *Bible Patterns of Good Women* (1867), and *Whisper to the Newly Married* (1850), the last of which proved so popular that it ran to twenty-three editions.

11. George Henry Lewes, in *The Edinburgh Review*, January 1850, vol. XCI, p. 155.

12. *A Regency Visitor: The English Tour of Prince Pückler-Muskau*, ed. E. M. Butler, London, 1957, p. 84. I am grateful to Nicholas Pickwoad for this reference.

13. E. W. Thomas, 'The Great Social Evil: a Natural Question', *The Magdalen's Friend*, etc., vol. III, 1862, p. 13.

14. W. R. Greg, 'Prostitution', *The Westminster Review*, vol. LIII, 1850, pp. 451–2 and 471.

15. See Hellerstein, Hume and Offen, eds, op. cit., p. 422–3.

16. Ruskin, op. cit., p. 117.

17. ibid., pp. 155–6.

18. See Chapter Seven, p. 242.

19. See F. K. Prochaska's excellent study, *Women and Philanthropy in Nineteenth-Century England*, Oxford, 1980.

20. Mrs Emma Sheppard, *An Out-stretched Hand to the Fallen*, London, 1860, p. 60, quoted in Prochaska, op. cit., p. 186, and note 21.

21. 'Charity in Women', *The Magdalen's Friend*, etc., vol. II, 1862, p. 173.

22. 'The Accepted Penitent', sermon preached before the Church Penitent Association by the Revd H. Drury, published in *The Magdalen's Friend*, etc., vol. III, 1862, pp. 159–60.

23. From 'Charity in Women', op. cit., p. 174.

24. John Angell James, *Female Piety: or the Young Woman's Friend and Guide through Life to Immortality*, London, 1852, p. 12. James (1785–1859) was an Evangelical nonconformist minister in Birmingham, and one of the leading projectors of the Evangelical Alliance which was set up in London in 1846 to 'concentrate the strength of an enlightened Protestantism against the encroachments of Popery and Puseyism, and to promote the interests of Scriptural Christianity'.

25. ibid., p. 17.

26. ibid., p. 18.

27. Dom Augustin Calmet, 'Dissertation sur les trois Maries', in *La Sainte Bible en latin et en français, avec des notes littérales, critiques et historiques*, etc., vol. XIII, Paris, 1773, p. 345.

28. *And She was called Magdalen. The Life of St Mary Magdalen, as revealed in the visions of the most outstanding stigmatist-mystic of the last century, Anna Katherina Emmerich*, ed. Robert Emmett Curtis, New York, 1962, p. 14.

29. E.-M. Faillon, *Monuments inédits sur l'Apostolat de Sainte Marie-Madeleine en Provence*, Paris, 2 vols, 1865, vol. I, cols 1148–60.

30. Réau, vol. III, 2, pp. 848 and 858.

31. Faillon, op. cit., vol. I, cols 1125–6 and 1142–4.

32. As was H. D. Lacordaire's *Sainte Marie Madeleine* (Marseille, 1984), first published in 1859, a poetical account of the saint and her cult at Ste Baume.

33. J. A. Farrer, *Literary Forgeries*, London, 1907, p. 211. My thanks to Nicolas Barker for referring me to this work.

34. Louis Duchesne, *Les Fastes épiscopaux de l'ancienne Gaule*, Paris, 1894; 2nd ed., 1907–15.

35. His book was translated as *The Life of Christ, Critically Examined*, 3 vols, London, 1846.

36. ibid., vol. III, p. 314.

37. Ernest Renan, *The Life of Jesus*, Book I of *The History of the Origins of Christianity*, London, 1889, p. 249. Renan in fact became director of the Collège de France in 1879.

38. *Les Apôtres*, Paris, 1866, p. 13.

39. Ernest Renan, *The Apostles*, New York, n.d., p. 49, quoted in William E. Phipps, *The Sexuality of Jesus. Theological and literary perspectives*, New York, 1973, p. 65.

40. John Angell James, op. cit., p. 44.

41. ibid., p. 45.

42. Clara Lucas Balfour, *The Women of Scripture*, London, 1847, pp. 320–1, 322–3 and 329–30.

43. ibid., p. 329.

44. Peter Gay, *The Bourgeois Experience. Victoria to Freud*, 2 vols, Oxford, 1986, vol. II, p. 374.

45. The Magdalen Society of New York was founded in 1830 to provide 'An Asylum for Females who have deviated from the paths of virtue, and are desirous of being restored to the respectable station in society by religious instruction and the formation of moral and industrial habits.' Gay, op. cit., vol. II, pp. 374–6. On 29 August 1868 Mr John Allen closed down his dance-house in New York, having been converted by a famous campaigning gentleman, the Revd Mr Arnold. A notice nailed to the door read: 'This dance-house is closed. No gentlemen admitted unless accompanied by their wives, who wish to employ Magdalens as servants.' Quoted in Herbert Asberry, *The Gangs of New York.*

An Informal History of the Underworld, New York and London, 1928, p. 58. My thanks to Nicholas Pickwoad for giving me this reference.

46. Prochaska, op. cit., pp. 189–90. There was also a Jewish Ladies Society for Preventive and Rescue Work, 1886. The Magdalena Centre in Seoul, S. Korea, gives counselling to thousands of prostitutes, helping those exploited by 'sexual tourism' in the Third World to make new lives. Alison Whyte, 'Korean losers in the world's oldest game', *Independent*, 26 September 1988. My thanks to Nicholas Pickwoad for this reference.

47. Samuel Warren, *Passages from the Diary of a late Physician*, 3 vols, London, 1838, vol. III. Warren (1807–77) studied medicine before taking up the law and then becoming a writer. *Passages from the Diary*, etc., was one of twenty-eight short stories which were published in *Blackwood's Magazine* between 1830 and 1837, and was enormously popular, going through several editions. It was also translated.

48. Frances Arnold-Forster, *Studies in Church Dedications, or England's Patron Saints*, 3 vols, London, 1899, vol. I, p. 91.

49. In 1846, A. B. Richards' poem 'Death and the Magdalen' was published in London in a volume of the same title. It concerned the demise of a fallen young woman: ''Twas her heart betray'd her,/ Her sad life hath paid her/ Foul impurities;/ Hot and bitter tears,/ Cold and ghastly fears,/ Ere, alone, she dies!/ God will never judge her./ As her fellow sinners here below,/ Though they wrought her woe:/ Seraphs will not grudge her/ Room mid

serried rank and shining row:/ Thither she will go!' (p. 11). In 1854 Mrs Oliphant's *Magdalen Hepburn: a Story of the Scottish Reformation* was issued; in 1857 *Magdalen Stafford: or a Gleam of Sunshine on a Rainy Day* (anon.) was published, as was Charles Miller's *Magdalen Nisbet.* Caroline Mary Smith's *Magdalen Havering* (1861; the pages of the British Library copy are still uncut) followed, as did, in 1872, Averil Beaumont's *Magdalen Wynyard.* *Madeleine* is also the title of the autobiography of a seduced middle-class girl in America who bore a child and became a prostitute rather than enter a reformatory. The book was published in 1919 with an introduction by Judge Ben B. Lindsey of the Juvenile Court of Denver, which included the poignant reminder to its readers: '. . . I have an intense appreciation of *Madeleine.* It ought to be read and pondered over. It is *true.* The Madeleines are right in your midst' (p. ii).

50. William Makepeace Thackeray, *The History of Henry Esmond*, 3 vols, London, 1852, Book II, chap. xiii. As a young girl in Brussels, Gertrude Maes is seduced by Captain Esmond, later Viscount Castlewood. He marries her just before Henry's birth, and later deserts her, leading her to believe that he has previously married. I am grateful to Nicholas Pickwoad for this reference.

51. William Wilkie Collins, *No Name*, in *The Works of Wilkie Collins*, New York, n.d. In Chapter I, having just described Magdalen's lively and wayward character, expressed in her vivacious appearance, the extraordinary mobility of her face, her being taller than average, and with a 'seductive, serpentine sinuousness' complemented by her 'brilliantly-striped morning dress, . . . her fluttering ribbons, . . . the large scarlet rosettes on her smart little shoes', and her lack of 'a sense of order', Collins then goes on to remark on the strangeness of her name: 'Surely, the grand old Bible name – suggestive of a sad and sombre dignity; recalling, in its first association, mournful ideas of penitence and seclusion – had been here, as events had turned out, inappropriately bestowed? Surely this self-contradictory girl had perversely accomplished one contradiction more, by developing into a character which was out of all harmony with her own christian name?' See Jenny Bourne Taylor, *In the Secret Theatre of Home: Wilkie Collins, sensation narrative, and nineteenth-century psychology*, London and New York, 1988, on the use of names, and importance of physiognomy and phrenology in the creation of Collins' characters.

52. The medieval tradition of naming illegitimate daughters Magdalen is referred to in Chapter Five, note 13, p. 427. Norah regains the family fortunes by marrying the cousin who inherits from Noel Vanstone, thereby regaining her name and position. See introduction by Virginia Blain to the World's Classics Edition of *No Name*, Oxford and New York, 1986, pp. vii–xxi.

53. William Wilkie Collins, *The New Magdalen*, London, 1883, p. 342.

54. ibid., pp. 14 and 15. *The New Magdalen* has an unsatisfactory ending, however, as Mercy Merrick and her Evangelical minister have to live abroad because of her tainted past, and

society's affront because of it.

55. *Madeleine Férat* was first written as a play, but not accepted. It was produced several years later at the Théâtre Libre in Paris, which put on plays bringing a slice of life to the theatre.

56. Georg Büchner, *Woyzeck*, in *Complete Plays and Prose*, trs. and introd. Carl Richard Mueller, New York, 1963, pp. 131–2. Alban Berg's *Wozzeck* was first produced in 1921.

57. Fromentin's novel concerns the passion of a young man for an older married woman. It was dedicated to George Sand. In correspondence of 1844, the author had promised the Creole wife of a stockbroker of La Rochelle, where he was born, to write the story of their love. Their passion, whilst spoken of, was, as in the novel, never consummated. Hebbel's play had a recent, very successful short run in London at the Gate Theatre (April–May 1990), where the nineteenth-century setting was imaginatively transformed into Fifties' Bible Belt America. My thanks to Stuart Proffitt, who informed me of the production.

58. Almeida Garrett's play was performed in 1991 at the Lilian Baylis Theatre in London.

59. Of the 91 images of the non-biblical Magdalen, 25 had such titles as 'sleeping' or 'reading Magdalen'; the rest were entitled 'A Magdalen', and not otherwise distinguished. 12 images were of Mary and Martha of Bethany. These figures were drawn from Liesbeth Heenk's 'The Iconographical Development of the Type of the Contemporary Fallen Woman in Nineteenth-Century English Art', unpublished M.A. thesis, University of Leiden,

1988. My thanks to Liesbeth Heenk for making her research available to me.

60. Vittorio Malamani, *Canova*, Milan, 1911, pp. 80–2. The sculpture was originally made for a Venetian patrician, a Monsignore Priuli, and was bought in Rome after his death by M. Juliot, a minister of the former Cisalpine Republic, who sold it to Sommariva. Stendhal is quoted in David Wakefield's *Stendhal: The Promise of Happiness*, Bedford, 1984, p. 155. My thanks to David Wakefield for a copy of his book. Eugène Beauharnais' version is in the Hermitage, St Petersburg. Canova also executed a *Fainting Magdalen*, now lost. In his own funeral monument, a *Pietà* cast in bronze after his death in 1822, the figure of Mary Magdalen is eloquently draped against that of Christ, which is in turn supported by the Virgin. It is in the Temple at Possagno in the Veneto.

61. Kenneth Clark, *The Nude*, Harmondsworth, 1976, p. 152.

62. C. Melnotte, 'La Maddalena nell'arte del XIX secolo', in *La Maddalena*, p. 241. See cat. no. 79 of the same catalogue for Hayez.

63. Henri Triqueti (1807–74). The sculpture is now in the Museo Civico Medievale e Moderno in Modena.

64. This is illustrated in *La Maddalena*, cat. no. 81, pp. 207–8.

65. See Lynda Nead, *Myths of Sexuality. Representations of Women in Victorian Britain*, Oxford, 1988, p. 69.

66. Melnotte, op. cit., p. 242.

67. *The Athenæum*, 1844, p. 157, quoted in Heenk, op. cit., Appendix, p. 13.

68. Nead, op. cit., p. 69.

69. Quoted in William Gaunt and F. Gordon Roe, *Etty and the Nude:*

The Art and Life of William Etty, RA, 1787–1849, Leigh-on-Sea, 1943, p. 17.

70. ibid., p. 22; Thackeray's appreciation is to be found in 'May Gambols; or Titmarsh in the Picture Galleries', *Fraser's Magazine*, June, 1844, reprinted in W. M. Thackeray, *Critical Papers in Art*, London, 1904, p. 218. My thanks to Nicholas Pickwoad for this reference.

71. From *Blackwood's Edinburgh Magazine*, vol. LII, July-December 1842, p. 27, quoted in Heenk, op. cit., Catalogue, p. 2. The painting went to the National Gallery, London, no. 365, then to the Tate Gallery, and was then lent to Stockport.

72. Lefèbvre's painting is illustrated in *La Maddalena*, cat. no. 126. p. 278.

73. Quoted in Heather Dawkins, 'The Diaries and Photographs of Hannah Cullwick', *Art History*, vol. X, no. 2, June 1987, pp. 180–1. I am grateful to David McKitterick for sending me a copy of this article.

74. Quoted in Dawkins, op. cit.

75. *The Pre-Raphaelites*, London, Tate Gallery, 1984, cat. no. 5, p. 1, illus. p. 51.

76. The subtitle of Averil Beaumont's novel *Magdalen Wynyard* (1872). 'The Provocations of a Pre-Raphaelite', underscores the perceived connection between the dangerously sexuate, liberated woman of Pre-Raphaelite paintings and the name Magdalen.

77. The drawing is in pen and Indian ink. Quoted in Virginia Surtees, *The Paintings and Drawings of Dante Gabriel Rossetti (1828–1882): a catalogue raisonné*, Oxford, 1971, cat. no. 109: *Mary Magdalene at the door of Simon the Pharisee*, p. 62. Rossetti also did a watercolour, *Mary Magdalene leaving the House of Feasting*, in 1857, which is now in the Tate Gallery, London.

78. The letter is quoted in Surtees, op. cit., p. 62; see also cat. no. 109N, p. 65.

79. Letter to W. Bell Scott, quoted in Surtees, op. cit., cat. no. 109J, p. 64.

80. Burne-Jones also designed a *Noli me tangere* (1877) for the windows of St Michael's Easthampstead, Berks., and a *Feast in the House of the Pharisee* at Allerton, Leeds (1885), and another for St Ladoca, Ladock, Cornwall (1863).

81. Thomas Hall Caine, *Recollections of Rossetti*, London, 1928, p. 221.

82. See Linda Nochlin's essay, 'Lost and Found: Once More the Fallen Woman', *Art Bulletin*, 60, March 1978, pp. 139–53, reprinted in *Feminism and Art History. Questioning the Litany*, ed. Norma Broude and Mary D. Garrard, New York, 1982, pp. 221–45, where she also suggests that Hunt may have used the figure of Charles Le Brun's *Repentant Magdalene renouncing All the Vanities of the World* (Paris, Louvre) 'for the relatively rare motif of upward mobility on the part of the fallen woman' (p. 232). The broken-winged bird, momentarily escaped from the tortures of the cat, mirrors the girl's position as victim if she does not herself escape from her cage. It was clearly a warning to young women not to stray from the virtuous path to which they had been assigned. Hunt's painting was criticised for its lack of signs of domesticity: the girl's surroundings were new, vulgar and flashy. To Ruskin there was 'nothing there that has the old thoughts of home upon it, or that is ever to become a part of home' (letter to *The Times*, 25 May 1854). Quoted in

Lynn Nead, 'The Magdalen in Modern Times: The Mythology of the Fallen Woman in Pre-Raphaelite Painting', *Oxford Art Journal*, 1984, vol. VII, no. 1, pp. 26–37. The following words are painted on the frame: 'As he that taketh away a garment in cold weather/ so is he that singeth songs to an heavy heart.' An ornate middle-class 'boudoir' book lies on the table beside the gentleman's top hat and cane, and a music sheet with the words 'Tennyson', *Lear* and '. . . *Tears*', alluding to the girl's future. Further signs of disorder are the unfinished tapestry and skeins of silk on the floor, and the time on the clock shown as five minutes to twelve midday.

83. Arnold-Forster, op. cit., p. 93.

84. A guild of St Mary Magdalen existed in the fifteenth century at the church at Pulham Market. A white English wine called Magdalen, made from the Rivaner grape, comes from Pulham St Mary. Holiday's figure was first used in a window made in 1880 for Salisbury Cathedral, where she represents Mary of Bethany. There are nine known uses of the figure, sometimes as Mary Magdalen, sometimes Mary of Bethany. I am extremely grateful to the Revd J. R. M. Cossar for sending me information about the window, and for permission to reproduce my photograph. An unusual scene of Mary Magdalen as Luke's sinner, surrounded by her friends and drinking, appears in the predella of a stained-glass window in the church of Mary Magdalen at Rodborough, Glos., executed in 1909.

85. In Goethe's *Faust* (1808 and 1832), Mary Magdalen becomes Magna Peccatrix, appearing in the final scene with Maria Aegyptica and Mulier Samaritana, a trio symbolising the Eternal Feminine, sinful and redeemed, counterparts to the Virgin on the one hand and, on the other, to Gretchen's earthly fragility. Mahler set the last scene of *Faust* in the second half of his Symphony in E Flat (1907), a hymn to the redemptive power of love.

86. Gérard de Nerval, *Journey to the Orient*, selected, trs. and introd. Norman Glass, London, 1984, p. 48.

87. 'Magdalena' in 'Poésies Diverses 1833–1838', in *Oeuvres de Théophile Gautier: Poésies*, Paris, 1890, pp. 306–13. Gautier (1811–72) was a friend of Nerval, and much influenced by both the latter and Flaubert in his pursuit of the Orient, part of his aesthetic quest, 'l'art pour l'art'. A painting of the crucifixion with Mary Magdalen, St John the Evangelist and the Virgin, by a sixteenth-century follower of Holbein, seen in 'une vieille église', apparently triggers off this 'Romantic' vision of the Magdalen, set in Gothic surroundings, so enthusing the poet that he self-deprecatingly described his enthusiasm as his 'maladie gothique'. He was an arch-exponent of the Romantic ideal of feminine beauty, and one of the creators of the *femme fatale*, who was carried to her extremes by writers and poets such as Swinburne, Baudelaire, Beardsley and Oscar Wilde.

88. In *Die Frau ohne Schatten* (1919), Richard Strauss's opera of transformation and reconciliation, the repentance formula/image of Mary Magdalen as Luke's sinner at the feet of Christ can be seen when the Empress, who can only receive her shadow, taking on her

human form through her repentance, prostrates herself at the feet of the gentle and saintly Barak the Dyer ('Baraka' means saintliness among the Berbers) who, in his transcendence through suffering, can be seen as a Christ-figure. Programme note, Richard Blackford, Royal Opera House programme, 14 July 1987.

89. Article 'Jules Massenet' in *The New Grove Dictionary of Music and Musicians*, ed. Stanley Sadie, London, 1980, vol. 11, p. 801.

90. Article 'Vincent D'Indy', in ibid., vol. 9, p. 223.

91. Giacomo Puccini, *Tosca*, Act I.

92. Richard Wagner, *Parsifal*. See Lucy Beckett, *Richard Wagner. Parsifal*, Cambridge, 1981, pp. 9ff, where it is suggested that Wagner's portrayal of Kundry was influenced by a scenario for a play called *Jesus of Nazareth*, which Wagner had worked on in 1848; and Northrop Frye, *Myth and Metaphor. Selected Essays, 1974–1988*, ed. Robert D. Denham, Charlottesville and London, 1990, pp. 340ff.

93. *New York Herald Tribune*, 19 October 1988. I am very grateful to Bill Underwood for sending me this reference.

94. See *Post-Impressionism: Cross Currents in European Painting*, exhibition catalogue, London, 1979–80, cat. no. 11, pp. 30–1.

95. The first etching is illustrated in Peter Webb, *Erotic Art*, London, 1973, p. 182, pl. 137.

96. See Gay, op. cit., vol. II, pp. 303–6. Kingsley (1819–75) was a social reformer and novelist; amongst his works are *Westward Ho!* (1855) in which a Spanish nobleman, Don Guzman Maria Magdalena Sotomayor de Soto, is taken prisoner by Amyas in Ireland, *The Heroes* (1856) and *The Water Babies* (1863). Kingsley's drawings of himself and Fanny as Christ and Mary Magdalen appear as plates 2 and 3 before p. 173 in Gay, ibid. In another case of self-identification, the Theosophist Mrs Anna Kingsford (1846–88) saw herself as Mary Magdalen and her husband as Christ. On converting to Roman Catholicism, she took the name Annie Mary Magdalen Maria Johanna.

97. See Catherine Lampert, *Rodin, Sculpture and Drawings*, London, 1986, cat. no. 117.

98. Rainer Maria Rilke, *Rodin & Other Prose Pieces*, trs. G. Craig Houston, London, 1986, pp. 75–6. Written *c*.1905.

99. See W. L. Graff, *Rainer Maria Rilke: Creative Anguish of a Modern Poet*, Princeton, 1956, p. 61.

100. See next chapter, pp. 374–5.

101. Graff, op. cit., pp. 178–9.

102. Quoted in Donald Prater, *A Ringing Glass: Life of Rainer Maria Rilke*, Oxford, 1986, p. 199.

103. Rainer Maria Rilke, 'Der Auferstandene', German text from Rainer Maria Rilke, *New Poems*, trs., introd. and notes, J. B. Leishman, London, 1964, pp. 202 and 204. My thanks to Julian Peach for providing me with the text; the translation is my own.

104. Rainer Maria Rilke, 'Pietà', from *Neue Gedichte*, Leipzig, 1911, p. 210. The translation is my own.

105. Maurice Maeterlinck, *Mary Magdalene*, London, 1910. See Miroslav John Hanak, *Maeterlinck's Symbolic Drama. A Leap into Transcendence*, Louvain, 1974.

CHAPTER X

1. Elisabeth Schüssler Fiorenza, *In Memory of Her. A Feminist Theological Reconstruction of Christian Origins*, London, 1983, p. 304.

2. *The Guardian*, 'Arts diary', 5 April 1990. In 1973 another film about Christ's sexual life was the subject of fire-bombing in Rome when the Danish Embassy was attacked after Pope Paul VI objected to the news that a film to be called *The Loves of Jesus Christ* was being made with the financial support of the Danish government. Christ was to be represented as a 'warlord, love apostle, erotomaniac, drunkard, idealist and revolutionary', and the film was to include 'direct and explicit portrayals of Jesus' relations with the women mentioned in the Bible in group sex scenes.' *New York Times News Service*, 30 June 1973. Quoted from Marina Warner, *Alone of All Her Sex*, London, 1976, chap. 15, note 5.

3. Martin Scorsese, interview in *La Repubblica*, 20 August 1988. The book had, incidentally, in its German edition, previously been subject to censorship, having been placed on the Index of Forbidden Books shortly after its publication in 1954. Twelve years later, the Index itself was abolished.

4. References to Nikos Kazantzakis' *Last Temptation* are taken from the 1988 reprint of the Faber edition, trs. P. A. Bien.

5. The pomegranate was said to have sprung from the blood of Dionysus. Eating it ensured that Persephone would return to the underworld each autumn. It is also the symbol of eternal life. The pomegranate tree at Mary Magdalen's door in *The Last Temptation* is the symbol of energy. The cut pomegranate sheds its seeds. Kazantzakis' *Last Temptation* inspired Geoffrey Cauley's ballet *Lazarus* in 1969. Revived at Sadler's Wells in January 1989, its central *pas de deux* is an unmistakably sexual encounter between Christ and Mary Magdalen. I am grateful to Jean Fraser and Nicholas Pickwoad for referring me to this work.

6. Kazantzakis, op. cit., p. 361.

7. ibid., Prologue, p. 7.

8. Leo Steinberg, *The Sexuality of Christ in Renaissance Art and in Modern Oblivion*, October, 25, Summer 1983; it was published in volume form by Faber, London, 1984. Steinberg illustrates on p. 191, fig. 229, a French *Pietà* of the late fifteenth century as an example of the 'enhanced loincloth' motif. I am inclined to agree with him that the female figure must be Mary Magdalen, despite its extremely unusual iconography – it is usually the Virgin who bears the dead Christ across her knees – simply by virtue of her elaborate costume and coiffure, the Magdalen's usual garb in French and northern art of the period (*c.*1490, Paris, Musée de Cluny).

9. Cavaliere d'Arpino, *Madonna and Child, with Saints John, Anne and Mary Magdalen* (Minneapolis Institute of Arts); illustrated in Steinberg, op. cit., p. 13 and fig. 16.

10. ibid., pp. 86 and 91.

11. D. H. Lawrence, 'The Man who Died' in *The Tales of D. H. Lawrence*, London, 1934; first published posthumously in 1931. The story was originally called 'The Escaped Cock'. I am grateful to M. R. D. Foot for referring me to this work. Despite the character metamorphoses, the old Lawrentian, and Freudian, male–female, active–passive principles still prevail in this novella. Although he rejects Madeleine, 'he felt gently towards

her humble crouching body'; of her reincarnation, the priestess, 'She is afraid of me, and my male difference . . . He crouched to her, and felt the blaze of his manhood and his power rise up in his loins, magnificent! "I am risen!"'

12. William E. Phipps, *Was Jesus Married? The Distortion of Sexuality in the Christian Tradition*, New York, Evanston, London, 1970, 1989. He refers to Mary Magdalen on pp. 64–7. I am grateful to Erwin Wright for all his help and for finding a copy of this book for me.

13. Michael Baigent, Richard Leigh and Henry Lincoln, *Holy Blood, Holy Grail*, London, 1983.

14. Denys Arcand, *Jesus of Montreal* (Canada, 1989). The story of Daniel in the lions' den was an Old Testament prefiguration of Christ, and the name Coulombe is close to 'colombe', or dove.

15. Krzysztof Kieślowski, *A Short Film about Love* (Poland, 1989). Kieślowski's film was the second of his ten-part series based on the Decalogue.

16. I am grateful to Geoff Brown, and to Lesley Troup, cataloguer at the National Film Archive, for providing me with a list of, and making it possible for me to see, early films of Christ's life in which the figure of Mary Magdalen appears. Among the films are *From the Manger to the Cross* (US, 1912), *King of Kings* (US, 1927), *Intolerance* (in the 'Judean Story', 1927), *Golgotha* (France, 1935), *Christus* (Italy, 1916), *INRI* (Germany, 1923), *Passion Play* (France, 1914), *Passion Play in Southern Italy* (Italy, 1912), *The First Easter* (Britain, 1939). I had hoped to find a kohl-eyed *houri* as Luke's sinner being

forgiven in the house of the Pharísee, but was unlucky.

17. Franco Zeffirelli, *Jesus of Nazareth*, Italy and Great Britain 1978.

18. 'I don't know how to love him. I don't see why he moves me . . . Just one more [man]. Don't you think it's funny – I am the one who has always been so calm, so cool, running every show. I never thought I'd come to this. I want him so. I love him so.' Tim Rice and Andrew Lloyd Webber, *Jesus Christ Superstar*, Leeds, 1970.

19. Eric Gill, *The Nuptials of God*, 1922.

20. Graham Sutherland also painted a *Noli me tangere* which is in the chapel of St Mary Magdalen, Chichester Cathedral.

21. These are referred to in Arianna Stassinopoulos Huffington's *Picasso. Creator and Destroyer*, London, 1988, p. 197. My thanks to my mother for this reference. See T. S. R. Boase, *The Sculpture of David Wynne 1949–1967*, London, 1968. I am very grateful to David Wynne for providing me with photographs at short notice.

22. Exhibition: *La Maddalena tra Sacro e Profano*, Florence, Palazzo Pitti, 24 May–7 September 1986. The article referred to is 'La Maddalena: un' identità velata e violata' by the exhibition's curator, Marilena Mosco.

23. Exhibition: *Marie-Madeleine. Figure inspiratrice dans la mystique, les arts et les lettres*, Musée Pétrarque, Fontaine-la-Vaucluse, 1988.

24. Exhibition: *Les Vanités dans la peinture au XVII siècle*, Musée des Beaux-Arts, Caen, 27 July–15 October 1990.

25. Exhibition: *Les Sculptures allemandes de la fin du Moyen-Age*, Paris, Musée du Louvre, 25 October 1991–16 February 1992. Domenichino's *Ecstasy of Mary*

Magdalen was used on the poster for the exhibition *Da Leonardo a Tiepolo*, Milan, Palazzo Reale, 6 June–30 September 1990, which showed Italian paintings from the Hermitage in St Petersburg. I am grateful to Judy Spours for giving me the poster for this exhibition.

26. Exhibition: *Martin Schongauer: maître de la gravure rhénane (vers 1450–91)*, Paris, Musée du Petit-Palais, 14 November 1991–16 February 1992.

27. Monica Furlong, review in the *Times Literary Supplement*, 6–12 November 1987, p. 1232.

28. Aurélie Briac, *L'Evangile selon Marie-Madeleine*, Paris, 1984. My thanks to Adele Airoldi for providing me with a copy.

29. Carolyn Slaughter, *Magdalene*, London, 1978.

30. Raymond-Leopold Bruckberger, *Marie-Madeleine*, Paris, 1952. English translation by H. L. Binsse, London, 1953.

31. Sholem Asch, *The Nazarene*, trs. M. Samuel, London, 1939. Here she is first seen in a Hellenised milieu, as an experienced 'mother type' with 'broad hips and full-developed breasts' visible between the 'red veils of her hair'. She distributes 'her favours as one distributes charity among the poor'. She also has religious seizures and dances, the nakedness of her body 'draped in a shower of flame-red hair'. After a dramatic conversion, she is seen lying outstretched below the cross, her hair now 'heavy and greying'. A similar background is used by Jean Josipovici in his *Catarsi di Maria Maddalena* (Rome, 1977), the story of her growing self-knowledge. Her spiritual journey begins while she is a black-haired courtesan dissatisfied with her life: through the agency of John the

Baptist, she opens up her house to the poor, dances, and feeds them out of her earnings. Called by the Master, she trudges through the desert and falls at his feet. When seen by Metellus, a former acquaintance, only her eyes are recognisable; her beauty has gone, the physical manifestation of her spiritual transformation. I am grateful to Gabriel Josipovici for lending me a copy of his father's book.

32. Jacqueline Kelen, *Un Amour infini: Marie-Madeleine, Prostituée sacrée*, Paris, 1982. I am grateful to Celia Jones for referring me to this book, and to Adele Airoldi for providing me with a copy. Some earlier novels about the life of Mary Magdalen are B. Montagu Scott, *Magdalen*, London, 1953; Edith Olivier, *Mary Magdalen*, London, 1952, and G. da Verona, *Sciogli la treccia, Maria Maddalena*, Florence, 1920. She is also the subject of an illustrated book, *Mary Magdalene. A Woman who showed her Gratitude*, in a series on 'Outstanding Women of the Bible', retold by Marlee Alex, illustrated by Jose Perez Montero, Grand Rapids, 1987, 1988, who is afflicted by demons and 'wicked fancies', sells her body to please men, until she is converted, and witnesses the resurrection. Anne C. Williman's novel *Mary of Magdala* (Nashville, 1990) is the most recent and presents a worthy if pedestrian account of the gospel character, expanding her story into an early marriage, widowhood and unrequited love for the disciple Matthew. After the crucifixion she returns to Magdala and a hinted second marriage to the worthy fisherman Jedidiah. I am grateful to Edith Hazen for finding me a copy of this book. A

further example of such celebrations of Mary Magdalen as the Eighties' liberated woman is in Sarah Maitland's 'Mary of Magdala', a monologue in which the Magdalen, at the crucifixion, ruminates over the past. She removes her veil, and shows off her red-gold hair. She remembers shocking Christ at the house of the Pharisee, 'giggling', 'grinning hugely', and letting down her hair. She becomes a friend of his mother – Jesus is not ashamed of her being a whore, as he found her 'beautiful, wise, funny and loving'. For three hours, she stands at the cross, her hair 'flaming', which she will never pin up again; in marvellous perversity, it is because of him that she is proud of her hair. (Read by Miriam Margolies, BBC Radio Four, Good Friday, 1987.)

33. Luise Rinser, *Mirjam*, Frankfurt-am-Main, 1987.

34. Marguerite Yourcenar, 'Mary Magdalene, or Salvation' in *Fires*, trs. Dori Katz, London, 1985. I am grateful to Mary Goodwin for referring me to this short story.

35. Before this date the mass for Mary Magdalen's feast-day (22 July), where the rubric denotes her as 'St Mary Magdalene, Penitent', contained readings from Luke 7:36–50, concerning the sinner, and the collect referred to Lazarus as her brother (*Missale Romanum*, London, 1949). In the revised Roman missal (1974), the mass has become a memorial, the least important category of mass.

36. Peter Ketter, *The Magdalen Question*, trs. Revd Hugo C. Koehler, Milwaukee, 1935.

37. See Chapter Nine, p. 328.

38. Marco Garzonio, *Gesù e le Donne, Gli incontri che hanno cambiato il Cristo*, Milan, 1990. I am grateful

to Adele Airoldi for bringing this book to my notice, and indeed for presenting me with a copy. I am grateful to her also for referring me to Jean d'Ormesson's novel of travel and adventure, *L'Histoire du juif errant*, Paris, 1990, the hero of which, Simon the Jew, had once been passionately in love with Mary Magdalen who had lost her head over Christ. No other woman can make him forget her, the cause of the curse which has forced him to wander for the rest of his life, to have ephemeral adventures, and, worse, not to be able to die.

39. Joseph A. Grassi, *The Hidden Heroes of the Gospels: Female Counterparts of Jesus*, London, 1989.

40. Elisabeth Moltmann-Wendel, *The Women around Jesus*, London, 1982.

41. Jean-Claude Barreau (*Les Memoires de Jésus*, Paris, 1978) suggested Christ was a widower. The idea that Christ was a philanderer and an adulterer was suggested to Luther by a friend, Pastor John Schlaginhaufen, in 1532. He wrote: 'Christ was an adulterer for the first time with the woman at the well, for it was said: "Nobody knows what he's doing with her" (John 4:27). Again with Magdalene, and still again with the adulterous woman in John 8, whom he let off so easily.' (Quoted in Phipps, op. cit., p. 12, from Martin Luther, *Works*, ed. H. T. Lehman, Philadelphia, 1957, 54, 154, Table Talk no. 1472.) Much along the same lines, Brigham Young, founder of the Mormons, suggested in a sermon that Christ had been a 'practical polygamist'; Mary and Martha had been his 'plural wives, and Mary Magdalene was another'. This was reported by one of Young's own wives, A. E. Young, in *Wife No 19*,

Hartford, Connecticut, 1876, p. 307, quoted in Phipps, p. 10.

42. Although each of these authors has more than one book to his or her credit, I have found the following works particularly interesting and useful: Ben Witherington's *Women in the Ministry of Jesus*, Cambridge, 1984; and Elaine Pagels' *Gnostic Gospels*, Harmondsworth, 1985. Susanne Heine's 'corrective' to the feminist angle, *Women and Early Christianity* (London, 1987), is perhaps the least weighted with bias, demanding an exegetical rather than eisegetical approach from feminist writers. See also Rosemary Radford Ruether, ed., *Religion and Sexism. Images of Woman in the Jewish and Christian Tradition*, New York, 1974, and *Womanguides. Readings toward a Feminist Theology*, Boston, 1985; and Leonard Swidler, *Biblical Affirmations of Woman*, Philadelphia, 1979. Carla Ricci's *Maria di Magdala e le molte Donne sul cammino di Gesù* , Naples, 1991, contains an excellent bibliography of works on the position of women in the early Church, and on Mary Magdalen herself. At the time of going to press my attention was brought to a new book about Mary Magdalen: Lilia Sebastiani, *Tra/Sfigurazione. Il personaggio evangelico di Maria di Magdala e il mito della peccatrice redenta nella tradizione occidentale*, Brescia, 1992. I am grateful to Aldo De Poli for telling me of this work, and to Adele Airoldi for obtaining a copy for me.

43. Warner, op. cit., pp. 338–9.

44. This was in the debate over abortion. Rosemary Radford Ruether, quoted in William Scobie, 'Virgin Territory', *Observer Magazine*, July 1987, p. 39. My thanks to Celia Jones for sending me this article.

45. Revd David Holloway, 'True Faith and the Virgin Birth', *The Times*, 20 December 1986.

46. Sarah Maitland, in 'Easter Night Thoughts: the Madonna and the Magdalen', broadcast by Thames Television, 26 March 1986.

47. Professor Geoffrey Parrinder, 'Myths of the virgin birth that obscure Jesus' family life', *The Independent*, December 1989. My thanks to Suzanne O'Farrell for sending this article to me.

48. *Mulieris Dignitatem. Apostolic Letter of the Supreme Pontiff John Paul II on the Dignity and Vocation of Women on the Occasion of the Marian Year*, published by the Catholic Truth Society, 1988.

49. 'Civil war in the Anglican Church', article by Andrew Brown, *The Independent*, 1 November 1988; also Andrew Brown, 'Schism looms over woman bishop's consecration', *The Independent*, 11 February 1989.

50. Quoted in a letter to *The Times*, 8 August 1991.

51. Henry C. Lea, *History of Sacerdotal Celibacy in the Christian Church*, London, 1932, p. 40.

52. See Mary Ann Rossi, 'Priesthood, Precedent, and Prejudice. On Recovering the Women Priests of Early Christianity', *Journal of Feminist Studies of Religion*, Spring 1991, vol. VII, no. 1, pp. 80–1. The article contains a translation of 'Notes on the Female Priesthood in Antiquity' by Giorgio Otranto. I am grateful to Mary Grey for sending me a copy of this article.

53. Rossi, op. cit., pp. 88–9.

54. *Mulieris Dignitatem*, p. 102. The pope was referring to such women as Phoebe, Prisca and

Euodias, mentioned in Paul's Epistles and Acts.

55. Revd John de Chazal, letter in *The Times*, 19 January 1989.

56. *Maria von Magdala: Initiative Gleichberechtigung für Frauen in der Kirche*, January 1989. I am grateful to Mary Grey for bringing this organisation to my attention. The Revd Ulla Monberg, curate at St James's Church, Piccadilly, London, also sees Mary Magdalen as a role model for women's ministry.

57. Mary Midgley, 'Sinister ideals', review of Nel Noddings, *Women and Evil* (Berkeley, University of California Press), in the *Times Literary Supplement*, 16–22 February 1990, and ensuing correspondence.

58. Peter Stanford, 'Devotion to another Mary', *The Weekend Guardian*, 9–10 September 1989, p. 7. The author was the then editor of the *Catholic Herald*. He has recently revised this view of Mary Magdalen in *Catholics and Sex*, written with Kate Saunders, London, 1992. The survival of the mythical Magdalen is also evidenced by the poster used to advertise the pontifical mass celebrating her feast-day in July 1992 in the church of S. Maria Maddalena in Tlaltelulco, Tlaxcala State, Mexico, where she is still described as the model of contemplation and of penitence ('Porque mucho a amado, mucho se e ha perdonado'). I am extremely grateful to Susan Tattersall for sending me the poster, together with photographs of scenes of Mary Magdalen's life in painted and gilded plaster which decorate the eighteenth-century church.

59. John S. Damm, sermon given on 22 July 1990 at St Peter's Lutheran Church, New York. I am very grateful to Ralph Price for bringing this sermon to my notice, and for providing me with a copy.

60. ibid.

61. Friedrich Nietzsche, *The Birth of Tragedy*, vol. 3 of *The Complete Works of Friedrich Nietzsche*, ed. Dr Oscar Levy, trs. William A. Haussmann, Edinburgh and London, 1909, Section 23, pp. 174–5. I am very grateful to Menno Lievers and Professor H. Philipse for directing me to this reference.

Select Bibliography

Alverny, Marie-Thérèse d', 'Comment les théologiens et les philosophes voient la femme', in *Cahiers de civilisation médiévale*, vol. XX, 1977, pp. 105–29.

Anderson, Bonnie S., and Zinsser, Judith P., *A History of their Own. Women in Europe from Prehistory to the Present*, vol. I, Harmondsworth, 1989.

Aquinas, St Thomas, *Summa Theologiae*, ed. C. Thomas Moore OP, London, 1976, vol. LV.

Aristotle, *The Generation of Animals*, trs. A. L. Peck, London and Cambridge (Mass.), Loeb Classical Library, 1943.

Atkinson, Clarissa W., Buchanan, Constance M. and Miles, Margaret R., eds, *Immaculate and Powerful. The Female in Sacred Image and Social Reality*, Wellingborough, 1987.

Augustine, St, *The City of God*, trs. Henry Bettenson, introd. John O'Meara, Harmondsworth, 1986.

Augustine, St, *The Confessions*, trs. and introd. R. S. Pine-Coffin, Harmondsworth, 1984.

Baker, Derek, ed., *Medieval Women*, Oxford, 1978.

Barocchi, Paola, ed., *Trattati d'Arte del Cinquecento. Fra manierismo e controriforma*, 3 vols, Bari, 1960–2.

Baron, S. W., *A Social and Religious History of the Jews*, 8 vols, New York, 1952–60.

Battisti, Eugenio, 'Maria Maddalena', in *Enciclopedia Cattolica*, vol. VIII, Florence, 1952, cols 138–43.

Beauvoir, Simone de, *The Second Sex*, trs. and ed. H. M. Parshley, London, 1988.

Bell, Rudolph M., *Holy Anorexia*, Chicago, 1985.

Bennett, R. F., *The Early Dominicans. Studies in Thirteenth-Century Dominican History*, Cambridge, 1937.

Blunt, Anthony, *Artistic Theory in Italy 1450–1600*, London, Oxford and New York, 1975.

Bonaventure, St, attrib., *Meditations on the Life of Christ. An Illustrated Manuscript of the Fourteenth Century*. Translated from Paris Bibliothèque Nationale MS Ital. 115 by Isa Ragusa, ed. Ragusa and Rosalie B. Greene, Princeton, 1961.

Børresen, Kari Elisabeth, *Subordination and Equivalence. The Nature and Role of Woman in Augustine and Thomas Aquinas*, trs. Charles H. Talbot, Washington, DC, 1981.

Bourgain, L., *La Chaire française au XII siècle d'après les manuscrits*, Paris, 1879.

Broude, Norma, and Garrard, Mary D., eds, *Feminism and Art History. Questioning the Litany*, New York, 1982.

Brown, Peter, *The Body and Society. Men, Women and Sexual Renunciation in Early Christianity*, London and Boston, 1989.

Brown, Peter, *The Cult of the Saints. Its Rise and Function in Latin Christianity*, London, 1983.

Brundage, James A., *Law, Sex and Christian Society in Medieval Europe*, Chicago and London, 1988.

Bugge, John, *Virginitas: An Essay in the History of a Medieval Ideal*, The Hague, 1975.

Bynum, Caroline Walker, *Holy Feast and Holy Fast: The Religious Significance of Food to Medieval Women*, Berkeley and London, 1987.

Bynum, Caroline Walker, *Jesus as Mother. Studies in the Spirituality of the High Middle Ages*, Berkeley and London, 1982.

Calmet, Dom Augustin, 'Dissertation sur Les Trois Maries' in *Sainte Bible en latin et en français, avec des notes littérales, critiques et historiques, des préfaces et des dissertations, tirées du Commentaire du Dom . . .* , vol. XIII, Paris, 1773.

Catholic Encyclopedia, The, ed. Charles G. Heilbermann et al, 15 vols, London and New York, 1907–14.

Chadwick, Henry, *The Early Church*, Harmondsworth, 1978.

Chadwick, Owen, *The Reformation*, Harmondsworth, 1964.

Chadwick, Whitney, *Women, Art and Society*, London, 1990.

Chérest, A., *Vézelay. Etude historique*, 3 vols, Auxerre, 1863–8.

Clark, Kenneth, *The Nude*, Harmondsworth, 1976.

Cole, William Graham, *Sex in Christianity and Psychoanalysis*, London, 1956.

Cole, William Graham, *Sex and Love in the Bible*, London, 1960.

Coulton, G. G., *Five Centuries of Religion*, 4 vols, Cambridge, 1923–50.

Coulton, G. G., *Medieval Panorama*, Cambridge, 1938.

Cropper, E., 'On Beautiful Women, Parmigianino, *Petrarchismo*, and the Vernacular Style', *Art Bulletin*, vol. LVIII, 3 September 1976, pp. 374–94.

Daly, Mary F., *The Church and the Second Sex*, London, 1968.

Dictionnaire de Spiritualité, Ascétique et Mystique, Doctrine et Histoire, ed. M. Viller et al, Paris (1932) 1978, fascs LXVI–LXVII.

Donehoo, J. de Q., *The Apocryphal and Legendary Life of Christ*, New York and London, 1903.

Duchesne, Louis, *Fastes épiscopaux de l'ancienne Gaule*, 3 vols, Paris, 1907–15.

Duperray, Eve, ed., *Marie Madeleine dans la mystique, les arts et les lettres*, Actes du Colloque International, Avignon, 20–2 July 1988, Paris, 1989.

Eliade, Mircea, *The Sacred and the Profane. The Nature of Religion*, trs. Willard R. Trask, New York, 1959.

Encyclopedia of Religion, ed. Mircea Eliade, 15 vols, New York, 1987.

Epstein, Louis M., *Sex Laws and Customs in Judaism*, New York, 1948.

Faillon, E.-M., *Monuments inédits sur l'Apostolat de Sainte Marie-Madeleine en Provence*, 2 vols, Paris, 1863.

Figes, Eva, *Patriarchal Attitudes. Women in Society*, London, 1978.

Filoramo, Giovanni, *A History of Gnosticism*, trs. Anthony Alcock, Oxford, 1990.

Fiorenza, Elisabeth Schüssler, *In Memory of Her. A Feminist Theological Reconstruction of Christian Origins*, London, 1983.

Fliche, A., and Martin, V., *Histoire de l'Eglise depuis les origines jusqu'à nos jours*, 13 vols, Paris, 1934–50.

Foucault, Michel, *The History of Sexuality. An Introduction*, trs. R. Hurley, Harmondsworth, 1987.

Garth, Helen Meredith, *Saint Mary Magdalene in Mediaeval Literature*, Johns Hopkins University Studies in History and Political Science, Series LXVII, no. 3, 1950.

Geary, Patrick J., *Furta Sacra: Thefts of Relics in the Central Middle Ages*, Princeton, 1978.

Grabar, A., *Christian Iconography: A Study of its Origins*, Princeton, 1968.

Graef, Hilda, *Mary: A History of Doctrine and Devotion*, 2 vols, London and New York, 1963 and 1965.

Grant, Robert M., *The Formation of the New Testament*, London, 1965.

Grant, Robert M., *Gnosticism: An Anthology*, London, 1961.

Grant, Robert M., *Gnosticism and Early Christianity*, New York, 1966.

Hall, James, *Dictionary of Subjects and Symbols in Art*, London, 1984.

Hall, James, *A History of Ideas and Images in Italian Art*, London, 1983.

Hansel, Hans, *Die Maria-Magdalena-Legende. Eine Quellen-Untersuchung*. Greifswald, 1937.

Harding, Esther, *Woman's Mysteries, Ancient and Modern*, London, 1971.

Haskell, Francis, *Patrons and Painters: A Study in the Relations between Italian Art and Society in the Age of the Baroque*, London, 1963.

Hawtrey, Valentina, trs., *The Life of St Mary Magdalen*, London and New York, 1904.

Heine, Susanne, *Christianity and the Goddesses. Systematic criticism of a feminist theology*, trs. John Bowden, London, 1988.

Heine, Susanne, *Women and Early Christianity. Are the feminist scholars right?*, trs. John Bowden, London, 1988.

Hennecke, E., *New Testament Apocrypha*, ed. W. Schneemelcher, Eng. edn. ed., R. McL. Wilson, 2 vols, London, 1963 and 1965.

Hollander, Anne, *Seeing through Clothes*, New York, 1979.

Hooke, S. H., ed., *Myth and Ritual. Essays on the Myth and Ritual of the Hebrews in relation to the Culture Pattern of the Ancient East*, London, 1933.

Huizinga, Johann, *The Waning of the Middle Ages. A Study in Forms of Life, Thought and Art in France and the Netherlands in the Fourteenth and Fifteenth Centuries*, Harmondsworth, 1972.

Ingenhoff-Danhäuser, Monika, *Maria Magdalena: Heilige und Sünderin in der italienischen Renaissance. Studien zur Ikonographie der Heiligen von Leonardo bis Tizian*, Tübingen, 1984.

James, M. R., trs. and ed., *The Apocryphal New Testament. Being the Apocryphal Gospels, Acts, Epistles, and Apocalypses*, Oxford, 1924.

Jameson, Anna, *Sacred and Legendary Art*, 2 vols, London, 1900.

Janelle, Pierre, *The Catholic Reformation*, London, 1971.

Janssen, Marga, 'Maria Magdalen in der abendländischen Kunst. Ikonographie der Heiligen von den Anfängen bis ins 16. Jahrhundert', unpublished Ph.D. dissertation, Freiburg-im-Breisgau, 1961.

Janssen, Marga Anstett, 'Maria Magdalena' in *Lexikon der christlichen Ikonographie*, eds E. Kirschbaum SJ and W. Braunfels, Rome, Freiburg, Basel, Vienna, 1974, vol. 7, cols 516–41.

Jedin, Hubert, *A History of the Council of Trent*, trs. E. Graf, 2 vols, London, 1957 and 1961.

Jerome, St, *Select Letters*, trs. F. A. Wright, London, 1933.

Jonas, Hans, *The Gnostic Religion*, Boston, 1958.

Kaftal, George, *Iconography of the Saints in Tuscan Painting*, Florence, 1952.

Kaftal, George, *Iconography of the Saints in the Central and South Italian Schools of Painting*, Florence, 1965.

Kaftal, George, *Iconography of Saints in the Painting of North-East Italy*, with the collaboration of Fabio Bisogni, Florence, 1978.

Ketter, Peter, *The Magdalen Question*, trs. Revd Hugo C. Koehler, Milwaukee, 1935.

Knipping, John B., *Iconography of the Counter Reformation in the Netherlands: Heaven on Earth*, 2 vols, Nieuwkoop and Leiden, 1974.

Künstle, K., *Ikonographie der Heiligen*, Fribourg, 1926.

La Maddalena tra Sacro e Profano, exhibition catalogue, ed. M. Mosco, Milan-Florence, 1986.

LaRow, Sister Magdalen, SSJ, 'The Iconography of Mary Magdalen. The Evolution of a Western Tradition until 1300', unpublished Ph.D. dissertation, New York University, 1982.

Lea, Henry C., *History of Sacerdotal Celibacy in the Christian Church*, London, 1932.

Little, A. G., *Studies in English Franciscan History*, Manchester, 1917.

Mâle, Emile, *L'Art religieux après le Concile de Trente*, Paris, 1932, 1951.

Mâle, Emile, *L'Art religieux de la fin du Moyen Age en France*, Paris, 1922.

Mâle, Emile, *L'Art religieux du XIIe siècle en France*, Paris, 1922.

Mâle, Emile, *L'Art religieux du XIIIe siècle en France*, Paris, 1925.

Malvern, Marjorie M., *Venus in Sackcloth. The Magdalen's Origins and Metamorphoses*, Carbondale and Edwardsville, 1975.

Martz, Louis, *The Poetry of Meditation*, New Haven, 1962.

May, Geoffrey, *Social Control of Sexual Expression*, London, 1930.

Meiss, Millard, *Painting in Florence and Siena after the Black Death. The Arts, Religion and Society in the Mid-Fourteenth Century*, New York, 1964.

Millett, Kate, *Sexual Politics. A Surprising Examination of Society's Most Arbitrary Folly*, London, 1970.

Moorman, John, *A History of the Franciscan Order*, Oxford, 1968.

Murray, Robert, SJ, *Symbols of Church and Kingdom*, Cambridge, 1975.

Musurillo, Herbert A., SJ, *Symbolism and the Christian Imagination*, Dublin, 1962.

Nag Hammadi Library in English, The, ed. James M. Robinson, Leiden, 1984.

Nelson, John Charles, *Renaissance Theory of Love. The Context of Giordano Bruno's* Eroici furori, New York, 1958.

New Catholic Encyclopedia, The, Editorial Staff of the Catholic University of America, Washington DC, 15 vols, New York and London, 1967.

O'Faolain, Julia, and Martines, Lauro, eds, *Not in God's Image. Women in History*, London, 1979.

Owst, G. R., *Literature and Pulpit in Medieval England*, Cambridge, 1933.

Owst, G. R., *Preaching in Medieval England c.1350–1450*, Cambridge, 1926.

Pagels, Elaine, *Adam, Eve, and the Serpent*, London, 1988.

Pagels, Elaine, *The Gnostic Gospels*, Harmondsworth, 1985.

Panofsky, Erwin, *Renaissance and Renascences in Western Art*, New York, Evanston, San Francisco, London, 1972.

Panofsky, Erwin, *Studies in Iconology. Humanistic Themes in the Art of the Renaissance*, New York, Evanston, San Francisco, London, 1972.

Phipps, William E., *The Sexuality of Jesus. Theological and literary perspectives*, New York, 1973.

Phipps, William E., *Was Jesus Married? The Distortion of Sexuality in the Christian Tradition*, New York, Evanston, London, 1970.

Pigler, A., *Barockthemen: Eine Auswahl von Verzeichnissen zur Ikonographie des 17. und 18. Jahrhunderts*, 2 vols, Budapest, 1974.

Power, Eileen, *Medieval Women*, ed. M. M. Postan, Oxford, 1975.

Prodi, Paolo, 'Riforma cattolica e Controriforma', *Nuove Questioni di Storia moderna*, vol. I, 1964, pp. 357–418.

Pullan, Brian, *Rich and Poor in Renaissance Venice*, Oxford, 1971.

Quéré-Jaulmes, F., *La Femme: Les grandes textes des Pères de l'Eglise*, Paris, 1965.

Réau, Louis, *Iconographie de l'art chrétien*, 3 vols, Paris, 1955–9.

Robb, Nesca, *Neoplatonism and the Italian Renaissance*, London, 1935.

Rochon, A., *Histoire mondiale de la Femme*, Paris, 1966.

Rossiaud, Jacques, *Medieval Prostitution*, trs. Lydia G. Cochrane, Oxford, 1988.

Rougemont, Denis de, *Myths of Love*, trs. R. Howard, London, 1964.

Rougemont, Denis de, *Passion and Society*, trs. M. Belgion, London, 1956.

Ruether, Rosemary Radford, ed., *Religion and Sexism. Images of Woman in the Jewish and Christian Traditions*, New York, 1974.

Ruether, Rosemary Radford, ed., *Womanguides. Readings toward a Feminist Theology*, Boston, 1985.

Saxer, Victor, *Le Culte de Marie Madeleine en Occident des origines à la fin du moyen âge*, Auxerre–Paris, 1959.

Saxer, Victor, *Le Dossier vézelien de Marie Madeleine. Invention et translation des reliques en 1265–1267*, Brussels, 1975.

Saxer, Victor, 'Les saintes Marie Madeleine et Marie de Béthanie dans la tradition liturgique et homilétique orientale', *Revue des sciences religieuses*, vol. 32, 1958, pp. 1–37.

Saxer, Victor, 'Maria Maddalena', in *Bibliotheca Sanctorum*, Rome, 1967, vol. VIII, cols 1078–1103.

Schiller, Gertrud, *Ikonographie der christlichen Kunst*, 5 vols, Gütersloh, 1966–91.

Shahar, Shulamith, *The Fourth Estate: A History of Women in the Middle Ages*, London, 1983.

Southern, R. W., *The Making of the Middle Ages*, London, 1959.

Southern, R. W., *Western Society and the Church in the Middle Ages*, Harmondsworth, 1970.

Swidler, Leonard, *Women in Judaism. The Status of Women in Formative Judaism*, Metuchen (NJ), 1976.

Szövérffy, J., 'Peccatrix Quondam Femina: A Survey of the Mary Magdalen Hymns', *Traditio*, vol. XIX, 1963, pp. 79–146.

Taylor, Gordon Rattray, *Sex in History*, London, 1959.

Thurston, Herbert, 'St Mary Magdalene and the early Saints of Provence', *The Month*, vol. XCIII, 1899, pp. 75–81.

Trudgill, E., *Madonnas and Magdalens. The Origin and Development of Victorian Sexual Attitudes*, London, 1976.

Voragine, Jacobus de, *Legenda Aurea vulgo historia lombardica dicta*, ed. Dr T. Graesse, Dresden and Leipzig, 1846.

Warner, Marina, *Alone of All Her Sex. The Myth and the Cult of the Virgin Mary*, London, 1976.

Warner, Marina, *Monuments and Maidens. The Allegory of the Female Form*, London, 1987.

Weinstein, Donald, and Bell, Rudolph M., *Saints & Society. The Two Worlds of Western Christendom, 1000–1700*, Chicago and London, 1982.

Williams, N. P., *The Ideas of the Fall and of Original Sin. A historical and critical study*, etc., London, 1927.

Wind, Edgar, *Pagan Mysteries in the Renaissance*, Oxford, 1980.

Wittkower, Rudolph, *Art and Architecture in Italy 1600–1750*, Harmondsworth, 1978.

Young, Karl, *The Drama of the Medieval Church*, 2 vols, Oxford, 1933.

Index